The Official Guide

Paradox 9

Power Programming

About the Author...

Mike Prestwood is the author of several computer books including *Paradox 7 Programming Unleashed*. Mike is the president of Prestwood Software & Consulting (PSC), a Sacramento, CA–based Company that focuses on Windows programming and Internet consulting. PSC also markets and distributes several commercial applications including Paradox Workbench and Prestwood Writing Suite, and is the keeper of the Prestwood Coding Convention (PCC) and the Prestwood Software Development Methodology (PSDM), two standards in wide use in the Paradox and Delphi communities.

Prior to founding PSC, Mike worked for a variety of industry leaders including NEC, The Money Store, and Borland International (now Inprise). At NEC, Mike helped to develop an n-tier application using Delphi, Tibco, and Oracle. At The Money Store, Mike was the Product Manager of the mortgage division and led three teams of developers in building client/server applications using Paradox, Delphi, C++, Interbase, and Informix. While at Borland, Mike was responsible for developing a training program for SQL and advanced ObjectPAL. He taught a five-day ObjectPAL course and worked with others to create 20+ courses for Paradox technical support—more than 100 engineers at the time.

You can send e-mail to Mike at mikeprestwood@prestwood.com. In addition, visit the World Wide Web site of Prestwood Software & Consulting at http://www.prestwood.net or Mike's personal site at http://www.prestwood.com/mike.

The Official Guide

Paradox 9

Power Programming

Mike Prestwood

Osborne McGraw-Hill

Berkeley New York St. Louis San Francisco
Auckland Bogotá Hamburg London
Madrid Mexico City Milan Montreal New Delhi
Panama City Paris São Paulo
Singapore Sydney Tokyo Toronto

Osborne/**McGraw-Hill**
2600 Tenth Street
Berkeley, California 94710
U.S.A.

For information on translations or book distributors outside the U.S.A., or to arrange bulk purchase discounts for sales promotions, premiums, or fund-raisers, please contact Osborne/**McGraw-Hill** at the above address.

Paradox 9 Power Programming: The Official Guide

1234567890 AGM AGM 90198765432109

ISBN 0-07-211936-5

Publisher: Brandon A. Nordin
Associate Publisher and
Editor-in-Chief: Scott Rogers
Acquisitions Editor: Megg Bonar
Project Editor: Mark Karmendy
Editorial Assistant: Stephane Thomas
Technical Editor: Mike Delaney
Copy Editor: Dennis Weaver
Proofreader: Stefany Otis
Indexer: Jack Lewis
Computer Designers: Ann Sellers, Michelle Galicia, Roberta Steele
Illustrators: Brian Wells, Beth Young, Robert Hansen

Dedication

To my parents, Lester and Leslie.

Contents

Foreword

With the release of Paradox® 9, Corel is demonstrating their commitment to the Paradox community with a best of breed product. Paradox 9 delivers relational database computing power for building robust database applications quickly and more easily than *any* other product on the market today. Whether you are a business owner who needs to manage some data or a professional Paradox programmer, you will appreciate the new ease of use and power features we've added to Paradox 9.

Large organizations that require a complete solution will appreciate the ultra-smooth integration with Corel® WordPerfect® Suite applications. Power that delivers. Data that connects. Performance made easy.

Corel has included exciting new features in Version 9 to make using, manipulating, storing, updating, and retreiving your data easier than ever. A myriad of features for new and existing users include Experts Wizards that guide you through the creation of tables, forms, reports, charts, and mailing labels; the Application Framework feature that allows the creation of Paradox database applications, giving the look and feel of a real Windows application; and the new Visual Database Modeler feature that offers you an easy way to create Paradox databases with a visual display. In addition, new data query tools are provided in Version 9 to make data retrieval turnkey. Never before has Paradox offered so many features with such power and ease of use!

In the same way that Paradox 9 provides a solution to enhance your productivity, *Paradox 9 Power Programming: The Official Guide* does the same. In your hands you hold a guide that was developed in conjunction with the Paradox 9 team at Corel—a guide designed to help you make the most of your software tools. This book will show you how to quickly upgrade to the Paradox working environment with its familiar interface, increased power, and new features.

Corel is excited about the new technologies now available with Paradox 9 and we invite you to follow along in this CorelPRESS™ Official Guide. Author Mike Prestwood, along with the Product Teams at Corel, spent many hours working on the accuracy and features of this book, and we think you'll appreciate our efforts.

The Official Guides to Corel software represent a giant step in the ability of Corel to disseminate information to our users with the help of Osborne/McGraw-Hill and the creation of the CorelPRESS series of books. Congratulations to the team at Osborne who have created this excellent book, and to the team at Corel who supported the creation of this book!

Dr. Michael C. J. Cowpland
CEO, Corel Corporation
Ottawa, Ontario
April 1999

Acknowledgments

A book of this nature demands input from as many different people as possible. I'm lucky enough to have worked with many talented engineers over the years, and their contributions and their openness to my inquiries are greatly appreciated. I'd like to make special acknowledgment to the Corel Paradox team for their support. The following Corel team members reviewed the book for technical errors: Dan Alder, Darrell MacKay, Fazel Haffejee, Frederic Gaudet, George Campbell, John Savone, Karen Whiteford, Kaveh Sohrabi, Ken Wong (he did the bulk of the work), Marc Laframboise, Mark Anderson, Monica Viktora, and Rajeev Reyal. A special thank you goes to Chip Maxwell and Jo-Anne Lussier for keeping me informed and responding to inquiries.

The technical editor for this book is Mike Delaney with whom I worked every day here at Prestwood Software & Consulting. His assistance and attention to detail are greatly appreciated. Thanks also go to my past mentors David Orriss, Jr., James Arias-LaRheir, Tarik Ghbeish, Randy Spitz, and Chuck Rehn.

A special thank you goes to the staff at Osborne/McGraw-Hill for giving me this opportunity and for the guidance. Project editor Mark Karmendy made sure the chapters flowed from one to another, copyeditor Dennis Weaver made sure I used English in a decent way, and editorial assistant Stephane Thomas kept documents going to the correct person.

I probably could go on for another page or two, but let me finish with a big thank you to Megg Bonar of Osborne/McGraw-Hill and Michelle Murphy Croteau of Corel (now with Corel Dublin) for their support and guidance. Without them, this book would not be.

Introduction

Paradox 9 Power Programming: The Official Guide is for anyone who wishes to build business database applications using Paradox 9. In these pages, you will tackle ObjectPAL with a hands-on approach. This book includes material for beginner, intermediate, and advanced ObjectPAL programmers. Through instruction and example, you will learn the intricacies of ObjectPAL and how to write a complete database application. Advanced topics such as software design, architecture, and coding conventions are covered too.

If you already know the basics of ObjectPAL, this book is a good source for ideas, tricks, tips, short code routines, and advanced concepts. The goal of this book is to add to the manuals with as little duplication as possible to present a complete study of developing business database applications. If you own several Paradox books, I'm confident you will find this book to be the most useful, with many more advanced examples and discussions presented in clear English.

What You Should Know Before Reading This Book

This book doesn't document every feature of Paradox—that's the job of the manuals and help file—nor does it show you how to use interactive features, except for occasional interactive solutions to programming problems. That is the job of beginner-level Paradox books. This book assumes that you understand the basics of interactive Paradox. If you can create a table, form, report, and query, you fall into this category. Although you don't need to know how to use every interactive feature of Paradox, you must be familiar with the majority of its interactive—non-ObjectPAL—features.

Internet Home Page for Book and Support Files

The Internet home page for this book is http://www.prestwood.com/forums/paradox/books/official/. Here you will find information on ordering more copies of the book, support files, PCC, PSDM, sample applications, a bonus chapter on distributing applications, and much more.

Throughout this book are references to specific files on the Internet. Rather than downloading each individual file, you might wish to download all the files compressed into a single file. Refer to the page listed above for more instructions.

Search This Book

Also available from the Internet home page is a searchable version of this book. The searchable version does not contain graphics, but it does contain all the text and is a great way to find help on a specific subject in this book. You'll want to bookmark this page.

CHAPTER 1

The Paradox Development Environment

The definition of the word *paradox* seems to fit the software rendition well. A paradox is something that appears to contradict itself or be contrary to common sense but might be true. The name applies well to the Paradox database development environment because it is very powerful, yet easy to learn and use. With Paradox, you can quickly prototype an application for a client and then turn the prototype into the full application; this is known as rapid application development (RAD). Paradox brings RAD development to a new height of simplicity and power.

ObjectPAL stands for Object Paradox Application Language. The acronym portion of the name (PAL) comes from the DOS version of Paradox. The term *Object* was added to the name because ObjectPAL is an object-based event-driven programming environment that is much more advanced than its PAL predecessor. What does this mean to you? It means you get to work with a development environment that uses the analogy of objects to represent programming elements such as windows, buttons, fields, and bitmaps. Why is this so important? It is important because humans perceive everything in life as objects—for example, cars, houses, trees, dogs, and cats. Furthermore, we naturally break down each of these objects into other objects. For example, a car object is made up of other objects, including tires, frame, engine, and steering wheel. This makes using a car a relatively simple experience. We do not need to know that a carburetor is an object contained within an engine. We don't even have to know that an engine is an object contained within a car. We simply have to know how to use the interface the designers of the car gave us to work with. We have to know how to use the door, key, steering wheel, gas, and brakes. We don't need to know the specifics of how the engine generates energy that is transferred to the wheels. The concept of just using the interface to an object and not knowing the details inside is called the black box component model. In other words, a designer creates something (an object) and gives the users of the object an interface. The term *black box* refers to not being able to see what is within the box. In Paradox, you do not need to concern yourself with the details of what happens when you push a button—you simply attach code to the pushButton event of a button (the interface given to us by the designers of Paradox). This is the basis for object-based and object-oriented programming—hot topics these days.

Before we continue our journey into object-based programming and ObjectPAL, you need to review a few concepts. The first few chapters deal with issues such as planning, table design, and interactive form design. These chapters also discuss interactive issues that an ObjectPAL programmer needs to keep in mind. The rest of this chapter gives you an overview of the design and development process. It begins with a discussion of why you should use Paradox. Then, it moves into a discussion of types of applications and which types of applications Paradox is suitable for, then follows by discussing how to design and develop a good database application.

Why Should You Use Paradox?

A *database* is an organized collection of information. For Paradox table users, this meaning is stretched to mean a set of related tables (usually in the same directory). Paradox allows you to access Paradox tables and other types of databases, and is much more than a simple database program. Paradox has made complex databases accessible to the average user. In my opinion, Paradox has three levels of usability: easy database access, complex database access, and custom database application development. Although this book touches on the first two levels of usability, it is primarily concerned with the third: custom database application development.

Easy database access enables you to create simple database tables and to enter and browse through data quickly with the traditional table window or a more flexible form. In addition, Paradox delivers easy database access by providing you with a plethora of experts available in Paradox. These Corel Paradox Experts allow non-programmers and programmers to easily accomplish tasks like creating a complete employee records database application or documenting an existing application.

Complex database access enables you to ask complex questions about your data. In Paradox, you can set a filter in a form or ask a question of your data with a query. After you find the answer, you can use crosstabs, graphs, and reports to communicate the answer to your users.

Custom database application development includes bringing all the elements that display data—such as table views, forms, and reports—into a cohesive presentation. The application development side of Paradox brings a friendly user interface to the end user and a powerful language called ObjectPAL to the programmer. These elements together enable you to better control the application environment.

Paradox is the best tool on the market for delivering these three levels of usability. This should be a major consideration when deciding what tool to develop a custom database application with, for yourself or a client. Deliver a custom database application in Paradox and you deliver the most powerful data manipulation environment available with a balance of easy and complex database access and custom database application development.

Types of Tables—Which Type to Use

Paradox is capable of using both local tables (such as Paradox or dBASE) and remote tables (such as Oracle and Sybase). This means that, as a Paradox or dBASE developer, you can read and write Paradox and dBASE tables and indexes without importing them. This is important. Some developers get confused about this issue and ask how to convert a dBASE table to a Paradox table or vice versa. The answer is, you don't. Paradox is a front end to any type of data that the database engine can access. If you need to copy the data from dBASE to Paradox format, or vice versa, then simply copy the table giving it a new extension (for example .DBF to .DB). The database engine takes care of the details.

In addition to local table structures such as Paradox and dBASE, you can use any of the SQL servers supported by the database engine. This includes InterBase, Oracle, Sybase, MS-SQL, DB/2, and Informix. Also, the database engine is ODBC compliant. This means that you can use almost any ODBC driver to connect to almost anything, including text files, Btrieve databases, Excel spreadsheets, and Access databases.

Types of Applications

There are many types of applications, but because Paradox is a database management system (DBMS), it's best suited for developing custom database applications. This doesn't mean that custom database applications are the only type of application you can develop. In fact, you can develop many types of applications with Paradox. Table 1-1 discusses how well suited Paradox is for developing various types of applications.

Category	Suitability	Comments
Manager system	Sometimes yes	Suitable when the applications are written in Paradox.
Business data	Yes	Paradox's strong point.
Informational	Yes	Paradox's strong point.
Kiosk	Yes	Paradox's strong point.
Educational	Usually yes	Educational software often uses tables.

TABLE 1-1 Types of Applications with Paradox

Category	Suitability	Comments
Desk accessory	Sometimes yes	Suitable only when a Paradox application is used.
Games	No	A few interesting games can be created, however.
Prototype	Yes	Prototyping applications in Paradox is very fast.
General utility	No	The exception is a database utility.
Graphic	No	Although Paradox has good graphics capability, it is not well suited to develop a graphic program.

TABLE 1-1 Types of Applications with Paradox *(continued)*

Usually, choosing a tool is easy. When you are asked to do a certain project or when you get an inspiration to develop an application, usually you know what tool you should use. Clearly, Paradox isn't the best tool for every category of software. For example, you probably would not wish to write a file utility with it. If a project involves extensive amounts of data, Paradox will likely be well suited for the job. ObjectPAL is the powerful backbone of Paradox and therefore can be the backbone of a large DBMS. Paradox also is useful for prototyping an application that you plan to write in Delphi or C++Builder. Prototyping is the process of application development in which small parts or the general structure of an application are designed and tested. These models are used as the basis for building the finished system. If you are going to develop applications, it is important to know what tool—or development environment—to use.

Where to See Various Types of Paradox Applications

Before jumping into the formal discussion, you should see what Paradox is capable of. Sometimes it's nice to see what a product can do. As they say, "Seeing is believing." Knowing what a product can do is half the battle. If you haven't done so already, take some time now to study the applications that shipped with Paradox and run the application experts, too. If you have Internet access, you can view many completed Paradox applications with source code at the following URL:

http://prestwood.com/forums/paradox/books/official

This Internet page is the support page for this book. It is part of the Paradox Online forum, which is hosted by Mike Prestwood. The Paradox Online forum is one of many forums contained on PrestoNet (a FREE worldwide Internet environment).

Multiprogrammer Developing

When developing a large application, you will need to program in a team environment. Programming in a team environment is dramatically different than programming by yourself.

Divide and Conquer

The most dramatic part of getting used to programming in a multiprogrammer environment is getting used to the fact that you are not in charge of all the code. The best way to create a successful multiprogrammer environment is to divide the responsibility of the program among all the programmers, with no overlapping assignments. This way, you establish pride of ownership, and each programmer can do his or her best to make modules complete and bug-free.

Establishing Programmer Roles

Depending on the size of the team created, you can have any of the following roles: grunt programmer, lead programmer, architect, project leader, QA tester, unit tester, business analyst, user interface expert, and so on. The role a particular programmer will fill depends on his or her programming skills, how well he or she gets along with others, his or her leadership capabilities, and finally his or her knowledge of the requirements, design specification, and database.

NOTE *Many Paradox developers act as the analyst, programmer, tester, and project manager—a single-person team. If you are a single-person team, this section still applies to you and you can still benefit from the information by adapting it to your environment. For example, you may be the only developer, but perhaps you can find someone on the business side that can do the testing or project management.*

Development Roles

Whether you are an individual developer or part of a team, you need to fully understand the various roles individuals play during the software development life cycle. No matter how many individuals are involved with a large project, the development team usually consists of a project manager, a business analyst, a system architect, and one or more lead programmers. Even in multiprogrammer development teams, an individual may commonly fill more than one role. If you are an individual developer, you fill all the development team roles.

Project Manager

The project manager is the grease that keeps the project moving. He or she may be a technical or nontechnical project manager. Although it is not usually recommended, the technical project manager often doubles as the system architect. In either case, the project manager is responsible for coordinating efforts among the user community and the development team. Usually, the programmers, analysts, and quality assurance personnel report directly to the project manager and the project manager reports indirectly to the executive sponsor.

Business Analyst

The business analyst can work either for the user community or the development team. This person coordinates, gathers, refines, defines, and prioritizes the various user requirements. This role is often filled by a lead programmer or the system architect.

Database Administrator

The database administrator (DBA) takes the business requirements and develops the database specification. The database specification contains all the table names, field definitions, data restrictions, trigger definitions, and stored procedure definitions. The DBA is also responsible for creating and modifying the database. On smaller projects, this role is often filled by the lead programmer or system architect.

System Architect

The system architect takes the business requirements and the database specification and develops the software specification at the highest level. The system architect is also responsible for selecting the tools used for development.

Lead Programmer

The lead programmer (often the same person as the system architect) works with the system architect to flush out the details of the software specification. The lead programmer understands the big picture; he or she understands the goals and high-level architecture of the application.

Programmer

A regular programmer works with the lead programmer or system architect to code specific tasks. This level programmer may not understand the whole picture. In fact, this person is usually told very specifically what and how to code.

User Community

As a software developer, you need to identify the key players in the user community for whom you are developing an application. Identify who will be using the software and get them involved in the design and testing of the software while it is being developed.

EXECUTIVE SPONSOR The executive sponsor is responsible for final decisions. Often, conflicts may arise among the development participants, and only the executive sponsor can resolve them. Also, the executive sponsor signs off on requirements, accepts the application, and usually pays for the application.

DEVELOPMENT PARTICIPANT A development participant is the person who at first deals with the business analyst and system architect to define and refine requirements. If you are using the rapid application development (RAD) process, the development participants also participate during development with the programmers, approving the features as they are implemented. Finally, the development participants are involved at the end of the process in testing (beta testing).

Versioning Software

Versioning software enables you to keep track of various versions of the same file. This way, you can roll back to any version of the file that you have checked into the versioning software. Versioning software tracks and organizes all revisions of all files associated with a project. It also enables developers in a multiprogrammer environment to lock files being developed to safeguard against duplicate development.

One such commercial versioning software program I recommend is PVCS. PVCS (Project Version Control System) is a third-party software program created to track the revisions of files associated with a project. It has become one of the standard versioning software applications in the industry.

Developing Large Applications

It's important to understand the elements of ObjectPAL, but if you don't keep the big picture in mind, the end product suffers. Gaining the ability to develop large applications as an individual or as a small or large development shop requires that you set up a process for developing software and then document it. Many methodologies for developing software exist. This section will introduce you to what is needed to develop large applications and will help developers of all levels create better, more elegant applications. Its intent is to start you thinking about the big picture and to spark your interest in the software life cycle. Whether you are an individual or part of a large development shop, I hope you will go out and pick up a few books on the software life cycle and software development methodologies.

NOTE *To see a complete software development methodology in use by Prestwood Software & Consulting (PSC), log on to the Internet and go to http://www.prestwood.net/psdm. There, you will find Prestwood Software Development Methodology. This is the methodology used by PSC to develop software for companies, and you can use it as a starting point to developing your own software development methodology.*

The Software Development Cycle

The software development cycle, also known as *full cycle development*, is the process of developing a software application. Without a set and documented process, the end application is likely to be buggy, not meet the users' needs, and take too long to develop.

The purpose of this section is to define the software development cycle as it affects the development team and the user community. The cycle itself is composed of a series of steps punctuated with milestones. These steps lead from the analysis of a new application to its development, testing, and eventual deployment. Each step is defined in detail.

An approximate duration for each step, if applicable, is given for example only; the estimation assumes five developers, one business analyst, one quality assurance tester, and a medium-sized application. The estimates are included only for reference. The actual duration will depend on many factors, including quality of business requirements analysis, complexity of the requirements, talent pool of programmers, and testing plan.

Remember that the application development cycle is a developing process that is revised on an ongoing basis. You should not consider it to be set in stone, but it should act as a guideline; you should use it in accordance with the needs of the current cycle.

Waterfall Versus RAD

With the *waterfall* approach to developing software, one phase of the development cycle follows the other and the user is involved only at the beginning during the requirements gathering phase and at the end during the acceptance phase. The requirements gathering in the waterfall approach is critical and unless it is 100 percent perfect, the project will fall short. With the rapid application development (RAD) approach to developing software, the user is heavily involved throughout the development process. In true RAD development, software is often very focused on a specific task. If you need to create several applications for a single client, then true RAD can lead to several independent applications that do not communicate and sometimes overlap in functionality.

My preference is for a modified RAD approach to development. In a modified RAD approach, emphasis is placed on thoroughly gathering requirements and involving the user in both the coding and testing phase of development to continuously validate that the product being developed is the product the client wants.

Overview of the Life Cycle of a New Application

The following is a list of the steps in the application development cycle:

1. Feasibility study
2. Requirements gathering
3. Requirements freeze
4. Requirements sign-off

5. Design session
    a. Database specification (logical design)
    b. Software specification (logical design)
6. Database freeze (logical DB specification implementation)
7. Development
    a. Module coding
    b. Programmer integration testing
    c. Resolution of existing bugs
    d. Code optimization
8. Development of help file and user manual
9. Application stabilization
10. Quality assurance building
11. Quality assurance iterations/discrepancy resolution
    a. Test data creation
    b. Unit testing by programmers and quality assurance
    c. Integration testing
    d. Regression testing
    e. Running test scenarios
    f. Stress testing
12. User acceptance
13. Application deployment
14. Maintenance

Except for this chapter, this book is primarily concerned with step 7 (development). This step involves the coding and debugging phases of the software development cycle. Occasionally I digress into another area when the subject is something that a programmer needs to know to be more productive, or is something that helps you understand how Paradox and ObjectPAL fit into the software development life cycle.

Gathering Requirements

Requirements are collected by the business analysts, system architect, and development participants. The average duration needed to gather requirements is directly proportional to the size of the application. Five days is usually sufficient for a small- to medium-sized application. New requirements for the application are gathered until the requirements freeze. The business analyst also needs to identify the requirements critical for the application to be accepted by the executive sponsor at an acceptance meeting. The executive sponsor is the person identified on the business side that has final decision authority on all development issues, and is often the person controlling the budget.

The requirements report should be broken down into logical categories—for example, business rules, validations, data input, data output, reports, external hardware and software requirements, user expected response times, security, and, finally, open issues. The project manager should create a set of questions to weigh the quality of the business requirements. Examples include "Are all the report formats specified?" "Are all the tasks the user wants to accomplish specified?" "Is success clearly identified?" "Are any of the programmers uneasy about any of the requirements?" and so on.

DEALING WITH BUSINESS RULES Creating a database isn't just about creating tables and linking them. It is also about implementing business rules on the data. For example, in an invoicing system, you need to multiply quantity times price to get each line total on an invoice. Then, you sum up the line total and multiply it by the local tax rate (and perhaps add shipping costs). These are all business rules. Another less obvious business rule might be to start charging interest on invoices that still have a balance due after 30 days. When gathering requirements, remember to ask your client about all the business rules and incorporate as many as appropriate into the application.

REVIEWING REQUIREMENTS The requirements freeze represents the point at which new requirements are moved to the next development cycle. Any new requirement after this point must be approved by the project manager if it is to be included in the current development cycle. The project manager is responsible for keeping the scope of the project within the boundaries agreed upon between him or her and the executive sponsor.

SIGNING OFF REQUIREMENTS After you have defined the user requirements, you should have the executive sponsor sign off on the requirements list.

TIP *When you're finishing an application for a client, nothing is more frustrating than the client telling you that the application is all wrong. Do yourself a favor: During or shortly after the planning stage, be sure to echo to the client what you heard him or her say. Also consider putting your general plan in writing and have both you and your client sign it. This approach makes you a more professional consultant.*

Deliverable: Functional Requirements Document

From the time your client agrees to hire you to create an application to the time you actually deliver the application can be a long time—in some cases, more than a year. Keeping your client in the loop and up to date is important. An excellent way to update your client is to have regularly scheduled status meetings. Another way is to give the client status reports as you reach each milestone. The functional requirements document is a great milestone and should be delivered to the client for review.

Deliverable: User Interface Requirements Document

The user interface requirements document represents how the application will look and feel. Although you have already received input from the user, a good next step is to prototype the application and demonstrate the prototype to the users with the goal of either having the users approve it or refine it.

Planning

To put it simply, involve every member of the team. Any programmer with any experience will tell you that planning an application is just as important as getting started on it. In other words, the first step in designing a database application is to sit down, take some time, and think through the process. Each assigned developer should estimate the time requirements for each task assigned to them (this estimation phase could take an additional day or two). The project manager then compiles all the information into a project plan. Each developer is also responsible for creating a test scenario for any requirements he or she implements.

DESIGNING THE DATABASE AND SOFTWARE In a session away from the user community, the development team creates the database and software specifications. The software specification lead is the system architect, and the database specification lead is the DBA (this is often the same person). Gather all the data components and categorize them into tables. After you gather the business rules and data components, you need to decide on table structures. Whether you're developing a complete invoicing system or an application that just keeps track of phone numbers, planning your table structures correctly can save you hours of work later. Although Paradox makes it easy to restructure your tables later, you can never recover the time and frustration wasted because of poorly designed table structures. If you have all the correct participants and the requirements analysis is good, you can usually nail down the initial database in a day or two.

Develop your tables with your primary keys in mind. (Chapter 2 discusses this point further.) Increasing or decreasing the length of your fields is easy in Paradox, so keep in mind the minimum size needed as you develop your field lengths. A little careful planning can save you hours of backtracking later.

DELIVERABLE: SOFTWARE SPECIFICATION The software specification document represents an interpretation of the functional requirements document and the user interface requirements document. This document represents how you are going to implement the software features. It is a detailed description of the required characteristics of the application.

DELIVERABLE: DATABASE SPECIFICATION The database design is also based on the requirements. Do not hide the database you are creating from your client. Show it to him or her. The Database Specification Document is a good place to do that.

DELIVERABLE: TEST PLAN The user should be involved with creating the test plan for the software. That way, the software will work the way the users want it to.

Freezing the Database

Freezing the database is the milestone where the DBA implements the database specification. This is an important milestone to reach on time because, in general, very little coding can occur until the database is stable.

Coding Software

You are probably most familiar with the coding phase of the software development life cycle. This book focuses on this phase, which includes module coding, programmer integration testing, resolution of existing bugs, and optimization of code. This phase can take anywhere from three to eight weeks on a medium-sized application.

Programmers develop new features as described in the development specification into the application. The business analysts and the development participants are enlisted by the programmers to verify that the new features are developed. This step ensures correctness. This point is also a good time to involve your quality assurance department (testers). The quality assurance team can test the software against both the user requirements and the software specification.

FREEZING THE USER INTERFACE The user interface freeze (UI freeze) is necessary so that the developer(s) developing the help file and manual can start finalizing the documentation on how to use the application. This milestone is also helpful for keeping the development process moving because it forces the decision makers (the developers, analysts, and business participants) to decide on the look and feel of the application and specific menu and window designs.

DEVELOPING THE HELP FILE AND MANUAL Once the UI freeze occurs, you can dedicate some resources to documenting how the user is going to use the application. If you are a single developer, this step obviously cannot start until after the development is done. In a single-developer environment, this is likely to delay the deployment of the application.

FREEZING FEATURES Put simply, no new features. This freeze date is the final deadline for functional changes to the application. Debugging continues until deployment.

DEBUGGING SOFTWARE In the final debugging phase, the development team thoroughly tests every feature and fixes any anomalies. These tests include unit and integration testing. In unit testing, each developer tests his or her own work. In integration testing, each developer tests his or her work integrated with everyone else's work, including the final help file.

Testing Software

In many shops, the project manager moves control of the software from the programmers to the quality assurance group, along with the user requirements and software manual. The quality assurance team conducts initial acceptance testing to verify that the application is stable enough to begin a formal test cycle. This development period is dedicated to resolving existing discrepancies in the application and verifying the application against the user requirements. (You learn more about testing later in this chapter.)

User Acceptance

The business analyst and project manager present the application to the executive sponsor. Usually, the system architect demonstrates the software for the executive sponsor. Development participants usually do not need to attend the acceptance meeting because they have seen the software all throughout the development cycle. At this point, you can have the executive sponsor sign an acceptance contract that lists the critical features needed for acceptance of the software gathered in the first steps.

Deploying the Application

Deploying the application is, of course, the final step in developing an application. Do yourself and your client a favor and take some time to develop a fallback plan in the event you deploy the software and something goes wrong. If, for example, the company for which you are developing software has an existing software application, create a backup plan to return to it in case the software you are developing fails for any reason. If your clients have a manual procedure, make sure that they are prepared to return to it if needed.

Conventions

You should develop or adopt a coding convention. Perhaps consider developing or adopting both a general coding convention and an ObjectPAL-specific coding convention. For more information on coding conventions, refer to Appendix A.

Documenting Your Application

You can employ many methodologies for documenting a large software project. The following sections describe some of the documentation I use when creating large applications. Should you create all these documents for every project? No. The size and importance of the project determines how much documentation is called for.

Business Proposal

Sometimes known as the project charter, the business proposal contains the general information about your company, values, mission, and very high-level information about the project or projects you are going to deliver for the client.

Project Plan

The project plan contains the detail steps needed to complete the project, who is assigned to each task, how much each task costs to complete, and more. One popular tool for creating such a plan today is Microsoft Project. Figure 1-1 shows a Gantt chart of a typical medium-sized custom database business application.

Creating a Software Developer's Guide

A software developer's guide is a manual written by programmers for programmers. Its intention is to aid the coding and debugging of the application. In addition, you can use this guide to document programmer procedures such as how to use whatever versioning software you use and overall design considerations. Additionally, the software developer's guide is a good place to put miscellaneous notes that do not belong in any other document.

The software developer's guide often includes a section titled "Application Style Guide," which documents how the application should look and feel. As you will learn in Chapter 3, you should be consistent in how you design software. In a multiprogrammer environment, consistency is difficult to accomplish without a style guide. Either as part of the software developer's guide or separately, you should document the user interface of your application. This is especially important on large applications.

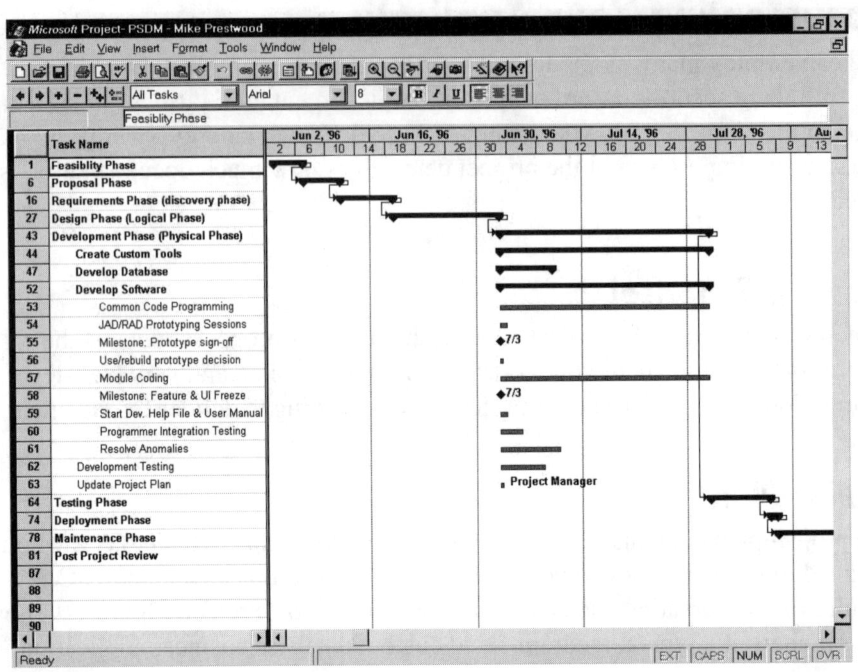

FIGURE 1-1 Microsoft Project showing a project plan in a Gantt chart view

Using Paradox's Visual Database Designer

Paradox comes with a very handy tool, the Visual Database Designer (select Tools | Data Model Designer). With it, you can easily document local and remote databases. Figure 1-2 shows a data model of an invoicing system using the sample tables that ship with Paradox. You can even print the data model and put it in a common location accessible by all programmers.

Creating a CRUD Matrix

CRUD is an acronym that stands for create, read, update, and delete. A *CRUD matrix* documents what objects (forms, reports, libraries, and scripts) access what data elements in a database. It can help you test your software on large projects and is critical for maintaining a large application. If you make changes in one form or script, a CRUD matrix can tell you what other forms, libraries, scripts, and reports will need to be tested.

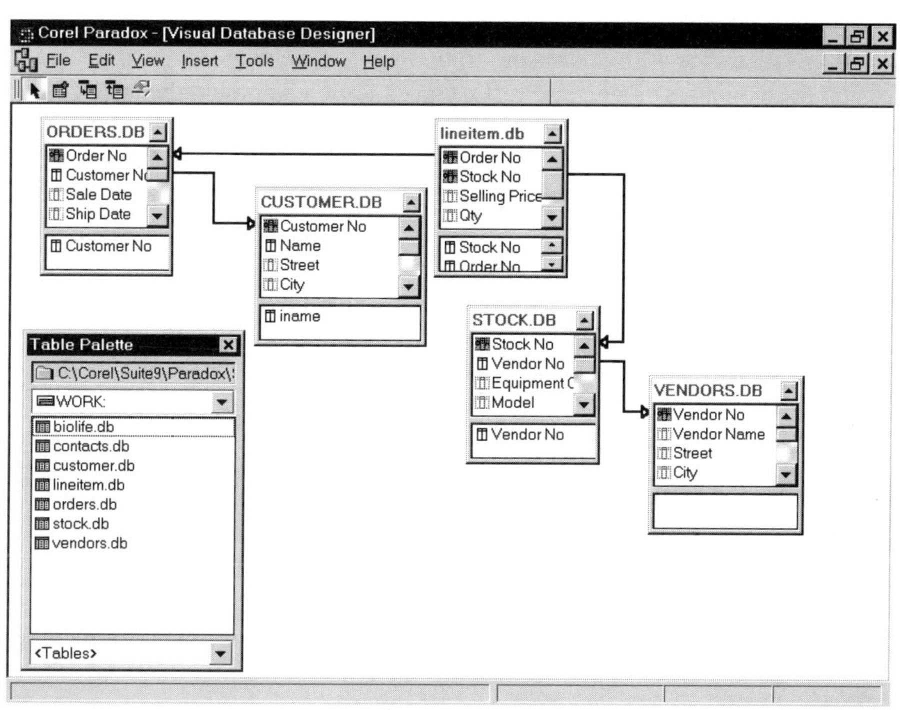

FIGURE 1-2 The data model from an invoicing system

Testing

The *alpha test* cycle is the preliminary testing of a new product in which research and development are still in progress. The *beta test* is a stage in product testing in which testing is done with actual users in the users' environment. The following sections offer some hints and tips on testing your completed application.

Creating Test Data

Test data is especially created to test the operation of a given program. Usually, one or more hand-calculated results or otherwise known results are associated with test data so that the program under testing may be validated. Also, data known to be invalid is used as test data.

Developing Test Scenarios

Develop test scenarios with your users so that you can standardize your tests. After you develop a set of standard tests, you can often automate the tests with automated testing software. This type of software is similar to the Windows recorder provided with Windows 3.0 and 3.1. Automated testing software can record mouse movements and keyboard presses.

Unit Testing

Unit testing is the testing of a unit. A unit is a recognized section of a program—for example, a form or group of forms. The programmer who programmed the unit usually performs the unit testing.

Integration Testing

After all programmers are done writing their modules, the modules need to be integrated and tested. This phase of testing tests how well all the units and modules fit together. On large projects, you often go through a build process where you bring all the application objects together for testing. This can include all the Paradox objects from the various programmers and a new database. This is where versioning software such as Intersolv's PVCS comes in handy because it can keep track of all the latest objects ready for the build process while the programmers continue coding.

Regression Testing

Regression tests are performed on a previously verified program whenever it is extended or corrected. In other words, you test all the bugs that were fixed. This step guarantees that previously identified bugs do not reappear in the program.

Testing the Boundaries

Testing boundaries is also known as *stress testing*. Stress testing is ensuring through trial operations that the program or system will continue to perform reliably in spite of data inaccuracies and extraordinary data volumes. Try your application with very large tables and empty tables. Run it on systems with the least amount of memory Paradox will run on—4MB. Log any errors you come across for final testing. Finally, play a game of "what if." For example,

- What if the user uses a corrupt table?
- What if the table gets moved or deleted?
- What if the user starts up using the wrong working directory?

Try to add your own questions to this list.

TIP *If you are a single developer, try to find someone else to exercise your program. As the programmer, you have certain ideas of how a user will use your application. These ideas probably apply to about half the users.*

Running Every Feature Three Times

Test each feature three times. Sometimes errors in logic don't show up until the second or even the third time through a sequence of events.

Protecting Your Application

Protecting your application means that users can't edit your application, even if they own Paradox. In addition, you want to restrict the users' movements through your application. You don't want users to exit without your permission. Also, you don't want users to be able to alter your applications. To protect your applications, you need to do only two things: password-protect your data tables and deliver your forms, reports, libraries, and scripts.

Delivering Your Application

The final step in the development cycle is to *deliver* all the forms, scripts, libraries, and reports. In ObjectPAL, it's the process of compiling an object for a special Paradox-only dynamic link library.

Summary

In this chapter you learned that Paradox is a database development front end with an object-based programming language added to it called ObjectPAL. You need to use the right tool for every job. If you're building a game, a tool other than Paradox would be better suited. Paradox is best left to developing custom business database applications.

You also learned that to successfully develop a large application means that you must have a defined process in place. Paradox is just a part of the complete software development life cycle. This chapter touched on many parts of the full software development life cycle and introduced you to many of the basic concepts needed to start developing your own software development methodology by encouraging you to plan, document, and fully test the software you develop.

CHAPTER 2

Tables and Developing

The *table* is a tool that you, the developer, use to store data. In your continuing quest to study the fundamentals of design, this chapter discusses constructing a database; that is, creating tables with relationships in mind. It discusses all three types of database relationships and their variations: the one-to-one (1:1) relationship, the one-to-many (1:M) relationship, and the many-to-many (M:M) relationship. For local table users, this chapter also helps you decide which table structure to use, namely, Paradox or dBASE. Finally, this chapter covers a few of the interesting characteristics of both dBASE and Paradox tables. First, however, consider the importance of aliases to the developer.

Aliases

In the past, when you developed an application and moved the data, you had to redefine all your links (a link establishes a relationship between tables by connecting corresponding fields). If you moved one of the tables to another directory path, you created a big problem. The usual solution was to break and then create the link again. An *alias* is the name you assign to a directory path and implement to solve this problem. Paradox uses aliases to refer to a location of files, such as a directory or to a specific database on a SQL server using either the BDE's native drivers or ODBC. You manage your aliases by selecting Tools | Alias Manager. In addition to using two types of native drivers (file-based and server-based), you can use ODBC drivers with the BDE.

In Paradox table terms, the location that is pointed to by the alias often is called a *database*. Although aliases might be new to you, they are a great time-saver. They make using hundreds of tables, queries, and forms in many different directories and on different servers manageable. There's tremendous value in having the capability to select File | Open | Table and browse through the aliases that you set up. In addition, you can use aliases in your code to refer to files. If you move the files, you just need to define the new path in the alias.

Using an alias offers the following benefits:

- Long pathnames are shortened to a single user-defined word.
- Your applications are instantly relocatable. ObjectPAL code can refer to objects by means of an alias. For example, when the path of your tables changes, redefine the alias to point to the new path.

- You can use multiple sets of data with the same application. After an application is set up with an alias, you can redefine your alias to point to a different path; instantly, you are working with a different set of data. This makes it possible to develop an application on your local drive and then switch the tables it uses to network tables and even to a SQL server with little modification.

You can set up aliases on a system by selecting Tools | Alias Manager or by using the *BDE Administrator*. You can use the Aliases tab of the BDE Administrator to easily browse through existing aliases and set the paths of existing aliases or add a new alias. I find it easier to use the BDE Administrator to add and alter aliases (see Figure 2-1).

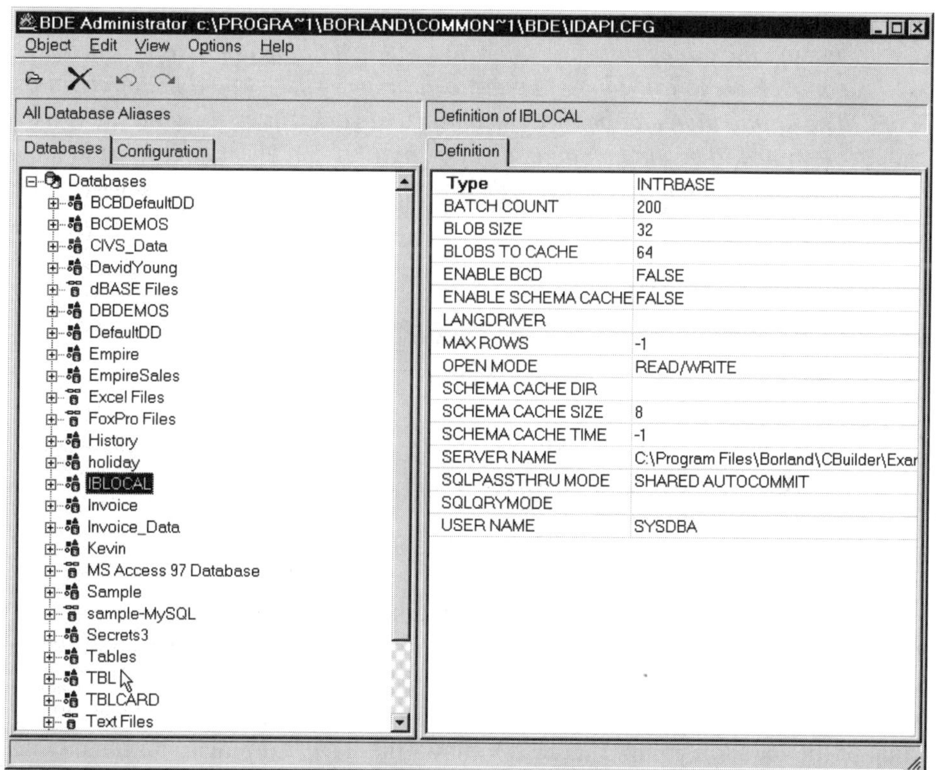

FIGURE 2-1 The Databases tab from the BDE Administrator

When you're ready to start creating your tables, you need to decide where you want to place them. You have two choices: the current working directory or another directory. If you're developing a single-user application, it makes sense to put all the files in the same directory if you will never need to move the tables to a network directory. If you are developing what might become a multiuser application, consider separating the tables from the rest of the application and using an alias to refer to the tables. Using an alias gives you the ability to move your tables to a network directory later, if needed. Because Paradox doesn't search for a table, you must develop your application with tables in the current working directory or use an alias. Hard-coding table paths usually is a mistake because it then becomes more difficult to move the tables.

TIP *Put your tables in a directory different from the one that contains the forms, reports, and libraries. Use an alias to refer to the tables. This makes your application instantly a network-compatible application by making the tables relocatable. When you install the application onsite, you simply have to ask where to put the data and where to put the application. The application can be local or on the network. Place the data files where they need to be, and change the alias path. If you eventually want to move your data onto a SQL server, then you will have less code to rewrite.*

Standard Aliases

When you create a standard alias (see Figure 2-2), you can use one of these driver types:

- **PARADOX** Paradox, for .DB tables
- **DBASE** dBASE and FoxPro, for .DBF tables
- **ASCIIDRV** ASCII text, for .TXT tables

The Alias Manager available within Paradox by selecting Tools | Alias Manager only allows you to configure the path attribute of a standard alias. To configure the other settings (for example, for a Paradox driver), you use the BDE Administrator. The BDE Administrator is available via a shortcut in the Utilities group of the Paradox group. Figure 2-3 shows the BDE Administrator displaying the Paradox driver settings.

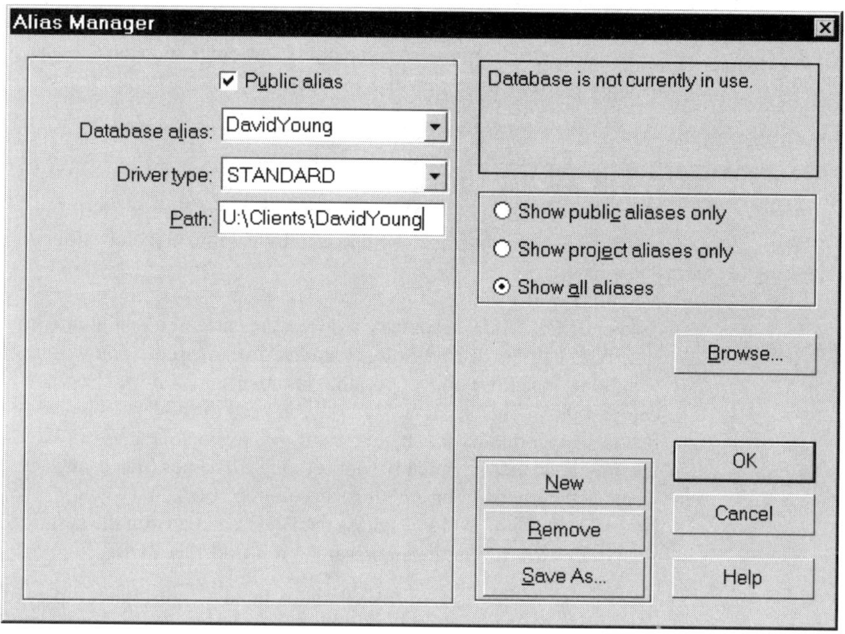

FIGURE 2-2 Alias Manager showing a standard alias

The following table lists the settings of the Paradox driver. For other driver settings, refer to the BDE Administrator help.

Parameter	Description
VERSION	Internal version number of the Paradox driver.
TYPE	Type of server to which this driver helps you connect. Can be SERVER (SQL server) or FILE (standard, file-based server).
NET DIR	The directory location of the Paradox network control file PDOXUSRS.NET. The active NET DIR parameter is stored in the Paradox section of the BDE configuration file and has precedence over any other NET DIR parameters that may be stored in older 16-bit configuration files, or in the System Init section of the current configuration file, or in the Registry. These other NET DIR entries will have no effect. To access a Paradox table on a network drive, the active NET DIR parameter in the Paradox section of the BDE configuration file must point to a network drive and folder in common to all users.

Parameter	Description
LANGDRIVER	Language driver used to determine table sort order and character set. [available drivers]. US default: 'ascii' ANSI (DBWINUS0).
LEVEL	Type of table format used to create temporary Paradox tables. Level 7 - Paradox for Windows 32-bit tables Level 5 - Paradox 5.0 tables Level 4 - STANDARD table format introduced in Paradox 4.0 Level 3 - Compatible table format used by Paradox 3.5 and earlier versions Default: Level 7 To use BLOB fields, secondary indexes, and strict referential integrity, specify either Paradox level 4 or Paradox level 5 tables. You will probably want to use the lowest level possible in order to maximize backward compatibility. Choose level 7 only if you need the advanced indexing features supported by that table format. For example, Paradox 7 tables are the only level that completely support long filenames (this is an issue when dealing with RI or lookups across directories). **Note:** The default level is 7 unless the BDE is already on the system. The setup will leave the settings unchanged if it finds the BDE.
BLOCK SIZE	Size of disk blocks used to store Paradox table records, in multiples of 1,024 bytes. Valid settings depend on the table format: Level 5 and 7 – 1,024, 2,048, 4,096, 16,384, and 32,768 Level 3 and 4 – 1,024, 2,048, and 4,096 Default: 2,048
FILL FACTOR	Percentage of current disk block that must be filled before Paradox will allocate another disk block for index files. Can be any integer ranging from 1 to 100. Default: 95. **Note:** Smaller values offer better performance but increase the size of indexes. Larger values give smaller index files but increase the time needed to create an index.
STRICTINTEGRTY	Specifies whether Paradox tables can be modified using applications that do not support referential integrity (such as Paradox 4.0). For example, if True you will be unable to change a table with referential integrity using Paradox 4.0; if False, you can change the table, but you risk the integrity of your data. Default: True.

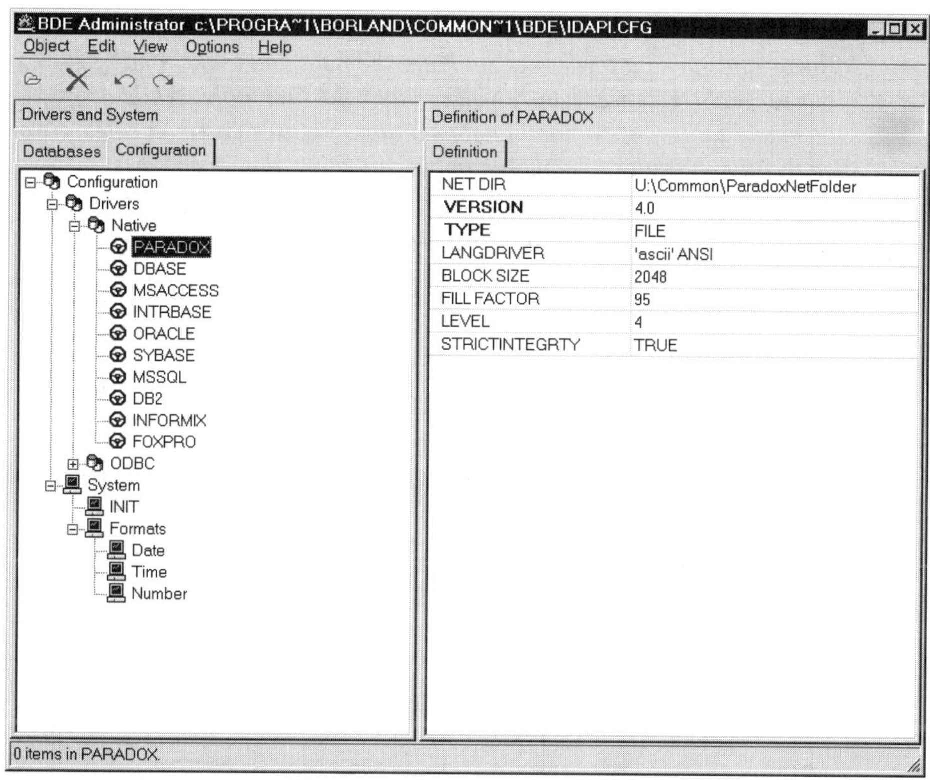

FIGURE 2-3 Paradox driver settings in the BDE Administrator

Public and Project Aliases

You can create either a *public* or *project* alias. Project aliases are stored in the PDOXWORK.CFG file, which is loaded whenever you change working directories. You can think of project aliases as aliases that belong to a certain project stored in a specific working directory.

TIP *If you are developing an application using local tables and you know you are eventually going to move the data onto a SQL server, then do yourself a favor and spend a few hours studying the field and table naming rules of your target SQL server before you create your first table. While creating your local tables, use a naming convention that uses common rules. If you use the naming rules in common between the two database types, then you will save yourself time when you move your data to the SQL server because SQL servers often have different naming rules from the naming rules in Paradox.*

SQL Aliases

The database engine provides several SQL native drivers including InterBase, Oracle, Microsoft SQL, Sybase, DB2, and Informix. These native drivers generally offer greater control and speed over many ODBC drivers. When both a native and several ODBC drivers exist for a SQL server (for example, as with Oracle), you might wish to do some experiments with them to determine which will perform best for your application architecture. Figure 2-4 displays an Oracle SQL alias in the Alias Manager.

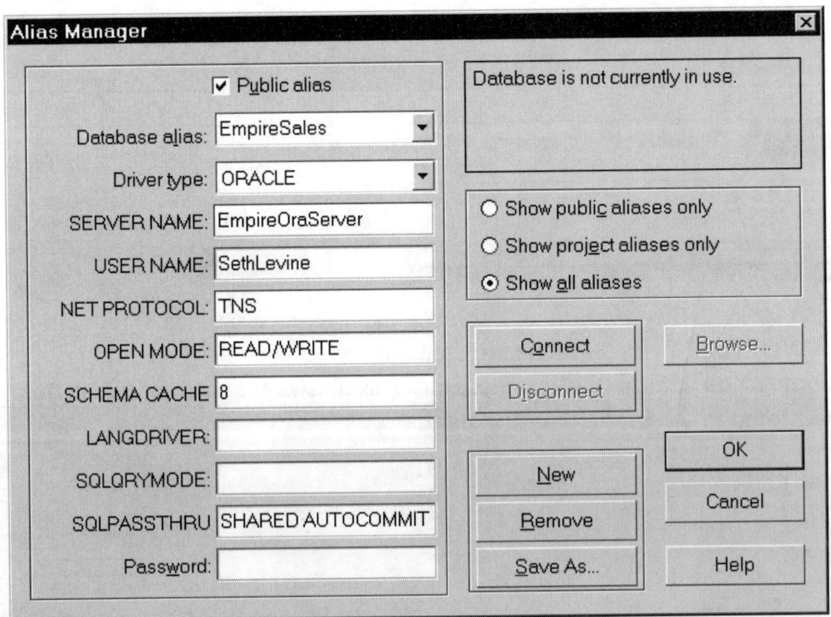

FIGURE 2-4 Alias Manager showing an Oracle SQL alias

ODBC Aliases

You can make use of any ODBC data source when you create an alias (see Figure 2-5). To create an ODBC alias, first you must use the ODBC Administrator to add, delete, and configure ODBC drivers or data sources. This command appears when you right-click an existing ODBC alias in the Databases tab of the BDE Administrator or the ODBC driver on the Configuration tab. It displays the ODBC administration utility provided by your ODBC driver vendor.

To make use of an ODBC driver, follow these steps:

1. Add the ODBC data source to your system using the ODBC Administrator.
2. Define the DSN (data source name). Note that if AutoODBC in the BDE Administrator (under Configuration | System | Init) is set to True, then any ODBC DSN automatically shows up as an alias in Paradox. The default is set to True when installing Paradox onto a machine that does not have the BDE already installed.
3. Set up an Alias that uses the data source.

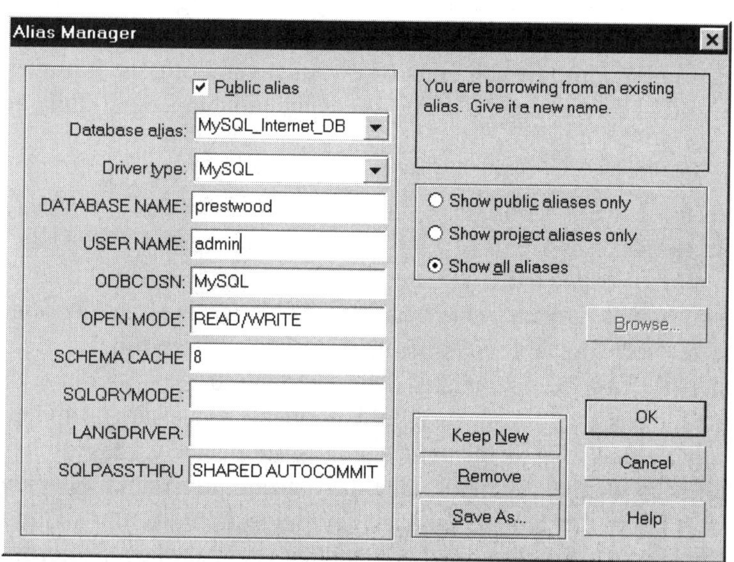

FIGURE 2-5 Alias Manager showing an ODBC alias

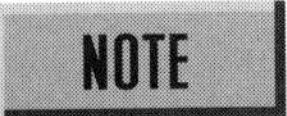

If you add an ODBC data source, you must define its DSN before you can connect to that database.

Primary Keys

Paradox tables enable you to manage many types of data in its fields. A *field* in Paradox terms is a single value in a record—for example, City. The entire City column of a table is considered the City field. In addition to standard types of data, such as text, number, date, and currency, you can store a variety of data, such as graphic, OLE, and binary. With Paradox table structures, you have a variety of data types including Time, TimeStamp, BCD, and Autoincrement.

The *structure* of a table is the arrangement of fields in a table: their data types, indexes, validity checks, and so on. Now, more than ever, deciding on table structure and relationships is a crucial element of developing an application. Develop tables in two steps: decide on data components and then decide on the table relationships. The first step in deciding table relationships is to decide which fields need to be a part of the primary key.

A *record* is the horizontal row in a Paradox table that represents a set of data for that item, such as a person's address information. A primary key sorts your table and makes each record unique. A primary key isn't required but it is highly recommended. In fact, I suggest that every table you create should contain a primary key. A key on a Paradox table orders records and ensures unique records, and allows *referential integrity*, which is a way of ensuring that the ties between similar data in separate tables can't be broken. Referential integrity is defined at the table level in Paradox. Establishing a key has several effects. It prevents duplicate records, sorts records, enables use of the table in a detail link, and speeds general access to the table.

A Paradox primary key can consist of more than one field (up to 16). These fields are treated as one—a composite. A *composite key* or *index* is a key or index composed of two or more fields of a table. A composite primary key must be made up of the first fields of the table. Use composite key fields when a table contains no single field in which every value is unique. Together, the combination of the fields in the key sorts the table. Define the primary key from the first field through however many fields it takes to make each record unique.

When a table has a composite key field, duplicate values are permitted in an individual key field as long as the values are not duplicated across all the key fields. In other words, the key fields, taken as a group, must uniquely identify a record. To sort tables that have composite key fields, Paradox starts with the first field and then sorts the following fields. Paradox's primary key also promotes normalized table structures (more on this later in this chapter).

Should you go crazy and key most or all the fields in a table? No. Your goal is always to find the least number of fields that will make each record unique.

Primary Keys and Secondary Indexes

An *index* is a file that determines the order in which a table displays records. It also enables objects such as UIObjects, TCursors, and Table variables to point to a specific record. A *secondary index* is an extra index primarily used for locating a specific record, linking two tables, querying, and sorting. Paradox tables can have a primary key and as many secondary indexes as you want, whereas a dBASE table can have only indexes—that is, files with .MDX or .NDX extensions. In general, you can refer to any file that sorts a table as an index.

Tables need indexes to speed them up. When using Paradox tables, get used to the idea of creating maintained and case-sensitive secondary indexes. Accepting and doing this simple step will greatly improve the overall speed of your application—especially queries. When you move up to writing applications that access SQL servers, remember that creating indexes also speeds them up.

Using a Primary Key

To demonstrate the proper use of primary keys and secondary indexes, we will develop a typical address table. In the following example development cycle, you will see how a table may change over time as you realize what truly makes each record unique. This is a natural process. Although it is a good idea to finalize your table structures as early in the development process as possible, you will learn from this example that you can finalize your table structures at any stage during the development process.

In a typical table consisting of addresses, you might index on the combination of first and last name. This combination of first name and last name makes every record in the table unique. The following is a typical address table with * representing the composite primary key:

```
1:  First Name*
2:  Last Name*
3:  Address
4:  City
5:  State
6:  Zip
7:  Phone
```

This table, however, first sorts by first name and then by last name. Ann Martinez will come before Bobby Brown. For a more standard sort, you might sort by last name and then first name. If you need to search by first name, create a secondary index that consists of first names so that you can search and sort by a person's last name, first name, or last and first names. The following is a typical address table with a more standard sort order. It has a secondary index represented by **.

```
1:  Last Name*
2:  First Name*     **
3:  Address
4:  City
5:  State
6:  Zip
7:  Phone
```

After entering records for a few days, you may discover that you have two identical names, such as John Smith. Because the combination of last name and then first name no longer makes each record unique, you come to the conclusion that it is a good idea to include the person's middle initial. With large amounts of data, you might even include the street address. This takes into account people with the same name, but who live at separate addresses. It also enables you to keep track of people's home and work addresses. Following is an example of a fully unique address table with a secondary index on First Name:

```
1:  Last Name*
2:  First Name*          **
3:  Middle Initial*
4:  Address*
5:  City
6:  State
7:  Zip
8:  Phone
```

In most cases, keying from the first field through however many fields needed to make each record unique, works. This technique is awkward at times, however. Consider the previous case in which you have included one's address to force each record to be unique. The unique primary key now contains two types of data (a person's name and address). The key now consists of four fields and therefore takes up more disk space then a key with fewer fields. A different approach, perhaps slightly more elegant, involves using a single, unique field entry, such as a Social Security Number field to make each record unique and using secondary indexes for alternate sorting and searching. Following is an example of a fully unique address table with two composite secondary indexes:

```
1:   SSN*
2:   Last Name              1 **        2 ***
3:   First Name             2 **        1 ***
4:   Middle Initial         3 **
5:   Address
6:   City
7:   State
8:   Zip
9:   Phone
```

If this table is developed for the government, then you might discover that the government actually reuses Social Security numbers. Therefore, if you need to keep a history, you may need to find another unique identifier, such as Birth Date:

```
1:   Social Security Number*
2:   Birth Date*
3:   Last Name              1 **        2 ***
4:   First Name             2 **        1 ***
5:   Middle Initial         3 **
6:   Address
7:   City
8:   State
9:   Zip
10:   Phone
```

If, for example, it is illegal to ask for a customer's Social Security number in your state, then the preceding table structure will not work. Because of a business rule, you might have to find another keying solution. The following presents a final solution, an autoincrementing key or artificial key:

```
1:   ID*
2:   Last Name              1 **        2 ***
3:   First Name             2 **        1 ***
4:   Middle Initial         3 **
5:   Address
6:   City
7:   State
```

```
8:  Zip
9:  Phone
10:  Social Security Number
11:  Birth Date
```

In this final solution, a random unique identifier is used to make each record unique. Although this artificial key is not preferred, the Autoincrement field would work well in this situation. The Autoincrement field type is a special field type that contains unique noneditable numbers. Paradox begins with the number 1 and adds one number for each record in the table. This field type can be very useful when designing tables. In particular, it is useful for adding an artificial, unique, primary key to a table.

NOTE *Autoincrement fields have the same type as a long integer. This is important to know when linking with detail tables.*

In general, try to avoid this final solution and use it only as a last resort. Using an artificial key generally is considered a bad idea. Have you ever gone into a store and been asked whether you know your customer number? Sometimes it's your phone number or your Social Security number, but sometimes it's a random number that you were expected to remember (and you probably didn't). If you use this last solution, make sure that you build an easy-to-use, effective way to quickly look up a customer's ID number.

As you can see, deciding which fields to include in a table is only half the battle. The other half of the battle is deciding what makes each record unique.

Relating Tables

The following material reviews the concepts and theories behind setting up table relationships. If you need help linking tables with the data model, refer to Paradox's manuals. Advanced database developers will appreciate this review of table relationships.

When you hear developers talk about table relationships, you hear things such as "the two tables are linked in a one-to-many." What they really are describing is the theoretical number of records possible in each table. The term *one-to-many* translates into the following: For every unique record in the first table, the second table can have one or more records. Examine a few cases to clearly understand relating tables, the terminology, and the theory behind relating tables.

The One-to-One Relationship (1:1)

Suppose that you're working with two tables that are both keyed on the Social Security number (the field name is SSN). One table contains personal information; the other contains medical information. You want to pull data from both of them and display that information as though it came from one database. You need to relate the two tables based on a common field or common fields—in this case, SSN.

After you relate these two tables in a 1:1 relationship, the medical database will display the correct record whenever you display a record from the personal database. Whenever you want to relate two tables, they must have one or more fields in common.

Now for the theory. Although you may not see a good reason that you can't dump all the information from both tables into a single table, there is one. In general database theory, it's a good idea to group data into smaller tables based on logical splits of the data such as address, employee, and medical information.

If you dump all the data into one huge table, managing the data can get out of control and the tables can grow unnecessarily. Imagine a table with address, employee, and medical information in it. It is a single table with perhaps 50 fields in it. Every time you create an entry and store just address information or work information, the database reserves room on your hard drive for all 50 fields, even though the majority of the fields are empty!

Now, imagine that this table is broken into three tables: ADDRESS.DB, EMPLOYEE.DB, and MEDICAL.DB. If you enter a record into the address table, no room is necessarily reserved in the employee and medical tables. Breaking large tables into several tables can save disk space and makes working with your data faster and easier to analyze.

An Example of a 1:1 Relationship

A 1:1 relationship is really just a large table split into multiple tables and linked on a common field or fields. In the following table relationship, for every record in Customer, there can be only one record in Custnote (see Figure 2-6).

The One-to-Many Relationship (1:M)

A *master table* in a multitable relationship is the primary table of your data model. If there is only one table in your data model, it is the master table. A *detail table* in a multitable relationship is the table whose records are subordinate to those of the

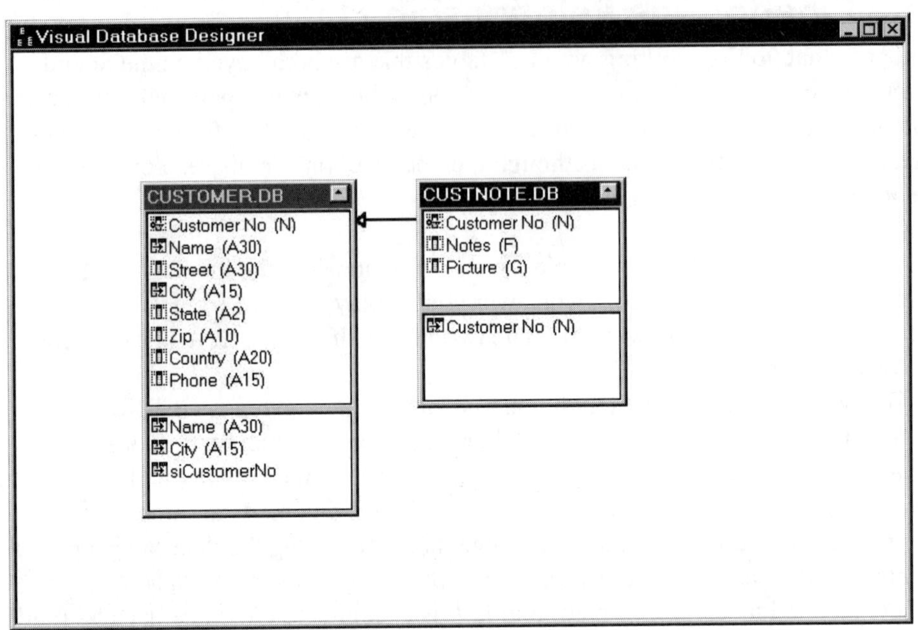

FIGURE 2-6 A 1:1 relationship in the Visual Database Designer

master table. A detail table is also called a *slave* table, a *child* table, or a *many* table. A clearer way to state this is as follows: for every record in the master table, there can be many records in the detail table.

An Example of a 1:M Relationship

When you look at an invoice from a store, you typically are seeing a master table and its detail records; the end product of tables set up in a series of 1:1 and 1:M relationships. This next example shows two tables from a typical invoicing system. For every order in the Orders table, there can be many line items in the Lineitem table. Note that the two tables are linked on Order No and that the Lineitem table uses a composite primary key.

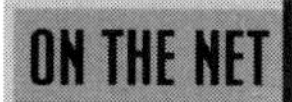

The form and data models that demonstrate this table relationship are at http://prestwood.com/forums/paradox/books/official/files/dm_1-m.fsl and http://prestwood.com/forums/paradox/books/official/files/dm_1-m.dm.

```
Orders.db                  Lineitem.db
1:  Order No* —>>          Order No*
2:  Customer No            Stock No*
3:  Sale Date              Selling Price
4:  Ship Date              Qty
5:  Total Invoice
6:  Amount Paid
7:  Balance Due
8:  Payment Method
```

The Many-to-One Relationship (M:1)

Usually when discussing table relationships, you're talking about the primary key. More specifically, however, you should be talking about the fields on which the tables are linked. The next example does not use an index on the first table; it demonstrates a M:1 relationship. At first glance, this may seem like a 1:1 relationship, but on closer inspection it actually is a M:1. You can have many records in Orders with the same Customer No for any one Customer No in the Customer table. The Customer No field in the Orders table in this case is called a *foreign key*.

The form and data models that demonstrate this table relationship are at http://prestwood.com/forums/paradox/books/official/files/dm_m-1.fsl and http://prestwood.com/forums/paradox/books/official/files/dm_m-1.dm.

```
Orders.db                  Customer.db
1:  Order No*
2:  Customer No <<—        Customer No*
3:  Sale Date              Name
4:  Ship Date              Street
5:  Total Invoice          City
6:  Amount Paid            State
7:  Balance Due            Zip
8:  Payment Method         Country
9:                         Phone
```

The Many-to-Many Relationship (M:M)

A many-to-many (M:M) relationship is when two tables share a common field or fields. Both can have multiple values based on the field(s) in common. Following is an example of a M:M relationship:

```
Phone.db                  Credit.db
1:  SSN*   <<—>>          SSN*
2:  Phone Desc*           Credit Card*
3:  Phone                 Number
4:                        Expiration
5:                        Credit Limit
```

The preceding M:M relationship becomes clearer when you add an intermediate table and make the relationship a M:1:M (see the "An Example of a M:1:M Relationship" section later).

Relating Three Tables

Now that you understand the basic three table relationships, let's add a third table to the scenario and study some case examples.

An Example of a 1:1:1 Relationship

Earlier in this chapter, I mentioned breaking a large table full of address, employee, and medical information into three tables: ADDRESS.DB, EMPLOYEE.DB and MEDICAL.DB. The following is that table relationship.

The files DM_1-1.FSL and DM_1-1.DM are available at http://prestwood.com/forums/paradox/books/official/. These files demonstrate this table relationship.

```
1:  Address.db         Employee.db              Medical.db
2:  SSN* —>           SSN* —>              SSN*
3:  Last Name          Department               Male or Female
4:  First Name         Desk Phone               Color of Hair
5:  Address 1          Manager SSN              Color of Eyes
6:  Address 2          Start Date               Weight (lbs)
7:  City               Salary (per year)        Height
8:  State              Shift Start Time         Blood type
9:  Zip                Shift End Time
```

An Example of a M:1:M Relationship

The next example is a follow-up to the M:M relationship presented earlier. This three-way table relationship is really just two 1:M relationships. For every record in the Address table, there can be many records in the Phone table and in the Credit table.

```
Phone.db                Address                 Credit.db
1:   SSN* <<—           SSN*             —>>    SSN*
2:   Phone Desc*        Last Name               Credit Card*
3:   Phone              First Name              Number
4:                      Address 1               Expiration
5:                      Address 2               Credit Limit
6:                      City
7:                      State
8:                      Zip
```

A Deceiving Example of a M:1:M Relationship

As stated earlier, a typical invoicing system is simply a series of 1:1 and 1:M table relationships. The next example is of a M:1:M relationship. More precisely, it is a M:1 between Orders and Customer and a 1:M between Orders and Lineitem. There can be many records in the Orders table for every one record in the Customer table. For every record in the Orders table, there can be many records in the Lineitem table. The Customer No field in the Orders table is a *foreign key;* that is, the key of another table.

```
1:   Orders.db                        Customer.db       Lineitem.db
2:   Order No* ——————----------——>>                    Order No*
3:   Customer No <<———                Customer No*      Stock No*
4:   Sale Date                        Name              Selling Price
5:   Ship Date                        Street            Qty
6:   Total Invoice                    City
7:   Amount Paid                      State
8:   Balance Due                      Zip
9:   Payment Method                   Country
10:                                   Phone
```

An Example of a 1:M:M Relationship

The next example is a 1:M:M (or more precisely, a 1:M with a 1:M). This example uses the same tables as the preceding example, but it views the data differently. A secondary index is used on the Orders table.

```
Customer.db         Orders.db          Lineitems.db
                    Order No*    —>>   Order No*
Customer No* ->>    Customer No**      Stock No*
Name                Sale Date          Selling Price
Street              Ship Date          Qty
City                Ship Via           Total
State               Total Invoice
Zip                 Amount Paid
Country             Balance Due
Phone               Payment Method
```

A good technique to use when you present this much data is to show the user only one or two identifying fields from each table and to use another page or form to show the details.

An Example of a 1:M:1 Relationship

Take a look at a table relationship that often throws developers off. In this scenario, you are developing the table structure for a clothing manufacturer. You have two tables: types of material and outfit patterns (MATERIAL.DB and PATTERNS.DB). You need to connect any one record in the Material table to any one record in the Patterns table. Initially, this sounds like a M:M, but it is not. After you start developing this table relationship, you will discover that you need a third intermediate table, as in the following:

```
Material.db         Outfits.db         Patterns.db
Cloth ID*  ->>      Cloth ID*
Cloth Desc          Pattern ID* <<—    Pattern ID*
Cost                Total cost         Pattern Desc
                                       Cost
```

This three-table relationship is a 1:M:1 relationship. For every record in the Material table, you can have many records in the Outfits table; and for every record in the Patterns table, you can have many records in the Outfits table.

The Recursive Relationship

The last table relationship to be demonstrated is a *recursive relationship*. A recursive relationship is when a single table is used as though it were two tables. In certain table structures, a single table contains all the fields needed to link to itself in a 1:M relationship. For example, take a look at the following table:

```
Employee.db
1:   SSN*
2:   Department
3:   Desk Phone
4:   Manager SSN     **
5:   Start Date
6:   Salary (per year)
7:   Shift Start Time
8:   Shift End Time
```

Any one Manager SSN field can link to many records defined by the SSN field. To do this relationship, you need a primary key and a secondary index. Putting a table multiple times in a data model enables you to do a recursive relationship. To aid in visualizing this relationship, use a *table alias* in the data model.

In a data model, a table alias is an alternate name for a table. A table alias enables you to rename a table in a data model. This enables you to refer to the table in the data model by the table alias rather than the table name. This is important in ObjectPAL when you need to refer to a table in a data model. Rather than referring to the table name, you can refer to the table alias. This way, if you change the underlying table, you do not have to change your code.

Table aliases are also helpful when using a recursive relationship in a data model. You can give the same table that appears multiple times in your data model different table aliases. This isn't required, but can have the advantage of clarifying your data model.

The recursive relationship is easier to understand if you look at a variation of it, as follows:

```
Emp2.db
1:   Manager SSN*
2:   Employee SSN*           **
3:   Department
4:   Desk Phone
5:   Start Date
6:   Salary (per year)
7:   Shift Start Time
8:   Shift End Time
```

Now you can easily see that the combination of Manager SSN and Employee SSN makes each record unique. In addition, there is a secondary index on Employee SSN, so you can still use the table in the same manner as the previous example.

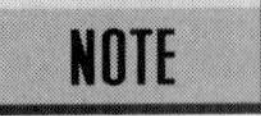

Another technique for doing a recursive relationship in Paradox is to use a live query in the data model and link from the query to the table. For more information about live queries, refer to Paradox's manuals.

Normalizing Data

Now that you have laid down a foundation for creating and relating tables, move onto normalizing data. The process of normalizing table structures arranges data to minimize data redundancy. This, in turn, usually leads to a database that uses less disk space, is easier to extract data from, and is sometimes faster. When you normalize data, you decompose one big flat file table into multiple relational tables. Each record includes the smallest number of fields necessary to establish a category. Rather than dumping all possible fields into a large table, normalized tables distribute information over many tables. This saves disk space each time a user doesn't need to use a particular set of fields. In addition, normalized tables provide more flexibility in terms of analysis and reduced errors in data since data is stored only once. Normalized data should be your goal at all times.

In this method of organizing information, you group fields into categories in which each category contains the least number of fields necessary to establish a unique group. A normalized data model is not required in Paradox, but it is highly recommended. The normalization process discussed next is broken into three steps: remove identical records, remove repeating groups, and move fields that do not relate to the key to another table. These three steps are commonly known as the first three normal forms. Although several other rules for normalizing data are common, it is generally agreed that the first three normal forms are sufficient for most database applications.

First Normal Form: Remove Identical Records

To put a table in first normal form, you remove all identical records. When you key a table in Paradox, you remove all duplicate records. (See the section, "Using a Primary Key," earlier in this chapter for a complete discussion.)

Second Normal Form: Remove Repeating Groups

To put a table in second normal form, you remove repeating groups—a process that is more difficult to explain. An example is used to help explain this step. In a traditional name and address table, you store a person's telephone number as part of the main table. In today's fast-paced, high-technology world, someone can have many telephone, fax, and communication numbers. A person can have several home and work numbers, as well as fax and modem numbers—perhaps even Internet and CompuServe account numbers. You could guess the maximum number of potential fields and put them in the table. (Typically, developers will put Home, Work, and Fax fields in their tables.) Some users might have no numbers, however, and some might have all three. Because when a record is created, database products allocate disk space for all fields defined, this can be a waste of disk space.

In addition, this scheme does not work when you need to have four or more numbers. Data with the potential for so many telephone numbers should be normalized. Again, the second rule to normalizing your data is to remove repeating groups. A traditional table with a Home field, a Work field, and a Fax field repeats a single field phone number three times. A good solution to this problem is to break apart the two bodies of information and link them in a 1:M relationship with a data model. In other words, for every one record in the parent table, there can be many records in the child table. Following is an example of using a second table for telephone numbers:

```
Rolodex.db                     Rolodx-p.db
1:  Last Name*    —>>          Last Name*
2:  First Name*   —>>          First Name*
3:  Middle Name*  —>>          Middle Name*
4:  Address 1                  Phone # Name*
5:  Address 2                  Phone Number
6:  City                       Phone Ext
7:  State
8:  Zip
9:  Zip Ext
10: Notes
```

Third Normal Form: Move Nonrelating Fields

The third and final normal form outlined in this chapter involves tables that have a composite primary key. If a nonkey field relies on only part of the total key, the nonkey field should be moved to a separate table. This means that every field in the table must be directly related to all the key fields—not just some of them. For example, in a typical invoicing system, the child or detail table consists of at least the following:

```
Lineitem.db
1:   Order No*
2:   Stock No*
3:   Description
4:   Selling Price
5:   Qty
```

Note that Description is related only to the Stock No field of the two-field composite index. Because Description does not directly pertain to Order No, it should be moved to another table and the two tables linked by the common field Stock No. The following structure accomplishes this:

```
Lineitem.db         Stock.db
1:   Order No*
2:   Stock No* ->   Stock No*
3:   Selling Price  Vendor No
4:   Qty            Description
5:                  Qty on Hand
6:                  Cost Price
7:                  Selling Price
```

If you study and learn the preceding three rules of normalizing data, you will be able to create larger databases that are optimized for disk space. In addition, the data will be better organized and therefore easier to analyze. I suggest that you reread this section—or this entire chapter—in a month or two in order to drive the point home. In addition, consider purchasing a book on normalizing databases.

Learn the Three Normal Forms in One Sentence

The three normal forms can be summed up in the following phrase: "All the fields of a table should relate to the key, the whole key, and nothing but the key."

dBASE Tables Versus Paradox Tables

After you decide to use Paradox as your front-end development tool, you still need to decide whether to use a local table structure, such as dBASE and Paradox, or move to a SQL server and use the client/server model for your software architecture. In general, use local tables when a smaller amount of data is being collected and use a SQL server when either a very large amount of data is being collected, a large number of concurrent users will be accessing the data, or when a SQL server offers a feature that Paradox and dBASE do not—for example, transactions, automatic backup, and recovery. After you decide on a local table structure, you still need to decide between Paradox or dBASE table structures. You can store tables on either your hard drive or a networked drive. Both have their advantages and disadvantages. Although single-user applications can store the data on either your local hard drive or the network, multiuser applications store the data on the network. What follows is intended to help you decide, but I must tell you up front that my strong preference is for the Paradox table structure.

The primary key in Paradox promotes normalized table structures. The BDE and Paradox now supports dBASE 7 tables and their new features such as primary keys, min and max values, defaults, and required fields. However, dBASE has not always used primary keys, and it is still optional (you can index a table without using a primary key). On the other hand, dBASE allows for the flexibility of non-normalized tables because it does not require the concept of a primary key. Both dBASE and Paradox offer flexible table structures. In addition, the Paradox table structure enables you to use spaces, lowercase characters, and special characters in the field's name. This feature along with primary keys decided the issue for me. The Paradox table structure enables you to humanize field names. For example, in the past with other database products you might have represented someone's first name with FNAME; now you can use First Name complete with a space.

The Paradox table structure supports so many advanced features that the choice seems clear. For example, the Paradox table structure has referential integrity and supports advanced field types, such as Formatted Memo, Graphic, Time, and Autoincrement. In addition, Paradox allows for unique and descending secondary indexes. dBASE, however, has the benefit of being supported on almost every platform, including DOS, Windows, OS/2, Macintosh, Amiga, and UNIX. Many products support the dBASE standard on many platforms. dBASE index expressions also permit tremendous flexibility. Refer to the "Using dBASE Expressions" section, later in this chapter.

Whether you use dBASE or Paradox tables is up to you. Each one has its advantages and disadvantages. dBASE gives you more flexible indexes and allows for compatibility across platforms. Paradox is faster, promotes normalized data structures, has referential integrity, and has more flexible field types. If after reading this short section, you still are not sure which table structure to use, I suggest you read the rest of this chapter carefully and experiment with both structures until you decide.

Paradox and dBASE Field Types

Why talk about Paradox and dBASE field types in a book on ObjectPAL? Partially because ObjectPAL is the backbone language to Paradox, and understanding the field types into which you can store data is important. The main reason to discuss these field types, however, is so that you can become familiar with which types of data can go into which types of fields. Later in this chapter, table field types and ObjectPAL data types will be discussed. For now, browse and study the following field types. Pay attention to the field types that are new to you. In particular, study what data can go in what field, and study each field type's maximum and minimum value limits. Understanding the type of data that can go into fields will help you better understand the ObjectPAL data types. The following list describes each field type.

- **Alpha** (A) A general-purpose field type that can contain up to 255 letters, numbers, special characters, and other printable ASCII characters.
- **Autoincrement** (+) This is a special field type that contains unique noneditable numbers. Paradox begins with the number 1 and adds one number for each record in the table. You can specify the starting number by specifying the minimum value during the creation of a table. Deleting a record does not change the field values of other records. This field type can be very useful when designing tables, and is especially useful for adding an artificial key to a table. (See "Primary Keys," earlier in this chapter.)
- **BCD** (#) Paradox BCD-type fields contain numeric data in a binary coded decimal (BCD) format. Use BCD fields when you want to perform calculations with a higher level of precision than that available with the use of other numeric fields (up to 32 digits after the decimal point). Calculations on BCD fields are not performed as quickly as those on other numeric fields. In Paradox, the BCD field type is provided only for compatibility with other applications that use BCD data. Paradox correctly interprets BCD data from other applications that use the BCD type. When Paradox performs calculations on BCD data, however, it converts the data to the numeric float type, and then converts the result back to BCD.
- **Binary** (B) This is a field type used by programmers to store custom data that Paradox cannot interpret. For example, a binary field can be used for sound and animation. You can store any type of binary data in a binary field type, but Paradox does not know what to do with data in a binary

field; you have to add routines to your program to use the binary data. You can specify the amount of the binary data stored in the table (0–240 characters).

- **Bytes** (Y) Only advanced users who need to work with data that Paradox cannot interpret should use the bytes field type because Paradox does not know how to interpret bytes fields. You can read and write the data in bytes fields with ObjectPAL—for example, to store bar codes or magnetic strips. However, you will have to rely on other routines to manipulate the data (for example, functions in DLLs). Unlike binary fields, bytes fields are stored in the Paradox table (rather than in the separate .MB file), allowing for faster access. You can specify from 1–255 bytes. This field type is valid for Paradox 5 and 7 tables.
- **Character** (C) A dBASE character field can contain up to 254 characters (including blank spaces). This field type is valid for dBASE III+, IV, and V. This field type is similar to the Paradox alpha field type.
- **Date** (D) Paradox date fields can contain any valid date from January 1, 9999 BC, to December 31, 9999 AD. This field type is valid for dBASE III+, IV, V, and Paradox 3.5, 4, 5, and 7.
- **Float** (F) dBASE provides two ways to store numeric data. The float number type contains numeric data in a binary floating point format. Use the float number type on fields that will not require precise calculations to be performed on them; some degree of precision is lost during calculation. Float number fields are best used to contain whole numbers or numbers of up to two decimal places. The size of a dBASE float number field can be from 1 to 20. This field type is valid for dBASE IV and V.
- **Formatted memo** (F) Paradox formatted memo fields are like memo fields except that you can format the text. You can alter and store the text attributes typeface, style, color, and size. You can also specify the amount of data stored in the table (0–240 characters).
- **Graphic** (G) Paradox graphic fields contain pictures in .BMP, .PCX, .TIF, .GIF, .JPG, and .EPS file formats. Not all graphic variations are available. Currently, for example, you cannot store a 24-bit .TIF graphic. When you paste a graphic into a graphic field, Paradox converts the graphic into the .BMP format. You can specify how much of the data is stored in the table (0–240 characters).

- **Logical** (L) Paradox logical fields contain values representing True or False (yes or no). By default, valid entries include T and F (case is not important).
- **Long integer** (I) Paradox long integer fields are 32-bit signed integers that contain whole numbers in the range -2,147,483,647–2,147,483,647. Long integer fields require more space to store than short fields.
- **Memo** (M) This is a special type of BLOB field used for storing text. *BLOB* is an acronym for *binary large object*. A BLOB is not a field type, but rather a data type. Field types that can contain BLOBs include binary, memo (both Paradox and dBASE), formatted memo, graphic, and OLE. You can specify how much of the binary data is stored in the table (1–240 characters).
- **Money** ($) Paradox money fields, like number fields, can contain only numbers. They can hold positive or negative values. By default, however, money fields are formatted to display decimal places and a money symbol. Regardless of the number of decimal places displayed, Paradox recognizes up to six decimal places when performing internal calculations on money fields.
- **Number** (N) This is a field that can contain only numbers from –10e307 to +10e308, with 15 significant digits. A number field can contain some valid non-numerical characters, such as a decimal point or a minus sign.
- **OLE** (O) Use the OLE field to store data generated by an OLE server, such as images, sound, documents, and so on. The OLE field provides you with a way to view and manipulate this data without leaving Paradox. Since version 5, Paradox has supported OLE 1 and OLE 2. You can specify how much of the binary data is stored in the table (0–240 characters).
- **Short** (S) This is a Paradox field type that can contain integers from -32,767–32,767. A short number field type uses less disk space than does the number field type. It's perfect for storing ages, years of employment, invoice numbers, item numbers, and so on.
- **Time** (T) Paradox time fields contain times of day, stored in milliseconds since midnight and limited to 24 hours.
- **TimeStamp** (@) Paradox TimeStamp fields contain a value comprised of both date and time values. Rules for this field type are the same as those for date fields and time fields.

To enter today's date, current time, or both into a date, time, or TimeStamp field, press the SPACEBAR *repeatedly until Paradox enters the data. Educate your users about this handy interactive feature.*

BLOB Field Types

The binary large object (BLOB) field types are binary, memo, formatted memo, graphic, and OLE. The value you specify in the Create Table dialog box refers to the amount of the BLOB data Paradox stores in the table. The entire BLOB is stored outside the table in a file with the same name as the table but with a .MB file extension. For example, the BLOB data for MYTABLE.DB is stored in My Table.mb.

Notes on the dBASE Table Structure

The following section contains notes on various important features of the dBASE table structure. The intent is to let you know about some of the key differences between the Paradox and dBASE table structures.

dBASE Tables Mark Records for Deletion

In dBASE, records are marked for deletion by the active index. They are deleted only after you pack the table. If you never pack the table, it will continue to grow. This is an advantage; however, it is also a disadvantage—but one that is easily overcome. You can put routines in your application to retrieve and purge deleted records. Just remember that dBASE tables must be purged of deleted records or they will continue to grow.

dBASE Allows Duplicates in the Main Index

Another difference is that with dBASE, you have the option of having duplicate key values in all the indexes except unique indexes. Even with a unique index, however, duplicate values are allowed in the table; duplicate values are prevented only in the index. Once a Paradox table is keyed, it will not allow duplicates.

dBASE Record Numbers Are Not Dynamic

When you delete a record in dBASE, the record still exists in the table until you pack the table from the Restructure Table dialog box. The record number sticks with the record until the deleted records are purged. To purge deleted records from a dBASE table, restructure the table and select the Pack Table check box.

In Paradox, the record numbers are put on a heap stack, and therefore, are dynamic; in dBASE, they are not. With Paradox tables, the record numbers reorder whenever you delete a record. To accomplish this, Paradox uses the concept of a *heap stack*. A heap stack is a technique to order a set of items in ascending order. In Paradox, the record number is a unique number that identifies each record and always starts with 1.

When you select Format | Filter for a Paradox table, the record numbers are reordered according to the new heap stack. When you do this same operation on a dBASE table, the record numbers for each record remain the same as before.

There are other less substantial differences between Paradox and dBASE tables. For example, the status bar and scroll bar behave differently, depending on which type of table you are displaying. For dBASE tables, the status bar shows you only what record number you are on—not what record number of how many, as in Paradox tables. Finally, the scroll bar behaves oddly when you use it with dBASE tables. The scroll box appears to stick to the center of the scroll bar. You can attribute this final oddity to the fact that dBASE tables do not use a stack heap and it is difficult for Paradox to estimate where the record pointer is in relationship to the whole table.

Using dBASE Expressions

One advantage that dBASE tables have over Paradox tables is that dBASE indexes are very flexible. You can write elaborate expressions using dBASE keywords in the Define Index dialog box (see Figure 2-7).

The dBASE expression engine allows you to code expressions that give you a unique view to a table. For a complete list of the dBASE functions that are allowed in expression indexes on dBASE tables, look in the Paradox help under "dBASE:expression indexes." You'll have to consult dBASE manuals and books for usage. What follows here are some common examples:

- DEPT+UPPER(LNAME) lists records by DEPT and LNAME fields. In this case, the index ignores case in the LNAME field.
- UPPER(Field1)+UPPER(Field2)+UPPER(Field3) lists records by the Field1, Field2, and Field3 fields. In the following index, case is ignored completely.
- SUBSTR(DEPT,1,3)+SUBSTR(UPPER(LNAME),1,3)
- DEPT+DTOS(DATE_HIRED)

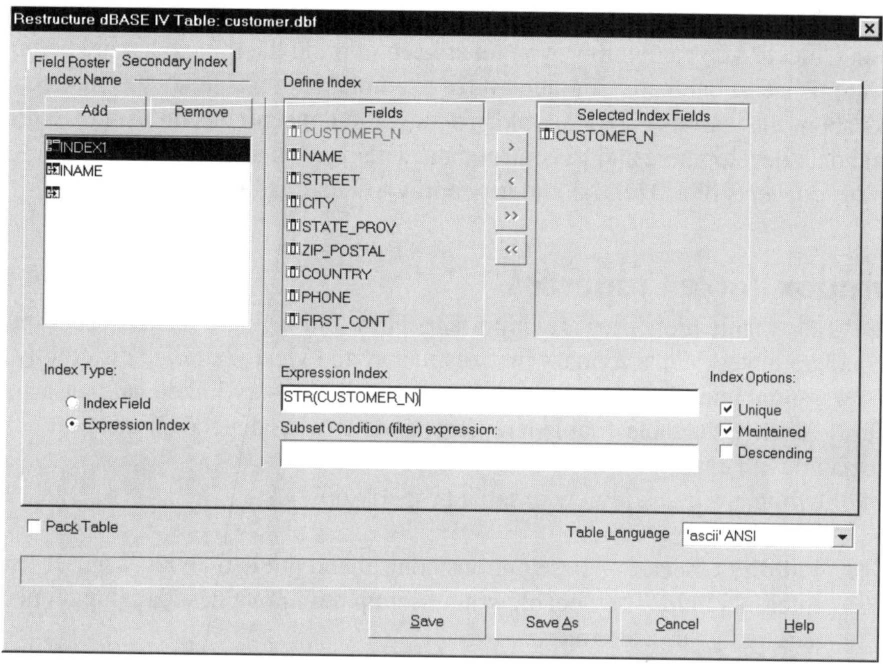

FIGURE 2-7 Entering dBASE expressions

- DEPT+STR(DATE()-DATE_HIRED,4,0)
- DEPT + STR(YEAR(DATE_HIRED),4,0) + STR(MONTH(DATE_HIRED),2,0) + STR(DAY(DATE_HIRED),2,0)
- IIF(DEPT="SALES",SUBSTR(LNAME,1,3),SUBSTR(CITY,1,3))
- IIF(STATE="AZ".OR.STATE="CA",STATE+"A",STATE)
- DEPT+STR(YEAR(DATE_HIRED),4,0)+STR(SALARY,7,0)
- DEPT+STR(MONTH(DATE_HIRED),2,0)+STATE
- DEPT+STATE+STR(100000-SALARY,8,0)

The preceding examples of index expressions show you how flexible dBASE indexes are. You are limited to expressions that have a length of no more than 220 characters and result in no more than 100 characters.

Notes on the Paradox Table Structure

As an ObjectPAL programmer, you must keep in mind the things that are better accomplished in interactive Paradox—for example, at the table level. This section talks about the various Paradox table properties. It concentrates on using pictures to aid data development and to control data. This section also discusses how various concepts of referential integrity apply to Paradox tables.

Paradox Table Properties

The Paradox table properties are important. They allow you to restrict data input, use lookup tables, add secondary indexes to sort and view your data differently, add referential integrity to ensure the data in two tables stay linked, add password security, change the table's table language, and view the dependent tables associated with a table.

Following is a quick review of table property options:

- **Validity Checks** These options control and guide the values a user can enter in a field. They enable you to set up default values, data input checks, required values, and more.
- **Table Lookup** This is a data entry tool that ensures that data from one table is entered correctly in another table.
- **Secondary Indexes** As discussed previously, secondary indexes are very useful in interactive mode and in ObjectPAL. Secondary indexes are useful for speeding up operations and viewing data in different ways, and have the following properties: Unique and Descending.
- **Referential Integrity** This enables you to ensure data across two tables. With referential integrity, you can make sure that ties between data will not be broken. For example, one option enables you to prohibit the deletion of a master table record if the child table has corresponding records.
- **Password Security** Full-password encryption at the table and field levels guarantees the security of your data.
- **Table Language** The language driver for a table determines the table's sort order and the available character sets. The default table language is set by the BDE Administrator. When you create or restructure a table, you can

override the default table language with the Table Language option in the Table Properties panel in the Restructure dialog box. Paradox offers many language drivers, including several ANSI language drivers, that enable you to store Windows ANSI high characters.

- **Dependent Tables** This table property shows all the tables that are recognized as children in a referential integrity link.

TIP

In the Restructure dialog box, you can use the Default column of the field roster to add a field called ModifyTimeStamp to every table in your project and set its Default value to NOW. These types of audit fields can be very helpful in business situations and are critical in many. Other types of audit fields you can add to the end of tables include CreateTimeStamp and EmployeeID.

Picture Strings

A *picture string* is a pattern of characters that defines what a user can type into a field during editing or data entry of a table or form. A picture string aids data entry and promotes—but does not ensure—consistent data. Picture strings are an input aid and a means of validating data.

Although picture strings can be implemented on a field at the table or form level, they are best implemented at the table level. When you add a picture to a table, any forms you create using that table will inherit the picture string. Every ObjectPAL programmer needs to keep this in mind. If you must limit what someone can enter into a field, implement the limiting factor at the table level with a validity check, if possible. You should use ObjectPAL on a form only when you determine that a picture won't work. Remember, ObjectPAL is on the form only. Unless you password-protect your table, nothing can prevent the user from selecting File | Open | Table and entering data directly into the table; in other words, bypassing your ObjectPAL code. This concept applies to all database backends, including SQL servers. One of the basic tenets of developing a good client/server application is to put as much processing on the database server as possible.

Use the Picture Assistant dialog box to enter new pictures (see Figure 2-8). To get to the Picture Assistant dialog box, select the Picture Assist button on the Restructure Table dialog box.

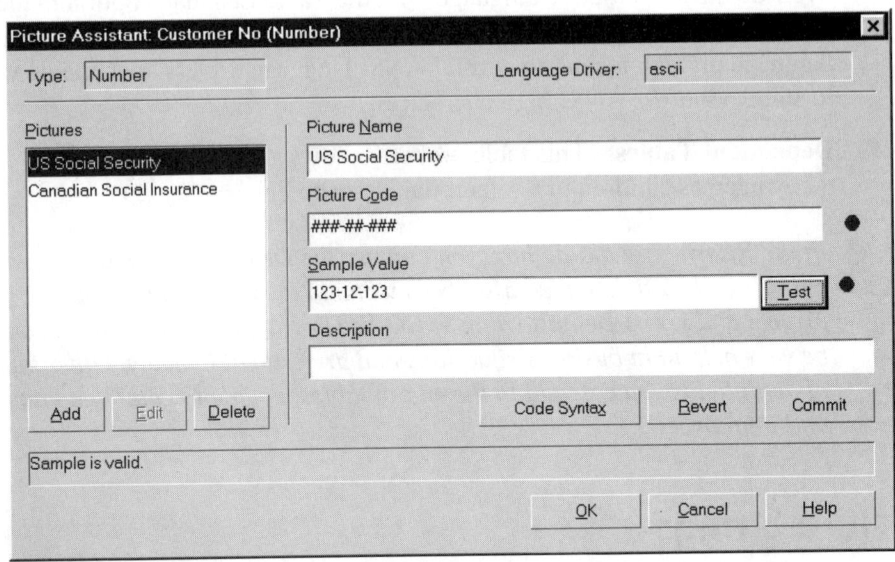

FIGURE 2-8 The Picture Assistant dialog box

Table 2-1 lists the picture string characters you can use to validate data.

Any other characters you use in a picture string are treated as a constant. Paradox automatically types the constant when the user comes to a point in the picture string in which that constant is specified. The exception is the first

Character	Description
#	A numeric digit
?	Any letter (uppercase or lowercase)
&	Any letter (converts to uppercase)
@	Any character
!	Any character (converts to uppercase)
;	Interprets the next character as a literal character, not as a special picture string character

TABLE 2-1 Picture String Characters

Character	Description
*	The character that follows can be repeated any number of times
[xyz]	The characters between square brackets are optional
{x,y,z}	Optional characters separated by commas
{}	Grouping operator
,	Alternative choices of values

TABLE 2-1 Picture String Characters *(continued)*

character, which figures since in life there are almost always exceptions. The user must tell Paradox that he or she wants to enter data by entering the first character or by pressing the SPACEBAR for autofill.

TIP *Remember, autofill is a great feature that you should promote to your users. To automatically fill in a date field with today's date, for example, just press the SPACEBAR a couple of times. Make sure you add this type of help to any manuals or help files you develop for your application. Autofill works with Date, Time, TimeStamp, and Logical fields and does not require a picture statement.*

Useful pictures include the following:

- Phone with autofill = *###-####*
- Phone with autofill (area opt) = *[(###)]###-####*
- Phone with 1-800 optional = *[{1-800-,(###)}]###-####*
- Flexible phone number = *[1 (*3{#})]*3{#}-*4#*
- US 5 or 9 ZIP Code = *#####[-####]*
- US 5, US 9, or Canada ZIP code = **5{#}[*4#],@#@ #@#*
- SSN with autofill = *###-##-####*
- SSN with no autofill = *###{-}##{-}####*
- Letters only (no spaces) = *?
- Letters only (capitalize first) = &*?

- Capital letters = *&
- Capital first letter = !*@
- Capitalize every word 1 = *[![*?][*]]
- Capitalize every word 2 = !*[* !,@]
- Capitalize every word 3 = *{ ,.}!*{{ ,.}*{ ,.}!,@}
- Capitalize every word 4 = *[[*#[ ]]![*?][@][ ]]
- Capital after = !*[{ ,.,(,;,}*{ ,.,(,;,}!,@]
- Time (HH:MM:SS:) = {0#,1#,2{0,1,2,3}}:{0,1,2,3,4,5}#:{0,1,2,3,4,5}#
- Time with SS optional = {0#,1#,2{0,1,2,3}}:{0,1,2,3,4,5}#[:{0,1,2,3,4,5}#]
- Time (HH:MM AM) or (HH:MM PM) = {1{:,{0,1,2}:},{2,3,4,5,6,7,8,9}:}{0,1,2,3,4,5}# {AM,PM}
- Date with autofill = {##/##/##,#/##/##}
- Date 2 = {##/01/##,#/01/##}
- Allow Miss, Ms., Mr., or Mrs. = M{iss,s.,r{.,s.}}
- Allow Dr., Doctor, Father, Miss, Mrs., Mr., Mr. & Mrs., Ms., Msgr., Pastor, and Reverend: = {D{r.,octor},Father,M{iss,r{s.,.[;& Mrs.]},s{.,gr.}},Pastor,Reverend}

NOTE *Available on the Internet at the following is PICTURES.TXT. You can use Notepad to open it and paste the settings into the Picture Assistant dialog box. The file is available at http://www.prestwood.com/forums/paradox/books/official/files/pictures.txt.*

Using Table Lookup Effectively

When the user presses CTRL-SPACEBAR to display a lookup table, the Lookup Help dialog box respects the table properties set for the table. You can use this feature to jazz up the way the Table Lookup dialog box looks. For example, you can change the colors of a table in a table window and the changes will carry over to the Table Lookup dialog box. The table properties you alter are stored in the TableView file with the same name as the table and a .TV extension. When you use that table in the lookup, it will appear with the new property values.

2

TIP *When users press CTRL-SPACEBAR to display a lookup table, remember to let them know that they can use CTRL-Q to locate a value. This is an interactive feature that can greatly enhance the user's perception of your application.*

Table Language and Sorting

How do you get support for special character sets in Paradox? For languages whose characters are written with an alphabet—not languages such as Chinese and Japanese—a language driver that supports the character set needs to exist.

In addition, the sort order of a table depends on the *language driver*. The three main language drivers with which we are concerned here in the United States are Paradox *ascii*, Paradox *intl*, and Paradox *ANSI INTL*. The Paradox intl (international) and Paradox ANSI INTL drivers sort alphabetically, mixing uppercase and lowercase; for example, aAbBBccC. The Paradox ascii (ASCII) driver sorts by the ASCII table, putting all the lowercase characters first; for example, aabbbcdAAABCCCD. It is important to know that the way in which Paradox sorts a table depends on the language driver.

Secondary Indexes

Earlier in this chapter, the importance of primary keys was addressed. A secondary index is used to sort a table by any of the fields in the table (not just by the primary key). A secondary index is a field or group of fields that you define as an alternate sort order for a table. You can use secondary indexes to view a table in a separate sort order, link a table on a field other than the primary key, and to speed up search and locate operations. A table can have more than one secondary index and each secondary index can be a composite of fields. When you use a secondary index, you change only the view order of the records. The physical location of the records in the table does not change. Secondary indexes are flexible and include the following options: Composite, Unique, Case-sensitive, Maintained, and Ascending/Descending.

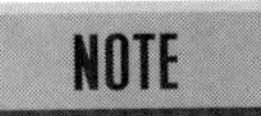

You cannot create a secondary index on a memo, formatted memo, binary, OLE, graphic, logical, or bytes field.

Referential Integrity

Referential integrity (RI) is extremely important. Point-and-click referential integrity enables you to set up relationships between tables so that your data is always valid. *Data integrity* is a guarantee that the values in a table are valid. You can use various features of Paradox tables to protect data from misuse including the required field option, the minimum and maximum options, and picture statements. For example, data integrity for autoincrementing might mean that no two records have the same key values. For referential integrity, data integrity might mean that the records in one table will always match the records in another table.

There are various types of referential integrity. Paradox supports Prohibit, Cascade, and Strict RI update rules. Figure 2-9 shows a referential integrity link

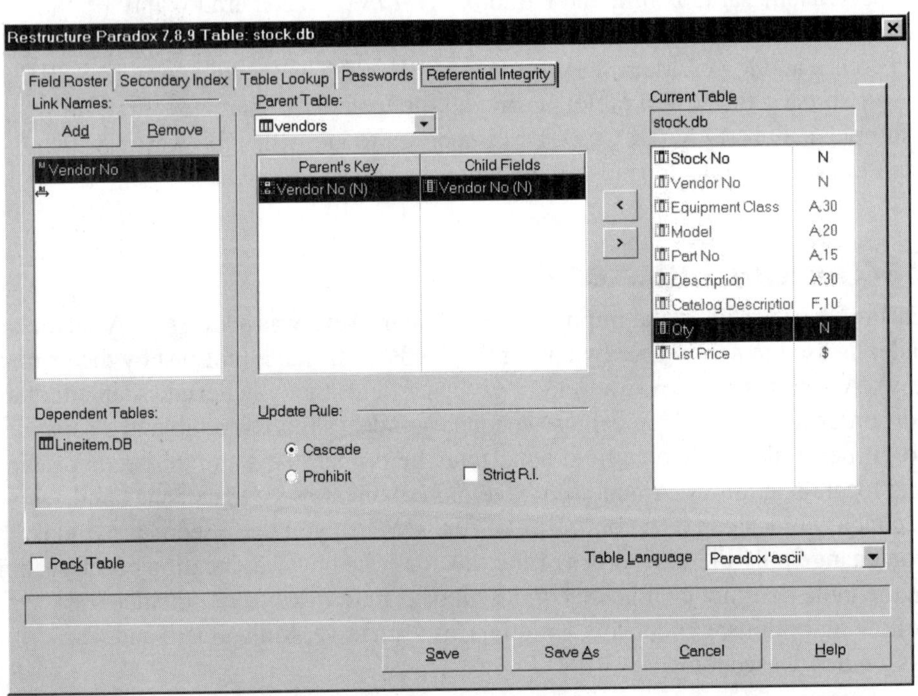

FIGURE 2-9 The Referential Integrity tab showing a link between LINEITEM.DB and STOCK.DB

being set up between LINEITEM.DB and STOCK.DB. To get to this dialog box, restructure the child table of a one-to-many, select the Referential Integrity tab, and select Add. Note the options selected in the Update Rule panel.

Setting Up Referential Integrity

You must be restructuring the child table to create a referential integrity link. In addition, you must make sure that the child table contains all key fields of the parent. Besides controlling data entry, the referential integrity link provides an update feature: either Cascade or Prohibit.

Cascade enables you to update child tables when a value changes in the parent table. With Cascade referential integrity, any changes that are made to the parent table's primary key are automatically made to the child table. Therefore, if you make a change to the parent table's primary key, the child table's foreign key also is updated. Referential integrity links don't need to be made on key fields in the child table. Whenever a change is made to the parent key, the change is cascaded to all the child records that match that key. If you change the spelling of a customer's name from Smith to Smythe, for example, the data in the reference field of all the child table records that consist of this key also will change.

Prohibit referential integrity prevents a change in the parent's key if any records match the value in the child table. You can use Prohibit in an invoicing system to prevent the invoice numbers in existing line-item entries from being changed or deleted.

Strict Referential Integrity Check Box

Strict referential integrity should have been called "Prohibit Paradox 4.0" because it prevents Paradox for DOS 4.0 and its earlier versions from writing to the table because they don't support referential integrity. When the Strict Referential Integrity option in the Update Rule panel is checked, Paradox 4.0 for DOS can't alter data (refer to Figure 2-9). This feature is designed entirely for interoperatability with Paradox for DOS.

When strict integrity is selected, Paradox for DOS sees the table as being write-protected. Therefore, the data can be viewed in Paradox for DOS, but can't be changed. If you are going to use referential integrity, and data security is important, then you should also turn on Strict Referential Integrity.

The Parent Must Use a Primary Key

One of the requirements to use referential integrity is that the parent table has a primary key. The child table must use all the fields of the parent table's primary key.

A parent table holds the master values for the link. It has the power to change these values, delete them, and add new values. A child table depends on the values in the parent table for its matching fields. Only the ones that exist in the parent table are available to a user to alter or view in a form.

Automatic Secondary Index

A referential integrity link can be defined between the primary key in a parent table and any index in a child table. The fields must match in number, type, and size. In other words, a parent table with two fields in its primary key must link to an index—primary or secondary—with two fields of the same type in the child table. You can use composite secondary indexes on the child table in a referential integrity link.

If Paradox needs to, it will automatically create any secondary indexes needed to establish a referential link. If Paradox needs a single field secondary index, it creates it Case-sensitive and Maintained and names it the same name as the field. If more than one field is needed, it names it the same name as the name you gave the referential integrity link.

Blank Field Caution

In referential integrity, blank fields are permitted to exist in the child, even when no matching blank field exists in the parent. Blank fields are considered to be outside the referential integrity link. This feature comes in handy when you want to enter a child record without matching it immediately to a parent record; you can add the link value later.

You should not blank out a primary-key value in the parent table, however. If you do, the corresponding fields in the child records are made blank as the change cascades from the parent. When you change the blank primary key to a nonblank value, the child records that were linked to it will remain blank. This is known as *orphaning records*. Remember, blanks in the master are considered to be outside the link.

To prevent orphaning of child records, restructure the table and use the Required Field validity check for all the key fields. In fact, it generally is considered good database design to make all the fields in a Paradox primary key Required Fields.

NOTE *Referential integrity and other settings stored in .VAL files sometimes interfere with the development of a project. This particularly is a problem when you are restructuring a child table in a referential integrity link. If this happens to you and you don't mind losing the validity checks for a table or for a set of tables, go ahead and delete or, better yet, rename them.*

Be careful, however. All the validity checks will be deleted. For example, the ORDERS.DB, CUSTOMER.DB, LINEITEM.DB, STOCK.DB, and VENDORS.DB tables in the SAMPLE directory that comes with Paradox are a wonderful starting point for an invoicing system. The .VAL files—or more precisely, the table validity checks and referential integrity—might interfere, however, with you using the tables.

Summary

No matter which table structure you choose, use aliases and make sure that your data model is correct. Aliases are your ticket to portability. No matter what type of relationship you set up, your data model is simply a series of 1:1, 1:M, M:1, and M:M relationships. When you study a complex data model, examine the relationship between any two tables.

The form is a wonderful tool, but it isn't the place where data is stored: the table is. Therefore, the table is a much better place to implement data integrity. Set up data validity checks at the table level if possible. You can use pictures, table lookups, and referential integrity to implement data integrity. Only after you determine that a data restriction can't be implemented at the table level should you move to the form level and use ObjectPAL to manipulate a user's input.

CHAPTER 3

How to Develop Forms

With Paradox, you can create forms and reports visually. You can create dazzling single or multiple forms for viewing, editing, and adding data. This chapter shows you how to begin integrating design elements into a complete application. It deals with issues, problems, solutions, and tips with design documents from a developing point of view. A *design document* is a form or a report that a developer uses to display data. This chapter also dives into special, summary, and calculated fields.

Study Applications for a Better User Interface

The user interface is the first element of your application that a user sees. Because first impressions are important, the user interface carries more weight than any other part of your application. It deserves much planning and effort. While developing Windows 95/98, Microsoft spent a great deal of money and time planning and testing the user interface. The efforts of Microsoft are apparent in the user-oriented design of the Windows 95/98 operating system. If you are a Windows 3.*x* developer and you are developing your first Windows 95/98 application, then you owe it to your users to study and learn the look and feel of the new operating system. When you deliver an application that has the look and feel of the operating system, the users are instantly familiar with your application and its user interface. Instead of trying to learn a new user interface, the user focuses on learning how to do the task your application is intended to deal with.

Often when you start a new form, you already have an idea of what you want it to look like. When you're inspired, go with it and harvest your inspiration. However, even when you are inspired, plan your user interface carefully—down to the most seamingly insignificant details. With large applications, document your look and feel in an application style guide.

When you're struggling to find the right look and feel for a form or application, however, why reinvent the wheel? Software companies spend millions of dollars studying the look and feel of software. You can benefit from all this effort by looking through the software right on your machine. Take some time—perhaps now—to open up and browse through your favorite Windows 95 software applications. In general, what does the application look like? Look for consistent features. Are all the buttons the same size? If the application deals with large amounts of data, how is that data handled? Does the application use any Windows 95-style gadgets? What color scheme did they develop? What things do you like, and what do you dislike? What would you change? Be really choosey. Closely examine the details of these professionally developed applications.

Your applications should look as professional as commercial applications. The closer you get, however, the more your users will enjoy your application. You should at least choose a design concept and stick to it. Select your colors, form size, button size and location, frame style, and fonts. Don't stray from the standard that you set for a particular project. If you don't know what the look and feel should be, design with a simple version of the Windows 95-style look and feel.

Do yourself a favor and purchase a good book on user interface design and concept. To really master the Windows 95 and Windows NT look and feel, consider a user interface book specific to Windows 95 and Windows NT.

Study Objects Before You Start Designing

Paradox comes with a plethora of objects and options. Browse through them and look at their many characteristics. Many people get caught up in a particular project and never explore the many visual features of Paradox. Spend some time studying the visual properties of objects. The objects from the toolbar tools that you can place in forms and reports are *design objects*. The better you know the design objects of Paradox, the better your applications will look. Make sure that you know what the properties do. For example, a field has several Run Time properties. What are the differences among Read Only, Tab Stop, and No Echo? Know the properties of design objects before you start programming in ObjectPAL.

Forms Are Your Application

A form in Paradox is used to present data, but it also doubles as the center of your application. A form has many objects that you can use to develop an application. It's important that you have a good grasp of what these objects can do. A table frame is an object used to display multiple records on a form. A field is a multipurpose object that enables you to display a single value from a table. It also enables you to show users extra bits of information, calculated values, and other values not stored directly in the table. An object such as a button, field, or box is an item that the user interacts with to create events. The more you know about Paradox's objects, the better your application will be.

A form stores the code for an application. For large applications, it is a good idea to break it into multiple forms or use libraries to store extra code. When you deliver your form, Paradox compiles it into what is actually a Windows DLL with a .FDL extension.

Screen Resolution

The main window in Paradox is the desktop. The desktop is the highest level of interaction with all Paradox objects. The desktop varies its size depending on your screen resolution. The desktop is also known as your application workspace. In ObjectPAL, there is an application variable type for manipulating Paradox's application workspace.

Forms designed for one screen resolution don't necessarily look good under a different resolution. If you will be porting applications from one machine to another, you should use the same resolution on both systems. (Also, be sure to use the same fonts on both systems.) If it's impossible to use the same resolution, develop the form for the lowest common resolution—for example, VGA (640 × 480) rather than SVGA (800 × 600).

Forms Versus Pages

A form can consist of multiple pages, and an application can consist of multiple forms. It's often difficult to decide when to add a page or start a new form. In general, think about adding a new page to the existing form first. If a new page won't work, add a new form. Because every page of a form must be the same size, usually size dictates whether to use a new page or form.

When all the forms and pages are the same size, then I let the data model dictate whether to add a new page or a new form. The general rule is one data model per form. When the data model gets in the way, then start a new form. For example, in a typical invoicing system, you might link Orders to Customers. You could use one form with this data model and simply add pages until another data model is indicated. For example, suppose that you need to have a page or form for the user to browse through the Customer table. The preceding data model does not work because the Customer table is the second table in a one-to-one relationship; it is restricted by the Orders table. Common sense tells you to create a new form with a new data model; that is, a data model with just the Customer table in it.

The Main Form

A typical application consists of tables, indexes, forms, reports, queries, and possibly scripts or libraries. This presents a problem to the user: how to start up the application. The common practice for developers is to give the main form the same name as the directory that contains it. If you stick with this practice, the users of your Paradox applications will soon learn how to start them up.

Getting the Most Out of Style Sheets

The prototyping of objects is a feature of Paradox that enables you to create great-looking and consistent forms and reports. This option enables you to save default settings, such as color, font information, ObjectPAL code, and so on. Use this feature to expedite the creation of consistent objects, complete with all the properties and ObjectPAL code. The following section discusses style sheets in general. If you need help changing the contents of the style sheet, consult Paradox's manuals.

Style sheets are powerful tools for design development. You can maintain several different looks and switch among them before you create a design document (either a form or a report). You can set up several screen and report style sheet files (with different fonts, colors, frame styles, and so on) and save them to your working directory.

You can even use custom color schemes, which are saved as part of the style sheet file. You also can create your own color schemes that are independent of the Windows color palette. The possibilities are limitless.

Keep in mind, however, that many users are still bound to only 16 colors. If you have a better video card, remember that the custom colors you define probably will be dithered on lesser video cards. Therefore, it is recommended that you test your work on a standard 16-color VGA card. It's also a good idea to test your application with at least three different Windows color schemes.

TIP *Design user interfaces using the default Windows color scheme. If you develop your applications using the default Windows color scheme, then your applications will look good with more of the predesigned Windows color schemes.*

If you get into the habit of choosing a style sheet before you create the first form for a project, you guarantee a consistent look and feel for your entire application—with little or no effort.

ON THE NET *The following zip file contains several style sheets ready for you to use: http://prestwood.com/forums/paradox/books/official/files/style.zip. If you have a style sheet to add to this zip file, email it along with a short description to mike@prestwood.com.*

The Six Steps to Create a Form

Everyone has his or her own technique for developing a form. This section explores one technique. Study this technique and use it to improve your own technique for developing forms. Following are the six steps of developing a form that I use:

1. **Create the data model.** This includes gathering data components and business rules, and planning and creating the tables.
2. **Prototype several forms.** Design several versions of one or two of the main forms of the application with the data models you created and the business rules you gathered in step 1. Let someone else decide which prototype form has the best look and feel. Create the rest of the forms.
3. **Test the built-in behavior.** Run the form and see whether the basic data model and fields are what you need. Make sure that you use the application the way that the user will. For example, search for values, insert a new record, change and delete records.
4. **Add objects and design elements.** After you decide on the prototyped forms and test the built-in behavior, the next step is to add text objects, graphics, buttons, and so on, to get the overall visual effect you want.
5. **Add ObjectPAL.** Decide what more you want an object to do and add the appropriate code.
6. **Test.** Large companies thoroughly test their software, and so should you. There are many types of tests you can run, including unit testing, integration testing, and regression testing.

Step 1: Create the Data Model

You can use Visual Database Designer to create your tables and links visually. You can even save and load data model files (.DM files). Whether you're working on forms, reports, or queries, all you do is draw lines between tables. The linking expert automatically does all the relational work for you by showing you how the tables can be linked. No matter how complex the relationship is, Paradox graphically displays the linked tables.

The first step in creating a form is to decide on a data model. The better you understand how the data model works and the theory behind relating tables, the easier it is for you to create forms and applications.

Step 2: Prototype Several Forms

Creating forms in Paradox is easy. Within a couple of hours, you could create nearly a dozen variations of a form. Design several versions of the main forms for your application and let someone else, such as the client, decide which prototype form he or she likes the look and feel of best.

When you prototype a form, set the form's properties, decide on a style sheet, create the form using either the data model or an expert, decide whether you want the form to be a window or a dialog box, set the title of the form, and so on.

Set the form's properties (see Figure 3-1). Get into the habit of setting the properties of a form whenever you create one. Give it a name, take the scroll bars off, and so on. Now is a good time to choose a look and feel for your application. Figure 3-1 shows the Window Style dialog box.

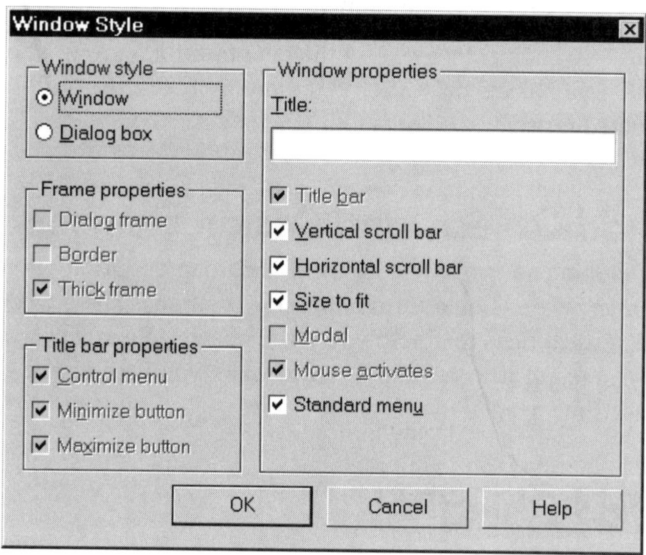

FIGURE 3-1 The Window Style dialog box

Step 3: Test the Built-In Behavior

Because Paradox has a tremendous amount of built-in functionality, exploring the built-in behavior of the form is important. Users often waste time because they don't know the built-in behavior. Sometimes, the built-in behavior is different from what they assume it is. After programming for many hours, they finally give up and either call for support or post a message on the Internet, only to be told that the default behavior already does what they were trying to do. In other words, if you don't know the default behavior, you might waste time duplicating it. Even worse, your added code may cause problems, prompting you to write more code to fix. This is a programming loop you must try to avoid.

Paradox provides experts that generate code at the field level, in the form open, etc. It is a good idea to study the ObjectPAL generated by these experts.

Testing your form before you begin to add to it also gives you an overall sense of what you're trying to accomplish. Developers often get caught up in one detail of an application and lose sight of the big picture. Use your forms the way your users will. Your applications will have a much better look and feel.

The next step is to add objects—calculated fields, lines, graphics, boxes used to contain fields (a wonderful way to set the tab order for a group of objects), and so on. You add more objects only after you thoroughly test the built-in behavior of your newly created form.

Step 4: Add Objects and Design Elements

When first developing a form, consider using the Snap To Grid option to help you quickly place many objects on a form in orderly positions. The *grid* consists of horizontal and vertical lines that help you place objects. You can show or hide the grid; you also can resize it. Use Snap To Grid when you first design a form. Doing so cuts down the time needed to design the form.

Step 5: Add ObjectPAL

If you have a detailed design specification, then the next step is to alter the default behavior of the objects to behave as specified. Before adding any code to alter or add to the built-in behavior, thoroughly test how your objects and design elements operate with the built-in behavior of Paradox. The next step is to decide what more you want the form to do. Do you want the form to automatically put values in fields? Do you want it to open another form? Do you want to add pull-down menus and a custom toolbar?

Whatever ObjectPAL you decide to add, develop in small steps and test as you go. If you add code and the code doesn't work, take it out! I can't tell you how many times I have talked to programmers who swear that the problem they have is a bug in Paradox and it turns out to be their overcoding. Often when faced with a task, you will experiment with code to see what happens. If you just keep adding code to your form in hopes of solving the problem, you will end up with a mess. Remember to remove code experiments. Also, remember to step back and remind yourself what you are trying to do, and try to think of different ways of accomplishing the same task.

NOTE *If you are already familiar with ObjectPAL, here is a tip. If, in experimentation, you use sleep(), doDefault, or DisableDefault to overcome some odd or misunderstood behavior, do not leave the commands in your code. If using the command didn't seem to make a difference, then take it out. Use commands only when they are called for. One great way to really learn the event model and the power of these and other commands is to experiment with adding them. Remember to take them out, however, if they do not do what you wanted.*

If you really think you have found a bug in Paradox, then don't waste any time on your complicated form. Instead, try to duplicate the problem on a brand new form with no extra code on it. Only after you have duplicated the problem on a new form should you notify Corel. I believe that you will find, more times than not, that the problem is not a bug in Paradox, however.

Step 6: Test

The final step in developing a form is to test your form as a whole. You'll see whether you are done or need to go back to steps 4 and 5. You should test your ObjectPAL code as you go. In this step, you test the whole application, not its individual elements. Does the form behave the way you thought it would? Does it behave the way your users will expect it to? Does it integrate with the rest of the application?

Notes on Creating Forms

Now that creating forms has been discussed in general abstract terms, the following section discusses specific design issues of creating forms.

Child Windows Versus Dialog Boxes

Put some thought into whether you want a form to be a child window or a dialog box. Forms that are child windows obey Microsoft's Multiple Document Interface (MDI). The MDI, for example, dictates that when you maximize one child window, all child windows are maximized.

A temporary window that requests or provides information is a *dialog box.* Many dialog boxes present options from which you must choose before you can perform an action. Other dialog boxes display warnings or error messages. Some are even utilities, such as the Paradox Workbench that is available from Prestwood Software & Consulting (www.prestwood.net).

A *model dialog box* is a dialog box that the user can't leave until he or she responds to it. In general, model dialog boxes are frustrating to the user and should be avoided. Reserve the use of model dialog boxes to situations when additional information is required to complete a command or when it is important to prevent any further interaction until satisfying a condition.

NOTE *If you leave the form as a child window to Paradox and hide the Paradox desktop, the child window hides with it. If you want to hide the Paradox desktop so that the form is the only visual object onscreen, you must define the form as a dialog box. Remember that a form is a dialog box only when it is opened in View Data mode. If you're in Design Form mode, running the form isn't the same as reopening it. You must reopen it.*

Spicing Up Your Forms

Windows is a wonderful color graphics environment. With the early versions of Windows, most applications had white backgrounds with black letters. Microsoft added three-dimensional buttons to version 3.1 to improve the look. Now with Windows 95, applications have come to life visually with stunning three-dimensional schemes. Keep this in mind, because your users will demand a high degree of visual appeal from your database applications. Just remember not to overdo it; keep your applications looking professional.

Spicing Up Your Applications

UIObjects are objects, such as circles, lines, fields, and buttons, that you can draw by using the toolbar. You can add pictures to spice up UIObjects. Use bitmaps whenever possible. Although small bitmaps are not part of the Windows 95 look and feel, many users consider them particularly attractive; they give your application a professional look. This illustration demonstrates adding graphics to buttons:

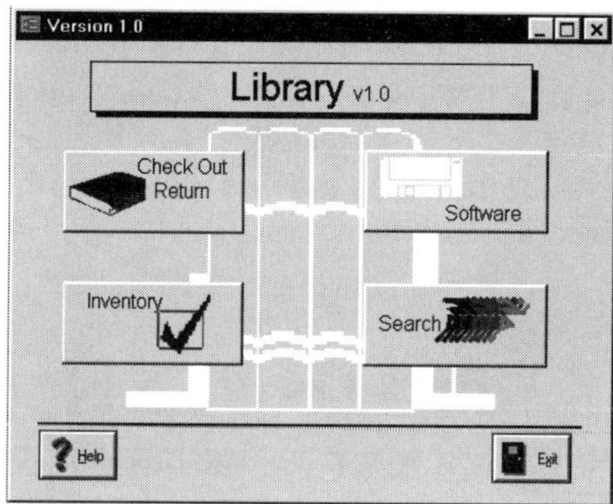

Do Not Crowd a Form

Many users use Paradox to duplicate printed forms: applications, records, and so on. Your natural inclination might be to put all the fields on a single 8.5 × 11-inch page—just like the real form. Try to resist this temptation, because it causes problems with the user interface.

Consistency Is the Key to Creating Good-Looking Forms

Choose consistent colors when you create and place objects. If you choose a white background for your forms, stick to it. If you choose another color or a special color scheme, such as a Windows 95 look, stick to it. When you design forms, a good approach is to set your colors to the Windows default by using the Control Panel.

To achieve a good user interface, you need to be consistent. Make similar objects the same size. Buttons are especially noticeable; try to use only one or two sizes for them and locate them on the right or bottom side of the form. Use a consistent line width and frame style.

At the same time, limit the number of visual elements in your application. A good-looking application doesn't have an abundance of colors or objects. Instead, good-looking applications use subtle design elements. Use patterns sparingly; only one or two styles for each application. When you select colors, feel free to choose as many as you need for the foreground, background, text, title, and user input—just be consistent. Realize, however, that just because your users have at least 16 colors, you don't have to use every color on a single form or in a single application.

Just as Microsoft has found a look and feel it likes (the Windows 95/98 look), you should strive to find your own style. You can create several looks and switch among them with each project, or you can develop a single look; your users may soon recognize your applications. Keep in mind, however, that the data is more important than the flashy objects around it.

Data Model and Table Lookup Notes

This section does not tell you how to use the data model; data model theory is discussed in Chapter 2, and it is assumed that you already know the basics of linking tables with the data model. Instead, this section points out some common pitfalls of the data model and table lookups with respect to forms.

Link the Correct Way

When using referential integrity, make sure that you link from the master to the detail. If you accidentally link from the detail to the master, the data model will attempt to update the child table before updating the master table; this causes the error message Master Record missing.

Do Not Hard-Code Table Lookups

When you hard-code a table lookup, you specify the drive, path, and table filename. As discussed in Chapter 2, aliases are not allowed on table lookups. This, unfortunately, limits the usefulness of table lookups. If your data needs to be portable, then put the table lookups in the same directory as the main data or a subdirectory below it. This second technique is called *relative directory addressing* (RDA). This enables you to move your entire data directory (along with its subdirectories) to a different location.

Special, Summary, and Calculated Fields

Many users have trouble understanding calculated fields. For this reason, and so that you don't try to duplicate this functionality by using ObjectPAL, this next section explores how to use special, summary, and calculated fields.

Using Special or Calculated Fields

To use a special or calculated field, select the field into which you want the value to go, inspect its properties, and choose Define Field. You can use the tools in the Define Field Object dialog box to set up a special or calculated field.

When you *define* a field object, you attach it to data from a table. For example, you define a field object in a form as a field in a table. You cannot define calculated fields to a field in a table. Do not confuse defining with binding. You *bind* or *associate* an object such as a table frame or multirecord object (MRO) with a table, whereas you *define* a field.

Special Fields and Summary Fields

A *special field* is a field, placed in a design document, that contains information about a table or design. These fields are predefined by Paradox, such as Now and Table Name. Table 3-1 describes special fields, Table 3-2 describes special table fields, and Table 3-3 describes the summary fields.

Field	Description
Now	Displays the current running time in the field. This is an excellent and easy way to add a clock to your application. Because you can't define a field to a table and also use it as a special Now field, use the time() method via ObjectPAL to time-stamp a record or use the TimeStamp field type.
Today	Displays the current date in the field.
TimeStamp	Displays the current time and date in the field.
Page Number	Displays the current page number of the form.
Number of Pages	Displays the total number of pages in the current form.

TABLE 3-1 Special Fields

Field	Description
Table Name	Displays the name of the table in the field. Table Name is particularly useful in reports.
Record Number	Displays the current record number in the field. Using a table's record number is particularly useful for autonumbering records in forms and reports when you don't need to store the number with the table. Record Number obeys restricted views. That is, if the number of records is restricted by the data model, Record Number reflects this and starts numbering at 1. This makes it useful for autonumbering items in a typical invoicing system.
Number of Records	Displays the total number of restricted records.
Number of Fields	Displays the number of fields in the table.

TABLE 3-2 Special Table Fields

Field	Description
Sum	Adds all the values.
Count	Displays a count of all the records.
Min	Displays the smallest value for this field in the table.
Max	Displays the largest value for this field in the table.
Avg	Displays the average value for this field in the table.
Std	Displays the standard deviation of the values in the set.
Var	Displays the statistical variance of the values in the set.

TABLE 3-3 Summary Fields

Example of Autoincrementing a Restricted View

Suppose that you wish to number the detail records in a typical invoicing system. To do this, you do not need ObjectPAL. The special table field Record Number can handle the task.

Step By Step

1. Launch Paradox, and set your working directory to the Paradox's sample directory.
2. Select File | New | Form and use the Data Model option to link ORDERS.DB to LINEITEM.DB in a 1:M relationship. Select OK.
3. At the Design Layout screen, select By Rows under the Field Layout section in the Layout tab, and select OK.
4. Add a column to the detail table frame by clicking below row 1 until the column is selected. Then press the INSERT key. Your form should now look similar to Figure 3-2.
5. To display the Define Field Object dialog box for the newly added column, select the undefined field of the column you added in step 4. Right-click (or press F6) to inspect the field. Select Define Field.
6. Select the drop-down arrow of the LINEITEM.DB table and then select "<Record Number>". Select OK.

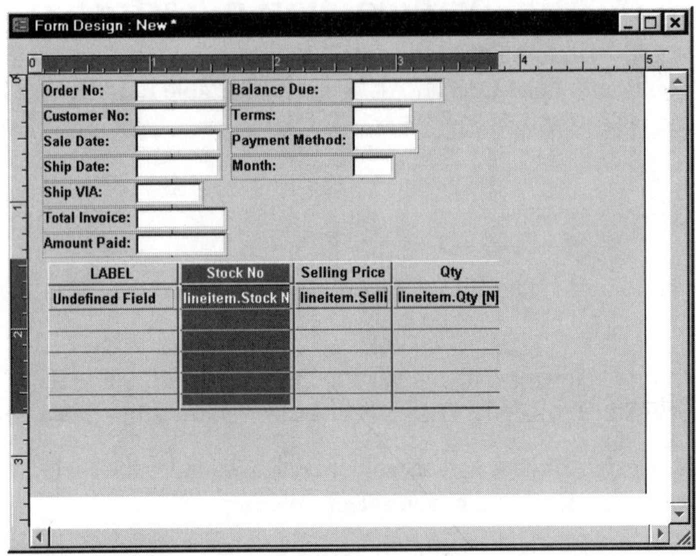

FIGURE 3-2 Adding a column to a table frame

7. Label the column Item Number if you want, and run the form. Optionally, you can change the format of the field to integer. The form, depicted here, shows the use of a table field for the line item in the first column.

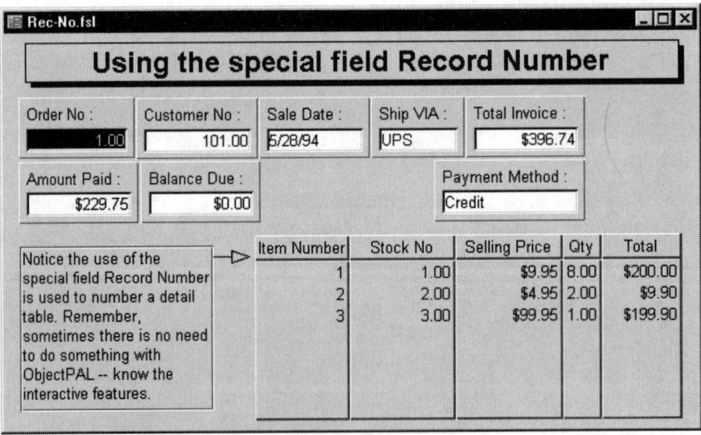

8. Save the form as REC-NO.FSL.

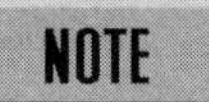

If you had any problems with this example (or any example in this book), you can download the completed files from the Internet at http://www.prestwood.com/forums/paradox/books/official/files.

Analysis

The first column is numbered 1 through however many records there are in the restricted view. The restricted view is determined by the table relationships set up in the data model. This operation is built into Paradox. You could do this same operation in ObjectPAL, but with difficulty.

Before you code in ObjectPAL, ask yourself two questions. Does Paradox already do this? Is there a better and easier way? Remember, simple solutions for simple problems.

You also can use the Record Number table field with reports—for example, when you want the records of a report to be numbered. Special and summary fields have many uses, so make sure that you know what all these field types do. The Now special field is particularly useful. To put a clock on a form, simply place an undefined field on the form and define it as the Now special field type. Voila! In an instant, you have created a running clock on your form.

Using Calculated Fields

Calculated fields use the Calculated panel of the Define Field Object dialog box to set up a user-defined formula or to display concatenated strings. When you combine two or more alphanumeric values, you *concatenate* them. An *operator* is a symbol that represents an operation to be performed on a value or values. For example, the + operator represents addition, and the * operator represents multiplication. The *arithmetic operators* in ObjectPAL are +, -, *, /, and (). Use these operators to construct mathematical expressions in queries and calculated fields. To concatenate two or more alphanumeric values in a calculated field (or ObjectPAL), for example, use the + operator. For example, the following formula

```
City.value + ", " + State.value
```

concatenates three strings to form a value, such as

```
Milpitas, CA
```

In addition to arithmetic operators, you can use in a calculated field any expression that returns a single value. This includes any ObjectPAL statement that returns a single value. Although you have not formally started your study of ObjectPAL, here are some fairly self-explanatory, single-command expressions you can use in a calculated field:

startUpDir()	privDir()
workingDir()	windowsDir()
windowsSystemDir()	isToolBarShowing()
getMouseScreenPosition()	version()
isDir("C:\\DOS")	fieldName1.value + fieldName2.value

Following are some combination-method expressions you can use in a calculated field:

size(startUpDir())	isLeapYear(today())
number(fieldName1.value) + number(fieldName2.value)	dow(today())
doy(today())	

Using *iif()*

You can use the iif (immediate if) statement in both calculated fields and ObjectPAL to make decisions. With an iif statement, you can in essence say, "If the following expression is true, this field's value is A. Otherwise, this field's value is B."

Syntax:

```
iif(Condition, ValueIfTrue, ValueIfFalse)
```

Examples:

```
iif(field1.value = blank(), today, field1.value)
iif(taxable.value = "Yes", ([LINEITEM.Selling Price] *
[LINEITEM.Qty]) * .06, blank())
```

TIP

If you ever have a calculated field on a form not update when you think it should, then you can use the ObjectPAL method forceRefresh() to make the calculated field display the correct values. This can occur, for example, when you update a field involved with a calculated field using a TCursor.

Special fields, special table fields, summary fields, and calculated fields are important to the ObjectPAL programmer. Many times, tasks are easier to accomplish with these fields than through ObjectPAL.

Summary

In addition to designing and creating tables, designing good forms makes your application more professional. Forms are the backbone of your application. In fact, in Paradox, forms are your application. The better you are at designing forms, the better your applications turn out.

CHAPTER 4

An Itroduction to ObjectPAL

Although interactive Paradox is powerful, it still can't do some things interactively. You have to accomplish some tasks using ObjectPAL (Object Paradox Application Language). Why would you need to use ObjectPAL? For example, you use ObjectPAL to automate or customize objects on a form. An example of a task that requires ObjectPAL is creating a custom menu system for a form. If you plan to develop a complete custom Paradox application, you probably will need to use ObjectPAL.

ObjectPAL is for both programmers and nonprogrammers. If you have experience with another language, especially an object-oriented programming language such as C++ or Delphi's ObjectPascal, you will find ObjectPAL especially interesting. If you have never programmed, ObjectPAL is a good language to learn first because it is easier to learn than C++ or ObjectPascal. With Paradox, you can paint objects onto a form and then attach bits of code to events on the object. You can learn as you go.

You use the user interface to design forms with objects on them, such as fields, tables, and buttons. When you're happy with the way the form works interactively, you attach ObjectPAL code to the objects that require it. The fact that you draw objects on a form and attach code to the objects allows even the nonprogrammer to create applications easily. This system of programming falls into the category of an event-driven language. It is event-driven because the objects you place on forms have predefined events attached to them. You attach code to the events and the user interacts with the events.

Features of ObjectPAL

ObjectPAL's features include an event handler, data types, strong program control, the run-time library, user-defined commands, support for dynamic link libraries, and delivery time binding.

The *event handler* is the part of Paradox that controls the events attached to objects. It decides when events are triggered. This type of programming cuts down the amount of time you spend programming.

Each ObjectPAL object is also known as an *object type*. ObjectPAL also has a long list of commands called *methods* and *procedures* that a programmer can use. These methods and procedures are organized by object types. For example, there is a set of methods and procedures associated with the TCursor object type (a TCursor allows you to access a table). A subcategory of object types is the data types which include String, Number, SmallInt, Date, Time, Array, DynArray, and others.

Each object type may also have properties associated with it. ObjectPAL also enables you to read or set all the properties that are associated with an object. You are already familiar with many of the properties such as Color, Tab Stop, and Next Tab Stop. For each object you work with in Paradox, you have a set of methods, procedures, and properties you can use to manipulate the object. Paradox's Object Explorer is your guide to each object type's properties and events. Paradox's ObjectPAL Reference help is your guide to each object type's methods and procedures.

The methods and procedures associated with each object type can either stand alone or work on the object they're associated with. Many of the commands are duplicated with the same name throughout the object types. Examples include open(), attach(), moveTo(), setTitle(), getPosition(), setPosition(), and searchRegistry().

To control all these object types, the language supports programming control—branching and looping—such as if, for, while, and scan.

As with C and Pascal, you can create your own commands with ObjectPAL. These user-created commands are called *custom methods* and *custom procedures*. Custom methods and procedures consist of methods and procedures from the run-time library and other user-defined routines. You also can make calls to dynamic link libraries (DLLs). DLLs contain functions and procedures that usually are written in C, C++, or Pascal. After you register the user-created function in ObjectPAL, you can use it as though it was included. Also, support for Delphi add-ins allows you to use menus and forms of the add-in within the Paradox desktop environment. These features offer you almost unlimited expandability.

A Powerful Programming Language

ObjectPAL is a complete programming language. Like Visual Basic's VBA, Delphi's ObjectPascal, and C++Builder's C++, ObjectPAL supports variables, control structures, loops, and more. The power of ObjectPAL pleases traditional programmers and has many features not found in other languages. You will appreciate ObjectPAL's flexible data typing (it isn't as strict as ObjectPascal, for example). It also has powerfull features not found in other languages. For example, ObjectPAL has a powerful switch statement that can match on strings, and ObjectPAL can manipulate databases with ease. The ObjectPAL language contains a rich array of functionality for managing data. You can find and manipulate values in a table. You can add records from one table to another. You can even scan a table, find every field that has a certain word, and change that word. No language can do it all, but ObjectPAL certainly comes close.

Sometimes, you might spend a few minutes in ObjectPAL, adding a few lines of code to an object on a form, and then you are done. Other times, you might spend hours coding many different objects that interact with one another. If you program in small steps and test as you go, programming in ObjectPAL can be fun and easy.

What Is Elegant Programming?

Before we continue our journey into ObjectPAL, this section diverges a little and discusses the ambiguous part of every programming language. Some programmers believe that what they write often approaches art because of its sheer elegance. Elegant programming is the best way to accomplish a particular task. It can mean many things, but most often, elegant programming means a routine that takes the least amount of code to complete a task fully. Try to resist overcoding a task. Recall from the last chapter: if you add some code that doesn't work, take it out!

The term *elegant code* has many meanings. Fast code, for example, is elegant. Code that uses a TCursor (a pointer to a table) can, in some situations, be more elegant than code that uses a UIObject (a user interface object). A TCursor is faster because it doesn't have the overhead of screen refreshes. (In many cases, however, you can accomplish the same objective by using a UIObject—especially if it's already there.)

Code that is free of bugs and takes into account all possibilities is elegant. The least amount of code is not always the most elegant. If code does not take care of all possibilities, then it is not adequate. This is the reason you need to let some of the users of your software test the software for functionality. This type of test is usually referred to as *beta testing* your software. For example, test the effect of putting blanks into date fields. Try putting negative numbers where you normally expect a positive number. If users can do it, they will!

Portable code is elegant. The capability to copy an object with code from one form to another with little modification is elegant. ObjectPAL is an object-based programming (OBP) language that enables you to create objects you can copy from one form to another. In most cases, this is not automatic, but with a little creative programming, you can create objects that are fully self-contained and that you can paste into other forms.

Even where you put code determines how elegant it is. The places—events—to which you attach ObjectPAL code is part of the event handler. The event handler handles all the events coming from Windows, such as key presses, mouse movements, and mouse button clicks. The event model that the event handler uses determines when your code will trigger. In ObjectPAL, *where* you code is as important as *what* you code.

Although no book can claim to have the correct answer for everything, this book does attempt to demonstrate elegant programming. This book won't always have the perfect solution for every problem; indeed, no book can make that claim. After typing in a routine, you might think of a more elegant way to code it. This is good: the challenging and fun part of programming is coming up with a better solution. The most elegant way isn't always obvious. As a programmer with limited time, you must balance your time between elegant and functional programming.

As you will see in later chapters, a problem often has several solutions that range from simple to complicated—and sometimes elegant. You learn the most by studying simple solutions first, and then more complicated solutions (rather than the other way around). You see the quickest and best way to complete a task. By seeing various levels of solutions to a problem, you learn more about elegant programming.

One form of elegant programming is structured programming—refer to Appendix A for more information on structured programming and how it applies to ObjectPAL.

Setting Your ObjectPAL Level

In this section, you are going to jump right in and write some ObjectPAL. First, make sure that your ObjectPAL level is set to Beginner. To do this, start Paradox. Select Tools | Settings | Developer Preferences to display the Developer Preferences dialog box (see Figure 4-1). This is where you set the developer preferences. From the ObjectPAL level panel of the General tab, select Beginner. Later, in the next chapter, you will switch to the Advanced level.

NOTE *Whether your ObjectPAL level is set to Beginner or Advanced, you can use all the ObjectPAL methods, procedures, properties, constants, keywords, and so on. The level panel is a help filter used just for learning purposes.*

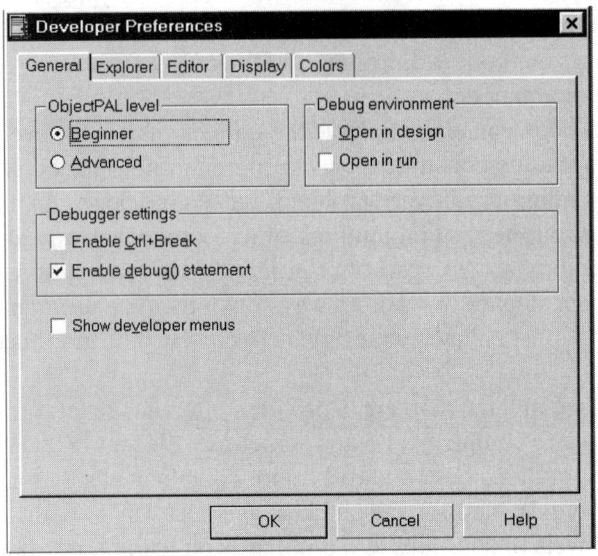

FIGURE 4-1 The Developer Preferences dialog box

Starting ObjectPAL

An object type's event is the location in a form, script, or library in which you place ObjectPAL code. This code is attached to the object and defines the object's response to that type of event. For example, pushing (clicking) a button triggers the pushButton event. If you wish to execute your code when a user clicks a button, then attach code to the button's pushButton event. Other examples include clicking on a box triggers the box's *mouseDown* event, and opening a form triggers the form's *init* event.

Code in ObjectPAL is attached to objects in the object's events. When the object you wish to work with is selected, select Tools | Object Explorer to display the Object Explorer. Figure 4-2 shows the Object Explorer in the Object Tree plus Tabbed Pane view displaying the events of a button. To add code to an event, simply double-click the event (this displays the ObjectPAL editor). The editor is closely tied to the compiler; you type commands—that is, text—into the editor that the compiler parses through and compiles into compiled PCode. This compiled PCode is what Paradox or the Paradox run time interprets when you run your application.

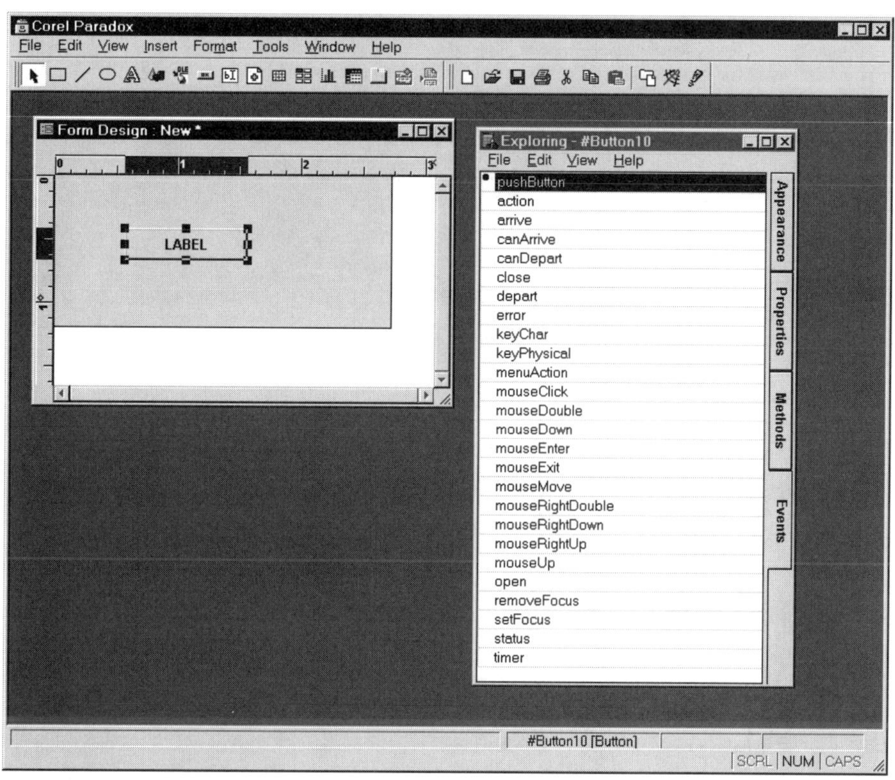

FIGURE 4-2 The Object Explorer

After you've opened the Object Explorer, you can edit any of the methods or events. For example, you can add code to the pushButton event of a button. The pushButton event is triggered when the user left-mouse clicks a button object. These events are what trigger your code. Figure 4-3 shows the ObjectPAL editor. With the Object Explorer open, select various objects and notice that the events for that particular object are displayed.

In the ObjectPAL editor, you enter code much as you would in other Windows editors, such as Notepad. The editor has the normal features of any Windows editor: cut, copy, paste, and so on. In addition, the editor has many features specific to ObjectPAL that check your syntax, help you build a line of code, color code your syntax, and debug your code.

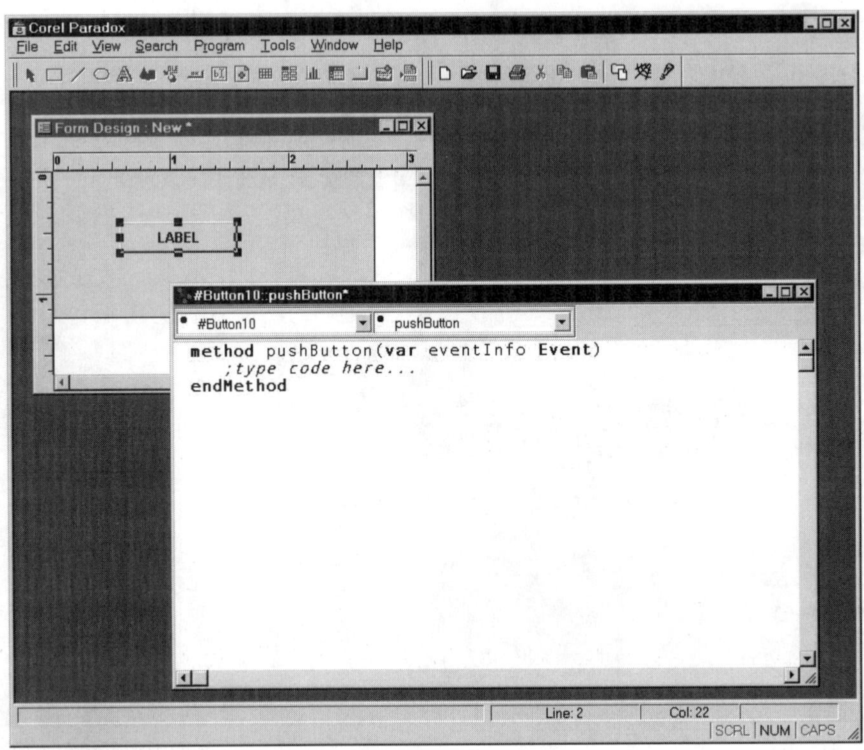

FIGURE 4-3 The ObjectPAL editor

Programming a Button to Send a Message to the Status Bar

A wonderful way to jump into ObjectPAL is to see what it can do. One type of command in ObjectPAL is called a *procedure*. Procedures generally are the easiest ObjectPAL commands to use because they usually are straightforward. The System object type has a message() procedure. You use it to display text on the status bar. The following is the syntax for message():

```
message ( const message String [, const message String]* )
```

To use this procedure, you type in the keyword **message** followed by an open parenthesis, and then type the string (in quotes) you want to show up on the status line followed by a close parenthesis, as in the following example (see Figure 4-4):

```
message("type String here")
```


You also can send a message composed of many different strings. Although the string concatenation symbol for ObjectPAL is the +, you can use a comma with the message() procedure. For example, the following lines of code display the same message on the status line:

```
message("Hello World")           ;Displays "Hello World".
message("Hello ", "World")       ;Displays "Hello World".
message("Hello " + "World")      ;Displays "Hello World".
```

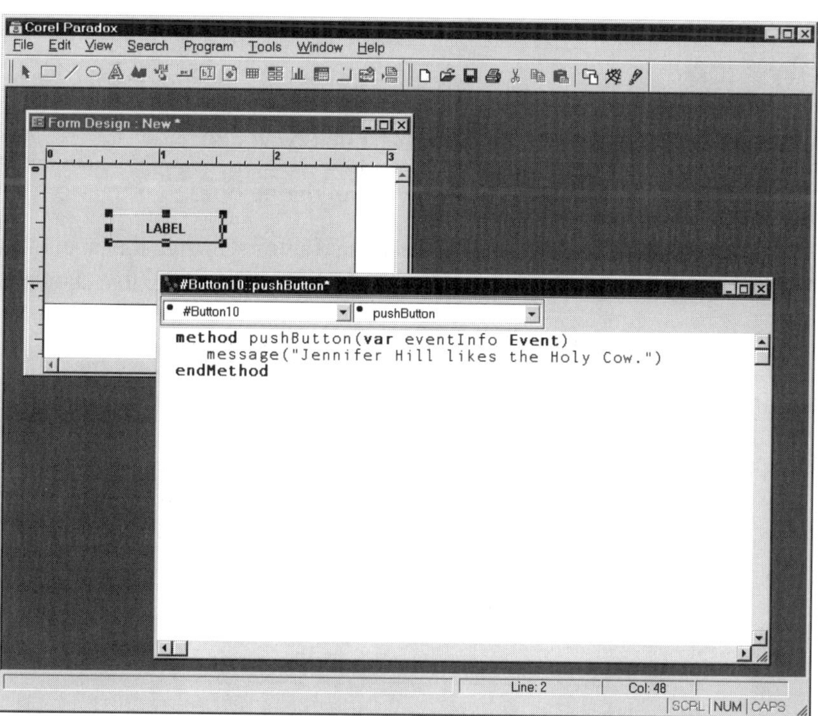

FIGURE 4-4 Using message() with a string

The first of the following few examples in ObjectPAL lead you step by step through the exercise. In most of the later examples, you are given only a setup description, the code for all the objects, and minimal instructions. It's important in these first few examples to understand how to get to the ObjectPAL editor, and how to enter code into methods and events.

Example of Sending a Message to the Status Line

Let's put the information we've learned so far to use and go through a step-by-step example. This example acquaints you with the pushButton event of a button and the System type's message() procedure. When you click on the button, a message is displayed on the status bar. Suppose that you want to send a message to the status bar when a user clicks a button.

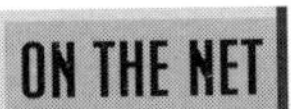

http://www.prestwood.com/forums/paradox/books/official/files/message.fsl.

Step By Step

1. Create a new blank form by selecting File | New | Form.
2. Select the Blank button on the New Form dialog box.
3. Place a button on the form with the Toolbar button. Change the label of the button to Display Message. Your form should now look like that shown here:

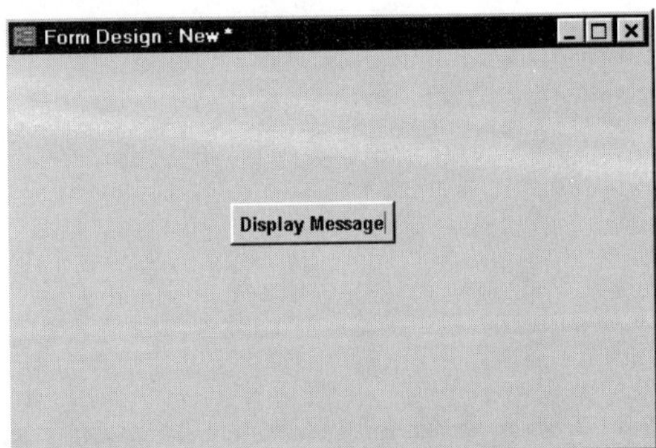

4. Make sure the button is selected and select Tools | Object Explorer to display the Object Explorer (see Figure 4-5).

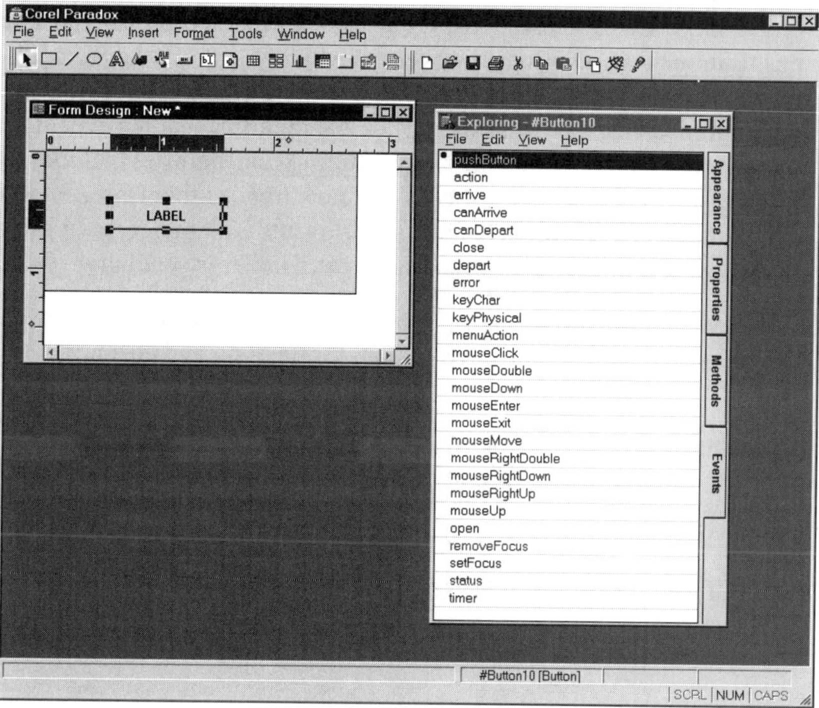

FIGURE 4-5 Select the Object Explorer option

5. To open the ObjectPAL editor for the pushButton event, double-click the pushButton event from the Events tab of the Object Explorer. Between method and endMethod, there is a blank line with a blinking cursor ready for you to type code.

6. In the pushButton event, type lines 2 and 3. Line 2 is a comment. You can tell it is a remark because it starts with a ;. Lines 1 and 4 signify the beginning and the end of the event. Line 3 does the actual work you want it to do.

```
1:    method pushButton(var eventInfo Event)
2:       ; Example of using System::message().
3:       message("The Holy Cow is a wild creature.")
4:    endMethod
```

All modifiable events and custom methods start with method and end with endMethod. Take a closer look at line 1. After method is the events name, pushButton. This identifies the event to which you are attaching code—in this case, pushButton. Following pushButton is the parameter that pushButton takes, var eventInfo Event. var signifies that the event is passed by reference (more on this later). eventInfo Event signifies that the eventInfo variable is of type Event. For now, realize that ObjectPAL is an event-driven type of language that sends events from object to object and line 1 identifies the type of event the event handler is sending.

7. Check your syntax by selecting Program | Check Syntax. If you have any syntax errors, correct them. (Watch out for opening and closing parentheses and quotation marks.)
8. Close the ObjectPAL editor window.
9. Save the form by selecting File | Save As. Save the form as MESSAGE.FSL.
10. Run the form by selecting Program | Run.
11. Click the Display Message button. The message appears in the status bar.

The Elements of ObjectPAL

Now that you have gotten your feet wet, take a closer look at ObjectPAL. ObjectPAL consists of many different elements. When you study a broad subject such as a programming language, it often is helpful to categorize what you are about to learn. The following paragraphs describe the elements of ObjectPAL.

An *event handler* is a type of programming language that has preset triggers to which the programmer can attach code. The idea of attaching code to triggers on objects puts Paradox in this category. Do not confuse the category of *event handler* with the term *event model*. An event model is the map that an event handler uses to process events. The *events* are the triggers that start your code, such as pushButton, open, and changeValue. Events are part of the event handler.

The actual words or building blocks of ObjectPAL are called *keywords*, such as doDefault, DisableDefault, method, endMethod, var, endVar, if, endIf, switch, and endSwitch. For example, an if statement is comprised of the following keywords: if, then, the optional else, and endIf. The ObjectPAL editor displays all keywords in bold. Consider keywords to be the skeleton of your code.

The *methods*—commands—act on and belong to objects, such as open(), setPosition(), and moveTo(). Examples of methods include formVariable.open ("form"), theBox.setPosition(100,100), and fieldName.moveTo(). Methods differ from *procedures*, which are commands that don't have a specified object on which they work, such as close(), setTitle(), and setAliasPath(). Examples of procedures include close(), setTitle("My Application"), and setAliasPath("MyAlias", "C:\\WORK\\DATA").

In ObjectPAL, you can manipulate the *properties*—the characteristics—of objects, such as value, color, and tabStop. Examples of properties include fieldName.value = "Angie Herbal", theBox.frame.color = Blue, and buttonName.tabStop = True. Most of the properties that you set interactively by typing in values or inspecting an object can be set using ObjectPAL.

Object variables are built into the language, such as self, container, and active. Examples of using object variables include self.color = Red, container.color = Blue, and message(active.Name).

A *constant* is a word that represents an unchanging value you can use in ObjectPAL. ObjectPaL has both predifined constants and user defined constants. Red, DataInsertRecord, and True are all constants that ObjectPAL already understands. With constants, the number the constant represents does not matter (and can change in a future version). This humanizes ObjectPAL; that is, it makes it easier to relate to. You use a meaningful word rather than a number in your code. Examples of using constants include box1.color = Red, action(DataInsertRecord), and fld3.tabStop = True. You also can use user-created constants; more on constants you create later in the section titled "Basic Language Elements and ObjectPAL."

Introducing the Event Handler

In the first example earlier in this chapter, you used the pushButton event of a button, but how do you know which event to add code to? One thing that makes ObjectPAL easy to learn is that it is an event-driven language. You can refer to the event-driven part of ObjectPAL as the event handler. In a traditional procedural language, you have to write everything, including the interface—one of the least favorite tasks for a developer.

In Paradox, you design the interface interactively with little trouble. In fact, it's fun to design forms with Paradox. With the interface out of the way, you simply attach code to enhance or restrict the interface and its built-in behavior. In most cases, you want to put the code on the object on which you want it to act. If you want a button to do something, put code on the pushButton event of the button. If you want to prevent a user from leaving a field, put code on the canDepart event of that field. Whenever you search for a place to put code, ask yourself, "What object am I working with or on?" Think of programming in ObjectPAL as attaching small bits of code to events or triggers. Table 4-1 lists some common events you can place code in. This table can be valuable for beginning ObjectPAL programmers.

Every object has a default behavior that you can modify with built-in events. Most objects share the same built-in events: action, menuAction, arrive, canDepart, mouseClick, and error. Some objects have unique built-in events, such as pushButton for a button.

The Six Beginner-Level Events

Whenever you're looking for a place to put code, consider ObjectPAL's six beginner-level events first. These core events are the events new users to ObjectPAL will use most. Table 4-2 provides a short description of each.

Object	Location	Example of Typical Use
Form	init	Initializes variables and sets up tables
Form	arrive	Maximizes a form and sets values in the form
Form	menuAction	Processes menu events
Form	action	Traps for key violations on a single table form
Form	mouseExit	Clears the status bar if you use mouseEnter
Page	arrive	Sets up a custom pull-down menu
Button	pushButton	Executes code when the user selects a button
Button	mouseEnter	Adds help by sending a message to the status bar
Field	changeValue	Checks a new value against an old value in a table

TABLE 4-1 Common Places to Put Code

Method	Description
action	Used when a user calls, or triggers, an event. Typically, action is used for trapping events and processing them. For example, action is useful for trapping database actions such as inserting a record, and moving in and out of edit mode.
menuAction	Called whenever a user selects a menu option. Put code in the menuAction method if you wish to trap for when the user selects an option from the menu, toolbar, or form control box.
arrive	arrive occurs whenever focus moves to a field. At first, arrive seems identical to setFocus, which occurs whenever focus moves to an object (and with fields, this appearance is somewhat accurate). With some objects, however, it is not. Look at a form opening to illustrate. First, the init event is called, followed by open and arrive, and finally setFocus. arrive occurs only after open, whereas setFocus occurs whenever the form becomes active—for example, with a multiple form application. You can use arrive to instruct the user what to enter. By the way, arrive only occurs after canArrive.
canDepart	Think of canDepart as the opposite of arrive. Typically, canDepart is used for data integrity. For example, if the value is less than 100, canDepart can prevent the user from leaving the field until the correct value is entered.
mouseClick	This is triggered whenever the logical left mouse button is pressed and released when the mouse is on an object.
error	This event is triggered whenever an error occurs. The error event is used to add to the event action (response).

TABLE 4-2 The Six Beginner-Level Events

Types of Commands

ObjectPAL has several types of commands you can use in an event. This section addresses procedures, methods, keywords, and properties, which are some of the commands you can use in an event.

Identifying Procedures

You already have used a procedure in your first example. A procedure is a powerful type of command; it can stand alone. In other words, a procedure would be complete on a line by itself. For example, each of the following is a procedure.

```
message("Press OK to continue")
msgInfo("Warning", "You are about to delete a record")
isFile("C:\\DOS\\COMMAND.COM") ;Note the double \.
```

Identifying Methods

A method is a weaker type of command. You must use an object of the same type as its class when using a method. For example:

```
TaxableField.isBlank()     ;TaxableField is a Field object.
f.open("FORM1")            ;f is a Form object.
```

Another way to look at methods versus procedures is to say that a procedure always knows the object it works on or with, but a method does not. To further confuse the issue, some commands can serve as both procedures and methods, as in the following example:

```
1:    close()      ;Procedure that closes the current form.
2:    f.close()    ;A method that closes the form associated
3:                 ;with f (f is a form variable).
```

Line 1 uses the close() command as a procedure—it knows to close the current form. If, however, you use close() as a method, you need to specify an object. In line 2, f is a form variable you have opened previously.

The Alternative Syntax

Do not confuse a command that can be both a method and procedure with the alternate syntax. Whenever you code object.method(), the alternate syntax enables you to code method(object), as in the following example:

```
f.close()    ;Regular syntax.
close(f)     ;Alternate syntax.
```

When a single command supports the alternate syntax, which syntax should you use? Although it doesn't really matter, the regular syntax object.doIt(), as seen in the preceding first line, is preferred. It's more consistent with the rest of the language. Don't worry too much about these variations in syntax at this point.

Identifying Keywords

Keywords are words reserved for use with certain commands in ObjectPAL. They are special language construct commands that are neither procedures nor methods. Keywords include Proc, endProc, method, endMethod, doDefault, iif, and

Database. At this point, just be aware that you shouldn't use keywords in ObjectPAL for the names of objects or variables.

Following is an example of keywords that are used properly:

```
;Button :: pushButton
method pushButton(var eventInfo Event) ;method is a keyword.
   if taxable.value = "Yes" then  ;if & then are keywords.
      tax.value = subtotal * .06
   else                            ;else is a keyword.
      tax.value = 0
   endIf                           ;endIf is a keyword.
endMethod                        ;endMethod is a keyword.
```


method, if, then, else, endIf, and endMethod are all keywords. You can't give objects or variables names that are the same as these keywords. In fact, it's a good idea not to give an object or a variable the same name as any element of the ObjectPAL language.

Altering Properties and Dot Notation

Objects that you place on a form have properties. You have already set many of the properties of objects—for example, when you change the color of a box on a form to blue. With ObjectPAL, you can alter an object's property with dot notation. Dot notation is the basic syntax structure used in ObjectPAL. It uses dots to separate elements in a complex statement. Following is the basic syntax structure:

```
ObjectName.property = Constant
```

The capability to alter properties while the form is running is powerful and sets Paradox above many other DBMS systems. Following are some examples of altering the properties of objects:

```
box1.color = Blue              ;Change box1 to blue.
box1.visible = False           ;Make box1 disappear.
Last_Name.color = Yellow       ;Change field color.
City.tabStop = False           ;Do not allow focus to City.
```

Dot notation also can represent a complete path to an object. The following examples set the properties of objects in other objects:

```
1: pge3.box1.Last_Name.color = DarkGray ;Change field to dark gray.
2: f.pge3.visible = False              ;Make a page disappear.
3: box1.Last_Name.Frame.Style = Windows3DGroup ;Change the style.
```

The example in line 3 of the preceding code represents a compound property. The path of the object is box1.Last_Name. The compound property is Frame.Style. This is confusing, especially when learning ObjectPAL. For now, understand that both the object path and the property can be composed of multiple values. The following are three instances for which dot notation is used in ObjectPAL:

- To separate an object and property, as in the following:

  ```
  Last_Name.value = "Santwier"
  ```

- To separate or indicate an object's path, as in the following:

  ```
  pge2.boxSection3.Last_Name.value = "Santwier"
  ```

- To separate an object and a method, as in the following:

  ```
  Last_Name.moveTo()
  ```

NOTE *For now, think of the containership path of an object as analogous to a directory path. When you open a file, you specify its path—for example, C:\PDOXWIN\DATA\MYFORM.FSL. You can think of a subfolder as being owned (or contained) within its parent folder just as objects are owned (contained) by owner objects. When referring to objects, you need to specify the path of the object with dots rather than a slash, as in the following example:*

```
pge2.boxSection3.Last_Name.
```

Properties are another type of code you can use in ObjectPAL to get or alter the attributes of an object. Think of objects as having a set of properties attached to them. Some of the properties of a field object are value, color, font.color, TabStop, Name, FieldName, TableName and Enabled. The next example demonstrates that you can alter the properties of objects with ObjectPAL.

Changing the Color of a Box

Suppose that you want to change the color of a box when the user clicks the box. This example uses the mouseClick method of a box to alter the property color. The object variable self is used to refer to the object to which the code is attached. This example also demonstrates using dot notation.

http://prestwood.com/forums/paradox/books/official/files/COLOR.FSL.

Step By Step

1. Create a new form and add a box to the form (see Figure 4-6).
2. Right-click the box and select Object Explorer to display its Object Explorer.
3. Select Events.

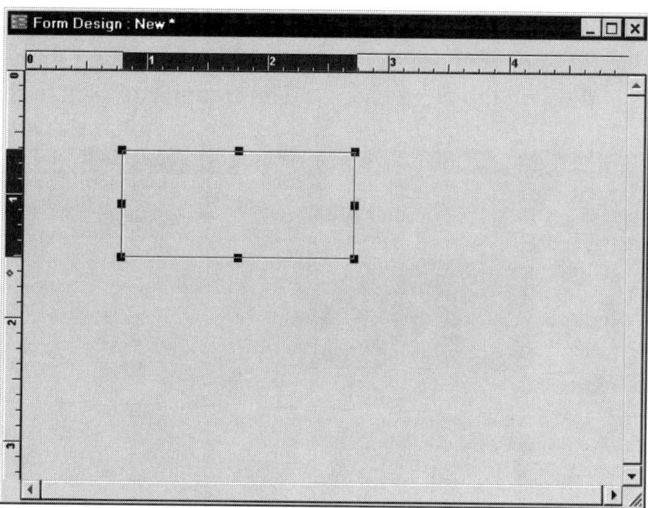

FIGURE 4-6 Setup form for example

4. Open the built-in mouseClick method.

5. In the mouseClick method, enter lines 3 and 4. Lines 2 and 5 begin and end the method attached to the event. These lines of code are always provided for you by ObjectPAL. In line 2, note that the eventInfo variable type in this case is MouseEvent. This is important to note and is discussed in more detail later. For now, understand an event of type MouseEvent was sent to the mouseClick event. Line 3 is a comment. Lines that start with a semicolon are stripped out when the form is compiled or run. Do yourself a favor and comment all your code heavily. You'll appreciate your efforts when you go back to the code a month later. The semicolon also is a good way to disable a line of code; it's useful when you debug code. Look at line 4, which uses a special built-in object variable, self, to refer to the object to which the code is attached. If you named the box box1, you could have used box1.color = Red rather than self.color = Red. color is a property of the object type Box; in this case, we set it to red.

```
1:    ;COLOR :: theBox :: mouseClick
2:    method mouseClick(var eventInfo MouseEvent)
3:       ;The following changes the color of self.
4:       self.color = Red
5:    endMethod
```

6. Check your syntax and save the form as COLOR.FSL.

7. Close the Edit box and run the form by selecting View | View Data. Click the box and watch the color change. The completed form is shown here:

One type of code that you write in ObjectPAL gets or alters the property of an object. Think of objects as having both attributes (properties) and code (methods and procedures) attached to them. Some of the properties of a field object are value, color, tabStop, name, fieldName, and tableName. A compound property involves another object in font.color. As demonstrated in the previous example, you can alter the properties of objects with ObjectPAL.

ObjectPAL Is Descriptive

In addition to altering an application's look by manipulating properties, there are many ObjectPAL commands that can have an effect on an application. For example, you can change the look of the desktop with the procedures hideToolbar() and showToolbar(). They hide and show the toolbar. For example:

```
hideToolbar()   ;Hide Toolbar.
sleep(1000)     ;Wait for 1 second.
showToolbar()   ;Show toolbar.
```

Notice how descriptive ObjectPAL is. It uses real words that describe what you're doing. Sounds easy so far, right? Well, that's because it is easy. The reason ObjectPAL has such a steep learning curve is that it's so rich in commands. Every procedure and method is as easy to understand as the previous examples; however, because there are so many procedures, methods, and properties, it takes a while just to get a handle on ObjectPAL.

Basic Language Elements and ObjectPAL

Now that you have looked at ObjectPAL from the big picture, this next section introduces basic programming elements common to most programming languages and relates these common elements to ObjectPAL. If you have programmed in another language before, then you will particularly like this section.

If you want to type and run the examples in this section, then use the pushButton method of a button and type the code, run the form, and select the button. (There is no need to type the comments.)

A *variable* is a place in memory used to store data temporarily. You first declare a variable and then you use it. For example, a *string* is an alphanumeric value or an expression consisting of alphanumeric characters. You can convert a number to a string with string(x) or you can declare a string variable and use it as the following code demonstrates. For example, line 2 that follows declares s as a string:

```
1:     var                                  ;Begin variable block.
2:        s     String                      ;Declare s as a String.
3:     endVar                               ;End variable block.
4:
5:     s = "Press OK to continue."          ;Set s to String value.
6:     message(s)                           ;Display value stored in s.
```

An *operator* is a symbol that represents an operation to be performed on a value or values. For example, the + operator represents addition, and the * operator represents multiplication. Line 8 in the code that follows multiplies x and y and then displays the result on the status line.

```
1:     var                     ;Start variable block.
2:        x     Number         ;Declare x as a number.
3:        y     Number         ;Declare y as a number.
4:     endVar                  ;End variable block.
5:
6:     x = 10                  ;Set x to 10.
7:     y = 5                   ;Set y to 5.
8:     message(x * y)          ;Displays 50 on the status line.
```

When you *concatenate* two values, you combine two or more alphanumeric values with the + operator. For example, line 9 that follows concatenates two strings and then assigns the value to s2:

```
1:     var                     ;Begin variable block.
2:        s1    String         ;Declare s1 as a String.
3:        s2    String         ;Declare s2 as a String.
4:     endVar                  ;End variable block.
5:
6:     s1 = "Enter name here"              ;Set s1 to String.
```

```
    s1.view("What is your name?")    ;View s1 in a view box.

    s2 = "Hello " + s1               ;Set s2 to String plus s1.
    message(s2)                      ;Display s2 on status line.
```

Comparison operators are symbols used to compare two values in a query, in a calculated field, or in an ObjectPAL expression. The comparison operators are ≤, ≥, <=, >=, and =. For example, lines 11–13 compare x and y. Depending on which value is greater, a different message is displayed.

```
 1:  var                                      ;Begin variable block.
 2:     x     Number                          ;Declare x as a number.
 3:     y     Number                          ;Declare y as a number.
 4:  endVar                                   ;End variable block.
 5:  x = 0                                    ;Set x to 0.
 6:  x.view("Enter value for x")              ;View x in a view box.
 7:  y = 0                                    ;Set y to 0.
 8:  y.view("Enter value for y")              ;View y in a view box.
 9:
10:  switch                                   ;Begin switch block.
11:     case x > y : message("x is bigger")       ;Is x > y?
12:     case y > x : message("y is bigger")       ;Is y > x?
13:     case x = y : message("They are equal")    ;Is x = Y?
14:  endSwitch                                ;End switch block.
```

A *constant* is a specific, unchanging value. ObjectPAL uses two types of constants: those used in calculations and defined in the Const window of an object and constants predefined by ObjectPAL. For example, line 2 that follows uses a user-set constant that sets the value of pi to 8 decimal points:

```
1:  const                      ;Begin constant block.
2:     pi = 3.14159265         ;Set the permanent value of pi.
3:  endConst                   ;End constant block.
4:
5:  ;Display the square root of pi.
6:  message("The square root of pi is ", sqrt(pi))
```

You already have used predefined constants; all property values are actually predefined constants. For example, in the previous example, you used self.color = Red. Red is a constant that represents a number ObjectPAL associates with the color red. You use constants as values that you pass to methods and procedures, such as DataNextRecord, DarkBlue, and FieldForward. Examples of passing constants to methods include fieldName.action(DataNextRecord), fieldName.font.color = DarkBlue, and active.action(FieldForward).

The following line of code shows the numeric equivalent to the constant Red:

```
message("The numeric value of Red is ", SmallInt(Red))
```

Although it is academically interesting to understand the numbers behind the built-in ObjectPAL constants, always use the constants in your own coding. Never use the numbers, for they get renumbered in a future version.

A *branch* transfers program control to an instruction other than the next sequential instruction. When you used the switch block in the example for comparison operators, you branched to one line of code or another depending on a comparison. Normally, a programming language executes line after line in sequential order. This is true whether the language is a line-oriented language, such as BASIC, or a statement-oriented language, such as ObjectPAL, Object Pascal, or C++.

In programming languages, a *control structure* is a set of keywords used to branch or loop. With control structures, you can alter the sequence of execution and add logic to your code. A *loop* is a set of instructions that is repeated a predetermined number of times or until a specified condition is met. For example, lines 6 and 7 in the code that follows are repeated 10 times as indicated in line 5.

```
1:    var                      ;Begin variable block.
2:       x     Number          ;Declare x as a number.
3:    endVar                   ;End variable block.
4:
5:    for x from 1 to 10       ;Begin loop.
6:       message(x)            ;Display x.
7:       sleep(500)            ;Wait 1/2 second.
8:    endFor                   ;End Loop.
```

A *logical value* is a True or False value that is assigned to an expression when it is evaluated. *Logical operators* are operators used in queries, in calculated fields, and in ObjectPAL methods. The three logical operators are and, or, and not. For example, line 2 in the code that follows declares l as a logical variable, and line 6 uses the not logical operator to display the opposite of l in a view box:

```
1:     var                      ;Begin variable block.
2:        l     Logical         ;Declare l as a logical.
3:     endVar                   ;End variable block.
4:
5:     l = True                 ;Set l to True.
6:     view(not l)              ;Display False in view box.
```


A *subroutine* is a sequence of instructions that performs a specific task, usually more than once in a program. The sequence may be invoked many times by the current program or by multiple applications. Although ObjectPAL doesn't have actual subroutines, you can think of custom methods and custom procedures as subroutines.

Hiding the Desktop

At one point or another, most users want to create a form that hides the Paradox desktop. To do this, the application type has two usefull methods: hide() and show(). To use them, you need to define an Application variable and use that variable with the hide() and show() methods, as in the following example:

```
1:     var
2:        app  Application    ;App is now an application variable.
3:     endVar
4:     app.hide()              ;Hide the desktop.
5:     sleep(5000)             ;Wait 5 seconds.
6:     app.show()              ;Show the desktop.
```

Unless you have defined your form as a dialog box and have reopened it, your form will disappear with the desktop. At first, hide the desktop only for a period of time; for example, five seconds. Note that even though hide() and show() don't have a parameter passed to them, you still use parentheses. Parentheses are part of the basic syntax for all methods and procedures. Contrast this with properties, which never use parentheses.

To cause a delay, you can use sleep() from the system type. In line 5, you use the sleep() procedure to sleep for 5,000 milliseconds (5 seconds). You can tell that sleep() is a procedure and not a method because it has no object on which to work. A method requires an object on which to work; a procedure does not.

After a variable is defined as an application, you can use any of the application-type methods on it. In addition to hide() and show(), you can use and manipulate an application variable with the following methods: bringToTop(), getPosition(), getTitle(), isMaximized(), isMinimized(), isVisible(), maximize(), minimize(), setPosition(), setTitle(), windowClienthandle(), and windowHandle().

First Database Routines

All this programming theory and manipulating properties and the desktop is necessary and useful, but it probably isn't the reason you purchased Paradox. This section discusses some of the basic commands used to edit data.

In ObjectPAL, you often have several ways to do something. For example, to go to the beginning of a table, you could use either a method or an action constant. The following two lines of code are equivalent:

```
MyField1.nextRecord()
MyField1.action(DataNextRecord)
```

These two methods represent two techniques for maneuvering through a table. Both of these methods move the pointer from the current record to the next record. The first line requires less typing and is my preferred usage. The second line represents more clearly what ObjectPAL is doing, however. The action() method sends a constant to the event action. When the constant DataNextRecord reaches the action event, action knows to move the table cursor to the next record. In addition to nextRecord(), there is a whole set of table-related methods, including home(), end(), and priorRecord().

In addition to using the object variable self, which refers to the object the code is attached to, you can use active, which represents the object with focus. You can combine these with the two distinctly different techniques for positioning the pointer, as in the following example:

```
self.nextRecord()              ;Move to the next record.
active.nextRecord()            ;Move to the next record.
self.action(DataNextRecord)    ;Move to the next record.
active.action(DataNextRecord) ;Move to the next record.
```

These two groups of code use the self and active built-in object variables. self refers to the object that executes the code and active refers to the object that has focus.

Using *edit()* and *endEdit()*

When you go into edit mode (with a command such as edit()), it is important to note that you put the whole form into edit mode. In other words, you can go to any field of any table on any page and enter or edit values. When you issue an endEdit() command, the whole form is taken out of edit mode. Since the edit() method is a method of an object (self) that also has a TableName property, the edit() method can use that property to put the correct table into edit mode. active refers to the object that currently has the focus. In a multitable form, you could use active to move the record pointer to the table that is attached to the selected object.

Basic Database Buttons

Suppose that you want to put eight buttons on a form that do simple database tasks: Top, Bottom, Previous, Next, Edit, Store, New, and Delete. This example introduces you to the following ObjectPAL methods: home(), end(), priorRecord(), nextRecord(), edit(), postRecord(), endEdit(), insertRecord(), and deleteRecord(). It also introduces the if structure.

http://prestwood.com/forums/paradox/books/official/files/OV-LIKE.FSL form.

Step By Step

1. Make your working directory Paradox's Samples directory and create a new form with the CUSTOMER.DB table in its data model.
2. Place eight buttons on the form. Change their labels to Top, Bottom, Previous, Next, Edit, Store, New, and Delete, as shown next:

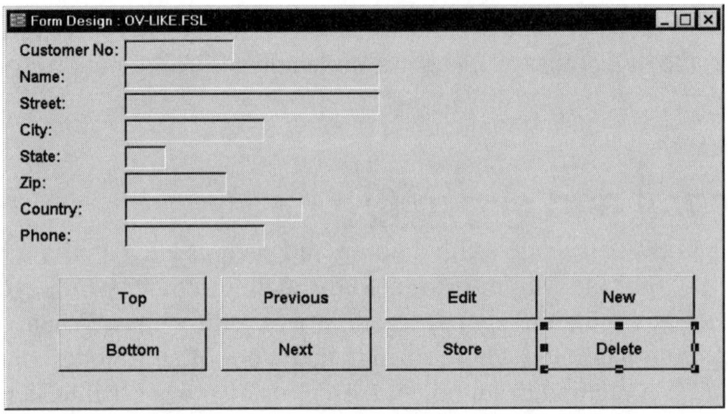

3. Add line 3 to the button labeled Top. Line 3 issues the home() command, which takes you to the beginning of the active table.

```
1:    ;OV-LIKE :: btnTop :: pushButton
2:    method pushButton(var eventInfo Event)
3:       active.home()   ;Move to the first record.
4:    endMethod
```

4. Add line 3 to the button labeled Bottom. Line 3 issues the end() command, which takes you to the last record in the table.

```
1:    ;OV-LIKE :: btnBottom :: pushButton
2:    method pushButton(var eventInfo Event)
3:       active.end()   ;Move to the last record.
4:    endMethod
```

5. Add line 3 to the button labeled Previous. Line 3 uses priorRecord() to move the pointer back one record.

```
1:    ;OV-LIKE :: btnPrevious :: pushButton
2:    method pushButton(var eventInfo Event)
3:       active.priorRecord();Move to the previous record.
4:    endMethod
```

6. Add line 3 to the button labeled Next. Line 3 uses nextRecord() to move the pointer forward one record.

```
;OV-LIKE :: btnNext :: pushButton
method pushButton(var eventInfo Event)
   active.nextRecord()   ;Move to the next record.
endMethod
```

7. Add line 3 to the button labeled Edit. Line 3 puts the form in edit mode with edit().

```
1:   ;OV-LIKE :: btnEdit :: pushButton
2:   method pushButton(var eventInfo Event)
3:      edit()                ;Put form into edit mode.
4:   endMethod
```

8. Add lines 3 and 4 to the button labeled Store. Lines 3 and 4 commit the user's changes to the record and end the edit session. Both postRecord() and endEdit() were used in this example to explicitly post the change to the table and end the edit mode. Note, however, that this was done just to introduce the method postRecord(). In a real application, ending edit mode with endEdit() automatically sends DataPostRecord to the built-in action event (changes, if any, to a record are committed when you end an edit session).

```
1:   ;OV-LIKE :: btnStore :: pushButton
2:   method pushButton(var eventInfo Event)
3:      active.postRecord()  ;Write the record to the table.
4:      endEdit()            ;End edit mode.
5:   endMethod
```

9. Add lines 3–5 to the button labeled New. With the New button, you want to get the form ready for the user edit. Move the focus to the upper-left field using the MoveTopLeft action constant with action(MoveTopLeft). Go into edit mode and insert a record with edit() and insertRecord().

```
1:   ;OV-LIKE :: btnNew :: pushButton
2:   method pushButton(var eventInfo Event)
3:      action(MoveTopLeft)     ;Move to first field on form.
4:      edit()                  ;Put form into edit mode.
5:      active.insertRecord()   ;Insert a new blank record.
6:   endMethod
```

10. Add lines 3–7 to the button labeled Delete. The syntax of the Delete button deserves special attention. There are times when deleteRecord() is not a valid command. Therefore, you need to do some error checking. deleteRecord() returns a logical True or False in an if structure. If deleteRecord() is successful, the message in line 4 is sent to the status bar. deleteRecord() sometimes fails—for example, when the user isn't in edit mode or when deleteRecord() interferes with referential integrity. Whenever deleteRecord() fails, a different message is sent to the message box in line 6.

```
1:     ;OV-LIKE :: btnDelete :: pushButton
2:     method pushButton(var eventInfo Event)
3:        if deleteRecord() then
4:           message("Record deleted")
5:         else
6:           message("Could not delete record. Perhaps detail
             ;records exist.")
7:         endIf
8:     endMethod
```

11. Check the syntax, save the form as OV-LIKE.FSL, and run it. Try out all the various buttons. The completed form is shown here:

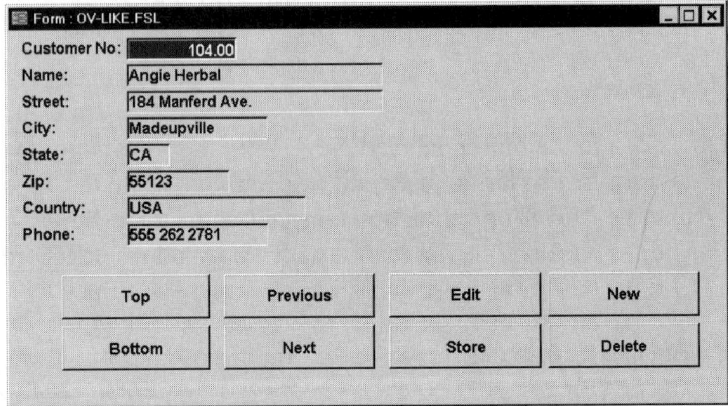

Referring to Objects with *active* and By Name

The techniques shown in the previous example used the object variable active and a method. They are useful for single-table forms. Most often, however, you'll create multitable forms. Therefore, you must be more precise. In the next example, you learn how to use a method on a single table in a multitable form.

Using *insertRecord()* and *deleteRecord()* with a MultiTable Form

Until now, you've seen how to use database-type methods on a form with a single table in the data model. But what if you want to delete a record from only one table in a 1:M relationship? You can use the name of an object to refer to the underlying table, as in the following example:

```
Last_Name.insertRecord() ;Insert a new blank record.
LineItem.DeleteRecord()  ;Delete current record.
```

Using the name of an object enables you to specify the table with which you want to work, which is crucial when you work with multiple tables. This example puts the commands together.

Example of Using a UIObject Name to Refer to the Underlying Table

Suppose that you wish to set up a button on a 1:M form that deletes only the currently selected detail record. This example shows you how to use dot notation in combination with a method. It also introduces the procedure msgQuestion(), which displays a message question dialog box.

http://prestwood.com/forums/paradox/books/official/files/DELETE.FSL.

Step By Step

1. Create a new form with a 1:M relationship between ORDERS.DB and LINEITEM.DB, and place a button on the form. Change the button's label to Delete Line Item, as shown here:

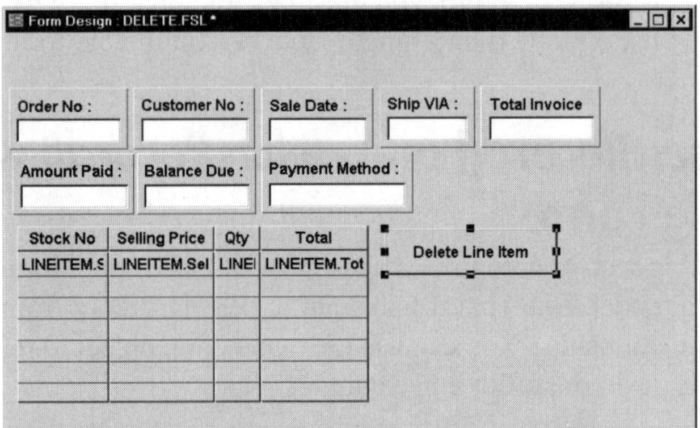

NOTE *All of the examples in this book that use tables, use the tables that come with Paradox. You need to change your working directory to the Samples subdirectory in the Paradox home directory.*

2. Alter the button's pushButton method to look like the following. In line 3, the msgQuestion() procedure is used to ask the user whether he or she really wants to delete the record. If the answer is yes, lines 4 and 5 delete the record. Otherwise, the if statement ends at line 6. To delete the record, you put the form into edit mode in line 4. In line 5, you use the name of an object to signify the table from which to delete a record. Just as easily, you could have used any other object that is connected to the table, or even the name of the table frame. Remember that when you use the name of an object with a method that uses a table, the method will use the table to which that object is connected.

```
1:    ;DELETE :: btnDeleteLine :: pushButton
2:    method pushButton(var eventInfo Event)
3:       if msgQuestion("Warning", " Are you sure you wish to
         ;Delete the current item?") = "Yes" then
4:          edit()
5:          Stock_No.deleteRecord()
6:       endIf
7:    endMethod
```

3. Test your syntax, correct any errors if necessary, save the form as DELETE.FSL, run the form, and click the button to delete a record in the detail table:

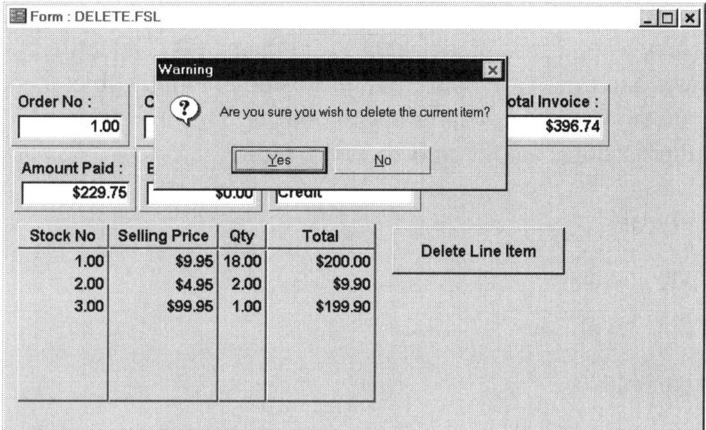

OOP and ObjectPAL

ObjectPAL isn't a true object-oriented programming language. It is, however, object-based programming (OBP). Take a look at objects, the three elements of object-oriented programming (OOP), and see how both relate to ObjectPAL. First up is a discussion of objects.

What Are Objects?

The biggest advantage of using object-based programming rather than procedural programming is that you can cut independent objects from one place or container and paste them to another place or container without affecting any other objects (at least in most cases). This makes your code highly portable. For example, if you create a button that launches the Windows Calculator, you can copy it from one form to another form without affecting other objects or code. With ObjectPAL, you can reuse code more easily than you can with a procedural language such as PAL, Basic, C, or Pascal. With ObjectPAL, you can develop self-contained smart objects once and reuse them.

Another advantage of object-based programming is that it is easier to maintain than a procedural programming language. Your code is contained in objects. Therefore, if something goes wrong, it generally affects only one module or part of your application. If you develop with a group of programmers, you will appreciate that each programmer's code is protected from the others' code. For example, code in one form generally will not affect code in another form.

The Six Categories of Objects

When you study a subject as broad as the more than 1,800 ObjectPAL methods and procedures and their variations, it helps to study them by object type. The ObjectPAL methods and procedures act on objects. The objects on which the methods and procedures act fall into six categories:

- Data types
- Display managers
- Data model objects
- Design objects
- System data objects
- Event objects

Following is an overview of each of the object categories. They are discussed in detail throughout this book.

Data Types and ObjectPAL

You use data type objects to store data. For example, Date, DateTime, Logical, Graphic, LongInt, and SmallInt are examples of data types that store specific types of data in memory. After you store data in a particular type of variable, you can manipulate the data by using the methods associated with that type of variable.

Display Managers

The display manager objects manage how objects are displayed. ObjectPAL has the following five display managers:

- Application object
- Form object
- TableView object

- Report object
- Script object

The Application display manager is the Paradox desktop. It manages the display of the other display managers: Form, TableView, Report, and Script. A Form display manager manages all the objects that you put on it. The form is the center of every ObjectPAL application. A TableView display manager manages and displays tables. A Report display manager manages the formatted display and how table information is printed. A Script is a special display manager that has no UIObjects on it but can display information on the status bar and in message boxes. In general, you deal with display managers in ObjectPAL as a complete unit. For example, you might maximize, minimize, or hide any of the display managers except for a Script.

Data Model Objects

You use data model objects to manipulate data in tables and databases. ObjectPAL has five types of data model objects:

- Database object
- Query object
- SQL object
- Table object
- TCursor object

You use the Database object's methods and procedures on a database—a set of tables in a directory. For example, with Database methods and procedures, you can open a database or delete a table. You use the Query object's methods and procedures to execute and manipulate queries.

The Table object's methods and procedures represent the table itself and are distinct from a TCursor's methods and procedures. A TCursor object is a pointer to the data while a Table object points to the whole table. It also is distinct from a TableFrame and a TableView, which are objects that display the data. Use the Table methods and procedures to add, copy, create, and index tables, to do column calculations, and to get information about a table's structure. Don't use Table methods to edit records, however. Use a TCursor or a table frame—a UIObject—instead.

Design Objects

Design object methods and procedures are commands used to manipulate menus, pop-up menus, and UIObjects. The three types of design objects are as follows:

- Menu
- PopUpMenu
- UIObject

You use Menu and PopUpMenu methods and procedures to build and manipulate menus. Similarly, you use UIObject—short for user interface object—methods and procedures to manipulate UIObjects. For example, when you change the color of a box to red or when you set the value of a field, you manipulate UIObject properties. UIObject methods and procedures add to this functionality. For example, they enable you to set the position of an object.

Scripts, libraries, forms, and UIObjects are the only objects that have events. The form, for example, is a display manager that is also a UIObject. A form has events to which you can attach code, and it responds to events. There also are methods and procedures that you can use to manipulate a form.

Many of the UIObject methods are duplicated among the TCursor methods. For example, insertRecord() works on both a UIObject and a TCursor. The UIObject methods that work with tables work on the underlying table by means of a visible object. Actions directed to the UIObject that affect a table are immediately visible in the object to which the table is bound. On the other hand, TCursor methods work with a table behind the scenes as if another user were making the changes.

System Data Objects

The types of system data objects are as follows:

- DDE object
- Library object
- FileSystem object
- Script object
- Session object

- System object
- TextStream object

You use the Dynamic Data Exchange (DDE) object's methods and procedures with DDE. DDE enables you to send and receive data between Windows applications. The Library object's methods and procedures work with libraries. A library is a place to store code. TextStream object's methods and procedures manipulate streams of text.

The other three categories—FileSystem, Session, and System—are used for objects outside Paradox, such as DOS-level or Windows-level procedures. FileSystem methods and procedures enable you to manipulate a FileSystem variable to provide access to and information about disk files, drives, and directories. A FileSystem variable provides a handle; that is, a variable you use in an ObjectPAL statement in order to work with a directory or a file. Session methods and procedures give you a channel to the BDE. For example, you can add and delete aliases by using Session methods. You use System procedures to display messages, find out about the user's system, get a filename with the file browser, and work with the help system.

Event Objects

Events are packets of information sent from one object to another. You use the methods and procedures to manipulate that packet. The following ten types of methods and procedures manipulate the various eventInfo variables:

```
Event                    MouseEvent
ActionEvent              MoveEvent
ErrorEvent               StatusEvent
KeyEvent                 TimerEvent
MenuEvent                ValueEvent
```

As an example, the following paragraphs discuss the Event, ActionEvent, ErrorEvent, and KeyEvent categories. The Event category is the base type from which the other event types are derived. Many of the methods listed in this section are used by the other event types.

You generate an ActionEvent primarily by editing and navigating in a table. ActionEvents and procedures enable you to get and set information in the action event.

An ErrorEvent eventInfo message is sent to the built-in error event. Use the error event to add to the built-in error-trapping behavior.

You use KeyEvents methods and procedures to manipulate and retrieve information about keystroke events in keyPhysical and keyChar.

MenuEvents methods and procedures enable you to retrieve and set data in the MenuEvent event packet that is related to menu selections in the application menu bar—in other words, menu constants. For example, when the user chooses an item from the toolbar, it triggers the menuAction event by sending it the appropriate menu constant. You use the methods in the MenuEvent class to manipulate the MenuEvent eventInfo packet.

To print your own reference sheet, create and run the following one-line script:

```
enumRTLMethods("RTL.DB")
```

This script creates a table that lists all the run-time library methods and procedures and their variations. That's more than 1,800 commands. By using the RTL.DB, you can create and print elaborate reports and use them as reference sheets. You also can query the table to view the methods in various ways.

Is ObjectPAL OOP?

Now that you have a firm grasp of the various objects used in ObjectPAL, look at the three elements of object-oriented programming (OOP) and see how they relate to ObjectPAL. The three elements are encapsulation, polymorphism, and inheritance.

Encapsulation and ObjectPAL

In OOP, *encapsulation* is the bundling of methods and variables within an object so that access to the variables is permitted only through the object's published interface. ObjectPAL supports encapsulation. It was used to create Paradox and is surfaced nicely in ObjectPAL. The TCursor has a lot of code associated with it that allows us programmers to manipulate data, but only the published interface is available to us. The details of how it does things is hidden within the TCursor object. The code you write is stored with the object that triggers it. The code is completely independent of other objects and other code. In other words, if the object is moved inside another object or to another form, the code goes with it. If you compile a form, the code is hidden and only the published interface is available to others. This is encapsulation.

The key benefit of encapsulation is that your code is self-contained and protected from other objects. If another object needs to access variables inside your object, you can grant access through a custom method. If a group of people develop an ObjectPAL application, each programmer needs to be concerned only with his or her particular section. A section in ObjectPAL means a group of objects (typically a form with objects on it). If an external object needs access to something in the current object, the current object must have a method to allow it to be accessed.

For example, a team of programmers could designate one programmer to be in charge of the library for an application. (The library is where generic code is put.) When another programmer wants a routine to be included in the library, that person gives the programmer in charge of the library the specifications for the custom method; that is, what the custom method should be passed and what it should do and return. When another programmer wants to add to or alter that custom method, the programmer in charge of the library decides whether the modification is possible given what the method already does.

Encapsulation makes it possible to bring foreign code together. With a traditional procedural language, a team of programmers must be sure not to use the same function and variable names. Because ObjectPAL supports encapsulation, you don't have to worry about the names of methods, procedures, objects, or variables. Each programmer can use his or her own variable-naming convention and not worry about the other programmers. When it comes time to bring all the sections of an application together, you simply have to worry about how the objects communicate. If you are an individual programmer, this means that you can reuse more of your code.

The capability to have duplicate names for variables and custom methods is a great relief to a programmer. For example, you can have a variable called Counter that belongs to two different objects or two objects could both have a custom method called cmRoutine().

Dot Notation and Encapsulation

The dot notation syntax of ObjectPAL supports encapsulation and enables you to grab values from other objects. For example, from an object of one form, you can open another form and (using the public or published interface) grab the value of one of its objects. For example:

```
var
  f2 Form
endVar

f2.open("form2")
field1.value = f2.field1.value
```

The rules for when you can use duplicate names and about which code can see other code refer to *scope*, which will be discussed in the next chapter.

Polymorphism and ObjectPAL

In OOP, the capability of the same command to be interpreted differently when used with or received by different objects is called *polymorphism*. In ObjectPAL, polymorphism is the capability of an object to act differently depending on the context in which it is being used. For example, methods require an object with which to work. Depending on the object's type, the method does different things. The following expression opens the object named Orders, depending on how varName is defined:

```
        varName.open("Orders")     ;varName is an object.
```

Orders can be a table, a form, a script, or many other objects. What ObjectPAL tries to open depends on what variable type you declare varName as. You can define varName to be a database, a DDE link, a form, a library, a report, a session, a TableView, a TCursor, a TextStream, or something else. As the programmer using this object-based language, you don't need to concern yourself with the details of opening these various objects. You write code that is based on this simple formula:

```
var
   object   ObjectType        ;First declare a variable.
endVar
 object.open ( parameterList)   ;Then use the variable.
```

ObjectPAL takes over and handles the details. For example, to open another form, you could use the following:

```
var
   tempVar   Form        ;tempVar is a form variable.
endVar

tempVar.open("Orders")  ;Open form.
```


TCursors and Polymorphism

A *TCursor* (table cursor) is a tool used to manipulate the data in a table and is a pointer to a record in a table. If you change the variable type of tempVar, the same open() method can open something else, such as a TCursor:

```
var
   tempVar   TCursor          ;tempVar is a TCursor.
endVar

tempVar.open("ORDERS.DB")     ;Open a TCursor to Orders.db.
```

In the future, when another type of object that can be opened is added, you won't need to learn the new syntax; you'll need to learn only the new characteristics of the object. This certainly beats learning syntax for 10 to 15 different open routines.

Inheritance; Well, Actually, Delegation

In OOP, a mechanism for automatically sharing methods and data types among objects is called *inheritance*. Typically, you would create a base class followed by creating descendant classes. Each descendant class would have all the properties, methods, procedures, and events of its parent class, plus added functionality. ObjectPAL does not support true inheritance. This is not a drawback, it just means ObjectPAL has its own mechanisms for storing and reusing code.

In ObjectPAL, an object inherits all the variables, types, and custom procedures of the objects by which it is contained. Also, the fact that methods and procedures from one object type are derived—inherited—from other types shows the existence of inheritance in ObjectPAL. In Paradox's online help for the **Report Type**, the help shows the methods and procedures for the report types that are derived (or inherited) from the Form object type.

Paradox UIObjects—objects you place on a form—inherit characteristics (default behavior) from the objects that the Paradox development team created. For example, when you place a TableFrame on a form, it has a lot of built-in properties, methods, procedures, and events that are inherited from the base TableFrame object. Since you can't inherit down another level, I call this delegation and not true inheritance. Every object in Paradox supports delegation. When you copy an object, the copy is delegated the properties and methods of the parent. Be careful when you use Design | Copy to Toolbar. If the object that you copy to the toolbar has ObjectPAL code on it, the code is copied, too.

Summary

This chapter introduced you to the basics of ObjectPAL. You learned a little about all the various aspects of programming in ObjectPAL. You learned that programming in an event-driven environment is about attaching code to objects. You learned the basics of ObjectPAL syntax and to refer to the properties and methods of objects using dot notation. In addition to containing properties and methods, you also learned that objects can contain procedures and events.

CHAPTER 5

Where To Put Code

Whether it's Paradox, Visual Basic, or Delphi, one of the toughest tasks for new programmers is deciding where to put code. All of these tools are event driven environments and allow you the programmer to attach code routines to objects that respond to events. This chapter will introduce you to containers, scope, bubbling, and other concepts and techniques that will aid you in placement of code.

Containers

Paradox employs what is called *containership*, which enables you to put a smaller object inside a larger object. You could say that the smaller object is contained by the larger object. In ObjectPAL, the built-in container variable refers to the object that contains the current object. A container object completely surrounds and controls the behavior of all the objects within it. The rules of a container dictate that when you move a container, its contained objects also move. Likewise, when you delete a container, its contained objects are also deleted.

When you have objects that can contain other objects, the containership, or path, has to stop somewhere. In ObjectPAL, the form is the highest level of container. A form contains at least one page, and the page contains design objects such as fields, buttons, table frames, and bitmaps, shown next. Note that the page contains the larger box, and that the larger box contains the circle, the smaller box, and the button. The field is contained by the small box.

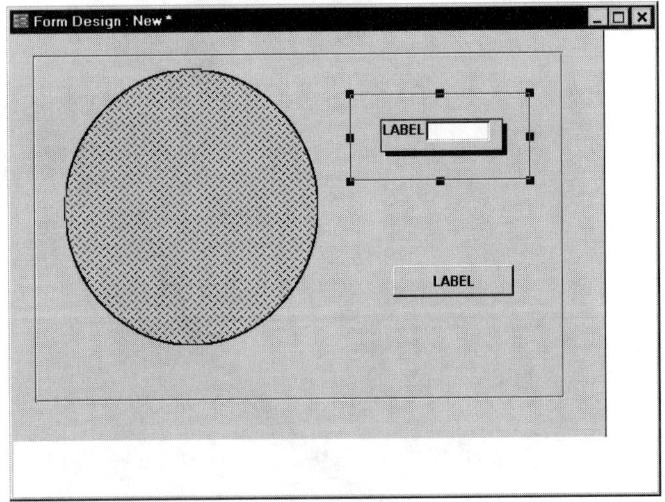

Remember that the form contains all these objects and that it is the highest level of container in Paradox. This creates special problems for programmers when you have an application that uses many forms. For example, if no two forms have a higher container, then how do you develop a common menu for use with all forms in an application? The Application Framework solves this problem and is discussed in a later chapter.

The keywords and object variables that you use with containers are as follows:

- **disableDefault** Stops the built-in behavior.
- **doDefault** Executes the built-in behavior now.
- **enableDefault** Allows the built-in behavior.
- **passEvent** Passes event up to the containership path to the parent container.
- **self** Refers to the object the code is on.
- **active** Refers to the object with focus.
- **container** Refers to the container of the object the code is on.
- **lastMouseClicked** Last object to receive a left mouse click.
- **lastMouseRightClicked** Last object to receive a right mouse click.
- **subject** Refers to another object.

You can refer to a container with the container variable. For example, message(self.container.name) displays the name of the object that contains self.

Containership Hierarchy: What Contains What

The Object Tree visually shows you the containership hierarchy of a form. It is one of the most important tools for developing forms and writing ObjectPAL code (see Figure 5-1). The Object Tree shows you what objects contain what other objects.

Use the Object Tree to rename objects quickly. Also, use it to see what contains what and to see which objects have code on them. Objects with code have a blue dot.

You can attach code to the objects that show up in the Object Tree. You can attach code to as many objects as you want, in any order that you want. Attaching code directly to the object with which you want to work makes ObjectPAL easier to use than many other development environments. For example, you can place a

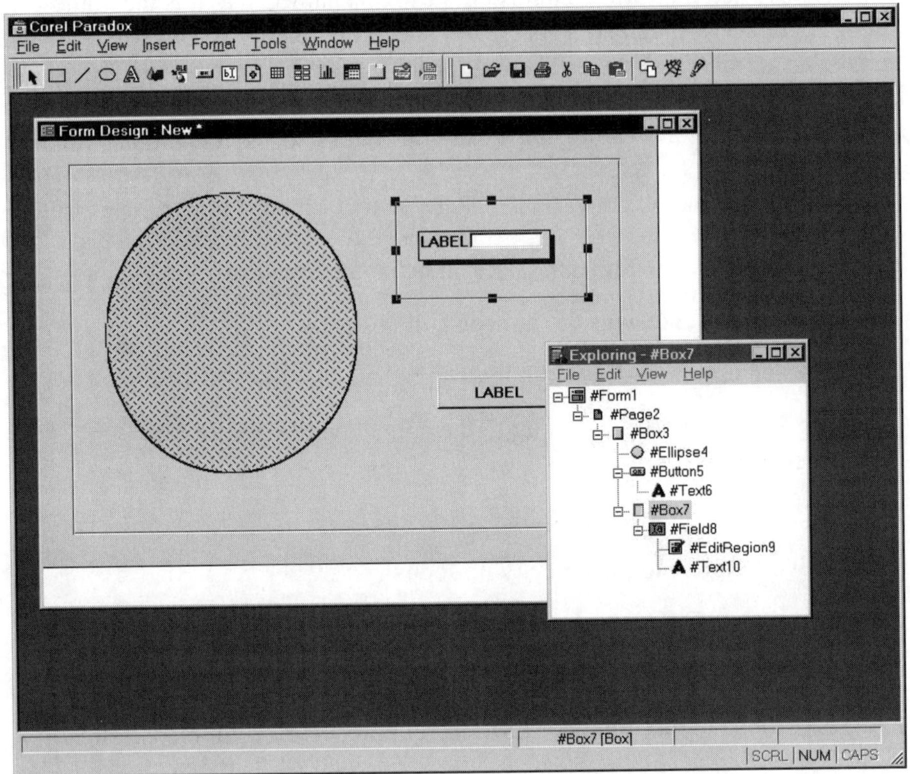

FIGURE 5-1 The Object Browser with only the Object Tree showing

box and a circle on a form and place code in the mouseClick event of both objects. Because the form and the other UIObjects you placed on the form contain built-in events, when you run the form, Paradox takes care of trapping a mouse click when the user clicks on either the box or the circle.

Containership Rules

The following are several rules dealing with containership:

- Deleting a container deletes all embedded objects.
- Containership determines dot notation.

- Containership enables you to have duplicate named objects in the same form.
- Noise names are not part of the containership path. A noise name is the default name Paradox gives new objects. Noise names always start with #.
- An object is embedded only if it is completely within the boundaries of the container.
- Objects inside a container can see the variables, custom methods, and custom procedures of its container (the ancestors all the way up the hierarchy path to the form object). The form object is the base object for UIObjects.
- A container cannot see the variables, custom methods, and custom procedures of its embedded (or descendant) objects.

Sometimes you may wish to have one object visually inside another object, but not have that object within the containership of it. Every object has a Contain Objects property which, by default, is checked. When checked, all objects within the visual boundary of the object are within the containership of the object. Uncheck the Contain Objects property of an object to break the containership path (the hierarchy path).

Scope: What Can See What

The *scope* of an object is the range of objects that have access to it. For example, if you declare a variable in the form's Var window, that variable may be used by any object in the form, but not by objects outside the form. Scope has a definite path determined by the containership hierarchy. An object can see all the variables or constants above it and within it, but not below it. In other words, an object can't see the variables, constants, and procedures of the objects it contains. Also, an object can't see variables, constants, or procedures that are on another branch of the Object Tree. Objects that are contained can see their containers' variables, constants, and procedures. That is, they "inherit" them (and can overwrite them with their own, an OOP feature).

For example, in Figure 5-2, the inner box is contained by the outer box. The inner box can see all its own variables and all the variables of its container (the outer box) as well as all the ancestor container objects—in this case, the page and

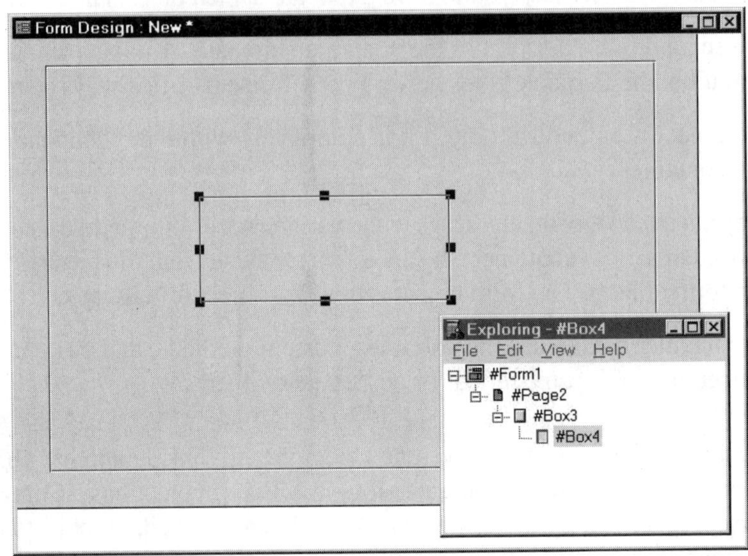

FIGURE 5-2 Scope is determined by containership hierarchy

form. The outer box, on the other hand, can see its own variables as well as the page and form variables. It can't see the variables of the inner box.

Scope can be summed up by the phrase "what can see what." A noise name is the default name that Paradox gives an object; noise names always start with a "#." Noise names don't interfere with scope, but real names do. Understanding this difference is absolutely crucial to understanding scope. When you view the containership hierarchy, you can find out which objects see which objects. You need to know where and when you can use duplicate names of objects on forms. The next example explores duplicate object names and duplicate variables.

ObjectPAL Is Event Driven

How does Paradox execute all these independent routines? ObjectPAL is an event-driven language, much like Delphi, Visual Basic, C++Builder, and JBuilder. You place UIObjects that have events already attached to them onto a form. The event handler monitors what events occur as the user interfaces with the running application and automatically executes the code attached to the event (both yours and the built-in default code). This mechanism of triggering events is known as an *event handler*. The plan or guideline that the event handler uses to trigger events is known as the event model.

To understand ObjectPAL, you first must understand the event model. Nothing else will make sense until you understand it. For now, keep the following points in mind:

- Every UIObject has a set of events already associated with it.
- All events are sent messages in the form of a variable.
- The variable that is passed from event to event is always named eventInfo.
- Although all messages passed to events are named eventInfo, the messages themselves come in several different types (for example: ActionEvent, MouseEvent, and MenuEvent). You can see what type of message is sent to any particular event within the event itself. For example, right after the pushButton event name is (var eventInfo Event). This means a message named eventInfo of type Event is passed to the pushButton event.
- Every message goes to the form object's event first. With the form prefilter, you can intercept an event before the target gets it. If you don't place code in the form's prefilter, the event is not affected by the prefilter. The form serves as a kind of dispatcher. An event goes to the form, and then the form sends the event packet to the target object.
- Every message has a target. This target is established in various ways. For example, when you click a field, it becomes the target of the event. Within the ObjectPAL editor for any event, you can find the target by inspecting the eventInfo variable with eventInfo.getTarget(ui). The current target is then assigned to the variable ui (you must declare ui as a UIObject variable type). The form sends the event to the target. Internal events stop after the target. Internal events such as open, close, and arrive go to the form and then to the target, and then they terminate.
- There are three types of events: external, internal, and special.
- Only external events bubble. The full path of an external event goes to the form's prefilter, then to the target object, and then it bubbles (is passed back up) the containership hierarchy. If an external event such as mouseDown, keyPhysical, and error are not trapped for at the form level or

the target level—in other words, no built-in code responds to the event—the object passes the event to its container. If the container has no built-in code that traps for that external event, it is passed to its container and so on until it reaches the form for the second time, where it stops.

- The form can see external events twice. If an external event has no built-in code that traps for it, the form sees it twice. The prefilter equals False when the form is the target of the event. The prefilter also equals False when another object is the target of the event and the form is seeing it for the second time.

Bubbling: The Path of Events

Bubbling of external events is a special topic that deserves more attention. An event has one of two definite paths: either form and then target, or form, target, and bubble back up to the form. *Bubbling* is when an event moves back up the containership path to the form. An external event such as mouseDown goes to the form, then to the target, and then it bubbles up the containership hierarchy until it reaches the form a second time, where it stops. The event might go through the entire path. If any of the objects in the path have built-in code that uses the event, the event might get cut short. (Your code does not stop bubbling; only built-in code does.) For example, mouseDown normally bubbles up to the form. If you left-click a field, however, the field knows what to do with mouseDown and the mouseDown event is not bubbled.

Most of the time, your code executes on the target. The target object executes an event such as mouseDown. The event goes first to the form. If the form doesn't have the appropriate code on the correct method, the event is returned to the target for execution. If the target doesn't have the appropriate code, the code is bubbled up through the containership path to the form, where it stops. The form sees the code twice—at the start and at the end—unless another object, such as the target's container, intercepts the event with built-in code, such as the preceding field example.

Now, follow what happens to a button's pushButton event when a user clicks it. The target object (the button) sends the pushButton event to the form. Because the form doesn't use a pushButton event, the event is returned to the target for execution. If the target (the button) doesn't have the appropriate built-in code, the event is bubbled up through the containership path to the form, where it stops. The form can see an event twice—at the start and at the end of its life cycle. You can place code anywhere on the containership path to trap for the event. In fact, you can place it several times on the path and all the code will execute.

Suppose that you want to trap for an event whenever the user arrives on a record. At the form's prefilter, you can trap for DataArriveRecord, as in the following:

```
1:   method action(var eventInfo ActionEvent)
2:      if eventInfo.isPreFilter()
3:         then
4:         ;This code executes for each object on the form
5:         if eventInfo.id() = DataArriveRecord then
6:            beep()  ;Do your stuff here
7:         endIf
8:      else
9:         ;This code executes only for the form
10:     endIf
11:  endMethod
```


If you are using a table frame, which has a record object, you can't move lines 5, 6, and 7 to the else part of the if structure because the record object of the table frame will use up the event and not allow it to bubble up to the else clause of the form. The action DataArriveRecord is never bubbled up to the form.

The event you're interested in applies to a table frame—one of the many other objects that are caught by the prefilter test. The comment after the then part of the if structure reads, This code executes for each object on the form. This refers to all the objects on the form except the form itself, which is tested in the else clause.

If you create a single record form—that is, a form with just fields on it—you can use the preceding else clause to trap for DataArriveRecord because it bubbles back up to the form.

Containership, Scope, and Bubbling Are Intertwined

The containership hierarchy is the branching tree represented in the Object Tree. The Object Tree enables you to see the containership hierarchy, or path, of objects. Containership hierarchy is closely related to bubbling and scope. Events go to the form and then to the target. Then, the event bubbles up the containership hierarchy. The event packet path is determined by the containership hierarchy. Scope is what can see what. Use the Object Tree to determine the scope of objects. If an object on the containership path has been renamed, then it has defined part of the scope path. If the object has not been renamed, then it is not part of the scope path.

Study the Events in Combination

An excellent technique for placing code on an object is to place code in "before and after" combinations. Many events have counterparts: for example, open and close, arrive and depart, canArrive and canDepart, and mouseEnter and mouseExit. If you need to code in a "before and after" maneuver, think and code in one of these method combinations. For example, occasionally you might need to create a table when a form is opened and delete it when the form is exited. The open and close combination is a good place to do this. Open and canDepart might be even better, but that's up to you as the programmer.

mouseEnter and *mouseExit*

Whenever you want something to occur when the pointer is within the boundaries of an object, use the mouseEnter and mouseExit combination.

Suppose that you want to display a message on the status bar whenever the mouse pointer is over a button. To do this, use the message() procedure in the mouseEnter and mouseExit events.

http://prestwood.com/forums/paradox/books/official/files/M-ENTER.FSL.

Step By Step

1. Create a new form with a button on it. Change the label of the button to **Close**, as shown here:

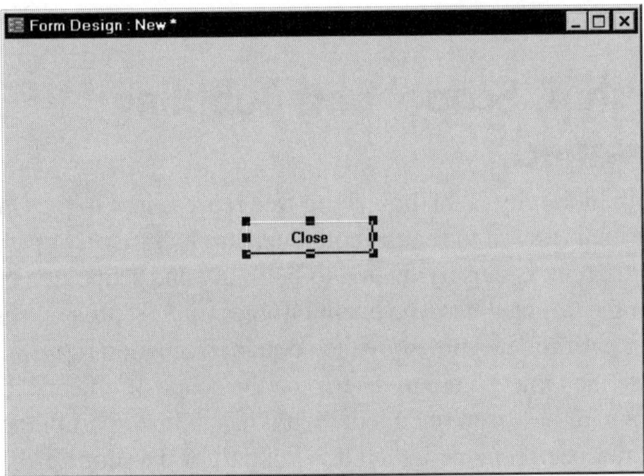

2. Add commands to the button. In this case, close the form by adding line 3 to the pushButton event. Line 3 closes the current form. Note that close() is used as a procedure in this case—it knows what object to work with.

```
1:   ;M-ENTER :: Button :: pushButton
2:   method pushButton(var eventInfo Event)
3:      close()
4:   endMethod
```

3. Place the message on the status bar by adding line 3 to the mouseEnter event of the button. Line 3, the mouseEnter event sends a message to the status bar whenever the mouse pointer enters the boundaries of the button.


```
1:   ;M-ENTER ::Button :: mouseEnter
2:   method mouseEnter(var eventInfo MouseEvent)
3:      message("This button closes the form")
4:   endMethod
```

4. Remove the message from the status bar by adding line 3 to the mouseExit event of the button. Line 3 posts a new message, the Null character.

```
1:   ; M-ENTER ::Button :: mouseExit
2:   method mouseExit(var eventInfo MouseEvent)
3:      message("")
4:   endMethod
```

5. Check the syntax, save the form as **M-ENTER.FSL**, and run it. Move your cursor over the button and keep an eye on the status bar (see Figure 5-3).

Rather than use the mouseExit method of every object, you can put code in the prefilter of the form's mouseExit method. Remember that external commands always bubble up. Therefore, putting message("") at the form level clears the status bar whenever the mouse leaves an object. Doing this will enable you to just add a message() procedure to the mouseEnter of all the objects you wish to provide this type of help for.

open Versus *arrive*

An object is always opened first, then arrived on. Therefore, open occurs before arrive. Remember that the default behavior happens last. When you open an object, the code on the form's built-in open method executes, and the form is opened. If you put code that deals with a UIObject in the open method, the code

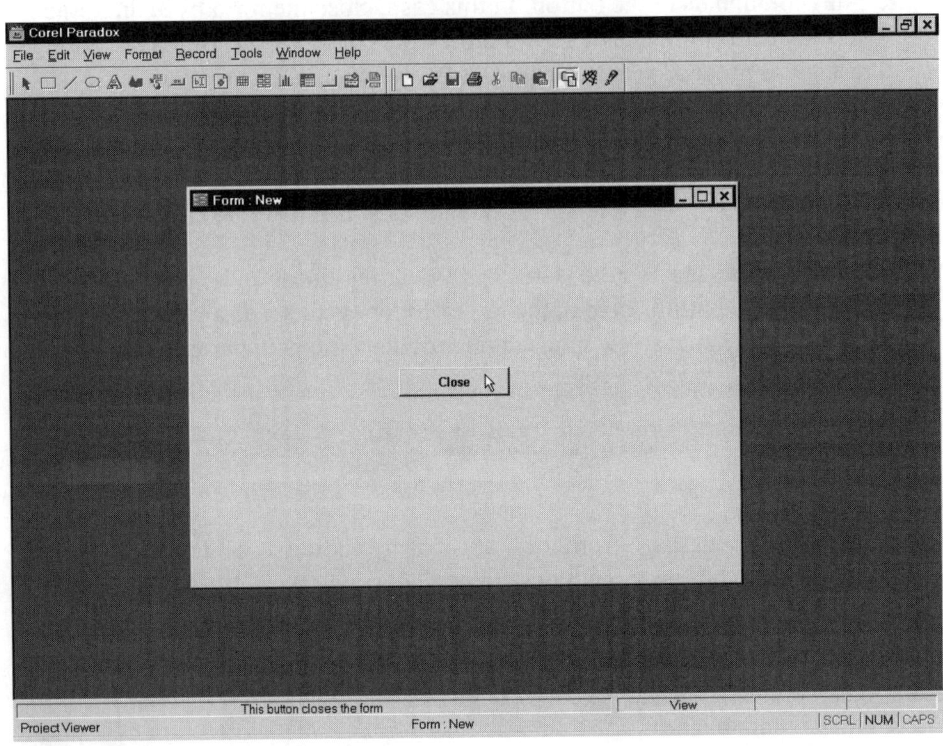

FIGURE 5-3 Completed mouseEnter/mouseExit example

might not execute correctly because the objects don't exist yet. You could put doDefault before your code to execute the default behavior, or you could move your code to the arrive event.

The open event is a good place to initialize a variable, create a table, and deal with the form—for example, to maximize or resize it. The arrive event is a good place to set the properties of the objects on the form—for example, the values of the field objects.

newValue Versus *changeValue*

The newValue event occurs whenever the value for an edit region changes value onscreen. This occurs whether or not the field is defined. The changeValue event occurs with both defined and undefined fields, but behaves quite differently for each. The changeValue event on an undefined field occurs whenever the value in it changes. With defined fields, however, it occurs only after a field is read from a table and changed by the user.

The changeValue event is a good place to do something based on a change in the table value. For example, you could perform some operation when payment type changes from cash to credit. If you want something to happen whenever a user changes a value in a field—undefined or defined—use changeValue.

keyChar Versus *keyPhysical*

The keyChar and keyPhysical events trap for the user pressing keys on the keyboard. The keyChar event traps for only the character keyboard keys; that is, the keys that print characters to the screen. keyPhysical traps for all the keyboard keys, both character keys and physical keys. The keyPhysical event filters the keyboard first and passes printable characters to the screen.

Use the keyChar event to trap for character keys, such as "A", "B", "1", "2", "(", and ";". Use the keyPhysical event to trap for keys such as ESC, F1, F8, and TAB. If you need to trap for both physical and character keys in a routine, use only keyPhysical because it can trap for both.

action, menuAction, and error

Use the action event to trap for table actions such as DataInsertRecord and DataPostRecord. Whenever a user does something related to the table, such as inserting a record or deleting a record, an action constant is sent to the action method. Use menuAction to catch user selection of menus, the Toolbar, and the control box. Whenever a user selects a menu option or clicks a button on the Toolbar, a menu constant is sent to the menuAction event of the form. You could use the error event to trap for errors, but because the built-in error event is always called after errors occur, use action instead. A good use for error is to add to the built-in error behavior—for example, to log all errors to a table.

About Coding

When new users to Paradox begin writing code in ObjectPAL, they often write tremendous amounts of code. The amount of code can become overwhelming if you don't understand the fundamentals of the product.

You usually follow certain steps whenever you develop an application. Before writing a single line of ObjectPAL code, you always should build the data model and arrange the form until it's similar to what you want. Then, run the form and work with it to see what it does and doesn't do. When you find something that you want to work differently, ask yourself, "What do I want to happen?" and "When do I want it to happen?" Try to do this for only one task or object at a time. In other words, develop in small steps.

Go back and forth between Design mode and Run mode and test your work incrementally. When you're done coding and testing a single object, move to the next. By refining your application in steps, you end up with functioning code in bite-sized chunks. If you try to tackle in one step all the work that an application requires, you can easily end up frustrated, with messy code. Remember, program and test one task at a time.

Watch Out for Spaghetti Code

BASIC, early Pascal, and early C promoted *spaghetti code*, which is intertwined code with many repeated parts. These procedural languages required you to write line after line of code. Although modern languages don't lend themselves to spaghetti code, it's still possible to write it. During the development process, you might copy a routine from one spot to another and later find a bug in it. You would have two pieces of code to correct. This is fine if you are perfect and can remember to change both pieces of code. But this method of programming is hard on upkeep, and it makes reusing code nearly impossible. You would have to start every new project from scratch. Instead of copying a routine to two different objects, consider placing the code in a custom method at the form level or in a library.

Use an Object-Oriented Methodology

Object-oriented programming involves compartmentalizing and reusing code. Although Paradox isn't fully object-oriented, it is object-based and supports many of the concepts of object-oriented programming. Your goal should be to avoid duplicating code by developing self-contained, reusable units. After a while, you will spend the majority of your developing time copying, pasting, and putting together previously developed units. When a bug in a certain unit turns up, you can debug that one unit, and every application from that point on that uses that unit is cleaned up or enhanced. In addition, when you enhance some code that many applications share, those applications are enhanced instantly.

Keep in mind that you can still write spaghetti code in ObjectPAL. If you duplicate parts, you inevitably introduce bugs into your application. ObjectPAL, however, promotes good programming. If you follow the rules of object-oriented methodology, develop in compartments, and avoid duplicating code, your programs will be clean.

Try to Localize Code

Because you're programming in ObjectPAL (an object-based programming language), the code should be as local to the object as possible. For example, if you're trying to decide to put code on a button or the form, then choose the button. If the situation warrants moving up to the form level, it will become obvious. There are many benefits for coding as low as possible, including the capability to copy objects with code on them from one form to another and still have it work. This requires a little extra thought on your part to create a fully self-contained object, but the benefits warrant the extra time.

TIP *Whenever you have a choice, try adding ObjectPAL code directly to the object to get the desired results. Do you ever want to not code locally? Yes—when you want to work with more than one of the same object. You can use a container above all the objects and put code on the object's container.*

Code as Low as Possible

Put code on the lowest possible container object. If you later need to use the same code elsewhere, move the code up the container path to the lowest container that both objects can see. If you follow this rule, your code will be compartmentalized and portable. By developing in compartments, you keep code segments apart. A bug introduced in one compartment is less likely to affect other parts of your application.

If you are programming a button, put all the code, including variables, on the button. This makes the button a self-contained unit that is easily copied and pasted to other forms. If you later need that same code on another button, convert it to a custom method and move it up the container path to the button's container object. A container object is an object that completely surrounds and controls the behavior of all the objects within it.

If you then decide you need to use the code with several pages within the form, then move the custom method to the form. If you need the same routine in several forms, consider putting it in a library. A library is an object that stores custom ObjectPAL code. Libraries are useful for storing and maintaining frequently used routines, and for sharing custom methods and variables among forms.

Using this general rule of coding as low to the object as possible gives you maximum access to your code and saves you time. In addition, if you later find a problem with the routine, you need to correct it in only one spot; instantly, all code that uses the routine benefits from the improvement.

Although you can write spaghetti code with an object-based language, ObjectPAL supports and promotes good object-oriented practices. By using contained objects and custom methods properly, you can keep your code clean. Develop in self-contained units whose code is protected from other objects.

When You Code, Think Levels

As I have hinted, in an ObjectPAL application, you put code on various levels. You can put code on objects, on the object's container, on the page, on the form, or even in a library. When you place code in your application, imagine that you are placing your code at various levels. The levels of coding are as follows:

- Application framework
- Script
- Library
- Form
- Page
- Container in a page (a box object, for example)
- Object on a page or in a container (a field object, for example)
- Elements of an object (the record object of a table frame, for example)
- The table level (picture strings and other validity checks, for example)

Application Framework Level

Because the form level is the highest container, creating applications that use multiple forms has special challenges. For example, how do you create a menu system that is in common with all forms? How do you create a separate menu system when displaying reports as opposed to forms? How do you retain a global menu when there are no forms displayed on the desktop? Do you have to duplicate code on every form? Duplicating code is one approach. Another is to pass control to a library and do the executing there. The application framework helps you do this and a whole lot more. When considering what level to place code on, you must consider the application framework levels, too.

Script Level

A script is an object consisting of ObjectPAL code that a user can run independently of a form or that can be called from ObjectPAL. Unlike forms and reports, scripts have no objects. Unlike libraries, scripts can be run without ObjectPAL. You will hardly ever use the script level in a project. It's useful, however, for enabling the user to execute code without opening a form. You occasionally might use the script level to start off an application—perhaps for setting up data for a form, such as adding or deleting records. Another use for scripts is to enable the user to run part of the code without launching the whole application. You will seldom use either of these techniques.

Library Level

A library is a good place to put code that you need to call from multiple forms. Many ObjectPAL programmers think of the library as a way to code above the highest container—the form. For now, just remember that a library is a place to put code that is shared among forms.

Three Form Levels

The form is the top-level UIObject to place code. When using the form level, I like to think of it as actually having three mental levels to place code: the init, the prefilter, and the form level. The init event occurs first and is the first place to consider placing code when you are placing code at the form level. All events go through the form's prefilter, and external events can go to the form twice. First, the event is prefiltered, and then it is sent to the target and can bubble back up to the form. If you want to intercept another object's event, use the form's prefilter. Think of the prefilter as a special level and the else part of the form's if statement as the form level. For example, if you want to do something after the form is opened, use the else portion of the form's arrive event.

If you want to trap for an error so that you can do something in addition to the built-in behavior, use the form's else portion of the error event. If you want to trap for an error before it happens, then most likely the action event is where you will want to code. If you want to write generic code that does something every time you arrive on any one of a set of fields, then use the prefilter of the form's arrive event.

Review of the *init, open,* and *arrive* Methods of a Form

The first event to receive a message when a form is opened is the init event, followed by the open event. The arrive event is special in that it occurs when the form is first opened and whenever it is selected. The form's arrive event is a good place to put code that you want executed when the form is first opened and whenever it is selected. For example, you could maximize the form and display a message upon arriving with the following code:

```
;Form :: arrive
method arrive(var eventInfo MoveEvent)
   if eventInfo.isPreFilter()
      then
      ;This code executes for each object on the form

   else
      ;This code executes only for the form
      maximize()
      msgInfo("Our database", "Welcome")
   endIf
endMethod
```

With this code, the form maximizes and displays the message every time the form is opened and selected. Compare the preceding routine to the following routine. They both accomplish the same thing: they maximize the application desktop and display a message when the form is opened. The following open version requires a doDefault, however:

```
;Form :: open
method open(var eventInfo Event)
   if eventInfo.isPreFilter()
      then
      ;This code executes for each object on the form

   else
```

```
 8:          ;This code executes only for the form
 9:          maximize()
10:          doDefault
11:          msgInfo("Our database", "Welcome")
12:       endIf
13:    endMethod
```

Note in line 10 that doDefault is added after the maximize line. Without the doDefault, the message would interrupt the opening of the form, and the form would look peculiar. For this reason, the arrive event is considered the better, more elegant location.

Review of the Form's Prefilter

People often have trouble using events prefiltered at the form level. If you have 50 fields on a form and want to set the colors on the arrive of each one, it doesn't make sense to add the code to every field's arrive event. Even if the code that sets colors is in a custom method, you don't need to call the custom method in each arrive event. The form's prefilter enables the programmer to write code that intercepts the arrive event for each object and performs the work for each object. Rather than modify 50 fields, the programmer has to deal with only one generic method at the form level. For example, if you want to set the color of every object in the Box class when the form opens, you could do the following:

```
;Form :: open
method open(var eventInfo Event)
   var UIObj UIObject endVar
   if eventInfo.isPreFilter()
   then
      ;This code executes for each object on the form
      eventInfo.getTarget(UIObj)
      if UIObj.class = "Box" then
         UIObj.color = Red
      endIf
   else
      ;This code executes only for the form

   endIf
endMethod
```

Using the form's prefilter to work on a group of objects is an important technique. With it, you can cut down on the amount of code you need to write.

http://prestwood.com/forums/paradox/books/official/files/GETTARG.FSL also demonstrates how to use the form's prefilter.

Prefilter Example

Suppose that you or your users are having a hard time seeing which field is currently active. One solution is to make the field highlight yellow while it is active. This section demonstrates how to use the form's prefilter to alter the appearance of a field whenever it has focus.

http://prestwood.com/forums/paradox/books/official/files/PREFILT.FSL.

Step By Step

1. Change your working directory to Paradox's Samples directory and create a form based on the CUSTOMER.DB table. Here's what the form should look like after you create it:

Form Design : New *

Customer No:
Name:
Street:
City:
State/Prov:
Zip/Postal Code:
Country:
Phone:
First Contact:

2. Add lines 3–5 and 8–11 to the form's arrive event. In line 4, a UIObject variable ui is declared. In line 8, a handle to the target object is put in the UIObject variable ui. Line 9 uses the handle to test whether it is a field by comparing the property class to the string Field. If they are the same, then a UIObject variable is used to change the field's color to yellow.

```
 1:    ;PREFILT ::Form :: arrive
 2:    method arrive(var eventInfo MoveEvent)
 3:       var
 4:       ui     UIObject                  ;Declare ui as a UIObject.
 5:       endVar
 6:       if eventInfo.isPreFilter() then
 7:          ;// This code executes for each object on the  form:
 8:          eventInfo.getTarget(ui)      ;Set ui to target.
 9:          if ui.class = "Field" then   ;Is ui a field, then
10:             ui.color = Yellow         ;change it to yellow.
11:          endIf
12:       else
13:         ;// This code executes only for the form:
14:
15:       endIf
16:    endMethod
```


3. Add lines 3–5 and 8–11 to the form's canDepart method. This step is the same as step 3 except for location—the code is in the form's canDepart —and it changes the color back to transparent.

```
 1:    ;PREFILT :: Form :: canDepart
 2:    method canDepart(var eventInfo MoveEvent)
 3:       var
 4:          ui     UIObject     ;Declare ui as a UIObject.
 5:       endVar
 6:       if eventInfo.isPreFilter() then
 7:          ;// This code executes for each object on the form:
 8:          eventInfo.getTarget(ui)     ;Set ui to target.
 9:          if ui.class = "Field" then  ;Is ui a field, then
10:             ui.color = Transparent   ;make it transparent.
11:          endIf
12:       else
13:         ;// This code executes only for the form:
14:
15:       endIf
16:
17:    endMethod
```

4. Check the syntax, save the form as PREFILT.FSL, and run it. Move from field to field using the TAB key or mouse and note that the active field changes color. Here's what they should look like:

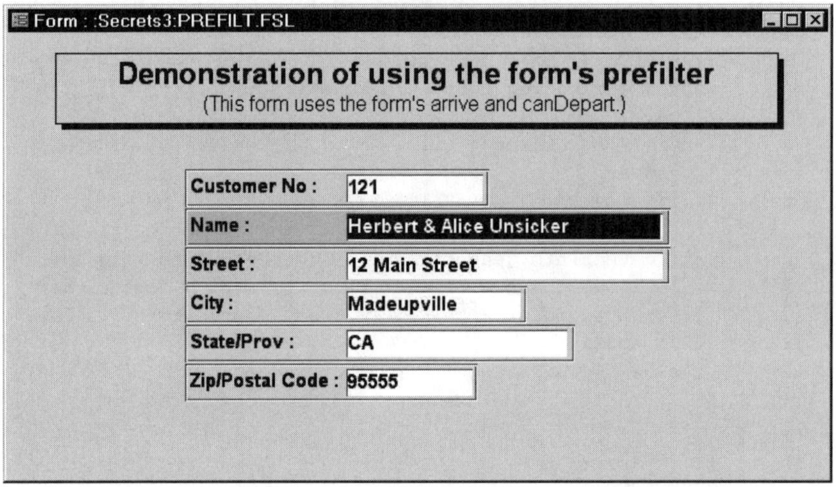

You can use the form's prefilter whenever you want to work with a group of objects. A group of objects can be categorized by class, color, font, and so on. You can check for all objects in a certain class or for objects with a certain name. You also can check for multiple criteria. For example:

```
;Form :: isPreFilter
if UI.class = "Field" then
   if UI.name <> "Last_Name" then
      UI.color = Red
   endIf
endIf
```

The prefilter of the form's arrive event is a good place for setting colors or other settings that need to be initialized at the beginning of a session, such as user configuration settings. You could write settings to a table or to an .INI file, read them in when the form is opened, and set all the object properties with this technique. More often, however, you will use the other events, such as the action and menuAction events, to manipulate a group of objects. Remember that all the form-level events have a prefilter you can use.

Prefilter and mouseExit

Have you ever noticed that the status bar continues to display the last message even when it's no longer needed? For most applications, this is what you want. Occasionally, however, you might want a cleaner look. You can put message("") in the form-level mouseExit event to turn off messages when a user leaves an object. In addition to cleaning up the status bar whenever you leave an object, this technique enables you to put a message on the mouseEnter event of objects you want to inform the user of. For example:


```
;Button :: mouseEnter
message("This button exits the application")
```

The Page Level

Normally, your first choice for high-level code should be either a library or the page level. Why not the form level? Because the form level forces the prefilter to fire for every object. In general, avoid the form-level else portion for faster applications. When you have a multipage form and you need to distinguish between pages, use the page level. A classic example of this is when building menus. Generally, an application will need a different menu for every page. In this case, the page's arrive event is the perfect location to build a menu.

In addition, use the menuAction event of the page when you build a custom menu and need to trap for the user's selection. This enables you to have different menus for different pages of a form. If you need the same menu choices on all the pages of a form, use the form-level menuAction event.

The Container Level: Using a Container to Hold Objects

Sometimes it's advantageous to put a container, such as a box object, in a page. Put objects inside the container, and put code at the container level that deals with the objects it contains.

The Container Level: Grouping Objects to Centralize Code

In addition to putting a box around objects, you could group them. This puts an invisible box-type object around the objects. If you want to test something about a group of objects, you can group them and test them with the arrive and canDepart events, for example. In a typical 1:M invoicing system, you might want to verify that a telephone number has been entered, but only when the user attempts to leave the header information. You can group the Header field objects and test the Telephone field on the canDepart event of the grouped objects. For example:

```
;Group :: canDepart
if Phone.isBlank() then
   beep()
   message("Enter a phone number.")
   eventInfo.setErrorCode(CanNotDepart)
endIf
```

Grouping Objects to Centralize Code Example

This example demonstrates how to return the values 0 through 9, depending on which object the user clicks. This example uses the technique of grouping objects to centralize code on the grouped object.

http://prestwood.com/forums/paradox/books/official/files/GROUP.FSL.

Step By Step

1. Change your working directory to Paradox's Samples directory, create a new form, and place 10 text objects with the values 0 through 9, as shown next. Then, group them by selecting all of them and choosing Format | Group.

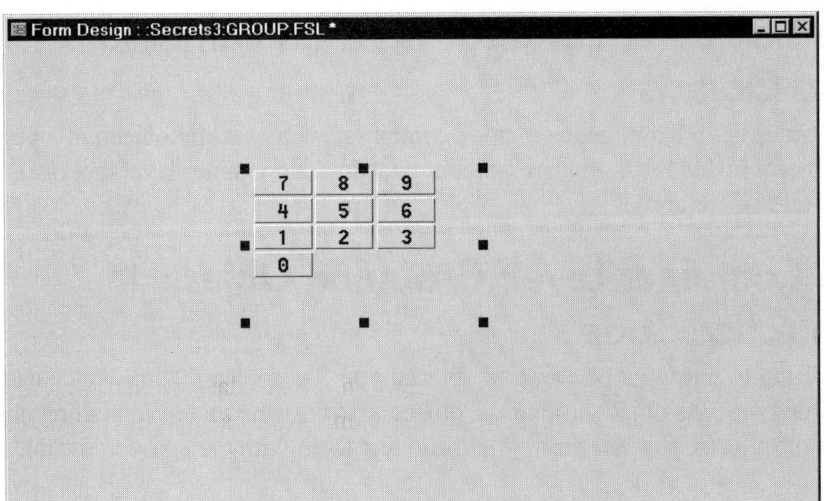

2. Add lines 3–11 to the mouseDown event of the grouped object. Line 4 declares a UIObject variable that is used in line 7 to get the intended object of a mouse action—in this case, the objects in the grouped object. Line 8 changes the object that is clicked to the color yellow, and line 9 notifies the user which object is hit. Line 10 sleeps for one-tenth of a second so that the user can see the object highlighted. Line 11 sets the color back to gray.

```
 1:    ;GROUP :: Group :: mouseDown
 2:    method mouseDown (var eventInfp MouseEvent)
 3:       var
 4:          obj  UIObject
 5:       endVar
 6:
 7:       eventInfo.getObjectHit (obj)
 8:       obj.color = Yellow
 9:       message ("You pressed the number ", obj.value)
10:       sleep (100)
11:       obj.color = Gray
12:    endMethod
```

3. Check the syntax, save the form as **GROUP.FSL**, and run it. When you click on one of the text objects, it changes color and displays the correct value in the status bar (see Figure 5-4).

Rather than use the message() procedure in line 9 of step 2 to notify the user of which object was clicked, you might want to use the data for something more practical. For example, you could turn this routine into a calculator.

The Object Level Often Is Best

The optimal place to put code—and also the first place you should think about putting code—is directly on the object itself. Most of the time, you put objects such as fields, buttons, and table frames within a page or in a container and attach code directly to them.

The Elements of Objects Also Is a Level

The lowest level for code is on the elements of an object. Many objects are actually composed of several objects. A field object is composed of a text label object and an

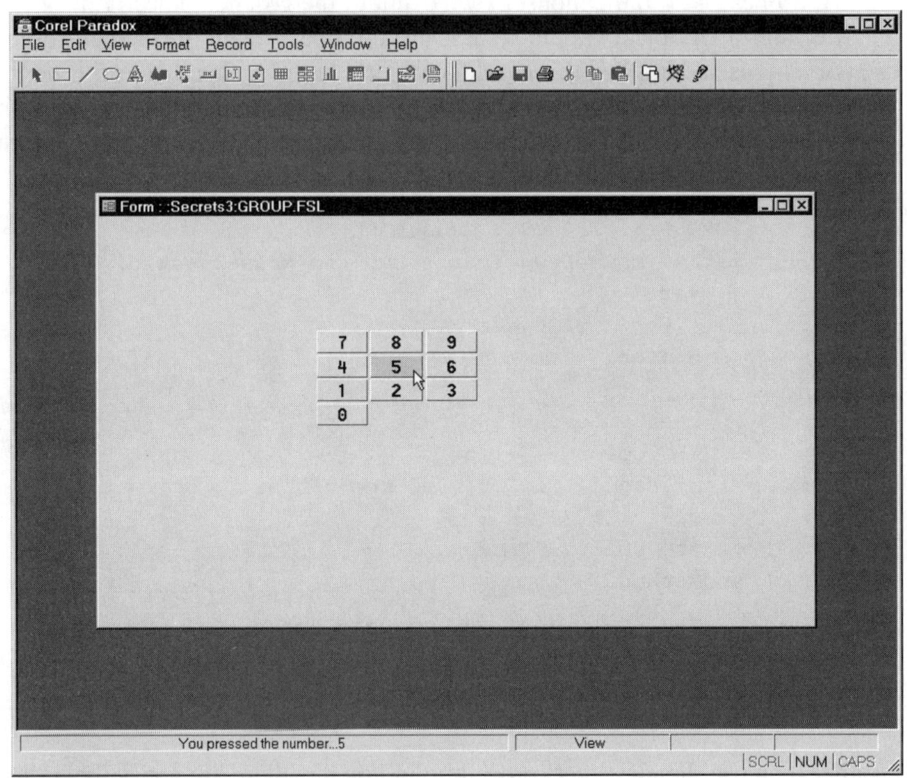

FIGURE 5-4 GROUP.FSL after an object has been clicked

edit region object (see Figure 5-5). When you put code on a field, you have a choice of 27 events at the field level, 10 at the edit region level, and 25 at the text label level. In the case of a field, you rarely use the edit region and text levels.

A button has two levels where you can attach code: the button object and the text object it contains. You usually use the pushButton event with buttons.

Figure 5-6 shows the Object Tree of a table frame. Note that a two-column table frame is composed of seven objects. Normally, you wouldn't place code on the header or on the column labels. That leaves three levels where you can place code on a table frame: the field level, the record level, and the table-frame level.

Figure 5-7 shows the Object Tree of a crosstab. A crosstab is composed of seven objects. Therefore, it has seven places where you can attach code.

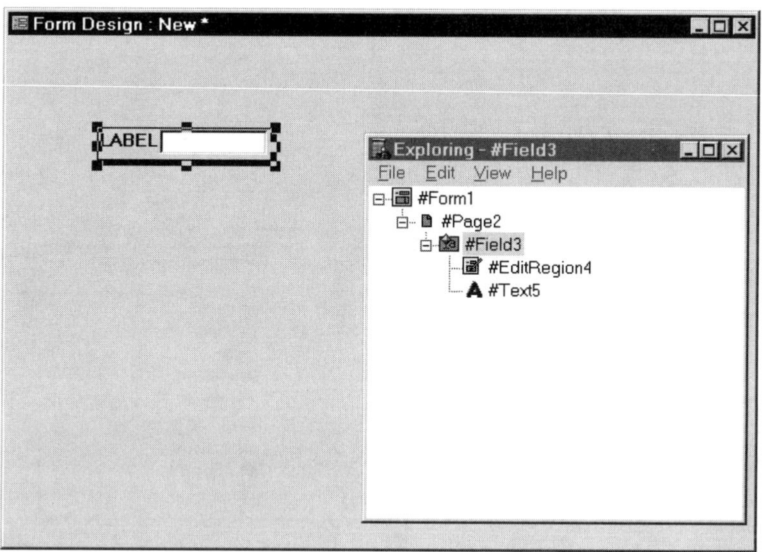

FIGURE 5-5 The Object Tree of a field

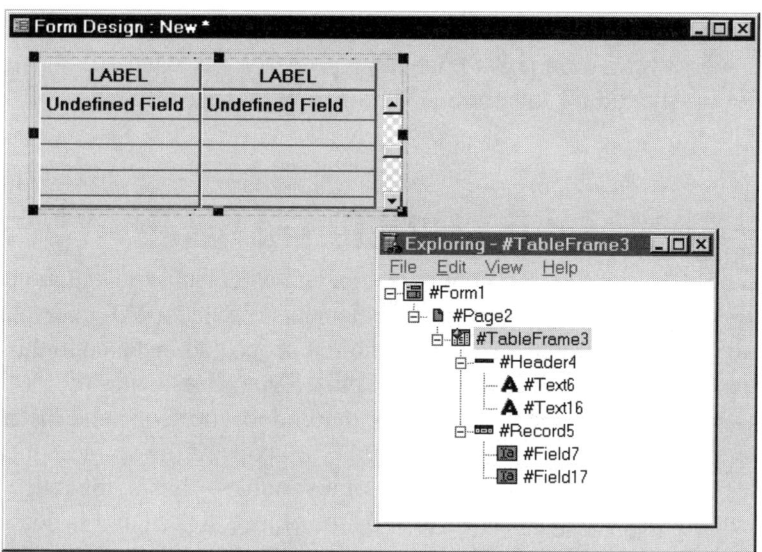

FIGURE 5-6 The Object Tree of a table frame

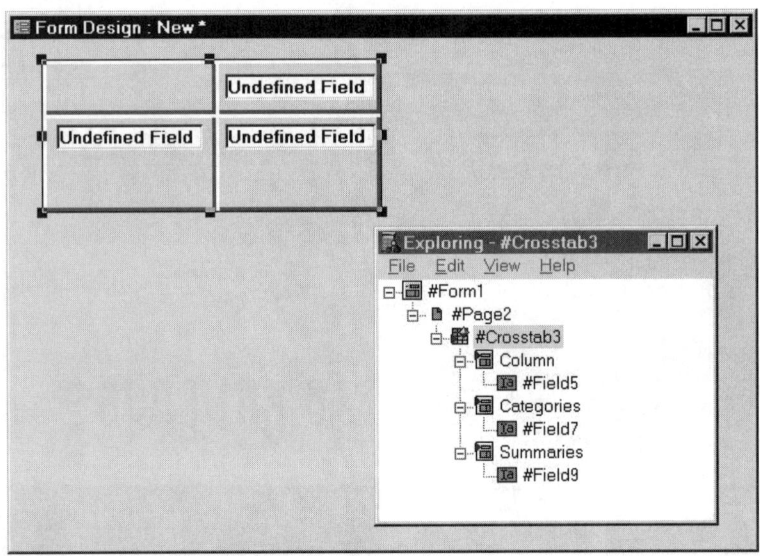

FIGURE 5-7 The Object Tree of a crosstab

Thinking of attaching code to various levels of an application or object is easier than randomly guessing where to put code. It gives you an idea of what can see what. Whenever a routine isn't behaving properly, ask yourself, "Is there a better level or location for this routine?" Sometimes, especially when you're dealing with multiple objects, the answer is yes.

Declaring Variables at Different Levels

The concepts of various levels, containership, and what can see what are important in ObjectPAL. One of the most important elements of ObjectPAL code placement is where to declare a variable. The discussion of scope and instance in this section also applies to the other object windows: Const, Type, Uses, and Proc.

The place where you declare a variable determines the scope and instance of a variable. The term *scope* means *accessiblity*. The scope of the variable means what other objects, if any, can see it. The scope of a variable—that is, the range of objects that have access to it—is defined by the objects in which it is declared and by the containership hierarchy. Objects can access only their own variables and the variables defined in the objects that contain them. The scope of a variable depends on where it is declared.

The *instance* of the variable means how long the variable exists. For example, if you declare a TCursor variable within a button and you want to use the same TCursor variable in another button, you could declare the TCursor in both buttons, which is a waste of resources. Or, you could move the declaration to higher ground—that is, to a place where both buttons can see and reuse one variable. In the case of two buttons on a page, the page level is a good choice. All the objects on the page, including the two buttons, have access to page-level variables.

Declare Private Variables Within a Method

After you choose which object to declare a variable on, you must decide whether you want the variable to be private to a method or global to the object. Variables declared within a method are visible only to that method and are dynamic; that is, they are accessible only while that method executes. They are initialized (reset) each time the method executes. A private variable can be seen only by the event in which it is declared. Its scope is limited. Therefore, if you want to use the variable in only a single method, use a variable that is private to the method.

If you declare a variable within a method (either within or above method...endMethod), then the variable is private to the method; that is, no other methods or objects can see or use the variable. In essence, the variable is private to the method.

Most often, the first place you choose to put a variable is inside method...endMethod. When you do this, the variable's scope is limited to the method and its existence is only for the duration of the method. Use this technique when no other objects need to use the variable and the variable can be initialized each time. For example, you can put both the variable declaration and the code in the same method window, as in the following:

```
;Btn1 :: pushButton
method pushButton(var eventInfo Event)
   var                          ;Private variables are declared
      s   String                ;inside method/endMethod.
   endVar

   s = "Hello World"
   msgInfo("", s)
endMethod
```

The first technique is easier to read; all code is located in the same place. In addition, the variable is private, or local. More specifically, the variable is local to only this method; no other events of this object or of another object can see the variable.

Declare Global Variables in the Var Window

The Var window of an object creates a variable that is global to the object. Variables declared in an object's Var window are visible to all methods attached to that object, and to any objects that object contains. A variable declared in an object's Var window is attached to the object and is static, accessible as long as the object exists.

A variable with broader scope in ObjectPAL is said to be global to the object. Any object can access it from that point down in the containership hierarchy. Do not confuse the concept of a variable being global to an object with a global variable in other languages. A variable that is global to an object in ObjectPAL is global only to that object and not to any other objects.

After you choose the object, you have three places in which you can declare a variable: in the Var window of the object, inside the method...endMethod structure of a method, or above the method...endMethod structure.

As an alternative to putting the variable declaration with the code, you can put the variable in the Var window and the code in the method, as in the following:

```
;Btn2 :: Var
var                     ;Global to an object variables
   s   String           ;are declared in the Var window
endVar                  ;of the object.
```

```
;Btn2 :: pushButton
method pushButton(var eventInfo Event)
   s = "Hello World"
   msgInfo("", s)
endMethod
```

This second technique uses a variable that is global to the object. It is more elegant if you need to use the variable elsewhere. The variable is global to the object; all the other methods of the object and of the objects it contains can see the variable. In other words, the scope you need for a particular variable is the determining factor. If no other object needs the variable, declare it privately.

Are there any exceptions to this rule? Yes. In the preceding example, either inside method...endMethod or in the Var window is equally elegant because the button's pushButton method occurs only once for each click of the button, which doesn't tax the system. In fact, you can declare a variable in any custom method or event that executes once. Methods such as pushButton, open, and arrive are prime candidates for declaring variables privately inside method...endMethod.

In the case of an event such as newValue, which is triggered many times by many different events, the second technique of separating the variable in the Var window from the code in the event is more elegant. Typically, the newValue event is triggered so many times during a session that redeclaring a variable each time doesn't make sense. A variable could be redeclared thousands of times in a newValue event.

Var window variables are declared for the instance of the object. Therefore, they are more elegant in most cases. It's better programming practice to declare your variables only once so that the system won't be taxed. The declaring of variables in the Var window occurs only once, and it occurs even before the open event of the object. If you want to see this for yourself, put the following code on a button and run the form. The message box will display the correct variable declaration.

```
;Button :: open
method open(var eventInfo Event)
   msgInfo("", dataType(o))
endMethod
```

```
;Button :: Var
var
   o   OLE
endVar
```

When you declare variables, you usually use one of the two techniques just discussed. The scope and instance of the variable are the determining factors. In general, it's a good rule of thumb to use the Var window as your first choice. Move the declaration from the Var window (which is global to the object) to within method...endMethod (which is private to the method) only when needed. By putting variables in the Var window of an object, more events have access to it.

Declaring Variables Outside a Method Block

What if you want the scope of a variable to be private to a method, but have its instance be for the duration of the object? Is this possible? Yes. Variables declared before the word "method" in a method...endMethod block are visible only to that method and are static. This technique has the benefit of declaring the variable only once—that is, when the object is created—yet the variable remains private to the method. In addition, its existence is for the duration of the object.

```
;Button :: pushButton
var
   O   OLE   ;Private variable declared only once.
endVar
method pushButton(var eventInfo Event)
   msgInfo("", DataType(O))
endMethod
```

This third technique is not used often enough. It is an elegant way to declare a variable private to a method, because the variable is declared only once. Declare permanent variables in either the Var window (scope that is global to the object with an instance of the duration of the object) or above the method...endMethod (scope that is private to the method with an instance of the duration of the object).

Variable Level Summary

After you decide that you need a variable that is global to an object—in other words, you have decided to use the Var window of an object—you must decide the level on which you want to declare the variable, such as the form, the page, the object's container, or the object. The answer depends on what you want the scope of the variable to be. In a way, it depends on how global you need the variable to be. In general, I declare the variable either at the form level or at the lowest possible container. If you declare a variable at the form level, you don't have to worry about the scope of the variable because the variable is global to the form. That is, all objects in the form can see it.

The better of these two approaches is to declare variables in the Var window of the lowest possible container. You can move them up the containership path when a broader scope is needed. For example, if you're going to use a variable on a button, declare it on the button. Declare the variable in the event itself—for example, within the pushButton event. If you use it in another of the button's events—for example, mouseEnter—move it to the button's Var window.

If you later need that variable for another object on that page or on another page in the form, move the variable back to the Var window of the page or form.

In general, declare the variable on as low a level as possible, and use the Var window whenever you need the same variable with two different events or two different objects.

Examples of Where to Put Code

Good examples are valuable. The following examples of where to put code might not be the most elegant, but they're good:

- **Field validation** Validate fields at the object level using the canDepart or changeValue events.
- **Record validation** Validate records at the record level with the action or canDepart events.
- **Initialize variables** Initialize variables in the form's init event. In general, avoid the form's open event except for routines that deal with every object in the form.
- **Universal constants** Declare often-used constants in a library and use the extended Uses syntax.
- **Universal custom types** Define often-used custom types in a library and use the extended Uses syntax.
- **Scripts** If you have a routine that needs to be called by code and run independently by a user, then use a script.

Summary

This chapter covered many aspects of ObjectPAL, including objects, containers, containership hierarchy, and bubbling. One of the hardest aspects of using ObjectPAL is deciding where to place code. Novice ObjectPAL programmers tend to place code everywhere. Rather than work with the default behavior, the event model, and the data model, beginners often tend to put code in the wrong place. Later, they add more code to try to fix an inelegant approach.

Taking the time to understand the default behavior of objects, the event model, and the data model can save you much time. If you don't fully understand how an object works, you could end up working harder and accomplishing less. Much of this book deals with this issue. This chapter concentrates on it and offers guidelines, tips, and techniques on where and when to code.

Where code is placed is important. When coding in any event-driven environment, think levels. In ObjectPAL this extends from the library through objects on a form. Ultimately, you must find the perfect place to put your code. Only through trial and error—and some experimentation—will you learn the good and bad places to put code. The guidelines presented in this chapter will get you started.

CHAPTER 6

The Event Model

The *event model* is an important aspect of ObjectPAL. The event model is the map of when events associated with UIObjects execute during Run mode. This chapter explores the event model in great detail.

The Event Model Makes Sense

As we have discussed, the form is the highest container in ObjectPAL. It always contains at least one page. You place objects, such as fields, table frames, and buttons inside a page. All UIObjects, including forms, pages, and UIObjects you place on pages, contain a set of events. All, for example, have an open event. The event model is not linear, but can be used in a linear fashion. Much like a procedural language, you can attach code to the open event of the form, page, box, field, and button. The code executes in order. First the code on the form executes, then the code on the page, box, and field executes. Finally, the code on the button executes.

If you place the following line of code in all the open events of the objects just mentioned, you'll notice the message information boxes you just saw are executed in a linear fashion:

```
MsgInfo("Open Event", self.name)
```

When the box and the button are on the same level, however, they both can't execute at the same time. What dictates the order of execution? The containership hierarchy determines which code is executed first. Generally, the order in which objects are placed on the page dictates which object is opened first. For an experiment, place a larger box around both of these objects and alternate moving them onto the page level. What do you expect to happen? Try it and find out.

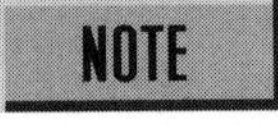

You can alter the path of objects by moving objects around in the containership hierarchy. Move objects on the same level by selecting Format | Order | Bring to Front and Format | Order | Send to Back.

Although events can execute in a linear fashion—that is, one event executes after another—you don't program ObjectPAL in a linear fashion. When you program in Paradox, think, "What object do I want to alter?" For example, if you want to check a value in a field after the user enters it, go to that field and put code on the canDepart event. You can use canDepart to check the field's contents before it permits the cursor to leave the field.

Default Behavior Occurs Last

The default behavior of the open event is to open the objects within it. When exactly does an object open? All default behavior occurs just before endMethod.

Take a closer look at the events open and arrive and when the default behavior occurs. An object is always opened before it is arrived on. Therefore, code in the open event always executes before code in the arrive event. Any code that you want to execute as a form opens or before a form opens goes in the open event. Any code that you want to execute after a form opens goes in the arrive event. The arrive event is a good place for code that requires user interface objects, because UIObjects aren't opened until the end of the open event (just before endMethod).

Events Are the Event Model

Objects in ObjectPAL come with events you can place code in. In addition to the code you can add to an event, each event has default built-in behavior. This behavior is executed just before endMethod. Sometimes an event is used by an object, and sometimes it's passed to another event. This using and passing of events is known as the *event model*, which is a map of the order in which events are executed. You cannot see this hidden code, but it is there and you can affect it, for example, with doDefault, disableDefault, and enableDefault.

Events can be generated by a user action, such as moving the mouse or pressing a key, or by ObjectPAL. An event generated by ObjectPAL usually is generated or called from a user's actions. So, in a sense, all events are started in one way or another by the user. Thinking of the event model in this simplified way is a good way to program. An open event occurs because the user chooses File | Open | Form. It's easier to think of a user opening a form, which causes the open event, than it is to think of the open event as receiving an internal event generated by ObjectPAL.

Likewise, when a user clicks a button, code in the button's pushButton event is executed, right? Wrong. pushButton is an internal event that is called by the external event mouseUp only when the cursor is inside the boundaries of the button. It's much easier, however, to think that when the user clicks a button, several events are executed in order: mouseDown, mouseUp, mouseClick, and pushButton. There are times when it's important to understand that mouseUp calls pushButton only when the cursor is within the boundaries of the button. Even so, most of the time you can think in terms of simple user actions.

Understanding when events are executed is key to understanding ObjectPAL. The better you know when code executes, the better and cleaner your applications will be. Although you usually use pushButton when you program a button, occasionally you will want to use mouseDown, mouseUp, or mouseClick. Understanding what the differences are is important.

The form http://prestwood.com/forums/paradox/books/official/files/BUTTON.FSL demonstrates the order of execution of a button's mouseDown, mouseUp, mouseClick, and pushButton events. In addition, it demonstrates mouseEnter and mouseExit.

Some Event Model Rules

There are many rules that govern the event model. The following are some introductory rules to keep in mind:

- All events generate a packet of information. This event packet contains information on what generated the event, the target of the next event, and more. Events are generated either by ObjectPAL or by a user interacting with a form. A few examples of events for which ObjectPAL generates events are open, arrive, and depart. A few examples of events for which a user generates events are mouseClick, keyChar, and menuAction.
- All events go to the form first. If the target is an object other than the form, the event goes through the form's prefilter and the event is sent to the target. This is important because the prefilter of the form is a great location to code certain types of generic code.
- Internal events are passed from the form's prefilter to the target object. Internal events, discussed in detail in the next section, are events called from within Paradox.
- External events, like internal events, are passed from the form's prefilter to the target object. Unlike internal events, however, external events can bubble back up to the form.

The Form's Init Event

The only object that supports this event is the form object itself; all other UIObjects within the form do not have this event. The chief benefit of this event, unlike all other form-level events, is that it does not have a prefilter clause. Now, you have control over what happens before the open event. In previous versions of ObjectPAL, the open event was called from a prewired C routine. When you access the ObjectPAL editor, you see the following:

```
method init (var eventInfo Event)

endMethod
```


How to Use the Init event

The init event is called once whenever a form is opened. The default behavior of init is to call open. It is important to note that when you use disableDefault in init, the form and all the objects within the form are still opened. However, any code in the open events of all objects does not execute. You have, in fact, disabled the code in the object's open events. To stop a form from opening, set an error code as in the following:

```
method init(var eventInfo Event)
   if cmSomeCondition() = True then
      ;In place of CanNotArrive, you
      ;can use any non zero value.
      eventInfo.setErrorCode(CanNotArrive)
   endIf
endMethod
```

The primary use for the init event is for initialization code. For example, if you want to set up some tables before the open event tries to open the tables, do it in init. If, after the tables are created, you want to use them in init, then call the open event with doDefault, as shown here:

```
method init(var eventInfo Event)
   cmBuildTables()
   doDefault
   ;Use the tables here.
endMethod
```

Categorizing Events: Internal, External, and Special

Events are categorized as internal, external, and special. These three categories of events follow very specific rules. Table 6-1 lists the events.

Internal Events

Internal events are events generated by Paradox. A good case study example of an internal event is open. The open event occurs from outer container inward. The form is opened, then the page, and then the objects in the page. Code in the canArrive, arrive, and setFocus events are also executed from outer container inward.

Like external events, internal events go first to the form and then to the target object. Unlike external and special events, internal events do not bubble. In simple

Internal	External	Special
init	mouseClick	pushButton
open	mouseDown	changeValue
close	mouseUp	newValue
canArrive	mouseDouble	
arrive	mouseRightDown	
setFocus	mouseRightUp	
canDepart	mouseRightDouble	
removeFocus	mouseMove	
depart	keyPhysical	
mouseEnter	keyChar	
mouseExit	error	
timer	status	
	action	
	menuAction	

TABLE 6-1 The Three Types of Events

terms, the event dies at the target. In other words, the complete path for an internal event is sent to the form and back to the object.

Take a closer look at the default behavior of each internal event. Internal events are always called either from other internal events or from an external built-in event. Paradox has many built-in default behaviors. The following sections describe the internal events and their default behaviors.

Rules Guiding Internal Events

Code placed in their counterparts close, canDepart, and depart execute from inner container out. To study this, suppose that you have a field inside a box on the first page of a form and you try to close the form. In what order does the code placed in various object's canDepart events execute? First, code in the canDepart for the field is executed. Then, code in its container—the box's canDepart—is executed; and then, finally, code in the box's container—the page canDepart—is executed. Code placed in the close, canDepart, and depart events are executed from inner container outward.

Like external events, internal events go first to the form and then to the target object. Unlike external and special events, internal events stop at the target. In other words, the complete path for an internal event is sent to the form and back to the object. Table 6-2 describes the internal events. The concept of bubbling back up to the form does not exist for internal events.

Event	Short Description
Init	Executed once when the form is opened
Open	Executed once for every object when the form is opened
Close	Executed once for every object when the form is closed
CanArrive	Executed before moving to an object
CanDepart	Executed before moving off an object
arrive	Executed after moving to an object
depart	Executed after moving off an object
setFocus	Executed whenever an object gets the focus

TABLE 6-2 Internal Events

Event	Short Description
removeFocus	Executed whenever an object loses the focus
mouseEnter	Executed whenever the mouse pointer enters an object
mouseExit	Executed whenever the mouse pointer exits an object
timer	Executed at a time interval specified by the programmer

TABLE 6-2 Internal Events *(continued)*

Default Behavior of Internal Events

Take a closer look at the default behavior of each internal event. Internal events are always called either from other internal events or from an external event. There is much built-in default behavior in Paradox. The following paragraphs describe the internal events and their default behavior.

Every object has to be opened. The open event is called only once for every object, starting with the form, then the page, then the objects contained by the page, and finally the objects contained within that container. After the first page is completely open, the process starts over with the next page in the form.

Remember that the prefilter of the form sees the open event before the target object sees it. The default code for open calls the open event for each of the objects it contains. Then, the open event for each one of those objects calls the open event for the objects it contains, and so on. The default behavior for the close event acts in the same way but in reverse. If a table is bound to the object, the object also opens the table. Any errors will abort the open process.

The form http://prestwood.com/forums/paradox/books/official/files/OPEN2.FSL demonstrates the open event and the prefilter section of the form's open event.

The canArrive event is interesting. It occurs before movement to an object is permitted. Think of canArrive as asking permission to move to the object. Contrary to what is implied in the manuals, canArrive is not used just for restricting entrance to a field. You can use this event to execute almost any kind of code just before arriving on an object. The canArrive event blocks arrival for records beyond the end of a table—except, of course, when you are in Edit mode and the Auto-Append option is checked in the data model. Any object whose tab stop property is unchecked also is blocked.

The arrive event is executed after movement has arrived on an object. An arrive event can be called only after a canArrive event. Pages, table frames, and multirecord objects move to the first tab stop object they contain. When you arrive on a field or a record, the object is made current; if you're in Edit mode, an edit window is created for the edit region of a field. If the object is a drop-down edit list, the focus moves to the list. If the object is a radio button, the focus moves to the first button.

The setFocus event occurs every time an object gets the focus. If the object getting the focus is contained in another object, setFocus is called for each container—from the outermost container inward. For example, if a page contains a box, which contains a field, code in setFocus is executed first for the page, next for the box, and then for the field. In an edit field, the default code highlights the currently selected edit region and causes the insertion point to blink. The focus property is set to True, and the status message reports the number of the current record and the total number of records. For buttons, if the tab stop property is set, a dotted rectangle is displayed around the label.

The canDepart event is executed before a move off an object. Field objects try to post their contents and trip changeValue. If the record is a changed record, the object tries to commit the current record. If the record is locked, the form tries to unlock it.

The removeFocus event occurs when an object loses the focus. On field objects, the flashing insertion point and highlight are removed. On a button, the dotted rectangle is removed. The object's focus property is set to FALSE. This is called for the active object and its containers.

After canDepart and removeFocus have executed successfully, the depart event is called. Field objects close their edit windows, then repaint and clean up the screen.

The mouseEnter event is generated whenever the mouse pointer enters an object. Form, page, and button objects set the pointer to an arrow. Field objects set the pointer to an I-beam. If a button is still down, its value toggles between TRUE and FALSE.

The mouseExit event is generated whenever the mouse pointer exits an object. Field objects set the pointer back to the arrow.

The Init Event

The init event is called once when a form is opened. The primary use for the init event is for initialization code. The only object that supports this event is the form object itself; all other UIObjects within the form do not have this event. The chief benefit of this event, unlike all other form-level events, is that it does not have a prefilter clause. Now, you have control over what happens before the open event. In previous versions of ObjectPAL, the open event was called from a prewired C routine that the developers of Paradox wrote.

DEFAULT BEHAVIOR The default behavior of init is to call open. You should note that when you use disableDefault in init, the form and all the objects within the form are still opened. However, any code in the open events of all objects does not execute. You have, in fact, disabled the code in the object's open events. To stop a form from opening, set an error code in the init event using eventInfo.setErrorCode(CanNotArrive).

The *open* and *close* Events

Every object has to be opened and is eventually closed. The open event is called only once for every object, starting with the form, then the page, then the objects contained by the page, and finally the objects contained within that container. After the first page is completely open, the process starts over with the next page in the form. Remember that the prefilter of the form sees the open event before the target object sees it.

DEFAULT BEHAVIOR The default code for open calls the open event for each of the objects it contains. Then, the open event for each one of these objects calls the open event for the objects it contains, and so on. If you use DisableDefault in the open of an object, the object and the objects it contains are still opened. The appearance is that DisableDefault has no effect; however, it does. DisableDefault in the open event prevents the code in the open event of the objects it contains from executing. If a table is bound to the object, the object also opens the table.

The default behavior for the close event acts in the same way.

EFFECT OF ERRORS Any errors abort the open process and put the object in Design mode. For example, eventInfo.setErrorCode(1) prevents an object from opening and puts the object in Design mode.

The *canArrive* Event

The canArrive event occurs before movement to an object is permitted. Think of canArrive as asking permission to move to the object. Contrary to what is implied in the manuals, canArrive is not used just for restricting entrance to a field. You can use this event to execute almost any kind of code just before arriving on an object.

DEFAULT BEHAVIOR The canArrive event blocks arrival for records beyond the end of a table—except, of course, when you are in Edit mode and the Auto-Append data model property is checked. Any object whose tab stop property is unchecked also is blocked. You can't disable the default behavior using DisableDefault. Instead, use the following:

```
eventInfo.setErrorCode(CanNotArrive).
```

EVENTINFO The eventInfo packet for the canArrive event is type MoveEvent. The reasons for a MoveEvent are PalMove, RefreshMove, ShutDownMove, StartupMove, and UserMove. Suppose that you want to know whether a move was made by ObjectPAL or by a user. You could use the following in canArrive:

```
Switch
  case eventInfo.reason() = PalMove
     : message("ObjectPAL move")
  case eventInfo.reason() = UserMove
     : message("move by user")
endSwitch
```

The MoveEvent eventInfo packet has a unique method called getDestination(), which enables you to know which object the user is trying to move to. Suppose that you want to know whether a user is going to move to either of two fields, such as Last_Name or First_Name, and you want to do this at the form level. You can use the following:

```
;Form :: canArrive prefilter
method canArrive(var eventInfo MoveEvent)
var
   ui UIObject
endVar
if eventInfo.isPreFilter() then
   ;// This code executes for each object on the form
```

```
else
   ;// This code executes only for the form
eventInfo.getDestination(ui)
if ui.name = "Last_Name" or  ui.name = "First_Name" then
   ;Execute code here.
endIf
endMethod
```

EFFECT OF ERRORS Any error denies permission to arrive on the object. Suppose that you want to stop movement to a field. You could use the following code in the canArrive built-in event:

```
eventInfo.setErrorCode(1)
```

ObjectPAL does provide the constant CanNotArrive to humanize the language a bit. As an alternative to using any nonzero value, you could use the following:

```
eventInfo.setErrorCode(CanNotArrive)
```

The *arrive* Event

The arrive event is executed after movement has arrived on an object. An arrive event can be called only after a canArrive event. You can use the inserting and blankRecord properties to tell when a record is being inserted and when a record is blank.

DEFAULT BEHAVIOR The arrive event calls the arrive event of the objects it contains. This process occurs inward; that is, from the outer container in—the form, the page, the objects in the page, and so on. Pages, table frames, and multirecord objects move to the first tab stop object they contain. When you arrive on a field or a record, the object is made current. If you're in Edit mode, an editing window appears when the field is touched, in FieldView or MemoView. If the object is a drop-down edit list, the focus moves to the list. If the object is a radio button, the focus moves to the first button.

EVENTINFO The eventInfo packet for the arrive event is type MoveEvent.

EFFECT OF ERRORS Any error prevents arriving on the object. Visually, an error means that no object gets focus. DisableDefault seems to have the same effect as setting an error. As usual, the preferred way to stop the behavior is to set an error.

The *setFocus* Event

The setFocus event occurs every time an object gets the focus.

DEFAULT BEHAVIOR If the object getting the focus is contained in another object, setFocus is called for each container—from the outermost container inward. For example, if a page contains a box, which contains a field, code in the setFocus event is executed first for the page, next for the box, and then for the field. In an edit field, the default code highlights the currently selected edit region and causes the insertion point to blink. The focus property is set to True, and the status message reports the number of the current record and the total number of records. For buttons, if the tab stop property is set, a dotted rectangle appears around the label.

The *canDepart* Event

The canDepart event is executed before a move off an object.

DEFAULT BEHAVIOR Field objects try to post their contents and trip changeValue. If the record is a changed record, the object tries to commit the current record. If the record is locked, the form tries to unlock it.

EVENTINFO The eventInfo packet for the canDepart event is type MoveEvent.

The *removeFocus* Event

The removeFocus event occurs when an object loses the focus.

DEFAULT BEHAVIOR On field objects, the flashing insertion point and highlight are removed. On a button, the dotted rectangle is removed. The object's focus property is set to FALSE. This is called for the active object and its containers.

EVENTINFO The eventInfo packet for removeFocus is type Event.

The *depart* Event

After canDepart and removeFocus have executed successfully, the depart event is called.

DEFAULT BEHAVIOR Field objects close their edit windows and then Paradox repaints and cleans up the screen.

EVENTINFO The eventInfo packet for depart is type MoveEvent. The reasons for a MoveEvent are PalMove, RefreshMove, ShutDownMove, StartupMove, and UserMove. All these event reasons are self-explanatory except perhaps for RefreshMove. An example of when RefreshMove is generated is when data is updated by scrolling through a table.

EFFECT OF ERRORS Any nonzero value stops the departure from a field or a page. For example, eventInfo.setErrorCode(CanNotDepart) in the depart event of a field or page keeps focus on the current field or page. In the case of a page, however, focus is lost. Therefore, a better location to execute this code for all objects is in canDepart. Setting the error code in the depart event of the form does not stop the form from closing.

The *mouseEnter* Event

The mouseEnter event is generated whenever the mouse pointer enters an object.

DEFAULT BEHAVIOR Form, page, and button objects set the pointer to an arrow. Field objects set the pointer to an I-beam. If a button has received a mouseDown but not a mouseUp, and is still down, its value toggles from False to True. You can disable this default behavior by using DisableDefault in mouseEnter.

The *mouseExit* Event

The mouseExit event is generated whenever the mouse pointer exits an object.

DEFAULT BEHAVIOR Field objects set the pointer back to the arrow. If a button has received a mouseDown but not a mouseUp, and is still down, its value toggles from True to False. You can disable this default behavior by using DisableDefault in mouseEnter.

External Events

External events are generated by the user interacting with a form. Keep in mind, however, that ObjectPAL can call some external events.

Now take a closer look at the default behavior of each external event. Both internal and external events go first to the form and then to the target object.

External events, however, unlike internal events, bubble back up to the form. Paradox has many built-in default behaviors. The default behavior for an external event is to pass the event to its container, which is how it bubbles up to the form. The following sections explain the default behavior of the external events that do something in addition to bubbling their events.

Rules Guiding External Events

External events are events generated by the user interacting with a form and by ObjectPAL. Both internal and external events go first to the form and then to the target object. External events, however, unlike internal events, bubble back up to the form. The default behavior for an external event is to pass the event to its container, which is how it bubbles up to the form. External events are generated when a user interacts with the user interface. Table 6-3 describes the external events.

Event	Short Description
MouseMove	Occurs whenever the mouse moves
MouseDown	Occurs when the left mouse button is pressed
MouseUp	Occurs when the left mouse button is released
MouseClick	Occurs when the pointer is inside an object and the left mouse button is pressed and released
MouseDouble	Occurs when the left mouse button is double-clicked
MouseRightDown	Occurs when the right mouse button is pressed
MouseRightUp	Occurs when the right mouse button is released
MouseRightDouble	Occurs when the right mouse button is double-clicked
KeyPhysical	Occurs whenever any key is pressed
KeyChar	Occurs whenever a character key is pressed
Action	Executes when a keystroke or menu option maps to an action
MenuAction	Occurs when a menu option or a toolbar icon is selected
Error	Occurs whenever an error is encountered
Status	Occurs whenever a message is displayed in the status bar

TABLE 6-3 External Events

Default Behavior of External Events

Now take a closer look at the default behavior of each external event. The following paragraphs explain the default behavior of the external events that do something in addition to bubbling their events.

The mouseDown event occurs when the left mouse button is pressed. The event packet for mouseDown contains the mouse coordinates in twips (1/1,440 of an inch) relative to the last object that executed a mouseEnter event. If the object is a field that is active, the field is put into Field view. If the object is a button, its value is toggled between True and False.

The mouseRightDown event occurs when the right mouse button is pressed. It is the same as the mouseDown event, except that it uses the right mouse button instead. If the object is a formatted memo, a graphic, OLE, or an undefined field, a pop-up menu is displayed.

The mouseUp event occurs when the left mouse button is released. mouseUp is called for the last object that received a mouseDown event. Therefore, an object always sees the mouseDown and mouseUp events in a pair. If you select text, mouseUp ends the selection. If the object is a button and the pointer is still inside the button, mouseUp calls the pushButton event. The mouseRightUp event is the same as the mouseUp event, except that it uses the right mouse button instead.

The mouseDouble event occurs when the left mouse button is double-clicked. A field object enters Field view. The mouseRightDouble event is the same as the mouseDouble event, except that it uses the right mouse button.

The movement of the mouse is tracked with the mouseMove event. Whenever the pointer is moved within an object, the mouseMove event is executed.

The keyPhysical event occurs whenever *any* key is pressed and each time a key is autorepeated. keyPhysical includes all the physical keys on the keyboard, including the character keys, the function keys, and the ALT, CTRL, and ESC keys. A keystroke goes first to Windows and then to Paradox, which gives it to the form's prefilter. The form sends it to the active object for processing. The object's keyPhysical determines whether the keystroke represents an action or a display character. Actions are passed to the action event, and display characters are passed to keyChar.

The keyChar event occurs whenever a character key is pressed. As discussed previously, the keyPhysical event for the active object sends action events such as DataNextRecord to the action event, and it sends characters such as "a" to keyChar. If the active object is a field in Edit mode, a lock is put on the table before the first character is inserted. If the active object is a button and the character is a SPACEBAR, the button's pushButton event is called. Remember, a button can be active only if its TabStop option is set to TRUE.

The action event is called frequently. It executes when it is sent an action keystroke from keyPhysical, when menuAction maps to a menu option, or when an event such as DataPostRecord calls for an action. The default behavior for action is extensive because all actions go through it. For example, Page Down moves to the next record, F9 toggles Edit mode, and Insert inserts a record only if the form is in Edit mode.

The menuAction event occurs when a menu option, a toolbar icon, or an option from the control box is selected. The option is sent first to the form's action event for processing and then to the active object.

The error event occurs right after an error is encountered. You shouldn't test for errors with the error event. Use action instead. An error is passed to its container until it gets to the form. The form might or might not display a message, depending on the severity of the error. You can trap for errors and alter the default behavior in the action event before the error gets to the error event. You can use the error event to add to the built-in default error behavior.

The status event occurs whenever a message is displayed on the status bar. The default behavior of status is too extensive to be described here. In short, any time you see a message in one of the four status areas, an event has gone through the status event.

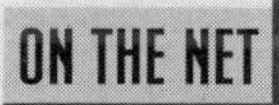

The form http://prestwood.com/forums/paradox/books/official/files/STATUS_F.FSL demonstrates filtering messages going to the status bar. It uses the status event to disable messages.

The *mouseDown* Event

The mouseDown event occurs when the left mouse button is pressed.

DEFAULT BEHAVIOR If the object is a field that is active, the field is put into Field view. If the object is a button with its tab stop property set to True, the button becomes active. A button's value is toggled from False to True. You can verify this value by typing the following code into the pushButton event of a button:

```
;Button :: pushButton
method mouseDown(var eventInfo MouseEvent)
   message(self.value)
   sleep(500)
   DoDefault
   message(self.value)
endMethod
```

EVENTINFO The eventInfo packet for mouseDown contains the mouse coordinates in twips relative to the last object that executed a mouseEnter event.

The *mouseRightDown* Event

The mouseRightDown event occurs when the right mouse button is pressed. It is the same as the mouseDown event, except that it uses the right mouse button instead.

DEFAULT BEHAVIOR If the object is a formatted memo, a graphic, OLE, or an undefined field, a pop-up menu appears.

The *mouseUp* Event

The mouseUp event occurs when the left mouse button is released. mouseUp is called for the last object that received a mouseDown event. Therefore, an object always sees the mouseDown and mouseUp events in a pair.

DEFAULT BEHAVIOR If you select text, mouseUp ends the selection. If the object is a button and the pointer is still inside the button, mouseUp calls the pushButton event.

The mouseRightUp event is the same as the mouseUp event, except that it uses the right mouse button instead.

The *mouseDouble* Event

The mouseDouble event occurs when the left mouse button is double-clicked.

DEFAULT BEHAVIOR A field object enters Field view.

The mouseRightDouble event is the same as the mouseDouble event, except that it uses the right mouse button.

The *mouseMove* Event

The movement of the mouse is tracked with the mouseMove event. Whenever the pointer is moved within an object, the mouseMove event is executed.

DEFAULT BEHAVIOR An active edit field checks the state of the SHIFT key. If the SHIFT key is down (or pressed), the selection is extended. If necessary, an active graphic field scrolls the graphic. When you press and hold the mouse button inside an object, the mouseMove event of the object is called until you release the button (even when the pointer moves outside the object).

The *keyPhysical* Event

The keyPhysical event occurs whenever any key is pressed and each time a key is autorepeated. keyPhysical includes all the physical keys on the keyboard, including the character keys, the function keys, and the ALT, CTRL, and ESC keys.

DEFAULT BEHAVIOR A keystroke goes first to Windows and then to Paradox, which gives it to the form's prefilter. The form sends it to the active object for processing. The object determines whether the keystroke represents an action or a display character. Actions are passed to the action event, and display characters are passed to the keyChar event.

The *keyChar* Event

The keyChar event occurs whenever a character key is pressed. Actually, the keyPhysical event for the active object sends action events such as nextRecord() to the action event, and it sends characters such as "a" to keyChar; if a keyPhysical does not map to an action, then it calls keyChar.

DEFAULT BEHAVIOR If the active object is a field in Edit mode, a lock is put on the record before the first character is inserted.

If the active object is a button and the character is a SPACEBAR, the button's pushButton event is called without calling mouseDown or mouseUp. In other words, your code in mouseDown and mouseUp does not execute. (Remember, a button can be active only if its tab stop is set to True.)

The *action* Event

The action event is called frequently. It executes when it is sent an action keystroke KeyEvent from keyPhysical, when a MenuEvent from menuAction maps to a menu option, or when an event calls for an action. An example of a event calling for an action is UIObject.postRecord(). In this case, the postRecord() calls for a DataPostRecord. The constant DataPostRecord is sent to the action event. You can send action commands to action using the action() method.

DEFAULT BEHAVIOR The default behavior for action is to perform the pending action. Its default behavior is extensive because all actions go through it. For example, Page Down moves to the next record, F9 toggles Edit mode, and ALT-TAB task-switches to another application.

The *menuAction* Event

The menuAction event occurs when a menu option or Toolbar icon is selected. You can send MenuCommands to menuAction using the menuAction() event.

DEFAULT BEHAVIOR The option is sent first to the form's menuAction event for processing and then to the active object.

The *error* Event

The error event occurs after an error is encountered. Because error is always called after an error, to prevent an error, trap for specific types of errors in the action event.

DEFAULT BEHAVIOR An error is passed to its container until it gets to the form. The form might or might not display a message, depending on the severity of the error; that is, depending on whether the error is a warning or critical level error. All critical errors produce the Error dialog box. Warning errors, on the other hand, may or may not display a message in the status bar. You can trap for errors and alter this default behavior in the form's action event.

The *status* Event

The status event occurs whenever a message is displayed in the status bar.

DEFAULT BEHAVIOR The default behavior of status is too extensive to be described here. In short, any time you see a message in one of the four status areas, it has gone through the built-in status event. For example, whenever a key violation occurs, a message is sent to the StatusWindow.

Special Events

Special events are specific to a few objects, such as a field's newValue event. The following sections explain the default behavior of the special events.

Introducing Special Events

Special events are specific to a few objects, such as newValue of a field. Table 6-4 describes the special events.

Default Behavior of the Special Events

The following paragraphs explain the default behavior of the special events.

The only UIObjects that have a pushButton event are buttons and fields displayed as a list box. The form has a pushButton event because it dispatches it with its prefilter clause. pushButton occurs when the pointer is inside an object for both the mouseDown and mouseUp events. In fact, mouseUp calls pushButton. Button objects visually depress and pop out. Check boxes check or uncheck. Radio buttons push in or pop out. If the Tab Stop property is set to True, the focus moves to it.

The newValue event is executed after the value in a field changes. Code in newValue is executed even if the value is changed only onscreen.

Code in the changeValue event on a defined field, on the other hand, is executed by a change in a table. Code in the changeValue event on an undefined field is executed when the value in the field changes.

The changeValue event is executed before a value in a table is changed. If you have code on both changeValue and newValue, the code on changeValue occurs first; that is, before the value changes. Code in the newValue event is executed after the value changes. Therefore, if you want to do validity checks on a field, changeValue is a good place to put them.

The *pushButton* Event

Only button objects and the form have a pushButton event. Some field display types are actually composite objects that include buttons; fields themselves never have a pushButton. For example, a field displayed as a check box is composed of a field, a button, and a text object.

Event	Description
pushButton	Executes whenever you click a button
newValue	Executes whenever the value in a field changes
changeValue	Executes whenever the value in a table changes

TABLE 6-4 Special Events

6

The form, which has all the events, acts like a dispatcher. The pushButton event occurs when the pointer is inside an object for both the mouseDown and mouseUp events. In fact, mouseUp calls mouseClick, which then calls pushButton.

DEFAULT BEHAVIOR Button objects visually depress and pop out. Check boxes check or uncheck. Radio buttons push in or pop out. If the tab stop property is set to True, the focus moves to it.

The *newValue* Event

Only fields and the form have a newValue event. The newValue event is executed after the value in a field changes. Code in the newValue event is executed even if the value is changed only onscreen. Code in the form's open event also executes the code in the newValue event for each field object in the form. Code in the changeValue event, on the other hand, is executed by a change in a table.

The *changeValue* Event

The changeValue event is executed before a value in a table is changed. If you have code on both changeValue and newValue, the code on changeValue occurs first, before the value changes. Code in the newValue event is executed after the value changes. Therefore, if you want to do validity checks on a field, do them in changeValue. To fully understand the relationship between DoDefault, self.value, and eventInfo.newValue(), enter the following code into the changeValue event of a field bound to a table and then change the value:

```
;Field :: changeValue
method changeValue(var eventInfo ValueEvent)
  ;Before default behavior.
  view(self.value, "self before DoDefault")
  view(String(eventInfo.newValue()), "newValue before
  ;DoDefault")

  DoDefault

  ;After default behavior.
  view(self.value, "self after DoDefault")
  view(String(eventInfo.newValue()), "newValue after
  ;DoDefault")
endMethod
```

Tracing Events Example

In this example, you study the events by using a feature of the debugger called the Tracer. Your goal is to use the Tracer to demonstrate the event model and default behavior.

Step By Step

1. Create a new form by selecting File | New | Form.
2. Open the Editor window for the action event of the form.
3. Open the Tracer by selecting View | Tracer.
4. From the Tracer window, choose Properties | Built-In Events.
5. The Select Built-in Event Methods for Tracing dialog box, shown here, lists all the events you can trace. In this dialog box, choose Select All and click on OK.

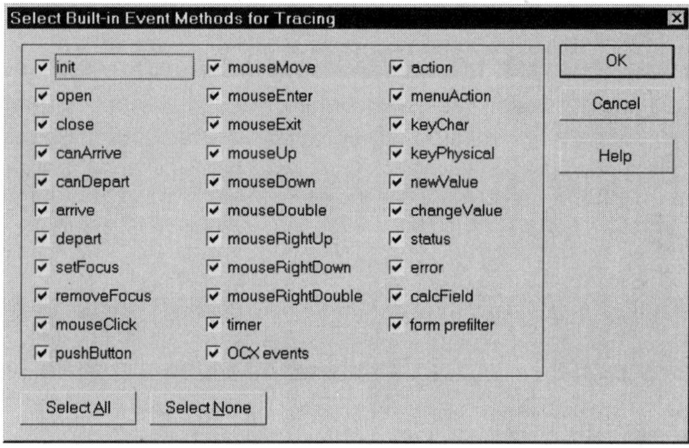

6. Make sure that Properties | Trace On is checked:

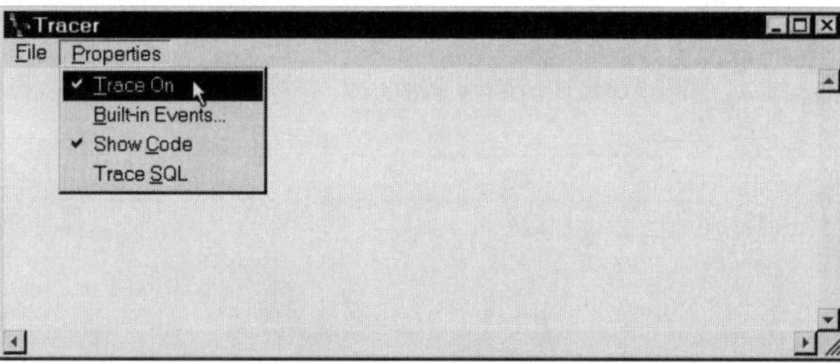

7. Run the form (there is no need to save the form). Note in Figure 6-1 how many events occur even on an empty form.

Tracing one or two events at a time is a great way to get acquainted with the event model. Take some time right now (about 30 minutes) to try tracing various combinations of events.

Tracing Your Own Code Example

This section demonstrates how to use the Tracer to trace just your code. Suppose that while you are developing an application, an error occurs and you have no idea what code is causing the error.

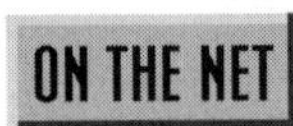

http://prestwood.com/forums/paradox/books/official/files/OV-LIKE.FSL.

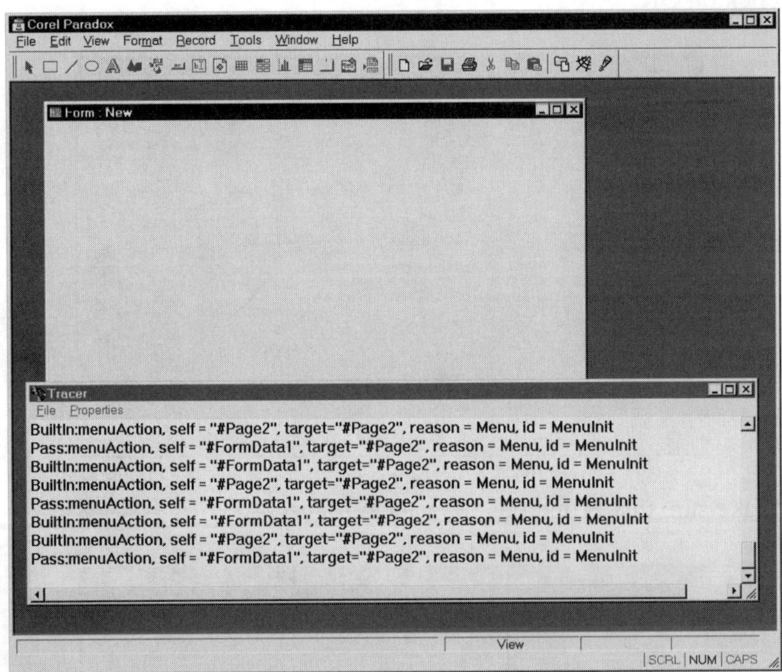

FIGURE 6-1 The Tracer tracing code

Step By Step

1. Change your working directory to Paradox's Samples directory and open the OV-LIKE.FSL form that you created in Chapter 3 (or any form that has ObjectPAL code added to it).
2. Open the Editor window for any event.
3. Select Program | Compile with Debug. This step is crucial. Selecting this option allows the compiler to generate the data needed by the run-time interpreter to display your code in the Tracer.
4. Select View | Tracer to open the Tracer.
5. Select Properties | Built-In Events and make sure that no events are selected for tracing.
6. Make sure that Properites | Trace On and Properties | Show Code are checked.
7. Run the form, select the various buttons, and see what happens (see Figure 6-2).

You can use the Tracer for two purposes: to analyze the events and/or to analyze your code. When analyzing or debugging your code, the Tracer is great for finding the location of bugs.

Tracing execution on a large form is very time-consuming. The Tracer updates the screen every time it executes a line of code. As usual in a GUI, screen updates dramatically slow you down. Shrink the Tracer execution window as small as possible. When you want to see the trace execution, then open the window. Following are the steps:

1. Run it.
2. Press CTRL-break.
3. Minimize it.

This solution works so well, you can now just leave the Tracer execution windows minimized on your screen.

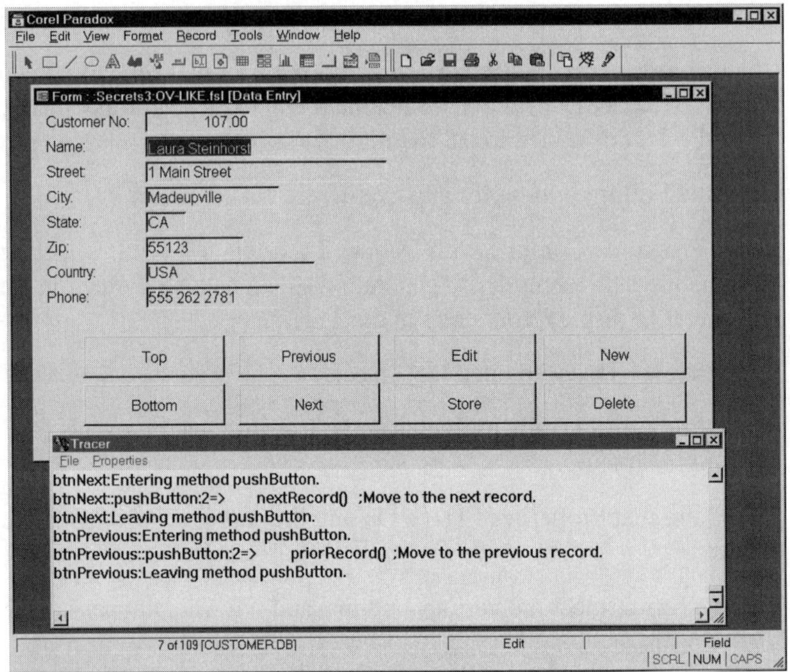

FIGURE 6-2 Using the Tracer to trace your own code

Introducing the Event Packet

When you open a form interactively, many events are generated by ObjectPAL. The form opens and then the prefilter tells the page to open by sending an event to it. Understanding the sending and receiving of events is understanding the event model.

Whenever an event is called, an information packet is generated. This information packet often is passed from one event to the next. This information is called the event packet. You can read any value in the event packet with the eventInfo variable. Table 6-5 describes the different types of events.

Type of Event	Information About	Events
ActionEvent	Editing and navigating a table	action
ErrorEvent	Errors	error
Event	Base event type from which all others are derived—inherited	init, open, close, setFocus, removeFocus, newValue, and pushButton
KeyEvent	Keystroke events	keyChar and keyPhysical
MenuEvent	Menu selections	menuAction
MouseEvent	The mouse and pointer	mouseClick, mouseDown, mouseUp, mouseDouble, mouseRightUp, mouseRightDouble, mouseMove, mouseEnter, and mouseExit
MoveEvent	Navigating from field to field	arrive, canArrive, canDepart, and depart
StatusEvent	Messages in the status line	Status
TimerEvent	Events at specified intervals	timer
ValueEvent	Changes to a field's value	changeValue

TABLE 6-5 Types of Events

The type of eventInfo an event generates is declared in its prototype syntax. Every time you open the ObjectPAL editor for an event, Paradox automatically prototypes the event for you: the first line of every event. For events, simply go into the event, and it will tell you on the first line the type of event the eventInfo variable is. Take a look at a button's pushButton event:

```
;Button :: pushButton
method pushButton(var eventInfo Event)

endMethod
```

Notice var eventInfo Event in parentheses. In this prototype, eventInfo is a variable that is declared as an Event. This is important because it tells you what types of events can be used to extract and set information in the eventInfo variable. With pushButton, all the events can be used.

Next, look at the keyPhysical event of a field.

```
;Field :: keyPhysical
method keyPhysical(var eventInfo KeyEvent)

endMethod
```

The eventInfo packet is defined as a KeyEvent type event. This indicates that you can use any of the KeyEvents to extract and deal with the event information. To see a list of all the events that work with KeyEvent, from within the ObjectPAL editor, select View | ObjectPAL Quick Lookup to bring up the ObjectPAL Quick Lookup dialog box, and then KeyEvent from the Types and Methods tab, shown here:

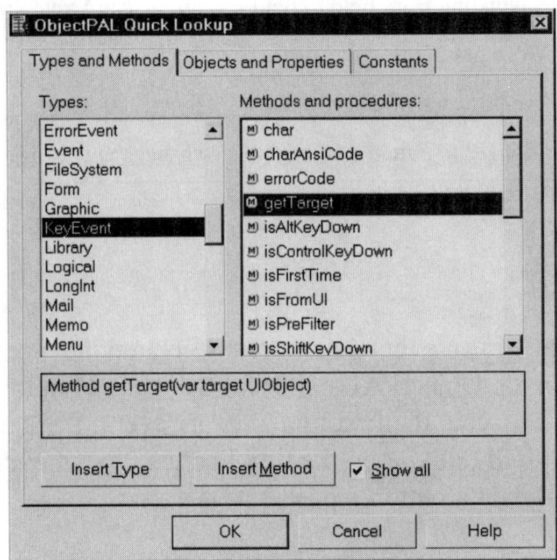

You can use any of the KeyEvents in the keyPhysical or keyChar events to deal with and alter an event created by the keyboard. For example, to prevent all CTRL keystroke combinations on a certain field, alter the field's keyPhysical as follows:

```
;Field :: keyPhysical
method keyPhysical(var eventInfo KeyEvent)
   if eventInfo.isControlKeyDown() then
      disableDefault
```

```
            msgInfo("", "Control key combinations are invalid
            ;here")
        endIf
    endMethod
```

In this routine, the CTRL key is trapped for, and disableDefault prevents the default behavior.

The Path of *eventInfo* from Field to Field

One important part of the event model is the sequence of execution from field to field. This illustration shows the sequence of execution of the events when moving from field to field:

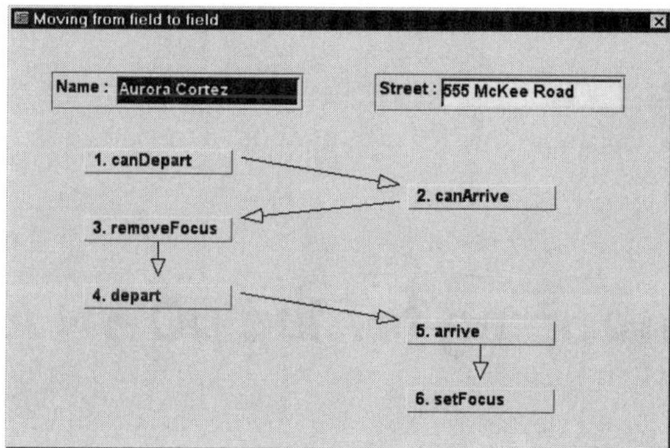

Controlling Default Behavior

The default behavior for events was described earlier in this chapter. The preceding section introduced you to the eventInfo packet. To use and manipulate the default behavior, you must understand the default behavior and the eventInfo packet. You can use the following keywords and variables to control the default behavior: disableDefault, doDefault, enableDefault, and passEvent.

disableDefault prevents the built-in behavior from executing. Normally, the default behavior is executed just before endMethod. The exception is if doDefault explicitly executes the default behavior ahead of time. Also, you can prevent the default behavior with disableDefault. If you have disabled the default behavior—at the beginning of the event, for example—you can reenable it with enableDefault. passEvent passes an event to the object's container.

Redirecting Status Messages

You can use reason() in the status event to trap for a particular category of messages and redirect either with setReason() or statusValue(), as shown in this table:

Constant	Description
StatusWindow	The left largest area on the status bar
ModeWindow1	First small window right of the status area
ModeWindow2	Second small window right of the status area
ModeWindow3	Third small window right of the status area (rightmost window)

To redirect status messages to a field, use the following code in the prefilter of the status event:

```
if eventInfo.reason() = StatusWindow then
  fldStatus.value = eventInfo.statusValue()
endIf
```

Case Study Trapping for the DOWN ARROW in *keyPhysical*

Trapping for the DOWN ARROW in keyPhysical presents some interesting problems when combined with doDefault and disableDefault. For example, suppose that you put the following code on the keyPhysical event of a field named Name. Figure 6-3 shows what happens when the code is executed.

```
;fldName :: keyPhysical
method keyPhysical(var eventInfo KeyEvent)
  if eventInfo.vCharCode() = VK_DOWN then
     Total_Invoice.moveTo()
  endIf
endMethod
```

What do you think will happen when the user presses the DOWN ARROW while on the Name field? The goal is to jump from the Name field to the Total_Invoice field when the user presses the DOWN ARROW key. The code, however, appears to

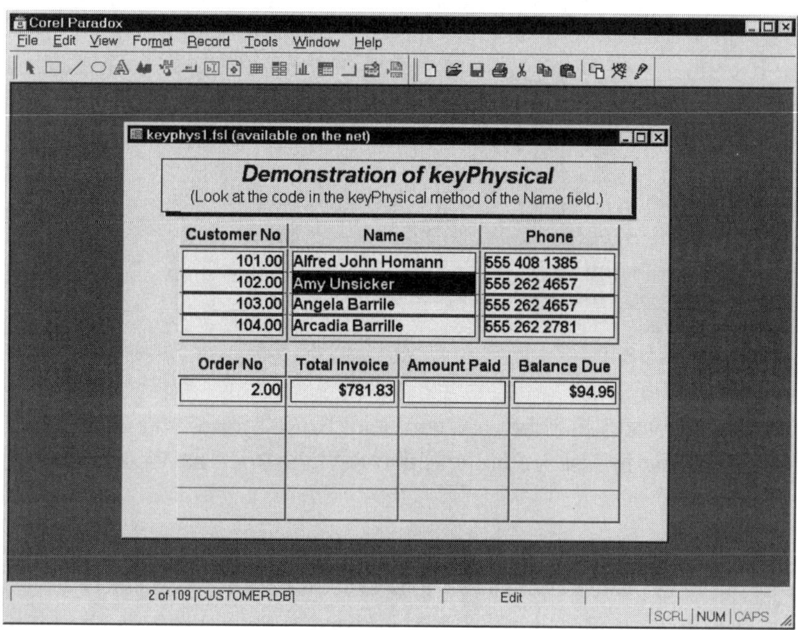

FIGURE 6-3 Demonstration of trapping for keyPhysical

have no effect. What actually happens is the focus does move to the Total_Invoice field, but immediately moves back to the Name field (this time on the next record down). This movement occurs because the default behavior executes after the move.

Now consider the following code:

```
;fldName :: keyPhysical
method keyPhysical(var eventInfo KeyEvent)
  if eventInfo.vCharCode() = VK_DOWN then
     doDefault
     Total_Invoice.moveTo()
  endIf
endMethod
```

Now, what do you think will happen when the user presses the DOWN ARROW while on the Name field? In this case, the code appears to do the job. The focus is indeed on Total_Invoice. What actually occurs, however, is that the focus moves first to the Name field of the next record and then to the destination; this move is invoked by doDefault.

What if you have code on the arrive of Name? It, of course, would execute.

Finally, consider the following code:

```
;fldName :: keyPhysical
method keyPhysical(var eventInfo KeyEvent)
  if eventInfo.vCharCode() = VK_DOWN then
     disableDefault
     Total_Invoice.moveTo()
  endIf
endMethod
```

Now the code works just the way you want. In this case, you disable the default behavior and in essence pretend that the keystroke never occurred.

Creating and Sending Your Own Events

You have already learned about action() and menuAction() to generate built-in Action and MenuAction constants. Now, you're ready to learn about broadcastAction() and postAction(), which work similar to action(). They send Action constants to the action event. broadcastAction() sends an Action constant to the action event of an object and all the objects it contains. postAction() sends the Action constant to a queue for delayed execution. postAction() is most useful when working with the newValue event.

In general, avoid placing code in newValue except when you're using postAction(). The newValue event is called when the data underneath a field changes, or when you click a list member (such as a radio button or list box). While you are in a newValue event, you are coming out of the heart of a recalc/repaint loop inside the newValue event. Therefore, you cannot modify the value of a bound field. The solution is to use newValue sparingly, and when you do use it, use postAction()—for example, self.postAction(UserAction + 1).

This line of code uses the constant UserAction, which offsets the standard action constants with a Corel set integer so that the actions defined by the programmer will never map to an existing Paradox action. This constant is similar to the UserMenu constant.

Using postAction() has the effect of queuing up a user-defined action call to the object receiving the newValue. As soon as the newValue is done executing and the system has completed the refresh loop, the built-in action() fires, and you can trap for this action with the following:

```
If eventInfo.id() = UserAction + 1 then
  ;Do here what you would have done in newValue.
endIf
```

The end effect is the same, but the code is much safer and easier to debug.

If you have a common set of code (such as a calculation), which you were putting in newValue, then you can execute this calculation from anywhere in your application simply by calling the action() or postAction() method for this object, thus making your code more reusable.

In a newValue event, you can do many tasks, such as writing to unbound fields or changing display properties. Many programmers try to do "database stuff" inside a newValue, and this kind of programming isn't good. When in doubt, use postAction() to send a custom action ID to self and trap for the custom action ID in the action event. Your safety will be guaranteed because the action code cannot execute until the recalc/repaint cycle is complete.

Events Can Cause Events

In an event-driven environment such as Paradox, an event often creates another event before the first event finishes. In effect, you can have several events occurring at the same time. (Some developers have mistakenly called this a *secondary event stream*. Furthermore, they have mistakenly referred to the first event as the *primary event stream*. I do not use that terminology here because it just confuses the issue.) Suffice it to say, just as Windows sends messages from application to application, Paradox passes messages from object to object. This message in ObjectPAL is always named eventInfo and has a particular type.

Using the Built-In Error Codes

Rather than always just setting the error code to a nonzero value, try using built-in error constants whenever possible. The following example enforces uniqueness in a table and checks whether the field is required. This example is interesting because it uses the peReqdErr and peKeyViol constants instead of just nonzero values.

```
;Record :: action
var
  tc TCursor
endVar

;check for required field
if isBlank(Ship_Via) and self.locked then
  eventinfo.setErrorCode(peReqdErr)
  return
endIf

;Key violation check
tc.attach(ORDERS)
if tc.locate("Order_No", Order_No.value) then
  if tc.recNo()<> self.recNo then
     eventinfo.setErrorCode(peKeyViol)
  endIf
endIf
```

Note that the preceding code works for both Paradox and dBASE tables.

Summary

This chapter formally introduced you to the event model. The event model is the core piece to understanding how and where to program in ObjectPAL. Events are categorized in three categories: internal, external, and special. Only external events bubble. You also learned that you can control the default behavior with doDefault, disableDefault, enableDefault, and passEvent. You will revisit the event model many times.

You learned that code in internal events is executed by Paradox. Like external events, internal events go first to the form and then to the target object. Unlike external and special events, internal events do not bubble. In general, external events are events generated by the user interacting with a form.

CHAPTER 7

More About Syntax

This chapter addresses syntax. Its intent is to make you feel more comfortable with ObjectPAL. After reading and entering in all the examples in this chapter, you will have a much better grasp on how to write ObjectPAL code.

ObjectPAL and Case Sensitivity

When is Paradox case sensitive? Paradox is case sensitive with string comparisons and locates. For example, Yes is not the same as YES when you compare strings. When you locate a record, Lupton is not the same as lupton or LUPTON. Case sensitivity applies even when you check against parts of the ObjectPAL language if the part is in a string. For example, box isn't the same as Box. You can check which class an object belongs to with the following:

```
var ui UIObject endVar
eventInfo.getTarget(ui)
if ui.class = "Box" then
   ;Put your code here. For example:
   message(ui.name)
endIf
```

If you accidentally typed box or BOX, the routine would fail. Therefore, you need to watch your string comparisons. You can use ignoreCaseInStringCompares() and ignoreCaseInLocate() procedures, however, to force case insensitivity, as in the following example:

```
var ui UIObject endVar
eventInfo.getTarget(ui)
ignoreCaseInStringCompares(Yes)
if ui.class = "box" then
   ;Put your code here. For example:
   message(ui.name)
endIf
```

Other than string compares and locates, ObjectPAL syntax is not case sensitive. The mixture of uppercase and lowercase characters you use when writing ObjectPAL keywords, methods, procedures, variables, and so on, is up to you. Appendix A goes into detail on this subject.

Further Details of Variables

Declaring variables already has been introduced by implication because variables have been used in many examples before now. What follows in this section is a formal introduction/review of declaring variables in ObjectPAL. You declare variables in a var block, as in the following example:

```
var            ;Start of variable block.
               ;Declare variables here.
endVar         ;End of variable block.
```

When you declare variables of the same type, you can either put them on the same line or separate lines. The choice is yours; it does not matter to the compiler. For example, the following declares four variables—two numbers and two strings.


```
var
   s1      String     ;You can declare like variables on
   s2      String     ;separate lines, or
   n1,n2   Number     ;on the same line separated by commas.
endVar
```

Following are some examples of how variables are declared:

```
si     SmallInt       ;Declare si as a small integer. This
                      ;is useful for smaller numbers.
s      String         ;Declare s as a String.
f      Form           ;Declare f as form.
app    Application    ;Declare an application variable
                      ;when you want to deal with the
                      ;desktop. For example,
                      ;to maximize or hide the
                      ;application.
t      Time           ;Declare t as type
                      ;time to deal with time.
```

Following are some examples of using variables in expressions:

```
x = x + 1
s = "Nicole Kimberly Prestwood"
```

```
s = "The new value is " + String(x)
s = "The time is " + String(t)
message(s)
```

The Built-In Object Variables

ObjectPAL offers built-in variables in addition to its events. These variables are predefined by Paradox for you to use in your ObjectPAL routines. The built-in object variables are an integral part of ObjectPAL. Like so much of ObjectPAL, they are self-explanatory. In fact, you've already used several of them. The built-in object variables are self, subject, container, active, lastMouseClicked, and lastMouseRightClicked. Use the built-in object variables as much as possible. They make your code very readable and more portable.

Using *self*

With one exception, self always refers to the object to which the code is attached. The exception is when self is used in a library. When self is used in a library, it always refers to the object that calls the custom method. For now, concentrate on using self within code on an object like a field.

Use self whenever possible; it makes your routines more generic. Use self whenever code refers to itself. If you have a choice between the following two lines of code, always choose the one that uses self:

```
fldName.value = " Sandy Kowalski "
self.value = " Sandy Kowalski "
```

If you later change the name of the Last_Name field, you don't have to change the name used in the code. In addition, if you copy or move the code to an object with a different name, it will still work. Finally, when you copy an object with code attached to it, the code is more likely to work if you use self.

Using *subject*

When self is used in a library, it refers to the calling object. Wouldn't it be nice if you could do the same with custom routines in a form? You can, with subject. With dot notation and subject, you can have a routine work on another object.

Using *container*

When you use container in your code, it refers to the object that contains the object to which the code is attached. If you have a small box inside a large box and you execute the following code attached to the small box, the large box turns red:

```
;SmallBox :: mouseClick
container.color = red
```

Using *active*

active refers to the object that is currently active; in other words, the last object to receive a moveTo() command. Usually, it's the object that currently has the focus; that is, the object ready to be edited. In the following example, active is used to indicate the object that has the focus:


```
active.nextRecord()
```

In a multitable form (a form with several tables bound to it), this line of code acts differently, depending on which object has the focus.

Using *LastMouseClicked* and *LastMouseRightClicked*

LastMouseClicked refers to the last object to receive a mouseDown/mouseUp combination. A mouseDown/mouseUp combination occurs whenever the user presses the left mouse button while the pointer is over an object. This variable enables you to deal with the user's most recent mouse clicks without writing special code. lastMouseRightClicked is the same as lastMouseClicked, except that the right mouse button is pressed.

The built-in object variables—self, subject, container, active, lastMouseClicked, and lastMouseRightClicked—are used in developing generic routines. Generic routines are important. The more generic routines you use, the less coding you have to do.

You can use any property that applies to the type of object with which you are working. Properties that don't apply won't work. For example, because buttons don't have frames or color properties, self.color = Red doesn't work on a button.

Data Types

What are data types? Data typing is the classifying of data into categories such as string, number, and date. This classification is necessary so that the compiler knows how to treat and store the data. For example, a number takes up more room in memory than a small integer. In ObjectPAL, you can declare a variable to be any of the many variable types.

How do you know the available types? You already know the answer to that question. When you browse through all the variable types and their methods by selecting View | ObjectPAL Quick Lookup. Those are the variable types you can declare a variable as. The methods and procedures that correspond to them are the methods and procedures you use to manipulate them.

To create an up-to-date table of class names, create and run the following one-line script:

```
enumRTLClassNames("RTLCLASS.DB")
```

This one line of code creates a table with all the current class names. Why should you do this if the preceding table has all the classes? When a new version of Paradox is released, you can run this same script and check to see whether any new classes of objects were added.

As soon as you find a variable type with which you want to work, you declare a variable as that type in a variable block. As soon as the variable is declared, you can use any of the methods in its class to manipulate it. For example, as soon as a TCursor is defined, you then can use any of the TCursor object type or class of methods to manipulate it:

```
var                         ;This is the start of a var structure.
   tc   TCursor             ;Set variable types in between.
endVar                      ;This marks the end of a var structure.
tc.open("ZIPCODES.DB")
```

The tc variable is a handle to a TCursor object. A TCursor is a type of object. How do data types relate to object types? Data types are simply a very important subset of all the variable types. Remember that in ObjectPAL there are more than 50 object types. All these object types are variables that you can manipulate with the appropriate method or procedure. For example, you use the data types to store data in memory. As soon as data is stored in a particular type of variable in memory, you can use the methods associated with the type or class of variable to manipulate it.

Although the Paradox table structure supports many data types, as you can see, ObjectPAL picks up where Paradox and dBASE tables leave off. There are more ObjectPAL data types than either Paradox or dBASE field types. If you wanted to store time in a dBASE table, what field type would you choose? dBASE, unlike the Paradox table structure, does not offer a time format. One technique is to use a character field of size 12 to store the characters and then use ObjectPAL to manipulate them. The important thing to note at this point is that the data types in ObjectPAL enable you to deal with more types of data than the set Paradox and dBASE field types allow. You declare or cast a variable as a particular type of variable. This is known as typecasting.

Using *AnyType*

AnyType is the catch-all variable type for the times when you can't predict what type of variable you'll need. After you declare a variable as an AnyType variable, you can use the seven AnyType methods and procedures to manipulate it. These methods are very important because most of them are the core methods for the rest of the data types. Following is a description of each:

- **blank()** Returns a blank value.
- **dataType()** Returns a string representing the data type of a variable.
- **isAssigned()** Reports whether a variable has been assigned a value.
- **isBlank()** Reports whether an expression has a blank value.
- **isFixedType()** Reports whether a variable's data type has been explicitly declared.
- **unAssign()** Sets a variable's state to unAssigned.
- **view()** Displays in a dialog box the value of a variable.

Implicit Casting with *AnyType*

Whenever the compiler comes across a variable or value in your code, it stores it in memory. If the value was not typecast, then the compiler casts it at that time. This can create problems. For example, if you type and run the following code, you'll get an error:

```
1:     ;Button :: pushButton
2:     method pushButton(var eventInfo Event)
3:        var
4:           n      Number        ;Declare n as a number.
5:        endVar
6:
7:           ;Set n to 40000.
8:           n = 2 * 20000        ;This gives an error.
9:           n.view()
10:    endMethod
```

Why? Isn't 40,000 within the range of a Number? Yes, but when ObjectPAL came across the equation 2 * 20000, it had to store the numbers in memory and, because the first number is an integer, the numbers were stored in temporary small integer variables. Small integers cannot store the value 40,000. To fix this, change the preceding line 8 to the following.

```
8:     n = 2.0 * 20000.0
```

More on implicit casting of numbers later when SmallInt, LongInt, and Number are discussed. For now, following are some examples of implicit casting that you can type into a button if you want:

```
x = 1                        ;x is cast as a SmallInt.
view(Datatype(x))            ;Displays SmallInt.

x = 1.1                      ;x is cast as a Number.
view(Datatype(x))            ;Displays Number.

x = 40000                    ;x is cast as a LongInt.
view(Datatype(x))            ;Displays LongInt.

x = "Clark Lupton"           ;x is cast as a String.
view(Datatype(x))            ;Displays String.
```

Using *AnyType*

In the next example, you use the same variable as a number and then as a string without declaring it again. It demonstrates using an AnyType variable. Suppose that you need to use x as both a number and a string. In this example, x is used first as a number, then as a string.

http://prestwood.com/forums/paradox/books/official/files/DATATYPE.FSL.

Step By Step

1. Create a new form and place a button on it.

2. Open the pushButton event of the button and add lines 3–13 to it. Line 4 declares *x* as an AnyType variable, which means that you can store many types of data in it without declaring it again. Line 7 sets *x* to the number 12.3. It is viewed with the Number class viewer in line 8. In line 9, msgInfo() uses dataType() to confirm that the type of *x* has been declared by ObjectPAL as type Number. Lines 11–13 are just like lines 7–9, except that in line 11, *x* is set to the string 12.3. In line 12, the string viewer is used when the user is shown the value. In line 13, msgInfo() confirms that, internally, ObjectPAL has changed the data type to a String type.


```
1:     ;DATATYPE :: Button :: pushButton
2:     method pushButton(var eventInfo Event)
3:        var
4:           x      AnyType       ;Declare x as AnyType.
5:        endVar
6:
7:           x = 12.3            ;First use x as a Number.
8:           x.view()            ;View x.
9:           msgInfo("DataType", dataType(x))
10:
11:          x = "12.3"          ;Then use x as a String.
12:          x.view()            ;View x.
13:          msgInfo("DataType", dataType(x))
14:    endMethod
```

3. Check your syntax, save the form as DATATYPE.FSL, and run it. Click the button. First, you see the number 12.3 in a number-style viewer. After you click OK, you see a message box confirming that the current data type for *x* is indeed Number. After you click OK to the message box, you see the characters 12.3, but this time they are in a string box. After you click OK to the viewer, a message box confirms that *x* indeed is now a String.

You Don't Have to Declare Variables, But You Should

Although *x* was specifically declared as an AnyType variable in the preceding example, declaring an AnyType variable isn't required. Whenever the ObjectPAL compiler comes across a variable that hasn't been declared, it declares it as AnyType. In general, it's good programming practice to always declare variables. Get in the habit of declaring variables so that the compiler can catch typing mistakes. If you declare a siCounter variable at the form and accidently type liCounter, the compiler will catch it when Program | Compiler Warnings is turned on (you must be in the ObjectPAL editor). Declaring variables also makes your code easier to read.

Is it a good idea to declare all variables as AnyType so that you don't have to worry about variable type? No. Avoid using AnyType variables because they slow your code down. Declaring a variable as an AnyType variable is the same as not declaring the variable at all. If you explicitly declare all your variables, your code will run faster. AnyType variables are useful when you don't know what the data type will be.

Declared Variables Run Faster

This example demonstrates that declaring variables makes your code faster. In this example, you will create two buttons. Both buttons will beep, count to 2,000, and beep again. You will notice that the button with the declared counter variable will have a shorter duration between the beeps.

http://prestwood.com/forums/paradox/books/official/files/DATATYPE.FSL.

Step By Step

1. Change your working directory to Paradox's Samples directory and create a new form with two buttons on it. Label them **Undeclared** and **Declared**.

2. Add lines 3–5 to the pushButton event of the Undeclared button.

```
1:    ;DATATYPE :: btnUndeclared :: pushButton
2:    method pushButton(var eventInfo Event)
3:       beep()
4:       for Counter from 1 to 2000 endFor
```

```
        beep()
    endMethod
```

3. Add lines 3–9 to the pushButton event of the Declared button.

```
 1:    ;DATATYPE :: btnDeclared :: pushButton
 2:    method pushButton(var eventInfo Event)
 3:       var
 4:          Counter SmallInt
 5:       endVar
 6:
 7:       beep()
 8:       for Counter from 1 to 2000 endFor
 9:       beep()
10:    endMethod
```


4. Check the syntax, save the form as **DATATYPE.FSL**, and run the form. Click both buttons. Note how much closer together the beeps are for the button labeled Declared.

Compile-Time Binding

Take a closer look at the preceding example, for two reasons: to explain compile-time binding and to review scope.

When the compiler compiles your source code, it casts all the variable types of the variables you have used. This process is called *binding*. When the compiler comes across a variable, it needs to find out whether the variable is declared. It first searches the method...endMethod structure in which the variable is used. Then, the compiler searches for a var...endVar structure above the current method...endMethod structure. After this, it searches the Var window of the object to which the code is attached, and then the Var window of the Object's container, and so on until it reaches the form. When the compiler comes across the first occurrence of the variable declaration, it stops searching. If the compiler goes all the way up to the Var window of the form and the variable is not declared anywhere, then the variable is declared as AnyType.

Many Methods Return a Logical

Nearly all methods and procedures return something. In many cases, they return a simple Logical True or False. You can use this return value to determine whether a method or procedure succeeded. For example, the following line of code displays True in the status bar if it can take the form out of Edit mode, and False if it can't:

```
message(endEdit())
```

This simple example shows you that almost every method and procedure returns something. In most cases, you can use this fact to add error checking to your routines. For example, the following line of code displays the error box, complete with an error message when the locate() method returns False:

```
if not fldName.locate("Name", "Sam Unsicker") then
   errorShow()
endIf
```

The Logical Data Type

A variable declared as Logical can contain only two values: True or False. It can, however, be at any one of four states/values: unassigned, blank, True, or False. For example, type the following code on the pushButton event of a button:

```
;Button :: pushButton
method pushButton(var eventInfo Event)
   var
      l      Logical       ;Declare l as a logical variable.
   endVar

   l.view("Unassigned")    ;View l.

   l = blank()             ;Set l to blank.
   l.view("Blank")         ;View l.

   l = True                ;Set l to True.
   l.view("True")          ;View l.

   l = False               ;Set l to False.
   l.view("False")         ;View l.
endMethod
```

A field that is either blank or zero is considered Null. Whenever you store an empty field, Paradox and dBASE actually store a Null. This condition for a field is called *blank* in Paradox. The ObjectPAL Logical data type is equivalent to the dBASE and Paradox Logical field types.

In your ObjectPAL code, you can use Yes/No or On/Off in place of True/False, but the value that is displayed to the user is still dependent on the display format, usually True or False. If you type the following code on the pushButton event of a button, you'll notice that, although l is specifically set to Yes in line 7, True is displayed when line 8 displays a Logical view box:

```
1:    ;Button :: pushButton
2:    method pushButton(var eventInfo Event)
3:       var
4:          l     Logical
5:       endVar
6:
7:       l = Yes
8:       l.view()
9:    endMethod
```

Why use a Logical data type when you could just as easily use a String? One reason is that a Logical variable occupies only 1 byte of storage, and in computer languages, smaller is faster.

The following example shows that most methods and procedures return a value. You can return a value to a Logical variable and then display the value of the variable.

Using isFile() Example

Suppose that you wish to find out whether a file exists. In this example, you use the fact that isFile() returns a Logical to determine whether a file exists.

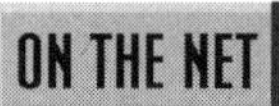

http://prestwood.com/forums/paradox/books/official/files/DATATYPE.FSL.

Step By Step

1. Create a form and add a button to it. Label the button **Using a Logical**.

2. Add lines 3–8 to the pushButton event of the Using a Logical button. Line 4 declares l as a Logical variable. isFile() returns True if the file exists and

False if it doesn't. In line 7, l is given this return value from isFile(). Line 8 displays the result. Note that you passed view() a title to display.

```
1:     ;DATATYPE :: btnLogical :: pushButton
2:     method pushButton(var eventInfo Event)
3:        var
4:           lFileExist    Logical
5:        endVar
6:
7:        lFileExist = isFile("C:\\AUTOEXEC.BAT")
8:        lFileExist.view("Does file exist?")
9:     endMethod
```

3. Check the syntax, save the form as **ISFILE.FSL**, and run it. Click the button. The Logical viewer will display True or False, depending on whether the file exists.

Dealing with Numbers

Often, you need to calculate and convert numbers, such as time, date, currency, and so on. You either manipulate them or convert them so that you can manipulate them. For example, a Number is different from a String. When you have number characters stored in a String variable or Alpha field, you need to convert the string to a Number before you can use it in a calculation. ObjectPAL offers many methods and procedures for accomplishing this task. When declaring a variable as a number, you actually have three choices: Number, LongInt, and SmallInt.

Using *Number*

A Number variable is the most flexible of the three number data types and takes up the most room in memory. A Number variable can contain up to 18 significant digits, and the power of 10 can range from $\pm 3.4 * 10^{-4930}$ to $\pm 1.1 * 10^{4930}$.

Using *LongInt*

A LongInt (long integer) variable can range from –2,147,483,648 to +2,147,483,647. Why use a data type that is limited by design when you have more powerful data types? Very simply, LongInt variables occupy only 4 bytes of storage, and in computer terms, smaller means faster.

Using *SmallInt*

A SmallInt (small integer) variable can range from –32,768 to +32,767. Again, the reason you may want to use a data type that is limited by design when you have more powerful LongInt and Number data types is because a SmallInt variable occupies only 2 bytes of storage, which is half of what LongInt variables take up. A SmallInt uses up the least amount of bytes to store small numbers. In computer terms, smallest is best.

As introduced earlier, whenever ObjectPAL comes across a number, it casts the number internally as the most appropriate type of number. If the number is an integer, ObjectPAL casts the number as either a small integer, a large integer, or a number, depending on its size, as the following code indicates. If the number contains a decimal point, it is cast as a Number. If you want, type the following in the pushButton event of a button:


```
msgStop("Datatype of 320", dataType(320))
```

This first example returns SmallInt, which takes up the smallest possible room in memory—only 2 bytes.

```
msgStop("Datatype of 33000", dataType(33000))
```

This second example returns LongInt because the data is too large to be a SmallInt.

```
msgStop("Datatype of 2200000000", dataType(2200000000))
```

This third example returns Number because the data is too large to be a LongInt.

```
msgStop("Datatype of 320.0", dataType(320.0))
```

This final example is rather interesting. Although the value clearly can fit into a SmallInt, the compiler puts it into a Number because of the decimal point.

Why is this concept so important? Doesn't ObjectPAL take care of this for you? Well, yes and no. In most cases, you don't have to worry about it. The following code passes a syntax check, but fails during run time. You could pull your hair out for hours trying to figure out why. Type lines 3–8 into the pushButton event of a button and see whether you can figure out how to solve the problem. Following is the answer:

```
1:    ;Button :: pushButton
2:    method pushButton(var eventInfo Event)
3:       var
4:          si    SmallInt
5:       endVar
6:
7:       si = 60 * 24 * 24
8:       si.view()
9:    endMethod
```

When ObjectPAL comes to line 7, it casts all the numbers in the expression as small integers. When the code is executed and the three numbers are multiplied, they result in a number larger than a small integer can handle, and a run-time overflow error occurs, as shown here:

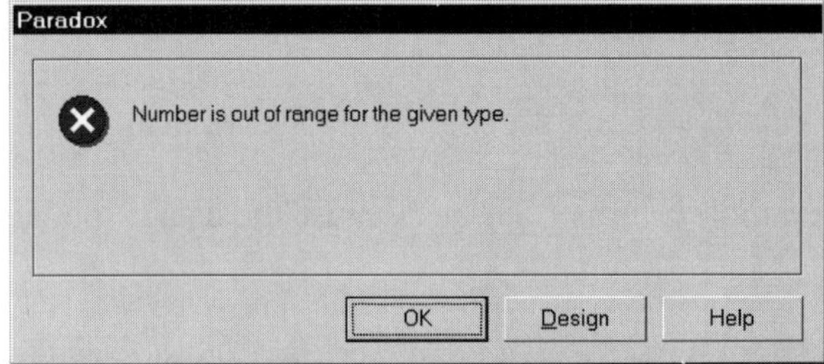

This problem has many solutions, all of which rely on the fact that ObjectPAL looks at an expression as a whole and sets the data types to the lowest common data type. You simply have to make any one of the elements involved with the calculation a larger number type (for example, LongInt or Number). Line 7 can be replaced with any of the following:

Solution 1

```
7:    si = Number(60) * 24 * 24
```

The first solution casts the first number in the calculation as a Number. ObjectPAL internally casts the other two numbers, and the result is the same type.

Solution 2

```
si = 60.0 * 24 * 24
```

The second solution simply uses a floating point number (indicated by .0).

Solution 3

```
si = 60. * 24 * 24
```

The third solution is a variation of the second solution. ObjectPAL checks only for the existence of a decimal point in a number. It doesn't check whether the number is a floating point number. The third solution uses this fact and simply adds a decimal point to the first of the three values.

Converting *Number* to *SmallInt* and *LongInt*

Suppose that you want to convert a Number variable first to a SmallInt and then to a LongInt. This example demonstrates how to do that. Often when you are assigning one variable to another, you will have to cast one variable as the other variable's type.

http://prestwood.com/forums/paradox/books/official/files/DATATYPE.FSL.

Step By Step

1. Change your working directory to Paradox's Samples directory. Open the DATATYPE.FSL form and put a button on it. Label the button **Number to SmallInt & LongInt**.

2. Add lines 3–18 to the pushButton event of the Number to SmallInt & LongInt button.

```
1:     ;DATATYPE :: btnNumber :: pushButton
2:     method pushButton(var eventInfo Event)
3:        var
4:           n      Number      ;Declare n as a number.
5:           si     SmallInt    ;Declare si as a SmallInt.
6:           li     LongInt     ;Declare li as a LongInt.
```

```
      endVar

         n = 3.8              ;Set number to 3.8.
         n.view()             ;Displays 3.80.

         si = SmallInt(n) ;Set si to SmallInt of n.
         si.view()            ;Displays 3.

         li = LongInt(n)  ;Set li to LongInt of n.
         li.view()            ;Displays 3.

         n.view()             ;Displays 3.80.
   endMethod
```

3. Check the syntax, run the form, and click the button.

The first viewer displays 3.80 in the Number viewer. Note that the number is formatted according to the Windows number format (the Windows default is two decimal points). When you click OK, the number is converted internally to a SmallInt variable and is displayed in a SmallInt viewer. Note that the number was chopped down to just 3 and not rounded up to 4. Click OK again. The number is again converted, this time to a LongInt. It's displayed one last time to show you that the original *n* Number variable is unchanged.

Whenever you need a number of a different type than is declared, cast it. In this example, you cast a number as both a long integer and a small integer, but you can go either way. Note, however, that converting a noninteger causes the decimal points to be stripped. For example, values of 1.1, 12.85, and .001 would be converted to 1, 12, and 0.

The Currency *Data Type*

A Currency variable can range from $3.4 * \pm 10^{-4930}$ to $1.1 * \pm 10^{4930}$, precise to six decimal places. The number of decimal places displayed depends on the user's Control Panel settings. The value stored in a table does not, however. A table stores the full six decimal places.

Currency variables are rounded, not truncated. Although internally, ObjectPAL keeps track of Currency variables to six decimal places, the values are rounded when they're displayed to the user. The number of decimal places depends on the user's Control Panel settings. Most users use the default of two decimal points.

If you type in the following code, ObjectPAL shows you a dialog box with the correctly rounded figure of 19.96 in a currency view box.

```
;DATATYPE :: btnPrice :: pushButton
method pushButton(var eventInfo Event)
   var
      nPrice     Number       ;Declare nPrice as a number.
   endVar

   nPrice = 19.9599           ;Set nPrice to a number.
   view(Currency(nPrice))     ;Displays 19.96.
endMethod
```

Although the number of decimal places depends on your Control Panel settings, the number will be rounded correctly. Also, note the alternative syntax used for view().

The *Date, Time,* and *DateTime* Data Types

Although Time and Date data types aren't related, each shares data and methods with the DateTime data type. When deciding between these three data types, ask yourself whether you need time in the same field as the date information. Whenever possible, separate date and time.

Using *Date*

There are differences between dates stored in a table and Date variables. The Date data type can be any valid date, whereas a Paradox table can store only dates from 01/01/100 to 12/31/9999. Use the methods and procedures to bridge the gap and manipulate date data.

You can store any valid date with the ObjectPAL Date data type. For example, type the following code into the pushButton event of a button:

```
;Button :: pushButton
method pushButton(var eventInfo Event)
   msgInfo("Beginning Date", Date(0))
endMethod
```

This displays the string 00/00/0000 in a dialog box. You can type in negative numbers that represent B.C. dates, too.

Subtracting Two Dates

If you subtract two dates, you get another date. For example, type the following code into the pushButton event of a button.

```
;Button :: pushButton
method pushButton(var eventInfo Event)
   message(date("01/15/94") - date("01/01/94"))
endMethod
```

This displays 01/14/0001 in the status bar. This information isn't very useful. Usually, you want the number of days or years between the two dates. The trick to getting the number of days between two dates is to cast the result as a number. For example, type the following code into the pushButton event of a button:

```
;Button :: pushButton
method pushButton(var eventInfo Event)
   var
      dBorn   Date
   endVar

   dBorn = Date("01/20/1967")
   dBorn.view("Enter your birthdate")
   msgInfo("Days since your birthdate", Number(Today() - dBorn))
endMethod
```

Calculating Years

To calculate years, simply cast the value as a year. For example, type the following code into the pushButton event of a button:

```
;DATATYPE :: btnBirth :: pushButton
method pushButton(var eventInfo Event)
   var
      dBorn   Date
   endVar

   dBorn = Date("01/20/1967")
```

```
        dBorn.view("Enter your birthdate")
        msgInfo("Your age", Year(Today() - dBorn))
    endMethod
```

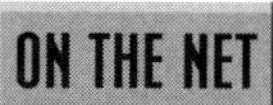

http://prestwood.com/forums/paradox/books/official/files/AGE.FSL uses a similar technique to the one just demonstrated to display the number of seconds, hours, days, and years since your birth.

The *Time* Variable Type

A Time variable is stored in the format HH:MM:SS AM/PM. You could use any of the following as separators: blank, tab, space, comma, hyphen, slash, period, colon, or semicolon. If you want, type the following code into the pushButton event of a button. (All the following strings are legal time strings in ObjectPAL.)


```
;DATATYPE :: btnTimeFormats :: pushButton
method pushButton(var eventInfo Event)
   var t Time endVar
      t = time("10:05:32 AM")
      t.view()

      t = time("10;05;32 AM")
      t.view()

      t = time("10 05 32 AM")
      t.view()

      t = time("10,05,32 AM")
      t.view()

      t = time("10/05/32 AM")
      t.view()
endMethod
```

Note that although you can type time value strings in any of the legal formats of ObjectPAL, the time in the displayed view box is the same because it is guided by the operating system. It's displayed to the user in the format specified in the Control Panel. The values the user inputs must be in accordance with his or her

Control Panel settings. Internally, ObjectPAL stores the time all the way down to the millisecond.

Using *Time*

Call Time() with no parameters to return the current time. For example, type the following code into the pushButton event of a button:

```
;Button :: pushButton
method pushButton(var eventInfo Event)
  msgInfo("Current time", time())
endMethod
```

Converting Regular Time to Military Time

The user's Control Panel settings determine whether the 12-hour time format (HH:MM:SS AM/PM) or the 24-hour (military) time format is used. Sometimes you want to convert 12-hour time to 24-hour time, however. The following routine casts a string as Time and then displays it in 24-hour format. You can type the code into the pushButton event of a button.

http://prestwood.com/forums/paradox/books/official/files/WORLD-T.FSL

```
;Button :: pushButton
method pushButton(var eventInfo Event)
  var
    s   String
    t   Time
  endVar

  formatSetTimeDefault("hh:mm:ss am")
  s = "2:20:00 PM"
  t = time(s)
  formatAdd("24", "to(%h:%m:%s)na()np()")
  formatSetTimeDefault("24")
  t.view()
endMethod
```

Subtracting Time

Suppose that you need to get the number of seconds between two times. Type the following into the pushButton event of a button:

```
1:     ;Button :: pushButton
2:     method pushButton(var eventInfo Event)
3:        var
4:           t1, t2 Time
5:        endVar
6:
7:        t1 = time("1:35:30 PM")
8:        t2 = time("2:10:15 PM")
9:        view(Number(t2 - t1) / 1000)           ;For seconds.
10:       view(Number(t2 - t1) / 1000 / 60)      ;For minutes.
11:       view(Number(t2 - t1) / 1000 / 60 / 60) ;For hours.
12:    endMethod
```


If this code does not work, you may need to reset the default display time to “hh:mm:ss am” in order for the sample to work. Hence, add the line below before line 7:

```
formatSetTimeDefault("hh:mm:ss am")
```

Testing the Speed of ObjectPAL

Because there are many ways in ObjectPAL to accomplish a given task, you often need to test the speed of two routines. ObjectPAL offers, in the form of the time() method, an easy way to do this. To calculate the amount of time a scan loop takes on the CUSTOMER table, type in lines 3–19 into the pushButton event of a button:

```
1:     ;DATATYPE :: btnSpeed :: pushButton
2:     method pushButton(var eventInfo Event)
3:        var
4:           tcCustomer  TCursor
5:           tBeg, tEnd  Time
6:           nDifftime   Number
7:        endVar
8:
```

```
      tcCustomer.open("CUSTOMER.DB")    ;Open CUSTOMER.DB table.

      tBeg = time()                     ;Grab current time.
      scan tcCustomer:
         ;Nothing here. Just testing scan time.
      endScan
      tEnd = time()                     ;Grab current time.

      ;The following calculates the number of milliseconds that passed.
      nDiffTime = number(tEnd) - number(tBeg)
      nDiffTime.view("Milliseconds to scan Customer table")
   endMethod
```

The preceding routine opens the CUSTOMER table, gets the current time, scans the CUSTOMER table, and then gets the current time again. Finally, it calculates the duration of the scan loop and displays it in milliseconds. Use the preceding technique whenever you need to know how fast a routine is in ObjectPAL—for example, when you discover two ways to accomplish the same task and need to determine which is faster.

Using *DateTime*

DateTime is a special data type that stores both date and time values in the same variable. DateTime stores data in the form of hour-minute-second-millisecond year-month-day. The DateTime() method returns the current date and time. For example, to return the current date and time in a message information box, type line 3 into the pushButton event of a button.

```
1:   ;Button :: pushButton
2:   method pushButton(var eventInfo Event)
3:      msgInfo("Current Date & time", DateTime())
4:   endMethod
```

As an interesting experiment, you can cast values with the procedure DateTime() and display the results. This experimentation helps you to understand the numbers behind the DateTime data type. For example, type line 3 into the pushButton event of a button:

```
1:   ;Button :: pushButton
2:   method pushButton(var eventInfo Event)
```

```
3:       msgInfo("Beginning Date/Time", DateTime(0))
4:    endMethod
```

Line 3 displays 12:00:00 AM, 00/00/0000 in a dialog box. This shows you that going back all the way to year 0 is legal in ObjectPAL. In fact, you can even use B.C. dates and times (negative numbers).

If you store data in an alphanumeric field type and later need to do a calculation on the value, you must cast the string in the field as a number. To cast a string as a number, use Number and DateTime() together. For example, type lines 3–8 into the pushButton event of a button:

```
1:    ;Button :: pushButton
2:    method pushButton(var eventInfo Event)
3:       var
4:          nBirth   Number
5:       endVar
6:
7:       nBirth = Number(DateTime("07:30:00 PM, January 20, 1967"))
8:       msgInfo("Lisa's Birthday", nBirth)
9:    endMethod
```


The preceding line 8 displays the number 62042700600000 in a dialog box. This isn't very useful, but you can use this code in a calculation with values (including another DateTime converted to a Number).

Dealing with Characters

When you're dealing with characters, your first choice should be the String data type. The String data type allows strings as long as 32,767 characters.

Using Quoted Strings

A quoted string typed into a method can't be more than 255 characters long. You can, however, concatenate many strings together and display the result. For example, the following assigns values to a string variable that together add up to more than 255 characters and then displays it. If you want to participate in a typing exercise, type in lines 3–11 to the pushButton event of a button:

```
1:    ;DATATYPE :: btnQuote :: pushButton
2:    method pushButton(var eventInfo Event)
```

```
      var
        sNote   String
     endVar

     sNote = "The final stage in the evolution of a star,"
       + " whose original mass was from 1.4 to 2.5 times greater than
       + " our Sun."
       + " Gravitational collapse caused the star to contract to a
       + " sphere with "
       + " a small radius of 10 to 20 kilometers, consisting mainly of
       + " free neutrons."
       + " The density of a neutron star is a hundred million million
       + " times "
       + "(10 to the 14) greater than the density of water."
       + " Some rotating neutron stars evolve into pulsars."
     msgInfo("Neutron Star", sNote)
  endMethod
```

Using Null Characters

Use "" to represent an empty string. This is equivalent to the Null character. Alternatively, you can use the blank() method to empty a string. For example, type lines 3–10 into the pushButton event of a button:

```
 1:   ;Button :: pushButton
 2:   method pushButton(var eventInfo Event)
 3:      var
 4:         s    String
 5:      endVar
 6:
 7:      s = "Bradley Scott Unsicker"
 8:      s.view()                ;Displays Bradley Scott Unsicker.
 9:      s.blank()               ;Set s to null.
10:      s.view()                ;Displays null.
11:   endMethod
```

Line 9 empties, or blanks out, the string. This is only one technique to empty a string. You also could replace line 6 with either of the following:

```
s = ""
s = blank()
```

Embedding Codes in Strings

Sometimes you might want to code some special characters or backslash codes to add to a string when it's displayed to the user. Special characters are ANSI characters not found on the keyboard. Backslash codes are the way to include some special characters in ObjectPAL. For example, \t represents a tab.

You use the string procedure chr() to display an ANSI code. Suppose that you're going to display a message to the user and you want to embed a few returns (ANSI character 13) into the text, as shown here:

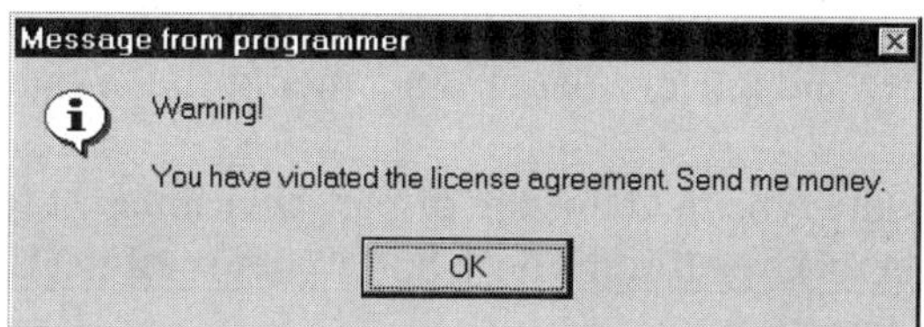

NOTE *CHR.FSL demonstrates the technique of using chr(13).*

You could use the following code:

```
;Button :: pushButton
method pushButton(var eventInfo Event)
   var
       sThreat   String
   endVar

   sThreat = "You have violated the license agreement. Send me
   ;money."
   msgInfo("Message from programmer", "Warning!" + chr(13) + chr(13)
   ;+ sThreat)
endMethod
```

This technique can add a little extra flair to your applications that other programmers might not think to include.

A *keycode* is a code that represents a keyboard character in ObjectPAL scripts. A keycode can be an ASCII number, an IBM extended keycode number, or a string that represents a keyname known to Paradox.

Many programmers prefer to use the following Windows and C++ standard escapes:

```
chr(13)  = \r = \n = <enter>
\t = <tab>
\b = <backspace>
```

The *Memo* Data Type

When you need to work with a string longer then 32,767 characters, use a Memo variable. As soon as you set up a Memo variable, you can use writeToFile() and readFromFile() to set and retrieve data from a memo file. Memo fields can be as large as 512MB!

Three of the Memo type methods are of particular interest for manipulating a Memo variable: memo(), readFromFile(), and writeFromFile(). Following are descriptions of the three:

```
memo()            ;Casts a value as a Memo
readFromFile()    ;Reads a memo from a file
writeToFile()     ;Writes a memo to a file
```

The Array Data Type

An *array* is a group or series of related items identified by a single name and referenced by an index. An array is a special type of variable. It enables you to store a group of elements identified by a single name. Arrays are stored in consecutive locations in memory. Think of each one of these locations as being a cell reserved for your data—very similar to a single-column Paradox table. If, for example, you declare an array with five elements, you can put a value directly in cell 3 and later pull it out. Following this analogy, an array is very similar to a one-field table. Arrays are limited to 65,535 elements.

Using a Static Array

There are two types of arrays: *static* and *resizeable*. A static array has a fixed number of elements and uses slightly less memory than a resizeable array. A resizeable array, however, can be resized. The size of a static array is set when you declare the array, and a resizeable array is set in code after you declare it. The following is the syntax model to declare a static array:

```
arrayName Array[size] dataType
```

For example, the following declares a three-element array ready to store three small integers:

```
var
   arNumbers   Array[3] SmallInt
endVar
```

As soon as the array is declared, you can reference any of the elements of the array directly:

```
arrayName[element] = value
```

For example, the following sets the second and third elements in arNumbers to 10 and 20:


```
arNumbers[2] = 10
arNumbers[3] = 20
```

As soon as the elements of the array have values, you can retrieve the values much like you retrieve values from regular variables and fields. For example, the following displays the second element in the array in the status bar:

```
message(arNumbers[2])
```

If you think that using an array is just like using multiple variables, you're right. One benefit of using arrays is that they group multiple variables into a single group of variables called an array. This gives you a way to address a set of values. For example, type the following piece of code into the pushButton event of a button. It uses a three-element array to store a user's first, middle, and last name. Then it displays all three variables with a single line of code.

```
;Button :: pushButton
method pushButton(var eventInfo Event)
   var
      arName Array[3] String   ;Declare a 3 element fixed array.
   endVar

   arName[1] = "Lester"        ;Set first element of array.
```

```
      arName[2] = "Earl"          ;Set second element of array.
      arName[3] = "Prestwood"     ;Set third element of array.

      arName.view()               ;View array.
   endMethod
```

Using a Resizeable Array

If you don't know the size of the array needed at declaration, use a resizeable array. The following is the syntax model to declare an array variable:

```
arrayName Array[] DataType
```

After you declare a resizeable array, use the setSize() method to set its size. As soon as the array is declared and its size is set, you can reference any of the elements of the array the same way you reference the elements of a static array. For example, type the following code into the pushButton event of a button. It declares a resizeable array, sets its size to 10, and fills it with numbers:

```
 1:   ;Button :: pushButton
 2:   method pushButton(var eventInfo Event)
 3:      var
 4:         myArray   Array[] SmallInt
 5:         Counter   SmallInt
 6:      endVar
 7:
 8:      myArray.setSize(10)
 9:
10:      for Counter from 1 to 10
11:         myArray[Counter] = Counter
12:      endFor
13:
14:      myArray.addLast(100)
15:
16:      myArray.view()
17:   endMethod
```

Note that line 14 uses the addLast() method to add one additional element to the array before displaying it.

The following example shows you how to loop through an array using a for loop with the size() method. This technique is important because an array can't use a forEach loop. (A forEach loop applies only to dynamic arrays.)

http://prestwood.com/forums/paradox/books/official/files/ARRAY.FSL demonstrates using sets of information.

Using an Array and *enumFormNames* to Find an Open Form

Suppose that you want to use an array with the enumFormNames() procedure to check for an open form. If the form is not open, display all the open forms in an array view box.

ON THE NET *http://prestwood.com/forums/paradox/books/official/files/ARRAYS.FSL.*

Step By Step

1. Change your working directory to Paradox's Samples directory and create a new form. Place a button labeled **Check for open form** on it.

2. In the pushButton event of the button, type lines 3–8. Line 4 declares a resizeable array—arForms—that is populated in line 8 with enumFormNames(). Note that you don't have to set the size of the resizeable array ahead of time. Line 5 declares a SmallInt variable named siCounter. Line 10 uses siCounter to scan through the array from the first element to however many elements are in the array. This is determined by arForms.size(). Line 11 checks to see whether the current array element is Arrays. If it is, a message information box is displayed in line 12, and execution stops in line 13 with the keyword return. If the element is not Arrays, the loop continues. This cycle continues until either Arrays is found or the end of the array is reached. If the routine is never exited, line 17 tells the user that the form isn't open. Line 18 shows the user all the currently open forms.

```
1:     ;Button :: pushButton
2:     method pushButton(var eventInfo Event)
3:        var
4:           arForms     Array[] String
5:           siCounter   SmallInt
6:        endVar
7:
```

```
      enumFormNames(arForms)

      for siCounter from 1 to arForms.size()
         if arForms[siCounter] = "Arrays" then
           msgInfo("Found", "Form 'Arrays' is open")
           return
         endIf
      endFor

      msgInfo("Not Found", "Form 'Arrays' is not open")
      arForms.view("Current forms open")
   endMethod
```

3. Check the syntax, save the form as **ARRAY.FSL**, and run it. Click the button. A dialog box indicates whether the form is open. After you click OK, the routine either stops or displays all the open forms. If a form with the name Arrays is open, the routine stops. Otherwise, an array view box displays all the open forms.

The Details of the *DynArray* Data Type

A DynArray (dynamic array) is very similar to a regular array, except that it uses address names rather than index numbers. Just as static and resizeable arrays are for using sets of data, so is the DynArray. If you can imagine an array is similar to a single-column Paradox table, then a DynArray is similar to a two-column Paradox table with the first column being the primary key. The number of elements (indexes) you can have in a DynArray is limited only by memory. An index can be up to 255 characters and is sorted in alphabetical order.

Of the many DynArray methods, the following are some of the most useful:

- **contains()** Searches a DynArray for a pattern of characters.
- **empty()** Removes all items from a DynArray.
- **getKeys()** Loads a resizable array with the indexes of an existing DynArray.
- **removeItem()** Deletes a specified item from a DynArray.
- **size()** Returns the number of elements in a DynArray.

The following is the syntax model to declare a DynArray:

```
DynArrayName    DynArray[] dataType
```

The following declares dyn1 as a DynArray:

```
var
   dyn1    DynArray[] SmallInt
endVar
```

As soon as the array is declared, you can reference any of the elements of the DynArray directly:

```
DynArrayName[ElementName] = value
```


The following creates two elements in dyn1 and sets their values:

```
myDynArray["Last_Name"] = "Megan"
myDynArray["First_Name"] = "Miles"
```

As soon as the elements of a DynArray have values, you can retrieve the values much like you retrieve values from a regular array. Rather than using a numbered index, however, you use named indexes. For example, the following displays the First_Name element in the array in the status bar:

```
message(myDynArray["First_Name"])
```

Now look at a completed example. Type lines 3–10 in the pushButton event of button.

```
 1:   ;Button :: pushButton
 2:   method pushButton(var eventInfo Event)
 3:      var
 4:         myDynArray    DynArray[] String
 5:      endVar
 6:
 7:      myDynArray["Last_Name"] = "Megan"
 8:      myDynArray["First_Name"] = "Miles"
 9:
10:      myDynArray.view()
11:   endMethod
```

When you run the preceding code, note that the indexes are in alphabetical order.

Using *forEach*

The forEach structure enables you to loop through a DynArray, much like scan enables you to loop through a table. The syntax for forEach is as follows:

```
forEach VarName in DynArrayName
     Statements
endForEach
```

For example:

```
forEach sElement in Dyn1          ;Scan through DynArray for sElement.
   message(DynArrayVar[sElement])     ;Display element on status bar.
   sleep(500)                         ;Wait for .5 seconds.
endForEach                            ;End for loop.
```

Suppose that you want to use a forEach loop to move through a DynArray of your system information, showing the user each element until you get to the IconHeight element. In addition to the forEach loop, this example also acquaints you with sysInfo(). Add lines 3–15 to the pushButton event of a button.

```
1:   ;Button :: pushButton
2:   method pushButton(var eventInfo Event)
3:      var
4:         dynSys    DynArray[] Anytype
5:         sElement String
6:      endVar
7:
8:      sysInfo(dynSys)
9:
10:     forEach sElement in dynSys
11:        if sElement = "IconHeight" then quitLoop endIf
12:        msgInfo(sElement, dynSys[sElement])
13:     endForEach
14:
15:     dynSys.view()
16:  endMethod
```

Check the syntax, run the form, and click the button. A message information dialog box appears for each element of the DynArray. Rather than cycle through all 30 bits of information, the program stops after the most important information is displayed. At the end of this parade of system information, a DynArray view box shows you all the elements at once.

In step 2, line 4 declares the DynArray dynSys. Note that no size is indicated in line 3 or in the body of the code. Line 5 declares sElement as a string variable. In line 8, the sysInfo() procedure is used to put information about your system into the DynArray. s is used in line 10 to store the index name, which is used in lines 11 and 12. Lines 10–13 comprise the forEach block, which moves through each element in the DynArray, checking to see whether the element name is equal to IconHeight. If it is equal, the loop is exited with the keyword quitLoop. If the loop hasn't reached IconHeight yet, the element name and value are displayed. Finally, line 15 shows the complete DynArray all at once. In this case, a view is a better way to see all the elements of the array than looping through and showing one element at a time.

This simple example merely shows you how to loop through a DynArray and acquaints you with sysInfo(). Normally, you will do much more than this example does, using or manipulating each element as you go.

Using Custom Data Types

A custom data type is a way for you to create your own data type. You do this in a Type structure in either the Type window or in the event, much like you declare variables and constants. That is, the scope and instance of a custom type follows the same rules as a var block. The following is the syntax model:

```
type
   UserType = ExistingType
endType
```

The old Currency type of Paradox tables is now called Money. However, ObjectPAL was left to the same old Currency data type. If you don't like this inconsistency, then you could declare a new variable type called Money and use it in place of Currency.

```
Type                        ;Begin type block.
     Money = Currency        ;Set custom types.
endType                     ;End type block.
```

After you do this, you could use either Currency or Money whenever you deal with money. You could use either line 2 or line 6 in the following code (lines 1–3 declare Total as a Currency data type).

```
1:    var
2:       Total     Currency
3:    endVar
4:    var
5:       Total     Money
6:    endVar
```

Another use of the type block is to define a data type as a set or record of existing types. For example, enter lines 3–23 into the pushButton event of a button:

```
1:    ;Button :: pushButton
2:    method pushButton(var eventInfo Event)
3:       type                                 ;Start type block.
4:          ctEmployee = Record               ;Start record block.
5:             Name       String              ;Set elements of record.
6:             Position   String              ;type employee.
7:             YearEmp    SmallInt
8:             SickDays   SmallInt
9:             VacDays    SmallInt
10:            endRecord                      ;End record block.
11:      endType                              ;End type block.
12:
13:      var                                  ;Begin var block.
14:         emp ctEmployee                    ;Set emp to employee.
15:      endVar                               ;End var block.
16:
17:      emp.Name = "Glenn Allen Unsicker"
18:      emp.Position = "Registered Nurse"
19:      emp.YearEmp = 34
20:      emp.SickDays = 312
21:      emp.VacDays = 72
22:
23:      emp.view()                           ;View emp record.
24:   endMethod
```

As soon as a custom type is defined as a record, you can deal with a set of variables all at once.

Understanding Properties

Paradox offers two sets of property names: end-user properties and ObjectPAL properties. The distinction is that the properties listed in the Explorer are the ObjectPAL Names for the properties you set interactively. In addition, there are many properties you can only set using ObjectPAL. If you see a property name listed in the Explorer and then look in the ObjectPAL Browser, you can paste the correct name into your code. For example, you can paste Design.SizeToFit as opposed to Size to Fit (from the Properties sheet). The properties displayed in the Properties sheets are end-user properties; the properties displayed in the Object Explorer are the ObjectPAL equivalents. This helps get you acquainted with the differences between the two sets of property names.

Using Constants

As already stated, an ObjectPAL constant is a value that represents a number. A constant is a specific, unchanging value used in calculations and defined in a const block very similar to a variable block. Just as variables have scope and instance in ObjectPAL, so do constants. The following declares a constant with private scope; the instance of the constant is for the duration of the object.

```
;Button :: pushButton
const
   youngest = "Veronica Renee Martinez"
endConst
method pushButton(var eventInfo Event)
   view(youngest, "New family member")
endMethod
```

The value of constants, of course, doesn't change. You use these constants in ObjectPAL statements to do a variety of tasks.

TIP

Two advantages of using constants are that they humanize your code and help make managing your code easier. They humanize your code by making your code easier to read. A constant named tax is easier to remember and understand than 8.125. Constants help you maintain your code by centralizing values. If the tax rate in your area changes from 8.125 to 8.5, you change the constant in one location. In the preceding example, when a new, younger member of my family arrives, I just change the one constant and the change is propagated throughout. Imagine having to change it throughout your code.

Using Methods and Procedures

The most often used types of commands are methods and procedures in the run-time library. The *run-time library* (RTL) is the predefined set of methods and procedures used for operating on objects. The Types and Methods tab, shown here, from the ObjectPAL Quick Lookup dialog box, is the run-time library. You'll remember you get to the ObjectPAL Quick Lookup dialog box by selecting View | ObjectPAL Quick Lookup. Methods and procedures differ from events in that they actually do something tangible that you specify. The primary use of an event is to execute code you add to it.

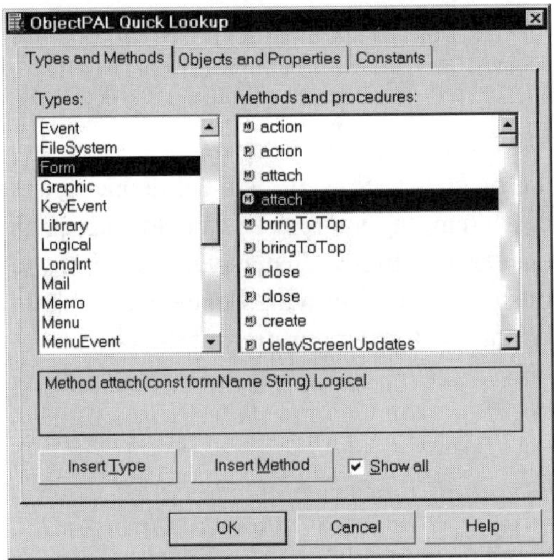

Here are two quick definitions to remind you about the difference between a method and a procedure:

- **method** A function or command in ObjectPAL that acts on an object. A method uses dot notation to work on an object, as in object.method().
- **procedure** A function or command in ObjectPAL that has no object to work on. The programmer doesn't specify an object.

The following is an example of using the open() method. You can type lines 3–7 into the pushButton event of a button (make sure that your working directory is set to Paradox's Samples directory):

```
;Commands :: btnMethod :: pushButton
method pushButton(var eventInfo Event)
   var
      f     Form
   endVar

   f.open("OV-LIKE.FSL")
endMethod
```

The open() is the method and the f form variable is the object. A procedure, on the other hand, has no object to work on.

http://prestwood.com/forums/paradox/books/official/files/COMMANDS. FSL contains all the code from this chapter. For practice, you should type in all the code from this chapter yourself. If you run into trouble, then open this form to see what went wrong.

The following is an example of using the isDir() procedure. Type line 3 into the pushButton event of a button.

```
1:     ;Commands :: btnProcedure :: pushButton
2:     method pushButton(var eventInfo Event)
3:        view(isDir("C:\\WINDOWS"))
4:     endMethod
```

isDir() is the procedure. It checks whether a directory exists.

It's not always necessary to keep in mind the difference between a method and a procedure. This book takes a formal look at the ObjectPAL language. It's enough to know that methods and procedures are two types of commands.

Using Properties

One reason ObjectPAL is powerful is that you can change the properties of an object. You are already familiar with various properties of objects; you have set them in previous examples and in interactive Paradox. This section explores the syntax used to manipulate them in ObjectPAL. You can set most of an object's properties while the form is running—another feature that sets Paradox apart from other database systems. You can set not only the value of a field and the color of a box, but also the size and position of objects, the alignment, the tab stop, and so on.

Just as you can set the values of properties using interactive Paradox, you also can set them using ObjectPAL, as shown here. All properties of an object are either read-only or read/write.

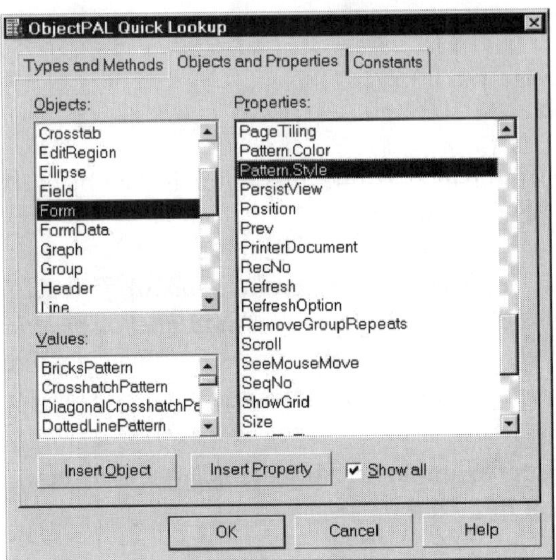

Read-Only Properties

Some properties are read-only. That is, you cannot set their value. You can only read it. For example, to display the record number of the active field in a message information box whenever a button is clicked, add line 3 to the pushButton event of a button.

```
1:    ;Commands :: btnReadOnly :: pushButton
2:    method pushButton(var eventInfo Event)
3:       msgInfo("Record number", active.recNo)      ;recNo is a property.
4:    endMethod
```

For this code to work, the tabstop property must be set to False. If the tabstop property is set to True, focus will move to the button before the pushButton event is called. Because a button does not have a recNo property, a critical error results.

Read/Write Properties

Another type of property is a read/write property. For example, to toggle the AutoAppend property of a table frame when a button is clicked, add line 3 to the pushButton event of a button.

```
1:  ;Commands :: btnReadWrite :: pushButton
2:  method pushButton(var eventInfo Event)
3:     Customer.autoAppend = not Customer.autoAppend     ;Customer is a
       ;table frame.
4:  endMethod
```

There are two categories of properties: read/write and read-only. The Objects and Properties tab of the ObjectPAL Quick Lookup is shown there:

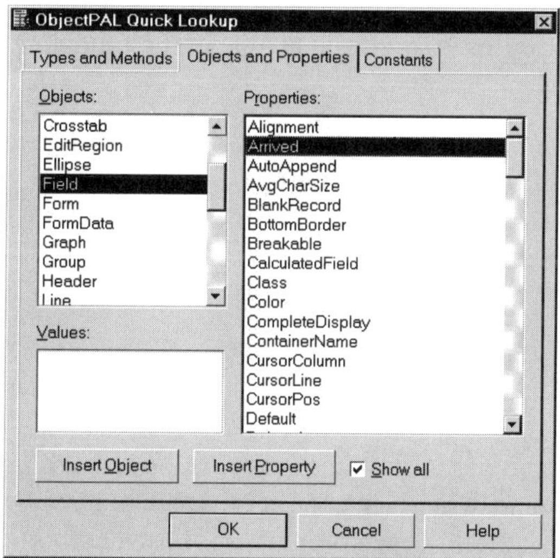

You're familiar with the read/write properties. The read-only properties include Arrived, BlankRecord, Class, ContainerName, FieldNo, FieldSize, FieldType, Focus, FullName, FullSize, IndexField, Locked, and Required. The following statement assumes that an object named theBox is on a form:

```
;Button :: pushButton
message("Full containership path is " + theBox.fullName)
```

If you're having trouble with scope or the containership hierarchy and you need to know the full containership path of an object, use the preceding statement.

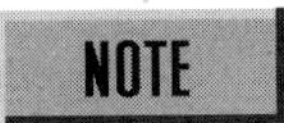

Only the subcategory of object types known as UIObjects have properties (UIObjects are visual controls you use to design forms). Objects such as TCursors and strings do not.

You read and set properties in ObjectPAL by means of dot notation, just as you do with the other aspects of ObjectPAL syntax. You are familiar with the basic syntax for properties. The following two examples should look familiar:

```
fldName.value = " Daphne Homann "
theBox.color = Red
```

Following are examples of setting the value for a read/write property. If you have a box named Box1 on a form, you could put the following code on a button:

```
;Button :: pushButton
method pushButton(var eventInfo Event)
   Box1.color = Red
   Box1.Frame.Color = Blue
   Box1.Frame.Thickness = LWidthHairLine
   Box1.Frame.Style = DashDotFrame
   Box1.Pattern.Color = Yellow
   Box1.Pattern.Style = LatticePattern
endMethod
```

No matter which property is set, the syntax is the same: *objectName.property = constant*. Use this syntax whenever you set the value of a read/write property. The previous examples set the values of properties. The syntax for reading an object's property value is similar. When you get the current value of a read/write or read-only property, you use the syntax objectName.property, which returns the current value of the object's specified property. The following code displays the current color of the object named theBox in the status bar. Usually, you use this technique to add logic to your application:

```
;Button :: pushButton
method pushButton(var eventInfo Event)
   message(theBox.color)
endMethod
```

In the following code, the value property of the field named GotoPage is used to determine whether it should display a message and move to Page2:

```
;Button :: pushButton
method pushButton(var eventInfo Event)
   if GotoPage.value = "Page2" then
      message("Moving to page two")
      Page2.moveTo()
   endIf
endMethod
```

Using the *first* Property of an Object

The first property returns the full containership path of the first contained object. You can display the string it returns in a message information dialog box. For example, type the following code in the pushButton event of a button. It displays the full path of the label the button contains.

```
;Button :: pushButon
method pushButton(var eventInfo Event)
   msgInfo("Button label", self.first)
endMethod
```

A more practical use of first is to write generic routines. Suppose that you want to change the font color of the label of a button. You could rename the button's label and use the font.color property of the object. If you change the name of an object, the name and its 4-byte address are stored in the symbol table. Therefore, use the following code instead.

```
;Button :: pushButon
method pushButton(var eventInfo Event)
   var
      f    Form
   endVar

   f.attach()
   f.(self.first).font.color = Red
endMethod
```

Note in the preceding code two things: the use of attach() and parentheses. first returns a string, not an object. In order to use the string in ObjectPAL, you need to dereference it. Dereferencing is when you put the name of something in a variable and then use the variable as if you were using the name. Dereferencing an object using dot notation in ObjectPAL requires two rules: an object preceding the dereference and the use of parentheses around the dereferenced value. You need to start back in the containership path one object and then put the string in parentheses (see the preceding line 7). The following section puts this technique to work.

Toggling the Font Color of the Label of a Button Example

Now you'll see a full example of using the first color in context. Suppose that you want to toggle the font color of the label of a button between red and black. In this example, you make use of the first property to write a generic routine that will work with any button.

http://prestwood.com/forums/paradox/books/official/files/TOGGLE3.FSL.

Step By Step

1. Change your working directory to Paradox's Samples directory and create a new form. Place a button on it.

2. Add lines 2–15 to the pushButton event. (As always, typing the comments is optional.) Line 4 declares f as a Form variable, which line 7 uses to attach to the current form. Lines 12–16 use the form variable with the object variable self and the first property to inspect and alter the color property of the button label's text.

```
1:    ;Button :: pushButton
2:    method pushButton(var eventInfo Event)
3:       var
4:          f   Form   ;Declare a Form variable.
5:       endVar
6:
7:       f.attach()    ;Attach to current form.
8:
9:       ;Notice the use of the Form variable and
10:      ;the use of parentheses to dereference
11:      ;the String.
12:      if f.(self.first).font.color = Red then
```

```
            f.(self.first).font.color = Black
        else
            f.(self.first).font.color = Red
        endIf
    endMethod
```

3. Check the syntax, save the new form as TOGGLE3.FSL (shown here), and run it.

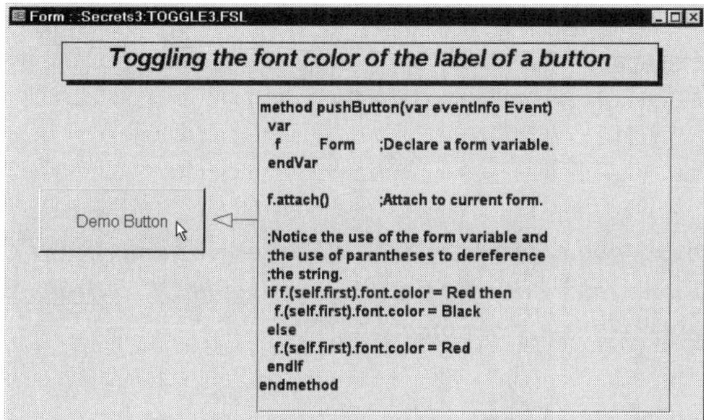

Using the *first* and *next* Properties Together

Sometimes while creating an application you need to manipulate a series of objects. Oftentimes, you can create generic routines to handle a group of objects. One such technique for handling a group of objects is to use the first and next properties. The following code, for example, displays an array of all the objects inside an object named Outside. It is important to note that this code does not list the objects inside of each object.

```
;First&Next :: btnTraverse :: pushButton
method pushButton(var eventInfo Event)
   var
      ui            UIObject
      arLayer1      Array[] String
      siCounter     SmallInt
   endVar

   ;Attach to the object.
   ui.attach(Outer)

   ;You must call first first.
```

```
   ui.attach(ui.first)
   arLayer1.addLast(ui.fullname)

   ;Now call next until next = next.
   siCounter = 1
   ui.attach(ui.next)
   while arLayer1[siCounter] <> ui.fullName
      arLayer1.addLast(ui.fullName)
      ui.attach(ui.next)
      siCounter = siCounter + 1
   endWhile

   arLayer1.view()
endMethod
```

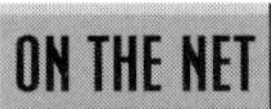

http://prestwood.com/forums/paradox/books/official/files/FIRST&NEXT.FSL demonstrates both the first/next and enumObjectNames() techniques for dealing with a set of objects.

Using *enumObjectNames()*

Oftentimes, it is much easier and quicker to use enumObjectNames() and work through the array using a for loop. The following code, for example, enumerates all the objects in the object named Outer, displays the objects in a view box, and then displays each object one at a time:

```
;First&Next :: btnEnum :: pushButton
method pushButton(var eventInfo Event)
   var
      arObjects   Array[] String
      siCounter   SmallInt
   endVar

   outer.enumObjectNames(arObjects)
   arObjects.view()

   for siCounter from 1 to arObjects.size()
      ;Manipulate arObjects[siCounter] here.
      view(arObjects[siCounter])
   endFor
endMethod
```

It is important to note that the preceding routine displays all the objects within an object (including the objects within the objects).

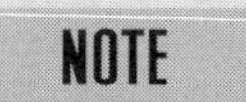

When possible, use enumObjectNames() rather than enumUIObjects(). enumUIObjects() enumerates object information to a table and, therefore, is much slower than enumObjectNames().

Adding Scroll Bars to a Graphic Field Example

A fun exercise is to use a property that you normally set interactively in your code. This next example toggles the horizontal and vertical scroll bars on a field. If you display large amounts of data or a bitmap, you may want to add this routine to your application.

Suppose that you want to add scroll bars to a graphic field when the user double-clicks it. To do this, you need to check whether the bitmap object currently has scroll bars. If it does, then remove them. If it doesn't, then add them.

http://prestwood.com/forums/paradox/books/official/files/SCROLL.FSL.

Step By Step

1. Create a new form bound to a table with a graphic field in it (for example, the BIOLIFE.DB table in the Samples directory). Place a field on the form and define the field to the graphic field, as shown here:

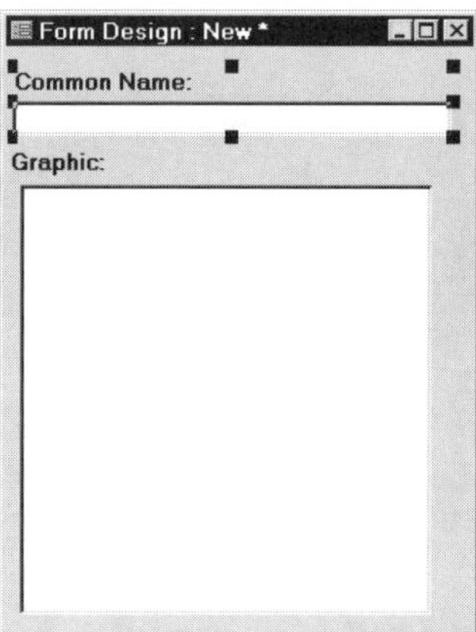

2. Add lines 3–15 to the mouseDouble event of the graphic field. Line 3 turns on a feature that delays the drawing of the screen until the operation is complete. Without this line of code, the graphic would refresh twice, once for each scroll bar added. To see this for yourself, put a semicolon in front of line 3. This disables the line of code. Run the form. Line 4 determines whether you need to add or remove both scroll bars by checking whether the horizontal scroll bar is on.

```
1:    ;Field :: doubleClick
2:    method mouseDouble(var eventInfo MouseEvent)
3:       delayScreenUpdates(Yes)
4:       if self.HorizontalScrollBar = On then
5:         message("Removing scroll bars...")
6:         self.HorizontalScrollBar = Off
7:         self.VerticalScrollBar = Off
8:         message("")
9:       else
10:        message("Adding scroll bars...")
11:        self.HorizontalScrollBar = On
12:        self.VerticalScrollBar = On
13:        message("")
14:      endIf
15:      delayScreenUpdates(No)
16:   endMethod
```

3. Check your syntax, save the form as SCROLL.FSL, and run the form. Click the graphic several times and watch the scroll bars come and go.

If the horizontal scroll bar is on in line 5, lines 5–8 remove both scroll bars. Line 5 tells the user that the scroll bars are being removed. Lines 6 and 7 turn off the horizontal and vertical scroll bars. Line 8 clears the status bar.

If the horizontal scroll bar isn't on in line 4, lines 10–13 add both scroll bars. Line 10 tells the user that the scroll bars are being added. Lines 11 and 12 turn on the horizontal and vertical scroll bars.

Using the *Enabled* Property

Enabled is a read/write property for all UIObjects. Enabled is an interesting and powerful property that ObjectPAL programmers can use. When the Enabled property is set to False, the object and the objects that are contained in the object appear to be disabled. Specifically, the following things happen:

- The object no longer responds to mouse clicks.
- You cannot move to the object.
- All text in the object becomes grayed.
- The Enabled property cascades to all the objects inside the given object.

7

Note the importance of this last item. For example, setting a Notebook object's Enabled property to False causes the Enabled property of every field, label, and record object inside that Notebook object also to be set to False. This makes it very easy to "disable" an entire collection of objects with one property set. Setting the Enabled property to True also cascades to all the child objects. The syntax for it is simple.

```
active.enabled = False
active.enabled = not active.enabled
```

http://prestwood.com/forums/paradox/books/official/files/ENABLED.FSL demonstrates the Enabled property on text, field, and button objects, as well as a box with all three contained within it.

About Compound Properties

Just as there are compound objects in ObjectPAL, there are also compound properties. A *compound property* is a property that has several parts to it separated by dots. For example, Table 7-1 lists some sample compound properties.

Compound Property	Sample Usage
design.SizeToFit	box1.design.SizeToFit = True
font.style	fld1.font.style = FontAttribBold
Background.Pattern.Style	grph1.Background.Pattern.Style = CrosshatchPattern
List.Value	fld1.lst1.list.value = "Bill Lupton"

TABLE 7-1 Sample Compound Properities

The Details of Branching

Branching involves testing a condition and doing something based on the result of that test. It enables you to code a Logical decision into your application. ObjectPAL has four types of branching: iif, if, switch, and try.

Control Structures

In programming languages, *control structures* are keywords used to alter the sequence of execution and add logic to your code. All programming languages contain control structures. They are a fundamental element of any programming language.

Normally, a programming language executes line after line in sequential order. This is true whether the language is a line-oriented language such as BASIC or a statement-oriented language such as C. A branch transfers program control to an instruction other than the next sequential instruction.

A set of instructions that is repeated a predetermined number of times or until a specified condition is met is called a *loop*. Control structures enable you to branch and loop based on whether a certain condition evaluates to True. They also enable you to add logic to your code. The techniques you learn in this chapter will help you when you learn other programming languages. Although the syntax might vary, the control structures in ObjectPAL apply to other languages.

Using *iif*

iif() (short for *immediate if*) returns one of two values, depending on the result of a Logical expression. iif() enables you to branch within a single statement. You can use iif() wherever you use any other expression. iif() is especially useful where an if statement is illegal, such as in calculated fields and reports. The syntax for an iif() is as follows:

```
iif (Condition, TrueValue, FalseValue)
```

For example:

```
ans = iif(Total > 100, Yes, No)
```

The true and false sections of iif() simply return a value. They don't execute commands.

The Details of the *if* Statement

You're familiar with the if statement because you have used it several times in the examples of this book. if executes one set of commands or another, depending on the result of a Logical expression. When ObjectPAL comes to an if statement, it evaluates whether the expression is true. If the expression is true, ObjectPAL executes the statements in the TrueStatements sequence. If the expression isn't true, ObjectPAL skips the TrueStatements sequence. Then, if the optional else keyword is present, ObjectPAL executes the FalseStatements sequence. In both cases, execution continues after the endIf keyword. For example:

```
if Condition then         ;If condition, then
   TrueStatements         ;execute these statements.
[else                     ;Otherwise,
   FalseStatements]       ;execute these statements.
endIf
```

The following is an example of an if statement using the else clause:

```
if self.value < 0 then              ;If negative, then set
   self.font.color = Red            ;the font color to red, &
   message("Value is negative")     ;display a message.
else
   self.font.color = Black          ;Otherwise, color is black
   message("")                      ;and clear message.
endIf
```

The if statement is highly flexible; you can nest if statements. Nesting an if statement means that any statement in TrueStatements or FalseStatements sequences also can be an if statement, as in the following example:

```
if Condition1 then            ;If condition1, then
     TrueStatements1          ;execute these statements.
else                          ;Otherwise,
     if Condition2 then       ;if Condition2, then
     TrueStatements2          ;execute these statements.
     endIf                    ;End inside if block.
endIf                         ;End outside if block.
```

The following is an example of a nested if statement:

```
if skillLevel = "Beginner" then
   if skillBox.color = "Red" then
      skillBox.color = "Green"
    endIf
endIf
```

The following two examples demonstrate how to use compound conditions with and and or:

```
;Example 1:

if Cond1 and Cond2 then       ;If both are true, then
     TrueStatements           ;execute these statements.
else                          ;Otherwise,
     FalseStatements          ;execute these statements.
endIf                         ;End of if block.
```

For example:

```
if self.value > 0 and self.value < 10 then
   self.font.color = Yellow
   message("Balance is low")
endIf
```

```
;Exmaple 2:
```

```
if Cond1 or Cond2 then        ;If either are True, then
     TrueStatements           ;execute these statements.
else                          ;Otherwise,
     FalseStatements          ;execute these statements.
endIf                         ;End of if block.
```

For example:

```
if x = 1 or x = 2 then
   message("True")
else
   message("False")
endIf
```


An earlier example used the following keyword sequence:

```
1:    if   deleteRecord() then
2:       message("Record deleted")
3:    else
4:       message("Could not delete record")
5:    endIf
```

Line 1 tries to delete a record. If the delete is successful, the code after the then keyword and before the else keyword is executed. If the delete fails, the code after the else keyword and before the endIf keyword is executed.

If you wanted to check the data of a field before the user leaves it, you could use an if statement in the canDepart event of the field that you want to check. Essentially, canDepart asks for permission to leave the field. In other words, code you add to the canDepart event is executed just before the cursor leaves the field, as in the following example:

```
1:    if self.value > 100 then
2:       eventInfo.setErrorCode(canNotDepart)
3:       msgStop("!!! Warning !!!","Value too large.")
4:    endIf
```

This example has more than one line of code between the if and endIf keywords. Take a close look at line 2. eventInfo is a variable. In essence, this eventInfo variable represents a packet that ObjectPAL sends from object to object. setErrorCode() is a method that works on this packet. In this case, setErrorCode() uses the CanNotDepart error constant to set the error code in the packet to the error code CanNotDepart. You can inspect this error code with the errorCode() method. Setting the error code in the packet in this way prevents the cursor from leaving the field.

The *switch* Block

You can use nested if statements to execute one set of commands out of many sets. ObjectPAL offers a better way, however, to make compound decisions: the switch block. switch executes a set of alternative statement sequences, depending on which of several conditions is met.

switch uses the values of the condition statements in each case to determine which sequence of statements to execute. Each case works like a single if statement, and the switch structure works like multiple, compound, or nested if statements.

As soon as the first case evaluates to True, the corresponding sequence of statements is executed and the remaining cases are skipped. If no case evaluates to True and the optional otherWise clause is present, the statements in otherWise are executed. If no case evaluates to True and no otherWise clause is present, switch has no effect. Following is the syntax:

```
switch
     case Condition1    :Statements1
    [case Condition2    :Statements2] ;Repeat as needed.
    [otherWise          :Statements3]
endSwitch
```

For example:

```
switch
   case AmountField < 0     : message("We're in the red")
   case AmountField < 10    : message("Balance is very low")
   case AmountField < 100   : message("Balance is low")
   case AmountField > 1000  : message("Go spend some money")
   otherWise                : message("Balance is looking good")
 endSwitch
```

This first example is formatted well because each resulting sequence of commands was short enough to fit nicely on a single line of code, but how do you keep your code readable when you need to use multiple lines of code in the resulting sequence? This next example shows how you can use compound expressions and execute multiple statements, and still keep the code very readable:

```
switch
    case Field1 < 0 and Field2 = True
        :  ans = 1
           message("One")
           Page1.moveTo()
    case Field1 < 0 and Field2 = False
        :  ans = 2
           message("Two")
           Page2.moveTo()
    case Field1 >= 0 and Field2 = True
        :  ans = 3
           message("Three")
           Page3.moveTo()
    case Field1 >= 0 and Field2 = False
        :  ans = 4
           message("Four")
           Page4.moveTo()
endSwitch
```


The *try* Block

Use try as your basic ObjectPAL error recovery tool. With try, you can attempt to execute a block of code. If all the commands succeed, execution skips to just after the endTry keyword. If any one command generates a critical error, the recovery block executes starting just after the onFail keyword. Following is the syntax:

```
try
     [Statements]        ;The transaction block.
     [fail()]            ;Optional.
onFail
     [Statements]        ;The recovery block.
     [reTry]             ;Optional.
endTry
```

You can call the keyword reTry to execute the transaction block again, as in the following example:

```
var
   nCounter   Number
endVar

nCounter = 1

try
   Last_Name.postRecord()
onFail
  sleep(250)
  if nCounter >= 5 then
     msgStop("Warning", "Could not post record")
  else
     nCounter = nCounter + 1
     reTry
  endIf
endTry
```

A method or procedure that generates a warning error or returns a False does not cause the onFail block to execute. You can raise warning errors to critical errors by using errorTrapOnWarnings(), as in the following example:

```
errorTrapOnWarnings(Yes)      ;Raise warning errors to critical
                              ;so try will catch them.
```

In addition, you can use the keyword fail() to force a branch to the onFail portion. Use this technique to force a block of code to fail, such as when a method or procedure returns a False. For example, type the following line of code in the pushButton event of a button:

```
;Button :: pushButton
method pushButton(var eventInfo Event)
   try
      if not isfile("C:\\NOFILE.TXT") then fail() endIf
```

```
          message("File exists.")
       onFail
          message("File does not exist.")
       endTry
    endMethod
```

You can nest fail() inside several procedure calls, far from where the block begins. If you decide in a recovery block that the error code is not what you expected, or if the error code is too serious to be handled in the current onFail block, call fail() again to pass it up to the next try block's onFail clause.

If no higher-level try block exists, the whole application fails. It cancels existing actions, closes resources, and causes a critical error. This is done by the implicit try block that ObjectPAL wraps around every method, as seen in this error message:

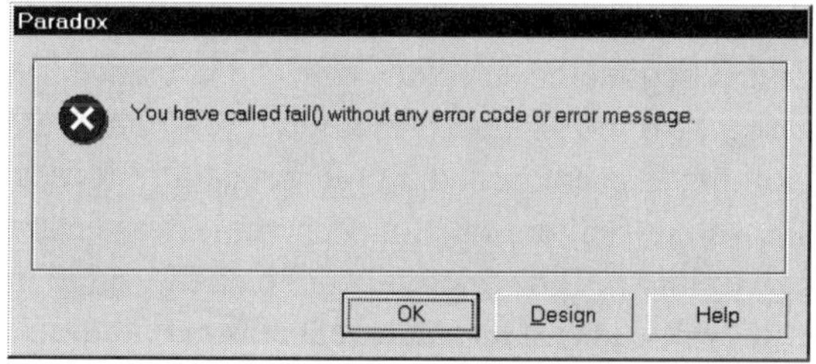

Using *try* to Test a Date in an Undefined Field

Suppose that you want to test whether the value in an undefined field is a valid date. How can you tell whether the user has typed a valid date into an undefined field? ObjectPAL doesn't have an isDate type method, so how do you test? One way to test whether the user typed in a valid date is to try to cast the value as a date. If the test fails, you know that the date isn't valid. Although blanks are normally a legal date, in this example, blanks are not allowed.

http://prestwood.com/forums/paradox/books/official/files/TRY.FSL.

Step By Step

1. Create a new form. Put an undefined field and a button on the new form. Label the button **Test Date** and name the field **fldDate**, and change its label to **Enter date**, as shown here:

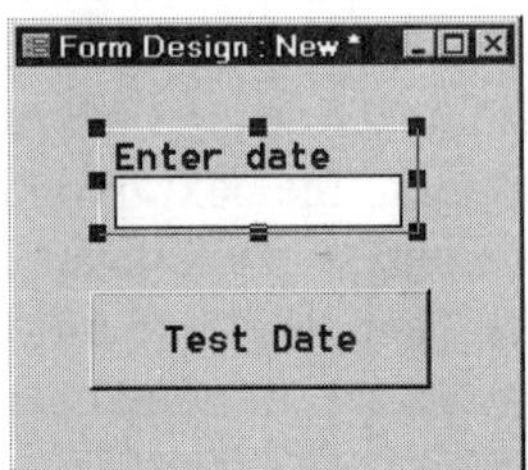

2. Add lines 3–9 to the pushButton event of the button. Lines 3–9 make up the try block. Line 3 begins the structure with the keyword try. Line 4 uses an if statement along with the isBlank() method to test whether something was entered. If nothing was entered, the fail() procedure forces a fail, and the execution skips to onFail in line 7. If something was entered, the execution drops through to line 5. Line 5 attempts to cast the value in the fldDate field as a date. If the value is cast as a date, execution continues to line 6, which displays a message information box. After line 6 displays the message, the execution skips to endTry in line 9. If the casting of the fldDate field with the Date() procedure in line 5 fails, the execution skips to onFail in line 7.

```
 1:    ;TRY :: Button :: pushButton
 2:    method pushButton(var eventInfo Event)
 3:       try
 4:          if fldDate.isBlank() then fail() endIf
 5:          date(fldDate.value)
 6:          msgInfo("", "Valid date")
 7:       onFail
 8:          msgInfo("Warning", "Invalid date")
 9:       endTry
10:    endMethod
```

3. Check the syntax, save the form as **TRY.FSL**, and run it. Enter various dates into the field. Test each date after you've entered it by clicking on the button. For example, try 1/8/65, 10/33/93, 001/1/1991, and a blank. This form uses isBlank() and a try structure to test whether the data typed into an undefined field is valid.

Remember that, in a try structure, if any command in the try portion generates a critical error, the execution skips to onFail. If you don't care about blank entries, you can leave out the if statement, as in the following example:

```
;Button :: pushButton
try                                   ;Begin try block.
   date(fldDate.value)                ;Cast fldDate as a date.
   msgInfo("", "Valid date")          ;Display a message box.
onFail                                ;Begin onFail block.
   msgInfo("", "Invalid date")        ;Display a message box.
endTry                                ;End try block.
```

You can use a try block to add function to ObjectPAL. For example, this section showed you how to add an isDate() type of method. A try block is also a great way to put error checking into your application. You could surround a piece of code with a try structure and display a generic message if any command fails.

The Details of Looping

When you program, you often need to repeat a number of commands. One of the most important aspects of a programming language is its capability to loop—that is, to go through a series of commands a certain number of times. ObjectPAL has four ways to loop: scan, for, forEach, and while.

Using the *loop* and *quitLoop* Keywords

Because all four loops have two keywords in common, loop and quitLoop, this section addresses these before getting into the four loops. loop passes program control to the top of the nearest loop. When loop is executed within a for, forEach, scan, or while structure, it skips the statements between it and endFor, endForEach, endScan, or endWhile and returns to the beginning of the structure.

quitLoop exits a loop to the nearest endFor, endForEach, endScan, etc. quitLoop immediately exits to the nearest for, forEach, endScan, or endWhile keyword. Execution continues with the statement that follows the nearest endFor, endForEach, endScan, or endWhile. quitLoop causes an error if it is executed outside a for, forEach, scan, or while structure.

The *while* Loop

A while loop enables you to execute a set of commands while a condition is true. Specifically, while repeats a sequence of statements as long as a specified condition evaluates to True. At the end of the set of commands, the condition is tested again. In a typical while loop, you must make the condition False somewhere in the set of commands.

```
while Condition    ;Test condition, if true
   [Statements]    ;execute these statements.
                   ;Don't forget to make
                   ;the condition false some place.
endWhile           ;Go back to while.
```

while starts by evaluating the Logical expression Condition. If Condition evaluates to False, the execution continues after endWhile. If Condition is True, Statements are executed. When the program comes to endWhile, it returns to the first line of the loop, which reevaluates Condition. Statements are repeated until Condition evaluates to False.

Using a *while* Loop Example

This example demonstrates a simple while loop that counts to 10. It uses a counter variable to keep track of how many times to cycle through the loop.

http://prestwood.com/forums/paradox/books/official/files/LOOPS.FSL.

Step By Step

1. Create a new form with a button labeled **While loop**.
2. Add lines 3–14 to the pushButton event of the While loop button. Line 4 declares Counter as a SmallInt variable. In line 7, Counter is initialized to 0. (All variables must be initialized before you use them.) Lines 9–13 form the while loop. When Counter is less than 10, lines 10–12 are executed. In line 12, the Counter variable is incremented. If you leave this line out, the counter will loop forever. (You'll have to use CTRL+break to exit the loop.) With while loops, you have to make the condition False at some point. This example uses a simple Counter variable that eventually makes the condition in line 9 False, which in turn ends the loop. Execution continues after endWhile.

```
1:    ;LOOPS :: Button :: pushButton
2:    method pushButton(var eventInfo Event)
3:       var
```

```
            Counter   SmallInt   ;Counter is a SmallInt.
         endVar

         Counter = 0             ;Variables must be
                                 ;initialized.
         While Counter < 10      ;Start of while loop.
           message(Counter)      ;Display Counter.
           sleep(250)            ;Sleep for 1/4 second.
           Counter = Counter + 1 ;Increments counter.
         endWhile                ;End of while loop.
         message("Final value for Counter is " +
         StrVal(Counter))
      endMethod
```


3. Check the syntax, save the form as **LOOPS.FSL**, and run the form. Click the While Loop button. Watch the status bar count from 0 to 9 in the loop and display the number 10 after the loop is finished.

This example uses a while loop as a counter. Normally, you would use a for loop for a loop that has a counter. while loops are useful for executing a set of commands as long as a condition is True. For example, you might execute a set of commands while the left character of a string is equal to Sm or while a box's color is red. The important thing to remember about a while loop is that it's your responsibility to make the condition False to exit the loop.

The *for* Loop

Use a for loop to execute a sequence of statements a specific number of times. You don't have to increment the counter in a for loop, as you must in a while loop.

```
for Counter [from startVal] [to endVal] [step stepVal]
   Statements
endFor
```

The three values startVal, endVal, and stepVal are values or expressions that represent the beginning, ending, and increment values. for executes a sequence of statements as many times as the counter specifies. The specific number of times is stored in Counter, and it is controlled by the optional from, to, and step keywords. You can use any combination of these keywords to specify the number of times that the statements in the loop should be executed. You don't have to declare Counter explicitly, but a for loop runs faster if you do. If you previously didn't assign a value to Counter, from creates the variable and assigns the value of startVal to it.

You can use for without the from, to, and step keywords. If startVal is omitted, the counter starts at the current value of Counter. If endVal is omitted, the for loop executes indefinitely—not too practical! Finally, if stepVal is omitted, the counter increments by 1 each time through the loop, as in the following example:

```
;Button :: pushButton
for Counter from 1 to 3          ;Count from 1 to 3.
   Counter.view()                ;Execute these statements.
endFor                           ;End for block.
```

Using the *for* Loop

This section demonstrates two for loops: with and without step. The first for loop counts to 5 and the second for loop counts to 20 by .5.

http://prestwood.com/forums/paradox/books/official/files/LOOPS.FSL.

Step By Step

1. Create a new form and place two buttons on the form and name one **Simple for loop** and the other **For loop using step**.

2. Add lines 3–9 to the pushButton event of the Simple for loop button. Line 4 declares Counter as a SmallInt variable. You also could use Number, LongInt, or AnyType. In fact, you could choose not to declare Counter at all, but that would be poor programming. Lines 6–8 make up the for loop. Line 6 sets up the Counter variable to count from 1 to 5 at the default increment step of 1.

   Between for and endFor, you put all the commands that you want to loop through five times. In this case, a message information dialog box is displayed. Line 8 ends the for loop. Remember that, in a for loop, all the commands between for and endFor are executed once every time the loop is executed. Line 9 displays the final value for Counter, which is always one increment beyond the CountTo value.

```
1:    ;LOOPS :: Button1 :: pushButton
2:    method pushButton(var eventInfo Event)
3:       var
```

```
        Counter    SmallInt            ;Declare Counter.
     endVar
     for Counter from 1 to 5           ;Start of for loop.
        msgInfo("Counter", Counter) ;Commands to loop.
     endFor                            ;End of for loop.
     message("Note the final value for Counter is " +
     String(Counter))
  endMethod
```

3. Add lines 3–15 to the pushButton event of the For loop using step button. Line 4 declares Counter and CountTo variables of type Number. Because of containership and encapsulation, you can use the same name (Counter) in both buttons. Line 7 initializes CountTo to 20, and line 8 displays it so that the user can either accept it or change it. Line 10 sets up the Counter variable to count from 0 to the value stored in CountTo at the increment step of .5.

   Lines 10–13 make up the for loop. Line 11 displays the Counter in the status bar, and line 12 sleeps for a quarter second. Line 15 reminds you that the Counter value is always one increment beyond the value used in the last loop.

```
 1:  ;LOOPS :: Button2 :: pushButton
 2:  method pushButton(var eventInfo Event)
 3:     var
 4:        Counter, CountTo    Number
 5:     endVar
 6:
 7:     CountTo = 20
 8:     CountTo.view("Enter a number")
 9:
10:     for Counter from 0 to CountTo Step .5
11:       message(Counter)
12:       sleep(250)
13:     endFor
14:
15:     message("Note the final value for Counter after loop
                 is " + String(Counter))
16:  endMethod
```

4. Check the syntax, save the form, and run it. Click the Simple for loop and For loop using step buttons. Watch the status bar as they loop.

Using the *forEach* Loop

A forEach loop works similarly to a for loop. You use a forEach loop to move through the elements in a DynArray.

Using the *scan* Loop

You bought Paradox so that you could view, enter, and manipulate data. For the ObjectPAL programmer, the scan loop is very easy to use, and it's a powerful tool for manipulating the data in a table. In many ways, using a scan loop is similar to using a query in Interactive mode. In fact, there are occasions when using a scan loop is faster than doing a complicated query.

The scan loop is an extremely powerful tool that you can use to manipulate a whole table or, with the for keyword, a subset of a table. The scan loop scans a TCursor and executes ObjectPAL instructions. The syntax for a scan loop is as follows:

```
scan tcVar [for booleanExpression]:
     Statements
endScan
```

The colon at the end of the first line is required. It separates the first line from the following statements. scan starts with the first record in a TCursor and moves from record to record, executing Statements for every record. scan automatically moves from record to record through the table, so you don't need to call action(DataNextRecord) within your statements. When an indexed field is changed by a scan loop, the changed record moves to its sorted position in the table. Therefore, it's possible to encounter the same record more than once. As with all the loops discussed in this chapter, be sure to put statements that occur only once before the loop.

The for expression is used to filter the records. Only the records that match the expression are acted on. All other records are skipped. When you use the for keyword with scan, it must be followed by a colon to differentiate it from a for loop.

Using a *scan* Loop to Make a Field Proper

Suppose that you want to use a scan loop to change a field to a proper format. This example uses a scan loop and the format() command to change a field named Name in the CUSTOMER.DB table to a proper format. Before you make drastic changes to a table, you should always make a backup copy. This section acquaints you with the script, the scan loop, and format().

ON THE NET *http://prestwood.com/forums/paradox/books/official/files/PROPER.SSL.*

Step By Step

1. Make the Paradox's Samples directory your working directory. Open the CUSTOMER.DB file. Change some of the last names to all uppercase or all lowercase.

2. Choose File | New | Script and type in lines 3–16. Line 4 declares tc as a TCursor variable. Line 7 asks for permission to continue using a message question box. If the answer is Yes, then line 8 opens the TCursor and puts it in Edit mode in line 9. In this code, the scan loop uses only three lines: lines 10–12. Line 13 ends the edit session, and line 14 closes the TCursor. Line 15 tells the user that the program is done.

```
 1:     ;Script :: Run
 2:     method run(var eventInfo Event)
 3:        Var
 4:           tc     TCursor
 5:        endVar
 6:
 7:        if msgQuestion("Question?",
            "Make Name field proper?") = "Yes" then
 8:           tc.open("CUSTOMER.DB")
 9:           tc.edit()
10:           scan tc:
11:              tc."Name" = format("cl,cc", tc."Name")
12:           endScan
13:           tc.endedit()
14:           tc.close()
15:           msgInfo("","All done converting Name field")
16:        endIf
17:     endMethod
```

3. Check the syntax, save the script as **PROPER.SSL**, and run the script. After the script has finished executing, reopen CUSTOMER.DB. Now the Name field is in a proper format.

Using the Form's Prefilter

The final type of command used in ObjectPAL I am going to demonstrate in this chapter is not a command, but a programming technique. It is revisited in this chapter because it is so important, and this example is particularly handy. If you have typed in all the code so far from this chapter, then continue doing so by adding lines 3–6 and 9–20 to the form's mouseRightDown event.

```
1:    ;Commands :: form :: mouseRightDown
2:    method mouseRightDown(var eventInfo MouseEvent)
3:       var
4:          ui       UIObject
5:          sCode    String
6:       endVar
7:       if eventInfo.isPreFilter() then
8:          ;// This code executes for each object on the form.
9:          eventInfo.getTarget(ui)
10:         if ui.class = "Button" then
11:            sCode = ui.methodGet("pushButton")
12:            sCode.view()
13:         endIf
14:         if ui.container.class = "Button" then
15:            sCode = ui.container.methodGet("pushButton")
16:            sCode.view()
17:         endIf
18:      else
19:         ;// This code executes only for the form.
20:      endIf
21:   endMethod
```

After you add this code, you can right-click any button to display the code in the pushButton event of it.

Summary

This chapter introduced you to control structures. Control structures are broken down into two categories: branching and looping in ObjectPAL. ObjectPAL offers the immediate if (iif), the if statement, the switch block, and the try block for branching. For looping, ObjectPAL offers the while, for, forEach, and scan loops.

This chapter reviewed the various types of commands available to the ObjectPAL programmer including methods, procedures, and properties. Methods need an object to act upon, while procedures know which object to work on. Properties come in two flavors: read-only and read/write. This chapter also reviewed the action() and menuAction() methods, which allow you to use constants as commands. Finally, this chapter reviewed three important places to put code: the action event, the menuAction event, and the form's prefilter. A common use for the action and menuAction events is to trap for user actions. Finally, use the form's prefilter to write generic code.

In this chapter you also learned that ObjectPAL is not case sensitive (except in string compares) and is very flexible. For example, you learned that you can use the apostrophe to separate an object and a property. The apostrophe is particularly useful when using compound properties. A programming language's syntax is something you learn as you go along. The syntax is the structure of the language. With the guidelines presented in this chapter, you now have a foundation of knowledge about ObjectPAL syntax on which to build. Whenever you type a routine, you are practicing and learning syntax.

CHAPTER 8

The Application Type

The Application type (or object) allows you to manipulate the application environment (such as changing the title displayed in Paradox's application title bar). This short chapter introduces you to the display managers (the application is a display manager) and shows you how to use the Application type.

Display Managers

A *display manager* is a group of ObjectPAL data types that includes the application, the form, the report, TableView, and the script. Except for the script, these object types are used to display data. This chapter tells you how to turn database ideas and concepts into full-featured applications, complete with buttons, that enable you to keep control of the application environment. This chapter covers handling the desktop, moving from one page in a form to another page, moving from form to form, and using a TableView window. You also learn about techniques that you can use to develop a complete Windows application.

Paradox uses display managers to display data. Display managers are objects that contain design objects. Following are the five types of display managers:

- Application
- Form
- TableView
- Report
- Script

This chapter deals with the Application display manager.

The Application Display Manager

In general Paradox terms, the term "application" can refer to a group of files in a directory. In ObjectPAL, the Application object refers to the Paradox desktop. Specifically, an Application variable in ObjectPAL is an ObjectPAL data type that provides a handle to the Paradox desktop. You can use the Quick Lookup dialog box to see the methods and procedures you can use with the Application object. Figure 8-1 shows the Types and Methods tab from the ObjectPAL Quick Lookup dialog box, showing the Application type.

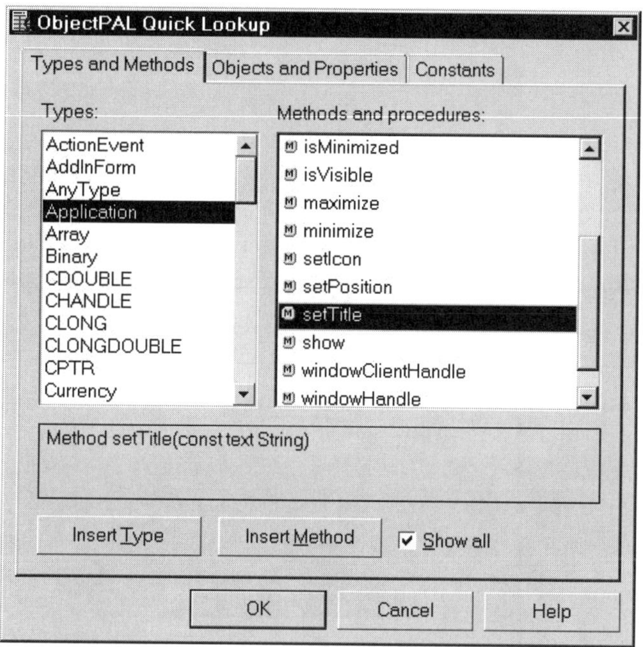

FIGURE 8-1 The Types and Methods tab from the ObjectPAL Quick Lookup dialog box

As you can see by Figure 8-1, Paradox enables you to manipulate the Application object. For example, you can open, close, minimize, maximize, and move them. The first step in manipulating a display manager is to define a variable as a display manager, as in the following example:

```
Var
    app     Application
    f       Form
    tv      TableView
    r       Report
    sc      Script
endVar
```

After you define a variable, you can manipulate it with any of the object methods that belong to that object type. To set the title of the application, for example, use the following (see Figure 8-2):

```
var
   app  Application
endVar

app.setTitle("My Custom Application")
```

After you define the Application variable app, you can manipulate the app variable with any of the application methods. To browse through the various application methods, from the ObjectPAL Editor, select View | ObjectPAL Quick Lookup and with the Types and Methods tab displayed, choose Application.

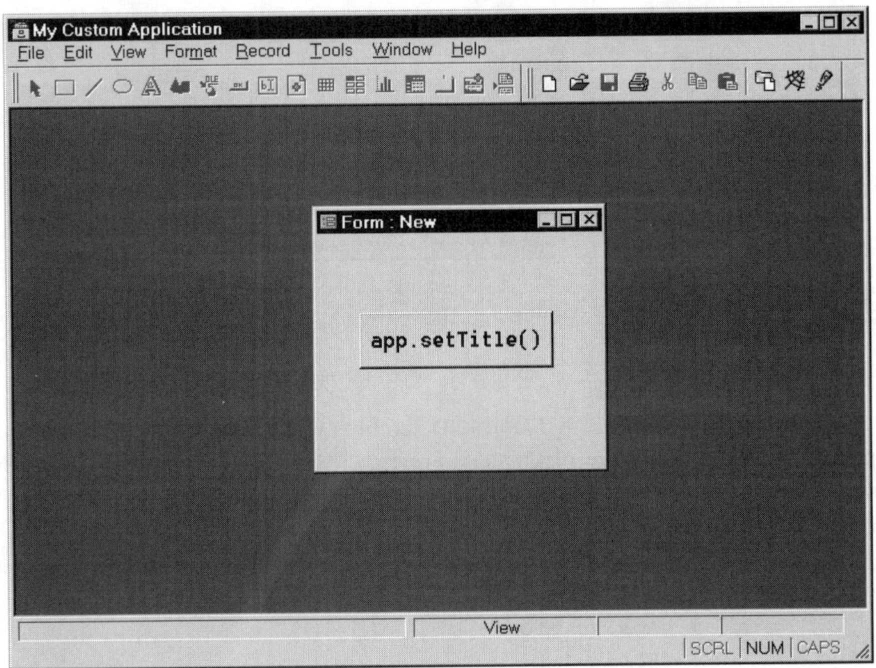

FIGURE 8-2 Setting the Application title

Using *hide(), show(), minimize(),* and *maximize()*

If you want to hide the desktop (for example, to hide the standard Paradox menu) and display a form, you must define the form as a dialog box. To do this, right-click on the form's title bar, select Window Style, and check the Dialog Box check box option in the Window Style panel. Figure 8-3 shows the Window Style dialog box.

If the form is not a dialog box, it is a child window. As with all Windows applications, when you hide the application, all the child windows are hidden too. Dialog boxes are not child windows, and therefore do not hide with the application.

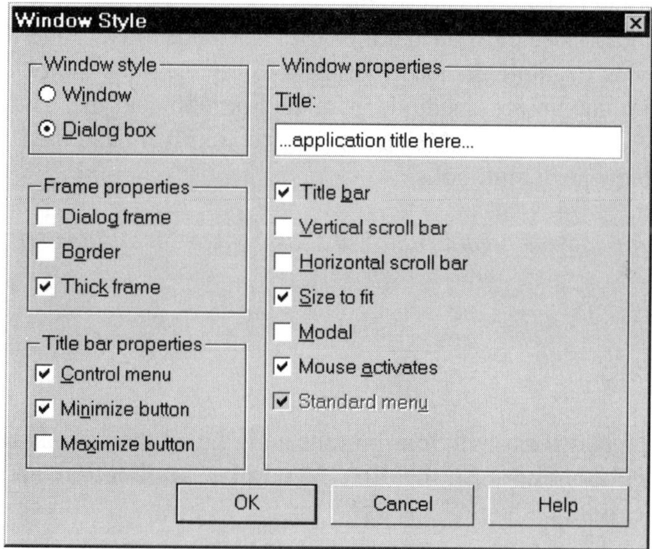

FIGURE 8-3 The Window Style dialog box

If you want to show a form and hide Paradox, then define a form as a dialog box. To define a variable of type Application, for example, use the following:

```
var
    app   Application
endVar
```

Now, you can hide or show the application in View Data mode, as in the following:

```
app.hide()
sleep(5000)
app.show(5000)
```

The form is a dialog box only when you open it in View Data mode. If you're in Design mode, running the form is not equivalent because the form is still a child window of Paradox. You must open it in View Data mode to view it as a dialog box.

The following example demonstrates how to use the hide(), show(), minimize(), and maximize() methods from the Form object type. These methods are important because they enable you to control your form and the Paradox desktop to achieve different looks.

http://prestwood.com/forums/paradox/books/official/files/HIDE.FSL.

Step By Step

1. Create a new form with four buttons on it. Label the buttons **Hide Application**, **Show Application**, **Maximize Application**, and **Minimize Application**. It should look like this:

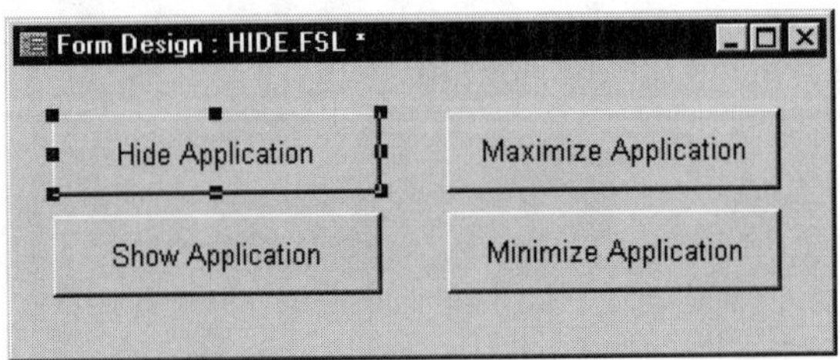

2. Select Format | Window Style, and choose Dialog Box from the Window style panel:

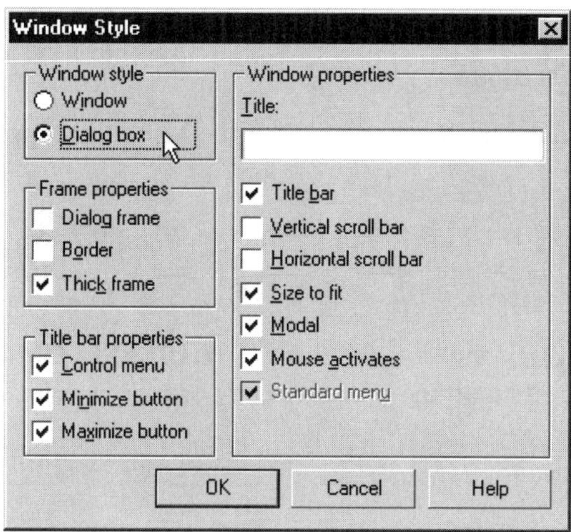

3. In the Var window of the form, add line 3. Line 3 declares the Application variable app. Because there is only one application—namely, the current application—you don't need to attach or open the Application variable. You can simply use it.

```
1:     ;Page2 :: Var
2:     Var
3:        app   Application
4:     endVar
```

4. Add line 3 to the pushButton event of the Hide Application button.

```
1:     ;Button :: pushButton
2:     method pushButton(var eventInfo Event)
3:        app.hide()
4:     endmethod
```

5. Add line 3 to the pushButton event of the Show Application button.

```
1:     ;Button :: pushButton
2:     method pushButton(var eventInfo Event)
3:        app.show()
4:     endmethod
```

6. Add line 3 to the pushButton event of the Maximize Application button.

```
1:    ;Button :: pushButton
2:    method pushButton(var eventInfo Event)
3:       app.maximize()
4:    endmethod
```

7. Add line 3 to the pushButton event of the Minimize Application button.

```
1:    ;Button :: pushButton
2:    method pushButton(var eventInfo Event)
3:       app.minimize()
4:    endmethod
```

8. Check the syntax and save the form as **HIDE.FSL**. Close the form and then open it. Click all the buttons in any order to see how they work.

Summary

This short chapter is important because it introduced the Application object, which gives you control over applications you create.

CHAPTER 9

Manipulating Forms

This chapter deals with the Form object, which is one of the display managers. This chapter covers moving from one page in a form to another page, moving from form to form, and sizing the form.

The Form Display Manager

Just as you can use the minimize(), maximize(), hide(), and show() methods with the Application object, you can also call these methods for the Form object. The only difference in syntax is that the form versions don't use the optional variable. You could use the name of the form or the built-in object variable self to refer to the form, but a variable is not needed with these methods. In addition, you could use attach() to attach a Form variable to the current form. To demonstrate this important technique, type the following into the pushButton event of a button:

```
;Button :: pushButton
method pushButton(var eventInfo Event)
   var
      f      Form          ;Declare f as a Form variable.
   endVar

   f.attach()              ;Attach f to the current form.
   view(f.getTitle())      ;Show title in a view box.
endMethod
```

The capability of controlling the application and the form during run time is an important part of Paradox. Use this form whenever you want to experiment with various combinations, such as minimizing and maximizing the form and the application. For example, you can hide the application and minimize the form.

Maximizing with *sysInfo()*

When designing a form, you need to consider screen size. You must decide whether your application is going to be full screen or smaller. If you choose full screen, you must decide for which resolution you're going to develop, such as 640 × 480, 800 × 600, 1,024 × 768, and so on. One solution is to check the user's screen size and to make a decision based on the answer. Use the sysInfo() procedure to get the current user's system information. The sysInfo() procedure supplies a great deal of information about your system. For example, type the following into the pushButton event of a button:

```
;Form :: Var
Var
   dynSys    DynArray[] AnyType  ;Variable for sysInfo()
endVar

sysInfo(dynSys)
dynSys.view()
```

After you get this information, you can extract the width of the monitor resolution and use it to decide what to do. The FullWidth index contains the horizontal working area in pixels in a maximized window. You can use this information to determine whether your form will fit on the screen. For example, if you develop a form for 800 × 600, you can use the following to let the user know:

```
;Form :: open
if dynSys["FullWidth"] < 800 then
   msgStop("Startup Error!", "Form requires 800 x 600 resolution")
   close()
endIf
```


This, unfortunately, eliminates standard VGA (640 × 480) users from using your form. A good solution to this problem is to develop all your forms with a 640 × 480 maximized resolution. In today's computer industry, most users have at least VGA. You can check whether the user is using VGA, then maximize if he or she is. If the user's resolution is higher than that, the default Size to fit setting centers the form on his or her screen (remember to check the Size to fit property of the form). This enables users of higher-resolution monitors to get the benefit of their larger screens and still use all the screen real estate of a VGA setup.

Maximizing If the Resolution Is VGA

Suppose that you want to develop a form for use on a VGA or higher-resolution monitor. If the form is open on a VGA system, then maximize the form. If the form is open on a higher-resolution system, let the default behavior take over centering the form on the desktop. This next example uses sysInfo() from the System class of methods and procedures and maximize() from the Form object type of methods and procedures.

http://prestwood.com/forums/paradox/books/official/files/VGA.FSL.

Step By Step

1. Create a form for which the size of the page is VGA, 6.67 inches by 4.11 inches. Make sure that the Size to fit option is checked for the form.

2. In the Var window of the form, type line 3. Line 3 declares dynSys as a DynArray variable that is ready to accept any type of data. In this case, you could declare dynSys private to the open event; but the data retrieved with sysInfo() is so useful, I like to make it global to the form for use throughout the form.

```
1:    ;Form :: Var
2:    Var
3:       dynSys    DynArray[] AnyType ;Variable for sysInfo()
4:    endVar
```

3. In the open event of the form, enter lines 3–6. Line 3 uses sysInfo() to grab system information and put it into the DynArray dynSys. Line 4 checks whether the FullWidth index in dynSys equals 640. If it does, line 5 maximizes the form.

```
1:    ;Form :: Init
2:    method init(var eventInfo Event)
3:       sysInfo(dynSys)
4:       if dynSys["FullWidth"] = 640 then
5:          maximize()
6:       endIf
7:   endMethod
```

4. Check the syntax, save the form as **VGA.FSL**, and run it. If you're using a VGA monitor, the form will maximize (see Figure 9-1). If you have another resolution, the form won't maximize (see Figure 9-2). The form is nicely fitted and centered on any screen larger than 640 × 480.

Another technique that is not too popular is to design a form for each resolution and to use a script to decide which version to load. You also can create a dynamic form that resizes itself depending on the resolution. This final technique

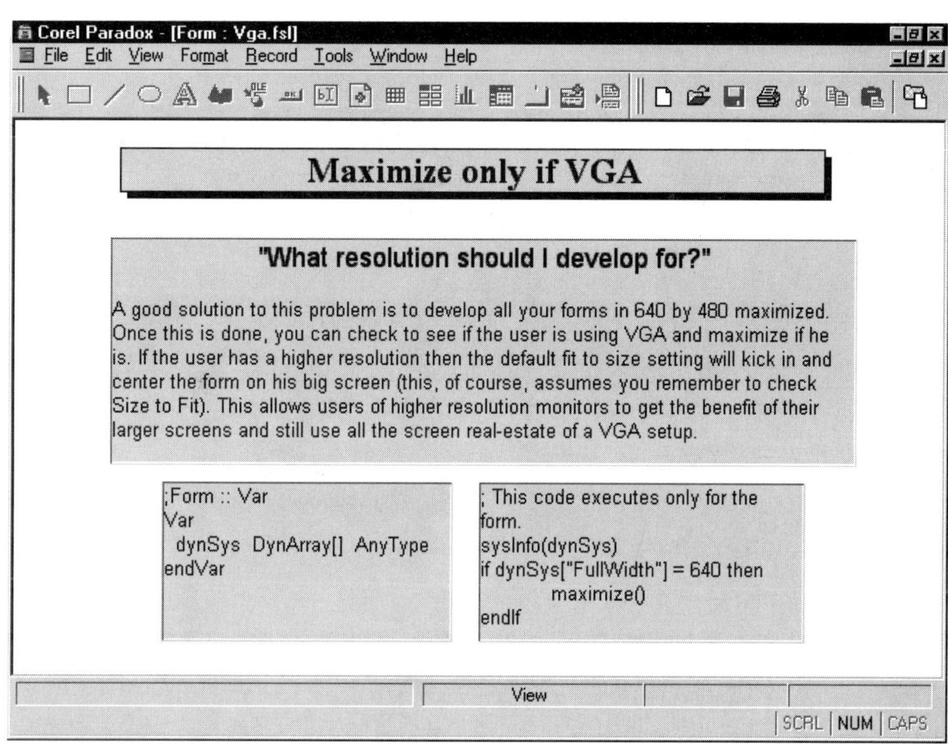

FIGURE 9-1 VGA.FSL on a VGA system uses the full screen

is my preferred way of handling screen resolution. See the following section, "Dynamic Forms."

Dynamic Forms

Suppose that you need to create a form that dynamically resizes the objects within the form when the user resizes the form. The following example demonstrates how to create a form where all the objects dynamically resize themselves when the user resizes the form. This example is particularly useful when developing an application for use with multiple screen resolutions.

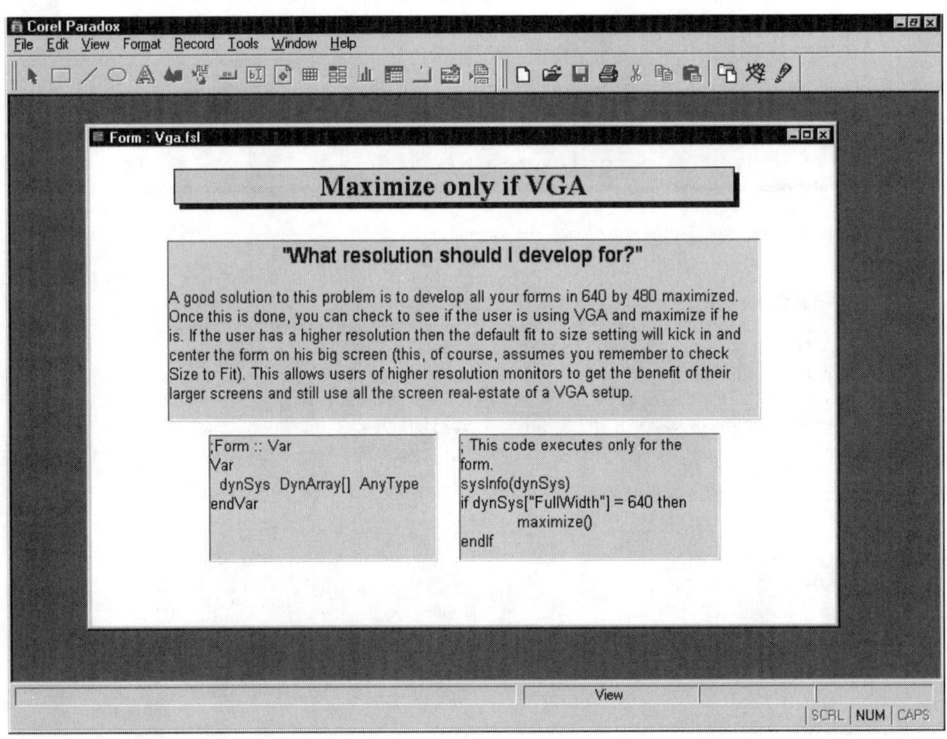

FIGURE 9-2 VGA.FSL on an 800 × 600 system

http://prestwood.com/forums/paradox/books/official/files/DYNAFORM.FSL.

Step By Step

1. Change your working directory to Paradox's Samples directory and create a new form.

2. In the setFocus event of the form, type lines 9 and 10. Line 9 executes a doDefault, which finishes bringing focus to the form. In line 10, the form is set to best fit. This is equivalent to the user selecting View | Zoom | Best Fit.

```
1:     ;Form :: setFocus
2:     method setFocus(var eventInfo Event)
```

```

      if eventInfo.isPreFilter() then
      ;// This code executes for each object on the form:

      else
      ;// This code executes only for the form:
         doDefault
         menuAction(MenuPropertiesZoomBestFit) ;Set zoom
                                               ;to best
                                               ;fit.
       endIf
    endMethod
```

3. In the menuAction event of the form, type lines 7–10. In step 3, the menuAction event of the form is used to trap for a menu event. In this case, you are trapping for MenuControlSize in line 7. This means that the user is resizing the form. Line 8 executes a doDefault so that the form will finish resizing and size the page because best fit is set. Finally, the form property sizeToFit is set to True in line 9 so that the form will match the aspect ratio of the newly resized page.


```
 1:  ;Form :: menuAction
 2:  method menuAction(var eventInfo MenuEvent)
 3:     if eventInfo.isPreFilter() then
 4:        ;// This code executes for each object on the form:
 5:     else
 6:       ;// This code executes only for the form:
 7:       if eventInfo.id() = MenuControlSize   then ;If user
          ;resizes the form,
 8:          doDefault                       ;make the form resize too.
 9:          self.sizeToFit = True
10:       endIf
11:     endIf
12:  endMethod
```

4. In the close event of the form, type lines 8–10.

```
 1:   ;Form :: close
 2:   method close(var eventInfo Event)
 3:      if eventInfo.isPreFilter() then
 4:         ;// This code executes for each object on the form:
 5:
 6:      else
 7:         ;// This code executes only for the form:
 8:         if not isMaximized() then show() endIf ;If _maximized,
            ;show.
 9:         menuAction(MenuPropertiesZoom100)    ;Set zoom to _100%.
```

```
            self.sizeToFit = True        ;Size the form to the page.
        endIf
    endMethod
```

5. Check the syntax, place a few objects on the form, save the form as **DYNAFORM.FSL**, and run it. Resize the form and notice how the page resizes itself to fit the form (see Figure 9-3).

Pages and Forms

Your data model dictates whether you should use a new page or a new form. If the page that you want to add uses a table in the current data model, first consider

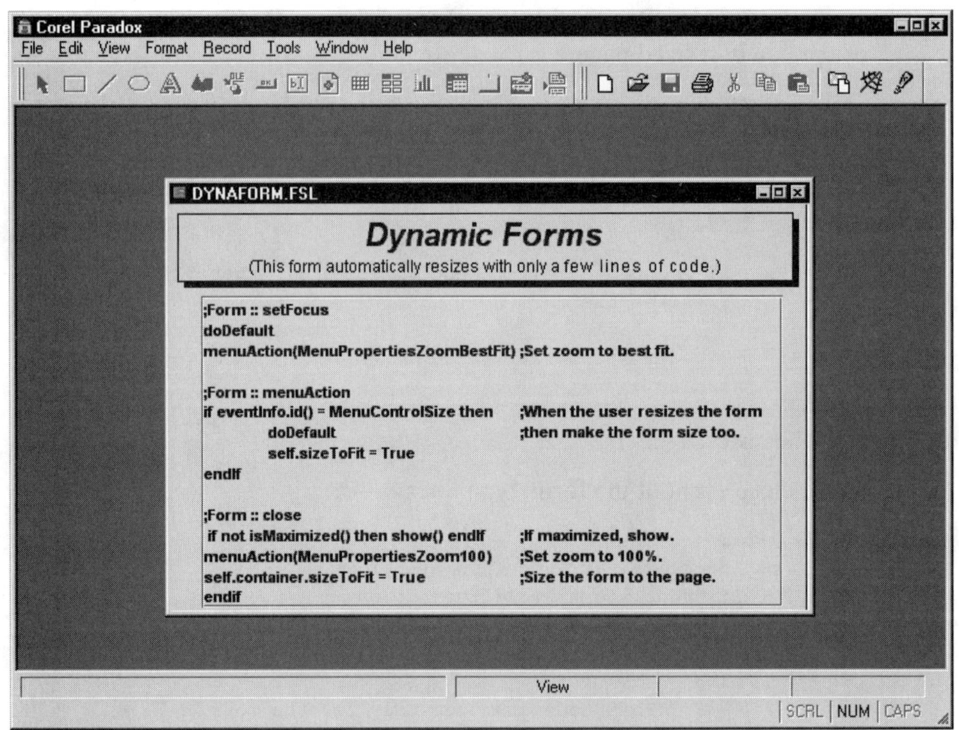

FIGURE 9-3 Completed example of a form that dynamically resizes

adding a page. If a new page won't work because of size or some other reason, add a new form.

If you add another form to your application, you need to know how to move from form to form and how to pass information between forms. These two issues are discussed later in this chapter. There are two techniques to move from page to page. The first technique uses moveTo() and the second technique uses moveToPage(). To use moveTo(), first rename the page. Then, use pageName.moveTo().

Moving from Page to Page

Suppose that you want to move back and forth from the first page in a form to the second by using buttons. This example acquaints you with moveTo().

http://prestwood.com/forums/paradox/books/official/files/PAGES.FSL.

Step By Step

1. Create a form with two pages on it. Name the first page **pge1** and the second page **pge2**. On pge1, create a button labeled **Page Two**. On pge2, create a button labeled **Page One**. Make sure that the pages are stacked and not tiled horizontally or vertically.

2. Add line 3 to the pushButton event of the Page Two button on pge1.

```
1:    ;Button :: pushButton
2:    method pushButton(var eventInfo Event)
3:       pge2.moveTo()
4:    endMethod
```

3. Add line 3 to the pushButton event of the Page One button on pge2.

```
1:    ;Button :: pushButton
2:    method pushButton(var eventInfo Event)
3:       pge1.moveTo()
4:    endMethod
```

4. Check the syntax, save the form as **PAGES.FSL**, and run it. Click the Page Two button to move to the second page. When you're on the second page, click on the Page One button to return to the first page.

In step 2, line 3 moves to the page named pge2, and line 3 of step 3 moves to the page named pge1. An alternative technique is to use the order of the pages instead of a page's UIObject name, as in the following:

```
moveToPage(2)
```

Using the *positionalOrder* Property

The page has a positionalOrder property you can use to know which page a user is on. Use this read/write property if you need to know which page the user is currently on or to set the position of a page. The following line of code, for example, moves a page named pgeConfig to the top of the positional order:

```
pgeConfig.positionalOrder = 1
```

Moving from Form to Form

To open a new form, you need to do two things: define a variable as a form and use the open() method, as in the following:

```
var
   f     Form
endVar

f.open(":ALIAS:FILENAME")
```

If you specify an alias, Paradox looks in only the alias directory for the file. If you don't specify an alias, Paradox looks in the working directory. Paradox doesn't search for a form that you want to open. If you specify the following, for example,

```
f.open("ORDERS.FDL")
```

Paradox looks in only the working directory for a delivered form. If you specify

```
f.open("C:\DATA\ORDERS.FDL")
```

Paradox looks in only the Data directory on drive C (it does not look in the working directory). If you specify

```
f.open(":DATA:ORDERS.FDL")
```

Paradox looks in only the directory specified in the Data alias.

Paradox looks first for the nondelivered version of a form, such as FILENAME.FSL, and then looks for its delivered version, such as FILENAME.FDL. The following searches first for ORDERS.FSL and then for ORDERS.FDL in the current working directory only:

```
f.open("ORDERS")
```

If you want to search only for a specific name, use an extension, as in the following:

```
f.open("ORDERS.FDL")
```

If you want to reverse the search order, use the following:


```
if not f.open("ORDERS.FDL") then
   f.open("ORDERS.FSL")
endIf
```

To move to a form that is already open, you must do three things:

1. Define a variable as a Form variable (if you haven't done so already).
2. Use the attach() method to attach to the form.
3. Use the moveTo() or bringToTop() method to go to the form.

Following is an example:

```
var
   f     Form
endVar

f.attach("Form : ORDERS.FSL")
f.moveTo()
```

First, check whether the form is open. If it is, attach and move to it. If the form isn't open, you can combine the preceding methods with an if method, as in the following:

```
var
   f    Form
endVar

if f.attach("Form : ORDER.FSL") then
   f.moveTo()
else
   f.open("ORDER")
endIf
```

The only other problem is the title of the form. You had to specify Form : ORDER.FSL. When you're ready to deliver your forms, you must rewrite all your code to reflect the new name. In other words, you must specify Form : ORDER.FDL, which is an unsuitable situation.

You can rename the form with the setTitle() method and use this name with the attach() method. For example, on the built-in open() method of the form, first set the title with the following:

```
;Form2 :: open
setTitle("Order Entry")
```

Then, you can open either the delivered (.FDL) or nondelivered (.FSL) forms without modifying your code at delivery time if you use the following:

```
;Form1.Button :: pushButton
if f.attach("Order Entry") then
   f.moveTo()
else
   f.open("ORDER")
endIf
```

To save yourself a line of code and some time, get into the habit of explicitly naming a form every time you create a new one. If you don't need to change the title of a form during run time, name the form. Doing so makes it easier to attach, and the form has a more professional appearance. Rather than Form : MYFORM.FSL, you can place a more meaningful title. You might, for example, use Order Entry System. With this title, the program tries to attach to a form called

Order Entry System and moves to it if attach() is successful. If attach() fails, the program attempts to open ORDER.FSL or ORDER.FDL. This is important—it's the best way to open another form. (The last example in this section adds a twist to this. It uses the if keyword to check whether the final open() method worked.)

Opening Another Form

Suppose that you want to open a second form or to move to that second form, depending on whether the second form is already open. The following steps demonstrate what I believe is the best way to open another form.

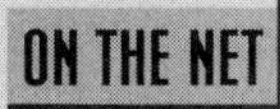

http://prestwood.com/forums/paradox/books/official/files/FORM1.FSL.

Step By Step

1. Create two forms. In the Window Style dialog box, shown here, set the form title of one form to **Form One**, and save it as **FORM1.FSL**. Name the other form **Form Two**, save it as **FORM2.FSL**, and close it. On Form One, put a button labeled **Other form** on it.

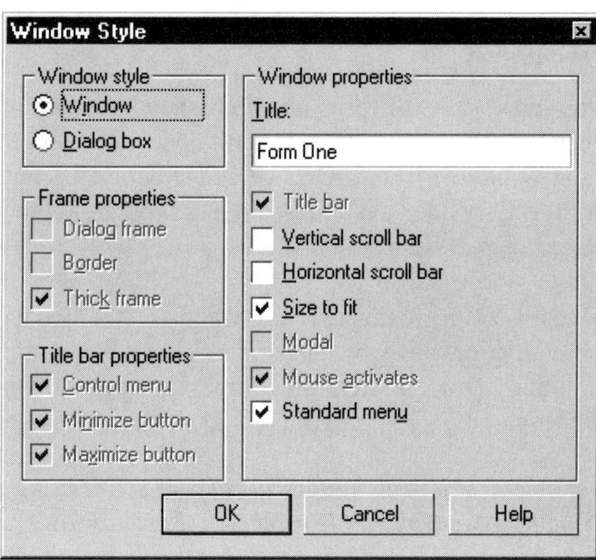

2. In the pushButton event of the Other form button on Form One, add lines 3–13. Line 4 declares f as a Form variable. Line 7 uses attach() to try and attach f to Form Two. If attach() is successful, line 8 moves control to the newly attached form. If attach() fails, the execution moves to line 10, where another if structure executes. Line 10 of the new if structure opens the FORM2 file on disk. If line 10 fails to open the form, line 11 displays the error stack with errorShow(). Line 10 uses only the name of the form; no extension is used. This enables ObjectPAL to try to open FORM2.FSL first. If FORM2.FSL doesn't exist, ObjectPAL automatically tries to open FORM2.FDL. No extra code is required.

```
 1:    ;Button :: pushButton
 2:    method pushButton(var eventInfo Event)
 3:       var
 4:          f    Form
 5:       endVar
 6:
 7:       if f.attach("Form Two") then
 8:          f.moveTo()
 9:       else
10:          if not f.open("FORM2") then
11:             errorShow("Form open error")
12:          endIf
13:       endIf
14:    endMethod
```

3. Check the syntax, save the form, and run it. Click the button labeled Other form. When the other form opens, leave it open and select the first form by selecting Window | 1 Form One. Click the button a second time. The second form isn't opened again. Instead, it's brought to the front very quickly (see Figure 9-4).

Using an if statement is a great way to test whether a method has been successful. Use if with errorShow() whenever you can. It helps safeguard your applications, and it makes them more professional. Using if with an errorShow() is another way of developing good programming skills.

TIP

Whenever you open a form, report, library, or script using the open() method and do not specify a file extension, Paradox always looks first for the nondelivered .?SL file and then for the delivered .?DL file. For example, with the following line of code, Paradox first tries to open FILENAME.FSL and then FILENAME.FDL:

```
f.open("FILENAME.")
```

Using *WinStyleDefault*

If you use WinStyleHidden, or any of the constants in the WindowStyles category, make sure that you also use WinStyleDefault. For example, do not do the following:

```
var
   f      Form
endVar

f.open("MYFORM", WinStyleHidden)       ;This is wrong.
sleep(1000)
f.show()
```


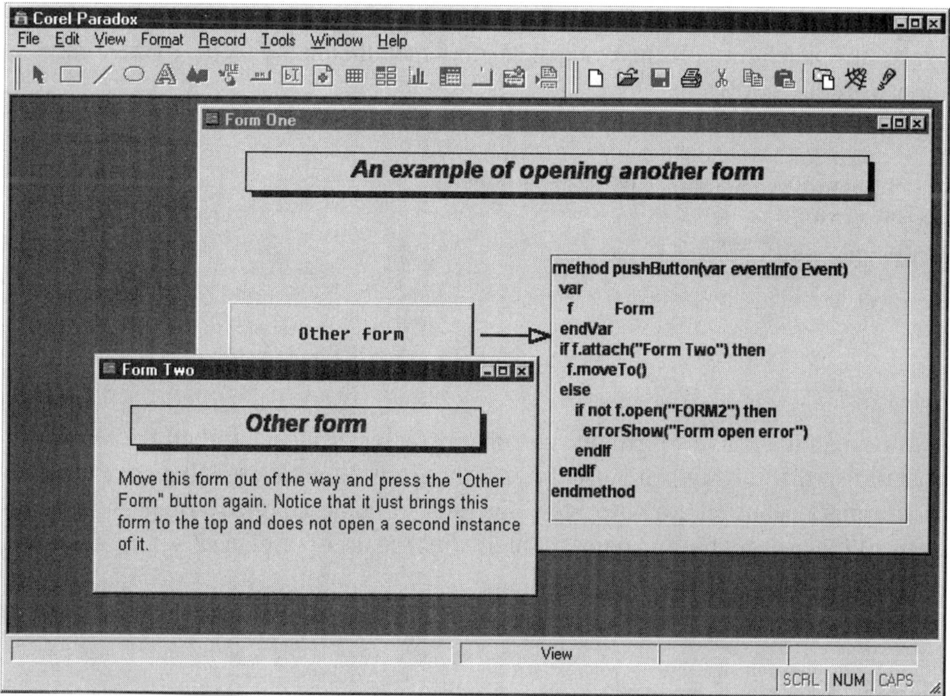

FIGURE 9-4 Opening another form

Instead, do the following:

```
var
   f      Form
endVar

f.open("MYFORM", WinStyleDefault + WinStyleHidden) ;Correct.
sleep(1000)
f.show()
```

To see why, try the preceding with a dialog box-style form or with a form with scroll bars. You'll notice that when you do not use WinStyleHidden, the screen refresh routines are messed up. This rule also applies to reports.

Using *openAsDialog()*

Here is an example of using openAsDialog() with the WindowStyles. Create a form and in the Window Style panel, choose the Dialog Box. In the Title Bar Properties panel, turn off the Control Menu. Open the dialog form from another form with the following:

```
;Button :: pushButton
method pushButton(var eventInfo Event)
   var
      f   Form
   endVar

   f.openAsDialog("MYFORM", WinStyleDefault + WinStyleModal +
   ;WinStyleControlMenu)
endMethod
```

A dynamic form is a form that automatically resizes itself and all the objects it contains so that it fits when a user resizes the form. When a user changes the size of a form, the constant MenuControlSize goes through the form's menuAction event. You can trap for this constant and, after the user is finished, set the form's sizeToFit property to True.

Getting User Input

With ObjectPAL, you have several ways to get input from a user. You could simply place an undefined field on the form for the user to type in to. This passive way of getting user input works for many situations. Another, more decisive technique is to use a view dialog box. You already have used view() several times. Following is one more example for you to type in to the pushButton event of a button:

```
method pushButton(var eventInfo Event)
   var
      sName     String
   endVar

   sName = "Enter your name"
   sName.view("Full name")
   if sName = "Enter your name" then
      ;Either user did not change text or clicked Cancel.
     return
   endIf
   message("Your name is " + sName)
endMethod
```


You also could use some of the simple built-in dialog boxes with msgQuestion(), msgYesNoCancel(), and so on, as in the following example:

```
if msgQuestion("Question", "Do you want to proceed?") = "No" then
   return
endIf
```

Using *formReturn()*

To get more complex data input from a user, you must use another form for input. After the user types a value into an undefined field on the other form, you need to return the value from the second form to the first. You can use formReturn() to return a value from one form to another.

Using formReturn() actually requires several steps. Suppose that you want to return a value from a form form2 to form1. First, you open form2 and wait for it from form1, as in the following example:

```
var
   f     Form
   s     String
endVar

```

```
f.open("FORM2")
s = String(f.wait())
```

Note that the variable s is set up to wait for a value from form2. On form2, use formReturn() to return a value to s, as in the following example:

```
formReturn("Hello first form")
```

After the form2 returns a value to form1, close form2 with close(), as in the following example:

```
f.close()
```

Following is the code for both forms:

```
;btnCallForm :: pushButton
method pushButton(var eventInfo Event)
   var
      f      Form
      s      String
   endVar

   f.open("FORM2")
   s = f.wait()
   f.close()
   s.view()
endMethod

;btnCalledForm :: pushButton
method pushButton(var eventInfo Event)
   formReturn("Hello first form")
endMethod
```

Note that the form is closed immediately after using wait(). Following are a couple of rules to keep in mind when using formReturn():

- If formReturn() has a wait() waiting on it, formReturn() returns a value but does not close the current form.
- If formReturn() does not have a wait() waiting, formReturn() closes the form.

As long as you keep the preceding rules in mind, formReturn() is easy to use.

Using *formReturn()* with Dot Notation

Suppose that you need to return more than one value from a called form. This example demonstrates how to use formReturn() in conjunction with dot notation to return three values from the called form to the calling form. In addition, it demonstrates that text objects have a value property that you can read (and set) from another form. In this case, the calling form reads two text boxes on the called form. Finally, it demonstrates that you do not have to close the called form immediately after using wait().

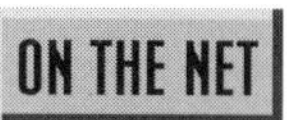

http://prestwood.com/forums/paradox/books/official/files/FORMRET1.FSL and FORMRET2.FSL.

Step By Step

1. Create two forms. On the first form, place a button labeled **Call Other Form** and save it as **FORMRET1.FSL**:

2. Place two button objects on the second form, and two text objects. Label the two buttons as **OK** and **Cancel**. Name the two text boxes **txt1** and **txt2**. Set the value of txt1 to **Hello** and set the value of txt2 to **World**, as shown here. Save this second form as **FORMRET2.FSL**.

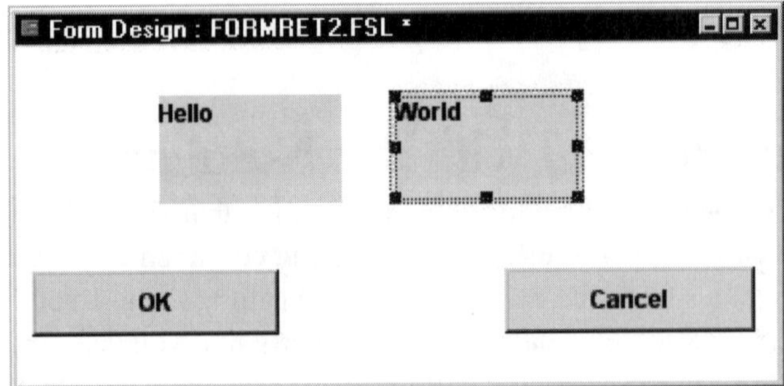

3. Make FORMRET2.FSL a modal dialog box. This forces the user to click one of the two buttons:

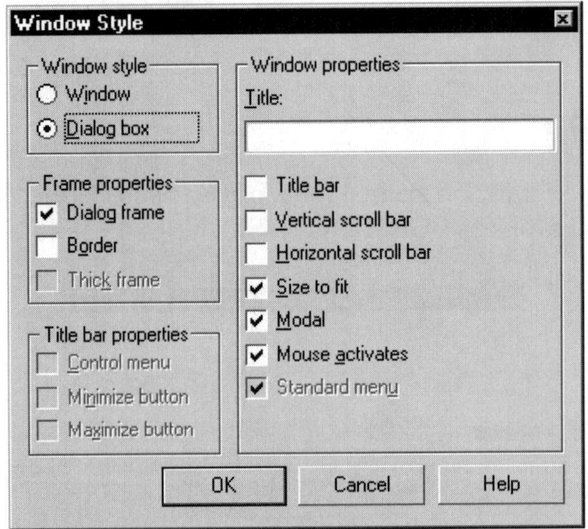

4. On the first form (FORMRET1.FSL), add lines 3–14 to the pushButton event of the button labeled Call Other Form. Lines 4 and 5 declare fFormRet2 as a Form variable and sReturnedValue, sTxt1, and sTxt2 as String variables. Line 7 uses the fFormRet2 variable with open() to open the second form. Line 8 waits for the second form to return a value (pay special attention to the syntax used in this line). After formReturn() returns a value and control back to the calling form, the wait() in line 8 returns a value to the String variable sReturnedValue. Lines 9 and 10 grab two values from two text objects on the second form. Finally, line 11 closes the second form only after you have grabbed two values from two of its text objects. Lines 12, 13, and 14 view the three values in view boxes.

```
;FORMRET1 :: btnCallForm :: pushButton
method pushButton(var eventInfo Event)
  var
     fFormRet2    Form
     sReturnedValue, sTxt1, sTxt2    String
  endVar

  fFormRet2.open("FORMRET2")         ;Open 2nd form.
  sReturnedValue = String(fFormRet2.wait())    ;Wait on 2nd form.
  sTxt1 = fFormRet2.txt1.value     ;Grab a value from txt1 object.
  sTxt2 = fFormRet2.txt2.value     ;Grab a value from txt2 object.
  fFormRet2.close()                ;Close 2nd form.

  sReturnedValue.view()     ;View returned value.
  sTxt1.view()              ;View txt1 value.
  sTxt2.view()              ;View txt2 value.
endMethod
```

5. On the second form (FORMRET2.FSL), add line 3 to the pushButton event of the button labeled OK. Line 3 in both uses formReturn() to return a value and control back to the calling form. It is interesting to note that, at this point, you could use formCaller() to find out which form is the calling form. formCaller() assigns the calling form to a Form variable.


```
1:  ;BtnOK :: pushbutton
2:  method pushButton(var eventInfo Event)
3:     formReturn("OK")
4:  endMethod
```

6. On the second form (FORMRET2.FSL), add line 3 to the pushButton event of the button labeled Cancel.

```
1:  ;BtnOK :: pushbutton
2:  method pushButton(var eventInfo Event)
3:     formReturn("Cancel")
4:  endMethod
```

7. On the second form (FORMRET2.FSL), add lines 7–10 to the form-level menuAction event.

```
1:  ;Form :: menuAction
2:  method menuAction(var eventInfo MenuEvent)
3:     if eventInfo.isPreFilter() then
4:        ;// This code executes for each object on the form
5:     else
6:        ;// This code executes only for the form
7:        if eventInfo.id() = MenuControlClose then
```

```
 8:            disableDefault
 9:            formReturn("Cancel")
10:         endIf
11:      endIf
12:   endMethod
```

8. Check the syntax, save both forms, and close the second form (FORMRET2.FSL). Run FORMRET1.FSL and click the button. On the second form, click either the OK or Cancel button:

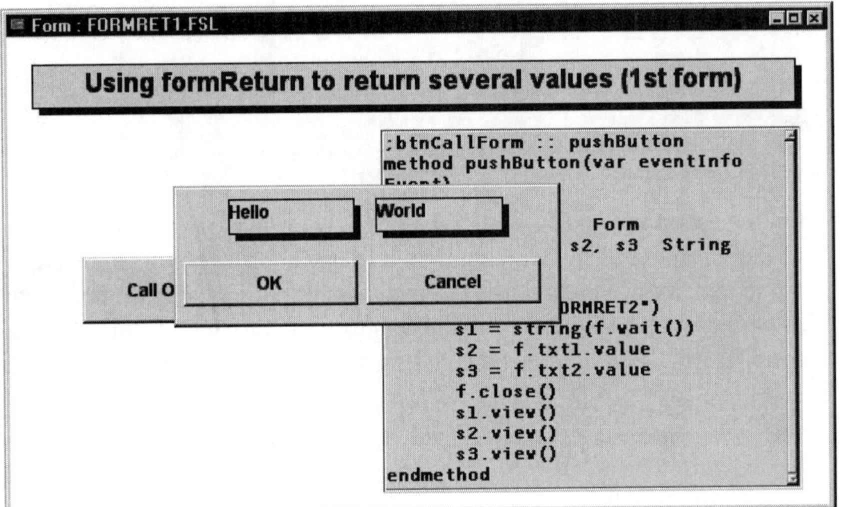

Passing Values with *close()*

If you do not need to keep the second form open, then do not use formReturn(). Instead, just use close() in its place. To see this in action, follow these steps:

1. In step 4, delete lines 10, 11, 12, 14, and 15.
2. In steps 5 and 6, change formReturn() to close(). For example, change formReturn("OK") to close("OK").

If you do not need to keep the second form open, this technique of using close() is the preferred technique. formReturn() is used too much.

Passing Values Between Forms

Often, you need to pass values from one form to another. As with many things in ObjectPAL, you have several ways of approaching this task. You can't pass a variable directly from one form to another; you must use a custom method or procedure that changes or sets a variable. You can, however, change the value of a field directly.

Passing Values Directly to a UIObject

With ObjectPAL, you can pass values directly from one object to another. Because a form is an object, you also can pass values directly from one form to another. You can use statements, such as the following:

```
fieldlName.value = field2Name.value
```

Likewise, you can declare a Form variable, attach it to another form, and use dot notation to transfer values. For example, to put the value in field1 on form1 into field2 on form2, use the following:


```
var
   f     Form
endVar

f.attach("Form : Form2.fsl")  ;Form titles can be tricky
field1.value = f.field2.value
```

This technique works well if both forms currently are open and the names of the form titles don't change. You use this technique to manipulate the value property of objects. After you've attached form2 to a variable, you can expand this technique to manipulate, call, and use any of the properties of the other form's objects:

```
f.box3.color = Red
f.line4.visible = False
f.maximize()
f.hide()
f.button3.pushButton()
f.ID_No.locate("ID No", ID_No)
```

The following is an example of opening a form and setting a field's value:

```
;Button :: pushButton
var
   f     Form
endVar

f.open("MYFORM2")
f.fldName = "Joe Santoro"
```

This example illustrates that a form is just another object, which can be manipulated like UIObjects. As soon as you have a handle to the other form, you can manipulate it.

Passing Variables with a Table

You can write values to a table from the first form and read in the values from the other form. You use a TCursor to write to and read from a table in either the working or the private directory. You even can include a mechanism for cleaning up, or deleting, the tables when you exit the application—perhaps on the canDepart event of the form.

This technique works well for passing large amounts of data, nontextual data, or data you want to hang around for the next time you enter your application. To pass a sound file or a picture from one form to another, for example, use this method.

Passing Variables Through a Library

You can use a library to store and pass values. Because external objects have access only to the custom methods of a library, you must use at least two custom methods. One custom method puts the value into the library's variables; the other custom method gets the value. This technique works well if you already are using a library with your application.

This technique is valuable if you're going to close and open forms. You could write one custom method that sets a variable in the library and another that checks it. As soon as you have the two custom methods in the library, you can call them from various forms.

Keeping Two Forms in Sync

With a relational database manager system such as Paradox, you often gather data into compartments. Usually, you display the data on a form in a 1:1 relationship. Occasionally, however, you need to display the data on separate forms. Having independent forms is a convenient way of displaying parts of a complete database a little at a time.

For example, in an address book application, you might separate personal information from business information. One table is connected to a form that shows personal information, such as home address, home telephone number, and so on. The other table is connected to a form that shows business information, such as title, work address, work telephone number, and so on. You might make the business form the main, or master, form and include on it a button that displays the person's home information.

When both forms are displayed, you need to keep them in sync. A form is a display manager, and display managers in Paradox are objects, just as a field is an object. Therefore, you can manipulate objects on another form. In this address book example, you can use a button to open a second form and position it on the same record or on the corresponding record. You can use two techniques to accomplish this.

You use the first technique if both forms use the same table or if they use different tables that are related. The following code represents an elegant and clean way to keep two forms in sync:

```
;button :: pushButton
var
   f2    Form
endVar

f2.open("homeinfo", WinStyleDefault + WinStyleHidden)
f2.Last_Name.locate("Last Name", Last_Name1, "First Name",
;First_Name1)
f2.bringToTop()
```

Last_Name1 and First_Name1 are two fields on the master business form.

The second technique assumes that you're using the same table in both forms. Its code is as follows:

```
var
   tc      TCursor
   f       Form
endVar

tc.attach( fldInCurrentForm )
f.open("form2", WinStyleDefault + WinStyleHidden)
f.fldInform2.reSync(tc)
f.bringToTop()
```

Keeping Two Forms in Sync

Suppose you have two forms that are connected to the same table, or two similar tables, and you need to keep them in sync. This technique can be useful when displaying two forms both of which show customer information. The following example uses dot notation and locate() to keep the forms in sync.

http://prestwood.com/forums/paradox/books/official/files/SYNC1.FSL.

Step By Step

1. Change your working directory to Paradox's Samples directory and create a new form with the CUSTOMER table in the data model. Add a button to the form and label it **View Notes**, as shown here. Save the form as **SYNC1.FSL**.

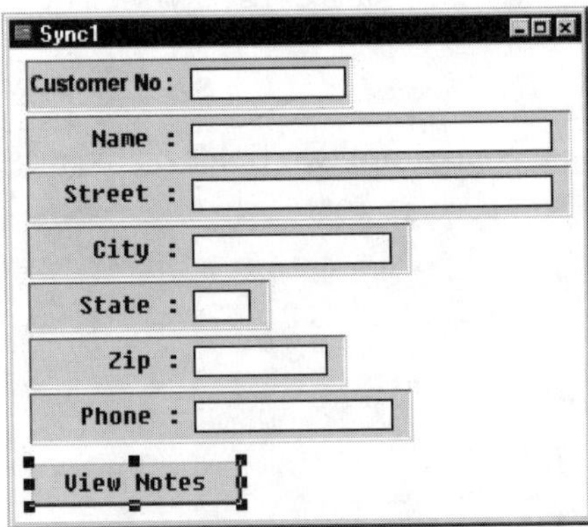

2. Create a table called Custnote with the following structure:

Field Name	Field Type	Key
Customer No	N	Y
Notes	F	
Picture	G	

3. Create a second form with the Custnote table in the data model. Add a button to the form and label it **Close**, as shown here. In the Window Style dialog box, change the title bar name to **SYNC2** and save the form as **SYNC2.FSL**.

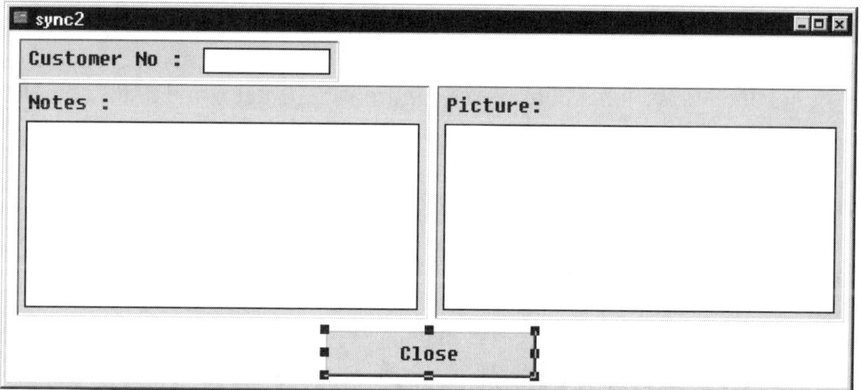

4. In the pushButton event of the View Notes button on SYNC1.FSL, enter lines 3–17. Line 4 declares f as a form variable for use in lines 7 or 8 to either attach to or open SYNC2.FSL. After a handle is opened, lines 11, 12, 13, and 14 use it to set what record the other form is on, and then line 17 shows the form.

```
1:    ;Button :: pushButton
2:    method pushButton(var eventInfo Event)
3:       var
4:           f    Form
5:       endVar
6:
7:       if not f.attach("Sync2") then
8:           f.open("SYNC2", WinStyleDefault + WinStyleHidden)
9:       endIf
10:
11:      if not f.Customer_No.locate("Customer No", Customer_No) then
```

```
            f.Customer_No.edit()
            f.Customer_No.insertRecord()
            f.Customer_No = Customer_No.value
        endIf

        f.bringToTop()
    endMethod
```

5. In the pushButton event of the Close button on SYNC2.FSL, type line 3. Line 3 closes the form and returns control back to the calling form. Also note that Edit mode is automatically ended and any unposted changes to the table are posted.

```
1:  ;Button :: pushButton
2:  method pushButton(var eventInfo Event)
3:     close()
4:  endMethod
```

6. Check the syntax, save the forms, and run it. Move to any record and then click the View Notes button (see Figure 9-5). Enter some notes and click the Close button.

The highest container level in an ObjectPAL application is the form. Often, you need to pass data from form to form. You can use any of the techniques outlined in this section to exchange data between forms or to sync forms.

Using *setWorkingDir()* and *setPrivDir()*

Two important procedures are setWorkingDir() and setPrivDir(). These two procedures are fairly straightforward except that the default behavior, when changing either your working or private directory, is to close all the open windows (forms, reports, etc.). To stop this, you can trap for either MenuChangingWork or MenuChangingPriv in the menuAction event. The following code, for example, traps for ObjectPAL changing the working directory, and stops it from closing the form to which this code is attached.

```
if eventInfo.id() = MenuChangingWork then
   eventInfo.setErrorCode(1)
endIf
```

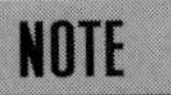

You can disable the warning prompts that are displayed when you change working or private directories. To do this, first display the Preferences

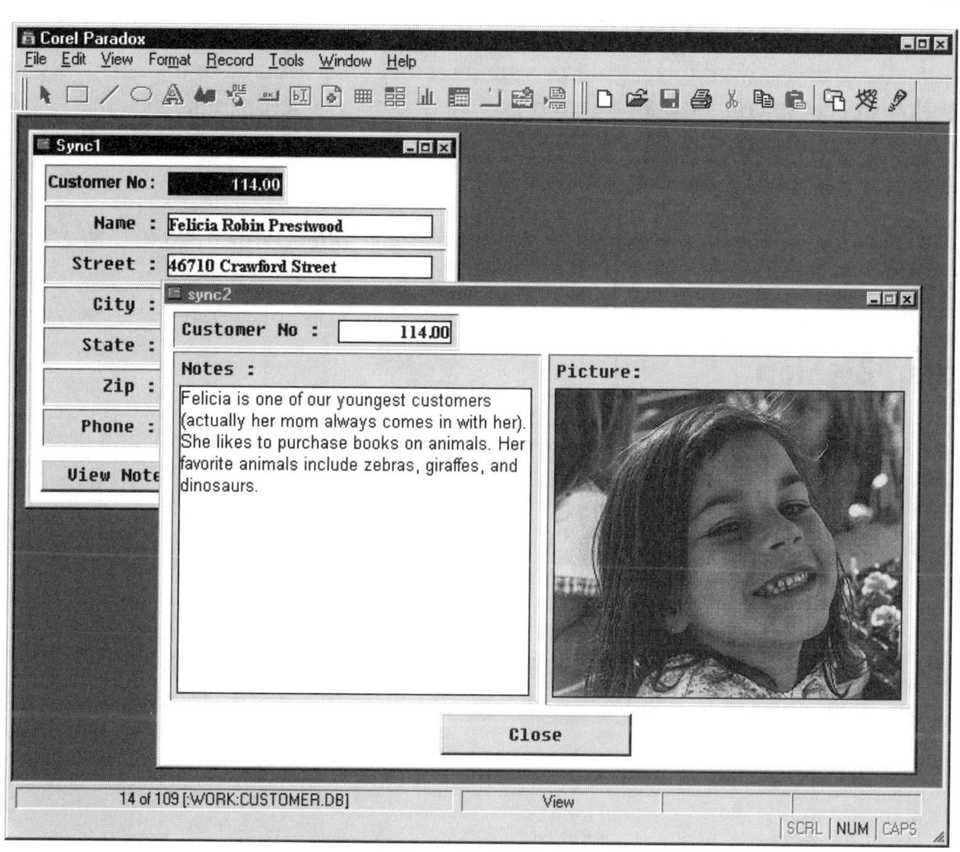

FIGURE 9-5 SYNC1.FSL calling SYNC2.FSL

dialog box by selecting Edit | Preferences. Then, select the Advanced tab and clear the check box for the Don't show warning prompts when changing directories option.

The next examples show you a good technique for using both setPrivDir() and setWorkingDir().

Setting Your Private Directory

Suppose that you want to set your private directory when you open a form—perhaps because you have a preferred private directory where you keep some favorite forms and tables. The following code will change your private directory only if needed and if the directory exists.

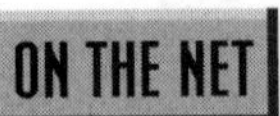

http://prestwood.com/forums/paradox/books/official/files/PRIV1.FSL.

Step By Step

1. Change your working directory to Paradox's Samples directory and create a new form.

2. In the init event of the form, type lines 3–11. Line 4 declares s as a string variable. Line 4 sets sDir to a string that points to my preferred private directory. The if statement in lines 9–11 starts off in line 9 by checking two conditions. First, it compares the current private directory with sDir. Then, it makes sure that the directory path sDir represents exists. If both of these conditions are True, line 10 changes the private directory to sDir.

```
1:    ;PRIV1 :: Form :: init
2:    method init(var eventInfo Event)
3:       var
4:           sDir    String
5:       endVar

6:       ;Set the String of your preferred private directory.
7:       sDir = "C:\\PDOXWIN\\PRIVATE"

8:       ;Change private directory if appropriate.
9:       if privDir() <> sDir and isDir(sDir) then
10:          setPrivDir(sDir)
11:      endIf
12:   endMethod
```

3. In the menuAction event of the form, type lines 9–11. Line 9 checks for the constant MenuChangingPriv. If it is detected, line 10 sets an error code to a nonzero value.

```
;Form :: menuAction
method menuAction(var eventInfo MenuEvent)

if eventInfo.isPreFilter() then
   ;// This code executes for each object on the form:

else
   ;// This code executes only for the form:
   if eventInfo.id() = MenuChangingPriv then
      eventInfo.setErrorCode(1);Prevents the form from closing.
   endIf

endIf

endMethod
```

4. Check the syntax, save the form as **PRIV1.FSL**, and close it. Change your private directory to a different directory (such as C:\) and open the form. After the form opens, check the current private directory by selecting File | Private Directory.

Setting Your Working Directory

Suppose that you have code that relies on objects that are in the same directory as the form, and you want to automatically change your working directory to that directory when the form is opened. This section shows you how to accomplish this.

http://prestwood.com/forums/paradox/books/official/files/WORK1.FSL.

Step By Step

1. Change your working directory to Paradox's Samples directory and create a new form.

2. In the init method of the form, type lines 3–14. Line 4 declares f as a Form variable and line 5 sets dynDir as a DynArray ready to accept string values. Line 8 is rather interesting. It uses attach() to attach f to the current form. When you attach to the current form, you do not have to include its title.

Line 9 checks to see whether the current working directory is the same directory the form is in. If it is not, then line 10 uses getFilename() and splitFullFileName() to extract the form's path. Line 11 sets the working directory.

```
1:    ;Form :: init
2:    method init(var eventInfo Event)
3:       var
4:          f          Form
5:          dynDir     DynArray[] String
6:       endVar

7:       ;Set working directory to this directory.
8:       f.attach()
9:       if not isFile(":WORK:ANSWERS.FSL") then
10:         splitFullFileName(f.getFileName(), dynDir)
11:         if not setWorkingDir(dynDir["Drive"] + dynDir["Path"])
            ;then
12:            errorShow()
13:         endIf
14:      endIf
15:   endMethod
```

3. In the menuAction event of the form, type lines 8–10. Similar to the previous example, in step 3, line 8 checks for the constant MenuChangingWork. If it is detected, line 9 sets an error code to a nonzero value.

```
1:    ;Form :: menuAction
2:    method menuAction(var eventInfo MenuEvent)
3:       if eventInfo.isPreFilter() then
4:          ;// This code executes for each object on the form:
5:
6:       else
7:          ;// This code executes only for the form:
8:          if eventInfo.id() = MenuChangingWork then
9:             eventInfo.setErrorCode(1)
10:         endIf
11:      endIf
12:   endMethod
```

4. Check the syntax and save the form as **WORK1.FSL**. Change your working directory to a different directory (such as C:\) and open the form. After the form opens, check the current working directory by selecting File | Working Directory.

Printing a Form

One of the first things you'll want to do is print a form. Unlike the Report type of methods, the Form object type does not have a print() command. You can print a form from ObjectPAL, however. Just as you can select File | Print, you can send a form to the printer with ObjectPAL. To print the current form, use either of these lines of code:

```
1:      menuAction(MenuFilePrint)   ;Emulates the menu.
2:      action(DataPrint)           ;Invokes an action constant.
```

You can use either of these techniques to print a form. The technique of using the menuAction() procedure in the preceding line 1 uses the technique to invoke a menu constant. The second invokes an action constant.

Preventing a User from Exiting

Two techniques work well for preventing the user from exiting your application. The first technique traps for the MenuControlClose constant with eventInfo.id() = MenuControlClose or eventInfo.id() = MenuCanClose in the menuAction event, and sets the CanNotDepart error code. The second technique uses canDepart of the form. Both of them use a flag. A flag is a variable used in a routine to indicate whether a condition has occurred. The next example demonstrates how to use menuAction to prevent exiting. The second technique of using canDepart is then demonstrated.

Using *menuAction* to Prevent Exiting

Suppose that you want to prevent a user from exiting a form unless you specify otherwise. In this example, however, the user can go into Design mode. The next example demonstrates trapping for MenuCanClose and MenuControlClose in the menuAction event.

http://prestwood.com/forums/paradox/books/official/files/NOCLOSE1.FSL.

Step By Step

1. Create a new form. On the form, place a radio button field named **fldFlag**. Add two choices to the radio button: **Allow Close** and **Do Not Allow Close**. Here's how the form should look:

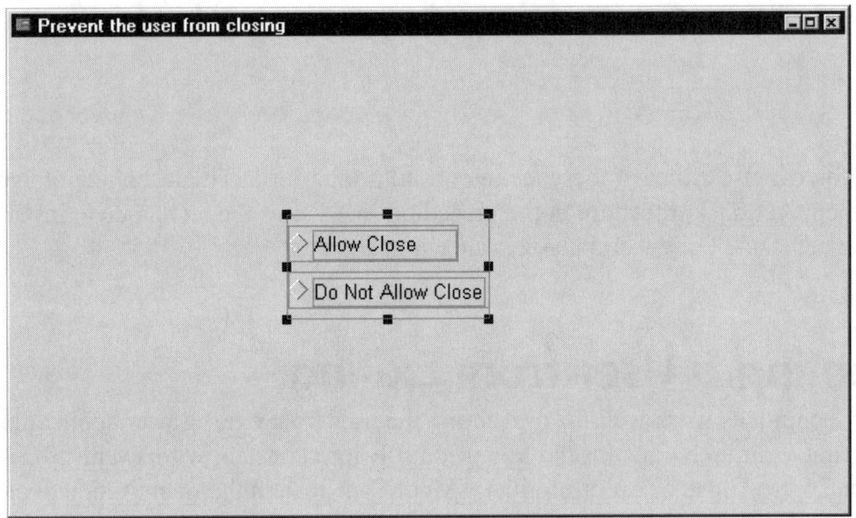

2. Add lines 7–12 to the menuAction event of the form. Lines 7 and 8 check for MenuCanClose and MenuControlClose. MenuControlClose is called when the user attempts to close the form, and MenuCanClose is called when the application tries to close or when the user selects Window | Close All. The menu control constants are listed online in the ObjectPAL Quick Lookup dialog. You can use this technique to trap for any of the menu command constants. Line 9 enables you to exit. (You need a way to exit at some point in your code.) Line 10 does the real work. It sets the CanNotDepart error code.

```
1:    ;Form :: menuAction
2:    method menuAction(var eventInfo MenuEvent)
3:    if eventInfo.isPreFilter() then
4:       ;This code executes for each object on the form
5:    else
6:       ;This code executes only for the form
7:       if eventInfo.id() = MenuCanClose or
8:          eventInfo.id() = MenuControlClose then
```

```
            if fldFlag.value = "Do not allow close" then
               eventInfo.setErrorCode(CanNotDepart)
            endIf
         endIf
      endIf
      endMethod
```

3. Check the syntax, save the form as **NOCLOSE1.FSL**, and run it. Set the fldFlag field to Do Not Allow Close, and try all the various ways of exiting. Then, set the flag field to Allow Close and exit or move into Design mode.

Using *canDepart* to Prevent Exiting

Suppose that you want to prevent a user from exiting a form (including going into Design mode). This next example demonstrates how to use canDepart to prevent exiting. You use the canDepart event of a form to prevent a form from closing, thereby preventing the application from closing. It also provides a way to toggle this effect on and off (perhaps with a flag field).

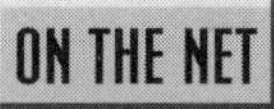

http://prestwood.com/forums/paradox/books/official/files/NOCLOSE2.FSL.

Step By Step

1. Create a new form. On the form, place a radio button field named **fldFlag**. The radio button field has two choices, which are Allow Close and Do Not Allow Close. The form should look like it did in the last example.

2. Add lines 8–10 to the canDepart event of the form. Line 8 checks the value of the fldFlag field. If the value is Do Not Allow Close, line 9 sets the error code to <u>CanNotDepart</u>.

```
1:     ;Form :: canDepart
2:     method canDepart(var eventInfo MoveEvent)
3:        if eventInfo.isPreFilter() then
4:           ;This code executes for each object on the form
5:
6:        else
7:           ;This code executes only for the form
```

```
        if fldFlag.value = "Do not allow close" then
           eventInfo.setErrorCode(CanNotDepart)
        endIf
     endIf
  endMethod
```

3. Check the syntax, save the form as **NOCLOSE2.FSL**, and run it. Set the fldFlag field to Do Not Allow Close, and try all the various ways of exiting. You cannot go into Design mode, as you could in the previous example. Set the fldFlag field to Allow Close, then exit.

Both the techniques presented in this section are important. Trapping for a constant in menuAction, or action, at the form level enables you to centralize your code. Using the canDepart event and setting the error code to CanNotDepart also is useful. Both these techniques have broad uses.

Summary

This chapter is important because it gives you the tools to control any form you create. Using the techniques presented in this chapter also gives you control over using multiple forms within an application.

CHAPTER 10

Using Table Windows

In Paradox, a *table window* is an object that displays data in its own window. A table window is what opens when you select File | Open | Table and choose a table. A TableView object (variable) in ObjectPAL is a handle to that window. Sometimes, you want to display a table and work with it in a TableView. Although a TableView is limited in functionality, you can open and manipulate it similarly to how you open and manipulate a form. Included in the list of methods and procedures for the TableView object type are open(), close(), action(), bringToTop(), and isMaximized(). Refer to Paradox's help for a complete list.

The *TableView* Object

Just as there are Application and Form variables, there is a variable for use with a table window. It is the TableView variable. As soon as you declare a variable as a TableView and open the TableView, you establish a handle to a table window. With that handle, you can open, wait, and close table windows.

You also can use ObjectPAL to manipulate TableView properties. For example, similarly to manipulating a form with a Form variable, you can manipulate the TableView object such as background color, grid style, and the value of the current record. You also can manipulate the field-level data in the table (TVData), such as font characteristics and display format. Finally, you can manipulate the TableView heading (TVHeading), such as changing fonts, colors, and alignment.

The following code declares a TableView variable named tv:

```
Var
    tv   TableView
endVar
```

Because this variable now exists, you can use it to open a table window, as follows:

```
tv.open("CUSTOMER.DB")
tv.wait()
tv.close()
```

The TableView action() method is powerful. It gives you access to many of the form methods and procedures. For example, to put a table window into Edit mode, use the following:

```
tv.action(DataBeginEdit)
```

The TableView object has several other methods and procedures you can use, including hide and show. For example:

```
tv.hide()
message("Table is hidden for 3 seconds")
sleep(3000)
tv.show()
```

To instruct the user in how to use a table window, you can use the TableView setTitle() method to set the title of the table window. For example, to tell the user how to start and end Edit mode, do the following:

```
TableViewVar.setTitle("F9 for edit mode :: Close to return")
```

The next example demonstrates opening a table window from a button.

Displaying a Table Window from a Button

Suppose that you want to have a button on a form bring up a table window. In this next example, you will declare a TableView variable and use the open() method to open up the CUSTOMER.DB table.

http://prestwood.com/forums/paradox/books/official/files/TVIEW1.FSL.

Step By Step

1. Set your working directory to Paradox's Samples directory. Create a new form and put a button on it labeled **CUSTOMERS.DB**.

2. Add lines 4–8 to the pushButton event of the button. This routine opens CUSTOMER.DB in a table window. Line 5 declares tv as a TableView variable, which line 8 uses to open the table.

```
1:     ;Button :: pushButton
2:     method pushButton(var eventInfo Event)
3:        ;This routine brings up a TableView
4:        var
5:           tv      TableView
6:        endVar
7:
8:        tv.open("CUSTOMER.DB")
9:     endMethod
```

3. Check the syntax, save the form as **TVIEW1.FSL**, and run it. Click the button. Figure 10-1 shows how the form and table window look when you click the button.

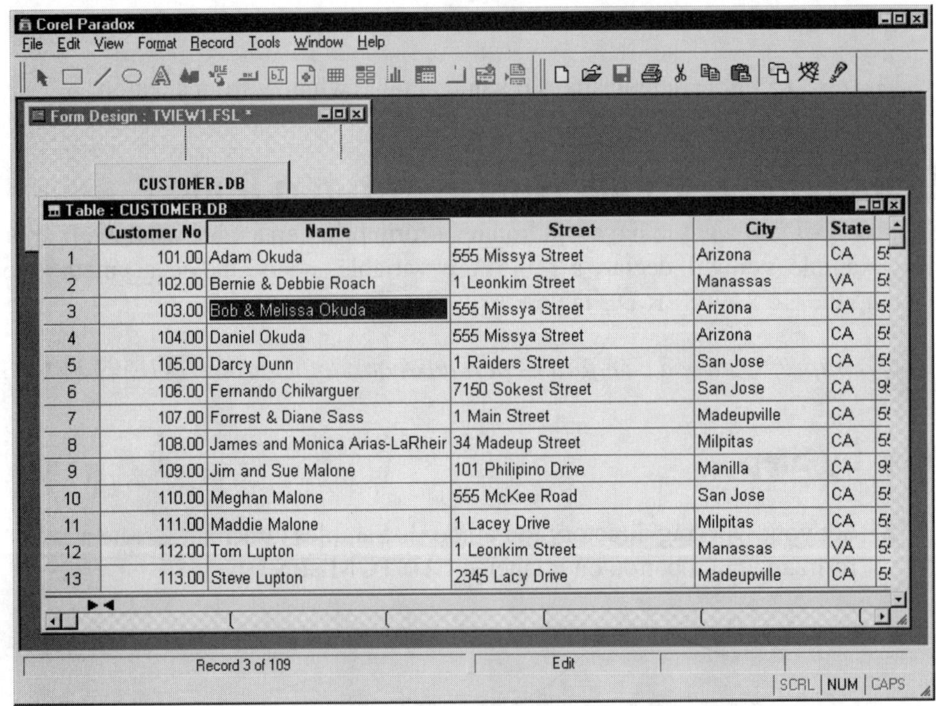

FIGURE 10-1 TVIEW1.FSL demonstrates how to open a table window

Getting a Table Window Ready for Input

The next logical step in learning how to handle a table window is to get it ready for data entry. You can use the action() method with constants to manipulate a table window. I like the technique presented in the next example because of its simplicity. It demonstrates how to get a table window ready for input. Suppose that you want to have a button on a form that opens a table window ready for input when the user clicks it. In this example, you will use the setTitle() method to set the text in the title bar of the table window, and action() to move to the end of the table, put it in Edit mode, and insert a record by moving past the last record.

ON THE NET *http://prestwood.com/forums/paradox/books/official/files/TVIEW2.FSL.*

Step By Step

1. Set your working directory to Paradox's Samples directory. Create a new form and place a button on it labeled **Add a Customer**.

2. Add lines 4–11 to the pushButton event of the button to open the CUSTOMER table window that is ready for input. Line 5 declares tv as a TableView variable. It's used in lines 8–11. Line 8 opens the CUSTOMER.DB table with the tv variable in a table window. Lines 9–11 use action constants to move to the end of the table, to switch into Edit mode, and to move to the next record. Now, the table window is ready for input.

```
1:     ;Button :: pushButton
2:     method pushButton(var eventInfo Event)
3:        ;This routine brings up a table view ready for input.
4:        var
5:           tv   TableView
6:        endVar
7:
8:        tv.open("CUSTOMER.DB")
9:        tv.setTitle("Enter a record and close Table Window")
9:        tv.action(MoveEnd)
10:       tv.action(DataBeginEdit)
11:       tv.action(DataNextRecord)
12:    endMethod
```

3. Check the syntax, save the form as **TVIEW2.FSL**, run it, and click the button. The TableView does exactly what you told it to do, and it's ready for input. Your form should look similar to Figure 10-2. The CUSTOMER.DB table is ready for input.

http://prestwood.com/forums/paradox/books/official/files/TVIEW3.FSL demonstrates using open(), wait(), close(), edit(), end(), and setTitle() with a TableView variable, as shown here:

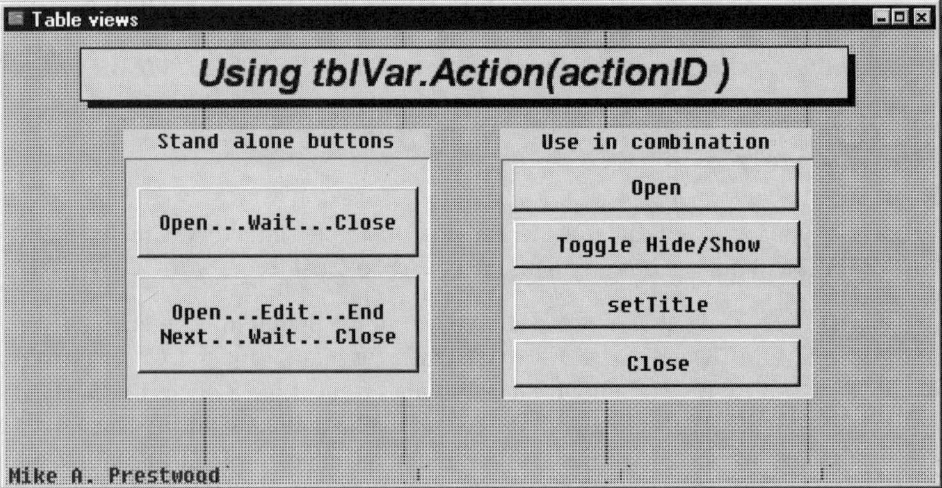

Summary

This short chapter is important because it gave you the tools to control the displaying of data to a user using a table window. Now you can easily add the ability to display the raw table data to your users in table windows using the ObjectPAL Table View object. This is particularly important when using the Paradox run time because the run time does not surface the File | Open | Table option to the user. It is important to note that these techniques do work with the run-time edition of Paradox.

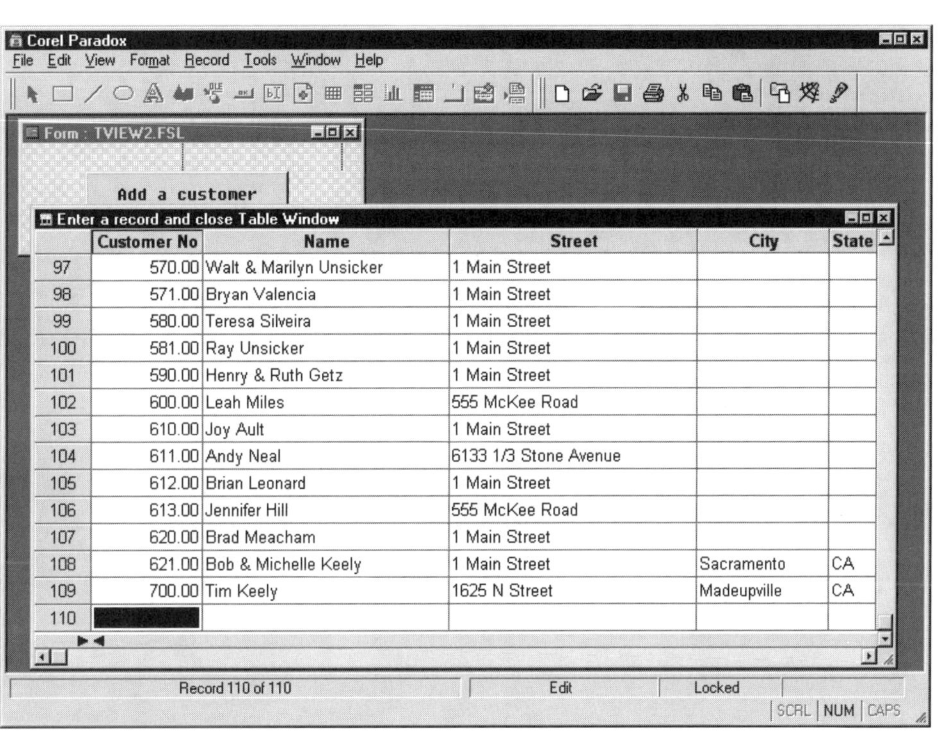

FIGURE 10-2 TVIEW2.FSL

CHAPTER 11

Programming with Queries

The technique of asking questions about data by providing an example of the answer you expect is called *query by example* (QBE). You can use this tool to ask questions about your data and analyze it. A query is a means of extracting sets of information from a database or table. You can base forms and reports on a subset of your data by using a query as the first table in your data model. You can even use a live query as this first table. And you can also create queries on the fly in ObjectPAL. The Query variable is a handle to a QBE query.

Queries

Queries are a very important part of any database. Having a large amount of data isn't useful unless you can analyze it. Queries are what you use to analyze your data. Sometimes they are the only way to get certain information about a product. Paradox delivers a graphical QBE that makes it easier than ever to create queries and get fast answers. You can access up to 24 tables in a single query. Join, outer join, inclusion, and set operations are available for full relational queries.

QBE has two functions—namely, as an end-user tool and as a way to use a subset of all the data. You can use QBE to develop specialized forms and reports. Important query methods and procedures include the following:

- **executeQBE()** Executes a QBE query.
- **QUERY** Begins a QBE statement or string.
- **readFromFile()** Reads a QBE file into a query variable.
- **readFromString()** Reads a string into a query variable.
- **writeQBE()** Writes a query statement to a specified file.

Displaying the Query Window

Suppose that you want to bring up the query window with a particular query. To do this, you can use sendKeys() from the system type. For example, change your working directory to Paradox's Samples directory and type line 3 into the pushButton event of a button.

```
1:  ;Button :: pushButton
2:  method pushButton(var eventInfo Event)
3:     sendKeys("%foqworld{ENTER}")  ;Emulates pressing keys.
4:  endMethod
```

sendKeys() emulates the user pressing keys. The first part of the preceding code emulates the user pressing ALT-F-O-Q, which is the same as selecting File | Open | Query. The second half, WORLD{ENTER}, specifies the name of the query to open and presses the RETURN key.

Executing a Saved Query

The term "query" in ObjectPAL refers to the Query variable. The Query variable is your handle to a query. Just as you can declare a Form variable and open it, you can declare a Query variable, read a file into it, and execute it. For example, change your working directory to Paradox's Samples directory and type lines 2–7 into the pushButton event of a button.

```
1:    method pushButton(var eventInfo Event)
2:       var
3:          q    Query                 ;Declare a Query variable.
4:       endVar
5:
6:       q.readFromFile("CUSTOMERLIST.QBE") ;Read in QBE.
7:       q.executeQBE()                 ;Execute QBE.
8:       ;Open up the answer table in your private directory.
9:    endMethod
```


Running a Query from a Button

Suppose that you have an existing query, CUSTOMERLIST.QBE, that you want to run, then show the results in a table window and enable Paradox to delete the answer table automatically when it exits.

1. Change your working directory to Paradox's Samples directory and create a query based on the CUSTOMER.DB table and check the Customer Name and Phone fields, as shown here. Save the query as **CustomerList.qbe**.

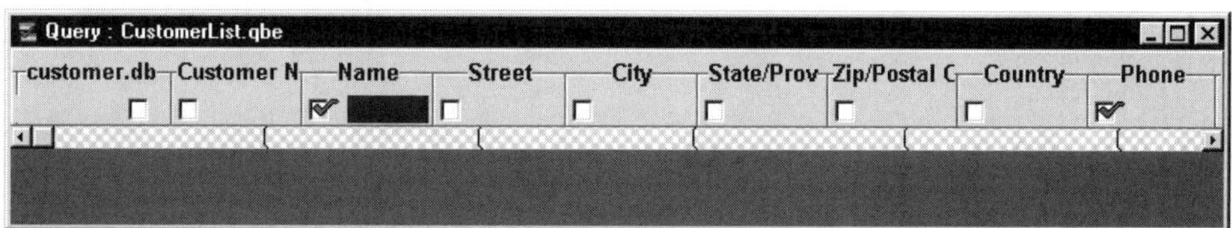

2. Create a new form. Add a button labeled **Run Query File** to it, as shown here:

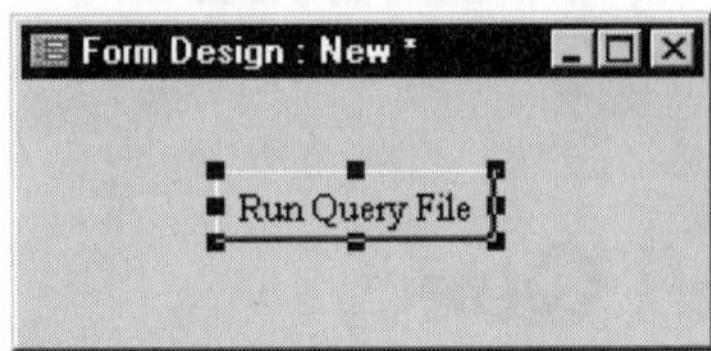

3. Add lines 3–10 to the pushButton event of the Run Query File button to execute the query. Line 4 declares a Query variable, and line 5 declares a TableView variable. Line 8 uses readFromFile() to read the QBE file CUSTOMERLIST.QBE into the q Query variable. Then, executeQBE() is used in line 9 to run the query and create a table named __ANS.DB in your private directory.

```
1:     ;Button :: pushButton
2:     method pushButton(var eventInfo Event)
3:        var
4:           q     Query              ;Declare query variable.
5:           tv    TableView
6:        endVar
7:
8:        q.readFromFile("CustomerList.QBE") ;Read in QBE.
9:        q.executeQBE(":priv:__ans") ;Optional: specify answer table.
10:       tv.open(":priv:__ans")
11:    endMethod
```

4. Check the syntax, save the form as **Query.fsl**, run the form, and click the button. The query runs and creates a table named __ANS.DB in your private directory. Then the table is opened (see Figure 11-1). When you exit Paradox, the table is deleted.

This last step of using two underscores at the beginning of a file in your private directory is important. It is also interesting, because it takes advantage of an undocumented feature of Paradox. Any file in the private directory that starts with two underscores is deleted when the program is exited. This is a normal part of the cleanup process of Paradox. In addition, the files are not listed in the browser or Project Viewer.

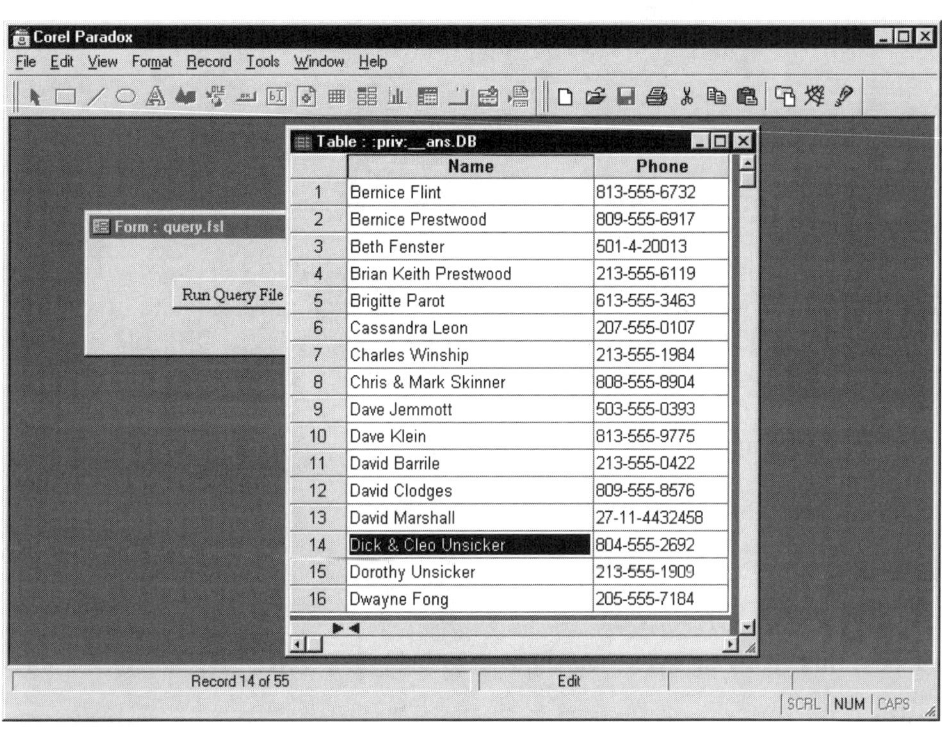

FIGURE 11-1 QUERY.FSL demonstrates how to run a query from ObjectPAL

Using a Query Statement with *executeQBE()*

In addition to executing a query file—for example, CUSTOMERLIST.QBE—you can code a query inside your code with ObjectPAL. First, you declare a Query variable.

```
var
     q    Query
endVar
```

Next, you use the defined Query variable to start the query section in your code. Then comes the actual Query string. For example:

```
q = Query
     WORLD.DB | COUNTRY | CURRENCY          |
              | Check   | Check ..Dollar..  |
EndQuery
```

Typing all these field names, checks, and values would be a hassle, to say the least. In essence, you have to learn a whole new programming language, the QBE language. Luckily, ObjectPAL provides an easier way. A saved QBE file is simply a text file. Therefore, you can use the Edit | Paste From option to paste the text file and alter it as needed. Then, use executeQBE() the way you did in the previous example. For example:

```
q.executeQBE(":PRIV:ANSWER.DB")
```

Using *executeQBE*

Suppose that you want to execute a query by using the ObjectPAL Query variable.

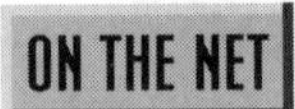

http://prestwood.com/forums/paradox/books/official/files/QUERY1.FSL.

Step By Step

1. Change your working directory to Paradox's Samples directory and create a new query based on CUSTOMER.DB. Check the Name and Phone fields and query for all the records with **Negril** in the City field, as shown here. Save the query as **CustomerQuery.QBE**.

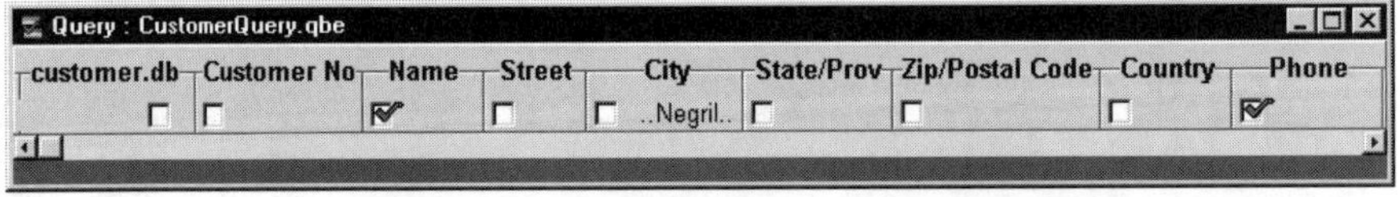

2. Create a new form and add a button labeled **Query Customer** to it.

3. The easiest way to a build a query in ObjectPAL is to build it interactively and paste it into the Editor. A QBE file is simply a text file, as you can see

in the illustration shown here. It can be pasted directly into the Editor. The easiest way to do this is to use the Edit | Paste From option of the editor.

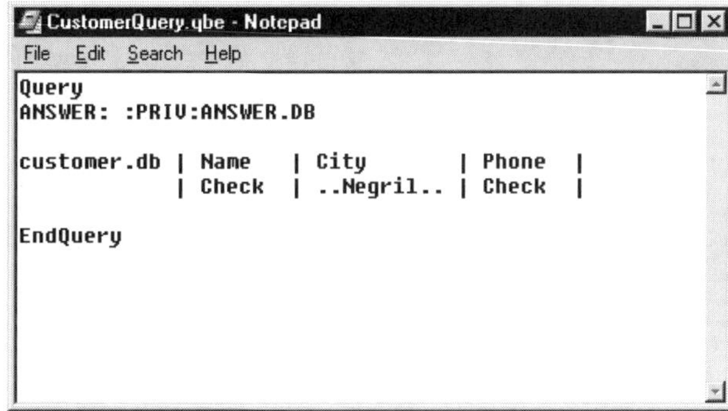


```
Query
ANSWER: :PRIV:ANSWER.DB

customer.db | Name    | City         | Phone  |
            | Check   | ..Negril..   | Check  |

EndQuery
```

4. Paste the text from CustomerQuery.qbe into the pushButton event of the Query Customer.DB button and alter as follows. This illustration shows how the code looks after you insert the QBE file:

```
QUERY1::#Button4::pushButton
#Button4    pushButton

method pushButton(var eventInfo Event)
   var
      q  Query
      tv TableView
   endVar

   q = Query
        ANSWER: :PRIV:ANSWER.DB

        customer.db | Name    | City         | Phone  |
                    | Check   | ..Negril..   | Check  |

       EndQuery

   executeQBE(q)
   tv.open(":priv:answer.db")
endmethod
```

Lines 4 and 5 declare the Query and TableView variables. Lines 8–14 contain the query that is pasted in. Only line 8 has been altered. Line 9 specifies where the answer table should be created. If you leave out line 9, the default is :PRIV:ANSWER.DB. In this case, if you delete line 9, you will get the same result. Line 16 uses executeQBE() to execute the Query variable, and line 17 displays the table that results.

```
;Button :: pushButton
method pushButton(var eventInfo Event)
   var
     q  Query
     tv TableView
   endVar

   q = Query
   ANSWER: :PRIV:ANSWER.DB

   customer.db | Name    | City        | Phone   |
               | Check   | ..Negril..  | Check   |

   EndQuery

   executeQBE(q)
   tv.open(":PRIV:ANSWER.DB")
endMethod
```

5. Check the syntax, save the form as **QUERY1.FSL**, and run it. Click the button. The query is run, and the table is shown in a table window, as seen here:

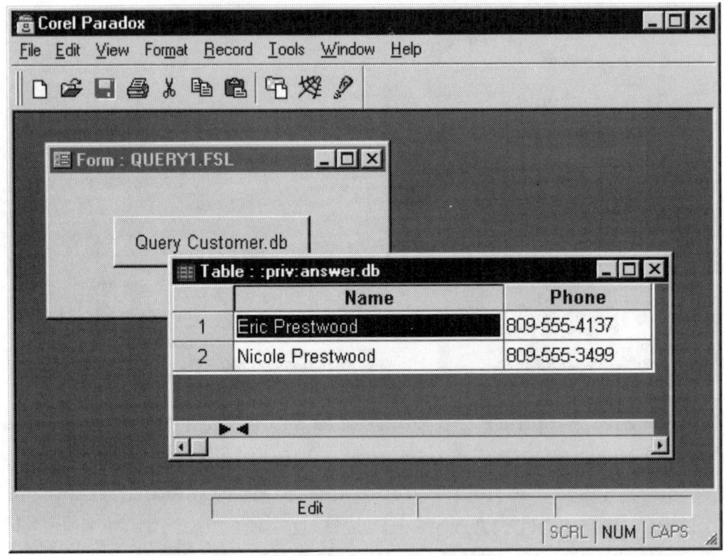

Passing a Value to a Query

You know how to execute a QBE file on disk and how to execute values stored in your code. The next step is to learn how to pass a value to a query. Often, you'll want to enable the user to enter values and to query the table for the values entered. In effect, you simulate the query editor. Use a tilde variable whenever you want to pass a value to a query.

Using a Tilde (~) Variable

Suppose that you want to pass a value to a query and have the query search for that value. The next example demonstrates how to use a tilde variable to set values for a query, run the query, and display the result.

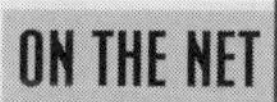

You can find this form on the disc; the location is http://prestwood.com/forums/paradox/books/official/files/QUERY2.FSL.

Step By Step

1. Change your working directory to Paradox's Samples directory. Create a new form. Place an unbound field named **Enter_City** and labeled **Enter search string**. Also, place a button labeled **Query Customer Table** on the form, as shown here:

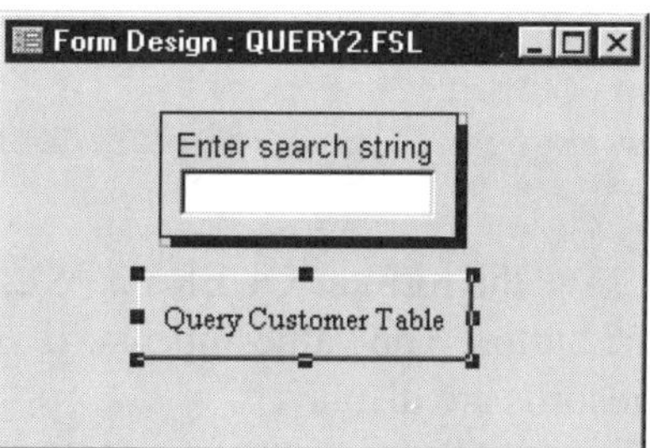

2. Before entering the code in step 3, open the CustomerQuery.qbe query you created in the previous example. Then, paste the query directly into your

code and alter it by replacing the **Negril** value with the tilde and variable name (see the next step).

3. The altered pushButton event should look like the following code listing. Lines 4–6 declare the variables. Line 9 passes the value in the Enter Search String field to the s variable. Lines 11–18 are the query that you pasted. Lines 11 and 16 have been altered from the value that was pasted in. Line 20 executes the Query variable, and line 21 displays the result.

```
 1:   ;Button :: pushButton
 2:   method pushButton(var eventInfo Event)
 3:      var
 4:         sName           String
 5:         qryCustomer     Query
 6:         tvAnswer        TableView
 7:      endVar
 8:
 9:      sName = Enter_City.value
10:
11:      qryCustomer = Query
12:
13:      ANSWER: :PRIV:ANSWER.DB
14:
15:      customer.db | Name    | City          | Phone   |
16:                  | Check   | ..~sName..    | Check   |
17:
18:      EndQuery
19:
20:      executeQBE(qryCustomer)
21:      tvAnswer.open(":priv:answer.db")
22:   endMethod
```

4. Check the syntax, save the form as QUERY2.FSL, and run it. Type a value, and click the button. The value appears. If you don't type a value into the field, all records are displayed.

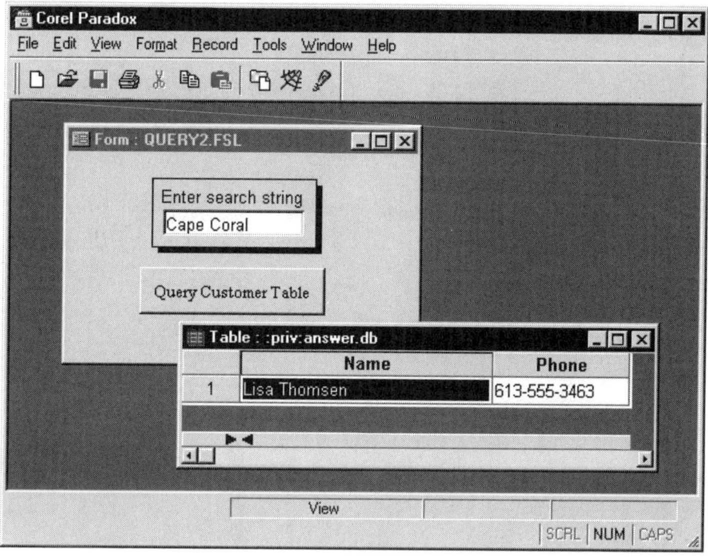

Rather than bring the query editor up for the user to use (as demonstrated previously), you can simulate the query editor on a form with an interface that is more specific than File | Open | Query.

Executing a Query Stored in a String

If you want, you can build a query in a string variable and then use readFromString() to read the string into a Query variable. After the query string is in a Query variable, use executeQBE() to execute it. Because you have tilde (~) variables, this technique is not really needed, but it can be useful. The following code executes the same CustomerQuery.qbe query you used in a previous example in this chapter.

```
;Button :: pushButton
method pushButton(var eventInfo Event)
   var
      sQuery      String
```

```
            s1            String
            s2            String
            s3            String
            s4            String
            s5            String
            qryCustomer Query
            tvAnswer      TableView
      endVar

      errorTrapOnWarnings(Yes)

      s1 = "Query\n"
      s2 = "ANSWER: :PRIV:ANSWER.DB\n"
      s3 = "customer.db | Name    | City           | Phone   |\n"
      s4 = "            | Check   | ..San Jose..   | Check   |\n"
      s5 = "EndQuery"

      sQuery = s1 + s2 + s3 + s4 + s5

      qryCustomer.readFromString(sQuery)
      qryCustomer.executeQBE()
      if not tvAnswer.open(":PRIV:ANSWER") then errorShow() endIf
   endMethod
```

TIP *Here is a tip if you are having problems with a query and you are not sure whether the problem is the query string itself or something else. Use writeQBE() to write the Query variable out to a file, and then try to run the query interactively. In addition, you can use isQueryValid(), which tells you if the query is valid. The benefit of using writeQBE() is that you can open the query and look at it.*

Another debugging technique is to use the errorShow() procedure, as in the following example:

```
if not qryCustomer.executeQBE() then errorShow() endIf
```

Points to remember about using readFromString() are as follows:

- End each line of the query with \n, which represents a line feed.
- A quoted string is limited to 255 characters.

- Use multiple quoted strings for quoted strings longer than 255.
- Use the errorShow() procedure to check whether the query executes.

Using an In-Memory TCursor

In-memory TCursors are interesting because they are fast and they are not connected to the live data. You can ask "what if" questions of the data before writing the data to the live database. The command wantInMemoryTCursor() is used when you want to specify how a TCursor is created resulting from a query. Following is the syntax:

```
wantInMemoryTCursor(const yesNo Logical)
```

NOTE *The procedure wantInMemoryTCursor(Yes) is only necessary for queries that would normally produce live query views. If the query doesn't meet the conditions for a live query, and the answer is a TCursor, the TCursor will be in memory nonetheless.*

Specify Yes (or Null) to build the TCursor in-memory; the TCursor is not connected to a table. Specify No to attach the TCursor to the live data. If you do not call wantInMemoryTCursor() before you execute a query to a TCursor, the default is the same as if you called it and passed it No; the resulting TCursor is live to the data. The exception is with multitable queries that specify an answer TCursor, which will always produce an in-memory TCursor. Here is how you use wantInMemoryTCursor() with a query to gain access to an in-memory TCursor:


```
;Button :: pushButton
method pushButton(var eventInfo Event)
   var
      qryCustomerQuery  Query
      tcCustomerQuery   TCursor
   endVar

   qryCustomerQuery.wantInMemoryTCursor(Yes)
   qryCustomerQuery.readFromFile("CustomerQuery.QBE")
   qryCustomerQuery.executeQBE(tcCustomerQuery)

   ;Utilize in-memory TCursor here.
endMethod
```

This command also works with SQL variables. In fact, SQL variables are very similar in nature to Query variables. You manipulate them with ObjectPAL using the same techniques. Other methods that are useful with in-memory TCursors include isInMemoryTCursor(), isView(), and instantiateView(). isInMemoryTCursor() returns True when the TCursor is an in-memory TCursor. isView() returns True if the TCursor is connected to live data. Finally, instantiateView() copies an in-memory TCursor to a physical table.

Query Methods

There are query methods to generate and modify queries using ObjectPAL. These methods include appendTable(), setCriteria(), setQuerySortOrder(), setCheck(), and setRowOp(). These methods are not as easy as they may seem. Here are a few pointers:

- You can set a row operator to check all the fields, but if you want to check all fields but one, you cannot use checkRow() and you need to setCheck() each field.
- To set the Answer table sort order, you must fill an array with every checked field; if you remove or add a field to the Answer table of the query, you must fix the array and reuse setAnswerSortOrder().
- setAnswerFieldOrder() interferes with Delete, Insert and Changeto queries. It also will inhibit removeTable().

This next example uses appendTable() to add a table to a query image, checkRow() to check all the rows of the query image, executeQBE() to run the query, and, finally, open() to open the answer table. Change your working directory to the Samples directory and type lines 3–14 into the pushButton event of a button. Figure 11-2 shows the final result.

```
1:   ;Button :: pushButton
2:   method pushButton(var eventInfo Event)
3:      const
4:         sAns = ":priv:__ans.db"  ;Path to answer table.
```

```
      endConst
      var
         qCustomers    Query
         tvCustomers   TableView
      endVar

      qCustomers.appendTable("CUSTOMER.DB")                 ;Add table to query.
      qCustomers.checkRow("CUSTOMER.DB", CheckCheck)        ;Check all fields.
      qCustomers.executeQBE(sAns)                           ;Execute query.
      tvCustomers.open(sAns)                                ;Display table.
   endMethod
```


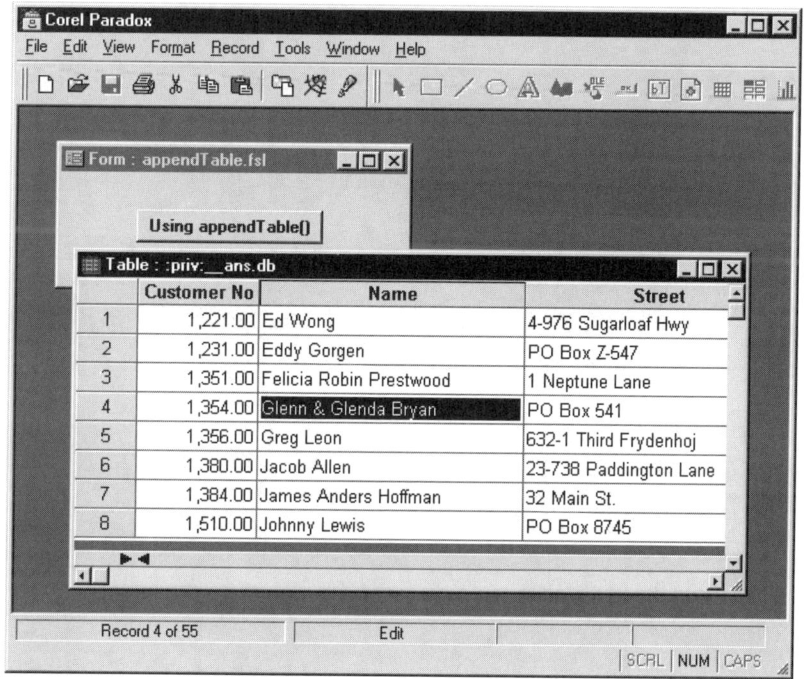

FIGURE 11-2 Example using appendTable()

Summary

In this chapter, you learned that a query is what you use to ask a table a question. You learned how to use sendKeys() to open up a query image for your users. You learned how to generate and use queries in ObjectPAL. You learned how to execute a saved query, and execute a query string with executeQBE(). You learned how to pass a value to a query using a tilde variable. Finally, you learned how to work with live queries, in-memory TCursors, and some of the Paradox query methods.

CHAPTER 12

Handling Reports

A report is a tool for printing data to get an organized, formatted hard copy of your data. You can communicate data with presentation-quality reports. Paradox's built-in report writer is a high-quality tool that will suffice for the majority of your printouts. With the combination of reports and queries—and the ObjectPAL commands that enable you to use them—you can add sophisticated printing capabilities to your applications.

Using Reports in ObjectPAL

For manipulating reports, ObjectPAL offers the report object. The report object (or variable) is a handle to a report window. With a report variable, you can attach to an already opened report or you can open a report. After the handle is established, you can manipulate the report. If you browse the online help and explore the Form object type, Report type, and TableView object type, you will see that many methods and procedures are shared among them.

Opening a Report

The next bit of code demonstrates opening a report and setting the title of the report. To achieve a smooth opening of the report, note that WinStyleDefault + WinStyleHidden is used along with the show() method. Change working directories to Paradox's Samples directory and type lines 3–9 into the pushButton event of a button.

```
 1:  ;Button :: pushButton
 2:  method pushButton(var eventInfo Event)
 3:     var
 4:        r Report
 5:     endVar
 6:
 7:     r.open("Customer", WinStyleDefault + WinStyleHidden)
 8:     r.setTitle("New report title")
 9:     r.show()  ;You can also use bringToTop().
10:  endMethod
```

Printing Reports

The first step in learning how to handle reports with ObjectPAL is learning how to print an existing report. The next two examples demonstrate how to use the print() and open() report methods.

Suppose that you want to create two buttons on a form. The first button directly prints an existing report with no interaction from the user. The second button previews the report and prompts the user with the Print File dialog box.

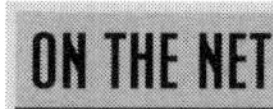

http://prestwood.com/forums/paradox/books/official/files/REPORT1.FSL.

Step By Step

1. Change your working directory to Paradox's Samples directory. Create a new form and place two buttons on it. Label the first button **Print Report** and the second **Open then Print Report**, as shown here:

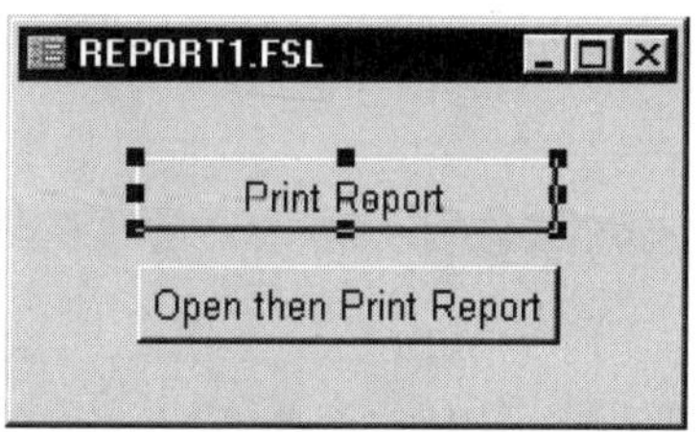

2. Add lines 3–7 to the pushButton event of the Print Report button. Line 4 declares r to be a Report variable. In this case, r is a temporary variable, alive only for the duration of the method. This is important to note because, with display managers, the existence of the object (the report, in this case) does not close when the variable is destroyed. This is not true with all objects. For example, OLE and TCursor objects automatically close when the variable is destroyed. To optimize this form, you can combine these two declarations into a single declaration higher up in the containership path. In line 7, print() is used to print the report without first previewing it. You do not need to open the report first.

```
1:    ;Button :: pushButton
2:    method pushButton(var eventInfo Event)
3:       var
4:          r     Report
5:       endVar
6:
7:       r.print("Customer")
8:    endMethod
```

3. Add lines 3–8 to the pushButton event of the Open then Print Report button. Lines 7 and 8 on the second button use open() to open the report to preview it, and use print() to display the Print File dialog box.

```
1:    ;Button :: pushButton
2:    method pushButton(var eventInfo Event)
3:       var
4:         r  Report
5:       endVar
6:
7:       r.open("Customer")
8:       r.print()
9:    endMethod
```

4. Check your syntax, save the form as **REPORT1.FSL**, run the form, and press the Open then Print Report button (see Figure 12-1).

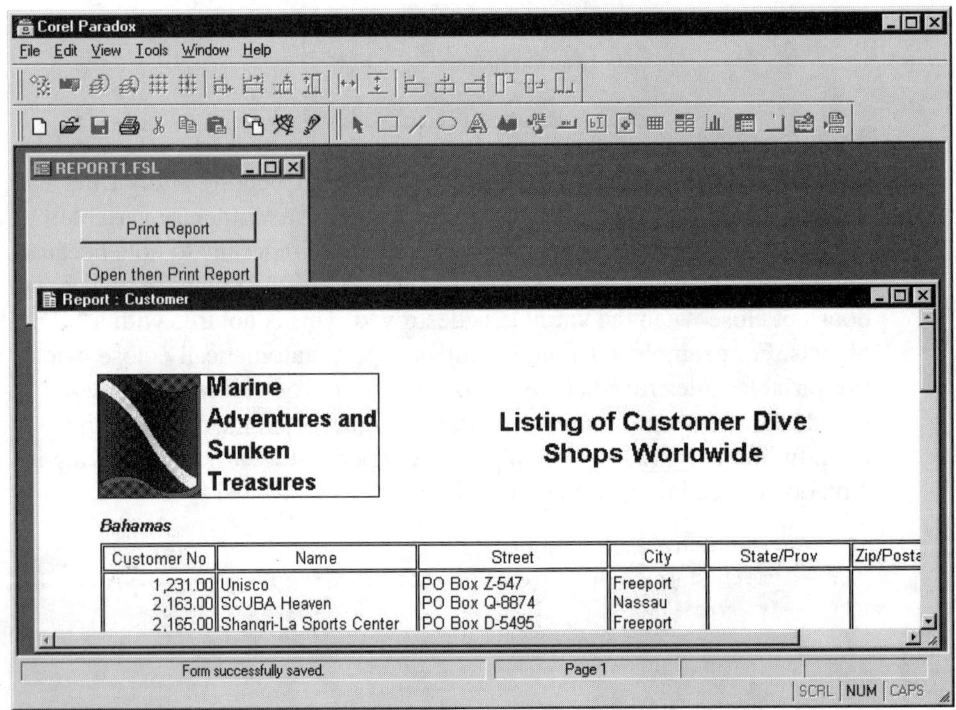

FIGURE 12-1 The Open then Print Report button previews a report

Printing a Report Based on the Current Record

In general, reports deal only with a set of data. They step through the master table one record at a time and print the report information once for every record. Often, you need to print a report based on a subset of the table or even just a single record. There are several techniques for doing this in Paradox, including using a query and using ObjectPAL. Both are demonstrated in this section. The query technique takes two steps. First, execute a query. Then, print a report that is based on the answer table for the query. In the following example, you print a report based on only the current record.

Using a Query to Print a Report Based on the Current Record

Suppose that you want to print a rcport bascd on thc current record. This example uses an embedded query to generate a table with a single record in it. It also demonstrates using a temporary table to control the report.

http://prestwood.com/forums/paradox/books/official/files/REPORT2.FSL.

Step By Step

1. Create a query with all the fields checked based on ORDERS.DB and run it. This generates an ANSWER.DB table in your private directory, which is used in step 2.
2. Change your working directory to Paradox's Samples directory and create a new form with the :PRIV:ANSWERS.DB, ORDERS.DB, and LINEITEM.DB tables in the data model.
3. Link the :PRIV:ANSWERS.DB table to the Orders table in a 1:1 relationship.
4. Link the Orders table to the Lineitem table in a 1:M relationship. Place a button on the form and label it **Print Current Invoice**. Note that you must initially create the :PRIV:ANSWER.DB table in order to link it.

5. Add lines 3–19 to the pushButton event of the Print Current Invoice button. If you would rather view the report on the screen than print it, substitute r.open("ORDER") for line 19 below. Line 9 takes the value from the Order_No field and puts it in the s variable. Lines 10–16 make up the query; line 14 uses the s variable. Line 18 executes the query, and line 19 prints the report. Because the report is based on the table created by the query executed in line 19, it consists of only one record.

```
1:   ;Button :: pushButton
2:   method pushButton(var eventInfo Event)
3:      var
4:        r  Report
5:        q  Query
6:        s  String
7:      endVar
8:
9:      s = Order_No.value
10:     q = Query
11:     ANSWER: :PRIV:ANSWER.DB
12:
13:     ORDERS.DB | Order No  |
14:               | Check  ~s |
15:
16:     EndQuery
17:
18:     executeQBE(q)
19:     r.print("ORDER") ;To see report, use r.open("ORDER") instead.
20:  endMethod
```

6. Check your syntax, save the form as **REPORT2.FSL**, and run it. Move to the record that you want to print, and click the button.

Fully Controlling a Report

An alternate and perhaps easier technique to print the current record and maintain full control of a report is to use setGenFilter(), setMenu(), and wait(). setGenFilter() is used to filter the data down to the current invoice. setMenu() is used to keep the user from using other menu options. Finally, wait() is used so that the user doesn't stray from the report. Following is the code in full for you to study:

```
;btn :: pushButton
method pushButton(var eventInfo Event)
```

```
3:     var
4:        r           Report
5:        m           Menu
6:        pop         PopUpMenu
7:        dynFilter   DynArray[] String
8:     endVar
9:
10:    ;Load the report hidden.
11:    if not r.load(":INVOICE:INVOICE", WinStyleDefault + WinStyleHidden) then
12:       errorShow()
13:       return
14:    endIf
15:
16:    ;Apply filter.
17:    dynFilter["Order No"] = String(Order_No.value)
18:    r.Order_No.setGenFilter(dynFilter)
19:    r.run()
20:
21:    ;Give the user only a simple menu.
22:    pop.addText("&Print...", MenuEnabled, MenuFilePrint)
23:    pop.addText("&Printer Setup...", MenuEnabled, MenuFilePrinterSetup)
24:    pop.addText("&Close", MenuEnabled, MenuControlClose)
25:    m.addPopUp("&File", pop)
26:    r.setMenu(m)
27:
28:    ;Show report and wait.
29:    r.maximize()
30:    r.wait()
31: endMethod
```


CAUTION *Line 17 in this code works fine if the field's display attributes do not display the thousands separator. If you are having trouble adopting this code to your application and cannot adjust the display attributes for the field, then strip out the thousands separator using ObjectPAL's format() method. For example, replace line 17 above with dynFilter["Order No"] = format("EI",Order_No.Value).*

Manipulating the Printer Before You Print

ObjectPAL offers the capability to manipulate the printer before you print. The System type procedures are printerGetInfo(), printerGetOptions(), printerSetCurrent(), printerSetOptions(), and enumPrinters(). For example, to get a listing of all the available printer setups, type lines 3–8 into the pushButton event of a button.

```
1:  ;btn :: pushButton
2:  method pushButton(var eventInfo Event)
3:     var
4:       arPrinters   Array[] String
5:     endVar
6:
7:     enumPrinters(arPrinters)
8:     arPrinters.view("Available Printer Setups")
9:  endMethod
```

In addition to these System type procedures, the Report type print() method can control the printer.

Using the *reportPrintInfo* Variable

Another option for changing printer orientation is to set reportPrintInfo.orient = PrintLandscape. The following code fragment prints a report called Customer.rsl in landscape orientation.

```
var
   r    Report
   rpi  ReportPrintInfo
endVar

rpi.orient = PrintLandscape

rpi.name = "Customer"
r.print( rpi )
```

Paper size cannot be set this way, but the number of copies, page incrementing, and starting and ending pages can be set—*if the printer driver supports these features*. To find out whether your printer driver supports these features, select File | Printer Setup: <Modify Printer Setup> <Setup>. If the Printer Setup dialog box provides fields for you to specify the number of copies, starting and ending pages, or page incrementing, then your printer driver does handle these features; otherwise, it does not.

You also can use this technique to change the master table of a report. The following code demonstrates this technique:

```
var
   r      Report
   rpi    ReportPrintInfo
endVar

rpi.name = "MYREPORT"

rpi.masterTable = "OTHER.DB"
r.print(rpi)
```

Using a Custom Toolbar with a Report

Other than menus that use the standard menu constants, you can't use user-defined pull-down menus with a report, because reports don't have ObjectPAL. Specifically, reports don't have a menuAction event to which you can add code. There is, however, an alternative solution. Create a small toolbar-style dialog box, then open the dialog box over the report. That is, after you preview the report, open the dialog box. Because dialog boxes are always on top, the options that you put on the dialog box are always seen; therefore, they are always active. In the following example, you launch a report and a dialog box from a button.

Adding a Toolbar to a Report

Suppose that you want to launch a report and a dialog box from a button and have the dialog box control the report. Because the second form is a dialog box, it always stays on top of the report and gives the user easy control over the report.

http://prestwood.com/forums/paradox/books/official/files/REPORT3.FSL.

Step By Step

1. Change your working directory to Paradox's Samples directory. Create a new form or open an existing one, and place a button on it. Label the

button **Go**, set the title of the form to **Report Form** (see the illustration shown next), and save the form as **REPORT3.FSL**.

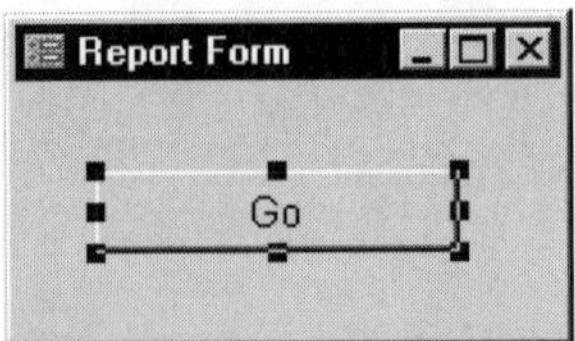

2. Add lines 3–19 to the pushButton event of the Go button on the main form and save it as **REPORT3.FSL**. Lines 4 and 5 on the Go button of the first form declare f as a Form variable and r as a Report variable. Lines 8–13 use a Report variable to either open the report or attach to it and bring it to the top if it's open. Line 12 specifically sets a title when the report is opened. This is done so that later you can attach a Report variable to the open report. Lines 15–19 either open the small dialog box form or attach a Form variable to it and move to the small dialog box.

```
 1:   ;Button :: pushButton
 2:   method pushButton(var eventInfo Event)
 3:      var
 4:         f    Form
 5:         r    Report
 6:      endVar
 7:
 8:      if r.attach("Report 1") then
 9:         r.bringToTop()
10:      else
11:         r.open("Customer")
12:         r.setTitle("Report 1")
13:      endIf
14:
15:      if f.attach("Options") then
16:         f.moveTo()
17:      else
18:         f.open("REP-MENU")
19:      endIf
20:   endMethod
```

3. Now, create another new form with four buttons on it, set the form title to **Options**, make it a dialog box, and save it as **REP–MENU.FSL**. Label the four buttons **Design**, **Maximize**, **Go to page 5**, and **Close**, as shown here:

4. Open the REP–MENU.FSL form that you created in step 2 and add line 3 to its Var window of the Page object. Line 3 on the dialog box form declares r as a Report variable. The r Report variable is used throughout the dialog box to deal with the open report.

```
1:    ;Page :: Var
2:    Var
3:       r  Report
4:    endVar
```

5. Add lines 3–8 to the open event of the page object of the REP–MENU.FSL form.

```
1:    ;Page :: open
2:    method open(var eventInfo Event)
3:       if r.attach("Report 1") then
4:          r.bringToTop()
5:       else
6:          msgStop("Startup Error!",
                "This form is only for use with Report3.fsl")
7:          close()
8:       endIf
9:    endMethod
```


6. Add line 3 to the pushButton event of the Design button on the REP–MENU.FSL form.

```
1:    ;Button :: pushButton
2:    method pushButton(var eventInfo Event)
3:       r.design()
4:    endMethod
```

7. Add line 3 to the pushButton event of the Maximize button on the REP–MENU.FSL form.

```
1:    ;Button :: pushButton
2:    method pushButton(var eventInfo Event)
3:       r.maximize()
4:    endMethod
```

8. Add line 3 to the pushButton event of the Move to page 5 button on the REP–MENU.FSL form.

```
1:    ;Button :: pushButton
2:    method pushButton(var eventInfo Event)
3:       r.moveToPage(5)
4:    endMethod
```

9. Add lines 3 and 4 to the Close button on the REP–MENU.FSL form.

```
1:    ;Button :: pushButton
2:    method pushButton(var eventInfo Event)
3:       r.close()
4:       close()
5:    endMethod
```

10. Add lines 3–5 and 12–16 to the depart event of the REP–MENU.FSL form.

```
1:    ;Form :: depart
2:    method depart(var eventInfo MoveEvent)
3:       var
4:         f  Form
5:       endVar
6:
7:       if eventInfo.isPreFilter() then
8:          ;This code executes for each object on the form
9:       else
10:         ;This code executes only for the form
11:         if f.attach("Report Form") then
12:           f.moveTo()
13:         else
14:           f.open("REPORT3")
```

```
            endIf
        endIf
    endMethod
```

11. Check your syntax and save both forms. Close the REP–MENU form and run the first REPORT3.FSL form. Click the Go button. The report opens first, and the dialog box opens on top of it. You can select either the pull-down menus or the buttons from the dialog box form that you created. It doesn't matter whether the report or the dialog box is active (see Figure 12-2).

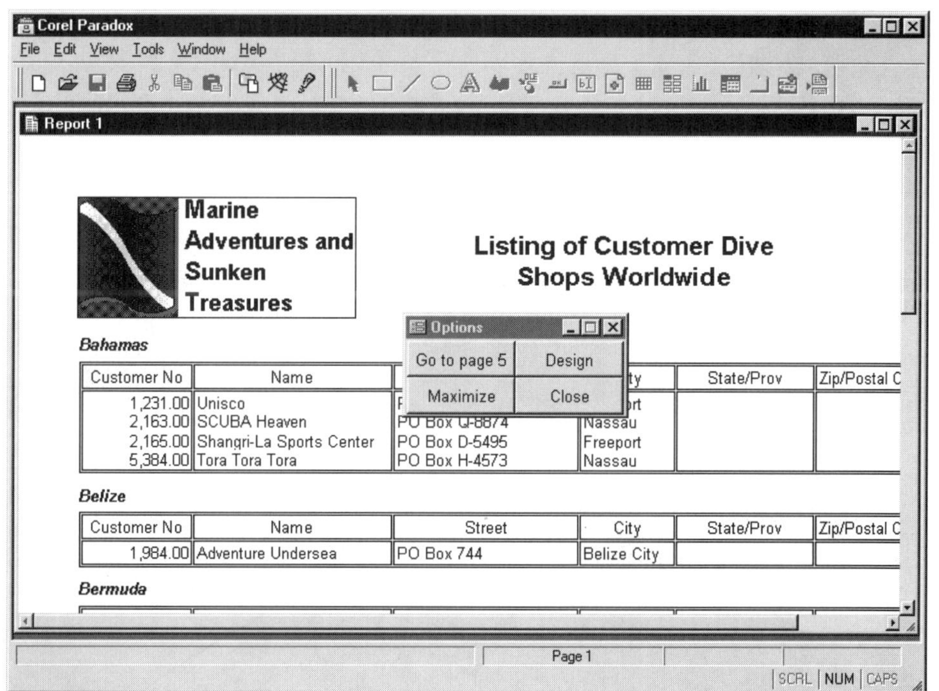

FIGURE 12-2 REP–MENU.FSL and a report; the form always stays above the report because it's a dialog box

Summary

In this chapter, you learned about using reports and integrating them into your application. You learned how to run a report using the open() method, how to print a report with the print() method, and how to control a report with a query and with setGenFilter() and setMenu(). You also learned how to manipulate the printer before you print.

CHAPTER 13

Crosstabs and Charts

Crosstabs and charts allow you to look at your data in various and creative ways. They allow you to focus on subsets of data. Often, you need to gather the data in your tables into a cross-tabulating summary. You can do this with either a crosstab or a chart. A crosstab shows you the raw data, while a chart displays the data graphically. This chapter delves into creating and using crosstabs and charts.

Using Crosstabs

Crosstabs give you a whole new way to analyze your data. A *crosstab* is an object you place on a form or report that enables you to summarize data in one field by expressing it in terms of two other fields. These spreadsheet-like structures are easy for the user to understand. Unfortunately, crosstabs aren't used enough by developers. So, keep in mind that another way to improve the look and feel of an application is to use crosstabs to show summaries of information. In today's technological world, people are bombarded with information. Users expect to be presented with neat little packages of information.

Just like queries, crosstabs are valuable for getting at hidden information in your tables. A crosstab does the following:

- Classifies data by one or more categories
- Sorts the summarized information
- Summarizes the data within these categories
- Displays information in a spreadsheet format with rows and columns

Crosstabs and Charts

A table's fields often represent separate sets, or categories, of data. Cross-tabulating data focuses on summaries of data from one or more fields of a table that are divided into the categories of unique values from one or more other fields of the table. A crosstab shows this data, while a chart presents the data graphically.

One-Dimensional Summary Crosstabs

A simple crosstab is one-dimensional. You analyze one type of data in light of another. For example, you can see how order amounts break down when classified by the method customers used to pay for them.

Creating Crosstabs

Crosstabs can be designed on either a form or report. To create a crosstab, use the Crosstab tool. The quickest way to get to the Crosstab tool is to open the table and select Tools | Quick Design | Quick Crosstab. The Quick Crosstab feature enables you to define your crosstab and places it on a form for the user to modify. The Quick Crosstab feature eliminates keystrokes for the user; however, it does not enable you to define a crosstab with a query—only with a table. Figure 13-1 shows a quick crosstab based on the VENDORS.DB table. In this case, the crosstab is a one-dimensional horizontal crosstab showing the count of vendors per state.

Using Quick Crosstab

To create the crosstab in Figure 13-1, follow these steps.

1. Open the VENDORS.DB table located in Paradox's Samples folder.

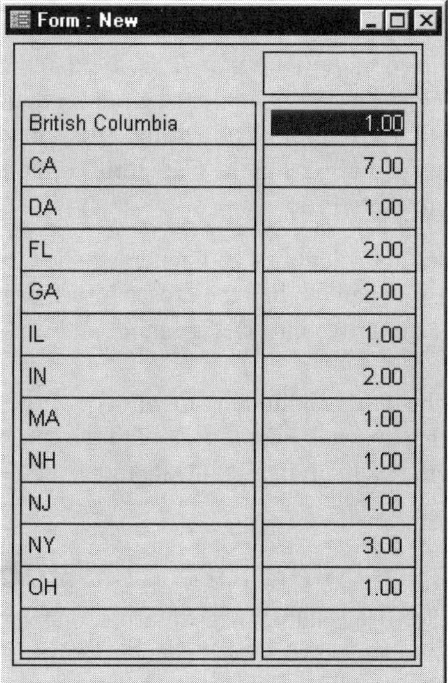

FIGURE 13-1 A 1-D horizontal crosstab

2. With the table open, open the Define Crosstab dialog box by selecting Tools | Quick Design | Quick Crosstab.

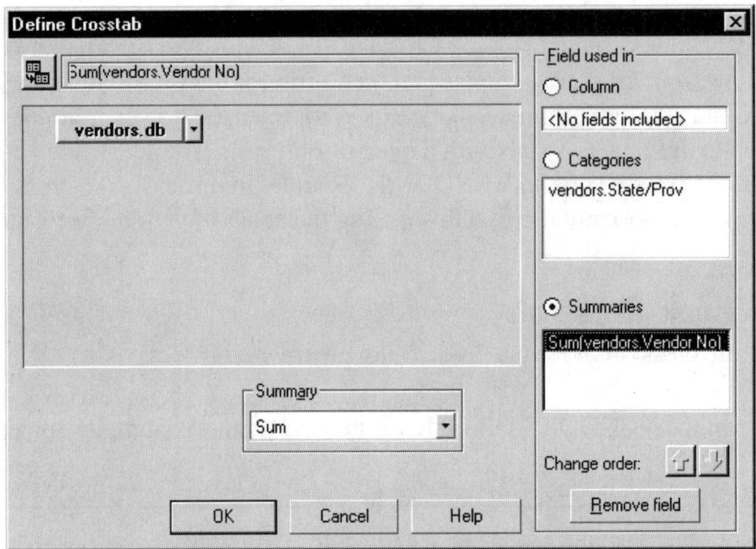

3. Set the Categories option to the State/Prov field and the Summaries option to Vendor No. Note that we skipped the Column option. If you want to change this crosstab from a 1-D horizontal crosstab to a 1-D vertical crosstab, then instead of setting the Categories option to State/Prov, set the Column option to State/Prov.

4. Choose OK. Paradox calculates and generates the crosstab in a new form. From this form, you can modify the crosstab further in the Form Design window. Press F8 to move into Design mode.

Paradox generates the data in a hidden table in your private directory and creates a new form with a crosstab object on it with the settings you indicated. Notice Paradox brings the form up in View Data mode, as Figure 13-1 shows.

Two-Dimensional Summary Crosstabs

A more complex type of crosstab summarizes information by more than one category. Two-dimensional crosstabs add an additional element to the design stage. This enables you to display a cross-reference to some other piece of information. For example, the Orders table contains a Month field, whose values are month-of-sale dates. With this field and the Payment Method field, you can generate a crosstab that presents the sum of orders by payment method and by month. The numbers are spread out to reflect both the months when the orders were placed and the method used to pay for them. Values from the Payment Method field appear across the top, and values from the Month field appear down the left side.

Creating a Two-Dimensional Crosstab Using the Crosstab Expert

Suppose you wish to know how many customers placed orders during each month, sorted by payment type. To do this, you need to create a two-dimensional crosstab that displays the months across the columns, payment methods down the rows, and sums the amount paid for each payment type by month.

Step By Step

1. Change your working directory to Paradox's Samples directory and create a blank form with ORDERS.DB in the data model.
2. In the Form Design window, use the Crosstab tool to place a blank crosstab on the form. The Crosstab Expert starts (see the following illustration). Select the Orders table and select Next.

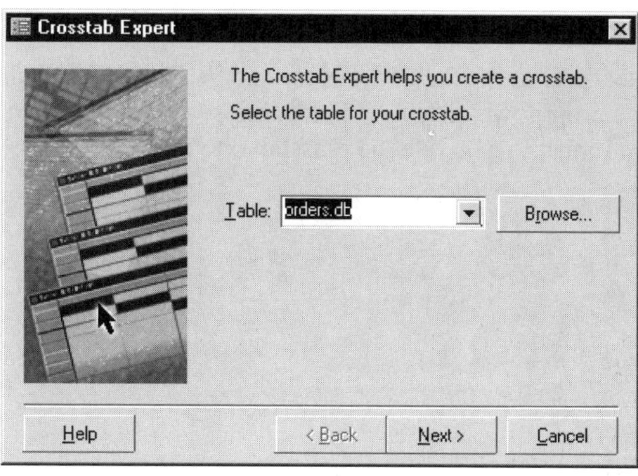

If the Crosstab Expert doesn't start, then you need to check the "Run experts when creating objects on documents" option on the Experts tab of the Preferences dialog box (see next).

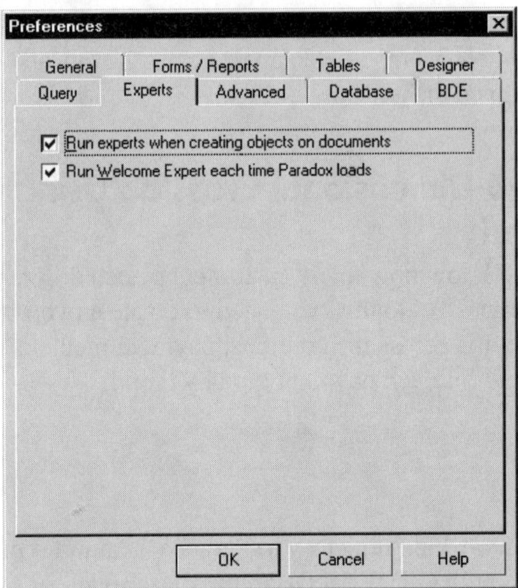

3. With the Month field selected, click the Add as Column Heading button. This adds the Month field to the crosstab's columns.
4. With the Payment Method field selected, click the Add as Row button. This adds the Payment Method field to the crosstab's rows.
5. Click Next and move the Order No to the Fields to Calculate on column. From the drop-down Calculate field, choose Count (see next). Select Next and then Finish to generate the crosstab on your form.

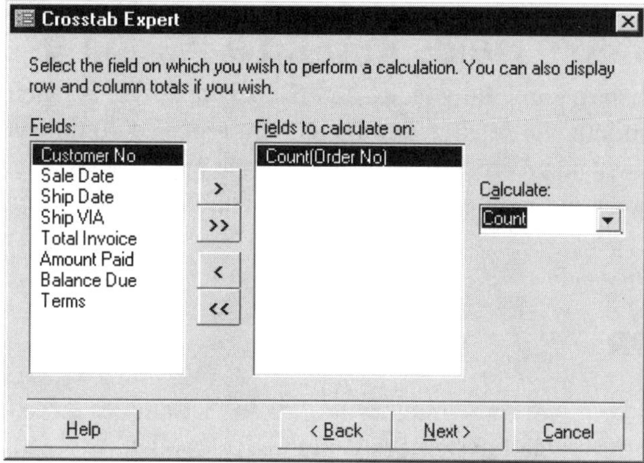

6. Switch the form to View Data mode (shown next). The summary information (count of orders) appears sorted in columns by Month (alphabetical order, not numerical order) and in rows by Payment Method. This is a convenient way of analyzing the payment habits of customers over a period of time.

Form : New

	Apr	Aug	Dec	Feb	Jan	Jul	Jun
AmEx			4			2	1
COD		3					
Cash	3	3		1	1	1	
Check	1	1	1	3		3	2
Credit	10	8	3	4	7	8	12
MC	5	2	1	3		5	7
Visa	5	4	2		2	6	3

Using Multiple Fields in a Row Heading

Suppose you wish to know how many orders each customer is placing, broken down by each month and separated into payment type. To do this, you need to create a two-dimensional crosstab that displays the payment type across the columns, customer and months down the rows, and counts the order number for each payment type.

Step By Step

1. Change your working directory to Paradox's Samples directory and create a blank form with ORDERS.DB in the data model.
2. In the Form Design window, use the Crosstab tool to place a blank crosstab on the form. The Crosstab Expert starts. Select the Orders table and select Next.
3. Add the Payment Method field to the column heading and add both Customer No and Month to the row heading (see next).

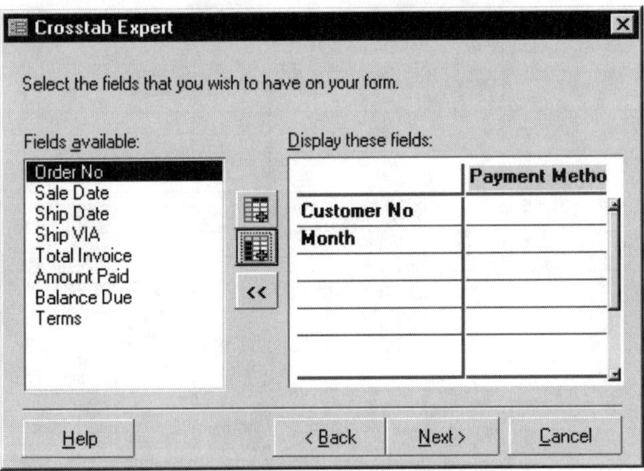

4. Click Next and move the Order No to the Fields to Calculate on column. From the drop-down Calculate field, choose Count (see next). Select Next and then Finish to generate the crosstab on your form.

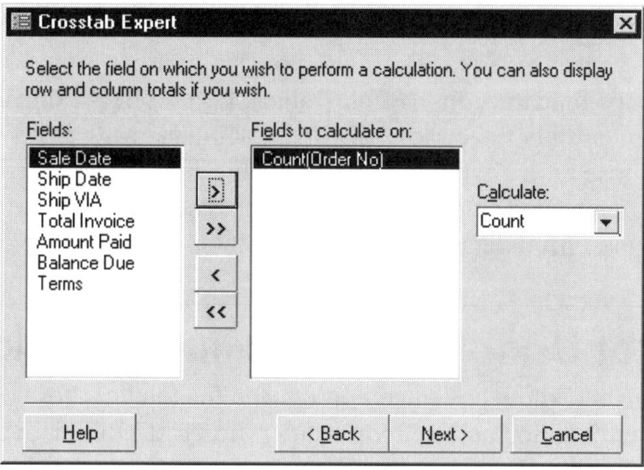

5. Switch the form to View Data mode (see next).

Form : New

	Cash	Check	Credit	MC
1,231.00 Apr			1.00	
1,231.00 Aug			1.00	
1,231.00 Feb		1.00		
1,231.00 Jan			1.00	
1,231.00 Jul			2.00	
1,231.00 May		1.00	1.00	

Using Multiple Summary Fields

Whether your crosstab is one-dimensional or two-dimensional, you need to specify the field(s) that contain the data you want to summarize in the crosstab. A one-dimensional crosstab summarizes just within each of the categories represented by the column headings or just within each of the row categories. A two-dimensional crosstab summarizes by the categories of both the column and the row.

Paradox distinguishes whether the field has summary features by the field type. For example, if you select a numeric field, you can perform Sum, Count, Min, Max, and Average functions on the field values. If you select a character or date field, Paradox gives only the options of Count, Min, and Max to be summarized.

You can choose as many fields as are available and that are valid from the tables of the data model. The order in which you choose them determines the order in which the summarized data appears in each block, or cell, of the crosstab.

Example of Using Multiple Summary Fields

Suppose you wish to know how many orders and the total of those orders broken down by Payment Method and categorized per month. To do this, you need to create a two-dimensional crosstab that displays the Payment Method across the columns, the Month down the rows, and then counts the Order No for each Payment Method and sums the Amount Paid.

Step By Step

1. Change your working directory to Paradox's Samples directory and create a blank form with ORDERS.DB in the data model.
2. In the Form Design window, use the Crosstab tool to place a blank crosstab on the form. The Crosstab Expert starts. Select the Orders table and then select Next.
3. Add the Payment Method field to the column heading and add Month to the row heading.

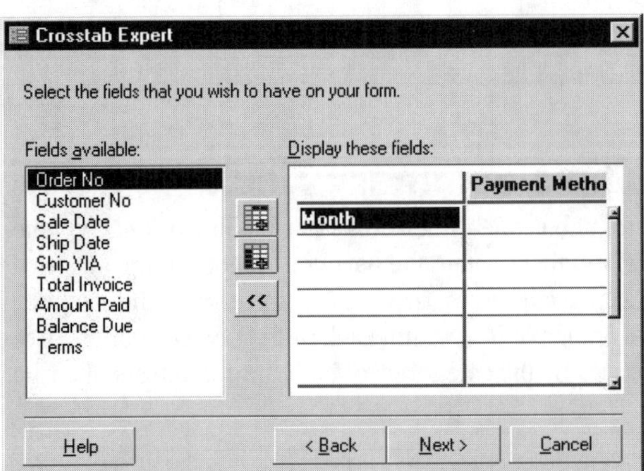

4. Click Next and move the Order No and Total Invoice fields to the Fields to Calculate on column. Change both to Sum using the Calculate field option (see next). Select Next and then Finish to generate the crosstab on your form.

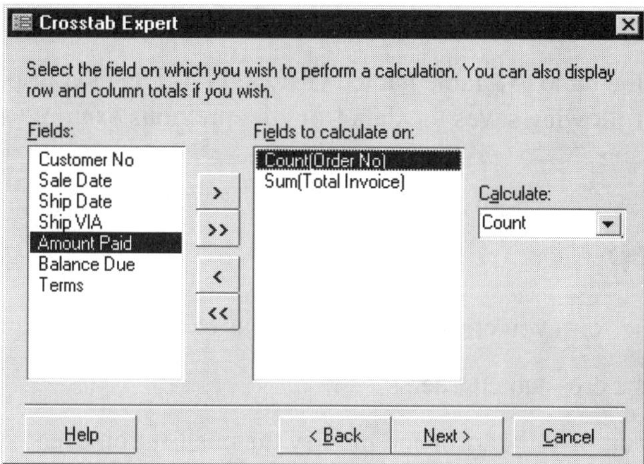

5. Switch the form to View Data mode (see next).

Form : New

	AmEx	COD	Cash	Check
Apr			3 $106,941.00	1 $3,525.00
Aug		3 $5,388.80	3 $51,107.70	1 $18,532.00
Dec	4 $56,839.95			1 $51,730.80
Feb			1 $33,540.00	3 $32,984.85
Jan			1 $1,701.00	
Jul	2 $3,850.00		1 $2,356.90	3 $59,984.15

Saving the Data of a Crosstab

You can save the data generated by a crosstab using the following line of code:

```
action(DataSaveCrosstab)
```

This saves the table to a table named CROSSTAB.DB in your private directory. The following saves the data from the previous example and opens the generated table.

Step By Step

1. Open the form you created in the previous example in Design mode.
2. Name the crosstab ctOrders.
3. Add a button to the form and modify the pushButton event as follows:

```
method pushButton(var eventInfo Event)
   const
      CROSSTAB = ":priv:crosstab.db"
   endConst
   var
      tvCrosstab TableView
   endVar

   ctOrders.action(DataSaveCrosstab)
   tvCrosstab.open(CROSSTAB)
endMethod
```

4. Switch the form to View Data mode and press the button.

Crosstab Errors

Paradox runs a query to calculate a crosstab's summary information. This hidden temporary table is put in your private directory. The process might fail if the resulting answer table contains more than 1,000 fields, or if you have inadequate disk space for the query. When the crosstab fails, an empty grid appears in its place.

Multitable Crosstabs

You can create a crosstab that takes its information from more than one table. A crosstab can draw information from any number of tables that are linked in a single-valued (1:1 or M:1) relationship. For example, if you want to view the number of items in stock by equipment class and the vendor that supplies them, you can link the Stock and Vendors tables. You're then free to define the rows, columns, and summary fields of the crosstab using any field from either table.

NOTE *You can use fields from multiple linked tables only if the link is single-valued. You can't crosstab information from fields of multiple tables linked in multiple-valued one-to-many relationships. In a one-to-many relationship, you can crosstab information from the master or child only. You cannot use fields from both.*

Using this type of crosstab, you can look at combinations of information in a new way and analyze your buying strategies accordingly.

Crosstabs of Detail Tables

Suppose you have a linked multiple-valued (one-to-many) relationship and you want to see a summary crosstab of only those records in the detail table that apply to a record of the master table. For example, you can link the Customer and Orders tables. In this relationship, each customer can have many orders. You can link the two tables and create a crosstab on the detail table, Orders. You can then place the Customer No or Name field (or both) from the master table, Customer, on the form. Because of the data model, Paradox knows that the information in the crosstab applies only to the current record of the master table.

Later in this chapter, you'll see a crosstab of the detail table Orders that sums the Total Invoice field by Payment Method and by Month for each Customer. This crosstab is derived from the fields of the detail table, Orders, that summarizes information by customer; that is, by the Name field from the master table, Customer. As you scroll through the Customer table, the crosstab is updated to show each customer's order information.

The following example will not function as just stated. The crosstab will only contain information about the first customer listed in the customer table and it is not scrollable.

Step By Step

1. Change your working directory to Paradox's Samples directory and create a blank form with the Customer and Orders table in the data model (link them in a one-to-many relationship from the Customer table to the Orders table). The following illustration shows what your form should look like.

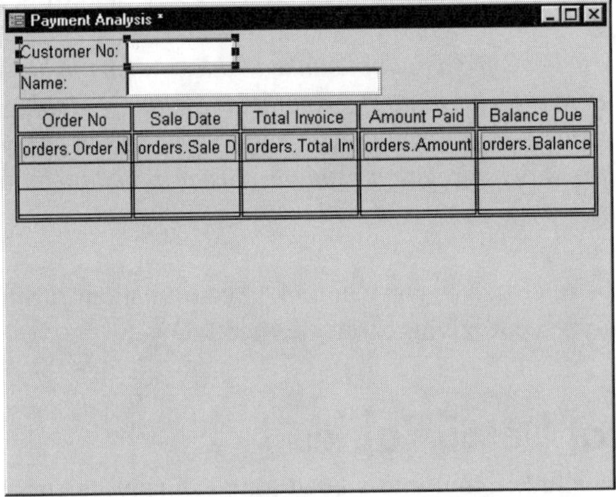

2. In the Form Design window, use the Crosstab tool to place a blank crosstab on the form. When the Crosstab Expert starts, select Cancel.
3. Right-click in the upper right of the crosstab and select Define Crosstab (see next).

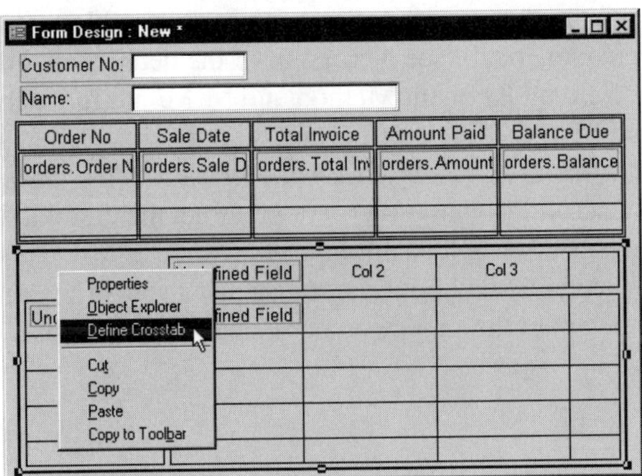

4. Add the orders.Payment Method field to the Column field, the orders.Month field to the Categories field, and summarize the orders.Total Invoice field (see next).

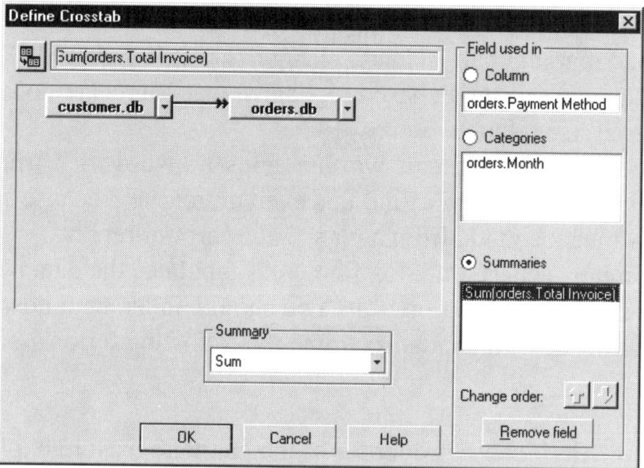

5. Save the form as **PaymentMethod.fsl** (you'll use this form in the next section). Switch the form to View Data mode (see below).

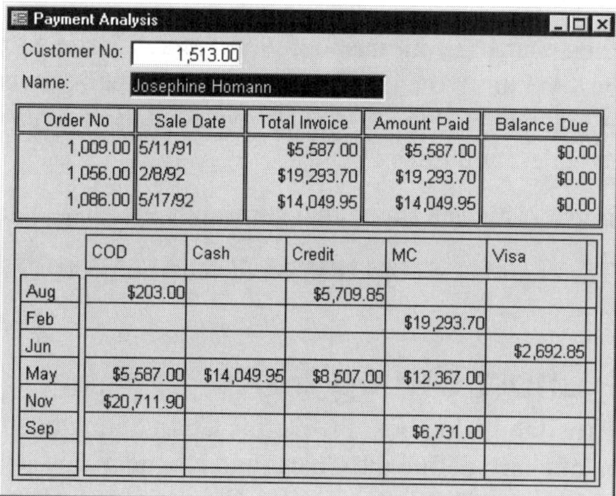

Using Charts

Charts add visual excitement and flair to your forms and reports. Using a chart to represent data visually is appealing to the eye and brain. You can use many types of charts, including line, bar, and three-dimensional pie charts. You can even combine line and marker charts. Charts change as data is changed. They are wonderful visual aids. Most database users agree that charts are not used enough, especially for analyzing data.

You have heard that a picture is worth a thousand words. It's true. If you are doing a business application, you find this even more true, because sometimes quick decisions must be made from a glance at a form or report.

When you create a chart, Paradox first cross-tabulates the data before it generates the visual representation of it. You should understand how crosstabs work before you work with charts. Examine the following terms associated with charting:

- **Title/subtitle** These properties of the chart are used to explain what the chart represents. Limited space is available, so keep it to the point.
- **Data series** This comprises the charted values, actual numbers.
- **Legend** This is a text description of the Data Series numbers.
- **Axis** When charting you must define a "versus." The X- and Y-Axes are essentially X versus Y on a chart, in which case the X-Axis is represented by a set of numbers and the Y-Axis is represented by a number. The axis has labels, scales, and titles.
- **Chart frame** This is a frame that surrounds the chart data.
- **Chart** The chart itself objects sit on the chart object.

The Define Chart Dialog Box

Like the Define Crosstab dialog box, the Define Chart dialog box enables the user to choose the type of chart, define the Chart field X- and Y-Axes values, and perform 2-D summaries on fields. The Define Chart dialog box is displayed when you use the Quick Chart, or if you use the Property Inspector on the Crosstab object, there's a Define Chart option. For those who like to do everything manually, you can avoid using this dialog box. Paradox helps create charts quicker when you are not completely sure how to define the field values with the Define Chart dialog box. In the Define Chart dialog box, you can do the following:

- Choose which type of data you're charting—tabular, one-dimensional summary, or two-dimensional summary.
- Specify the field whose values you want to use as X-Axis values.
- Specify the field(s) whose values you want to chart against the Y-Axis (the different series of the chart).
- If you're creating a two-dimensional summary chart, specify an additional field whose values you want to group the charted summary data by.
- If you're creating either a one-dimensional or two-dimensional summary chart, specify the type of summary operation to perform on each Y value field you choose.

The "Fields used in" options are similar to those of the crosstabs. Choose the radio button of choice and select the field from the table drop-down box. Both the X- and Y-Axes values of the "Field used in" option must be defined to continue to the Define Chart dialog box. What makes this dialog box different from the Define Crosstab dialog box is the data type options. The data type options enable you to define charts differently. Descriptions of each of the data types are in the following sections.

Adding a Chart to a Form

In this next example, we will add a pie chart to the PaymentMethod.fsl form you created in the last example.

1. Open the PaymentMethod.fsl form from the previous example in Design Form mode.
2. Add a chart to the form (you may need to resize the page of the form). When the Chart Expert starts, select Cancel (you may want to explore the Chart Expert on your own; it makes creating charts very easy).
3. Right-click in the upper-right corner of the chart and select Define Chart (see Figure 13-2).

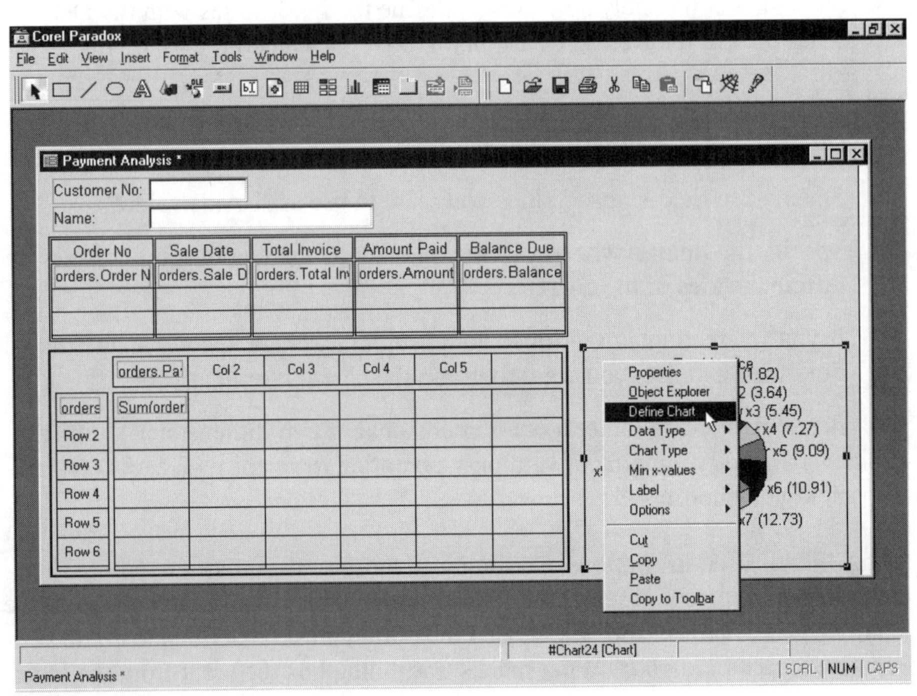

FIGURE 13-2 Opening the Define Chart dialog box

4. Select 1-D Summary in the Data type panel, add the orders.Payment Method to the X-Axis, and sum the orders.Total Invoice in the Y-Value (see next).

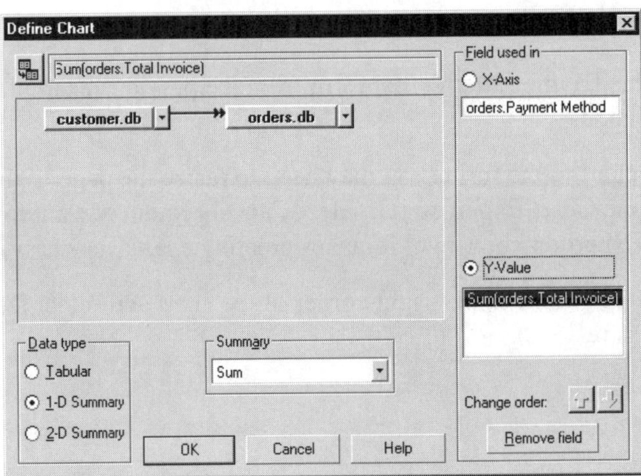

5. Switch the form to View Data mode (see next).

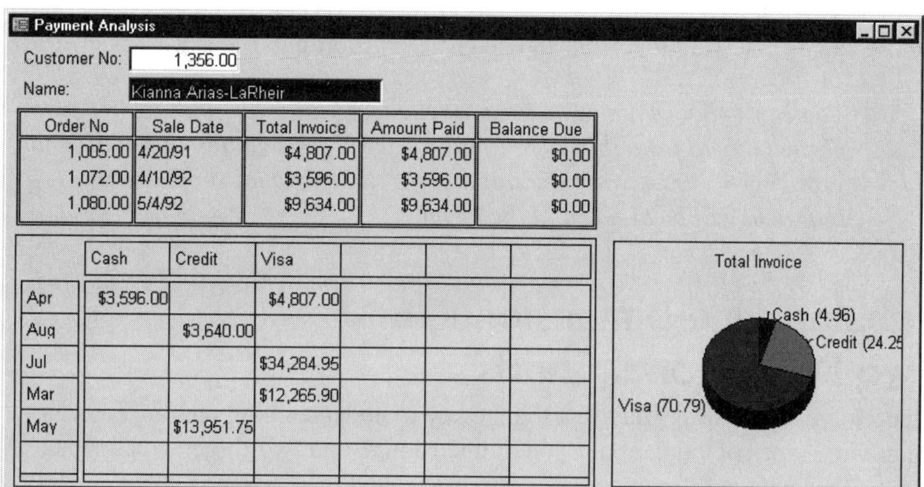

Choosing the Chart's Data Type

In the lower-left corner of the Define Chart dialog box, select the data type of the chart:

- Tabular (the default)
- 1-D Summary
- 2-D Summary

The "Field used in" panel on the right side of the dialog box changes, depending on which data type you choose.

Specifying X-Axis Values

When you first open the Define Chart dialog box, X-Axis is selected by default in the "Field used in" area. With X-Axis selected, choose a field from the drop-down menu of the table whose unique values you want to be the X-Axis values. You can only choose one field to supply X-Axis values for all three data types—tabular, one-dimensional summary, and two-dimensional summary.

Specifying the Y-Axis Values

With Y-Value selected, choose the field(s) from the drop-down menu of the table whose values you want to define and be charted according to the Y-Axis measure.

NOTE *You can't choose the same field for X and Y values. If you've already chosen a field from this table to supply the X-Axis values—or additional grouping values if you're creating a two-dimensional summary chart—that field will be dimmed in the menu.*

Tabular, One-Dimensional, and Two-Dimensional Charts

Understanding the three data types is the key to understanding charts. You can chart three types of data: tabular, one-dimensional, and two-dimensional. Once you understand the differences between these data types, charting specific data becomes easier.

Tabular Charts

A tabular chart measures the values in one numeric field within each category represented by the unique values in another field. The Tabular Chart type enables the designer to plot the data in the X-field value versus the Y-field value. There are no Summaries on any of the fields. The tabular format enables you to add many fields to the Y-field value area so that you can compare other field values side by side. In a tabular format, the Y-field values must be numeric. Paradox grays out all other fields that are not numeric. You must specify the following for a tabular chart:

- One field for X-Axis values.
- One or more fields for the Y-Value (each field becomes a series in the chart).

Step By Step

1. Change your working directory to Paradox's Samples directory and create a blank form with the Customer and Orders tables in the data model (link them in a one-to-many relationship from the Customer table to the Orders table). Your form should look like the one shown here.

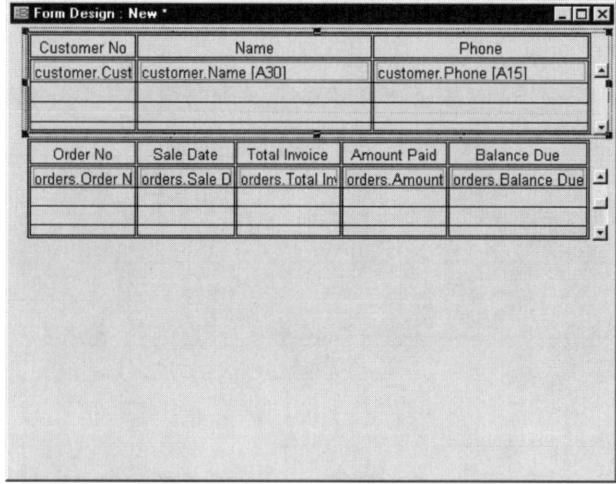

2. In the Form Design window, add a blank chart on the form. When the Chart Expert starts, select Cancel.

3. Right-click in the upper right of the chart and select Define Chart.

4. In the Data type panel, select Tabular. Add the orders.Customer No field to the X-Axis area. Next add orders.Total Invoice, orders.Amount Paid, and orders.Balance Due to the Y-Value area (see next).

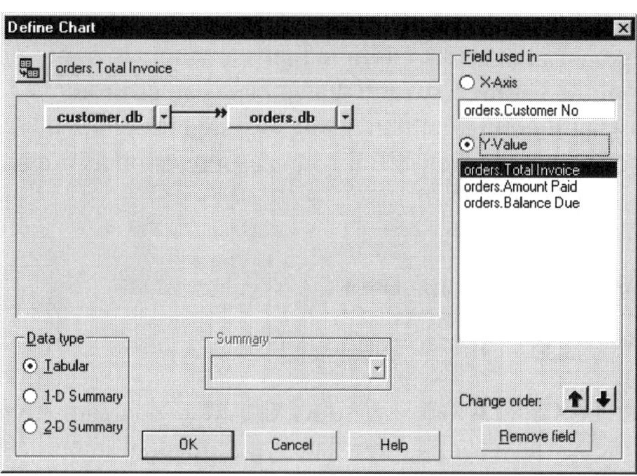

5. Switch the form to View Data mode (see next).

Balance Due Analysis

Customer No	Name	Phone
1221	Lisa Anne Prestwood	808-555-0269
1231	Matthew Martinez	809-555-3915
1351	Soren Hoffman	357-6-876708
1354	Valentine Hoffman	809-555-8576

Order No	Sale Date	Total Invoice	Amount Paid	Balance Due
1001	4/3/91	$7,320.00	$7,320.00	$0.00
1023	7/1/91	$1,414.00	$0.00	$1,414.00
1059	2/24/92	$33,540.00	$33,540.00	$0.00

One-Dimensional Summary Charts

The 1-D (one-dimensional) Summary is similar to the tabular format, except you can summarize on the Y-field value, which cannot be done in the Tabular format. In addition to the default value of the Sum operator, you can perform additional functions on the Y-field value, such as Count, Min, Max, and Average. Like the Tabular data type, you can select multiple fields to summarize on. Similar to what you learned about the Define Crosstab dialog box, you can remove fields from the Y-Value area by highlighting the field and choosing the Remove Field button. You must include the following when defining a one-dimensional summary chart:

- One field for the X-values
- One or more summary fields for the Y-value(s)
- The summary operation to perform on each Y-field

SPECIFYING THE X-AXIS IN A 1-D SUMMARY CHART You can only choose one field to supply the X-value for all three data types: tabular, one-dimensional summary, and two-dimensional summary.

SPECIFYING THE Y-VALUE IN A 1-D SUMMARY CHART If the data type of the chart is one-dimensional summary, you can choose as many of the table's available and valid fields to define the Y-value as you need. When you choose a Y-value field, Paradox automatically couples it with a default summary operation.

If you don't want the default summary operation Paradox chooses by default, select the summary field in the Y-Value panel whose summary operation you want to change. Then, choose one of the available summary operations for that field from the Summary drop-down list.

Two-Dimensional Summary Charts

In the previous examples, you've learned about the basics behind building a chart in a 1-D view, so take a look at designing and running a 2-D chart. You must define the following for a two-dimensional summary chart:

- One field for the X-values
- One field to group by (each unique value will be a series)
- One summary field for the Y-value
- The summary to perform on the Y-value

The 2-D (two-dimensional) summary has the same features as the 1-D summary with the addition of a Group By radio button. The Group By option allows a second grouping addition to the X-Axis of the charted data. The Group By option only allows one field selection; if the 2-D summary data type has been selected, Paradox requires a field value to be defined. To define the group field, select one of the available fields from the table drop-down button.

In addition to these options, the Define Chart dialog box includes the Data Modeling button in the top-left corner. If you select this option, Paradox brings up the Data Model dialog box and enables you to redefine your data model. As I mentioned earlier, you can avoid the Define Chart dialog box by using the Property Inspector and manually defining the field values. You will probably save time, though, designing your crosstab if you use the Define Chart dialog box. Paradox tries to help steer you in the right direction if you are unsure of the defining of values.

SPECIFYING THE X-AXIS 2-D SUMMARY CHART You can only choose one field to supply X-Axis values for all three data types—tabular, one-dimensional summary, and two-dimensional summary.

SPECIFYING THE GROUP BY IN A 2-D SUMMARY CHART While the data type of the chart is two-dimensional summary, the title area's menu contains Define

Group. This choice isn't on this menu when the data type is tabular or one-dimensional. If you're creating a two-dimensional summary chart, choose Define Group to choose one field whose unique values you want to group the summary data by. The summary data is also grouped by the categories of the X-Axis values.

If the data type of the chart is two-dimensional summary, you can choose any one of a table's available and valid fields to group the summary data by. The data is also grouped by the X-Axis categories. With Grouped By selected, choose from the drop-down menu of the table field you want to group the summary data by.

SPECIFYING THE Y-VALUE IN A 2-D SUMMARY CHART If the data type of the chart is two-dimensional summary, you can choose any one of a table's available and valid fields to define the Y-Axis. When you choose the Y-Axis field, Paradox automatically couples it with a default summary operation. See the previous section for a description of the default summary operations Paradox chooses for specific field types and how to change the summary operation.

While the data type of the chart is two-dimensional summary, you can only choose one field for the single series allowed for this data type. The Y-Axis menu contains Define Y-Value. Choose Define Y-Value to choose one field whose values you want to define and be charted according to the Y-Axis.

Charts and ObjectPAL

For information on creating and manipulating charts using ObjectPAL, refer to the "Creating a Chart from Scratch" and "A Simple Example of Manipulating a Chart Property" sections in Chapter 17.

Summary

Today's users expect applications to be sophisticated. Using color wisely, adding charts, and sticking with the 32-bit Windows paradigm will go a long way to creating easy-to-use applications. Adding charts and crosstabs to your business database applications will give them true sophistication.

CHAPTER 14

Using Table and TCursor Variables

A *table* is an object that consists of rows of records and columns of fields. In ObjectPAL, a Table variable is a handle to a table on disk or to a table located on a SQL server. It's different from a TCursor variable. A TCursor variable looks at the data in a table, whereas a Table variable looks at the whole table. Table variables enable you to manipulate tables as a whole. For example, you can add records from one table to another, copy a table, and get the average value for a field. Table object type methods and procedures deal with the table as a whole.

A TCursor (table cursor) is a pointer to a record (or row) in a table. A TCursor is a tool used to manipulate a table directly without going through a UIObject. After you declare a TCursor variable, you can use it to open a handle to the first row of a specific table. Once open, you then have a handle to the data in the table.

The Table Object

An open() method is conspicuously absent from the table methods. The attach() method associates a Table variable with a table's filename. The extension .DB and .DBF specify the type of table. To use a Table variable, you need to declare it, as in the following:

```
var
   tbl  Table
endVar
```

After you have a Table variable with which to work, you open it by attaching directly to a table on disk, as in the following:

```
tbl.attach("CUSTOMER.DB")
```

For example, to display the total number of customers in the Customer table, alter the pushButton event of a button as follows:

```
method pushButton(var eventInfo Event)
   const
      CUSTOMER = ":work:Customer.db"
   endConst
   var
      tblCustomer Table
   endVar
```

```
   tblCustomer.attach(CUSTOMER)
   msgInfo("Number of Customers", tblCustomer.cCount("Customer No"))
endMethod
```

Using Table Methods and Procedures

Many of the table methods deal with data in the table and are duplicated in the TCursor class. After you declare a Table variable and open it with attach(), you can use the Table methods on it. The following statements, for example, are valid:

```
tbl.attach("DEST.DB")
tbl.cMax("Total")
tbl.delete()
```

The next example puts the cAverage() method to work with a Table variable.

Using *cAverage()* with a Table Variable

Suppose that you want to find the average sale for all invoices in the Customer table. You can do this by using cAverage() and a Table variable.

Step By Step

1. Change your working directory to Paradox's Samples directory. Open a form or create a new one. Place a button labeled **Average Order** on it.

2. Alter the pushButton event of the button as follows:

```
;Button :: pushButton
method pushButton(var eventInfo Event)
   const
      ORDERS = ":work:Orders.db"
   endConst
   var
      tblOrders Table
   endVar

   tblOrders.attach(ORDERS)
   msgInfo("Average Order", tblOrders.cAverage("Total Invoice"))
endMethod
```

3. Check the syntax, save the form as **TableExamples.fsl**, and change the mode to View Data. Click the button. After a short time, the answer appears onscreen:

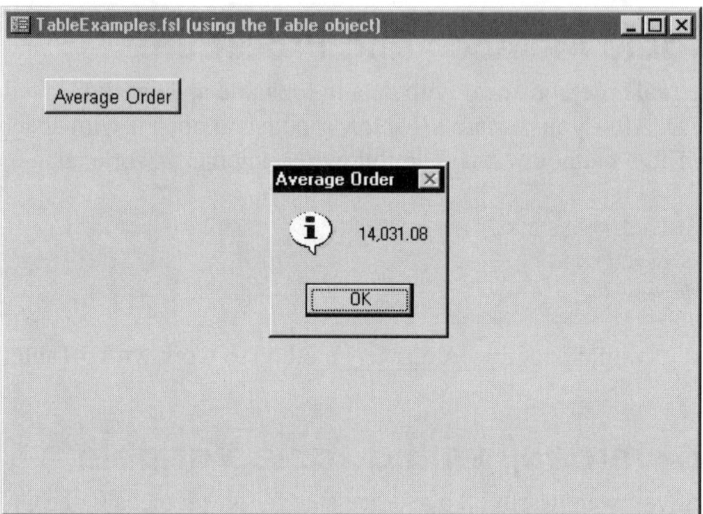

Compacting dBASE and Paradox tables

Deleted records are not immediately removed from a dBASE table. Instead, they are flagged as deleted and kept in the table. In addition, if you delete records from a Paradox table, they cannot be retrieved. However, the table file and associated index files contain dead space where the record was originally stored. To compact a Paradox table, alter the pushButton event of a button as follows:

```
method pushButton(var eventInfo Event)
   const
      ORDERS = ":work:Orders.db"
   endConst
   var
      tblOrders Table
      regIndex  Logical
   endVar

   tblOrders.attach(ORDERS)

   try
```

```
      regIndex = True
      if not tblOrders.compact(regIndex) then errorShow() endIf
   onFail
      ;There probably is a lock on the table.
      errorShow()
   endTry
endMethod
```

For dBASE tables, the optional argument regIndex specifies whether to regenerate or update the indexes associated with the table. When regIndex is set to True, this method regenerates all indexes associated with the table. If you use compact() with a Paradox table, all indexes are regenerated and dead space is removed. This method fails if any locks have been placed on the table or the table is open. This method returns True if successful; otherwise, it returns False.

Creating Tables

You can use the Create keyword to create a table. The following example demonstrates creating a Paradox table:

```
method pushButton(var eventInfo Event)
   const
      CUSTOMERNOTES = ":work:CustomerNotes.db"
   endConst
   var
      tblCustomerNotes   Table
      tvCustomerNotes    TableView
   endVar

   if isTable(CUSTOMERNOTES) then
      if msgQuestion("Confirm", "Table exists. Overwrite it?") <> "Yes"  then
         return
      endIf
   endIf

   errorTrapOnWarnings(True)

   tblCustomerNotes = create CUSTOMERNOTES
   with   "Customer No"     : "N",
          "Notes"            : "F",
          "ModifyTimeStamp"  : "@"
```

```
        key     "Customer No"
        endCreate

        tvCustomerNotes.open(CUSTOMERNOTES)
    endMethod
```

The TCursor Object

When you use a TCursor, it works in the background similar to another user. You can manipulate a TCursor variable just like any other variable using any of the TCursor object type methods. In fact, a TCursor has many of the same methods as a UIObject. The Table object type doesn't have nearly as many methods as a TCursor does. Its functionality is more limited because it operates only for the table as a whole, whereas a TCursor works directly on the data.

Think of a TCursor as a channel you open to a table. Typically, you open a TCursor with the following:

```
tc.open("TABLE.DB")
```

tc is a TCursor class variable. All further references to the table can be represented by the TCursor as in the following:

```
tc.FieldName = Today()
```

In this example, quotation marks aren't used around the field name in the table. Quotation marks aren't needed for field names that have no special characters. If, however, a field name contains a special character, such as a space or a hyphen, quotation marks are required. For the sake of consistency, you might put quotation marks around all field names when you use a TCursor, as in the following example:

```
tc."FieldName" = Today()
```

A TCursor works in the background. Therefore, when you manipulate a database, movement through the table doesn't appear onscreen. Because the screen isn't refreshed, changes are made quickly.

Using a TCursor

Treat a TCursor variable like other variables. Declare it in the Var window of the object. If the method executes only once (like pushButton), or if you need a private version of the variable, declare it within the method.

In general, opening and closing a TCursor can be time-consuming because opening and closing a file on a disk is slower than leaving it open. Therefore, it's best to minimize the number of times you open and close these objects. If the method you use occurs once, such as pushButton, it's okay to declare it inside the method:

```
;Button :: pushButton
method pushButton(var eventInfo Event)
   var
      tc    TCursor
   endVar

   tc.open("Customer.db")
   msgInfo("Current Customer", tc."Name")
   tc.close()
endMethod
```

Referring to Fields in a Table with a TCursor

ObjectPAL offers three ways to use a TCursor to refer to fields in a table: without quotes, with quotes, and dereferencing. For example:

```
1:  tc.Last_Name     ;Without quotes.
2:  tc."Last_Name"   ;With quotes (allows special characters).
3:  tc.(2)           ;Dereferencing with parentheses.
```


Line 1 refers to the field with just the field name of the field as it appears in the table. If you have a field with spaces in it—for example, Last Name—then you cannot use this first technique. Line 2 surrounds the field name with quotes and works with all field names. The preferred usage is to always use quotation marks, because it will always work. Line 3 shows how to dereference a field by surrounding it with parentheses. Line 3 is referring to the second field in the table. You could also dereference a field by using a variable. For example:

```
var
   sField       String    ;Declare a variable.
   tcCustomer   TCursor
endVar
tcCustomer.open("Customer.db")
sField = "Name"   ;Assign a field name to the variable.
view(tcCustomer.(sField))       ;Dereference the variable using parentheses.
```

Dereferencing with parentheses is a general ObjectPAL concept and is used in other places in ObjectPAL. For example, dereferencing is used with UIObjects. You can store the name of a UIObject in a variable and use it as part of your dot notation listing the object path. For example, if you name a page of a form pge1 and place a box on it named box1, you can do the following:

```
var
  sObject     String         ;Declare a variable.
endVar

sObject = "box1"             ;Assign an object name to the variable.
pge1.(sObject).color = Red   ;Dereference the variable using parentheses.
```

Example of Using a TCursor to Refer to a field

Suppose that you want to find a row based on one field and then display a different field from that record. This next example uses the Biolife table to demonstrate moveToRecord() and locate().

http://prestwood.com/forums/paradox/books/official/files/TCursorExamples.fsl.

Step By Step

1. Set your working directory to Paradox's Samples directory. Create a new form, place a drop-down field and a button labeled **Display Species** on it:

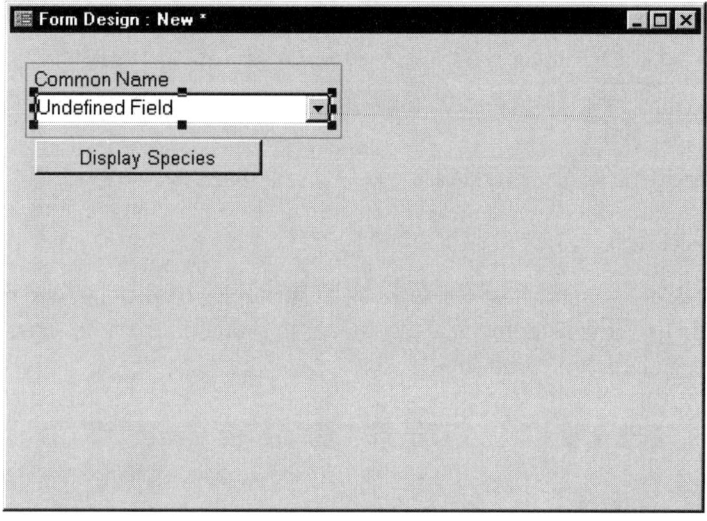

2. Name the drop-down field **fldCommonName**.
3. Alter the open event of the list object of the drop-down field as follows (use the Object Tree to get to the list object of the drop-down field).

```
method open(var eventInfo Event)
   DoDefault
   Self.datasource = "[:work:biolife.\"Common Name\"]"
endMethod
```

4. Alter the pushButton event of the button as follows:

```
;Button :: pushButton
method pushButton(var eventInfo Event)
   const
      BIOLIFE = ":work:biolife.db"
   endConst
   var
      tcBiolife   TCursor
   endVar

   if fldCommonName.isBlank() then
      msgStop("Error", "First select a common name.")
      return
   endIf
```

```
      if not tcBiolife.open(BIOLIFE) then
         errorShow()
         return
      endIf

      tcBiolife.locate("Common Name", fldCommonName.value)
      msgInfo("Species", fldCommonName.value + " = " + tcBiolife."Species Name")
   endMethod
```

5. Check the syntax, save the form as **TCursorExamples.fsl**, and change the mode to View Data mode. Select a common name from the drop-down field and click the button:

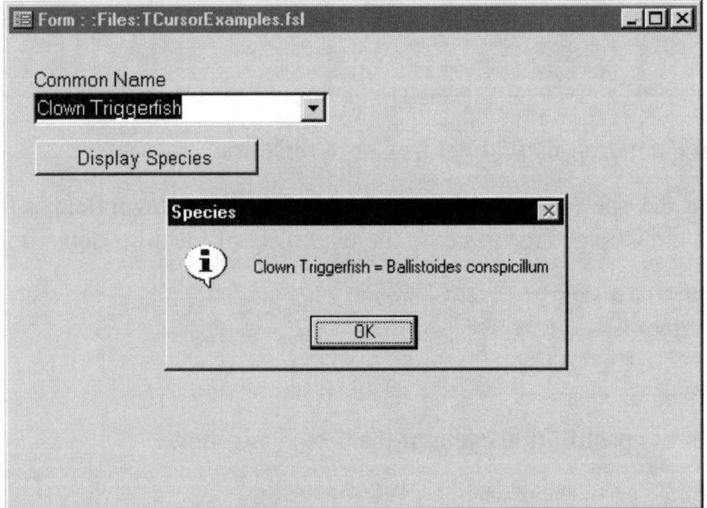

Inserting a Record with a TCursor

With a TCursor, you can manipulate and add data directly to a table with no interaction on the form, just as you can use a UIObject to put the table connected to it into Edit mode, insert a record, and post a value. Suppose that you want to insert a new record into the Customer table. To do this, open a TCursor to the Customer table and insert a new record. You can do the same tasks with a TCursor, as the following example demonstrates.

http://prestwood.com/forums/paradox/books/official/files/tc1.fsl.

Step By Step

1. Set your working directory to Paradox's Samples directory. Open the TCursorExamples.fsl form you created in the last example and add a button labeled **Add your Name**.

2. Alter the pushButton event as follows:

```
;Button :: pushButton
method pushButton(var eventInfo Event)
   const
      CUSTOMER = ":work:Customer.db"
   endConst
   var
      tcCustomer    TCursor
      sName         String
      tvCustomer    TableView
   endVar

   tcCustomer.open(CUSTOMER)
   tcCustomer.edit()
   tcCustomer.insertRecord()

   ; Enter a new customer name.
   sName = ""
   sName.view("Enter your name")
   if sName = "" then
      beep()
      message("No name entered. Aborted")
      tcCustomer.cancelEdit()
      return
   endIf
   tcCustomer.Name = sName

   ; Generate a new customer number.
   try
      tcCustomer."Customer No" = tcCustomer.cMax("Customer No") + 1
   onFail
      sleep(1000)
      retry
   endTry

```

```
    ; Post new record.
    tcCustomer.postRecord()
    tcCustomer.endEdit()
    tcCustomer.close()

    ;View table.
    tvCustomer.open(CUSTOMER)
    tvCustomer.action(MoveEnd)
    tvCustomer.action(MoveScrollLeft)
    tvCustomer.action(MoveScrollLeft)
    tvCustomer.action(MoveBeginLine)
endMethod
```

3. Check the syntax, save the form, run the form, and click the button. Nothing seems to happen. Open the Customer table. Now the first record is 100, and it displays your name.

Using *switchIndex()* with a TCursor

When you want to change the active index on a TCursor, use the switchIndex() method. The switchIndex() is in both the UIObject and TCursor object types. The syntax for switchIndex() is the same, as in the following:

```
switchIndex( [const IndexName_String][, const_stayOnRecord Logical ] ) Logical
```

To switch a table frame to a secondary index named secCity, for example, use the following:

```
CUSTOMERS.switchIndex("secCity")
```

To switch back to the primary key, leave out the secondary index, as in the following example:

```
CUSTOMERS.switchIndex()
```

You can use switchIndex() on a TCursor just like on a UIObject. You can even synchronize a UIObject connected to the same table with resync(). The next example demonstrates the technique of switching an index on a TCursor using ObjectPAL, and then resyncing it to the UIObject.

Example of Using *switchIndex()*

Suppose that you want to be able to quickly sort the Customer table by Name, City, Zip/Postal Code, or Phone Number. This is very handy for quickly looking up a customer who has forgotten their Customer No. To do this, we will have to add a secondary index for each sort we want.

http://prestwood.com/forums/paradox/books/official/files/CustomerList.fsl.

Step By Step

1. Change your working directory to Paradox's Samples directory. Create a new form with the Customer table in the data model, as shown next. Choose Tabular in the Style panel in the Design Layout dialog box.

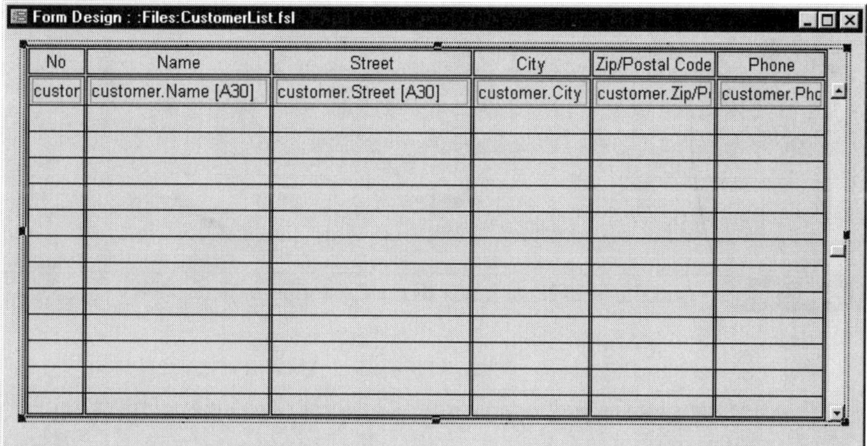

2. Name the TableFrame **tfCustomer**.

3. Restructure the Customer table and add a secondary index called **secPhone** (See Figure 14-1 for the settings).

4. Restructure the Customer table again, this time adding a secondary index called **secStreet** (see Figure 14-2 for the settings).

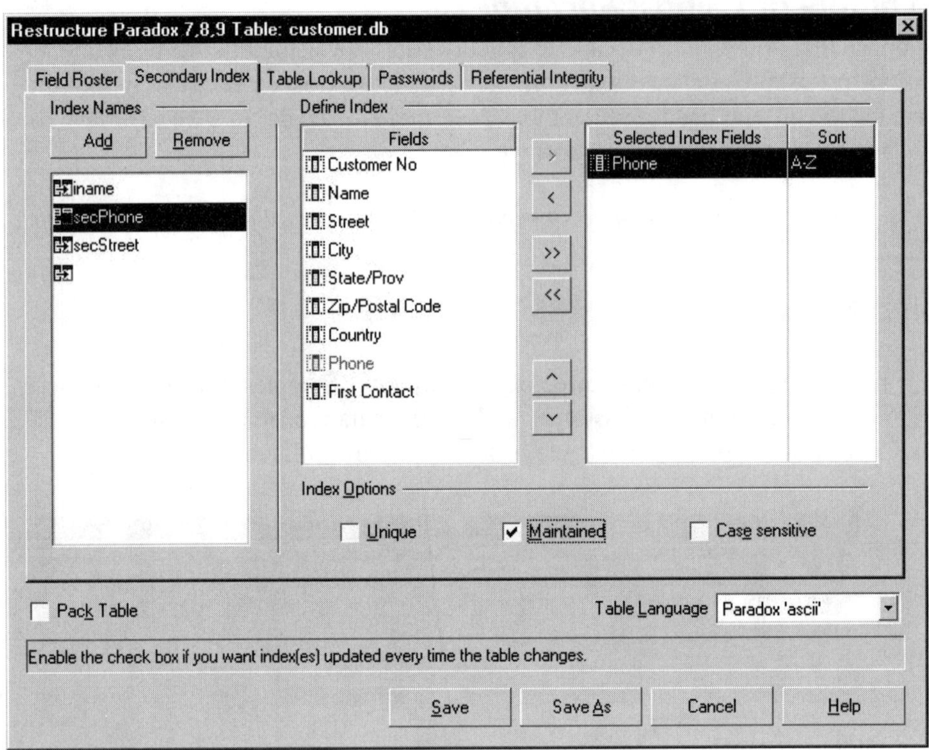

FIGURE 14-1 Add this secPhone index to the Customer table

5. Alter the mouseClick event of the Customer No heading text object as follows:

```
method mouseClick(var eventInfo MouseEvent)
   tfCustomer.switchIndex()
endMethod
```

6. Alter the mouseClick event of the Street heading text object as follows:

```
method mouseClick(var eventInfo MouseEvent)
   tfCustomer.switchIndex("secStreet")
endMethod
```

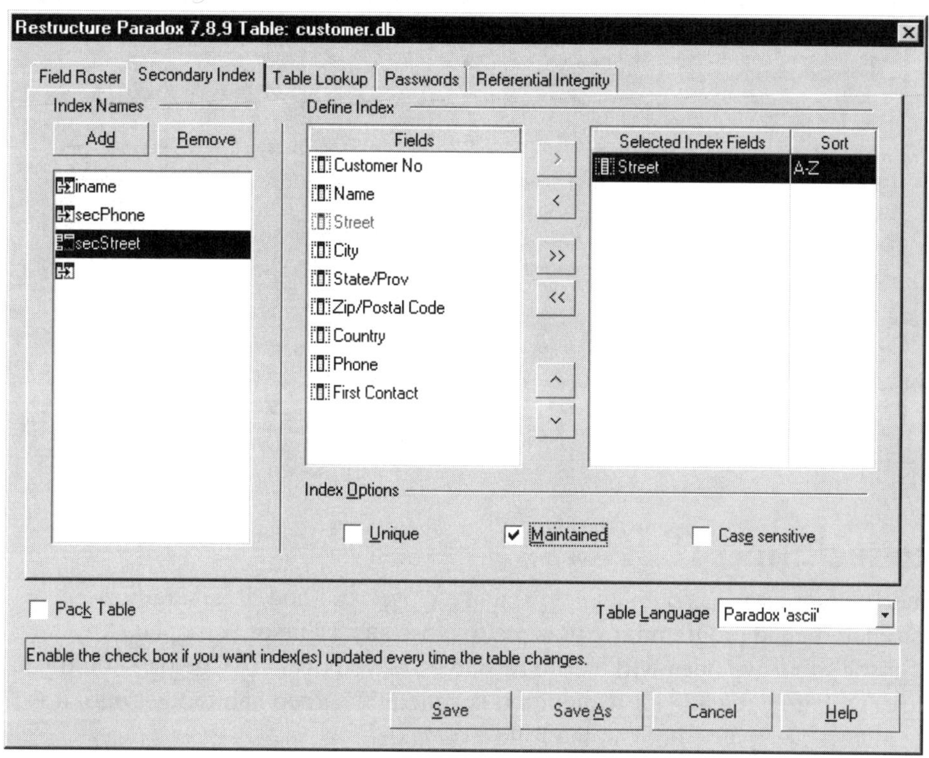

FIGURE 14-2 Add this secStreet index to the Customer table

7. Alter the mouseClick event of the Phone heading text object as follows:

```
method mouseClick(var eventInfo MouseEvent)
   tfCustomer.switchIndex("secPhone")
endMethod
```

8. Check your syntax, save the form as **CustomerList.fsl**, and switch it to View Data mode. Click the Street, Phone, and Customer No fields. This illustration shows the table sorted by street:

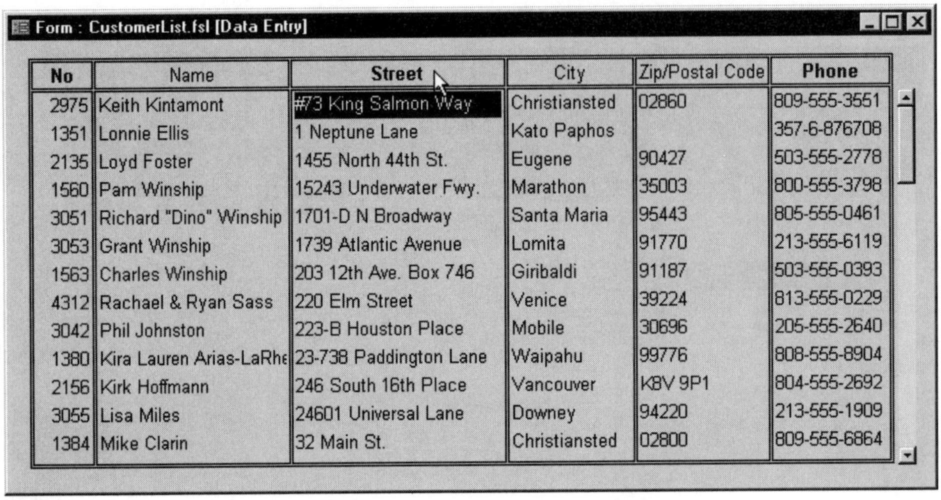

Form : CustomerList.fsl [Data Entry]

No	Name	Street	City	Zip/Postal Code	Phone
2975	Keith Kintamont	#73 King Salmon Way	Christiansted	02860	809-555-3551
1351	Lonnie Ellis	1 Neptune Lane	Kato Paphos		357-6-876708
2135	Loyd Foster	1455 North 44th St.	Eugene	90427	503-555-2778
1560	Pam Winship	15243 Underwater Fwy.	Marathon	35003	800-555-3798
3051	Richard "Dino" Winship	1701-D N Broadway	Santa Maria	95443	805-555-0461
3053	Grant Winship	1739 Atlantic Avenue	Lomita	91770	213-555-6119
1563	Charles Winship	203 12th Ave. Box 746	Giribaldi	91187	503-555-0393
4312	Rachael & Ryan Sass	220 Elm Street	Venice	39224	813-555-0229
3042	Phil Johnston	223-B Houston Place	Mobile	30696	205-555-2640
1380	Kira Lauren Arias-LaRhe	23-738 Paddington Lane	Waipahu	99776	808-555-8904
2156	Kirk Hoffmann	246 South 16th Place	Vancouver	K8V 9P1	804-555-2692
3055	Lisa Miles	24601 Universal Lane	Downey	94220	213-555-1909
1384	Mike Clarin	32 Main St.	Christiansted	02800	809-555-6864

Redeclaring TCursors

The TCursor class has both an open() and a close() method. It generally is considered good programming practice to close any TCursor you open. Any TCursor you leave open will use up resources. If you open a TCursor, should you close() it before reusing it? Although it is generally a good habit to get into, it is not always necessary. Look at the following code:

```
var
      tc TCursor
endVar

tc.open(t1)
tc.open(t2)
```

In this simple example, a TCursor is declared and used twice in a row, without ever closing the first TCursor. The question is, "Does the first instance of the tc variable close when you reopen it?" Yes.

Now take a look at the following example. The following code is in a Var window at the form level.

```
; Var Window of form
var
      tc TCursor
endVar
```

This code is in the pushButton event of a button on the form.

```
; Button1 :: pushButton
tc.open(t1)
```

The question is, should you close the TCursor with tc.close() after using it? The answer is, it depends. You could leave the TCursor open just in case you're going to use it again. This would save the time needed to reopen it. If, however, you are only going to use the TCursor once, then you should close it to save resources.

attach() Versus *open()*

Many people confuse attaching and opening. You can attach a TCursor to a table window, to a UIObject, or to a TCursor variable that is already attached. This establishes an association between a new TCursor variable and an already open channel. This new TCursor variable inherits all the characteristics that apply from the attached variable. This includes Edit mode, record number, and range.

When you open a TCursor, its view is the entire table. When you attach a TCursor, its view is restricted. In a multitable form, the first table in the data model is the master and controlling table. All other linked tables are detail tables. The second table shows only those records that match the current master record, and are said to have a *restricted view*. When you attach a TCursor to a detail table, the TCursor inherits the restricted view of the detail table.

A TCursor Can Respect a Restricted View

A table is in restricted view when it is filtered down to a subset of records. When you establish a 1:M relationship between the order numbers in the ORDERS.DB table and the records in the LINEITEM.DB table, the subset of records in the LINEITEM.DB table is restricted or filtered.

In addition to opening a TCursor in the background, you can attach a TCursor to a UIObject, which forces the TCursor to respect the restricted view of the object. For example, in a 1:M relationship, or in an active setRange(), you can attach a TCursor variable to any UIObject and the TCursor will be restricted, just as the original UIObject is, on the same record that the UIObject is and in the same Edit mode.

The next example shows you how to open a TCursor by attaching it to an object already connected to the table.

Implementing Cascade Delete Using ObjectPAL

A *cascade delete* is a setting you can set with many database products. Cascade delete deletes all the child records of a parent record. Because Paradox doesn't support cascade deletes, you must delete the child records. In a 1:1 relationship, this isn't a big deal. Simply delete both records in each table, as in the following:

```
ObjectConnectedToTableTwo.deleteRecord()
ObjectConnectedToTableOne.deleteRecord()
```

This technique works quite well. You just have to remember to do it.

In a 1:M relationship, deleting child records is trickier. You have to loop through the children and delete them one at a time. You shouldn't use a scan loop to delete records from a table. Instead, use either a while loop with eot() (end of table) or for loop with nRecords(). The following is an example using a for loop:

```
var
   Counter   Number
   tc        TCursor
endVar

tc.attach(ChildUIObjectName)
tc.edit()

for Counter from 1 to tc.nRecords()
   tc.deleteRecord()
endFor
```

In this code, you attach the TCursor to the UIObject, which ensures that the TCursor will have the same restricted view that the object has. Therefore, tc.nRecords() returns the number of records in the restricted view—not the whole table.

Another technique is to use a while loop with eot(). The following code, for example, works great in versions 1.0 and 4.5:

```
method pushButton(var eventInfo Event)
   var
      tc         TCursor
   endVar

   errorTrapOnWarnings(Yes)
```

```

    tc.attach(LINEITEM)       ;Attach to detail table.
    tc.edit()

    ;Delete all children records.
    while not tc.eot()
       tc.deleteRecord()
    endWhile

    edit()                    ;Make sure form is in edit mode.
    Order_No.deleteRecord()   ;Then delete the parent record.
endMethod
```

The preceding technique is not complete with version 5.0 and above of Paradox because of the interactive filter settings introduced with version 5.0. The following represents the preferred way to implement cascade delete in Paradox 9:

```
;btnCascadeDelete :: pushButton
method pushButton(var eventInfo Event)
     var
          tc          TCursor
     endVar

     tc.attach(LINEITEM)       ;Attach to detail table.
     tc.dropGenFilter()        ;Drop any user set filters.
    tc.home()                 ;Put TCursor on first record.
     tc.edit()

     while not tc.eot()       ;If there are any child
        tc.deleteRecord()      ;records, delete all of them.
     endWhile

     edit()                    ;Make sure form is in edit mode.
     Order_No.deleteRecord()   ;Delete the parent record.
endMethod
```


Why show you three different ways to accomplish the same task? For several reasons, first, to get you acquainted with the various ObjectPAL commands; and second, to show you that in ObjectPAL, there often are many ways to accomplish a single task. Which one is best? The best technique usually is the fastest or the one that uses the smallest amount of code. In this case, I believe all three are about equal.

Using *setRange()*

setRange() specifies a range of values (contrasted with setGenFilter(), which provides true filters—discussed next). setRange() is always preferred over setGenFilter(), because setRange() uses the active index. This makes setRange() faster than setGenFilter().

Suppose that you want to allow the user to specify a range of records they want to see—similar to a live query. The technique presented in this example uses setRange() on a TCursor with the resync() method.

You can find this form at http://prestwood.com/forums/paradox/books/official/files/SetRange.fsl.

Step By Step

1. Change your working directory to Paradox's Samples directory and create a new form with the Customer table in the data model and displayed in a table frame. Add two buttons labeled **All Cities** and **Set Range of Cities** as shown next. Finally, add two fields named **fldStart** and **fldEnd**.

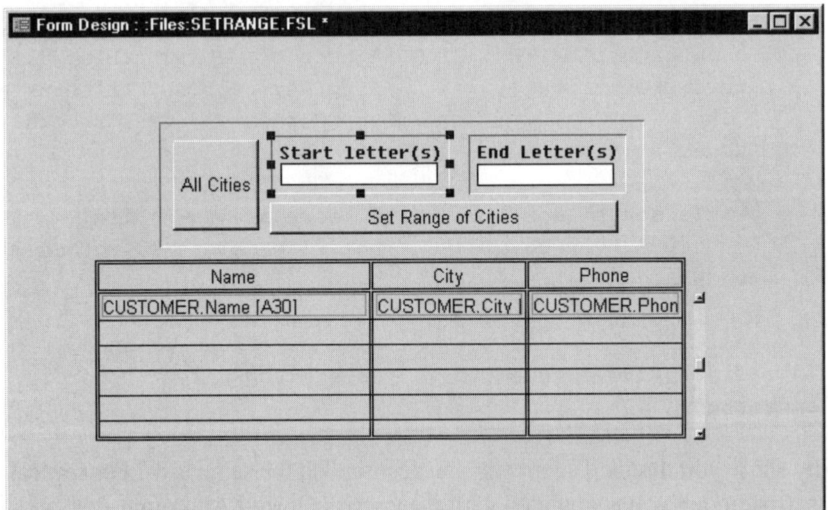

2. Restructure the Customer table and add a secondary index called **City** (see Figure 14-3 for the settings).

3. Alter the pushButton event of the Set Range of Cities button as follows:

```
;btnRange :: pushButton
method pushButton(var eventInfo Event)
   var
      tcCustomer TCursor
   endVar

   if not tcCustomer.open("CUSTOMER") then      ;Open TCursor.
      errorShow()
   endIf

   tcCustomer.switchIndex("City")                          ;Switch index on TCursor.
   tcCustomer.setRange(fldStart.value, fldEnd.value) ;Set range of records.

   CUSTOMER.resync(tcCustomer)                             ;Update the table frame.
endMethod
```

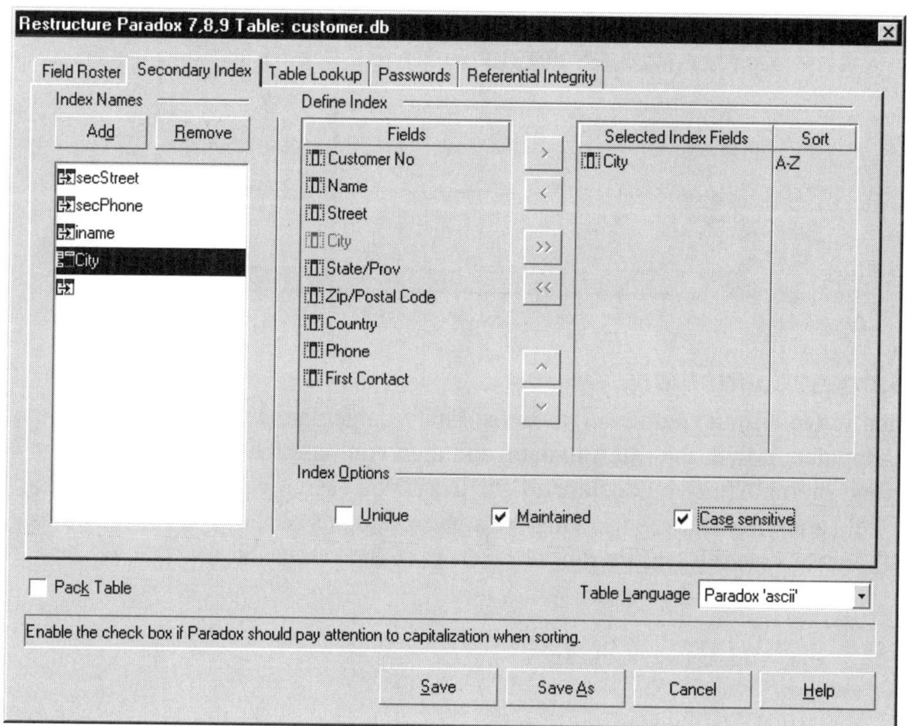

FIGURE 14-3 Add this City index to the Customer table

4. In the pushButton event of the All Cities button, enter line 3.

```
1:  ;btnAll :: pushButton
2:  method pushButton(var eventInfo Event)
3:     CUSTOMER.switchIndex()
4:  endMethod
```

5. Check the syntax, save the form as **SetRange.fsl**, and run it. This illustration shows the completed example. Your form should look similar:

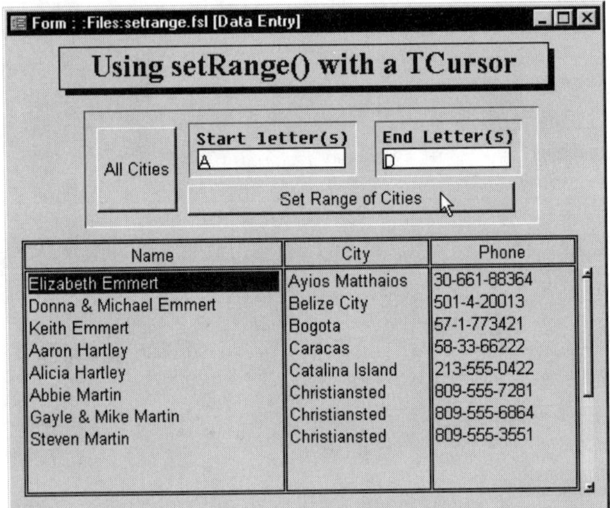

Using *setGenFilter()*

Using setGenFilter() requires two steps. First you declare a DynArray variable and populate it with the filtering data, and then you pass the DynArray to setGenFilter(). After you declare a DynArray, you assign values to it specifying the field and the values. Following are some examples of the types of formulas you can use with setGenFilter():

```
var
   dyn  DynArray[] String
endVar

dyn["State"] = "CA"               ;State field equals 'CA'.
dyn["Total"] = "< 0"              ;Negative numbers in Total field.
dyn["Total"] = "> 100, < 1000"  ;Greater than 100 & less than 1000.
dyn["Total"] = ">= 4, <= 8"
```

For example, to view all orders with a Balance Due over $100.00 and less than $1,000.00, enter the following on the pushButton event of a button on a form bound to the Orders table.

```
;btnShowMiddle :: pushButton
pushButton (var eventInfo Event)
var
   dyn  DynArray[] String            ;Declare DynArray.
endVar

dyn["Balance Due"] = "> 100, <1000" ;Assign filter to it.
ORDERS.setGenFilter(dyn)            ;Use it with setGenFilter().
```

Using Temporary Files

Sometimes, you need to create temporary tables to store information. Temporary tables are temporary because the data is needed only while the program is running. When you're done, you can delete them. One technique for deleting the tables is to use the canDepart event of the form.

A better technique is to use a little-known feature built into Paradox. Whenever you quit Paradox, it deletes all the tables in the private directory whose names start with two underscores and stores them in your private directory. You can use this feature to your advantage. Whenever you create tables for temporary use in ObjectPAL, give them names that start with two underscores. Paradox takes care of deleting them for you.

This technique isn't limited to tables. In fact, it isn't limited to Paradox files. Whenever it exits, Paradox deletes all files in the private directory whose names start with two underscores. Use this feature to your advantage. Put all scratch files into your private directory and give them filenames that start with two underscores.

Manipulating Data in a Table

There are four basic approaches to manipulating tables and records with ObjectPAL:

- Attach a Table variable to a table on disk. Then, use the Table object type methods to manipulate the table. (The table methods deal with the table as a whole.)

- Open a TCursor or attach it to a UIObject. Then, use the TCursor class methods to manipulate the table. No manipulations are updated to the screen. If you want to update the screen, use resync().
- Use the UIObject methods to manipulate the data. Each manipulation updates the screen as it occurs.
- Send action commands to the UIObjects, such as active.action (DataNextRecord). The action commands simulate what a user does.

TIP *You can speed up a TCursor by using update(), setBatchOn(), or copyToArray(). If you use setBatchOn(), make sure to follow it with setBatchOff() every time you use it because it places an exclusive lock.*

Copying an Entire Record with a TCursor

You can copy an entire record in a table frame by using the ObjectPal method copyToArray(). For the sake of simplicity, create a button on the form. In the pushButton event, use the following code:

```
method pushButton(var eventInfo Event)
   var
      recArr    Array[]    AnyType
   endVar

   tFrameObject.edit()
   tFrameObject.copyToArray(recArr)
   tFrameObject.insertAfterRecord()
   tFrameObject.copyFromArray(recArr)
endMethod
```

In doing this, a complete duplicate of the record will be entered after the current record. Another approach would be to attach the preceding code to the table frame object using the keyPhysical event to monitor which key was pressed.

Autoincrementing

So far, this chapter has only touched on the power and capabilities of the Table and TCursor variables. A whole book could be devoted to just these two variable types. This final section of this chapter addresses autoincrementing with the TCursor.

In this section, you learn how to autoincrement using ObjectPAL. First, you autoincrement a simple field. Second, you autoincrement a nonkey field. Third, for the most elegant solution, you add locking to the routine. By studying simple and elegant methods, you learn how to implement different routines under different situations and functional programming.

Autoincrementing a field involves inserting a new record, finding the highest value, adding 1 to it, and storing the new value. You already know how to insert a new record, as in the following:

```
active.insertRecord()
Line_Item.insertRecord()
self.action(DataInsertRecord)
tc.insertRecord()
```

To get the current highest value, either move to the end of the table and put the value in a variable, or use the cMax() method. Either way, after you get the highest value, you need to put it into a variable.

Autoincrementing and Locking

Now you have just one more loophole to close. Theoretically, it's still possible for two users to end up with the same number. You can use autoincrementing with locks to make sure that this doesn't happen. A *lock* is a feature of the BDE that prevents other users from viewing, changing, or locking a table or a record while one user has a lock on it. The next example uses autoincrementing with locks.

Example of Autoincrementing with Locks

Suppose that you want to autoincrement a field in a multiuser environment. To do this, you need to work with locks.

http://prestwood.com/forums/paradox/books/official/files/Auto3.fsl.

Step By Step

1. Set your working directory to Paradox's Samples directory. Create a new form with the Customer table in the data model:

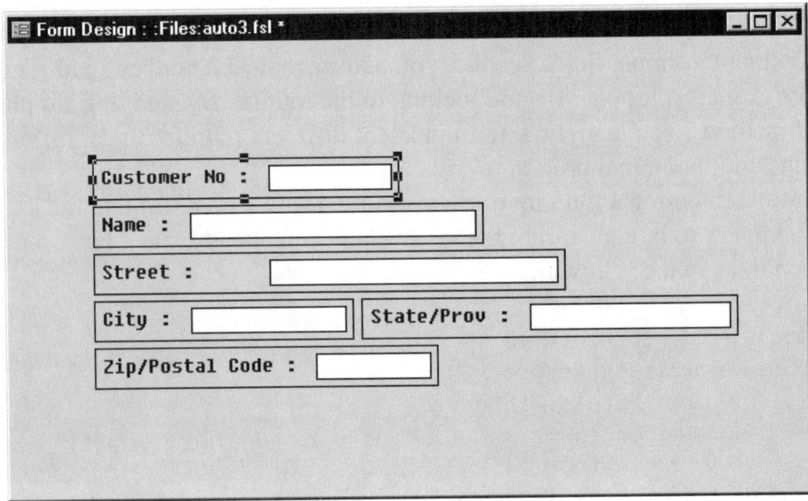

2. Create a table called **incremnt.db** (see Figure 14-4 for the structure).
3. Open the incremnt table and add one row to it with the current highest Customer No value from the Customer table. This should be 9,841 unless you've altered the data in the table.
4. Add lines 3 and 4 to the Var window of the page. Lines 3 and 4 declare a TCursor and SmallInt variables for use in the action event.

```
1:  ;Page :: Var
2:  Var
3:     tc            TCursor
4:     siCounter     SmallInt
5:  endVar
```

5. Alter the action event of the page as follows:

```
;Page :: action
method action(var eventInfo ActionEvent)
   if eventInfo.id() = DataInsertRecord then
      if not tc.open("incremnt.db") then errorShow() endIf
      siCounter = 0
      while not tc.lock("Full")
         siCounter = siCounter + 1
         message("Attempting to establish lock: " + String(siCounter))
         sleep(1000)
         if siCounter = 10 then
```

```
            DisableDefault
            msgStop("Warning", "Could not establish lock.")
            return
         endIf
      endWhile
      edit()
      DoDefault
      tc.edit()
      tc."Customer No" = tc."Customer No" + 1
      tc.postRecord()
      Customer_No = tc."Customer No"
      tc.unLock("Full")
      Name.moveTo()
      tc.close()
   endIf
endMethod
```

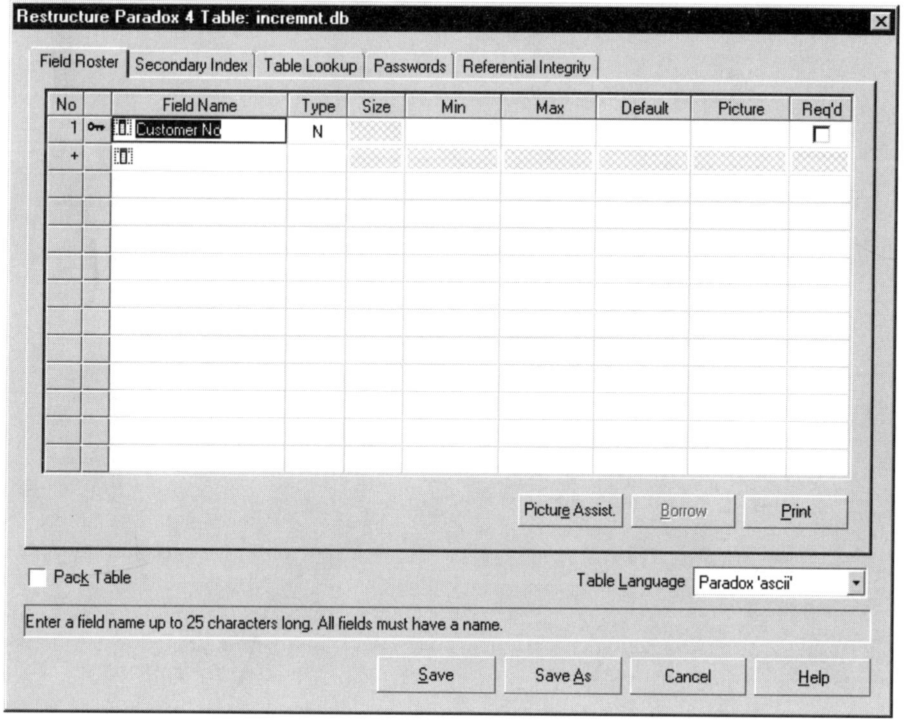

FIGURE 14-4 The incremnt table

6. Check the syntax, save the form as **Auto3.fsl**, and run the form. Insert a record.

Summary

In this chapter, you learned about ObjectPAL's Table and TCursor objects. You learned they differ in fundamental ways. Table objects give you a handle to a table and, in general, its methods and procedures deal with the table as a whole. A TCursor object gives you a handle to a specific record (or row) in a table and, in general, its methods and procedures deal with the data inside the table. When utilizing TCursor and Table variables, remember that you are utilizing another channel to the database. Table variables can lock out regular users by putting write and exclusive locks on the table. When programming a TCursor, think of the open TCursor as another user and code accordingly.

CHAPTER 15

Fields, Table Frames, and MROs

Fields, table frames, and multirecord objects (MROs) all display data. Table frames and MROs both have a record object and fields, of course, do not. You can, however, add a record object around a set of fields by using a 1-by-1 MRO. Using a record object's events is a good technique for managing inserts, updates, and deletes. Although there are several programming techniques you can use with all three, there are programming differences you need to keep in mind.

Fields

As a developer programming a database application, you need to manipulate fields and the data in the fields. This section deals with modifying fields, setting the tab order of fields, and manipulating Combo fields.

Automatically Entering Memo View

Memo view enables you to easily edit fields defined to a memo field. For example, the RETURN key takes you to the next line in a memo field when in Memo view. To manually enter Memo view, press SHIFT-F2. To automatically enter Memo view, put the following code in the arrive event of a standard or formatted memo field:

```
method arrive(var eventInfo MoveEvent)
   doDefault
   self.action(EditEnterMemoView)
endMethod
```

The following code can be used in a pushButton event to move to a memo field and put the memo field into Memo view:

```
method pushButton(var eventInfo Event)
   MyMemoField.moveto()
   MyMemoField.action(EditEnterMemoView)
endMethod
```

Setting the Tab Order of a Form

There are three commonly used techniques to set the tab stop order of a form: setting the Next Tab Stop property, using ObjectPAL, and using the concept of containership. The most elegant of these three solutions is the Next Tab Stop feature. The Next Tab Stop property is an interactive and easy solution. However, for the sake of demonstrating containership, and because it is very useful, I'll show you the third technique here: using containership.

Paradox has containership, which enables you to put a smaller object inside a larger object. You can say that the larger object contains the smaller object. You can use containership to dictate the tab order of fields by grouping them or putting them inside another object.

Suppose that you have a two-column form (a form with fields on the left and right). You put a box around the fields on the left; the box will contain those fields. Likewise, you can select all the fields and group them by selecting Design | Group (see Figure 15-1). In this case, when you tab to the first field in the group on the left, the tab order goes through all the other fields in the group before it exits to the fields on the right.

It is also a good idea to group the fields on the right side of the form, too. This way, the user goes through all the fields on the right, even if some of the fields on the left are empty.

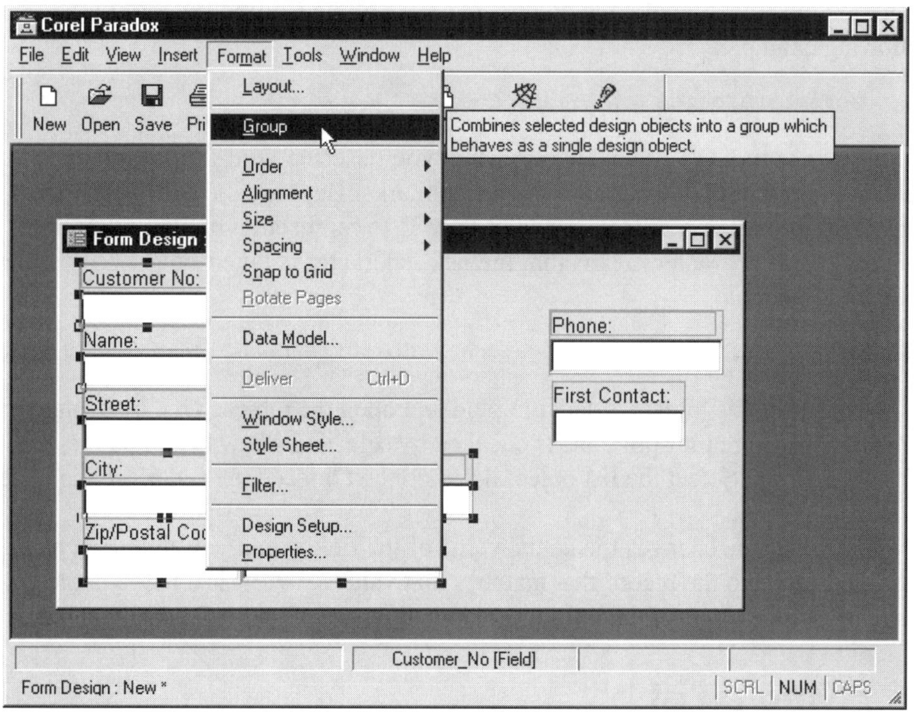

FIGURE 15-1 Grouping objects

Combo Fields

Often, you want to have a pick list or a Combo field available in your form when you're editing. A list field enables you to restrict the values entered into a field to those on the list. The following table lists the pertinent properties of the list object:

Property	Description
Datasource	Fills a list object with the values in a field in a table
list.count	Specifies the number of elements in the list
list.selection	Use to specify the currently selected item in the list
list.value	Sets the value of an item in a list

With the properties in the table, you can control a list object. Suppose that a user needs ID numbers or items of a specific type in a list and doesn't want to have to type hundreds of ID numbers. To fill a list object, use the dataSource property. You can place this line of code on the list object of the Combo field, as in the following example:

```
self.DataSource = "[tablename.fieldname]"
```

If you use the .DB file extension when you describe your table name, you need to embed the table name in quotation marks. Because the expression is already in quotation marks, you need to use \" to represent a quotation mark. The backslash character means that the next character is taken literally, as in the following example:

```
self.DataSource = "[\"tablename.db\".fieldname]"
```

To reach the list object, select the field and open the Object Tree by using the toolbar. Make sure the split pane is checked by selecting View | Both on the Object Explorer. Select the list object listed on the Object Tree and place the code on the open event.

This technique changes the actual value of the field when you're in Edit mode. It doesn't move to the record that matches that value. The list is a list of choices that changes the value of the current field to which the Combo field is attached.

Emptying a List

Setting a list's count property to 0 will blank the list. For example, the following code empties the list object called lst1:

```
lst1.list.count = 0
```

Using a Combo field to move to a new record, rather than changing the value of the current record in that field, requires a few extra steps:

1. Make the Combo field an undefined field. Name it Drop.
2. Add the self.DataSource code to the list object.
3. On the Combo field object (not the list object), change two methods as follows:

```
;lst1 :: open
self.value = fieldname.value   ;This sets the
                               ;initial value
```

```
;lst :: newValue
if eventInfo.reason() = EditValue then
   fieldName.locate("fieldname", DROP.value)
endIf
```

4. Save and execute this code. Now the Combo field acts as a data navigator for your table. I don't recommend this technique for large tables because a Combo field with more than a few hundred options is unmanageable. In addition, ObjectPAL limits the number of items in a list to 2,500.

The next example demonstrates how to populate a Combo field.

Populating a *Combo Field*

To activate a Combo field when a user arrives on it (tabs or clicks), you need to use the arrive event of the field and use the action() method. For example:


```
;fldList :: Arrive
method arrive(var eventInfo MoveEvent)
   if self.isBlank() then
      action(EditDropDownList)
   endIf
endMethod
```

Adding Automatically to a Combo Field

Suppose that you want to populate a Combo field and automatically add new entries to it. This next example demonstrates how to add automatically to a Combo field.

http://prestwood.com/forums/paradox/books/official/files/LIST2.FSL.

Step By Step

1. Set your working directory to Paradox's Samples directory. Create a new form with two undefined fields on it. Make the first field a Combo field. This example uses only the first undefined field. The other field is on the form so that you can move on and off the first field.

2. In the arrive event of the list object of the field, add line 3. It is important to use the arrive event of the list object and not the field (see Figure 15-2).

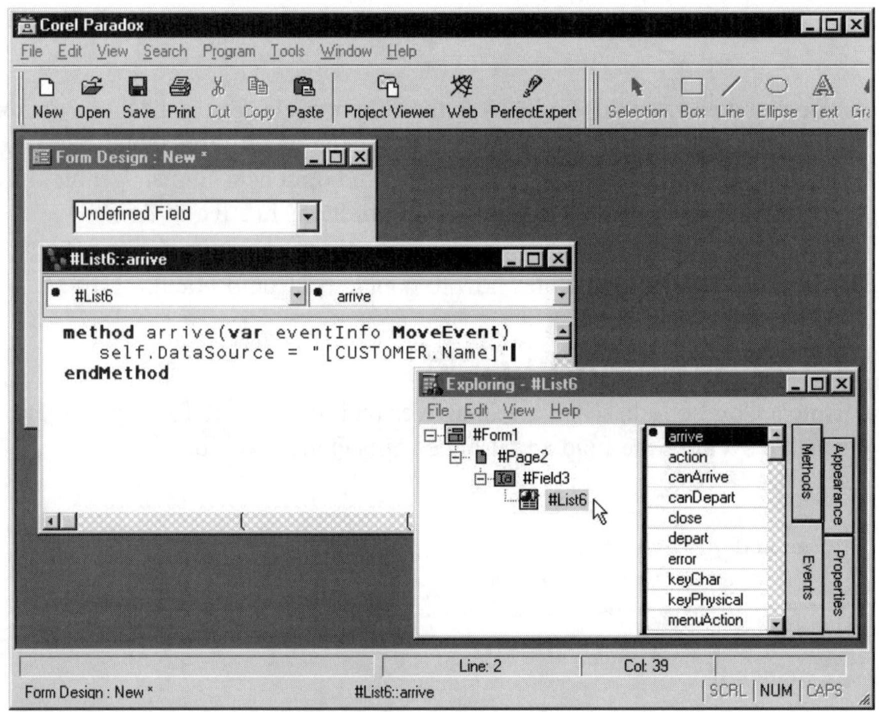

FIGURE 15-2 Getting to the list object of a field

The arrive event was selected for this task because you need the list to repopulate with the latest information every time it is selected.

```
;field.list :: arrive
method arrive(var eventInfo MoveEvent)
   self.DataSource="[CUSTOMER.Name]"
endMethod
```

3. In the canDepart event of the field, add lines 3–18. Line 4 declares a TCursor variable. (A better place to declare the variable is before the method or in the Var window. To keep the code visually close together, the code in this example puts the variable inside the method.) Line 8 tests whether the field has a value in it. If it does, line 9 opens a TCursor that will be used in lines 10–15. Line 10 tests whether the value is already in the table. If it isn't, line 11 puts the TCursor into Edit mode. Line 12 inserts a new record. Lines 13 and 14 set the values, and line 15 posts the record. Line 17 closes the TCursor.

```
 1:      ;fldList :: canDepart
 2:      method canDepart(var eventInfo MoveEvent)
 3:         var
 4:            tc    TCursor
 5:         endVar
 6:
 7:         ;Add a value if necessary.
 8:         if not self.isBlank() then
 9:           tc.open("CUSTOMER.DB")
10:           if not tc.locate("Name", self.value) then
11:              tc.edit()
12:              tc.insertRecord()
13:              tc."Name" = self.value
14:              tc.(1) = tc.cMax("Customer No") + 1
15:              tc.postRecord()
16:           endIf
17:           tc.close() ;Not needed, but good form.
18:         endIf
19:     endMethod
```

4. Check the syntax, save the form as **LIST2.FSL**, and run it. Add a new entry to the Combo field. Move off the field. Move back and drop down the edit list. Your entry has been added to the list.

Verifying Validity Checks

If you want to prevent the user from moving off a field when a validity check fails or when a key violation occurs within a field, use the following code:

```
;Field :: depart
doDefault
if self.edit() then
  if not self.postRecord() then
     errorShow()
     self.moveTo()
  endIf
endIf
```

Table Frames

A *table frame* is a design object for forms and reports that represents a table and consists of columns and rows. This section discusses how you can add sorting capabilities to table frames, how to highlight records, and how to manipulate table frames using ObjectPAL.

Preventing the User from Going Past the End of a Table

You can use the Auto-Append feature of the data model to always restrict the user from going past the last record in a table frame. Suppose that you want to prevent new records from being inserted into a table that is being accessed by means of a table frame embedded in a form. You can prevent a new record from being inserted by first trapping the DataInsertRecord action constant and then disabling the code of the default event. If you just want to stop the user from inserting a new record by moving past the last record, however, then uncheck the Auto-Append property of the table in the data model.

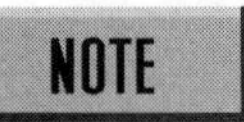

PAST-END.FSL demonstrates using ObjectPAL to prevent a user from moving past the last record in a table frame.

Selecting Multiple Records from a Table Frame

Sometimes it is useful to mark a set of records permanently. dBASE does this when you delete a record. The record is marked for deletion, and it is permanently deleted when you pack the table. When you program, you often want to mark a set of records permanently. I call this mechanism a *marked list.*

To implement a marked list, include a field in the database structure called Marked. Make the field type A1. With code, you enable the user to select the record (such as with the SPACEBAR or by clicking it). In turn, you place a character into the Marked field of the record (such as the letter Y for Yes or X for marked).

At this point, you can do a variety of things with queries. For example, by interrogating the Marked field and looking for your character that signifies that the field is marked, you can save the answer query in another directory or do simple housekeeping chores. This is an important technique for permanently marking records. It has a broad range of uses in your applications, such as the following:

```
;Routine to mark field.
;Field :: mouseDown
disableDefault
if self.isBlank() then
   self.value = "X"
else
   self.value = ""
endIf
```

After a user marks records, you can query for the X, or you can use a scan loop to loop through the table and do something with each record marked, as in the following example:

```
;Routine to handle marked field.
var
   tc    TCursor
endVar

tc.open("TABLE.DB")
scan tc for tc."Marked" = "X":
   ;Do something here.
endScan
```

Remember that you also need to clear out the Marked field at some point, as in the following example:

```
;Routine to clear marked field.
var
   tc   TCursor
endVar

tc.open("TABLE.DB")
tc.edit()
scan tc:
   tc."Marked" = ""
endScan
```

Redefining a Table Frame with the *TableName* and *FieldName* Properties

This section discusses redefining table frames in Run mode. This next example demonstrates how to define which table is bound to a table frame.

Suppose that you want to define an undefined table frame when the user presses a button. To do this, set the tableName property of the table frame in the pushButton event of a button.

http://prestwood.com/forums/paradox/books/official/files/DMADD1.FSL.

Step By Step

1. Change your working directory to Paradox's Samples directory. Create a new form with no tables in its data model.

2. Place a button labeled **Set** on the form and an undefined table frame named **tfCustomer** on the form (shown here).

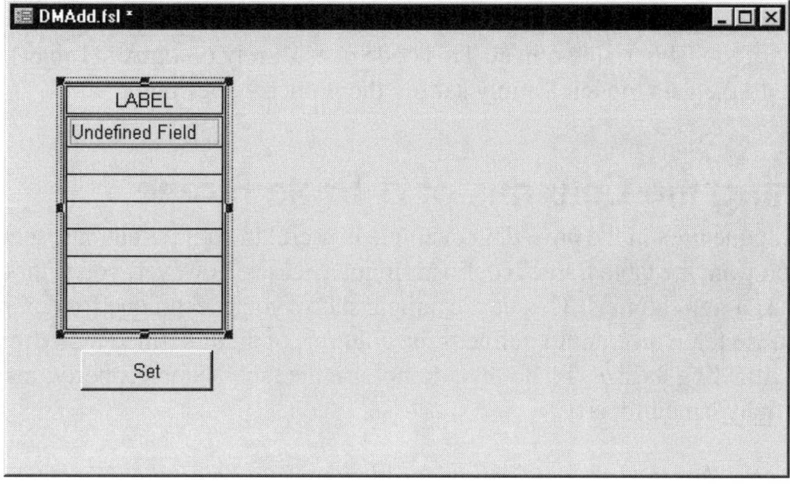

3. Add line 3 to the pushButton event of the Set button.

```
1:     ;Button :: pushButton
2:     method pushButton(var eventInfo Event)
3:        tfCustomer.tableName = "Customer.db"
4:     endMethod
```

4. Check the syntax, save the form as **DMADD1.FSL**, and run it. Click the Set button. The table frame has exploded from one column to all the fields in the table, as the following illustration shows.

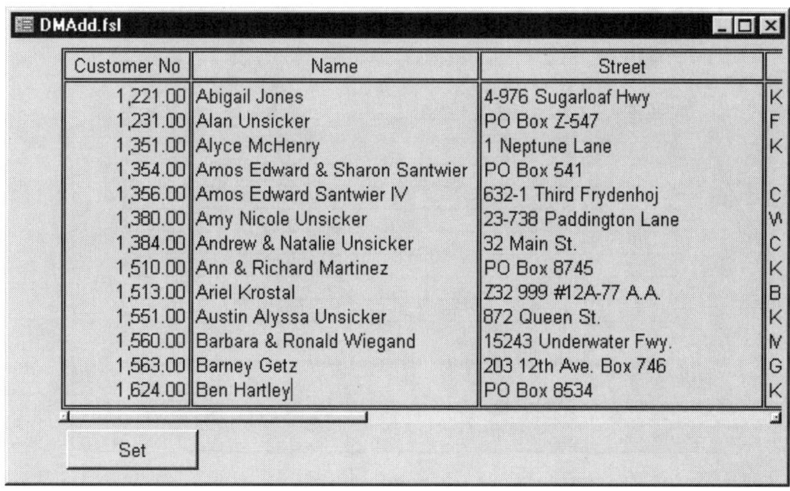

tfCustomer is the name of the table frame on the form. TableName is a property of the table frame object. This code doesn't rely on dmAddTable() to add the table to the data model. Simply setting the property does that.

Defining the Columns of a Table Frame

The technique used in the preceding example is useful in some situations, such as when you want the table frame redefined. In many cases, however, you want to define just a few columns. This next example shows you a technique for doing that.

Suppose that you want to define three columns of an undefined table frame without affecting its size. To do this, do not use the tableName property; instead, use the fieldName property.

http://prestwood.com/forums/paradox/books/official/files/DMADD2.FSL.

Step By Step

1. Change your working directory to Paradox's Samples directory. Create a new form with no tables in its data model. Place a button labeled **Show Customers** on the form.

2. Add an undefined table frame to the form with three columns (shown next). Name the fields of the columns as follows: **Col1**, **Col2**, and **Col3**.

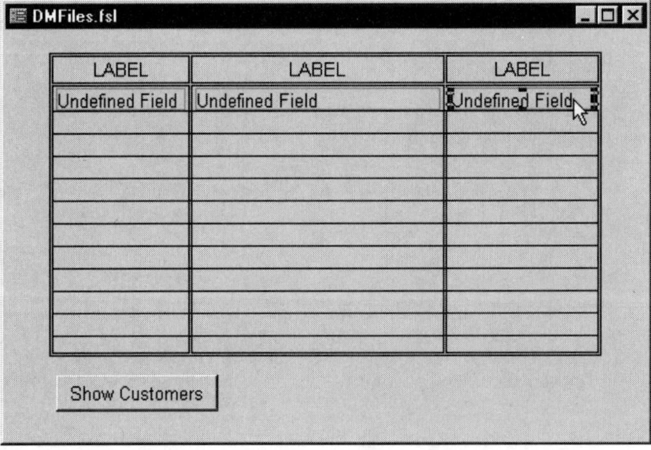

3. Add lines 3–5 to the pushButton event of the Set button. Lines 3–5 set the FieldName property of all three columns.

```
1:    ;Button :: pushButton
2:    method pushButton(var eventInfo Event)
3:       Col1.FieldName = "Customer.Customer No"
4:       Col2.FieldName = "Customer.Name"
5:       Col3.FieldName = "Customer.Phone"
6:    endMethod
```

4. Check the syntax, save the form as **DMFILES.FSL**, and run it. Click the Set button. Now the columns of the table frame are defined (shown here).

You can use this technique to redefine a table, too. The trick is to redefine the table frame to the Null character before trying to assign a new table to it. In the following code, tfCustomer is the name of the table frame.


```
tfCustomer = ""
```

Then, you can redefine the columns without a problem, as in the following example:

```
Col1.FieldName = "LINEITEM.Order No"
Col2.FieldName = "LINEITEM.Stock No"
Col3.FieldName = "LINEITEM.Total"
```

Resizing a Table Frame

The following code snippet demonstrates how to redefine and resize a table frame:

```
;DMADD3 :: btn :: pushButton
method pushButton(var eventInfo Event)
   delayScreenUpdates(Yes)            ;This is for a smooth look.
   tfTemp.verticalScrollBar = False   ;Turn off vertical scrollbar.
   tfTemp.TableName = "X.DB"          ;One column dummy table.
   tfTemp.design.sizeToFit = True     ;Tell the table frame to resize.
   tfTemp.TableName = "ZIPCODES.DB"   ;Bind table to table frame.
   tfTemp.verticalScrollBar = True    ;Turn on vertical scrollbar.
endMethod
```

Validating Fields at the Record Level of a Table Frame

Earlier we discussed using the record level of a table frame to validate fields. This next example demonstrates how to use this important technique.

Suppose that you want to make sure that the user hasn't entered a date beyond today's date in the Contact Date field of the Customer table. To do this, use the canDepart event of the table frame's record object. Compare the field's value with today's date using today(). If the value is greater than today's date, use setErrorcode() to prevent the user from posting the value.

http://prestwood.com/forums/paradox/books/official/files/RECORD1.FSL.

Step By Step

1. Set your working directory to Paradox's Samples directory. Create a new form with the Customer table in the data model and displaying the columns displayed next.

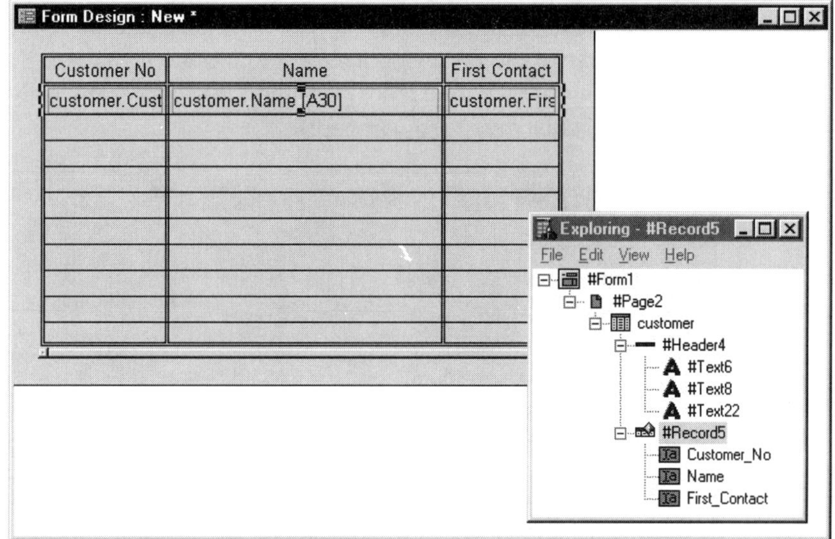

2. Add lines 3–9 to the canDepart event of the record object of the table frame bound to the Customer table (the record object is highlighted in the previous illustration). Line 3 checks whether the date entered in the Sale_Date field is later than today's date. If it is, line 4 sets the CanNotDepart error code. Lines 5–8 notify the user of the inaccurate date by changing the color of the record object to yellow, displaying a warning, and moving back to the field. You can customize your own warning system if you want.

```
1:    ;TableFrame.Record :: canDepart
2:    method canDepart(var eventInfo MoveEvent)
3:       if First_Contact.value > today() then
4:          eventInfo.setErrorCode(CanNotDepart)
5:          self.color = Yellow
6:          msgStop("Invalid Date!", "Contact date is invalid.")
7:          self.color = Transparent
8:          First_Contact.moveTo()
9:       endIf
10:   endMethod
```

NOTE *You also can use a validity check at the table structure level. When you restructure a table, you can use Today in the maximum validity check field. In fact, this should be your first choice for data validity.*

3. Check the syntax, save your work, and run the form. Press F9 to enter Edit mode, and try to change the First Contact field to tomorrow's date. You get a message indicating that the date is invalid, and the record turns yellow while the message is displayed (shown here).

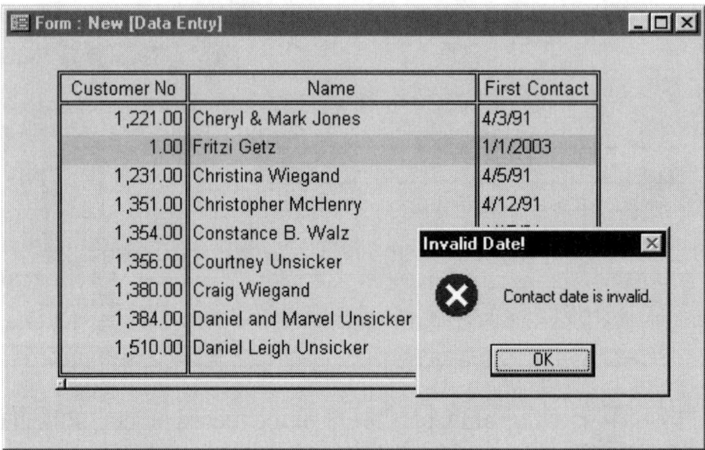

Multirecord Objects

Using the record object of a table frame to manipulate data at a record level is great, but what do you do when you have several fields? You use a 1-by-1 multirecord object (MRO) and surround the fields, which causes the MRO to bind to the underlying table.

A *multirecord object* (MRO) is an object that displays several records at once in a box. It is used with forms and reports. You can use a 1-by-1 MRO to add a record object to fields on a form. This enables you to perform field validation by using the record object of the MRO in a way similar to how you use the record of a table frame. This is because the fields in the MRO are contained by a record object. Having a record object means that you can use the canDepart event to trap for record departs, among other record-oriented tasks.

The first step in using this technique is to place an MRO over the fields you want to validate (shown here).

Don't panic as your screen becomes jumbled. Next, change the MRO to a 1-by-1 MRO and resize it so that the fields fit within it. This cleans up your screen and automatically binds the record object to the underlying table (shown here).

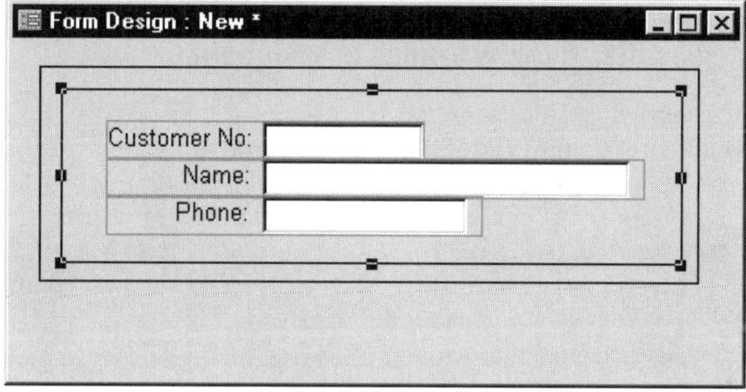

After you set up the record object, you can use the MRO object's methods to manipulate the data at the record level.

The next example demonstrates the important technique of using a 1-by-1 MRO.

Validating Fields at the Record Level by Using a Multirecord Object

Suppose that you want to make sure that the user doesn't leave the Telephone Number field of the Customer table empty. You can do this on a group of fields by surrounding the fields with a 1-by-1 multirecord object and using the record object to trap for when the user moves from record to record.

http://prestwood.com/forums/paradox/books/official/files/RECORD2.FSL.

Step By Step

1. Set your working directory to Paradox's Samples directory. Create a new form with the Customer table in the data model. Create field objects and define them to the Customer table's Customer No, Name, and Phone fields.

2. Add a 1-by-1 MRO around the fields (refer to the illustrations in the previous example to help set up the 1-by-1 MRO).

3. Add lines 3–9 to the canDepart event of the record object in the multirecord object. Line 3 checks whether the Phone field is blank. If it is, line 4 sets the CanNotDepart error code. Lines 5–8 notify the user by turning the box yellow, displaying a warning, and moving back to the field. You can customize these warnings to your own liking.

```
1:  ;MRO.Record :: canDepart
2:  method canDepart(var eventInfo MoveEvent)
3:     if Phone.isBlank() then
4:        eventInfo.setErrorCode(CanNotDepart)
5:        self.color = Yellow
6:        msgStop("Warning!", "Phone number required on this form.")
7:        self.color = Transparent
8:        moveTo(Phone)
9:     endIf
10: endMethod
```

4. Check the syntax, save your work as **RECORD2.FSL**, and run the form. Press F9 to enter Edit mode, and try to leave the Phone field blank. You get a message indicating that the phone number is required, and the record turns yellow while the message is displayed (shown here).

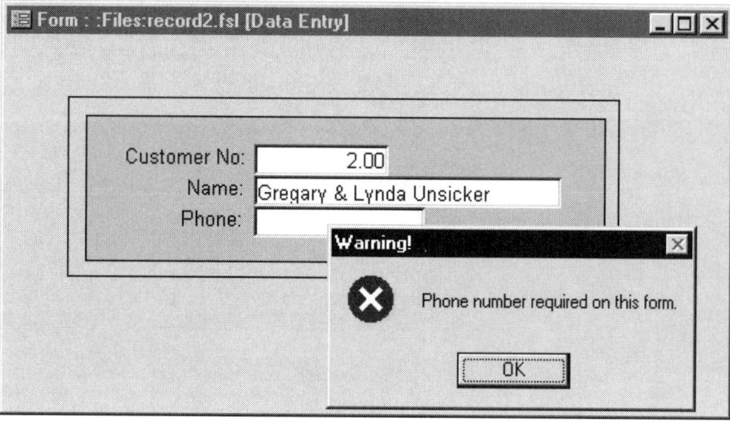

Summary

In this chapter you learned how to manipulate fields, table frames, and multirecord objects. You learned about the power and ease of use of the record object for validating records and fields. You also learned that it is preferred to do field validation at the table structure level; in that case, you don't use ObjectPAL at all. Proper field validation should be at the table or database level. Otherwise, your users could open the table directly and enter bad data. If you want to restrict input only on a particular form, however, you can use the techniques discussed in this chapter.

CHAPTER 16

Handling the Keyboard

This short but important chapter will introduce you to handling user input via the keyboard. Key concepts covered include what events are triggered when a user presses a key and how to limit the user's input. Also covered is a Paradox trick for interrupting a loop and sendKeys().

The Path of a Keystroke

A *keycode* is a code that represents a keyboard character in ObjectPAL. A keycode can be an ASCII number, an IBM extended keycode number, or a string that represents a keyname known to Paradox. When a user presses a key on the keyboard, one of two things occurs. Either Windows processes it, or Paradox processes it. Windows processes it, for example, when the sequence CTRL-ESC is used. When Paradox processes it, the keyPhysical event always sees it, and in the case of a character, the keyPhysical event passes the event to the keyChar event (see Figure 16-1).

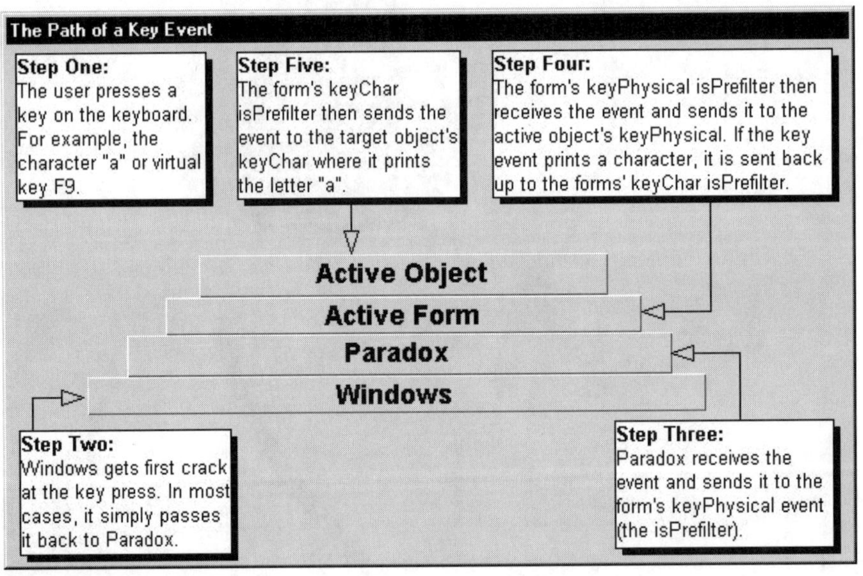

FIGURE 16-1 The path of a key event

The steps to trapping a keystroke are as follows:

1. Decide whether you need to trap for a character or virtual key. If you want to trap for a character such as a, A, b, B, 1, !, or @, then use either the keyPhysical event or the keyChar event. If you want to trap for virtual keys such as F1 or ESC, then you must use the keyPhysical event.
2. Decide at which level you need to trap for the keypress. The two usual places are the form's prefilter or directly on the field.
3. Inspect the eventInfo packet with either char() or vChar() to trap for the keystroke. If case does not matter, then use vChar(). If case does matter, then use char().

NOTE *As long as a field has focus, keystrokes do not bubble because the field uses up the keystroke. Therefore, the two best choices to trap for keystrokes are the form's prefilter or on the field itself.*

Using *KeyEvents* Methods and Procedures

The eventInfo passed to both the keyChar and keyPhysical events is of type KeyEvent. This means you can use the KeyEvent methods and procedures to enable you to get and set information about keystroke events. The keyEvent object type inherits some methods and procedures from the event object type. For example, the following traps for CTRL-SHIFT-F1 using several keyEvent methods.

```
; Field :: keyPhysical
method keyPhysical(var eventInfo KeyEvent)
   ;Start by disabling all keys, then we'll
   ;either do our processing or enable the
   ;keystroke at the end of this method.
   DisableDefault

   switch
      case eventInfo.isControlKeyDown()    :
         switch
            case eventInfo.isShiftKeyDown()   :
               switch
```

```
                    case eventInfo.vCharCode() = VK_F1 :
                       msgInfo("", "You pressed cntrl + shft + F1")
                       return
                    otherwise :
                       ;Another key was pressed.
                 endSwitch
              otherwise  :
                 ; No shift keystroke.
           endSwitch
        otherwise  :
           ; No control keystroke.
     endSwitch

     enableDefault ;Allow all other keystrokes.
  endMethod
```

Refer to KeyEvent Type in the ObjectPAL Reference help file for a complete list of methods.

Interrupting a Loop

Sometimes you may want to give the user the option of interrupting a loop. For example, if you are scanning through a large table, you could allow the user to abort the procedure in midstream. This type of control adds a touch of professionalism to your application. The following example demonstrates how you can enable the user to interrupt a loop by pressing the ESC key.

Suppose that you want to loop to 1,000 and display the counter in the status bar as the loop increments. The twist on this example is that you need to enable the user to press ESC to interrupt the loop. This example uses the form's prefilter with vChar() to trap a keystroke.

http://prestwood.com/forums/paradox/books/official/files/QUITLOOP.FSL.

Step By Step

1. Create a new form and place a button labeled **Count to 1000** and a text box on the form as shown next.

2. Add line 3 to the Var window of the form.

```
1:   ;Form :: Var
2:   Var
3:      lFlag Logical
4:   endVar
```

3. Add lines 5–7 to the keyPhysical event of the form.

```
1:   ;Form :: keyPhysical
2:   method keyPhysical(var eventInfo KeyEvent)
3:   if eventInfo.isPreFilter() then
4:      ;This code executes for each object on the form
5:      if eventInfo.vchar() = "VK_ESCAPE" then
6:        lFlag = True
7:      endIf
8:   else
9:      ;This code executes only for the form
10:  endIf
11:  endMethod
```

4. Alter the mouseDown event of the text box as follows:

```
;Text :: mouseDown
method mouseDown(var eventinfo MouseEvent)
   lFlag = True
endMethod
```


5. Add lines 3–16 to the pushButton event of the Count to 1000 button. Line 4 declares a variable private to a method for use in the for loop (lines 9–16). Line 7 sets the flag to False in case the user presses ESC, setting the

flag to True. Line 10 displays the value of siCounter in the status bar. Line 11 sleeps for the minimum amount of cycles (about 52 milliseconds), which is plenty of time to yield to Windows. This enables the ESC key to sneak in. Line 12 checks whether the flag has changed to True. If the flag is True, line 13 displays a message, and line 14 quits the loop.

```
1:    ;Button :: pushButton
2:    method pushButton(var eventInfo Event)
3:       var
4:          siCounter SmallInt
5:       endVar
6:
7:       lFlag = False
8:
9:       for siCounter from 1 to 1000
10:         message(siCounter)
11:         sleep()
12:         if lFlag = True then
13:            message("Counting interrupted")
14:            quitloop
15:         endIf
16:      endFor
17:   endMethod
```

6. Check the syntax, run the form, and click the button. As the computer counts to 1,000, the counter is shown in the status bar. Press ESC or click the text box to interrupt the loop (see Figure 16-2).

NOTE *Sometimes programmers use sleep(1) to indicate they want to release control to windows, but for the least amount of time. In place of sleep(1), you can use sleep() without a parameter—sleep(). In that case, Windows automatically permits about two events to occur.*

Using *keyPhysical*

As already discussed, use the keyPhysical event when you want to trap for all keyboard keys. Use the keyChar event when you want to trap for only characters that are printable to the screen.

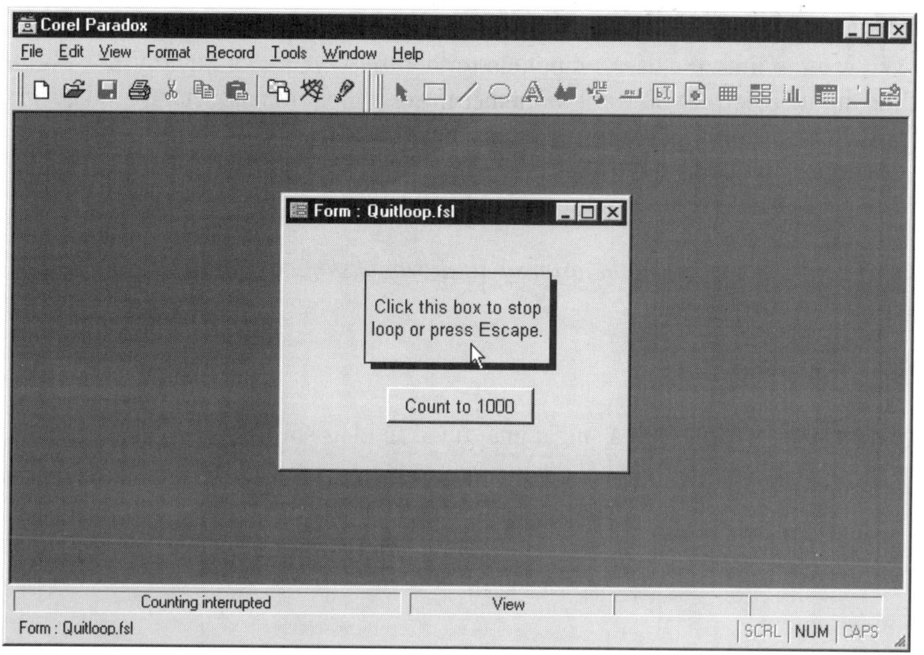

FIGURE 16-2 Finished example of interrupting a loop

Suppose that you created two field objects: field1 and field2. You want field2 to echo whatever you type into field1—including BACKSPACE, DELETE, and ENTER—as though you were typing directly into field2. How do you do this?

A problem that often confronts users is that values aren't committed to the field until endMethod. Remember that the default behavior occurs last in a method. Therefore, when you use the keyPhysical and keyChar events, invoke the default behavior to commit the last keystroke, as in the following example:

```
;Field1 :: keyPhysical
doDefault
field2.value = self.value
```

Limiting Keyboard Input

If you want to limit the user's input, use either the keyChar or keyPhysical events of the input object. If you want to limit the user's input to characters, use keyChar. If you want to control all keystrokes, use keyPhysical.

Suppose that you want to limit the user's input to a list of specified keys. The technique presented here can be used to control any keys.

http://prestwood.com/forums/paradox/books/official/files/ONLYKEYS.FSL.

Step By Step

1. Create a form with a single undefined field as shown here:

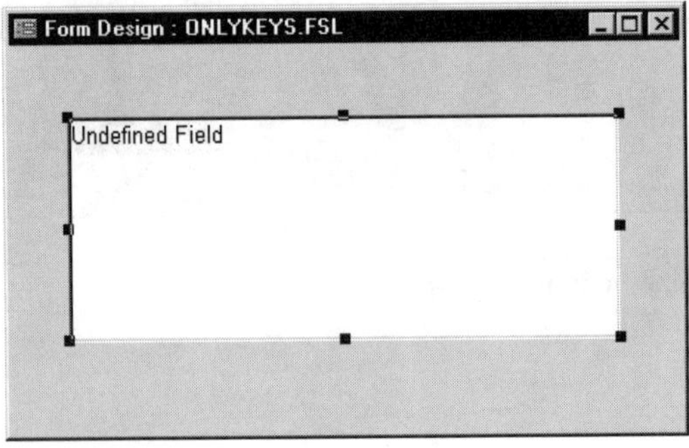

2. Alter the keyPhysical event of the field as follows:

```
method keyPhysical(var eventInfo KeyEvent)
   var
      sChar String
   endVar

   disableDefault

   sChar = eventInfo.char()

   switch
      case eventInfo.vCharCode() = VK_DELETE : enableDefault
      case eventInfo.vCharCode() = VK_BACK : enableDefault
      case eventInfo.vCharCode() = VK_F8 : enableDefault
```

```
            case sChar >="A" and sChar <="z" : enableDefault
            case sChar >="0" and sChar <="9" : enableDefault
            case sChar = "." : enableDefault
            case sChar = "," : enableDefault
            case sChar = " " : enableDefault
        endSwitch
    endMethod
```

3. Check the syntax, save the form as **ONLYKEYS.FSL**, and run it. Type some characters. Be sure to try numbers, letters, and special characters (see Figure 16-3).

This is a good routine to turn into a custom method that you can call whenever you need to limit user input. Alter this routine in other ways to suit your needs—perhaps develop three or four custom methods for limiting user input. You can't trap for everything, however. Some keys and key combinations are reserved by Windows, such as CTRL-F4.

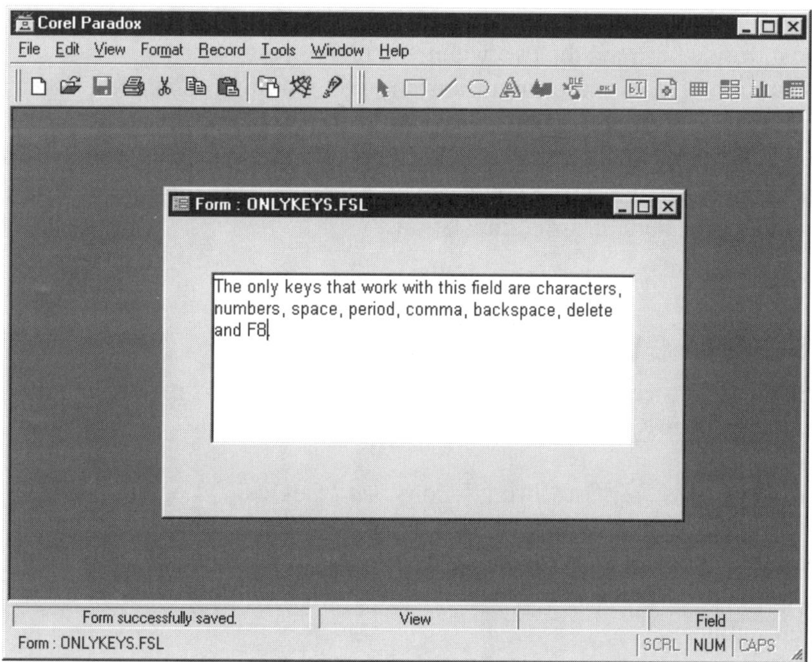

FIGURE 16-3 ONLYKEYS.FSL limits the user's input to numbers, letters, and spaces

Character Sets

You can't store all characters in a Paradox table. This is a limitation of current computer technology. The issue is what Paradox should store to a table. For example, should it store Windows ANSI characters or OEM DOS characters? *ANSI* is an acronym for American National Standards Institute. The ANSI set consists of 8-bit codes that represent 256 standard characters, such as letters, numbers, and symbols. The ANSI set is used by Windows applications. *Extended ASCII* is a character set designed by IBM. IBM extended the standard ASCII set from 7-bit codes to 8-bit codes and added more characters. The extended ASCII set contains 256 characters.

As a Windows product, the Paradox table structure has to be able to store Windows ANSI characters. Paradox supports dBASE and Paradox tables, however, and traditionally these table structures store OEM DOS characters. Therefore, Paradox must be able to deal with both character sets: the character set traditionally used by other products that used the table structures before Paradox and the character set used by Windows. In Paradox, the table language driver determines the character set. The problem is that although Microsoft controls both DOS and Windows, the two character sets, OEM and ANSI, are incompatible. You must decide between the two when you create your table.

One solution is to use the strict translation option of the Link tool. When strict translation is checked (the default), only the first 128 characters are stored. If you uncheck it, you enable your users to add characters that may not be supported by a different table language. There are disadvantages, however. For more information, refer to the online help on strict translation.

Using *sendKeys()*

The sendKeys() procedure sends keystrokes to the Windows message queue. The syntax for sendKeys() is as follows:

sendKeys(const ***keyText*** String [, const ***wait*** Logical]) Logical

The *wait* argument indicates whether to send the keys immediately (True), or to wait until the current method has finished (False). In most cases, False is the preferred setting.

Now type in an example to make sure you fully understand the principles of using sendKeys(). For example, the following simulates a user selecting File | Open | Table, typing Customer, and pressing ENTER. Type in the fourth line into the pushButton event of a button.

```
1:    ;Button :: pushButton
2:    method pushButton(var eventInfo Event)
3:       ;% = ALT key.
4:       sendKeys("%FOTCustomer{ENTER}")
5:    endMethod
```

Refer to the ObjectPAL Reference help file for more information.

Summary

Trapping for keystrokes is done in either the keyChar or keyPhysical events. The keyPhysical event passes the eventInfo to keyChar only if a printable character was pressed. The best location to trap for keys is either directly on the field in question or at the form's prefilter. If you wish to create a generic keyboard trapping routine, consider passing the eventInfo in the form's prefilter to a library routine that processes it.

CHAPTER 17

Manipulating Objects At Run Time

Objects that you place on forms and reports are UIObjects (user interface objects). Only UIObjects that you place on forms contain events. The form itself is also a UIObject—it has events and responds to events.

Pixels and Twips

A *pixel* is an abbreviation for picture element. Pixels vary in size depending on your monitor. One physical pixel is one dot on your screen, regardless of resolution. Contrast this with a *twip*, which is a physical unit where 1,440 twips are equal to one inch, regardless of resolution. Most ObjectPAL properties that manipulate size are in twips, not pixels.

Using the UIObject Variable

ObjectPAL offers tremendous flexibility in manipulating UIObjects during run time. You can either directly refer to a UIObject or attach to it and refer to it with the UIObject variable. For example, assuming a box named box1 is on a form, you can change its color with the following:

```
method pushButton(var eventInfo Event)
   box1.color = Red
endMethod
```

or with

```
method pushButton(var eventInfo Event)
   var
      ui UIObject
   endVar

   ui.attach(box1)
   ui.color = Red
endMethod
```

Obviously, in most situations the first single line of code is simpler, but the second technique is a particularly useful technique that you will often use when you do not know the name of the object a routine will be working with.

Moving a Text Box During Run Mode

Enabling the user to move objects around during View Data mode is very useful. In ObjectPAL, you can enable the user to move an object around to reveal something behind it, or you can enable the user to move an object to a new location. The following example shows you how to move an object around. When you let go of the mouse button, the mouseUp event occurs and the code in it snaps the object back to its original position. You could use this technique for many tasks. For example, you could use this technique in a game to reveal answers or offer clues in an educational game.

http://prestwood.com/forums/paradox/books/official/files/Mover.fsl.

Step By Step

1. Create a form with several text boxes on it. Give them various frames and colors (see Figure 17-1).

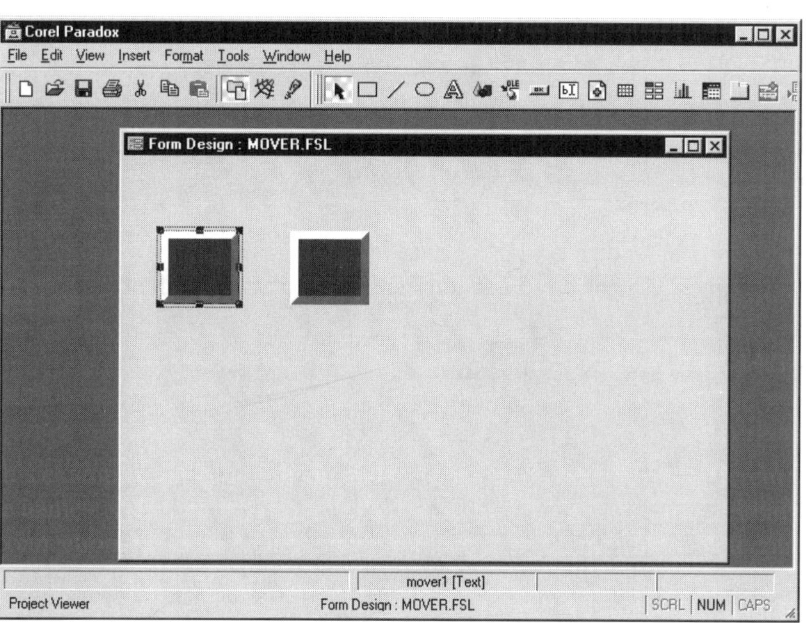

FIGURE 17-1 Setup form

2. Add lines 3–5 to the Var window of the form.

```
1:    ;Form :: Var
2:    Var
3:       x,y,x1,y1,w,h  SmallInt
4:       ui             UIObject
5:       sTargetClass   String
6:    endVar
```

3. Add line 3 to the Init event of the form.

```
1:    ;Form :: init
2:    method init(var eventInfo Event)
3:       sTargetClass = ""
4:    endMethod
```

4. Add lines 8–10 to the mouseDown event of the form:

```
1:    ;Form :: mouseDown
2:    method mouseDown(var eventInfo MouseEvent)
3:       if eventInfo.isprefilter() then
4:          ;This code executes for each object on the form
5:
6:       else
7:          ;This code executes only for the form
8:          eventinfo.getTarget(ui)
9:          ui.getPosition(x1, y1, w, h)
10:         sTargetClass = ui.class
11:      endIf
12:   endMethod
```

5. Add lines 3–5 and 11–17 to the mouseMove event of the form:

```
1:    ;Form :: mouseMove
2:    method mouseMove(var eventInfo MouseEvent)
3:    var
4:       liX, liY   LongInt
5:    endVar
6:       if eventInfo.isprefilter() then
7:          ;This code executes for each object on the form
8:
9:       else
10:         ;This code executes only for the form
```

```
        if eventinfo.isLeftDown() and
           sTargetClass = "Text" then
           liX = eventinfo.x()
           liY = eventinfo.y()
           ui.getPosition(x, y, w, h)
           ui.setPosition(x + liX - 400, y + liY - 400, w, h)
        endIf
     endIf
  endMethod
```

6. Add line 8 to the mouseUp event of the form:

```
1:   ;Form :: mouseUp
2:   method mouseUp(var eventInfo MouseEvent)
3:      if eventInfo.isprefilter() then
4:         ;This code executes for each object on the form
5:
6:      else
7:         ;This code executes only for the form
8:         ui.setPosition(x1,y1,w,h)
9:      endIf
10:  endMethod
```

7. Check the syntax, save the form as **MOVER.FSL**, and run the form. Click and drag any text box you placed on the form to move it. When you let go (mouseUp), the object snaps back to its original location (see Figure 17-2).

Creating UIObjects

ObjectPAL enables you to create objects in run time. To create objects on the fly, you need to use the create() method, and you need to know about things such as points and twips. As stated earlier, a twip is what you use to measure points on the screen. A point has a x value and a y value, both of which are measured in twips. A twip is 1/1,440 of an inch, or 1/20 of a printer's point. The following two examples use the create() command and a point variable to create and delete a line. The create() method does just what its name implies—creates objects. The type of object, where the object is created, and the dimensions of the object are all specified as part of the parameters for create().

The properties (frame, color, font, and so on) of the object produced by create() default to whatever the object defaults happen to be at the time the object is created. To modify the properties, you must change each individually, after the

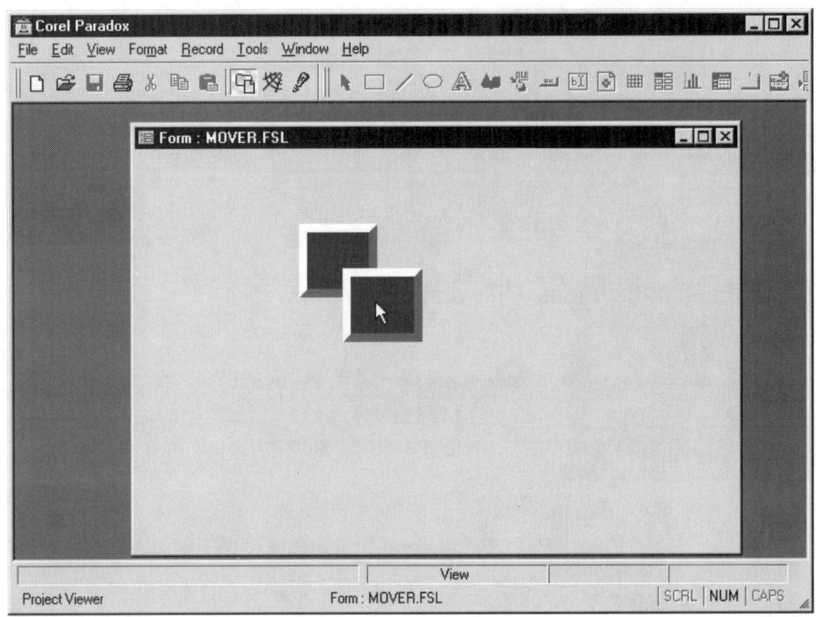

FIGURE 17-2 MOVER.FSL demonstrates moving objects during run time

object has been created. The notation and properties specific to graphs are discussed later in this chapter.

The parameters for create() are as follows:

objectType	Corresponds to the type of object being created. For graphs, this will be ChartTool.
x	The x coordinate (in twips) of the upper-left corner of the object.
y	The y coordinate (in twips) of the upper-left corner of the object.
w	The width (in twips) of the object to be created.
h	The height (in twips) of the object to be created.
container	This is an optional parameter. If present, container must be a UIObject capable of containing the created object. In other words, you cannot place a 1,000 × 1,000 object within a 500 × 500 container.

A Note on Working with Groups

Normal object creation goes from the outside to inside. For example, first the page is created and then you place a box on the page. Within the box, you place a table frame. Obviously, you cannot create the box without first creating the page. Likewise, you cannot create the frame without first creating the box. Unfortunately, groups work the opposite way. You cannot place a group on the page and then place objects within the group. You must first place the two objects and then place a group around these two objects.

Working with Frames

Because frames can vary in thickness, you need to allow for a border on the containing object. As a general rule of thumb, it is a good idea to give 15-twips distance between the inner object and its containing object.

Creating a Line

Suppose that you want to allow the user to create and delete a line. To do this, you use two buttons on a form. One button creates a line, and the other deletes it.

http://prestwood.com/forums/paradox/books/official/files/CreateLine.fsl.

Step By Step

1. Create a new form and place two buttons on it. Label the buttons **Create Line** and **Delete Line** (see Figure 17-3).
2. Add line 3 to the Var window of the page.

```
1:     ;Page :: Var
2:     Var
3:        ui UIObject
4:     endVar
```

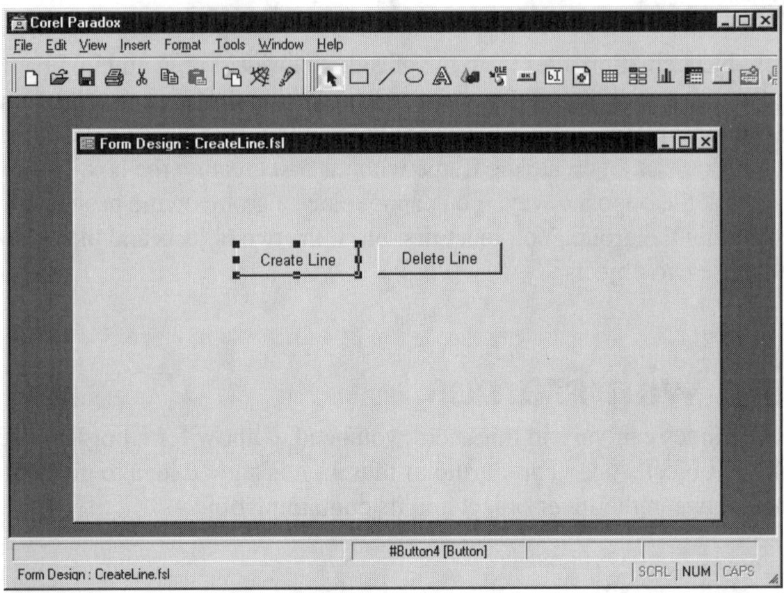

FIGURE 17-3 Setup form for the example

3. Add lines 3–6 to the pushButton event of the Create Line button.

```
1:    ;Button :: pushButton
2:    method pushButton(var eventInfo Event)
3:       const
4:          INCH = 1440
5:       endConst
6:
7:       ui.create(LineTool, 15, 15, 1.5 * INCH, 2 * INCH, self.container)
8:       ui.visible = True
9:    endMethod
```

4. Add line 3 to the pushButton event of the Delete Line button.

```
1:    ;Button :: pushButton
2:    method pushButton(var eventInfo Event)
3:       ui.delete()
4:    endMethod
```

5. Check your syntax, save the form as **CreateLine.fsl**, switch to View Data mode, and click the Create Line button. After the line is created, click the Delete Line button to remove it (see Figure 17-4).

Having Fun with Lines

Now let's have a little fun with creating lines. This next example randomly creates lines of varying length, position, color, and thickness in a box.

Step By Step

1. Create a new form and place two buttons, two fields, and a box on it (see Figure 17-5).
2. Label one button **Draw Lines** and the other **Clear Lines**. Change the upper field name to **fldLines** and label it **# of Lines**. Change the lower field's name to **fldDelay** and label it **Delay** (see Figure 17-5).

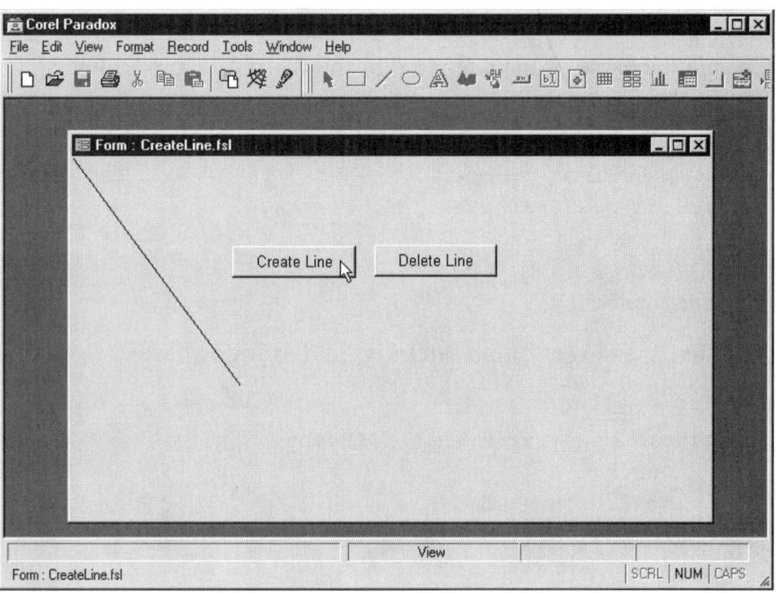

FIGURE 17-4 CreateLine.fsl demonstrates creating and deleting a line

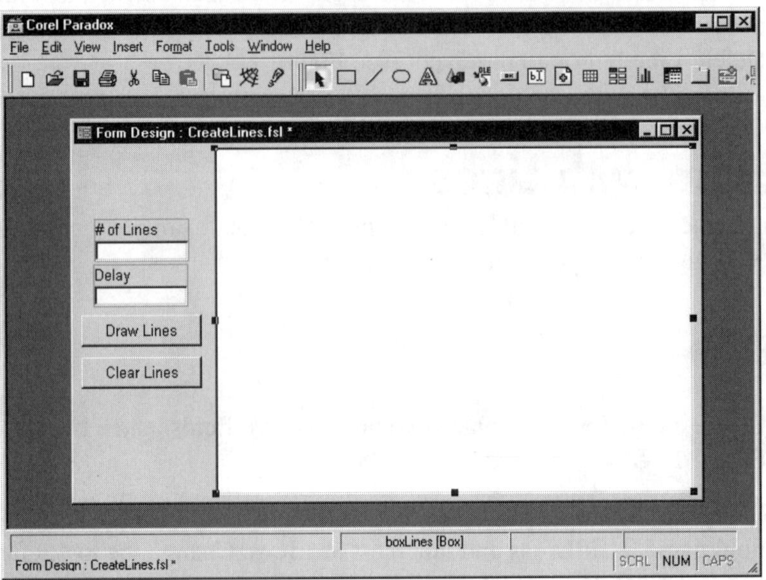

FIGURE 17-5 Setup form for the example

3. Change the name of the page to **pge** and the box to **boxLines**.
4. Alter the open event of the fldLines field as follows:

```
    ;fldLines :: open
method open(var eventInfo Event)
    DoDefault
    self.value = 100
endMethod
```

5. Alter the open event of the fldDelay field as follows:

```
    ;fldDelay :: open
method open(var eventInfo Event)
    DoDefault
    self.value = 50
endMethod
```

6. Alter the pushButton event of the Draw Lines button as follows. (As a programming exercise, try adding various line properties to this routine.)

```
;btnDraw :: pushButton
method pushButton(var eventInfo Event)
  var
     uiLine        UIObject
     pBox          Point
     siCounter     SmallInt
     xTemp, yTemp, wTemp, hTemp  LongInt
     x, y, w, h  LongInt
     siFrameSize SmallInt
     siColor       SmallInt
     siThickness SmallInt
  endVar

  setMouseShape(MouseWait)

  ; Get thickness of box's frame (plus a little for margin).
  siFrameSize = boxLines.Frame.Thickness + 15

  ; Get coordinates of box.
  pBox = boxLines.fullSize
  x = pBox.x() - siFrameSize
  y = pBox.y() - siFrameSize
  w = pBox.x() - siFrameSize
  h = pBox.y() - siFrameSize

  for siCounter from 1 to fldLines.value
     ;Set value for xTemp.
     xTemp = 0
    while (xTemp <= siFrameSize)
        xTemp = smallInt(rand() * x)
    endWhile

     ;Set value for yTemp.
     yTemp = 0
     while (yTemp <= siFrameSize)
```

```
         yTemp = smallInt(rand() * y)
      endWhile

      ;Set value for wTemp.
      wTemp = w
      while (xTemp + wTemp) >= w
         wTemp = smallInt(rand() * w)
      endWhile

      ;Set value for hTemp.
      hTemp = h
     while (yTemp + hTemp) >= h
         hTemp = smallInt(rand() * h)
     endWhile

     try
         ; Delay then create line.
         sleep(fldDelay.value)
         uiLine.create(LineTool, xTemp, yTemp, wTemp, hTemp,
         ; boxLines)

         ; Set line color.
         siColor = (smallInt(rand() * 5))
        switch
           case siColor = 1 : uiLine.color = Red
           case siColor = 2 : uiLine.color = DarkRed
           case siColor = 3 : uiLine.color = Blue
           case siColor = 4 : uiLine.color = DarkBlue
           otherwise : uiLine.color = Black
         endSwitch

          ; Set line thickness.
          siThickness = (smallInt(rand() * 40))
          uiLine.Thickness = siThickness

          uiLine.visible = True
      onFail
          beep()
```

```
            message("Could not create a line")
        endTry
    endFor

    setMouseShape(MouseArrow)
endMethod
```

7. Alter the pushButton event of the Clear Lines button as follows:

```
;btnClear :: pushButton
method pushButton(var eventInfo Event)
    var
        uiBox       UIObject
        uiLine      UIObject
        arLines     Array[] String
        siCounter   SmallInt
    endVar

    setMouseShape(MouseWait)
    DelayScreenUpdates(True)

    uiBox.attach("BoxLines")
    uiBox.enumObjectNames(arLines)

    for siCounter from 1 to arLines.size()
        if arLines[siCounter] <> "pge.boxLines" then
            uiLine.attach(arLines[siCounter])
            uiLine.delete()
        endIf
    endFor

    DelayScreenUpdates(False)
    setMouseShape(MouseArrow)
endmethod
```

8. Check your syntax, save the form as **CreateLines.fsl**, switch to View Data mode, and click the Draw Lines button. After the lines are created, either click the Draw Lines button again or click the Clear Lines button to remove them (see Figure 17-6).

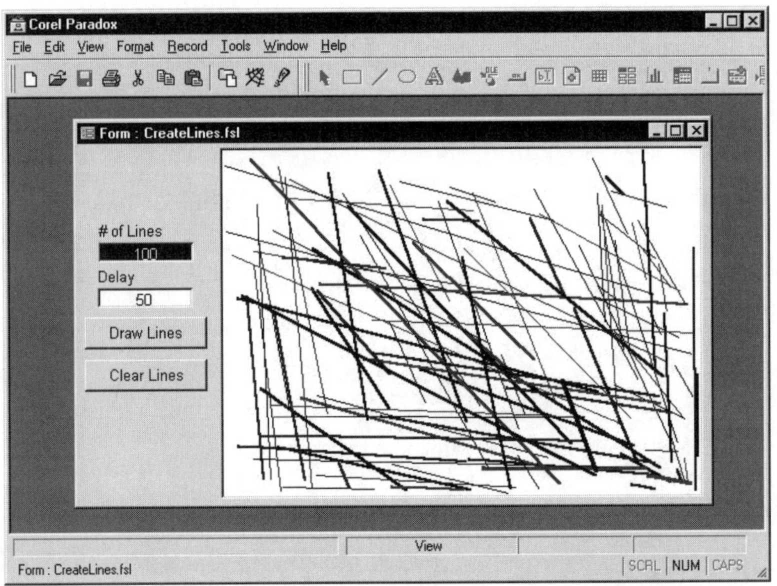

FIGURE 17-6 CreateLine.fsl demonstrates creating and deleting a line

Creating a Chart from Scratch

Now that you've seen how easy the create() method is, type the following code into the pushButton event of a button:

```
;Button :: pushButton
method pushButton(var eventInfo Event)
   var
     ui    UIObject      ;Declare a UIObject variable.
   endVar

   ui.create( ChartTool, 100, 100, 3000, 3000 ) ;Create the graph.
   ui.tableName = "ORDERS.DB" ;Set graph properties.
   ui.visible = True          ;Display graph.
endMethod
```

The preceding code creates a graph from scratch on a form. ObjectPAL is powerful; it enables you to create all types of objects while the object to which the code is attached is running. You also can alter the properties of graphs already created.

A Simple Example of Manipulating a Chart Property

This next example is similar to the preceding example, but adds the manipulation of the bindType and graphType properties to set the graph type. Following is another example you can type into the pushButton event of a button:

```
;Button :: pushButton
method pushButton(var eventInfo Event)
   var
      ui   UIObject
   endVar

   ui.create( ChartTool, 20, 20, 3000, 3000 )
   ui.bindType = GraphTabular
   ui.graphType = Graph2DPie
   ui.tableName = "Orders.db"
   ui.visible = True
endMethod
```

Using *designModified*

Sometimes you need to open another form, alter it, and close it from ObjectPAL. When you do, you are prompted to save the changes to the form; this is a very undesirable feature for a finished application. You could deliver the form and the problem would go away, or you could use the designModified property of the form, as in the following example:


```
f.designModified = False
```

In essence, you are telling the form that nothing was changed, when in fact it was.

This technique also works with reports. For example, the following code snippet is from our Paradox Workbench commercial utility—the code snippet opens a report and alters it:

```
var
   r   Report              ;Declare r as a report variable.
   ri  ReportOpenInfo      ;Declare ri as a ReportOpenInfo variable.
endVar

ri.name = "SOURCE"               ;Specify report name.
ri.masterTable = "SOURCE.DB"     ;Set master table for report.
r.open(ri)                       ;Open report.

;Set the value property of a text object.
r.txtTitle.value = "Source Code for " + fldFileName.value
r.show()
r.designModified = False         ;Tell report it has not changed.
r.wait()
```

Dereferencing a UIObject

You can create, move, size, and generally change any property of a UIObject. But how do you reference a UIObject with a variable? As discussed previously, you do so through dot notation and the use of parentheses. Referencing objects without hard-coding their names in the application adds flexibility to your routines.

When you work with several objects on a form, you might want to perform the same actions on each of the objects at different points in the code. One technique that saves many lines of code is to use a variable to reference an object. Remember the following three rules when you use a variable to reference an object:

- The statement that references an object must include a containership path. In the example that follows, Page refers to the name of the actual page in which the (Y) object resides.
- The first object in the path must not be a variable.
- Parentheses must surround the name of the variable.

Following is an example of how these rules are applied:

```
for X from 1 to 10
   Y = "Box" + strVal(X) ;This evaluates Y = "Box1" for
   Page.(Y).color = Blue ;the first iteration of the
                         ;for loop
endFor
```

This code changes the color of the objects named Box1 through Box10 to the color blue. Remember that it's easier to access the objects if you rename them yourself. If the name of the object is the previous name suffixed by a number, such as Box1, you can use code.

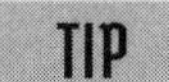

If you need to rename many objects one right after the other, use the Object Tree. By selecting and inspecting each object on the Object Tree, you can quickly rename many objects.

Using Timers to Animate a UIObject

Timers in ObjectPAL offer a powerful way to manipulate your environment. A timer enables you to execute an event every so many milliseconds. To set a timer, use setTimer(), as in the following:

```
setTimer(milliSeconds [,repeat])
```

For example, on the open event of any object, you can set a timer to trigger every 10 seconds:

```
self.setTimer(10000)
```

After you set the timer, add the code that you want to execute on the timer event of the object, as in the following example:

```
method timer(var eventInfo TimerEvent)
  msgInfo("10 second timer", "Press OK")
endMethod
```

You can use timers for a multitude of tasks, such as the following:

- Executing a set of commands every *n* milliseconds
- Checking the system time or date to set scheduled events
- Looping every *n* milliseconds for a multitasking looping technique
- Animating objects by moving and resizing them

Animating a Box Across the Screen

This next example demonstrates how to move an object across the screen. It uses the timer event and the position property to move a box across the screen. When the Box object has reached the other side, it starts over.

http://prestwood.com/forums/paradox/books/official/files/AnimateWithTimer.fsl.

Step By Step

1. Create a new form with a box measuring approximately one-inch by one-inch (see Figure 17-7).

2. Add lines 3 and 4 to the Var window of the box.

```
1:    ;Box :: Var
2:    Var
3:       posPt  Point
4:       x,y    LongInt
5:    endVar
```

3. Add lines 3–6 to the open event of the box.

```
1:    ;Box :: open
2:    method open(var eventInfo Event)
3:       self.setTimer(100)
4:       posPt = self.position
5:       x = posPt.x()
```

```
        y = posPt.y()
    endMethod
```

4. Add lines 3–7 to the timer event of the box.

```
1:  ;Box :: timer
2:  method timer(var eventInfo TimerEvent)
3:     x = x + 50
4:     self.position = Point(x, y)
5:     if x > 5800 then
6:        x = 200
7:     endIf
8:  endMethod
```

5. Check your syntax and run the form. The pull-down menus still work even though the code is executing (see Figure 17-8).

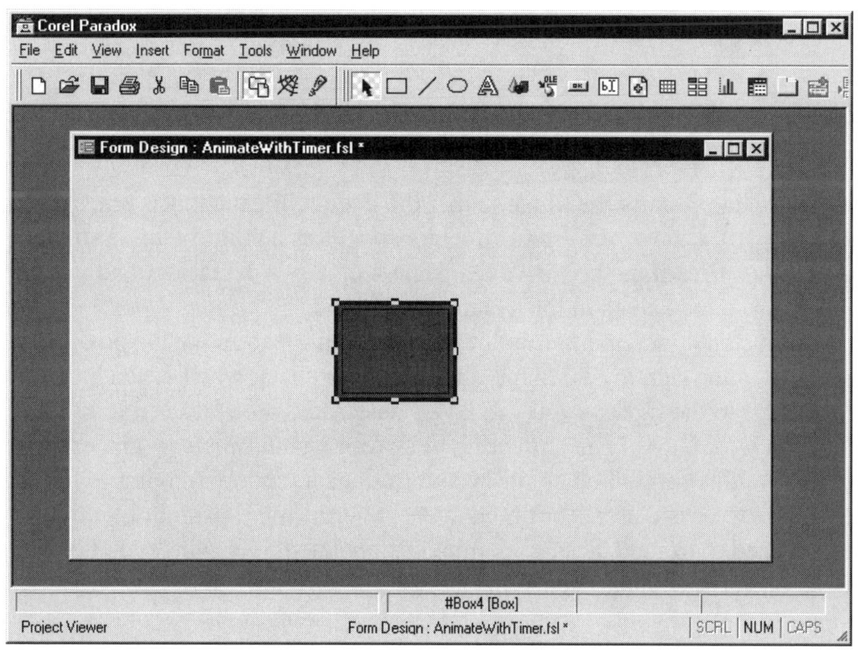

FIGURE 17-7 Setup form for the example

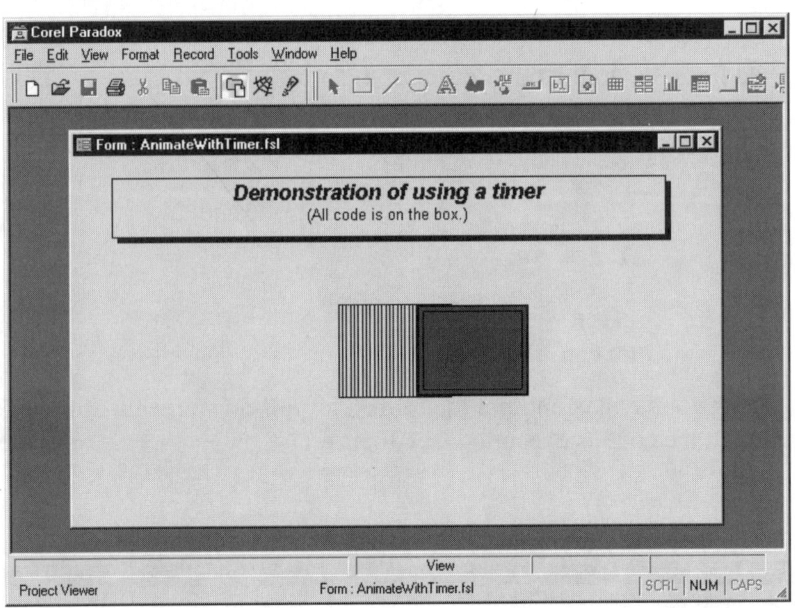

FIGURE 17-8 Demonstration of animating a UIObject

In step 3, line 3 starts the timer so that the code will execute 10 times a second (100/1000 = 10). Line 4 from step 2 declares posPt as a point variable so that you can get the position of the box in line 3. Line 4 in step 2 declares x and y long integers to store the values in lines 5 and 6 of step 3.

Line 3 in step 4 increments *x* by 50 for use in line 4 to move the box horizontally to the right by 50 twips. Lines 5 and 6 check whether the box has traveled as far to the right as you want. If it has, line 6 repositions it to the left.

You can have a lot of fun animating your forms with timers. As an exercise, add objects to this form. You could even introduce a random moving of objects. Timers have two basic uses: for timed events and for multitasking. Use timers when you need to execute a set of commands repeatedly, or when you need to multitask one task with another.

Looping with a Timer

Suppose that you want to enable a user to continue using his or her computer during a while loop that will take a long time to complete. To do this, you need to return control to Windows 95 or Windows NT. You won't see function calls in

ObjectPAL that are equivalent to WaitMessage in the Windows SDK. How do you handle this situation? Because it's part of the Windows API, you can call WaitMessage directly. To do this, declare it in a Uses statement and call it. There are, however, two better and easier techniques.

You can use two techniques, depending on how much control you want to give back to Windows. You can insert a sleep() statement in your while loop, which yields to Windows events. Depending on how complicated the while loop is, this might give you enough of a yield. You can add more sleep() statements to your code, or you can recode it to use the built-in timer event.

Set a timer event on a UIObject to fire every *x* milliseconds. You set *x*. Then, place one iteration of the while loop on the timer event. The iteration of the loop will process. You can vary how much you do on each timer event; a single iteration is the simplest example. Of course, you'll remove the while statement because the timer event controls the repetitive processing.

Example of Looping with Timers

Suppose that you want to add three fields to a form that count up while still enabling users to use the form and Windows. You can use this technique to create loops that enable users to continue their work. In this example, you set up three independent loops that use timers and three buttons that control the three loops as a set. The first button starts the looping process. The second button causes the three loops to pause. The third button kills all three loops. To show that these three loops are multitasking, you add a table frame connected to a table. That way, you can add records while the three loops count.

http://prestwood.com/forums/paradox/books/official/files/LoopUsingTimer.fsl.

Step By Step

1. Set your working directory to Paradox's Samples directory. Create a new form, based on the Customer table, and add three buttons on it. Label the buttons **Start Timers, Pause Timers**, and **Kill Timers**. Add three unlabeled undefined fields. Name them **Field1**, **Field2**, and **Field3**. Figure 17-9 shows how the form should look. In this figure, the three undefined fields and font sizes have been enlarged, and most of the columns have been deleted from the table frame.

17

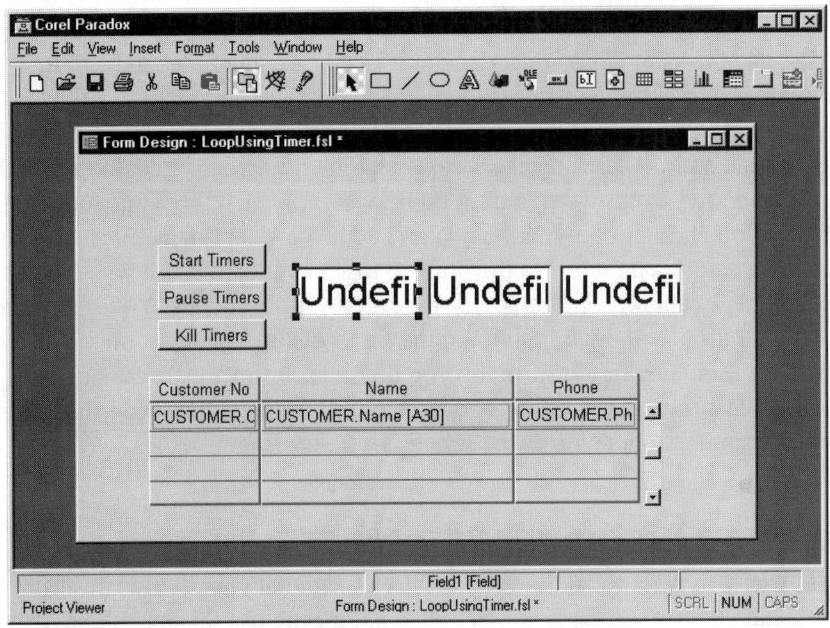

FIGURE 17-9 Setup form for the looping with timers example

2. Type line 3 in the Var window of the form.

```
1:    ;Form :: Var
2:    Var
3:       Counter1, Counter2, Counter3 SmallInt
4:    endVar
```

3. Type lines 3–5 in the open event of the page.

```
1:    ;Page :: open
2:    method open(var eventInfo Event)
3:       Counter1 = 0
4:       Counter2 = 0
5:       Counter3 = 0
6:    endMethod
```

4. Add lines 3–10 to the timer event of the Field1 field.

```
1:    ;Field :: timer
2:    method timer(var eventInfo TimerEvent)
3:       if Counter1 < 100 then
4:         Counter1 = Counter1 + 1
5:         self = Counter1
6:       else
7:         Counter1 = 0
8:         self = 0
9:         self.killTimer()
10:      endIf
11:   endMethod
```

5. Add lines 3–10 to the timer event of the Field2 field.

```
1:    ;Field :: timer
2:    method timer(var eventInfo TimerEvent)
3:       if Counter2 < 200 then
4:         Counter2 = Counter2 + 1
5:         self = Counter2
6:       else
7:         Counter2 = 0
8:         self = 0
9:         self.killTimer()
10:      endIf
11:   endMethod
```

6. Add lines 3–10 to the timer event of the Field3 field.

```
1:    ;Field :: timer
2:    method timer(var eventInfo TimerEvent)
3:       if Counter3 < 1000 then
4:         Counter3 = Counter3 + 1
5:         self = Counter3
6:       else
7:         Counter3 = 0
8:         self = 0
9:         self.killTimer()
10:      endIf
11:   endMethod
```

7. Add lines 3–5 to the pushButton event of the Start Timers button.

```
1:   ;Button :: pushButton
2:   method pushButton(var eventInfo Event)
3:      field1.setTimer(1000)
4:      field2.setTimer(250)
5:      field3.setTimer(50)
6:   endMethod
```

8. Add lines 3–5 to the pushButton event of the Pause Timers button.

```
1:   ;Button :: pushButton
2:   method pushButton(var eventInfo Event)
3:      field1.killTimer()
4:      field2.killTimer()
5:      field3.killTimer()
6:   endMethod
```

9. Add lines 3–13 to the pushButton event of the Kill Timers button.

```
1:   ;Button :: pushButton
2:   method pushButton(var eventInfo Event)
3:      field1.killTimer()
4:      Counter1 = 0
5:      Field1 = 0
6:
7:      field2.killTimer()
8:      Counter2 = 0
9:      Field2 = 0
10:
11:     field3.killTimer()
12:     Counter3 = 0
13:     Field3 = 0
14:  endMethod
```

10. Check the syntax, save the form as **LOOP-T.FSL**, and run the form. Click the Start Timers button and let it run a while. All three loops run at different speeds. You can use this effect to prioritize tasks. Click on the Pause Timers button; all three loops pause. When you click the Start Timers button a second time, the loops continue from where they paused. Now, use the table frame. For example, scroll up and down a few records, insert a record, and so on. Click the Kill Timers button to stop and reset all three loops. Figure 17-10 shows how the form should look after you finish this example.

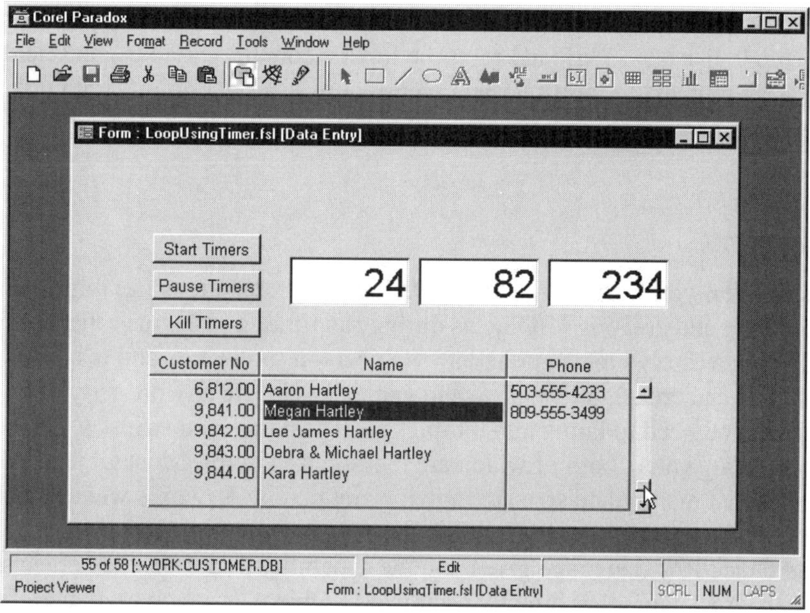

FIGURE 17-10 Using timers to create multitasking

In step 2, line 3 declares the three variables used in the three timers.

In step 3, lines 3–5 initialize the variables declared in step 2, sline 3 when the form is opened.

Except for the number of times that the timers loop, the three timers are the same. In step 4, line 3, the first loop checks whether the counter variable is less than 100. If it is, line 4 increments it by 1. Line 5 sets the value of self to the value of the counter variable. This shows progress through the loop; normally, you would do something more productive. If the counter variable in line 3 isn't less than 100, line 7 sets it to 0. Line 8 sets the value of the field to 0 to indicate visually that the loop is over. Line 9 destroys the timer.

In step 7, lines 3–5 on the Start Timer button start the looping process. They dictate which loop has priority—that is, the loop speed. Line 3 sets the first timer to fire once every second and starts it. Line 4 sets the second timer to fire once every quarter second and starts it. Line 5 sets the third timer to fire once every one-twentieth of a second and starts it.

In step 8, lines 3–5 on the Pause Timer button kill the timers but don't reset the counter variables. This enables the three loops to pause and restart.

In step 9, lines 3–13 kill and reset the timers, counter variables, and field values. Using timers to multitask and pause loops is an important technique. It often will come in handy.

Summary

In this chapter, you learned that ObjectPAL offers tremendous flexibility in manipulating and creating UIObjects during run time. You learned that the form itself is both a display manager and a UIObject—it has events and responds to events. You can create, move, size, and generally change any property of a UIObject. You need to know about things such as points and twips. A point has a x value and a y value, both of which are measured in twips. Most ObjectPAL properties that manipulate size are in twips, not pixels. A twip is what you use to measure points on the screen.

The ObjectPAL language gives you the capability to dereference objects and use timers. You can either directly refer to a UIObject or attach to it and refer to it with the UIObject variable. Referencing objects without hard-coding their names in the application adds flexibility to your routines. Timers in ObjectPAL offer a powerful way to manipulate your environment. Timers have two basic uses: for timed events and for multitasking. Use timers when you need to execute a set of commands repeatedly, or when you need to multitask one task with another.

CHAPTER 18

Reusing Code

Paradox provides several ways for you to reuse code, including custom methods, custom procedures, and scripts:

- **Custom methods** The most common way is to create custom methods and add them to specific objects (for example, a button, form, or library). These custom methods are public and can be accessed from other objects. For example, a custom method on a form can be accessed using dot notation from another form.
- **Custom procedures** Custom procedures are very closely related to custom methods but vary in scope. Custom procedures are private to the object. For example, a custom procedure on a form can *not* be accessed from another form.
- **Scripts** Scripts can be called from within an application using play() or run by a user from within the Paradox environment.

When deciding where to place reusable code, think about what object this code belongs to. Does it belong to the current Form object? Does it belong to more than one Form object? If it belongs to more than one form, then decide if it belongs to this application or all applications you develop. Finally, decide if the reusable code is reusable only within this object or will be called using dot notation from other objects. If there is a chance it will need to be called from another object, make it a custom method. Make the reusable code a custom procedure only if there is no chance the code will need to be called from another object.

Categorize and name your libraries carefully—perhaps creating one library for each application that stores application-specific information (give it the same name as the main form). Then, create libraries for specific purposes. For example, you might wish to create the following libraries: constants.lsl, strings.lsl, files.lsl, toolbars.lsl, internet.lsl, science.lsl, and printer.lsl. This list is here just for examples and is intended to encourage you to create your own. The better you become at reusing code, the better programmer you will become.

NOTE *If you create a particularly useful generic routine you wish to make available to others, then send it to me at mikeprestwood@prestwood.com. Be sure to document each custom method's public interface. Document how to use the custom method, not how you wrote it. Notes on how you wrote it are important and should be integrated as comments within the code itself. I'll integrate the routine with the appropriate library and make it available to others on www.prestwood.com. Also, if you create a whole library of generic routines, then zip it up and send it to me and I'll make it available to others.*

Custom Methods and Inheritance

In ObjectPAL, custom methods and procedures are code routines that you add to objects. You can even use the Copy to Toolbar option to make the code (and property changes) part of the current style sheet. In essence, you can inherit from the base class, add functionality, and save the new default object in the current style sheet. If you maintain one style sheet for each application, you can have default application-level code for each object. This isn't true inheritance because when you create a new object, the code is simply copied to the new object. If you change the generic routine by altering the code and select the Copy to Toolbar option, the changed code will apply only to newly created objects (the old objects will have the old code). Even with that said, this is still a useful way to customize the code attached to each object for each application you build.

Scope of Custom Methods

A custom method is always public. The object to which the custom method is attached and all the objects contained by it can call the custom method directly. With dot notation, objects can use the custom methods of other objects. For example, if a button has a custom method called cmMsg() on it, it can be called from another button.

Scope of Custom Procedures

Custom procedures, on the other hand, are more limited in scope (they are private to the object to which they are attached). Custom procedures have the same scope as variables. Only the object and objects contained by that object can call the custom procedure directly. In addition, dot notation doesn't work with custom procedures.

Custom Procedures Private to a Method

A custom procedure can be private to an object or private to a single method on that object. This is important if you want to reuse a bit of code within an event or custom method but not allow other events or objects to have access to the custom procedure. You do this by adding your own proc...endProc statement above or below the method line. When a custom procedure is private to a method, no other objects can call it. Likewise, no other events within the object can call it. The following is an example of a private custom procedure. The proc structure goes either above or just below the built-in method line. For example, create a button and alter the pushButton event as follows (be sure to add lines 2–4 above the method):

```
1:  ;Button4 :: pushButton
2:  proc cpMsg()
3:     message("A primary index can consist of up to 255 fields")
4:  endProc
5:  method pushButton(var eventInfo Event)
6:     cpMsg()
7:  endMethod
```

Passing by Value Versus Passing by Reference

Custom methods can receive and return values. You can pass a value by value or by reference. When you pass a value to a custom method by value, you pass a copy of the value. If the custom method alters the copy, nothing happens to the original. When you pass a value to a custom method by reference, you pass a reference to the location where the value is currently stored. In other words, you are actually referring to the original value. If the custom method alters it, it is altering the original value.

Passing by value and passing by reference are common to custom methods and procedures. Take a look at the following custom method prototypes:

```
1:  method cmCode(var s String)     ;Pass by reference.
2:  method cmCode(s String)         ;Pass by value.
3:  method cmCode(Const s String)   ;Pass by reference,
4:                                  ;but not changeable.
```

Line 1 uses the var keyword to pass the s value by reference. In other words, a pointer to the location of the original value is being passed. If the custom method alters s, then it is altering the original value.

In line 2, s is passed by value. In other words, a copy with its own memory address is created and the address to this new memory location is passed. If the custom method alters s, then the original is not altered.

In line 3, the value is passed by reference, but because the value is a constant, the custom method can't change it. The following examples demonstrate these concepts.

My First Custom Procedure

In this next step-by-step example, you create and use a simple custom procedure. It demonstrates creating and using a simple custom procedure that doesn't receive or return a value. Use this type of custom procedure to compartmentalize your code into easy to understand segments of code in custom procedures.

Step By Step

1. Create a new form and place a button labeled **Trivia** on it, as shown here:

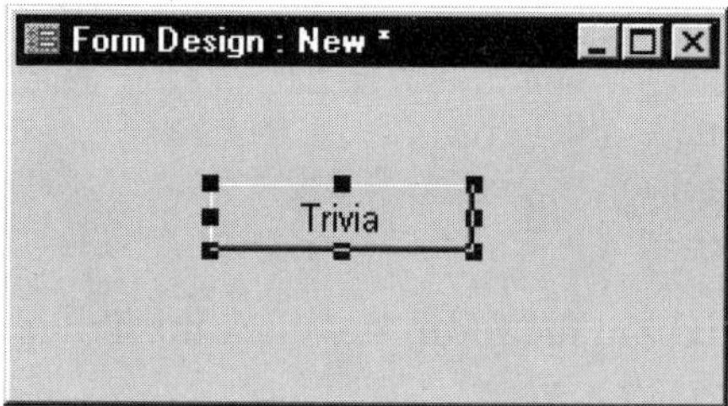

2. Open the Proc window for the form. To do this, make sure the form is selected and open the Object Explorer. Select the Methods tab and open the Proc window by selecting Proc, right-click, and select Edit Method, as shown here:

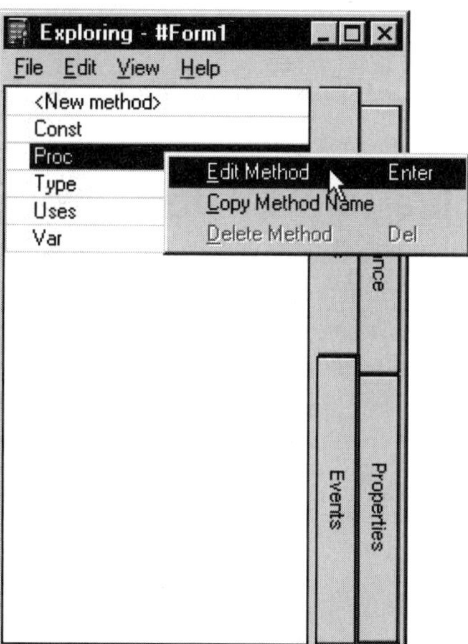

3. Alter the Proc window of the form to look like the following. Line 2 prototypes (sets up) the custom procedure. Nothing is in the parentheses, which indicates that the custom procedure expects to be passed nothing. The lack of code after the closing parenthesis indicates that the custom procedure returns nothing. Line 3 does the actual work.

```
1:     ;Button :: Proc
2:     proc cpMsg()
3:        msgInfo("PDoxWin Trivia",
                   "You can use up to 24 tables in a query.")
4:     endProc
```

4. Add line 3 to the pushButton event of the myMsg button.

```
1:     ;Button :: pushButton
2:     method pushButton(var eventInfo Event)
3:        cpMsg()
4:     endMethod
```

5. Check the syntax, run the form, and click the Trivia button. When the message appears, click OK:

Passing by Value to a Custom Procedure

This next step-by-step example demonstrates creating and using a custom procedure that receives, but doesn't return, a value. This category of custom procedure is important when writing generic custom procedures. For example, rather than referring directly to objects on forms, you can pass a UIObject variable to a custom procedure. Doing this makes the custom procedure work in more situations.

Step By Step

1. Create a new form (or use the form from the previous example) and place a button labeled **Pass by value** on it.
2. Add line 3 to the Proc window and alter line 2 of the "Pass by value" button.

```
1:     ;Button :: Proc
2:     proc cpMsg(s String)
3:        msgInfo("PDoxWin Trivia", s)
4:     endProc
```

3. Add lines 3–7 to the pushButton event of the "Pass by value" button.

```
1:     ;Button :: pushButton
2:     method pushButton(var eventInfo Event)
3:        var
4:          s     String
5:        endVar
6:        s = "Numeric fields are accurate to 15 significant digits"
7:        cpMsg(s)
8:     endMethod
```

4. Check the syntax and save your work. Run the form and click the "Pass by value" button. When the message appears, click OK.

The custom procedures are starting to get interesting. This discussion begins with the pushButton event in step 3. Line 4 declares s as a String variable, and line 7 calls the custom method. This time, a string is passed to it.

In step 2, line 2 prototypes the custom procedure. s String, which is between the parentheses, indicates that the custom procedure expects to be passed a string. The lack of code after the closing parenthesis indicates that the custom procedure returns nothing. Line 3 does the actual work of the custom procedure. It uses the variable s.

In this example, both the calling code and the custom procedure use a String variable called s. This shows the connection between the two. In reality, both variables need only to be of the same type; they don't need to have the same name.

Passing by Reference to a Custom Procedure

This example demonstrates creating and using a custom procedure that receives a reference to a variable but doesn't return a value.

Step By Step

1. Create a new form (or use the form from the previous example) and place a button labeled **Pass by reference** on it.

2. Add line 3 to the Proc window and alter line 2 of the "Pass by reference" button.

```
1:    ;Button :: Proc
2:    proc cpMsg(var s String)
3:       msgInfo("Windows Trivia", s)
4:    endProc
```

3. Add lines 3–8 to the pushButton event of the "Pass by reference" button.

```
1:    ;Button :: pushButton
2:    method pushButton(var eventInfo Event)
3:       var
4:         sMsg     String
5:       endVar
6:
7:       sMsg = "The Registration Database replaced INI files."
8:       cpMsg(sMsg)
9:    endMethod
```

4. Check the syntax and save your work. Run the form and click the "Pass by reference" button. When the message appears, click OK.

This discussion begins with the pushButton event in step 3. Line 4 declares sMsg as a String variable. Line 8 calls the custom method that uses the variable sMsg. This time, a variable is passed to the custom procedure.

In step 2, line 3 prototypes the custom procedure. In this case, var sMsg String in parentheses indicates that the custom procedure expects to be passed a variable. The lack of code after the closing parenthesis indicates that the custom procedure returns nothing. Line 2 does the actual work of the custom procedure. It uses the variable sMsg.

In this example, the calling code and the custom procedure use different variable names: sMsg and s. This shows that, although the two variables have a direct connection, the connection is by reference to the same value. You could have used the same variable name.

Returning a Value from a Custom Procedure

This next step-by-step example demonstrates how to create and use a custom procedure that doesn't receive a value by reference but does return a value. After the procedure is created, the return value is used in a message information dialog box.

Step By Step

1. Create a new form (or use the form from the previous example) and place a button labeled **Return a value** on it.
2. In the Proc window of the "Return a value" button, add line 3 and alter line 2.

```
1:     ;Button :: Proc
2:     proc cpNever() String
3:        return "Never duplicate a line of code!"
4:     endProc
```

3. In the pushButton event of the "Return a value" button, add line 3.

```
1:     ;Button :: pushButton
2:     method pushButton(var eventInfo Event)
3:        msgInfo("Message from guru", cpNever())
4:     endMethod
```

4. Check the syntax and save your work. Run the form and click the "Return a value" button. When the message appears, click OK.

Line 2 of step 2 prototypes the custom procedure. The lack of code in the parentheses indicates that the custom procedure expects to be passed nothing. The data declaration after the closing parenthesis indicates that the custom procedure returns a string. Line 3 does the actual work of the custom procedure. It uses the return keyword and passes back a string.

In step 3, line 3 calls the custom procedure and passes it nothing. Because the run-time library procedure msgInfo() expects a string, the custom procedure must return a value.

Sending and Returning a Value from a Custom Procedure

This example demonstrates how to create and use a custom procedure that receives a value by a reference and returns a value. After the procedure is created, the return value is used in a message information dialog box.

Step By Step

1. Create a new form (or use the form from the previous example) and place a button labeled **Pass & return a value** on it.

2. Alter the Proc window of the "Pass & return a value" button as follows:

```
1:    ;Button :: Proc
2:    proc cpAge(var d Date) Number
3:       var
4:          n    Number
5:       endVar
6:
7:       n = year(today() - d) - 1
8:       return n
9:    endProc
```

3. Add lines 3–9 to the pushButton event of the "Pass & return a value" button.

```
1:    ;Button :: pushButton
2:    method pushButton(var eventInfo Event)
3:       var
4:         dBorn     Date
5:       endVar
6:
7:       dBorn = date("01/08/65")
8:       dBorn.view("Enter your birthdate")
9:       msgInfo("Your age", cpAge(dBorn))
10:   endMethod
```

4. Check the syntax and save the form as CUSTPROC.FSL. Run the form and click the "Pass & return a value" button. When the first dialog box appears, type your birthdate and click OK. When the message displays your age, click OK.

In step 2, line 2 prototypes the custom procedure. var d Date in parentheses indicates that the custom procedure expects to be passed a reference to a Date variable. The data declaration after the closing parenthesis indicates that the custom procedure returns a number. Line 4 declares n as a Number variable. It is used in line 7 to accept the result of the calculation of the number of years between today and the date passed to the custom procedure. Line 8 returns n.

In step 3, line 4 declares dBorn as a Date variable. dBorn is given a value in line 7. Line 8 enables the user to change the value with a Date View dialog box. Line 9 calls the custom procedure inside a msgInfo() procedure.

The previous six examples represent the various types of custom procedures. In a nutshell, a custom procedure can be private to the method or public. Values can be passed to the custom procedure by value or by reference. Custom procedures can return a value, or not. After you master these elements, you can begin optimizing your code. Try never to duplicate a line of code. If you need to duplicate code on two objects, then consider putting the common code in a custom method or procedure and call it from both objects.

Custom Methods

Custom methods don't differ from custom procedures in any way except for scope. Although already stated, it is worth repeating. Custom procedures are private to a method or object and custom methods are always public. A custom method on an object can be called directly from any event on the object or from any event lower in the containership hierarchy. With dot notation, any object can call another object's custom method.

My First Custom Method

This next step-by-step example demonstrates how to create and use a custom method that simply executes a block of code; the custom method does not accept or return a value. In this case, the custom method asks a question.

Step By Step

1. Create a new form and place a button labeled **A Question** on it.
2. Create a new custom method for the form. To do this, make sure the form is selected and open the Object Explorer. Select the Methods tab and double-click the New Method option or right-click and select Edit Method, as shown here:

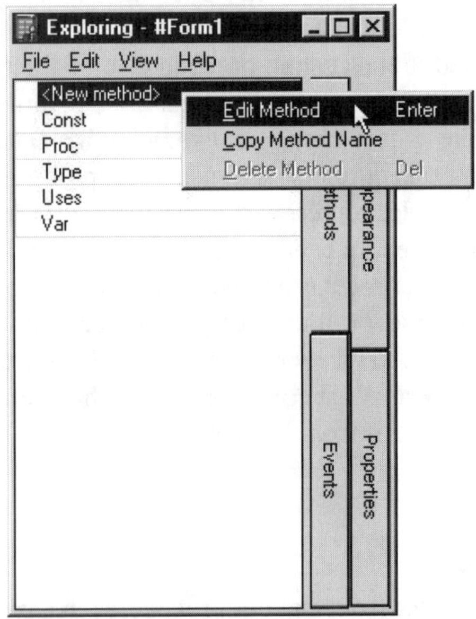

3. Name the custom method **cmQuestion**, and select OK.
4. Add lines 3–7 to the newly created custom method.

```
1:    ;Form :: cmQuestion
2:    method cmQuestion()
3:       if msgQuestion("Question?",
              "Is ObjectPAL full of features?")= "Yes" then
4:         message("When you're right, you're right!")
5:       else
6:          message("How much more do you want?")
7:       endIf
8:    endMethod
```

5. Add line 3 to the pushButton event of the A Question button.

```
1:    ;Button :: pushButton
2:    method pushButton(var eventInfo Event)
3:       cmQuestion()
4:    endMethod
```

6. Check the syntax and save the form as CUSTMETH.FSL (you will use this form for the next several step-by-step examples). Run the form and click the A Question button. When the first dialog box appears, answer the question.

In step 4, line 3 uses the message question dialog box to ask a question. If the user clicks Yes, the condition of the if structure is satisfied and the message in line 4 appears in the status bar. If the user clicks No, the message in line 6 appears.

In step 5, line 3 starts the whole process. The syntax for calling a custom method is the same as the syntax for calling a custom procedure. Therefore, you can't use the same name for a custom procedure and for a custom method in the same object. You can, however, use the same name for both as long as they are in different objects; the scope determines whether the procedure or method is called.

For example, if you put a custom procedure named cmQuestion on the page level of the form created in this example, it's called from the button rather than the cmQuestion form-level custom method. If you look at the Object Tree, you'll notice that the page is closer to the button than the form is.

Adding Private proc and var Structures to Custom Methods

As we have already discussed, custom procedures have the same scope as variables. They are private to the object or method and can be called from any event, custom procedure, or custom method contained within that object. This next example demonstrates adding both a private custom procedure and a private static variable to a custom method.

```
;Form :: cmUsingProc
var
   siCounter   SmallInt
endVar

Proc cpCounter()
```

```
      siCounter = siCounter + 1
   endProc

   method cmUsingProc()
      siCounter = 9
      cpCounter()
      siCounter.view()
   endMethod
```

After you create this custom method at the form level, you can call it from a button as follows:

```
   ;Button :: pushButton
   method pushButton(var eventInfo Event)
      cmUsingProc()
   endMethod
```

At this point, you should be understanding that reusing code using both custom procedures and custom methods is an important part of your ObjectPAL programming. To create truly reusable code (custom methods), you need to plan your application design well. When stepping back from your specific programming task and delving into application design, keep the application objects in mind (primarily forms and libraries).

Using *subject* to Dereference an Object

You can pass a subject to a custom method. With dot notation, you can tell a custom method to act on another object. To do this, you use the keyword subject. The code inside the custom method can use subject to refer to the object that preceded the calling of the custom method using dot notation. This next step-by-step example demonstrates how to use subject and dereference an object.

Suppose that you want to toggle the pattern of one of two ellipses, depending on the value in a field. This next step-by-step example dereferences a field and uses subject in a custom method to refer to the dereferenced value.

http://prestwood.com/forums/paradox/books/official/files/Subject.fsl.

Step By Step

1. Create a new form with two ellipses on it named **Ellipse1** and **Ellipse2** and name the page **Pge1**.
2. Add a radio button field named **choice** with the two values Ellipse1 and Ellipse2.
3. Add a button labeled **Toggle pattern**, as shown here:

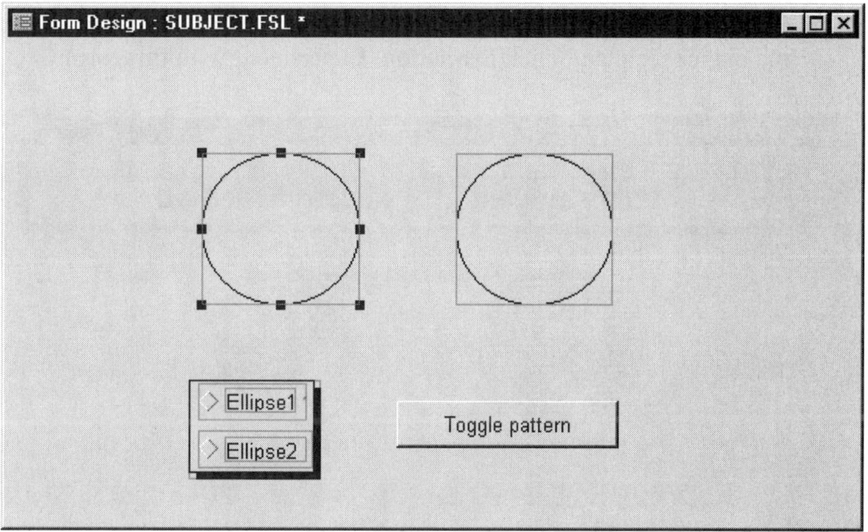

4. Create a custom method at the form level called cmToggleBackground() and add lines 3–7 to it.

```
1:  ;Form :: cmToggleBackground
2:  method cmToggleBackground()
3:     if subject.Pattern.Style = BricksPattern then
4:       subject.Pattern.Style = WeavePattern
5:     else
6:       subject.Pattern.Style = BricksPattern
7:     endIf
8:  endMethod
```

5. Add lines 3–7 to the pushButton event of the button.

```
1:    ;Button :: pushButton
2:    method pushButton(var eventInfo Event)
3:       if choice.isBlank() then
4:         return
5:       else
6:         pge1.(choice).cmToggleBackground()
7:       endIf
8:    endMethod
```

6. Check the syntax and save your work. Run the form. Select an ellipse from the choice field and click the button. Experiment with this form:

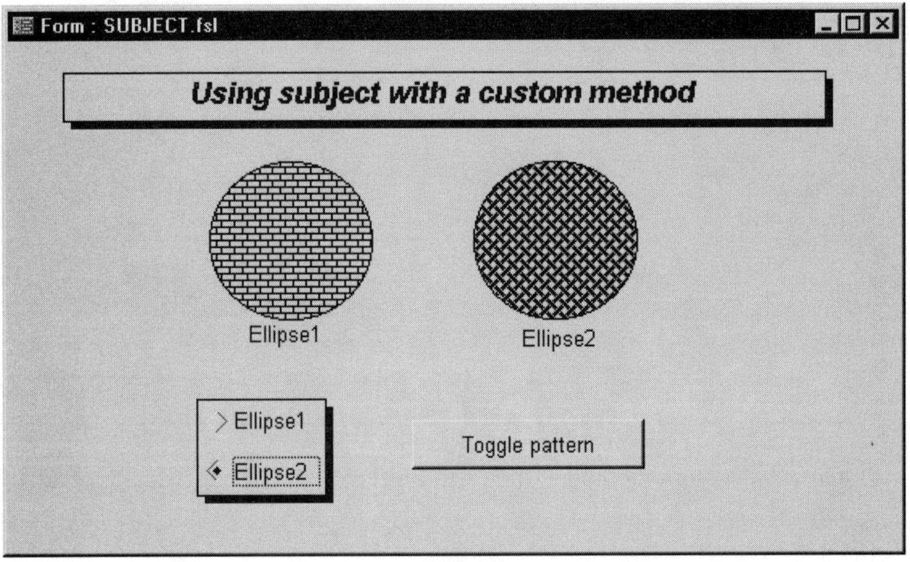

In step 4, line 2 prototypes the custom method. Line 3 checks whether the pattern of subject is a brick pattern. If it is, line 4 changes it to a weave pattern. If it isn't, line 6 sets it to a brick pattern. Note the use of subject. By not hard-coding the name of the object, you can make your routines more generic and flexible.

In step 5, line 3 ensures that the choice field has a value. Otherwise, an error would occur whenever the field is left blank. If the choice field is blank, the method returns control. If a choice was made, line 6 calls the custom method. Parentheses are used around the field name, and an object is specified before the first parenthesis.

Passing Arrays and Dynamic Arrays

To pass an array or a dynamic array to a custom method or procedure, you need to set up a Type statement. The syntax checker doesn't enable you to declare an array directly, so you have to create a custom type of the array or dynamic array. For example:

```
Type
   ctPassDyn = DynArray[] String
endType
```

Once you create the custom type, you can use the custom type when you prototype your custom method (usually the first line of your custom method). For example:

```
method (dynSystem ctPassDyn)
   ;Use dynSystem here.
endMethod
```

This next step-by-step example demonstrates how to pass an array to a custom method.

Passing an Array to a Custom Method

Suppose that you need to pass an array with two elements in it to a custom method for display. To do this, you have to create a custom type of an array. Then, use the custom type in the prototype line (usually the first line) of the custom method.

http://prestwood.com/forums/paradox/books/official/files/PassArray.fsl.

Step By Step

1. Create a new form and put a button labeled **Pass Array** on it.

2. Add line 3 to the Type window of the Pass Array button.

```
1:    ;Button :: Type
2:    Type
3:       ctPassAr = Array[2] String
4:    endType
```

3. Create a custom method called cmDisplayArray() on the Pass Array button and alter as follows:

```
1:   ;Button :: cmDisplayArray
2:   method cmDisplayArray(var ar ctPassAr)
3:      ar.view("Childhood friend")
4:   endMethod
```

4. Add lines 3–9 to the pushButton event of the Pass Array button.

```
1:   ;Button :: pushButton
2:   method pushButton(var eventInfo Event)
3:      var
4:        arName Array[2] String
5:      endVar
6:
7:      arName[1] = "Grant"
8:      arName[2] = "Winship"
9:      cmDisplayArray(arName)
10:  endMethod
```

5. Check the syntax and save your work. Run the form and click the button. The name "Grant Winship" appears in an Array view dialog box, as shown here:

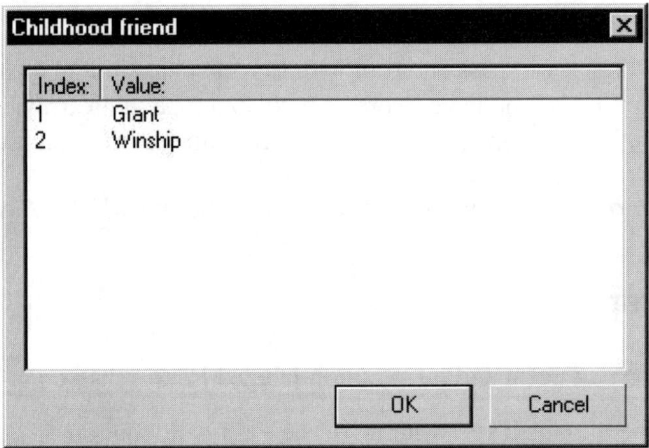

In step 2, line 3 declares a new data type: a two-element array that is ready to receive string elements.

In step 3, line 2 uses the new data type in the custom method's prototype. The var keyword indicates that the array is passed by reference. If you leave out the var keyword, the array is passed by value. Line 3 displays the array.

In step 4, line 4 declares arName as a two-element private array that is ready to receive string values. Lines 7 and 8 populate the array. Line 9 passes an array reference to the custom method.

With the knowledge you gain in this chapter, you can start to reuse and compartmentalize your code. Remember to try never to duplicate a line of code and to put often used code into custom procedures. These techniques work well for reusing code in a form. For reusing code across forms, ObjectPAL provides an object that is used only for storing code—the library.

Review of Custom Methods and Custom Procedures

Is there a good rule of thumb to use as to when to use a custom procedure? Functionally, the rule of thumb should be to always use custom procedures unless the code is called from outside of the containership hierarchy. Unfortunately, however, the real-world reality is that it's too much of a pain for most people to do this because of Paradox's incapability to present a list of custom procedures and jump directly to a specific one. Any procedure or method window is limited to 32K, which is dedicated to one method as opposed to being shared among many. This limits the wide use of custom procedures to just 32K per Proc window.

One advantage custom procedures have over custom methods is that they are faster. The extra speed of procedures is not execution speed, but access speed. This implies that the advantage of procedures decreases as the size of the procedure increases. The biggest advantage of custom procedures—and a motivation for their use—is their slightly faster access speed. However, speed is not that much of an issue in the decision because the difference in access time between custom methods and custom procedures is negligible. In addition, the scope is easily controlled by containership.

Libraries

A *library* is a Paradox object that stores custom ObjectPAL code. A library is useful for storing and maintaining frequently used routines and for sharing custom methods and constants among forms, scripts, and other libraries.

In a library, you can store custom methods, custom procedures, variables, constants, and user-defined types. Think of a library as a place to store often-used routines. It's the key to reusing your code and therefore, is a timesaver. The more you use libraries, the more time and energy you will save. You code a library similar to the way in which you code a form. In fact, you can think of a library as being a form with no user interface.

Characteristics of a Library

You never run a library. With ObjectPAL, you open and use the custom methods in a library, but you never run a library. A library doesn't contain objects. It contains compiled code.

The object variable *self* has different meanings, depending on when it's used. When it's used in a library, self refers to the calling object. When it's used in a form, self refers to the object to which the code is attached.

self refers to the calling object, not the library. This makes sense, although it's different than when another object's custom methods use self.

The scope of a library is determined by where you declare its variable and by how you open it (with or without the constant PrivateToForm). Although you can open a library from any point in the containership path, the placement of the Library variable determines which objects can see it. The form's Var window is a good place to declare a library's variable.

Every library has a built-in open, close, and error event. The open and close methods work just like a form's open and close methods. Open is a good place to initialize variables. error is called when code in the library generates an error. The error event is a good place to trap for errors that the library itself might generate. By default, the error event calls the built-in error event of the form that called that particular custom method.

A library is a complete unit, just like a form. With a library, however, external objects have access only to the library's custom methods. Although a library can't contain objects, it has Var, Const, and Type windows for declaring, setting, and defining variables. A library also has Procs and Uses windows for writing procedures and accessing other libraries and DLLs. You access all these items by writing custom methods that utilize them.

The custom methods you write in a library can be self-contained—that is, each method contains all the commands within its own code. By using custom methods, you can access variables, constants, types, and procedures inside a library. You can even get to a library's Uses window to call functions from other libraries or DLLs.

Libraries enable you to do the following:

- Reuse your code
- Centralize your code
- Set and retrieve variables in the Var window
- Call custom procedures in the Procs window

When should you use a library? Whenever you repeat code, create a custom method. Whenever you want to use a custom method on more than one form, put it in a library.

Opening a Library with *open()*

Use open() to give access to a library. You must declare a library first. As soon as you declare a variable, you use the open() command to open it. The syntax is as follows:

libvar*.open(** ***libName String [GlobalToDesktop | PrivateToForm]) Logical

Following are two examples:

```
lib.open("LIBRARY")
lib.open("LIBRARY", PrivateToForm)
```

GlobalToDesktop Is the Default

If you leave the second parameter of the open() method blank, Paradox opens the library global to the desktop (the default). This is important because this means you can share code and variables among the forms of an application. You could, for example, have one form set a variable in a library and another read that variable—in effect, setting and getting the variable as needed. We'll revisit passing variables through a library later in this chapter.

Closing a Library with *close()*

Closing a library frees up memory. Although it's not always necessary, you can close a library with the close() method. For example, the following closes the lib library variable:

```
lib.close()
```

Steps to Use a Library

This next section takes you on a short guided tour of how to create and use a library.

1. Create a custom method in a library. By means of custom methods, you can access all the various components of a library.
2. Declare the Library variable. You need to declare a Library variable on every form with which you want to use a particular library. A good place to declare a Library variable is on the Var method of the form, as in the following:

```
;Form :: Var
var
  libStrings Library
endVar
```

3. Open the library. After you declare the Library variable, you can use it to open the library. The syntax for opening a library is as follows:

```
library.open(Filename)
```

A good place to open a form's library is in the form's init method, as in the following:

```
;Form :: init
method init(var eventInfo Event)
   lib.open("Strings")
endMethod
```

Note that this statement doesn't specify an extension. Paradox automatically looks for LIBRARY.LSL first and then for LIBRARY.LDL.

NOTE *Use the open() command on all the forms in an application. Libraries don't have an attach() command. It is implied by open().*

4. Declare the custom method or methods in the Uses window or use the extended Uses syntax discussed later in this chapter. If you don't use the

extended Uses syntax, then every method you want to use from a library must be declared in the Uses window of the object you want to use it in. The syntax to prototype each custom method follows:

```
Uses ObjectPAL
   methodName( [[var | const] argList]) [returnType]
endUses
```

A good place for this is in the form's Uses window:

```
Uses ObjectPAL
  cmMsg()
endUses
```

5. To use Paradox's extended Uses, all you need to do is this:

```
Uses ObjectPAL
   "LIBRARY1.LSL" "LIBRARY2.LSL"
endUses
```

All the custom method prototypes, types, and constants from both LIBRARY1 and LIBRARY2 are bound at compile time. More information on extended Uses later in this chapter.

6. Use the custom method. After the custom method is set up for use, you must use proper dot notation to call it. The syntax for using a custom method from a library is as follows:

***libraryVariable*.customMethod([*argList*]) [ReturnValue]**

For example:

```
lib.cmMsg()
```

NOTE

The syntax of object.method() is consistent throughout ObjectPAL. If an object with the name box has code on its mouseClick event, you can access that code with box.mouseClick() method from any other object. When this code executes, the UIObject method mouseClick() calls the mouseClick event.

How do you know when you can call the code in a built-in method of an object? Easy, if the run-time library has a method equivalent, then you can use it—for example, mouseClick() and pushButton().

Passing *eventInfo*

Just like you can pass variables to a custom method, you can pass the eventInfo variable to a custom method. You can use this technique to centralize your code further by passing eventInfo to a custom method in a library. For example, you can pass the eventInfo up to a library routine to handle all errors.

Inspecting *eventInfo*

You can use the technique of passing eventInfo to inspect the eventInfo by creating your own custom method. For example, the following custom method displays information about an ActionEvent when passed eventInfo. Create a form based on the Customer table, shown next, and add the following custom method to the form level (name the custom method cmActionEvent()).

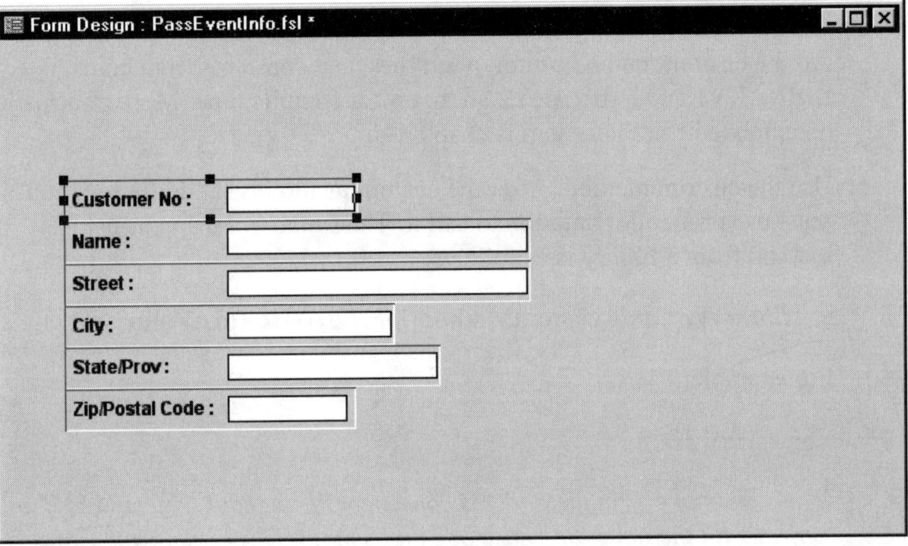

ON THE NET *http://prestwood.com/forums/paradox/books/official/files/PassEventInfo.fsl.*

```
;Form :: cmActionEvent
method cmActionEvent(var eventInfo ActionEvent)
  var
     ui              UIObject
     dynEventInfo    DynArray[] Anytype
```

```
   endVar
   eventInfo.getTarget(ui)

   dynEventInfo["actionClass"]                 = eventInfo.actionClass()
   dynEventInfo["errorCode"]                   = eventInfo.errorCode()
   dynEventInfo["getTarget Name"]              = ui.name
   dynEventInfo["getTarget Value"]             = ui.value
   dynEventInfo["getTarget Container Name"]    = ui.container.name
   dynEventInfo["id"]                          = eventInfo.id()
   dynEventInfo["isFirstTime"]                 = eventInfo.isFirstTime()
   dynEventInfo["isprefilter"]                 = eventInfo.isprefilter()
   dynEventInfo["isTargetSelf"]                = eventInfo.isTargetSelf()
   dynEventInfo["Reason"]                      = eventInfo.reason()

   dynEventInfo.view("View Eventinfo")
endMethod
```

Next, pass it an ActionEvent eventInfo variable. For example, type the following code into the action event of the form:

```
;EVENT1 :: Form :: action
method action(var eventInfo ActionEvent)
  if eventInfo.isprefilter() then
     ;// This code executes for each object on the form
     ;//
     if eventInfo.id() = DataUnlockRecord or
        eventInfo.id() = DataPostRecord then
        DoDefault
        if eventInfo.errorCode() = peKeyViol then
           msgStop("Warning",
                  "Key violation\n\nLet's inspect the action event eventInfo.")
           cmActionEvent(eventInfo)
        endIf
     endIf
  else
     ;// This code executes only for the form
     ;//
  endIf
endMethod
```

Next, run the form and cause a key violation (see Figure 18-1).

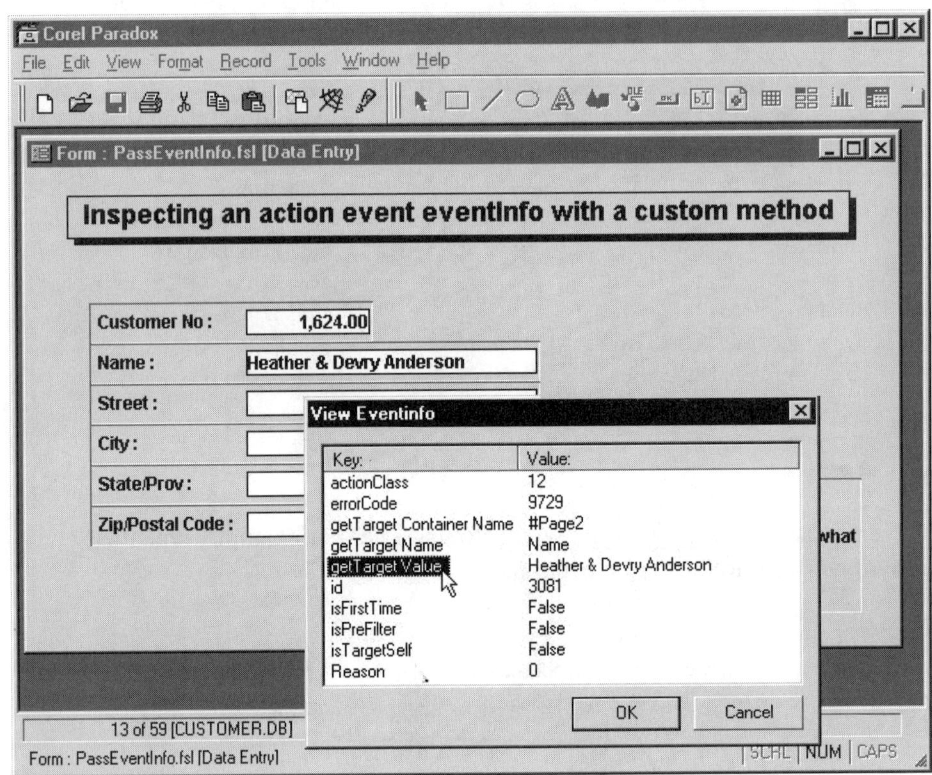

FIGURE 18-1 Passing EventInfo.fsl showing the contents of eventInfo

Passing Variables Through a Library

Passing variables from form to form and from form to library comes close to making up for the lack of a true global variable in ObjectPAL. Occasionally, you need a system-wide control mechanism, or you need to store a piece of data from a form in a library for later use. A variable in a library enables you to emulate a true global variable. The next example shows you how to put variables into and get variables from a library.

Passing a Variable Between Forms

Suppose that you want to pass a value from one form to another through a library. Because you are using a library, both forms don't have to be open at the same time.

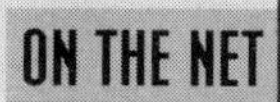

http://prestwood.com/forums/paradox/books/official/files/LIB1.FSL, http://prestwood.com/forums/paradox/books/official/files/LIB2.FSL, and http://prestwood.com/forums/paradox/books/official/files/LIB.LSL.

Step By Step

1. Create two forms and save the forms as **LIB1.FSL** and **LIB2.FSL**, respectively. Put a button labeled **Put** on the LIB1.FSL and a button labeled **Get** on the LIB2.FSL. Create a library and save it as **LIB.LSL** (see Figure 18-2).

2. Create a new library and add lines 3 and 4 to the Var window of the library.

```
1:    ;Library :: Var
2:    Var
3:       sFirstName String
4:       sLastName  String
5:    endVar
```

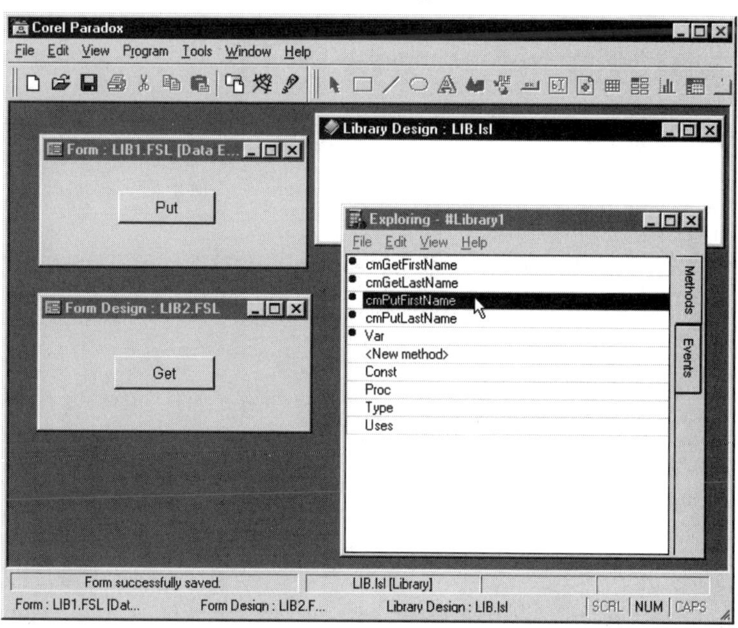

FIGURE 18-2 Set up forms, library, and custom methods

3. Create a new custom method in the library called cmPutFirstName() and add line 3 to it.

```
1:     ;Library :: cmPutFirstName
2:     method cmPutString1(AFirstName String)
3:        sFirstName = AFirstname
4:     endMethod
```

4. Create a new custom method in the library called cmPutLastName() and alter it as follows:

```
1:     ;Library :: cmPutLastName
2:     method cmPutString2(ALastName String)
3:        sLastName = ALastName
4:     endMethod
```

5. Create a new custom method in the library called cmGetFirstName() and alter as follows:

```
1:     ;Library :: cmGetFirstName
2:     method cmGetFirstName() String
3:        return sFirstName
4:     endMethod
```

6. Create a new custom method in the library called cmGetLastName() and alter it as follows: Save the library as **LIB.LSL**.

```
1:     ;Library :: cmGetLastName
2:     method cmGetLastName() String
3:        return sLastName
4:     endMethod
```

7. Create a new form and add lines 3 and 4 to the Uses window of the first form.

```
1:     ;Form :: Uses
2:     Uses ObjectPal
3:        "lib.lsl"
4:     endUses
```

8. Add line 3 to the Var window of the first form.

```
1:     ;Form :: Var
2:     Var
```

```
3:        lib Library
4:     endVar
```

9. Add lines 3–5 to the pushButton event of the Put button on the first form. Save the form as **LIB1.FSL**.

```
1:     ;Button :: pushButton
2:     method pushButton(var eventInfo Event)
3:        lib.open("LIB")
4:        lib.cmPutFirstName("Keith")
5:        lib.cmPutLastName("Kinnamont")
6:     endMethod
```

10. Add lines 3 and 4 to the Uses window of the second form. This is an example of using ObjectPAL's extended uses, which is discussed in the next section.

```
1:     ;Form :: Uses
2:     Uses ObjectPAL
3:        "lib.lsl"
4:     endUses
```

11. Add line 3 to the Var window of the second form.

```
1:     ;Form :: Var
2:     Var
3:        lib Library
4:     endVar
```

12. Add lines 3 and 4 to the pushButton event of the Get button on the second form. Save the form as **LIB2.FSL**.

```
1:     ;Button :: pushButton
2:     method pushButton(var eventInfo Event)
3:        lib.open("lib.lsl")
4:        msgInfo("Childhood friend", lib.cmGetFirstName() +
          ; " " + lib.cmGetLastName())
5:     endMethod
```

13. Check the syntax and save all the various elements (the forms and the library). Close the library and run both forms. Click the Put button on the first form, then click the Get button on the second form, as shown here:

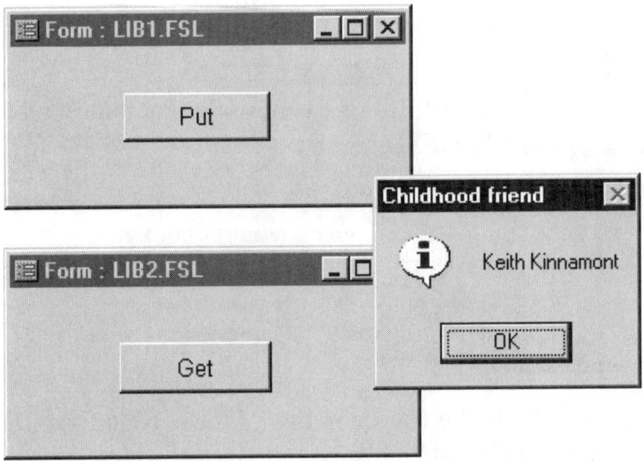

If you close LIB1.FSL before you open LIB2.FSL, the library is closed and reopened, losing any variables that were set. Also, if you press the Get button without first pressing the Set button, you'll get an error. You can avoid this error by initializing the variables in the library to Null in the library's open event.

Since custom methods are public, a library can access the custom methods in other libraries.

Extended Uses Syntax

Extended Uses enables ObjectPAL to use compile-time binding. Compile-time binding enables the compiler to resolve code at the time the code is compiled. Extended Uses enables you to utilize libraries easier as well as do some things you couldn't do before. Following are the three things it enables you to do:

- You can utilize the custom types you have defined in a library or form in another library or form without having to write the code again.
- You can utilize the constants you have defined in a library or form in another library or form without having to write the code again.
- You can utilize the custom methods from a library or form from another library or form without having to prototype the custom methods.

In C, compile-time binding is accomplished with the #include command. In Pascal, it is accomplished with the Uses statement (similar in nature to

ObjectPAL's Uses statement). Following is the syntax for doing compile-time binding in ObjectPAL:

```
Uses ObjectPAL
   ["fileName"]*
endUses
```

For example, assume that you have a library you use just for constants, a library just for custom types, and a library for custom methods. Following is the code you need in the Uses window of the form to give your code the capability to utilize all the constants, types, and custom methods from the libraries:

```
;Form :: Uses
Uses ObjectPAL
   "constants.lsl"
   "types.lsl"
   "methods.lsl"
endUses
```

Now in your code, you can utilize the constants from the CONSTANTS.LSL library, and the types from the TYPES.LSL library. In addition, although the two files, CONSTANTS.LSL and TYPES.LSL, need to be around while you deliver the form that utilizes them, the libraries do not need to be around after you deliver the form. The types and constants have been bound at delivery time.

The custom methods from the METHODS.LSL library are not quite that easy to use, but they almost are. You still have to open the library just as you learned earlier in this chapter; however, you do not have to prototype each method—the compiler does that for you at compile time. Following is an example of using an imaginary cmMyMethod() custom method in METHODS.LSL:

```
Uses ObjectPAL
   ;Step 1 - specify library.
   "methods.lsl"
endUses
method pushButton(var eventInfo Event)
   var
      libMethods Library
   endVar
```

```
   ;Step 2 - Open library.
   libMethods.open("methods")    ;Can be methods.lsl or methods.ldl.
   ;Step 3 - Call method using dot notation.
   libMethods.cmMyMethod()
endMethod
```

When you deliver your application, you still need to distribute a copy of the library (either .LSL or .FDL).

Creating a Library from Scratch

The last example in this chapter will demonstrate creating a library from scratch and then using it. This example is included to show you the flexibility and power of ObjectPAL. Following is the pertinent code from the pushButton event:

http://prestwood.com/forums/paradox/books/official/files/CreateLibrary.fsl.

```
;Button :: pushButton
method pushButton(var eventInfo Event)
   var
      lib  Library
   endVar

   ;Create library.
   lib.create()
   lib.methodSet("cmMessage", "method cmMessage() msgInfo(\"From new library\",
   ; \"Hello World!\") endMethod")
   lib.save("test")
   lib.close()

   ;Use library.
   lib.open("test")
   lib.cmMessage()
endMethod
```

Now, here is the pertinent code from the button's Uses method:

```
;Button :: Uses
Uses ObjectPAL
```

```
    cmMessage()
endUses
```

Summary

In this chapter, you learned that custom procedures, custom methods, libraries, and scripts are devices you can use to compartmentalize and organize your code. When your code is well organized, you can reuse more of it.

In ObjectPAL, custom methods and procedures are attached to objects. ObjectPAL comes with a set of methods and procedures already attached to objects, called the run-time library. A custom method consists of methods and procedures from the run-time library, as well as registered functions from dynamic link libraries (DLLs). Think of the set of custom methods and custom procedures that you develop as either enhancements you make to existing objects (like forms and buttons) and as your own private run-time library of code.

A custom procedure is similar to a custom method, except that a custom procedure is private to the object or method. A custom method is always public.

A library is a Paradox object that stores custom ObjectPAL code. A library is useful for storing and maintaining frequently used routines and for sharing custom methods, constants, and custom types among forms, scripts, and other libraries.

CHAPTER 19

Imitate Users with Action, PostAction, and MenuAction

Whenever you interact with Paradox, you generate either an Action or MenuAction constant. For example, when you select a menu item, a constant is sent to the built-in menuAction event. If the constant maps to an Action constant, an equivalent Action constant then is sent to the built-in action event. For example, when you select File | Print, the constant MenuFilePrint is sent to the form's menuAction event. Since MenuFilePrint maps to the action constant DataPrint, DataPrint is sent to action. In the events action and menuAction, you can trap for nearly every user interaction. In addition, using the action() and menuAction() methods you can invoke or imitate nearly any user interaction by sending Action and MenuAction constants to the built-in action and menuAction events.

Action() and PostAction()

Both action() and postAction() performs a specified action. The difference is that action() executes the action right away and postAction() posts an action to an action queue for delayed execution. With postAction(), the action is posted to an action queue at the time of the method call; Paradox waits until a yield occurs—for example, by the current method completing execution or by a call to sleep(). This is an important distinction to keep in mind while executing actions from within your code.

Using the *action()* and *postAction()*

These methods open up a whole bunch of commands. As an ObjectPAL programmer, you're interested in five action constant classes: ActionDataCommands, ActionEditCommands, ActionFieldCommands, ActionMoveCommands, and ActionSelectCommands. Use these commands with the action() method. The syntax for action constants is as follows:

```
ObjectName.action(ActionConstant)
```

ObjectName is the name of the object on which you want the action to occur, such as theBox or Last_Name. The actionConstant can be any constant category whose name starts with action. If you want, you can precede this expression with an object path, as in the following:

```
f.pge3.tf.action(DataNextRecord)
```

In this example, f is a handle to another form, and pge3 and tf are the names of two objects contained in the form (the third page and its table frame). The constant DataNextRecord moves the cursor forward one record (if possible).

Using *Action* Constants

The constants in the ActionDataCommands category deal with data in a table as a whole, as shown here:

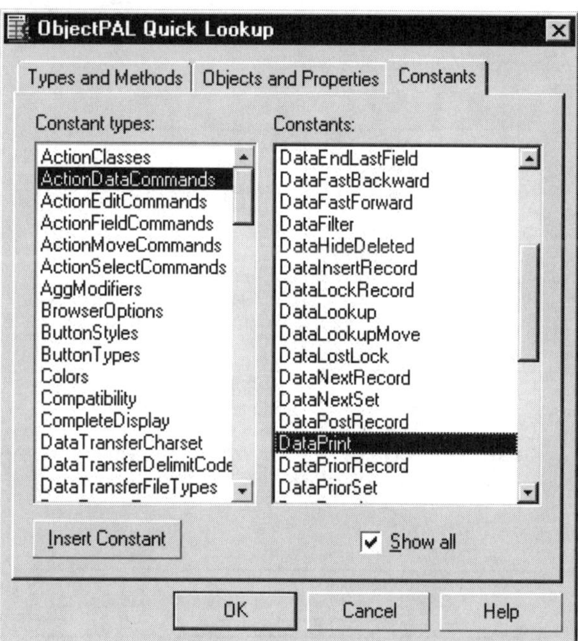

They are used for navigating the pointer in a table, locking a record, posting a record, toggling Edit mode, and positioning the record pointer. Following are three examples:

```
action(DataPrint)          ;Prints a form or table view.
action(DataTableView)      ;Open the master table in a window.
action(DataSaveCrosstab) ;Writes the crosstab data
                           ;to :PRIV:CROSSTAB.DB.
```

ActionEditCommands

In general, the constants in the ActionEditCommands category are used for altering data within a field, as shown here:

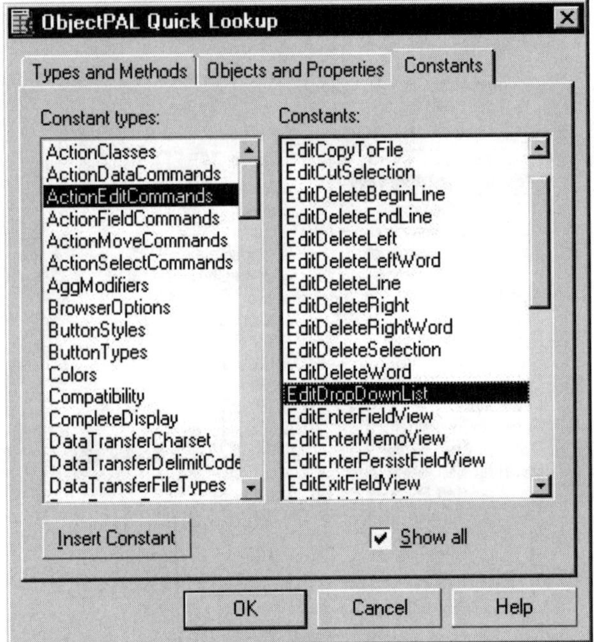

With these constants, you can copy text to the Clipboard, enter persistent field view, access the help system, and search your text. Following are three examples:

```
action(EditDropDownList)  ;Drops down pick list.
action(EditEnterMemoView) ;Enters memo view.
action(EditPasteFromFile) ;Pastes from file into
                          ;current field.
```

ActionFieldCommands

The constants in the ActionFieldCommands category are used for moving between field objects, as shown here:

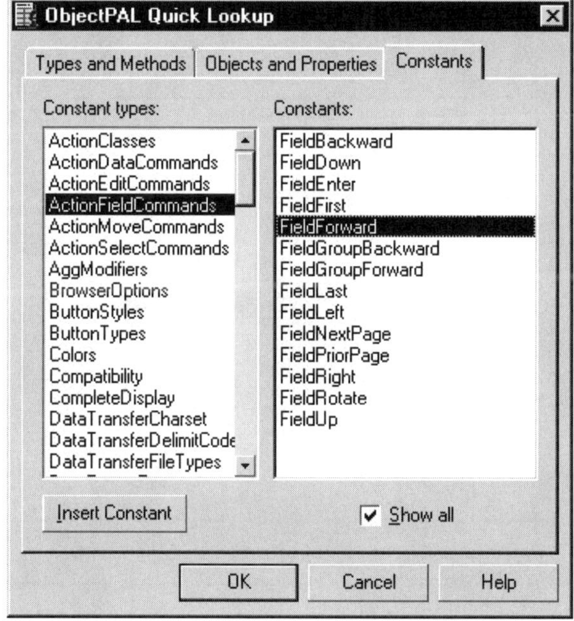

With these constants, you can invoke and control tab order. You can move the focus forward or backward in the tab order. You can ignore the tab order and move up, down, left, or right. You can even move from one table frame to another. Following are three examples:

```
action(FieldRotate)      ;Rotates columns in a table frame
action(FieldNextPage)    ;Moves to the next page in a form
action(FieldForward)     ;Moves one field forward
```

ActionMoveCommands

The constants in the ActionMoveCommands category are used for positioning within a field object, as shown here:

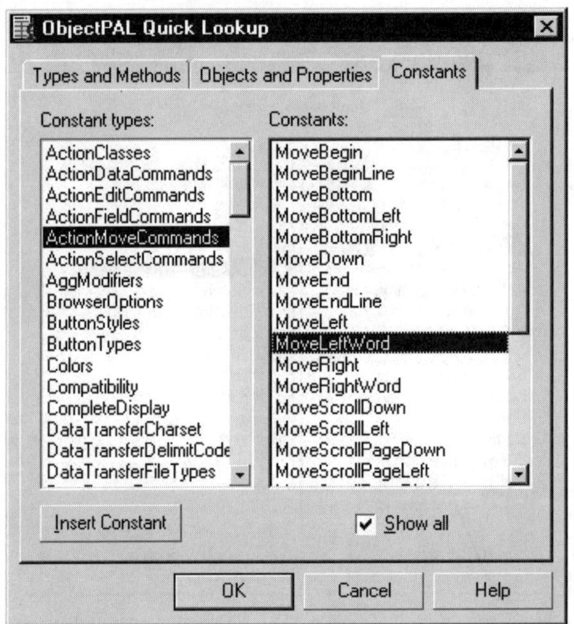

With these constants, you can move to the beginning or end of a field, move left one word, or scroll a field up or down. In general, these commands behave differently in a Memo field than they do in a set of fields. Following are three examples:

```
action(MoveEnd)               ;Moves to the end of the document or
                              ;to last field.
action(MoveLeftWord)          ;Moves cursor to word on the left.
action(MoveScrollPageDown)    ;Scrolls the page image down.
```

ActionSelectCommands

The ActionSelectCommands constants are similar to the ActionMoveCommands constants, but you use them to select data within a field object, as shown here:

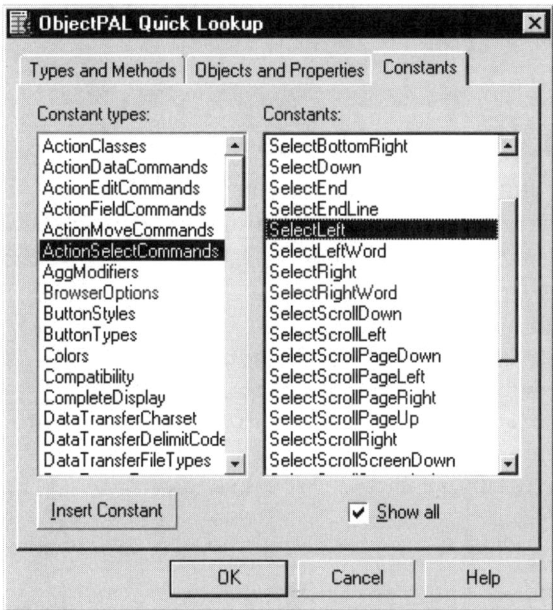

With these constants, you can select from the current position to the beginning of the document. Following are three examples:

```
action(SelectEnd)       ;Select to the end.
action(SelectLeft)      ;Selects one character to the left.
action(SelectSelectAll) ;Selects the entire document.
```

Browse through the online constants section by selecting View | ObjectPAL Quick Lookup and selecting the Constants tab. Select the categories whose names start with action. These constants are your gateway to more powerful data manipulation and, therefore, to more powerful applications.

If you find a constant that is not self-explanatory, search in the help for types of constants for a complete list of the constants along with a description for each.

Trapping *Action* Constants

In addition to executing action constants, you can trap for them. The basic idea is to use the action event and inspect the eventInfo variable. For example, to trap for when the form enters Edit mode, type lines 3–6 in the page's action event.

```
1:    ;Commands :: Pge1 :: action
2:    method action(var eventInfo ActionEvent)
3:       if eventInfo.id() = DataBeginEdit then
4:         DoDefault    ;Finish moving into edit mode.
5:         beep()
6:         msgInfo("Careful", "You are now in edit mode.")
7:       endIf
8:    endMethod
```

Using *MenuAction* Constants

Another method in ObjectPAL that opens up a whole world of power is menuAction(). The menuAction() method enables you to execute any of the MenuCommand constants, shown next. Any time you want to execute or trap a menu-equivalent task, consider using the menuAction() method or menuAction event.

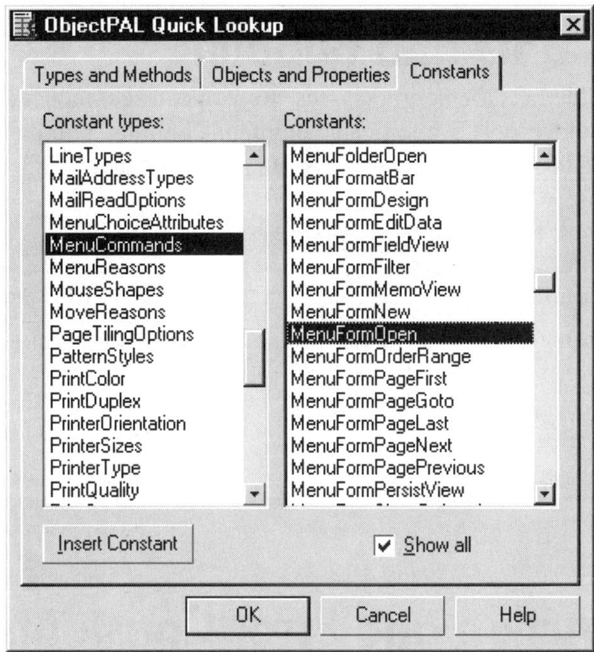

To display the Form Open dialog box, for example, add line 3 to the pushButton event of a button.

```
1:    ;Commands :: btnMenuAction :: pushButton
2:    method pushButton(var eventInfo Event)
3:       menuAction(MenuFormOpen)
4:    endMethod
```

Trapping *MenuAction* Constants

Just as you can trap for action constants, you can trap for MenuCommand constants. For example, to trap for the user pressing the Form Maximize button, add lines 3–5 to the menuAction event of a page.

```
1:    ;Commands :: Pge1 :: menuAction
2:    method menuAction(var eventInfo MenuEvent)
3:       if eventInfo.id() = MenuControlMaximize then
4:          disableDefault
5:       endIf
6:    endMethod
```

Action Constants and Bubbling

The following table lists the action classes. As you can see, most action events do not bubble. In fact, only ActionDataCommands bubble. You can use eventInfo.actionClass() to return the class of an action event.

ActionEvent	Bubble?	Description of Action
ActionDataCommands	Yes	Deal with the whole form
ActionEditCommands	No	Deal with editing data
ActionFieldCommands	No	Move from field to field
ActionMoveCommands	No	Move the cursor within a field
ActionSelectCommands	No	Select data within a field

Identifying Action and Error Constants

Sometimes it is necessary to identify a constant. Either you need to trap for it or you want to execute it. Either way, finding the action constant that maps to a specific task can be daunting. Using constantValueToName() enables you to extract the name of a constant from a number. The syntax for constantValueToName() is as follows:

constantValueToName (const ***groupName*** String, const ***value*** AnyType, var ***constName*** String) Logical

This method is very helpful in developing an application when you want to know which actions are being triggered. The one weakness of this method is that you have to specify the group type. For example, you have to specify ActionDataCommand, ActionMoveCommand, Error, and so on.

The following code snippet from http://prestwood.com/forums/paradox/books/official/files/ID_Actions.fsl demonstrates how to extract the name of an action or error constant from eventInfo, as shown next. For demonstration purposes, this code is called from the action event of the form; this code displays every action generated and every error generated. It uses actionClass() to extract the class of action constant. It also demonstrates using a list object to scroll values.

It uses a private custom procedure, which helps make it structured. (For more on structured programming, refer to Appendix A.)

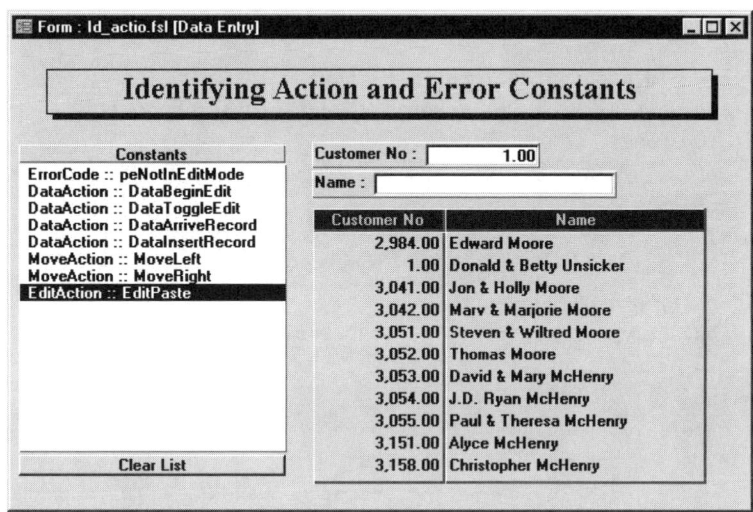

You can follow the actions I took in this illustration above. I first tried to insert a record and couldn't because I wasn't in Edit mode. This generated a peNotInEditMode error. I then toggled into Edit mode, moved to the Customer No field, entered a number, moved to the Name field and pasted a name in. Read through the code and see whether you can follow the logic; start from the method prototype line.

```
;ID_Actions :: Form :: cmIdentifyConstant
proc cpDisplayConstant(sConstantType String, sConstant String)
   ;Display constant class & constant in list field.
   ;This procedure is used by cmIdentifyConstant.
   beep()
   ;lstConstant is a list object of a list field placed on the form.
   lstConstant'list.selection = lstConstant'list.count + 1
   lstConstant'list.value = sConstantType + " :: " + sConstant
endProc

method cmIdentifyConstant(var eventInfo ActionEvent)
   ;Identify constant.
   var
      sConstant      String
      siConstantType SmallInt
```

```
      sConstantType  String
      siID           SmallInt
   endVar

   ;Check for an error.
   if eventInfo.errorCode() <> peOk then
      constantValueToName("Errors", eventInfo.errorCode(),
      sConstant)
      cpDisplayConstant("ErrorCode", sConstant)
      return
   endIf

   ;Identify action constant.
   siConstantType = eventInfo.actionClass()
   siID = eventInfo.id()
   switch
      case siConstantType = DataAction
      :  sConstantType = "DataAction"
         constantValueToName("ActionDataCommands", siID, sConstant)
      case siConstantType = EditAction
      :  sConstantType = "EditAction"
         constantValueToName("ActionEditCommands", siID, sConstant)
      case siConstantType = FieldAction
      :  sConstantType = "FieldAction"
         constantValueToName("ActionFieldCommands", siID, sConstant)
      case siConstantType = MoveAction
      :  sConstantType = "MoveAction"
         constantValueToName("ActionMoveCommands", siID, sConstant)
      case siConstantType = SelectAction
      :  sConstantType = "SelectAction"
         constantValueToName("ActionSelectCommands", siID, sConstant)
      otherwise
      :  ;This should never get called.
         sConstantType = "unknown"
         sConstant = "unknown"
   endSwitch

   cpDisplayConstant(sConstantType, sConstant)
endMethod
```

The following code calls the custom method. Notice that doDefault is called before eventInfo is passed to the custom method.

```
;ID_actions.fsl :: Form :: action
method action(var eventInfo ActionEvent)

   if eventInfo.isPreFilter() then
      ;// This code executes for each object on the form
      ;//
      DoDefault
      cmIdentifyConstant(eventInfo)
   else
      ;// This code executes only for the form
      ;//

   endIf

endMethod
```

You might want to put a variation of the preceding custom method into your standard library—perhaps alter it to return the action constant. After you do this, you can use it from time to time when you code to determine an action constant name that is giving you problems.

TIP

To send a list of all the constants to a table, create and run the following one-line script:
enumRTLConstants("CONST.DB")
This script creates a table that has all constants, including all the error constants. Use this table to create reports in any order you like.

Manipulating a Memo Field

To manipulate the font attributes and text of a Memo field use the action() method. The basic technique is to pass the action() method an action constant:

object.action(ActionConstant)

For example, the following selects all the text in a Memo field:

```
;Form :: Var
method pushButton(var eventInfo Event)
  fldMemo.action(SelectSelectAll)
endMethod
```

Time and Date Stamping a Memo Field

To time stamp and add a note to the end of a Memo field, use lines 3–7.

```
1: ;Button :: pushButton
2: method pushButton(var eventInfo Event)
3:   edit()
4:   Notes.moveTo()
5:   Notes.value = Notes.value + chr(13) + String(DateTime()) + chr(13)
6:   Notes.action(EditEnterMemoView)
7:   Notes.action(MoveEnd)
8: endMethod
```

To time stamp and add a note to the beginning of the Memo field, use lines 3–8.

```
1: ;Button :: pushButton
2: method pushButton(var eventInfo Event)
3:   edit()
4:   Notes.moveTo()
5:   Notes.value = String(DateTime()) + chr(13) + chr(13) + Notes.value
6:   Notes.action(EditEnterMemoView)
7:   Notes.action(MoveBegin)
8:   Notes.action(MoveDown)
9: endMethod
```

Identifying menuAction Constants

Steps for using the MenuID form:

1. Select a menu option to generate a menu constant.
2. Put the constant or number in the MenuAction field (the constant is always preferred). You can just click on the constant displayed below the Execute Menu Constant button.
3. Press the button to make sure it works.

You can use the form http://prestwood.com/forums/paradox/books/official/files/MenuID.fsl to browse and test menu constants, as shown here:

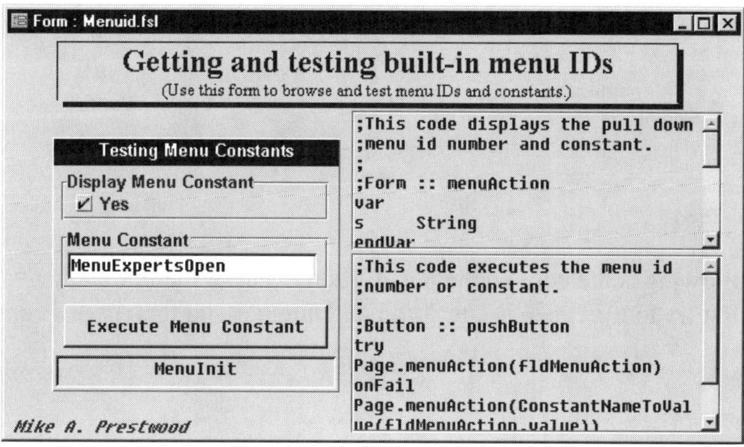

The interesting bit of code is in the page's menuAction event and in the pushButton event of the button. The following is the code in menuAction that traps the menu constants:

```
;MENUID :: page :: menuAction
method menuAction(var eventInfo MenuEvent)
var
   s   String
endVar

if eventInfo.isPreFilter() then
   ;// This code executes for each object on the form:

else
   ;// This code executes only for the form:
   switch
      case eventInfo.id() = MenuInit
         :  ;Occurs when the menu option is selected.
            ;Do nothing.
      case eventInfo.id() = MenuBuild
         :  ;Occurs when the menu is first built.
            ;Do nothing.
      case eventInfo.id() = MenuControlKeyMenu
         :  ;Menu selected via a key press.
            ;Do nothing.
      otherwise
         :  if fldDisplay.value = "Yes" then
```

```
                 constantValueToName("MenuCommands", eventInfo.id(), s)
                 msgInfo(eventInfo.id(), s)
              endIf
      endSwitch
      constantValueToName("MenuCommands", eventInfo.id(), s)
      fldStatus.value = s
   endMethod
```

The following is the code in the pushButton event of the button that uses a try block to first try to execute a MenuCommand number and then uses a constant.

```
;MENUID :: btnExecute :: pushButton
method pushButton(var eventInfo Event)
   ;Try to execute number.
   try
      menuAction(fldMenuAction)
   onFail
      ;Convert String to number.
      try
         menuAction(ConstantNameToValue(fldMenuAction.value))
      onFail
         msgStop("Warning", "Invalid menu constant.")
      endTry
   endTry
endMethod
```

Summary

In this chapter, you learned you can imitate nearly any user interaction by sending action and menuAction constants to the action and menuAction events using the action() and menuAction() methods. In addition, you learned how to trap for most user interactions in the action and menuAction events. Finally, you learned how to use the ID_Action and MenuID forms to identify action and menuAction constants.

CHAPTER 20

Menus

A *menu* is a set of options. Typically, a menu is a list that appears horizontally across the menu bar of an application. Menus in ObjectPAL also can take the form of buttons on a form, pull-down menus, or pop-up menus. A *pull-down menu* is a list of items that appears when you choose a menu item from the horizontal menu list. Pull-down menus display further options for you to choose.

This chapter will introduce you to creating both menus and pop-up menus. If you are going to create an application-wide menu, then I strongly recommend you use Paradox's Application Framework. This chapter will instruct you how to create menus for non-Application Framework applications and pop-up menus you can use with both.

Pop-Up Menus

A *pop-up menu* is the vertical list of options that usually becomes attached to a menu; however, it does not have to be attached. In other words, you can use pop-up menus without a menu. Most applications use pop-up menus heavily. When you right-click an object in Paradox, the Property Inspector that appears is a pop-up menu. This section explores how to use pop-up menus with a menu variable.

Stand-alone pop-up menus do not trigger menuAction. That is, when a user selects an option from a stand-alone pop-up menu, no event is sent to the menuAction event. Therefore, you cannot trap for stand-alone pop-up menus with menuAction. How, then, do you trap for the user's selection? You use show() to display the pop-up menu. Fortunately, show() returns the user's selection in a string. Therefore, use the following syntax:

```
s = pop1.show()
if s = "Option1" then
  ;Execute option1 code here.
endIf
```

The following is a complete example you can type into the mouseClick event of a box:

```
;Box :: mouseClick
method mouseClick(var eventInfo MouseEvent)
   var
      popColor   PopUpMenu
      sAns       String
   endVar
```

```
   ;Build menu.
   popColor.addText("Red")
   popColor.addText("White")
   popColor.addText("Blue")
   popColor.addSeparator()
   popColor.addText("Transparent")

   ;Show & capture choice.
   sAns = popColor.show()

   ;Use selected value.
   self.color = sAns
endMethod
```

Using *menuSetLimit()*

Normally, pop-up menus are limited to 32 options. If you wish to include more, you need to use the menuSetLimit() procedure. Create a new form and place an undefined field on the form. Alter the right mouse click of the undefined field as follows:

```
; Field :: mouseRightDown
method mouseRightDown(var eventInfo MouseEvent)
   var
      si1Counter    SmallInt
      si2Counter    SmallInt
      popChose      PopUpMenu
   endVar

   si2Counter = 0

   menuSetLimit(110)

   for si1Counter from 1 to 100
      popChose.addText(si1Counter)

      si2Counter = si2Counter + 1
      if si2Counter = 20 then
         popChose.addBar()
         si2Counter = 0
      endIf
   endFor
```

```
   self.value = popChose.show()
endMethod
```

Change the form to View Data mode, right-click on the field, and select a value.

Pull-Down Menus

Maneuvering within Windows applications has become quite elaborate. With Paradox, the user can use the built-in pull-down menus, the toolbar, and the Property Inspector. As a programmer, you can leave the Paradox default menu in place, trap for the menu constants in the menuAction event, and execute your own code in place of the default behavior. You also can remove the toolbar with hideToolbar(). You even can get rid of the built-in menus and use your own menus instead.

You can add pop-up menus that are similar to the Property Inspector, and the menus can pop up anywhere onscreen. Although Paradox doesn't offer balloon help—which is becoming popular—it does offer the programmer a great deal of control.

Where to Put Code

When you use custom menus in ObjectPAL, you must do two things: build the menu and process the user's input. The usual place to define a menu is in the arrive event of the form or page.

If you plan to change the menus in a particular form when you move from one page to another, however, create your menus on the arrive event of each page. In fact, a good rule of thumb is always to build and show menus on the arrive event of the page. That way, if you ever need to add a menu to the form, you can add it to another page, which is the most logical breaking point.

To process user input, use the menuAction event of the page. The following steps outline a good technique for capturing and processing user input:

1. Declare a String variable that catches the constants you trap for in the menuAction event.
2. Use sAns = eventInfo.menuChoice().
3. Use a switch structure to process the user's choice.

Unique Entry Menus

It's simple to set up a menu that always has a unique entry. For example, File | Save and Record | Save selections wouldn't work together, because Save is duplicated in two pull-down menus. If you need duplicate menu options, use a menu ID number.

The following steps outline how to set up a unique entry menu:

1. Define your variables. You need to define a Menu variable for the menu itself and a PopUpMenu variable for each pull-down menu you want. For example, you might use the following code on the Var window of the page:

```
var
  m     Menu
  pop   PopUpMenu
endVar
```

2. Build the menu. Construct the pull-down menus, attach them to entries in the menu, and show the menu. Use the addText() method to add entries to the PopUpMenu variable. For example, you might use the following code on the arrive event of the page:

```
pop.addText("Cut")
pop.addText("Copy")
pop.addText("Paste")
```

3. Add PopUpMenu to a menu bar item. Attach the constructed PopUpMenu variable to an entry on the Menu variable. For example, you might use the following code immediately after the code shown in step 2:

```
m.addPopUp("Edit", pop)
```

4. Display the menu. You display the Menu variable with the show() method:

```
m.show()
```

5. Trap for user responses. After you construct the menu, you must decide what each menu option does. In the menuAction event—usually the menuAction event of the page—you trap for the selection and act on that selection. For example, you can declare a String variable, trap for menuChoice() with eventInfo.menuChoice(), and use the switch statement to act on that selection.

```
var
   sAns String      ;Declare sAns as a String variable.
endVar

sAns = eventInfo.menuChoice() ;Capture user selection.

;Process user selection.
Switch
   case sAns = "Cut"    : active.action(EditCutSelection)
   case sAns = "Copy"   : active.action(EditCopySelection)
   case sAns = "Paste"  : active.action(EditPaste)
endSwitch
```

The next example uses the Customer table from the files that come with Paradox.

Duplicating the Paradox Menu

There are times you need to create your own menu system, yet retain a few of the Paradox menu options. You can duplicate the Paradox menu and send the correct constant to the built-in menuAction event in one step, as in the following:

```
pop.addText("&Tile", MenuEnabled, MenuWindowTile)
```

This technique is particularly important now that you can add a menu to a report, because menus can respond only to menu constants. You can read more about this technique later in this chapter.

Building a Unique Entry Menu

Suppose that you want to build a functional, two-entry, pull-down menu. File | Exit closes the form, and Edit | Cut, Edit | Copy, and Edit | Paste cuts, copies, and pastes text, respectively. This next step-by-step example uses the methods from the Menu and PopUpMenu types to build and use a pull-down menu.

http://prestwood.com/forums/paradox/books/official/files/Menu-1.fsl.

Step By Step

1. Create a form based on the Customer table located in Paradox's Samples directory. You can make it as fancy as you want, but a simple form is all that you need:

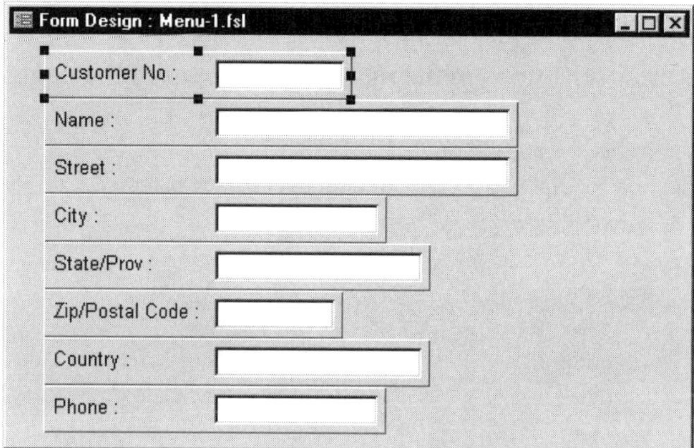

2. Define the variables in the Var window of the page.

```
;Page :: Var
Var
   m                     Menu
   sAns                  String
   popFile, popEdit      PopUpMenu
endVar
```

3. Build and show the menu in the arrive event of the page.

```
;Page :: arrive
method arrive(var eventInfo MoveEvent)
   ;Build File menu.
   popFile.addText("Exit")
   m.addPopUp("File", popFile)

   ;Build Edit menu.
   popEdit.addText("Cut")
```

```
      popEdit.addText("Copy")
      popEdit.addSeparator()
      popEdit.addText("Paste")
      m.addPopUp("Edit", popEdit)

      ;Display menu.
      m.show()
   endMethod
```

4. Trap for user selections in the menuAction event of the page.

```
;Page :: menuAction
method menuAction(var eventInfo MenuEvent)
   sAns = eventInfo.menuChoice()

   switch
      case sAns = "Exit"  : close()
      case sAns = "Cut"   : active.action(EditCutSelection)
      case sAns = "Copy"  : active.action(EditCopySelection)
      case sAns = "Paste" : active.action(EditPaste)
   endSwitch
endMethod
```

5. Check the syntax, save the form as **Menu-1.fsl**, and run it:

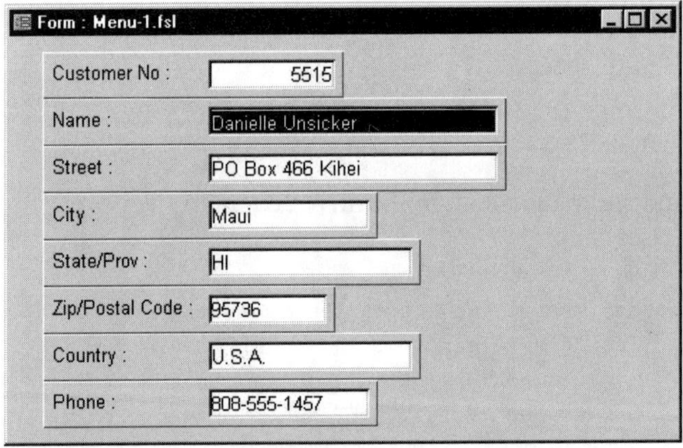

In step 2, lines 3–5 declare the variables. A good place in which to declare the menu variables is in the Var window of the page. If you declare the String variable sAns in the menuAction event, it is redeclared every time a user chooses a menu option. It makes only a minor difference here, but it can make a significant difference in a large application. It is slightly more elegant to declare the variable static, as in the Var window of the page.

Step 3 builds and shows the menu. Line 4 adds text to the popFile variable, and line 5 attaches popFile to the menu variable. Lines 8–11 add text to the popEdit variable. Line 10 adds a line to the menu between Copy and Paste with the addSeparator() method. Line 12 attaches the popEdit variable to the m menu variable. Now, two pop-up menus are attached to m. Line 15 uses the show() method.

Step 4 processes the user's selection. Line 3 grabs the user's selection and puts it into the sAns String variable. Lines 5–10 check which selection the user has selected and responds accordingly.

Dressing Up a Menu

Most programs use hot keys, bars, and other features to enhance the look of their menus. To dress up a menu in Paradox with ObjectPAL, you use a combination of ObjectPAL methods and embedded ASCII codes. For example, you can use the following to dress up a menu:

```
& = accelerator (underlines character)
\008 = all the way to the right like Help
\009 = tab use only on a sub menu
addSeperator()
addBreak()
addBar()
```

Using Menu ID Numbers

Menu IDs enable you to have identical menu options. This next step-by-step example shows you how to build a menu by using menu IDs. In it, you build a menu that is identical to the one in the previous example, but this time the menu uses menu IDs.

http://prestwood.com/forums/paradox/books/official/files/Menu-2.fsl.

Step By Step

1. Change your working directory to Paradox's Samples directory and create a new form.

2. Define the variables in the Var window of the page.

```
;Page :: Var
Var
   m                   Menu
   popFile, popEdit    PopUpMenu
   siAns               SmallInt
endVar
```

3. Build and show the menu in the page's arrive event.

```
;Page :: arrive
method arrive(var eventInfo MoveEvent)
   ;Build File menu
   popFile.addText("Exit", MenuEnabled, UserMenu + 101)
   m.addPopUp("File", popFile)

   ;Build Edit menu
   popEdit.addText("Cut", MenuEnabled, UserMenu + 201)
   popEdit.addText("Copy", MenuEnabled, UserMenu + 202)
   popEdit.addSeparator()
   popEdit.addText("Paste", MenuEnabled, UserMenu + 203)
   m.addPopUp("Edit", popEdit)

   ;Display menu
   m.show()
endMethod
```

4. Trap for the menu selection in the page's menuAction event.

```
;Page :: menuAction
method menuAction(var eventInfo MenuEvent)
   siAns = eventInfo.id()

   Switch
     case siAns = UserMenu + 101
        :  close()
     case siAns = UserMenu + 201
```

```
9:            : active.action(EditCutSelection)
10:         case siAns = UserMenu + 202
11:           : active.action(EditCopySelection)
12:         case siAns = UserMenu + 203
13:           : active.action(EditPaste)
14:       endSwitch
15:    endMethod
```

5. Check the syntax, save the form as **Menu-2.fsl**, and run it.

The only lines analyzed here are those that deal with using menu IDs. For analysis of the other lines, refer to the analysis section in the preceding example.

In step 2, line 5 declares a small integer for use in step 4.

In step 3, line 4 and lines 8–11 use the third syntax variation to assign return values to the menu options. They use the UserMenu built-in constant, which gives you the base value allowed in this version of Paradox. The numbering system used here and in the manuals is only by convention; with this version, you can use any numbers—up to 2,000—that you want. To verify the maximum number you can use with the constant UserMenu, type line 3 into the pushButton event of a button.

```
1:    ;Button :: pushButton
2:    method pushButton(var eventInfo Event)
3:       view(UserMenuMax - UserMenu)     ;Displays 1999.
4:    endMethod
```

It's a good idea to use the first digit of the menu ID for its left-to-right position and the next two digits for its top-to-bottom position. MenuEnabled is used because syntax 3 of addText() requires a MenuChoiceAttributes constant.

In step 4, lines 5–14 processes the user's selection in the menuAction event. Lines 6–12 must use UserMenu because UserMenu was used earlier.

Using the MenuInit Constant

When you activate a menu, the first event isn't MenuChoice(); it's MenuInit. This occurs just before the item or pull-down menu is displayed. It's your last-minute chance to change the status of the menu items. You might want to add the following code:

```
if eventinfo.id() <> MenuInit then
   sChoice = eventInfo.menuChoice()
   view(sChoice)
endIf
```

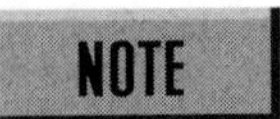

Use MenuEnabled only when you're creating menus. Use setMenuChoiceAttributes() later to modify them.

Cascading Pull-Down Menus

A *cascading menu* is the object that pops up when a pull-down menu or a pop-up menu displays another pop-up menu. This next step-by-step example shows you how to build a cascading menu.

http://prestwood.com/forums/paradox/books/official/files/Menu-3.fsl.

Step By Step

1. Change your working directory to Paradox's Samples directory and create a new form.
2. Define the variables in the page's Var window.

```
;Page :: Var
Var
   m                          Menu
   popFile, popEdit, popCut   PopUpMenu
   sAns                       String
endVar
```

3. Build the menus in the page's arrive event.

```
;Page :: arrive
method arrive(var eventInfo MoveEvent)
   ;Build File menu
   popFile.addText("Exit")
   m.addPopUp("File", popFile)

   ;Build Cut sub menu
   popCut.addText("Text")
   popCut.addText("Record")
   popEdit.addPopUp("Cut", popCut)

   ;Build Edit menu
   popEdit.addText("Copy")
   popEdit.addSeparator()
   popEdit.addText("Paste")
```

```
    m.addPopUp("Edit", popEdit)

    ;Display menu
    m.show()
endMethod
```

4. Trap for user input in the page's menuAction event.

```
;Page :: menuAction
method menuAction(var eventInfo MenuEvent)
   sAns = eventInfo.menuChoice()

   Switch
     case sAns = "Exit"
        : close()
     case sAns = "Text"
        : active.action(EditCutSelection)
     case sAns = "Record"
        : active.action(DataDeleteRecord)
     case sAns = "Copy"
        : active.action(EditCopySelection)
     case sAns = "Paste"   : active.action(EditPaste)
   endSwitch
endMethod
```

5. Check the syntax, save the form as **Menu-3.fsl**, and run it. Here's how the Menu-3.fsl form looks:

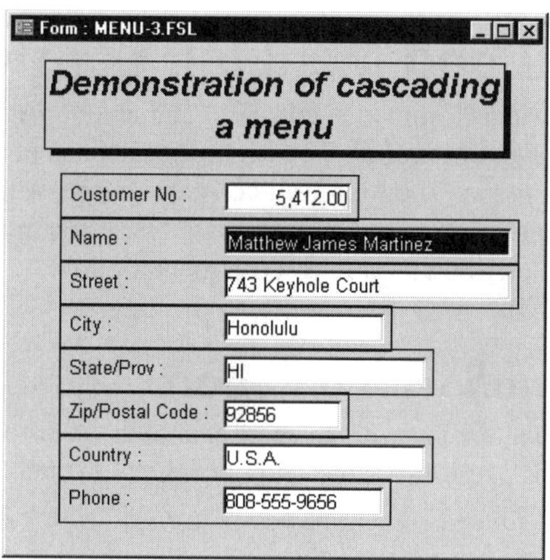

The only lines analyzed here are those that deal with using cascading menus. For analysis of the other lines, refer to the analysis sections in the previous two examples.

In step 2, line 4 uses an extra pop-up menu variable, popCut.

In step 3, lines 8 and 9 add two entries to the pop-up menu variable popCut. Line 10 adds popCut to popEdit. Lines 13–15 construct the rest of the popEdit pop-up menu. Line 16 adds this cascaded menu to the m menu variable. Line 19 displays the results.

Step 4 processes the user's menu choice.

You can use this technique to cascade as many times as you need. However, don't overuse cascading menus. You can use one or two cascades, but anything more becomes cumbersome for the user and takes up memory.

Menu Constants Have Duplicates

ObjectPAL is a very rich language. In fact, you often can accomplish a single task in two or three different ways. Many menu constants have duplicate constants in other classes. The menu constant MenuFilePrint, for example, has a DataAction constant, DataPrint.

Don't confuse the menuAction() procedure with the menuAction event. The menuAction() procedure is used to execute a MenuCommands constant while the menuAction event is used to trap for MenuCommands constants.

The BuildMenu and MenuInit Constants

You can trap for all MenuCommands constants in the menuAction event, including MenuBuild and MenuInit. The MenuBuild constant reports when the desktop is building a menu. The MenuInit constant reports when the user selects a menu option from a pull-down menu. With these two constants, you can trap for when a menu is built or when a user selects a menu option.

Using *setMenu()* with a Report

The default menus that display with a report enable the user to do many tasks you may not want, such as opening a table. Suppose that you want to use just a limited set of menu options with a report. This next example uses setMenu() to add menus to a report.

http://prestwood.com/forums/paradox/books/official/files/SetMenu.fsl.

Step By Step

1. Change your working directory to the Paradox's Samples directory, create a new form, and place a button on it.
2. In the pushButton event, type lines 3–17:

```
 1:   ;Button :: mouseClick
 2:   method pushButton(var eventInfo Event)
 3:      var
 4:         r     Report
 5:         m     Menu
 6:         pop   PopUpMenu
 7:      endVar
 8:
 9:      r.open("Customer", WinStyleDefault + WinStyleMaximize)
10:
11:      pop.addText("&Print...", MenuEnabled, MenuFilePrint)
12:      pop.addText("Printer &Setup...", MenuEnabled,
         ;MenuFilePrinterSetup)
13:      pop.addText("&Close", MenuEnabled, MenuControlClose)
14:      m.addPopUp("&File", pop)
15:
16:      r.setMenu(m)
17:   endMethod
```

3. Check the syntax, save the form as **SetMenu.fsl**, and run it (see Figure 20-1).

In step 2, line 9 opens the REPORT.RSL with the r Report variable declared in line 4. Lines 11–14 build the menu and line 16 attaches it to the report using the r Report variable. It is important to note the use of menu constants in lines 11–13. You can add menu options only to reports that call existing menu constants. Therefore, using menus on reports is somewhat limited.

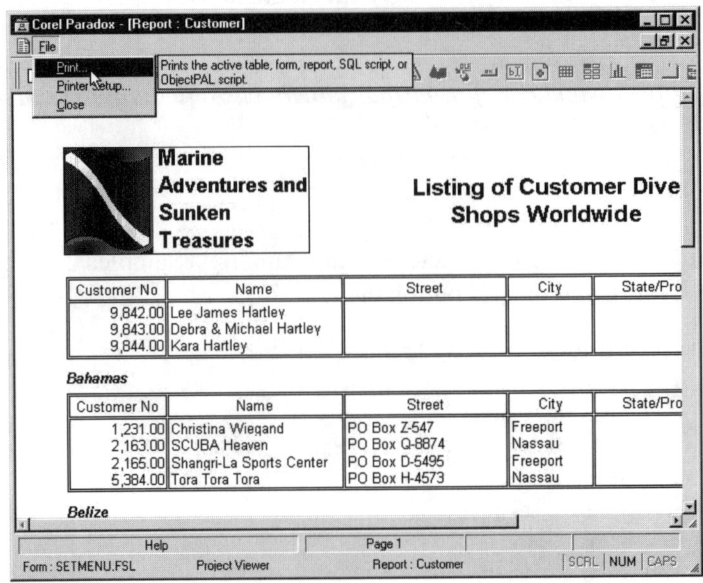

FIGURE 20-1 SetMenu.fsl adding a menu to a report

Summary

In this chapter, you learned about pop-up and pull-down menus. With the techniques you learned in this chapter, you can give your users control over your applications.

CHAPTER 21

Toolbars

Using ObjectPAL, you can modify an existing toolbar or create a new one. This short chapter introduces you to these concepts and demonstrates a trick for simulating a toolbar on a form.

Modifying Existing Toolbars

You can use the new Toolbar type to alter existing toolbars or create your own. You can use the Toolbar class attach() to bind a variable to an existing toolbar. After you have a handle to a toolbar, you can remove buttons with removeButton() and add them with addButton(). The following is the syntax for attach():

```
attach ( const toolbarName String ) Logical
```

The attach() method binds the Toolbar variable toolbarName to a variable. You can attach to any toolbars you create or to the standard toolbar. To attach to the standard toolbar, specify Standard for toolbarName. The following example demonstrates using attach() to bind a Toolbar variable to the standard toolbar:

```
var
   tbStandard    Toolbar
endVar
tbStandard.attach("Standard")
```

After you attach to a toolbar, you can remove buttons with removeButton(). The following is the syntax for removeButton():

```
removeButton ( const idCluster SmallInt, const idNum SmallInt ) Logical
```

You specify which cluster of toolbar buttons with idCluster. The cluster is specified left to right, starting from 0. The position of the button within a cluster also is specified left to right, starting with 0. For example, the Run button, which is five buttons over, is in cluster 2, and button 0. Type in the following code snippet into the pushButton event of a button:

```
;Button :: pushButton
method pushButton(var eventInfo Event)
```

```
 3:      var
 4:         tbStandard  ToolBar
 5:      endVar
 6:
 7:      tbStandard.attach("Standard")
 8:      tbStandard.removeButton(0, 0) ;New.
 9:      tbStandard.removeButton(0, 1) ;Save.
10:      tbStandard.removeButton(0, 0) ;Open.
11:      tbStandard.removeButton(0, 0) ;Print.
12:   endMethod
```

The preceding short program attached to the standard toolbar with line 7, and removed several buttons with lines 8–11. The buttons it removed you probably don't want, because they give the user too much control in a data access form.

Just as you can remove buttons, you also can add your own using addButton():

1. **addButton** (const ***idCluster*** SmallInt, const ***buttonType*** SmallInt, const ***idCommand*** SmallInt, const ***grBmp*** Graphic, const ***buttonHelp*** String) Logical
2. **addButton** (const ***idCluster*** SmallInt, const ***buttonType*** SmallInt, const ***idCommand*** SmallInt, const ***idBmp*** SmallInt, const ***buttonHelp*** String) Logical

The idCluster parameter is the same as for removeButton(). The buttonType parameter enables you to specify the type of button to add to the toolbar, such as the following:

- ToolbarButtonPush
- ToolbarButtonRadio
- ToolbarButtonRepeat
- ToolbarButtonToggle

The idCommand parameter specifies which menu constant to send to the active form's menuAction event. The only difference between the two versions of syntax is the fourth parameter, which enables you to specify either a bitmap or a constant that maps to an existing bitmap, as seen here:

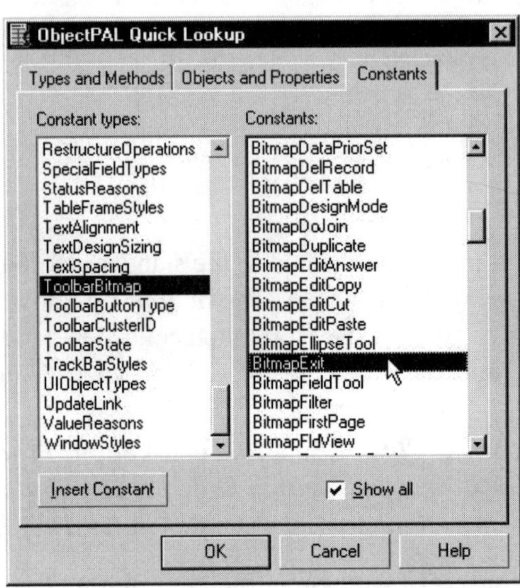

The final parameter is a string for the pop-up hint that appears when the mouse moves over the button. The following adds a button to the Standard toolbar in the eighth cluster that displays the Add Table dialog box.

```
;Button :: pushButton
method pushButton(var eventInfo Event)
   var
      tbStandard  ToolBar
   endVar

   tbStandard.attach("Standard")
   tbStandard.addButton(8, ToolbarButtonPush,
   ;MenuFileTableAdd,
      BitmapAddTable, "Add Table")
endMethod
```

Creating New Toolbars

You also can create your own toolbars with create(), using the following syntax:

```
create ( const toolbarName String [, const parentToolbarName String ]) Logical
```

The toolbarName parameter can be any string you want except for Standard, Property, Text Formatting, Align, Design Object, and ActiveX Control. The toolbarName identifies the toolbar and appears in the title bar when the toolbar is not docked. The following example creates a toolbar that includes one button:

```
;Button :: pushButton
method pushButton(var eventInfo Event)
   var
      tbMyToolbar  ToolBar
   endVar

   tbMyToolbar.create("MyToolbar")
   tbMyToolbar.addButton(0, ToolbarButtonPush, MenuFileTableAdd,
      BitmapAddTable, "Add Table")


   ;Add more buttons here.

EndMethod
```

Paradox's standard bitmap size is 22 pixels wide and 21 pixels high. Winword's is 22 pixels wide and 20 high. It doesn't really matter which you use—it is up to you. However, when adding icons to the Standard toolbar, use bitmaps that are 22 by 21 pixels.

Simulating a Toolbar on a Form

Toolbars don't exist at the form level, but you can simulate one. One technique is to create a screen shot of the Paradox desktop (with the toolbar). Open Paintbrush and cut out Paradox's toolbar. Add it to your form and add methods to each button.

The following steps give you an overview of how to create a form-level toolbar:

1. Click the Print Screen button on your keyboard while Paradox is showing. This sends a bitmap to the Clipboard.
2. Launch Paintbrush and paste the image into it.
3. Cut out only the toolbar (or only the parts that you want).
4. Paste the image into your form.
5. Add a transparent box over every toolbar option.
6. Add code to the mouseClick event of each transparent box.

This technique works, but no option on the toolbar has the appearance of pressing in as with normal toolbar buttons. If you want to go through the trouble, you can use two bitmaps and toggle their visible properties or place a bitmap inside a real button.

One final technique is to use a graphic as a button by toggling its frame between Inside3DFrame and Outside3DFrame. Add a bitmap to a form and add the following code:

```
;Bitmap :: mouseDown
method mouseDown(var eventInfo MouseEvent)
   self.Frame.Style = Inside3DFrame   ;Make frame pop in.
endMethod
;Bitmap :: mouseUp
method mouseUp(var eventInfo MouseEvent)
   self.Frame.Style = Outside3DFrame  ;Make frame pop out.
endMethod
```

The interesting thing about using the mouseDown, mouseUp, and mouseClick events is that mouseClick is called only when the pointer is inside the boundary of the object for both the mouseDown and mouseUp events. Using all three events makes your custom-created button behave just like a real button. You can execute any code you want in the mouseClick event. For example, add a bitmap to a form and alter its mouseClick event as follows:

```
;Bitmap :: mouseClick
var
   siQuestion   SmallInt
endVar
method mouseClick(var eventInfo MouseEvent)
   if not siQuestion.isAssigned() then
      siQuestion = 1
   endIf

    switch
       case siQuestion = 1
          :  msgInfo("About this screen", "This screen is the main
          ;screen.")
             siQuestion = 2
       case siQuestion = 2
          :  msgInfo("Keyboard Short Cuts", "Ctrl+M = Paradox Desktop
          ;Menu")
             siQuestion = 3
       case siQuestion = 3
          :  msgInfo("Tip / Hint", "Run multiple instances to increase
          ;your productivity.")
             siQuestion = 1
    endSwitch
 endMethod
```

Summary

In this chapter, you learned about toolbars. With the techniques you learned in this chapter, you can now add toolbars to your applications. Remember to be consistent within an application. If you develop a particularly attractive look and feel for one application, you might want to use it with all your applications. This applies to toolbars, too.

CHAPTER 22

Handling Files

This chapter demonstrates some of the FileSytem methods and procedures. Specifically, you are about to learn how to find the path of a file, find sets of files, and how to import and export files.

FileSystem Methods and Procedures

With the FileSystem commands, you can change your working directory, manipulate files on a disk, get the time and date from a file, and so on. Shown here are the FileSystem methods and procedures:

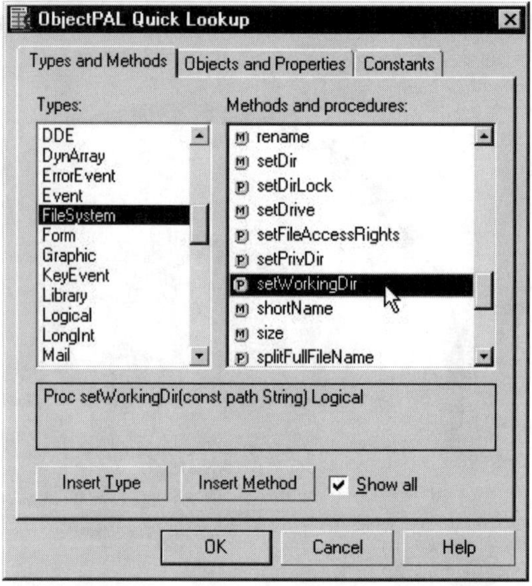

Finding the Path of a File

Suppose that you want to add a routine to a button that opens up the Paradox browser, browse for a file, select a file, and place its full path in a field. (This task is harder than it should be.)

http://prestwood.com/forums/paradox/books/official/files/FindPath.fsl.

Step By Step

1. Create a new form with a field and a button on it. Label the button **Browse**, as shown here, and name the field **fldFile**.

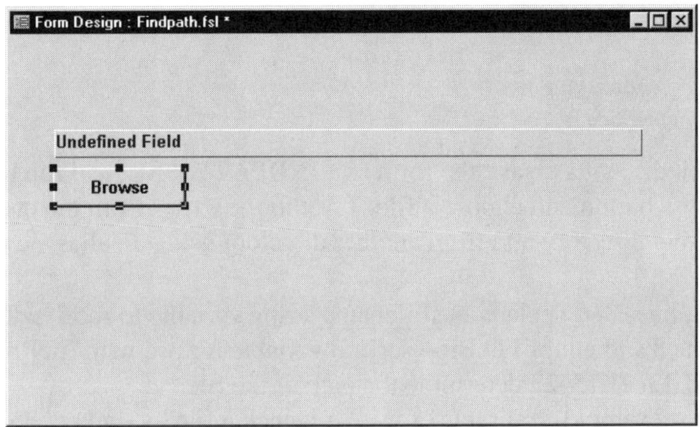

2. In the pushButton event, type lines 3–23.

```
1: ;Button :: pushButton
2: method pushButton(var eventInfo Event)
3:    var
4:      sFilename  String
5:      fbi        FileBrowserInfo
6:    endVar
7:
8:    if fileBrowser(sFileName, fbi) then
9:                ;A File was selected.
10:   else        ;If no file is selected,
11:      return   ;then return.
12:   endIf
13:
14:   ;Find path of file.
15:   switch
16:      case isDir(fbi.alias)
```

```
17:             : fldFile.value = fbi.alias + fbi.path + sFilename
18:         case sFilename.subStr(1,6) = ":PRIV:"
19:             : sFilename = sFilename.subStr(7, sFilename.size()-6)
20:               fldFile.value = getAliasPath(":PRIV:") + "\\"
                      + sFilename
21:         otherwise
22:             : fldFile.value = getAliasPath(fbi.alias) + "\\"
                      + fbi.path + sFilename
23:     endSwitch
24: endMethod
```

3. Check the syntax, save the form as **FINDPATH.FSL**, and run it. Click the Browse button and choose a file. Try choosing files from the current working directory and from another directory using an alias.

In step 2, lines 3–6 declare an sFilename string variable to receive the name of the file in line 8 and an fbi FileBrowserInfo variable for use with fileBrowser(), also in line 8. Lines 15–23 determine the path of the file.

In the next example, you set up a way to launch a file by double-clicking on its filename.

Finding a Set of Files

Suppose that you want to create a form that lists all the files in a directory and enables the user to launch a file by double-clicking its filename. This next step-by-step example uses the FileSystem methods to search your Windows directory for .EXE files and puts them in a list field. When the user double-clicks on a filename, the .EXE file is launched.

http://prestwood.com/forums/paradox/books/official/files/FindFile.fsl.

Step By Step

1. Create a new form with two undefined fields. Label the first undefined field **Search for**, as shown here, and change its name to **SearchForField**.

22

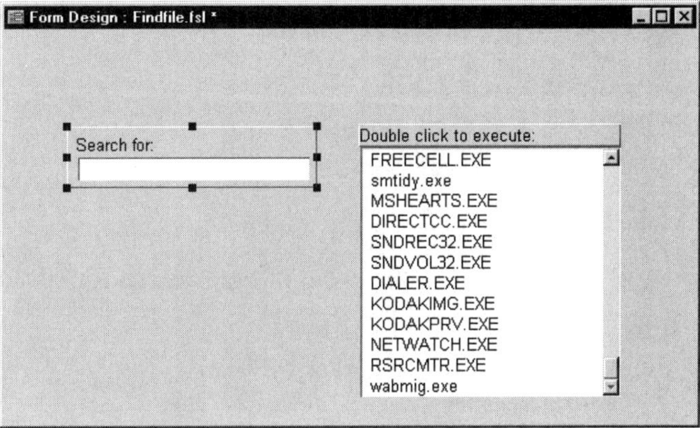

2. Make the second undefined field a list field; change its name to **fldResult**, and its list to **FileList**. Shown next is the Object Tree of the list field. The list object is inside the field object.

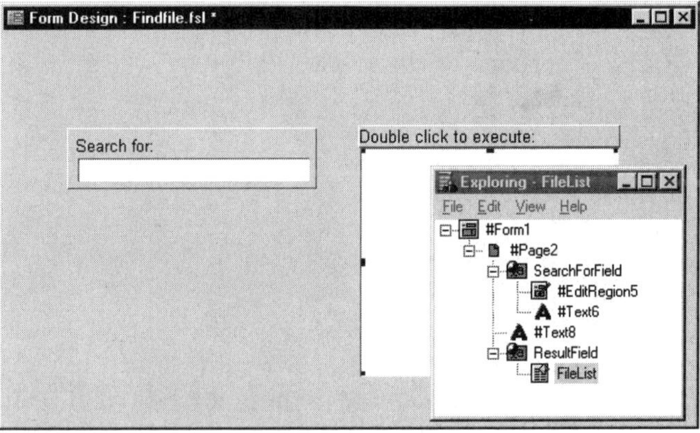

3. Place a text object above the fldResult field with the text **Double click to execute**.

4. Add line 3 to the Var window of the "Search for" field.

```
1:    ;SearchForField :: Var
2:    Var
3:       fs FileSystem
4:    endVar
```

5. Add lines 3 and 4 to the open event of the "Search for" field.

```
1:    ;SearchForField :: open
2:    method open(var eventInfo Event)
3:       doDefault
4:       self.value = windowsDir() + "\\*.EXE"
5:    endMethod
```

6. Add lines 3–17 to the newValue event of the "Search for" field.

```
 1:    ;SearchForField :: newValue
 2:    method newValue(var eventInfo Event)
 3:       if not SearchForField.isBlank() then
 4:         if fs.findFirst(SearchForField) then
 5:            fldResult.FileList.list.count = 0
 6:            fldResult.FileList.list.selection = 1
 7:            fldResult.FileList.list.value = FS.name()
 8:            while FS.findNext()
 9:               fldResult.FileList.list.selection =
               fldResult.FileList.list.selection +1
10:              fldResult.FileList.list.value = FS.name()
11:           endWhile
12:        else
13:           fldResult.FileList.list.count = 0
14:           fldResult.FileList.list.selection = 1
15:           fldResult.FileList.list.value = "File not found"
16:        endIf
17:      endIf
18:   endMethod
```

7. Add lines 3–7 to the mouseDouble event of the fldResult field.

```
1:    ;fldResult :: mouseDouble
2:    method mouseDouble(var eventInfo MouseEvent)
3:       try
4:         execute(fldResult.value)
5:       onFail
6:         msgStop("Warning", "Could not launch file")
7:       endTry
8:    endMethod
```

8. Check the syntax and save the form. Run the form. All the .EXE files from your Windows directory are listed. If you double-click a file, it will execute. Change the extension to .HLP. If .HLP is associated with WINHELP.EXE like the Windows default, you can double-click any Help file to launch it. Now, type in an invalid extension, such as .XYZ. The words "File not found" appear.

In step 4, line 3 sets up fs as a FileSystem variable. It's used later in step 6.

In step 6, line 4 populates the "Search for field" after invoking the default behavior.

In step 6, line 4 checks the value, and line 10 uses it and the fs System variable to find the first occurrence of the search criteria. If nothing is found, the execution skips to line 15. Lines 13–15 clear the list and set the first value to "File not found." If line 3 finds a file, lines 5–7 clear the list and set the initial value, and lines 8–12 loop through and populate the rest of the list.

In step 7, lines 3–7 attempt to launch the value that you double-click. These lines use a try block. If you don't use a try block, ObjectPAL will display abstract errors when the file isn't found. In other words, many ObjectPAL errors are meant for the programmer. You might want to use a try structure to test your code. If it fails, display a more meaningful message to the end user.

Importing and Exporting Data with DataTransfer

With the DataTransfer type, you can create, delete, import, and export data. With Paradox, you can import and export data interactively with File | Import and File | Export options. These options are very thorough and powerful. To import and export data with ObjectPAL, use the DataTransfer type.

Importing and Exporting Spreadsheets

You can import or export Quattro, Excel, or Lotus spreadsheets with ObjectPAL. You pass these procedures a few parameters and it takes over. You can use importSpreadSheet() to import and exportSpreadSheet() to export.

Use exportSpreadSheet() when you wish to export any of the following spreadsheets to a table: Quattro Pro for Windows, Quattro Pro DOS, Quattro, Lotus 2.*x*, Lotus 1.A, and Excel 3.0/4.0/5.0. Following is the syntax:

exportSpreadsheet (const ***tableName*** String, const ***fileName*** String [, const ***makeRowHeaders*** Logical]) Logical

The parameters are fairly straightforward. Specify the input spreadsheet filename with the *fileName* parameter. Specify the output table name with *tableName*. Finally, specify whether you want the spreadsheet's column labels to determine the field names of the table with *makeRowHeaders*. If successful, exportSpreadSheet() returns True; otherwise, it returns False. For example, the following single line of code exports an Excel spreadsheet named SALES.XLS to a Paradox table named SALES.DB:

```
method pushButton(var eventInfo Event)
   if exportSpreadsheet("SALES.DB", "SALES.XLS", True) then
      message("Export successful")
   else
      message("Export not successful")
   endIf
endMethod
```

NOTE *You are specifying the spreadsheet format (type), with the extension on the* fileName *parameter. Valid extensions are: .WB1, .WB2, and .WB3 for Quattro Pro for Windows, .WQ1 for Quattro Pro for DOS, .WKQ for Quattro, .WK1 for Lotus 2.*x*, .WKS for Lotus 1.A, and .XLS for Excel.*

Importing and Exporting ASCII files

ASCII is the acronym for American Standard Code for Information Interchange. The ASCII set consists of 7-bit codes that represent 128 standard characters—letters, numbers, and symbols. The characters in the ASCII set are the same as the first 128 characters in the extended ASCII and ANSI sets.

The meaning of the term "ASCII file" has expanded from its strict technical definition to something more generic. Today, ASCII can refer to any file that is composed of readable characters, even if it contains characters other than the 128 of the original set. Most programmers still restrict the definition of ASCII, however. They use the term "text file" when they need a more generic term.

ASCII files are important because they are the means by which file-incompatible programs (especially from different computer platforms) can exchange data. More and more programs can import and export dBASE tables. More and more applications are adding Paradox to their list of import and export routines. If the program you want to bring data from or port data to supports either Paradox or dBASE, use either of those formats. You might have to work with programs that can't import or export Paradox or dBASE tables, however. In those cases, you can fall back on ASCII text files. ASCII text files are in the one format that nearly all applications on all platforms can use. Text files are the common thread that enables applications and platforms to share data.

Exporting ASCII Files

To *export* a file is to convert it from a native format—either Paradox or dBASE—to a foreign format, such as ASCII. When you need data stored in either a Paradox or dBASE table in a text file, you export it. You can use the following procedures to export data:

```
exportASCIIFix()
exportASCIIVar()
exportParadoxDOS()
exportSpreadSheet()
```

Using *exportASCIIFix()*

You use the command exportASCIIFix() when you want to export a table to a delimited text file. The syntax for it follows:

exportASCIIVar (const ***tableName*** String, const ***fileName*** String [, const ***separator*** String, const ***delimiter*** String, const ***allFieldsDelimited*** Logical, const ***ansi*** Logical]) Logical

Specify *tablename* with the *tableName* parameter and specify the destination file with the *fileName* parameter. The separator and delimiter are optional parameters. Specify True with the allFieldsDelimited parameter to specify whether all fields including number and date fields should be delimited. Specify whether to use the ANSI or OEM character set with the ansi parameter.

The following example exports the data from the Customer table to the text file CUSTOMER.TXT. This example uses tabs to delimit field values, double quotes to enclose each value, delimits only character fields, and uses the ANSI character set.

```
;Button :: pushButton
method pushButton(var eventInfo Event)
   exportASCIIVar("customer.db", "customer.txt", "\t", "\"", False, True )
endMethod
```

This command is similar to exportASCIIFix(), which exports tables to a fixed-length field. exportASCIIFix() uses a specification file that specifies the exported field's name, type, start position, and length.

exportASCIIVar() does not export the following field types: memo (Paradox or dBASE), formatted memo, graphic, OLE, Byte, or binary, to delimited text.

Importing ASCII Files

When you *import* a file, you convert the data from a foreign format, such as ASCII, to a native format—either Paradox or dBASE. Importing data is the process of bringing data into dBASE, Paradox, or a variable. Normally, you can import just about anything into ObjectPAL. At the least, you can read in a file and dump it into a memo field.

You can use any of the following easy-to-use procedures to import files:

```
dlgImportAsciiFix()    ;Displays the Import Fix Data dialog box.
dlgImportAsciiVar()    ;Displays the Import Variable Data dialog box.
importASCIIFix()       ;Import data from a fixed length ASCII file.
importASCIIVar()       ;Import data from a variable length ASCII file.
appendASCIIFix()       ;Append fixed length ASCII data to a table.
appendASCIIVar()       ;Append variable length ASCII data to a table.
```

Both appendASCIIFix() and appendASCIIVar() dramatically increase the speed of importing of text files by importing them directly to existing tables.

Using the TextStream Type

Sometimes, a client or another user will give you a table whose format isn't consistent and expect you to translate it to Paradox or dBASE. Usually, you can use a while loop to loop through the text file and convert the text. Occasionally, however, the data won't permit this. When you run into this type of data, don't waste your time. Return the table and tell the person to give you consistent data. If the user pushes, explain the specifics of why the data cannot be imported.

Suppose that you have a text field with a date field and dates such as 1193, 121293, 42593, and 12193. If the text has four or six characters, you can easily break it into 1/1/93 and 12/12/93. If the text file has five characters, you might not be able to tell what the date is supposed to be. Clearly, 42593 is 4/25/93, but 12193 could be 1/21/93 or 12/1/93. There's no way to know. The moral of the story is to make sure that the original program exports data properly.

To import data, follow these steps:

1. Open a TextStream to the text file. It can be read-only.
2. Use a while loop to loop through the text file. You can use eof to check for the end of the file.
3. Use readLine() to read one line at a time to a String variable.
4. Use the match() method to look for the names of fields, or use the breakApart() method to break each line into logical components.
5. Close the TextStream variable.
6. The next two examples demonstrate routines from the IMPORT.FSL program, which is on the disc that comes with this book. The form demonstrates how to import text files into ObjectPAL, manipulate them, and store them in a Paradox table.

NOTE *Rather than use eof() to check for the end of the file, you can check whether readLine() was successful. If readLine() returns False, you're at the end of the file.*

Using *breakApart()*

The breakApart() method from the String type is useful for both importing and exporting because it enables you to split a string into an array of substrings based on one or more separators. Following is the syntax:

breakApart (var ***tokenArray*** Array[ ] String [, const ***separators*** String])

Notice the separators parameter is optional. If you do not specify a separator, then the string is split based on spaces. The tokenArray is an Array variable you provide. Type in lines 3–10 into the pushButton event of a button. This short program uses breakApart() to split a string based on spaces and periods.

```
1:   ;Button :: pushButton
2:   method pushButton(var eventInfo Event)
3:      var
4:         s     String
5:         ar    Array[] String
6:      endVar
7:
8:      s = "Mr. Daniel Raymond Unsicker"
9:      s.breakApart(ar, ". ")
10:     ar.view("Token Strings")
11:  endMethod
```

By combining breakApart() with subStr(), you can extract any form of data you want from strings. The next example adds the breakApart() method to the routine. breakApart() is a powerful method. It can split a string into substrings based on a separator.

Changing Your Working Directory

To change working directories, use the setWorkingDir() method. This is particularly useful when you open a form. On the init event of the form, type the following:

```
var
   f        Form
```

```
      dynPath  DynArray[] String
   endVar

   f.attach()
   splitFullFileName(f.getFileName(), dynPath)
   setWorkingDir(dynPath["Drive"] + dynPath["Path"])
```

The default behavior when you change working directories is to close all the objects that are open on the Paradox desktop. To prevent the currently opened objects from closing, use the following in the form's menuAction:

```
if eventInfo.id() = MenuChangingWork then
   eventInfo.setErrorCode(1)
endIf
```

It is important to note that you cannot execute any code after calling setWorkingDir() in the open event. If you want to execute code after changing working directories, then trap for the MenuChangedWork constant in menuAction, as in the following:

```
if eventInfo.id() = MenuChangedWork then
   ;Execute more code here.
endIf
```

Both setWorkingDir() and setPrivDir() are posted actions. Therefore, the logical value returned by them reports whether the action was posted (placed in the event queue)—not whether the directory was changed. Instead, use a try block to see whether the directory changed. Do not depend on the return value.

Changing the Working Directory of a Form

Suppose that you want to automatically change working directories when a form opens. In this case, you want to change the working directory to the same directory the form is in.

http://prestwood.com/forums/paradox/books/official/files/Work1.fsl.

Step By Step

1. Change your working directory to Paradox's Samples directory and create a new form.

2. Add lines 3–13 to the init event of the form.

```
1:  ;Form :: init
2:  method init(var eventInfo Event)
3:     var
4:        f     Form
5:        dyn1 DynArray[] String
6:     endVar
7:     f.attach()
8:     if not isFile(":WORK:WORK1.FSL") then
9:        splitFullFileName(f.getFileName(), dyn1)
10:       if not setWorkingDir(dyn1["Drive"] + dyn1["Path"]) then
11:          errorShow()
12:       endIf
13:    endIf
14: endMethod
```

3. Add lines 9–11 to the menuAction event of the form.

```
1:  ;Form :: menuAction
2:  method menuAction(var eventInfo MenuEvent)
3:
4:     if eventInfo.isPreFilter() then
5:       ;This code executes for each object on the form:
6:
7:     else
8:       ;This code executes only for the form:
9:       if eventInfo.id() = MenuChangingWork then
10:         eventInfo.setErrorCode(1)
11:      endIf
12:    endIf
13: endMethod
```

4. Check the syntax, save the new form as **WORK1.FSL**, and close it. Change your working directory to another directory and open up the form by browsing for it. When it opens, notice what your working directory is set to.

In step 2, line 7 attaches to the current form with the Form variable declared in line 4. Line 8 checks to see whether the current file is in the working directory, and if it is not, proceeds with lines 9–12. Line 9 grabs the current path and puts it into the dyn1 DynArray that was declared in line 5. Line 10 uses the DynArray to set the working directory and displays an error in line 11 if it fails.

In step 3, line 9 checks the eventInfo ID for the constant MenuChangingWork. If the current ID is MenuChangingWork, then a nonzero error code is set in line 10.

One other constant of interest when you're changing working directories is MenuChangedWork. This constant flows through menuAction after the working directory has successfully changed. You can use this, for example, to let the user know what the new working directory is whenever the working directory has changed. For example:

```
;Form :: menuAction
if eventInfo.id() = MenuChangedWork then
   message("New working directory: " + workingDir())
endIf
```

Summary

In this chapter you learned that importing and exporting of data with ObjectPAL can be a single line of code or, if needed, can be a complex routine.

CHAPTER 23

Multimedia and Paradox

This chapter discusses two ways in which you can add sound to your Paradox applications—with built-in ObjectPAL methods and procedures, and with the Windows multimedia DLL. The beep() command in ObjectPAL enables you to beep your PC's speaker; it sounds the Windows default beep. The sound() command enables you to play sounds by using a sound card. It creates a sound of a specified frequency and duration. You use the Windows multimedia DLL to play .WAV files and other MCI files.

Using the *beep()* Procedure

The simplest way to create sound in ObjectPAL is to call the beep() procedure. Type the following into the pushButton event of a button:

```
; Button :: pushButton
method pushButton(var eventInfo Event)
   beep()
endMethod
```

The *sound()* Procedure

sound() belongs to the System class of procedures. It creates a sound of a specified frequency and duration. The syntax for the sound procedure is as follows:

```
sound (const freqHertz, const durationMilliSecs LongInt)
```

sound() creates a sound of a specified frequency in hertz (freqHertz) for a specified length of time in milliseconds (durationMilliSecs). The frequency values can range from 1 to 50,000Hz. The audible limit for the human ear is approximately 16Hz to 20,000Hz.

The following table lists eight tones that you can use to construct your own melodies:

Tone	Description
sound(130,240)	130 is C1
sound(146,240)	146 is D1
sound(164,240)	164 is E1

Tone	Description
sound(174,240)	174 is F1
sound(195,240)	195 is G1
sound(220,240)	220 is A2
sound(249,240)	249 is B2
sound(265,240)	265 is C2

NOTE *In MIDI terminology, each note is given a number. For example, C2 is the same note as C1, but an octave higher.*

The following table lists the duration for each type of note. Use the values when you create melodies:

Note	Duration in Milliseconds
Whole note	960
Half note	480
Quarter note	240
Eighth note	120
Sixteenth note	60

The following code plays a C major scale in eighth notes except for the final C, which is a half note. Type lines 3–10 in the pushButton event of a button.

```
 1: ;Button :: pushButton
 2: method pushButton(var eventInfo Event)
 3:      sound(130,120)
 4:      sound(146,120)
 5:      sound(164,120)
 6:      sound(174,120)
 7:      sound(195,120)
 8:      sound(220,120)
 9:      sound(249,120)
10:      sound(265,480)
11: endMethod
```

You can use other elements of ObjectPAL to create interesting effects. See the following section for an example.

Another *sound()* Example

The following step-by-step example uses the ObjectPAL method rand() with the sound() procedure to play a random melody whenever the user presses a button.

Suppose that you want to create a random note played for a random duration. To do this, use the rand() method to play a random note for a random duration. You should make sure that the note is within hearing range and has at least a certain minimum duration.

Step By Step

1. Create a new form and place a button on it. Label it **Using sound() with rand()**.

2. Add lines 3–20 to the pushButton event of the "Using sound() with rand()" button.

```
1:    ;Button :: pushButton
2:    method pushButton(var eventInfo Event)
3:       var
4:         freq, dur Number
5:       endVar
6:
7:       freq = 0
8:       dur = 0
9:
10:      while freq < 110
11:        freq = rand()*1000
12:      endWhile
13:
14:      while dur < 60
15:        dur = rand() * 300
16:      endWhile
```

```
17:
18:       sound(freq, dur)
19:       sound(freq + 65, dur)
20:       sound(freq + 70, dur * 2)
21:    endMethod
```

3. Check the syntax, run the form, and click the button.

In step 2, line 4 declares Number variables that will be used with rand() and sound(). Lines 7 and 8 set the variables you need. All variables must be set to a value before you can use them. Lines 10–12 generate a number that produces an audible tone. Lines 14–16 generate a reasonable duration. Anything shorter than 60 milliseconds is too short to be used in the routine in lines 18–20. Lines 18–20 play the first, third, and fifth notes of a major scale. These are the same notes in a major chord.

Displaying Graphics

Graphics add flair and visual excitement to your forms. Pasting static graphics is fairly straightforward. In fact, Chapter 3 encouraged you to use graphics this way. Switching graphics while a form is running adds even more visual excitement to your applications and makes them more fun to use.

ObjectPAL offers several methods you can use to read and write graphics from the Clipboard or directly from a file.

Bringing Bitmaps from Disk Directly into a Form

If a table is too large because too many graphics have been pasted into it, you can use the graphic readFromFile() method in a form to read the files in directly from disk. This has the benefit of storing the images outside of a table.

This example demonstrates listing files on a disk and selectively reading them in with readFromFile(), and then displaying them on a form.

http://prestwood.com/forums/paradox/books/official/files/BMP.FSL.

Step By Step

1. Create a new form with a list field, a labeled field, and a button.
2. Label the button **Display bitmap**. Name the list field **BMPField** and its list object **FileList**. Name the labeled field **SearchForField** and change its label to **Directory**, as shown here:

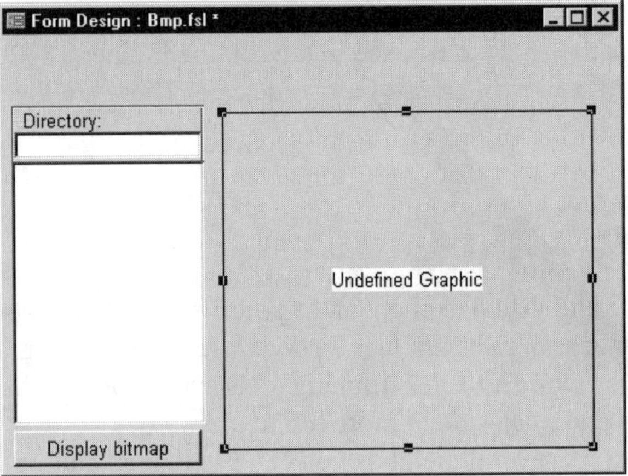

3. Add line 3 to the Var window of the form.

```
1:    ;Form :: Var
2:    Var
3:       fs   FileSystem
4:    endVar
```

4. Add line 3 to the open event of the SearchForField field.

```
1:    ;Field :: open
2:    method open(var eventInfo Event)
```

```
3:      self = windowsDir() + "\\*.BMP"
4:   endMethod
```

5. Add lines 3–18 to the newValue event of the SearchForField field.


```
1:    ;Field :: newValue
2:    method newValue(var eventInfo Event)
3:       if not SearchForField.isBlank() then
4:         if fs.findFirst(SearchForField) then
5:            BMPField.FileList.list.count = 0
6:            BMPField.FileList.list.selection = 1
7:            BMPField.FileList.list.value = fs.name()
8:            while fs.findNext()
9:              BMPField.FileList.list.selection =
10:             BMPField.FileList.list.selection +1
11:             BMPField.FileList.list.value = FS.name()
12:           endWhile
13:        else
14:           BMPField.FileList.list.count = 0
15:           BMPField.FileList.list.selection = 1
16:           BMPField.FileList.list.value = "File not found"
17:        endIf
18:      endIf
19:  endMethod
```

6. Add lines 3–10 to the pushButton event of the "Display bitmap" button.

```
1:    ;Button :: pushButton
2:    method pushButton(var eventInfo Event)
3:       var
4:         g Graphic
5:         s1, s2, s3, s4 String
6:       endVar
7:
8:       splitFullFileName(fs.fullName(),s1, s2, s3, s4)
9:       g.readFromFile(s1 + s2 + BMPField)
10:     GraphicField = g
11:  endMethod
```

7. Check the syntax, save your work, and run the form. Select a bitmap and click the button to display it. Your form should look similar to the one shown here when you're done with this example.

In step 6, line 4 declares a graphics variable for use in lines 9 and 10. Line 5 declares four String variables for use with splitFullFileName() in line 8. Line 8 splits the current file system variable into its four components: drive letter, path, filename, and file extension.

Line 9 uses the drive letter (stored in s1), the path (stored in s2), and the user's selection to read in a bitmap from a disk. Line 10 sets the value for the GraphicField object to the bitmap brought into g.

You can use the technique you learned in this example to load files from a disk. You even can apply this technique to a table frame by following these steps:

1. Create a table with an alphanumeric field.
2. In each record, place the name of the graphics file with the full path.
3. Create a tabular form that is bound to the table that you created.
4. Place a graphics object.
5. In the arrive event of the tableFrame field object, place the following code:

```
;TableFrame.Field :: arrive
method arrive(var eventInfo MoveEvent)
```

```
      var
         g Graphic
         s String
       endVar

      s = tableframeFieldObjectName
      g.readFromFile(s)
      graphicObjectName = g
   endMethod
```

As you scroll through the records, the graphics file is read into the graphics object. You don't need to be in Edit mode. You also might check the read-only property of the tableFrame field object.

Sound and graphics add flair to your applications and make them fun to use. You might not always have the time to add these extra features to your applications, but your users will appreciate it when you do.

Another technique to read a file in from diskette is to use the value property of a graphic field. The interesting piece of code is a procedure that is part of the timer event of the bitmap. Note that line 6 below uses the value property of the graphic object.

```
1:     Proc cpFindBitmap()
2:        if not fs.findNext() then
3:           fs.findFirst(windowsDir() + "\\*.BMP")
4:        endIf
5:
6:        self.value = windowsDir() + "\\" + fs.name()
7:     endProc
```

Using *readFromClipboard()* and *writeToClipboard()*

You can read from and write to the Windows Clipboard using readFromClipboard() and writeToClipboard(). The following example demonstrates using these two methods:

```
;Button :: pushButton
method pushButton(var eventInfo Event)
  var
     bmpOriginal Graphic
```

```
      bmpTemp      Graphic
   endVar

   bmpOriginal = bmp1.value
   bmpOriginal.writeToClipBoard()

   bmpTemp.readFromClipboard()

   bmp2.value = bmpTemp
endMethod
```

Animation

There are many ways to create and play animation in ObjectPAL. You can animate with a TCursor and a graphic field by cycling through the table. You can animate using the visible property, making one picture or element visible at a time. A similar technique is to use bringToFront(). Finally, you can use OLE to play AVI files (short movies). (See Figure 23-1.)

ON THE NET *See the file http://prestwood.com/forums/paradox/books/official/ files/ OLE2.FSL for an example of playing an AVI file. After you embed the OLE object, you can use the following code to play any Media Manager object. In this example, the user just clicks the object.*

```
;Object :: Var
Var
  o  OLE
endVar
;Object :: mouseClick
method mouseClick(var eventInfo MouseEvent)
  o = self.value
  o.edit("", 0)
endMethod
```

TIP *My favorite way to animate in ObjectPAL is to read in all the graphics from a table into an Array and then cycle through the graphics.*

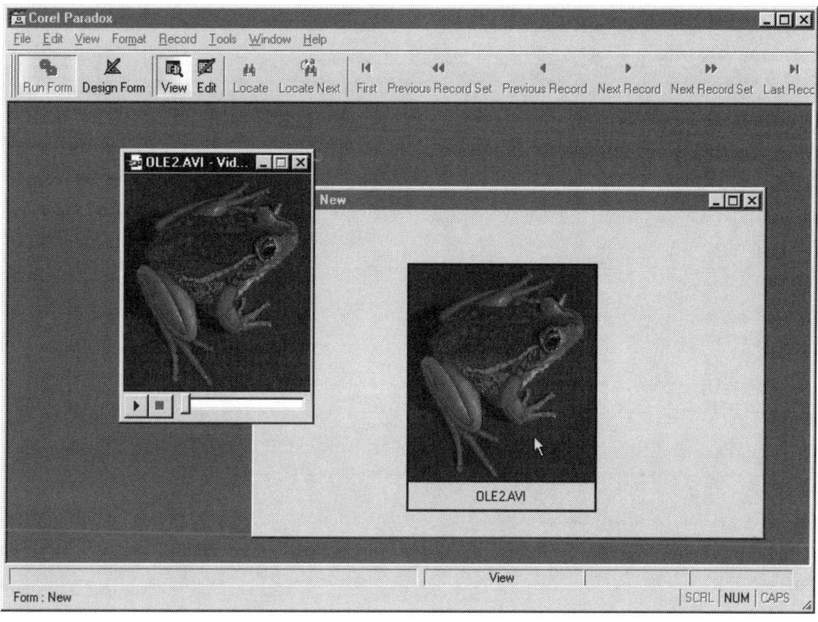

FIGURE 23-1 OLE2.FSL playing an AVI animation file with Media Player

Using a Table to Animate

Suppose that you want to add a spinning animation to your application to add that extra bit of flare. This next step-by-step example uses a table with graphics in it to store the images. The images are then read into an array of graphics (now, all the images are in memory). Once the images are in memory, a timer event is used to cycle through and display the images.

http://prestwood.com/forums/paradox/books/official/files/Animate.fsl and Animate.db.

Step By Step

1. Create a table named **ANIMATE.DB** (refer to Figure 23-2 for the table structure).

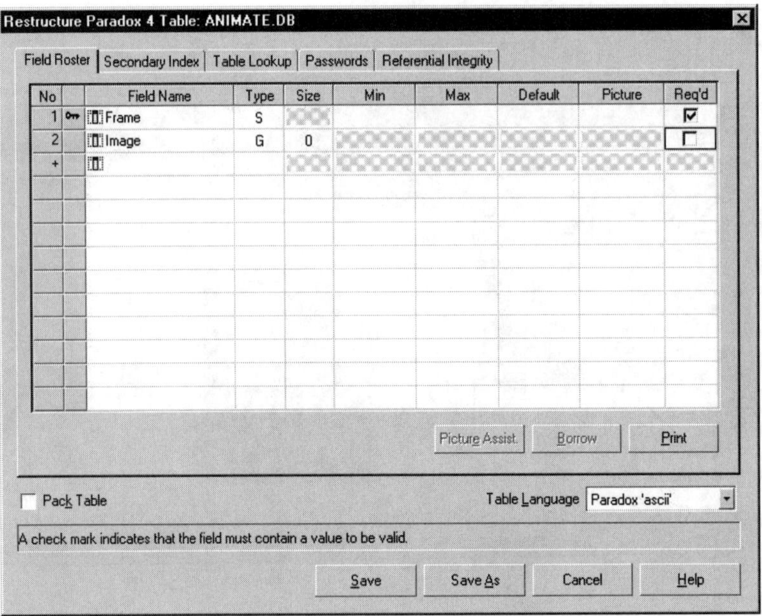

FIGURE 23-2 Setup form for using a table to animate example

2. Populate the table with the graphics you wish to animate.
3. Create a new form with an undefined graphic field on it.
4. In the Var window of the undefined graphic field, type lines 3–5:

```
1:  ;fldGraphic :: open
2:  Var
3:     lDirectionFlag   Logical
4:     lPosition        SmallInt
5:     arAnimation      Array[] Graphic
6:  endVar
```

5. In the open event of the undefined graphic field, type lines 3–18:

```
1:   ;fldGraphic :: open
2:   method open(var eventInfo Event)
3:      var
```

```
         tc TCursor
      endVar

      DoDefault               ;Finish opening object.

      tc.open("ANIMATE.DB")

      scan tc:
         arAnimation.setSize(arAnimation.size() + 1)
         arAnimation[tc.recNo()] = tc.(2)
      endScan

      lPosition = 1           ;Set starting position.
      lDirectionFlag = True ;Set start direction.
      self.setTimer(100)    ;Set speed of animation.
   endMethod
```

6. In the timer event of the undefined graphic field, type lines 3–19:

```
1: ;fldGraphic :: timer
2: method timer(var eventInfo TimerEvent)
3:    switch
4:     case lDirectionFlag = True :            ;Forward direction.
5:      if lPosition = arAnimation.size() then;If at end,
6:         lDirectionFlag = False              ;move backward.
7:      else
8:         self = arAnimation[lPosition]
9:         lPosition = lPosition + 1
10:      endIf
11:
12:     case lDirectionFlag = False :   ;Backward direction.
13:      if lPosition = 1 then
14:         lDirectionFlag = True       ;Next time move forward.
15:      else
16:         self = arAnimation[lPosition]
17:         lPosition = lPosition - 1
18:      endIf
19:    endSwitch
20: endMethod
```

7. Check the syntax, save the form as **ANIMATE.FSL**, and run it:

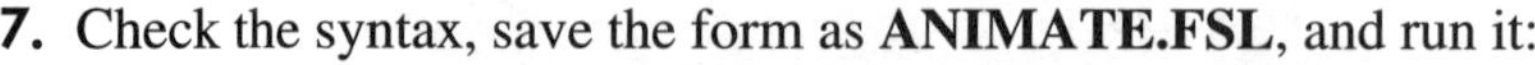

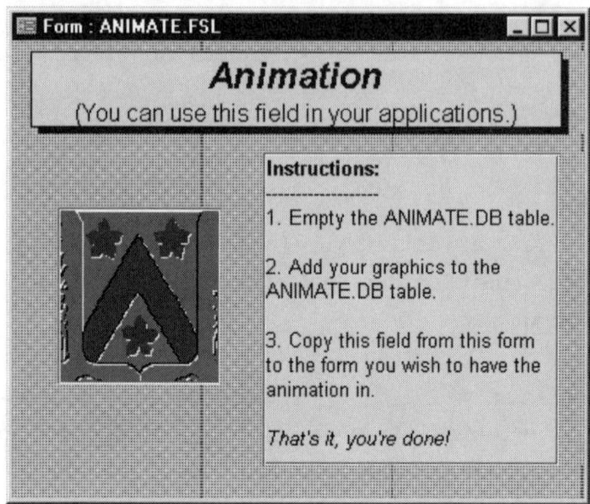

Step 5 uses a TCursor and a scan loop to read in all the graphic images into an array of graphic variables.

Step 6 cycles through the Array forward and then backward. This gives the images a sense of animation.

Summary

In this chapter, you learned two ways in which to add sound to your Paradox applications with beep() and sound(). The beep() command in ObjectPAL enables you to beep your PC's speaker. The sound() command enables you to play sounds by using a sound card. You also learned about how to add animation to your applications using a TCursor and a Graphic field by cycling through graphics. Finally, you learned how to use OLE to play AVI files (short movies).

CHAPTER 24

SQL and Client/Server Applications

This chapter focuses on using Paradox as a client/server development tool. It does not talk about connecting; it is assumed you have already connected. If you are having trouble connecting to a particular SQL server, then refer to the Connection Guide for that particular server. This chapter does review what a user can do interactively with Paradox and how to use ObjectPAL with SQL servers.

Who should read this chapter? Anyone interested in getting started with SQL and client/server applications. This chapter also covers using SQL on local tables—Paradox and dBASE tables.

About SQL

Structured Query Language (SQL) was developed to create a standard for accessing database information. The ANSI standard for SQL allows a user to become familiar with the commands needed to query many different types of data. After you learn ANSI SQL, you then can query many different databases.

Is SQL a solid standard? The answer is yes and no. Yes, the core ANSI SQL commands are solid and consistent from vendor to vendor. Every vendor, however, adds capability to its version of SQL. These improvements are expected because ANSI SQL does not go far enough to cover every feature of every high-end DBMS.

Many companies use the SQL standard for their high-end products. They include Oracle, Sybase, Microsoft SQL, Informix, and InterBase. Paradox also provides the capability to use standard ANSI SQL commands on local Paradox and dBASE tables.

Using SQL on Local Tables

Although SQL by definition is a standard, various flavors are on the market. Paradox, too, has its own flavor of SQL. Local SQL is built on a modified version of the InterBase SQL parser. The parser turns the SQL statements into QBE syntax, and then executes or translates it into BDE function calls.

Supported Syntax

Local SQL (sometimes called *client-based SQL*) is a subset of ANSI 92 SQL enhanced to support Paradox and dBASE (standard) naming conventions for tables and fields (columns in SQL terminology).

Local SQL and ANSI 92

Paradox is fairly SQL ANSI 92 compliant. This means that you can use most ANSI 92-compliant SQL statements. This is great for learning SQL because you can go out and buy any SQL primer book that is compliant to ANSI 92. However, the SQL-92 language standard is large and not all SQL-92 language elements are supported. The following SQL-92 language elements are not used in local SQL:

ALLOCATE CURSOR (Command)	ALLOCATE DESCRIPTOR (Command)
ALTER DOMAIN (Command)	CASE (Expression)
CHECK (Constraint)	CLOSE (Command)
COALESCE (Expression)	COMMIT (Command)
CONNECT (Command)	CONVERT (Function)
CORRESPONDING BY (Expression)	CREATE ASSERTION (Command)
CREATE CHARACTER SET (Command)	CREATE COLLATION (Command)
CREATE DOMAIN (Command)	CREATE SCHEMA (Command)
CREATE TRANSLATION (Command)	CREATE VIEW (Command)
CROSS JOIN (Relational operator)	CURRENT_DATE (Function)
CURRENT_TIME (Function)	CURRENT_TIMESTAMP (Function)
DEALLOCATE DESCRIPTOR (Command)	DEALLOCATE PREPARE (Command)
DECLARE CURSOR (Command)	DECLARE LOCAL TEMPORARY TABLE (Command)
DESCRIBE (Command)	DISCONNECT (Command)
DROP ASSERTION (Command)	DROP CHARACTER SET (Command)
DROP COLLATION (Command)	DROP DOMAIN (Command)
DROP SCHEMA (Command)	DROP TRANSLATION (Command)
DROP VIEW (Command)	EXCEPT (Relational operator)
EXECUTE (Command)	EXECUTE IMMEDIATE (Command)
FETCH (Command)	FOREIGN KEY (Constraint)
GET DESCRIPTOR (Command)	GET DIAGNOSTICS (Command)
GRANT (Command)	INTERSECT (Relational operator)
MATCH (Predicate)	NATURAL (Relational operator)

NULLIF (Expression)	OPEN (Command)
OVERLAPS (Predicate)	PREPARE (Command)
REFERENCES (Constraint)	REVOKE (Command)
ROLLBACK (Command)	Row value constructors
SET CATALOG (Command)	SET CONNECTION (Command)
SET CONSTRAINTS MODE (Command)	SET DESCRIPTOR (Command)
SET NAMES (Command)	SET SCHEMA (Command)
SET SESSION AUTHORIZATION (Command)	SET TIME ZONE (Command)
SET TRANSACTION (Command)	TRANSLATE (Function)
UNIQUE (Predicate)	USING (Relational operator)

NOTE *For an updated list of SQL-92 language elements that are not supported in local SQL, open the LOCALSQL.HLP help file included in your BDE directory and search for* ***Unsupported Language****. The BDE directory is usually installed in C:\ Program Files\Borland\Common Files\.*

Naming Tables

ANSI SQL confines each table or column name to a single word consisting of alphanumeric characters and the underscore. Local SQL, however, is enhanced to support more comprehensive names. Local SQL supports full file and path specifications for table names (including alias support).

Enclose table names with path or filename extensions in single or double quotation marks. For example,

```
select * from 'customer.db'
select * from ":work:customer.db"
```

NOTE *If you omit the file extension for a local table name, the table is assumed to be the Table object type specified in the Default Driver setting in the System page of the BDE Administrator.*

Column Names

Local SQL also supports Paradox's field names (characters such as space, dash, etc.) as long as these names are enclosed in single or double quotation marks and prefaced with a SQL table name or table correlation name. For example,

```
select o."Order No"
from Orders o
```

If the column you are using in a SQL statement contains only characters, then quotes are not required. For example,

```
select o.City
from Orders o
```

Even though quotes are optional, it is a good idea to always include them.

Column Names and PCC

With local SQL statements, should you use single quotes or double quotes? Since single quotes are not allowed when referring to fields using a TCursor, the "Prestwood Coding Convention" (PCC) standard for referring to fields using both local SQL or a TCursor is to use double quotes. The following SQL statement abides by the PCC standard:

```
select o."City"
from Orders o
```

The following usage of a TCursor abides by the PCC standard:

```
var
tcCustomer TCursor
endVar

tcCustomer.open("Customer")
msgInfo("", tcCustomer."City")
```

Notice the use of double quotes to refer to the City field even when quotes (single or double) were not required. For more information on standards and Prestwood Coding Convention, refer to Appendix A.

Supported SQL Statements

As outlined in Table 24-1, the SQL statements are broken into Data Manipulation Language (DML) and Data Definition Language (DDL). DML statements are used for handling data (selecting, inserting, updating, and deleting), and DDL statements handle the creating, altering, and dropping of tables, and the creating and dropping of indexes.

SQL Query Properties

Figure 24-1 shows the Answer tab of the Query Properties dialog box for SQL queries. The following is a short description of each feature:

- **Live query view** This option enables you to work with the live data generated from an SQL statement (see "Constrained Updates" for related information).
- **Answer table** This option enables you to specify if you want a Paradox or dBASE answer table. In addition, it enables you to specify the name of the table.

Category	Supported Keywords
DML statements	SELECT, INSERT, UPDATE, and DELETE
DML clauses	FROM, WHERE, ORDER BY, GROUP BY, HAVING, and UNION
Aggregate functions	SUM(), AVG(), MIN(), MAX(), COUNT(), and COUNT(*)
String functions	UPPER(), LOWER(), TRIM(), and SUBSTRING()
Operators	+, –, *, /, <, >, =, <>, IS NULL, IS NOTNULL, >=, =<, AND, OR, NOT, ||, and LIKE
DDL statements	CREATE TABLE, ALTER TABLE, DROP TABLE, CREATE INDEX, DROP INDEX, and CREATE VIEW

TABLE 24-1 Supported SQL Keywords

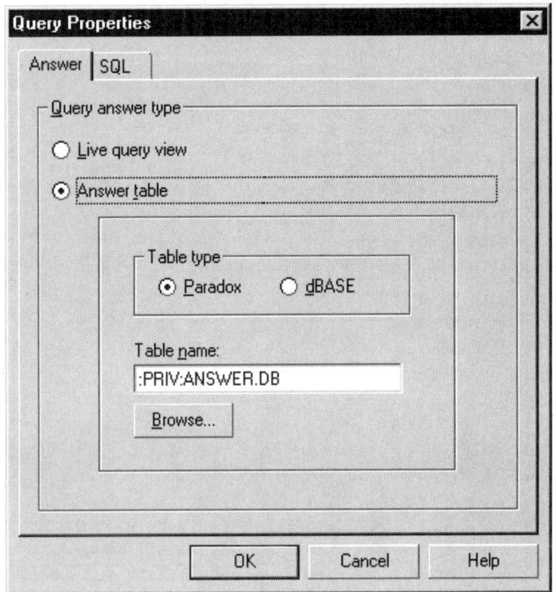

FIGURE 24-1 The Answer tab of the Query Properties dialog box

Figure 24-2 shows the SQL tab of the Query Properties dialog box for SQL queries. The following is a short description of each feature:

- **Queries against remote tables** This panel affects only remote SQL data. It enables you to specify whether a SQL statement is run locally or on the remote server. The "Run query remotely" option is the fastest.
- **Auxiliary table options** This panel enables you to specify whether auxiliary tables are created. For faster queries, select "Fast queries." To retain the ability to undo a SQL statement, select "Generate auxiliary tables" to create the necessary tables.
- **Constrained Updates** This option affects live queries only. If it is checked, you can enter values that match the select criteria only.

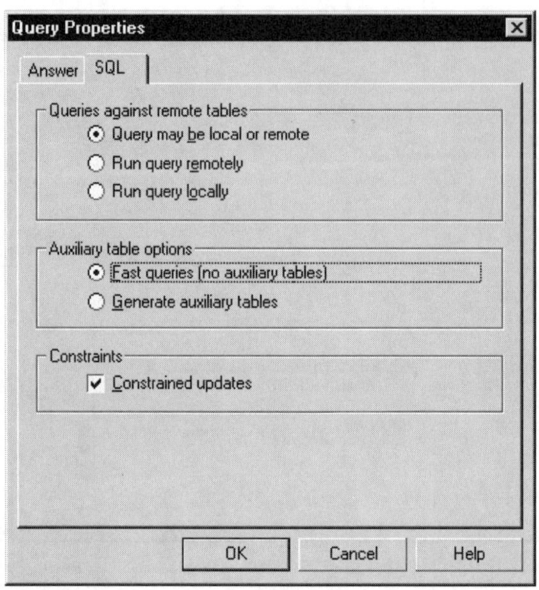

FIGURE 24-2 The SQL tab of the Query Properties dialog box

SQL and the QBE

If you are already familiar with building queries using Paradox's Query by Example (QBE), then an invaluable tool for learning SQL is the Show SQL option available from within the QBE. Figure 24-3 shows a simple QBE query on the customer table and the SQL Editor after selecting the Show SQL option.

Figure 24-4 shows a more complicated QBE query joining five tables and the SQL equivalent generated by the database engine.

The Visual Query Builder

Available while any SQL Editor is showing is the Visual Query Builder (see Figure 24-5). This brings the available techniques for building queries in Paradox to three: the traditional Query by Example (QBE), the industry standard Structured Query Language (SQL), and the new Visual Query Builder (VQB).

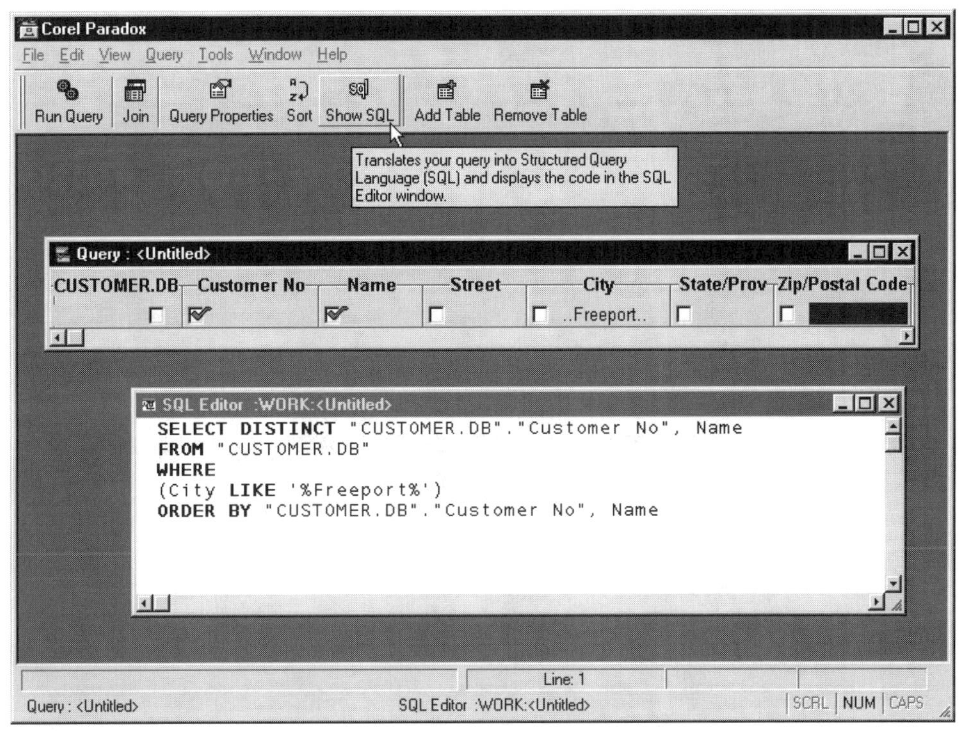

FIGURE 24-3 The Show SQL option translates your QBE into SQL

An SQL Primer

In this section, you learn about ANSI SQL as it applies to local Paradox and dBASE tables in a step-by-step example format. ANSI SQL is a rich query language. Each command supports many different keywords and parameters. To really learn SQL, you need to get a good ANSI SQL book. You can get started with this section and some of the Paradox and dBASE local tables located in the

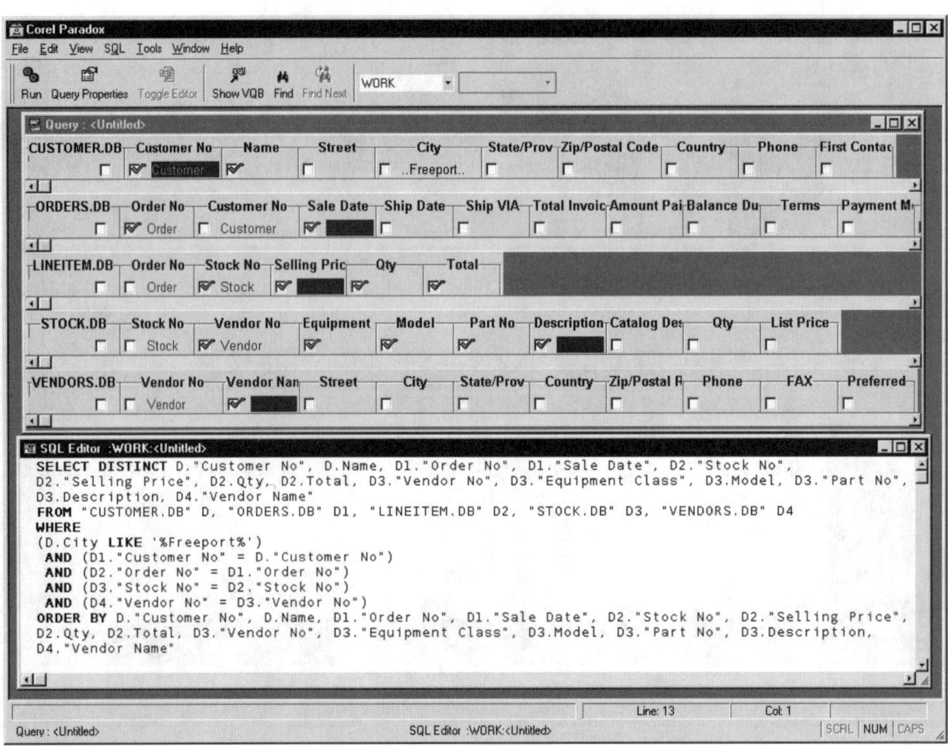

FIGURE 24-4 The Show SQL option works with sophisticated queries

Example directory. After you learn this core syntax, you can use it with any SQL DBMS, including Oracle, Sybase, MS SQL, Informix, and Gupta.

Using *select*

In this first step into SQL, you learn how to query your local Paradox tables with SQL. Here, you query the Customer and Orders tables using the SQL select command. The syntax for select is quite elaborate. For now, the basic syntax you need is as follows:

```
select criteria
from tablename
[where whereCriteria]
[order by orderBy]
```

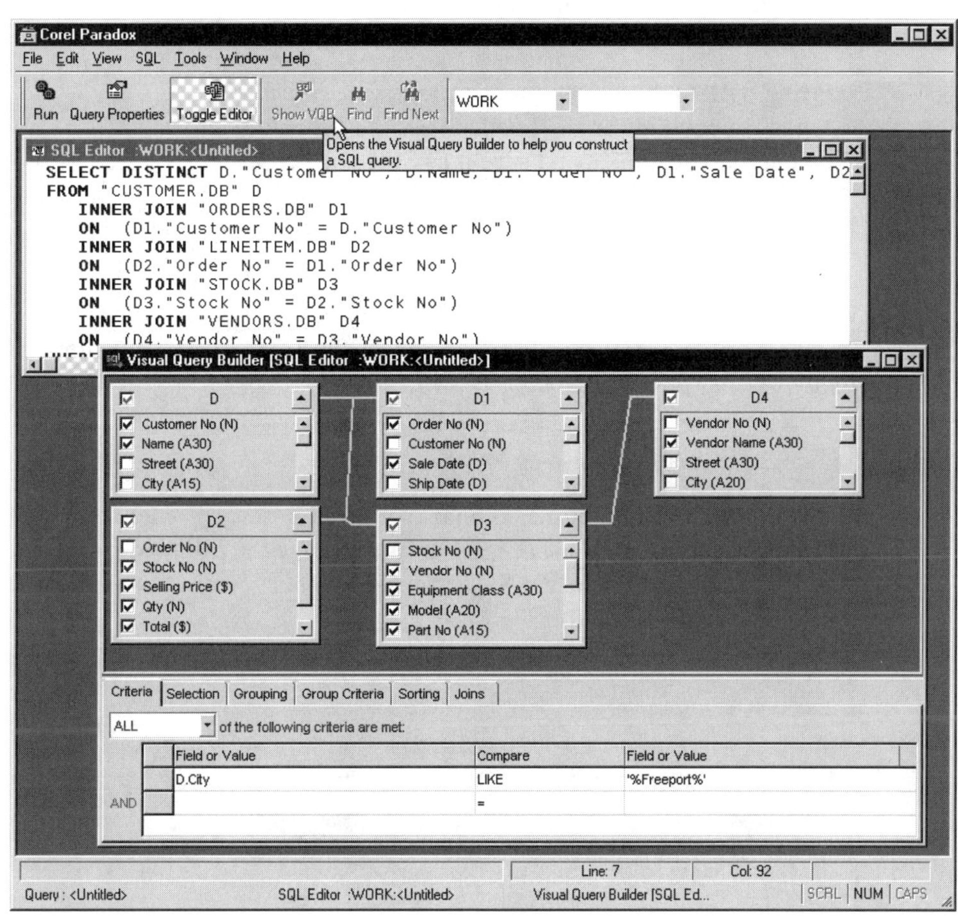

FIGURE 24-5 The Visual Query Builder

Step By Step

1. Change your working directory to Paradox's Samples directory, and select File | New | SQL File. From the New SQL dialog box, select the Blank

Editor option. The SQL Editor opens, ready for you to type and execute a single SQL statement.

2. Referring back to the syntax for select, in place of criteria, you can place the names of columns or an *, which signifies all columns. Type the following SQL statement and save it as **SQL-LS1.SQL** (see Figure 24-6).

```
select *
from Customer
```

Notice that the .DB extension for the Customer table above is not specified. If you do not specify an extension, Paradox uses the default database type (Paradox tables).

3. Run the SQL query by pressing F8.

4. Next, specify the names of the columns you want to see, separated by commas and ending with a space. For example, type the following, save it as **SQL-LS2.SQL**, and run the SQL statement. Your screen should then look similar to Figure 24-7.

```
select Name, Phone
from Customer
```

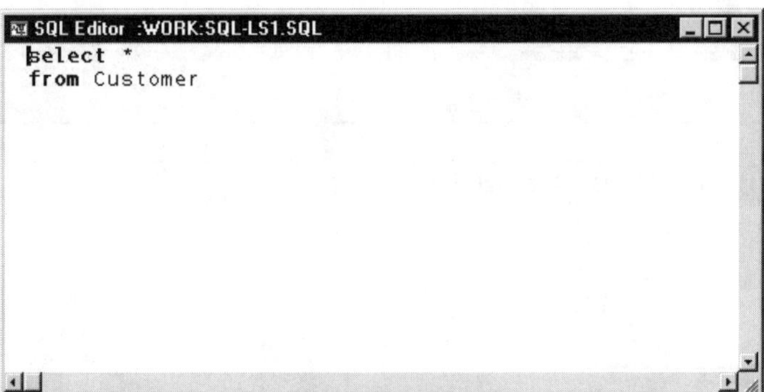

FIGURE 24-6 Using the select command

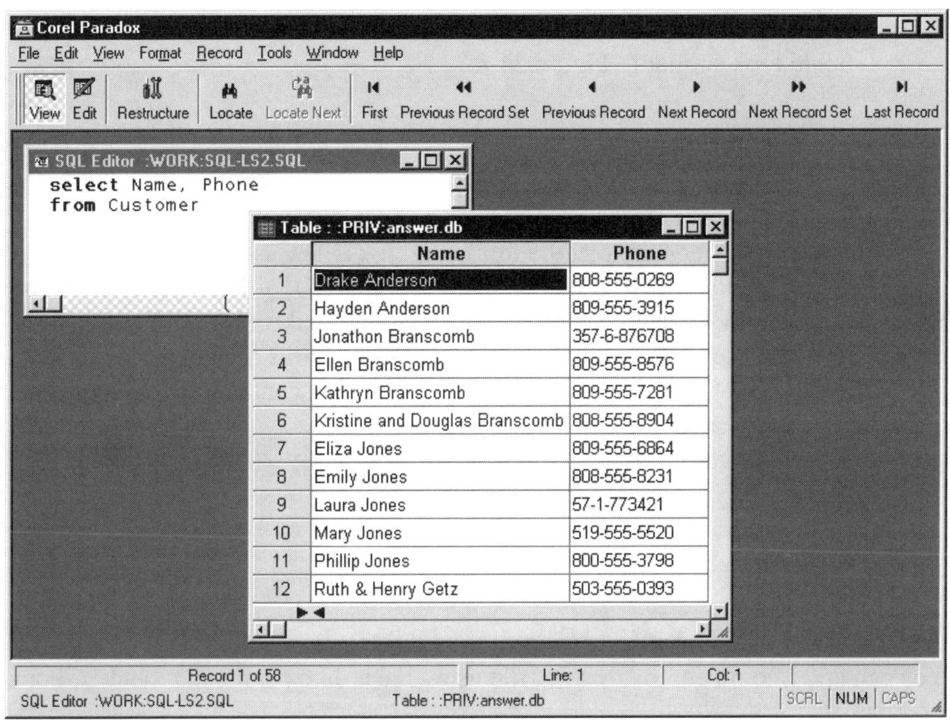

FIGURE 24-7 Specifying columns using select

5. The count clause enables you to count records. For example, type the following SQL statement into the SQL Editor to find out how many records are in the Customer table:

```
select count(*)
from Customer
```

6. The where clause enables you to narrow down your search criteria. Using this clause is similar to specifying example elements in Paradox's QBE. Refer to Table 24-1 to see which of the many aggregates and operators are supported by local SQL. Next, use the where clause to specify that you

want to see only the records where *City* is equal to *Madeupville*. To do this, type the following, save it as **SQL-LS3.SQL**, and run it. Your screen should look similar to Figure 24-6.

```
select3*
from Customer
where City = "Madeupville"
```

7. You also can use the where clause to link tables similar to how the data model does. For example, the following links the Customer and Orders tables. Type in the SQL statement and save as **SQL-LS4.SQL**, and run the following SQL statement. Your screen should look similar to Figure 24-7. (Note the use of the table name and quotation marks around the fields in line 1 in the following code. Any field name that contains spaces requires quotation marks.)

```
1:  select Customer."Customer No", Customer."Name", Orders."Order No"
2:  from Customer, Orders
3:  where Customer."Customer No" = Orders."Customer No"
```

Commenting SQL Files

You can add a comment to any SQL file using the C-like comment /* and */. For example,

```
/* This is a comment. */
```

Using *distinct, union,* and *order by*

The distinct keyword prevents duplicate values. The union clause enables you to combine one or more select statements to produce a single result. The order by clause specifies how to order the data. Here is an example of using all three:

```
select distinct p.Name from 'Customer.db' p
union select d.Name from 'Customer.dbf' d
order by p.Name
```

Step By Step

1. This next example uses a where clause and the and clause. It links the Customer and Orders table on Customer No and displays the five columns (some from each table) where the *Balance Due* is not 0. Save as **SQL-LS5.SQL**, and run the following SQL statement:

```
/* SQL-LS5.SQL */
select Customer."Customer No", Customer."Name",
     Customer."Phone", Orders."Order No", Orders."Balance Due"
from Customer, Orders
where Customer."Customer No" = Orders."Customer No"
     and Orders."Balance Due" <> 0
```

2. This next example introduces the order clause, which enables you to sort the answer table. Type the following and save as **SQL-LS6.SQL**, and run the following SQL statement.

```
/* SQL-LS6.SQL */
select Customer."Customer No", Customer."Name",
Customer."Phone"
from Customer
order by Name
```

3. This next example demonstrates linking two tables and ordering by one of the fields. Type the following and save as **SQL-LS7.SQL**, and run the following SQL statement:

```
/* SQL-LS7.SQL */
select Orders."Order No", Orders."Balance Due",
     Lineitem."Stock No"
from Orders, Lineitem
where Orders."Order No" = Lineitem."Order No"
order by Orders."Balance Due"
```

4. This next example demonstrates sorting in a descending order. When you use descending, you must also use distinct. Type the following and save as **SQL-LS8.SQL**, and run the following SQL statement:

```
/* SQL-LS8.SQL */
select distinct Orders."Order No", Orders."Balance Due",
     Lineitem."Stock No"
from Orders, Lineitem
where Orders."Order No" = Lineitem."Order No"
order by Orders."Balance Due" descending
```

Heterogeneous Joins

As previously mentioned, local SQL supports aliases when referencing table names. This way, you can execute heterogeneous joins; that is, joins of more than one Table object type. For example, you could create a SQL statement that joins Paradox, Oracle, and Informix tables in a single SQL query.

Heterogeneous joins are table links between two or more different types of tables. Because Paradox uses the BDE, you can easily link various heterogeneous tables. For example, the following joins a Paradox table to a dBASE table:

```
select p."Name", p."Customer No", d."Name" from
"Customer.db" p,
"Customer.dbf" d
where p."Name" = d."Name"
```

Finally, here are some more select statements you can try. Keep your working directory set to Paradox's Samples directory, and then type and run any or all of them.

Using *insert*

The syntax for insert is not nearly as elaborate as the syntax for select, but it is still fairly substantial. Paradox supports only a small subset, however. For now, the basic syntax you will use is as follows:

```
insert into tableName
([columnName1 [, columnName2] [, columnName3]...])
values ([value1 [, value2] [, value3]...])
```

Step By Step

1. The next SQL statement uses insert to insert a new record into the Customer table. Type the following, save it as **SQL-LI1.SQL**, run the SQL statement, and then open the table. Your screen should look similar to Figure 24-8. Notice that Paradox generates an inserted.db table. You can use these auxiliary tables to undo any changes you need to.

```
insert into Customer
(Customer."Customer No", Customer."Name")
values (0, 'Aurora Cortez')
```

2. The next SQL statement uses insert with a nested select statement to add the records from Customer.dbf into Customer.db.

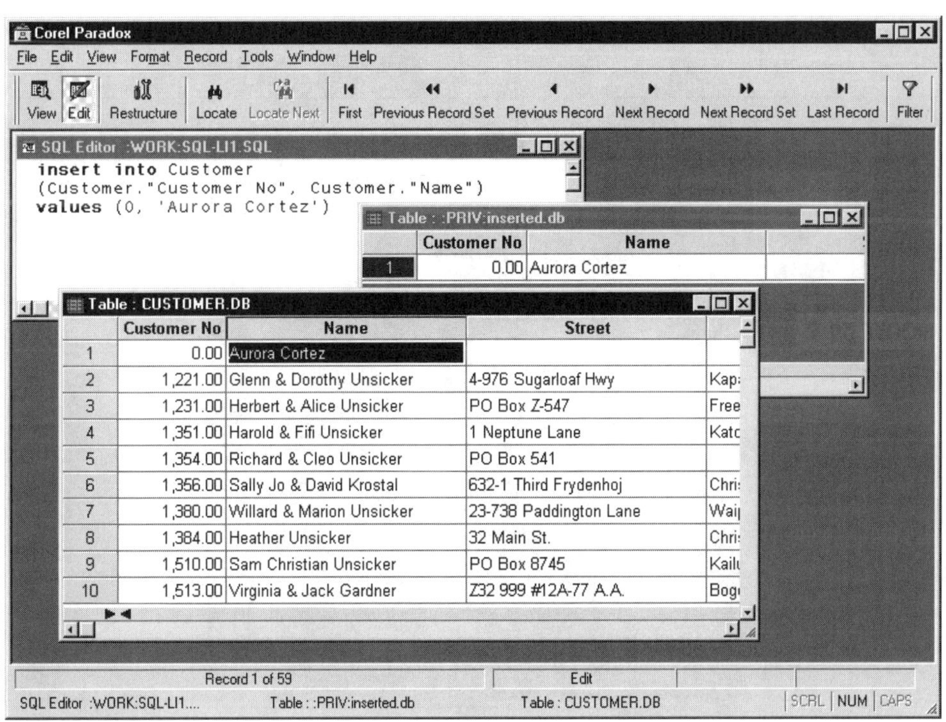

FIGURE 24-8 Using insert on a local table

```
/* Add one table to another. */
insert into "Customer.db"
select * from "Customer.dbf"
```

As briefly mentioned earlier, to increase the speed of the SQL statements, you can turn off the generating of auxiliary tables. From the SQL Editor, select SQL | Properties. Select the SQL tab and change the "Auxiliary table options" (see Figure 24-9). Remember that although the queries run faster, you will not have the benefit of the auxiliary tables. Without the auxiliary tables, it is harder to recover from data problems. This technique works for QBE queries, too.

Using *update*

The syntax for update also is not as elaborate as the syntax for select, but it is still fairly substantial. For now, the basic syntax you will use is as follows:

```
update tableName
set setcriteria
where wherecriteria
```

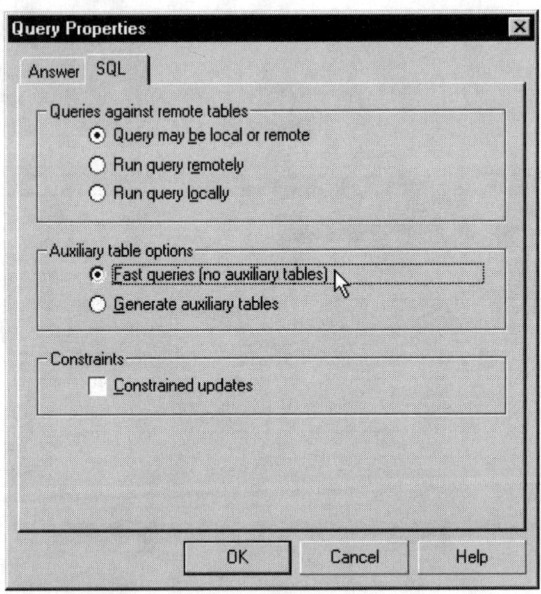

FIGURE 24-9 Auxiliary table options

The update command is very powerful, so be cautious when using it. One mistyped word can change all the data in your table.

Step By Step

1. For your first example, suppose that Sandy Jones and her husband got a divorce and she now wants to use her maiden name. The update command enables you to change the Customer table. Type the following SQL statement, save it as **SQL-LU1.SQL**, and execute it:

```
update Customer
set Name = "Sandy Kowalski"
where Name = "Sandy Jones"
```

2. The next update statement assumes the entire town of *Madeupville* was magically moved to Illinois. Type the following SQL statement, save it as **SQL-LU2.SQL**, and execute it:

```
update Customer
set Customer."State/Prov" = "IL"
where City = "Madeupville"
```

3. This next update statement accomplishes a similar task as step 2, but this SQL statement demonstrates how to specify and update multiple columns. Type the following SQL statement, save it as **SQL-LU3.SQL**, and execute it:

```
update Customer
set City = "SJ", Customer."State/Prov" = "IL"
where City = "San Jose" and Customer."State/Prov" = "CA"
```

Using *delete*

The syntax for delete is fairly straightforward. The basic syntax you will use is as follows:

```
delete from tableName
where whereCriteria
```

Step By Step

1. Suppose that you want to delete a record or set of records from a database. The delete command enables you to do so. Type the following SQL statement, save it as **SQL-LD1.SQL**, and execute it:

```
delete from Customer
where Name = "'Aurora Cortez'"
```

2. This final delete example adds a comment and the and clause. Suppose that you want to delete all the customers from a table where the customers are in Sacramento, CA. Type the following SQL statement, save it as **SQL-LD2.SQL**, and execute it:

```
/* SQL-LD2.SQL */
delete from Customer
where City = "Sacramento" and Customer."State/Prov" = "CA"
```

Using *create table* and *drop table*

The create table SQL commands enable you to create tables. The interesting thing about creating tables with create table is that the create table statement is often portable to other database servers. For example, all the create table SQL statements in this section work on Local InterBase and on Oracle. The syntax for create table is as follows:

```
create table tableName (fieldName fieldType [, fieldName fieldType...])
```

Use the following field types: SMALLINT, INT, DECIMAL(x,y), NUMERIC(x,y), FLOAT(x,y), CHAR(n), DATE, BOOLEAN, BLOB(n,s), TIME, TIMESTAMP, MONEY, AUTOINC, and BYTES(n).

Step By Step

1. Create a table, as follows:

```
create table test
(field1 char(20))
```

2. Delete it, as follows:

```
drop table test
```

3. Create one more table for use with the following index examples:

```
create table Contacts
(Name char(20), Phone char(15), Age SmallInt)
```

Using *create table* with the Primary-Key Constraint

You can create primary keys with the primary-key constraint. The syntax for create table using the optional primary-key constraint is as follows:

create table tableName (***fieldName*** fieldType [, ***fieldName*** fieldType...]
[, primary key (***fieldName*** [,fieldname…]])

Step By Step

1. The following is a create table example using the optional primary-key constraint:

```
/* Create emp table with a primary key. */
CREATE TABLE "emp"
   (
   SSN char(11),
   Last_Name char(20),
   First_Name char(15),
   Salary numeric(10,2),
   Dept_No smallint,
   PRIMARY KEY (SSN)
   )
```

2. To delete the primary key, execute the following SQL statement:

```
drop index emp.primary
```

3. To drop the table, execute the following SQL statement:

```
drop table emp
```

You cannot create a primary key using create index; you must create the primary key at the time you use create table.

Using *create index* and *drop index*

Step By Step

1. Create the emp table again (refer to step 1 of the previous "Step By Step" section).
2. To add a secondary index, execute the following SQL statement:

```
create index secLastFirst
on emp (Last_Name, First_Name)
```

3. To delete the newly created secondary index, execute the following SQL statement:

```
drop index emp.secLastFirst
```

Using Embedded SQL on Local Tables

Just as you can embed query code into your ObjectPAL code and execute it using executeQBE(), you can embed SQL code and execute it using executeSQL(). What is interesting is that embedded SQL statements work on local tables, too. For example, type the following code into the pushButton event of a button:

```
;Button :: pushButton
method pushButton(var eventInfo Event)
   var
        q     SQL
        tc    TCursor
        db    Database
        tv    TableView
   endVar

   q = SQL
        select Customer."Customer No", Customer."Name",
        ;Customer."Phone"
        from Customer
```

```
            where not Phone is null
        endSQL

        db.open("WORK")
        q.executeSQL(db, ":PRIV:ANSWER.DB")
        tv.open(":PRIV:ANSWER.DB")
    endMethod
```


That's it for the SQL primer. As stated earlier, to learn ANSI SQL really well, you should purchase an ANSI SQL book dedicated to ANSI SQL.

The Client/Server Model

In a client/server model, the database processes are shared between the client and the server. This is called *distributed processing*. In the case of Paradox, Paradox is the client, and any of the SQL servers that BDE can use can be the server. Oracle, Sybase, Informix, and InterBase are examples of SQL servers. For example, when you connect Paradox to an Oracle server, the database processes are divided between the server and Paradox.

Paradox provides access to SQL servers through SQL Links for Windows. When Paradox communicates with a SQL server, queries (commands) from Paradox need to be in the dialect of the particular server. The link provides this translation and sends the appropriate commands to the server. Because the link is fairly transparent, you do not have to learn SQL.

Back End/Front End

In a client/server model, the SQL server is called the *back end*. A client application, such as Paradox, is called the *front end*. When you set up a very large database, you generally have two software-buying considerations: the back end and the front end. Typical back-end servers include InterBase, Oracle, Sybase, Microsoft SQL, and Informix. Typical front-end servers include Paradox, Paradox for DOS, Access, and dBASE for Windows.

Columns and Rows

Sometimes, just getting used to the terminology of a new subject helps you to understand it. In SQL server terms, a *column* is the same as a Paradox table field's name, and a *row* is the same as a record.

Overview of Database Application Architectures

Database application architecture has more to do with the software development life cycle than it has to do with Paradox. However, understanding database application architecture is important because it will have a major impact on any large application you develop. Deciding the basic architecture of any application you develop is one of the final steps you undertake when you do your system analysis. You need to decide between a single-user and multiuser application. If you decide that you need a multiuser application, you need to decide between a multiuser network application and a client/server application. Finally, if you decide on a client/server application, you need to decide among a two-tier, three-tier, or multitier application.

Single-User Applications

A single-user application contains both the data and application on the same machine. Local tables include Paradox and dBASE and Local InterBase. This type of application is also known as one-tier development because both the application and data reside on the same machine.

NOTE

Local InterBase is a cross between the local table and the client/server concepts. Although you can develop client/server applications with Local InterBase, one processor processes both the application requests and manages and serves data. The great thing about Local InterBase is that it enables you to develop a client/server application on a single machine and move the data to another processor such as a Windows NT server, NLM server, or UNIX server. Personal Oracle is similar to Local InterBase.

Multiuser Applications

Multiuser one-tier applications are similar to single-user applications. The main difference is that the data is moved to the network. This way, multiple users can access the data. However, this setup is not client/server because the data is still processed by Paradox on a single machine—a single tier.

Client/Server Applications (Fat Client Versus Thin Client)

Client/server applications (two-tier development) split the processing needed to set and retrieve data between two processors, or two tiers. In general, client/server applications are either fat or thin.

A *fat client application* contains most of the business rules and data integrity on the client (in this case, in Paradox using ObjectPAL). Sometimes program architects like to use this model because they have very strong clients. This design architecture is sometimes referred to as the muscular client model because a typical client machine today runs at over 200MHz and has more than 32 megabytes of RAM.

A *thin client application* moves as much of the business rules and data integrity to the server as possible—for example, calculations, required fields, and data link enforcement. This process is accomplished by using data integrity rules such as referential integrity, stored procedures, and triggers. In general, thin client architectures are considered better because they spread more of the processing onto the server, and server machines are generally more powerful than client machines. Most companies today creating client/server applications try to create thin client applications.

Multitier Development

A hot topic in database development today is multitiered development. You are already familiar with two-tier or client/server development. Two-tiered development separates the application and data management to two computers (a client and a server). Multitiered development takes this to the next logical step by moving more of the processing to another server. It breaks up the application into more than just two logical separations.

Paradox is good at developing the presentation layer, and servers including InterBase, Oracle, and MS SQL are good for developing the database layer. Room is left for the middle layer (some refer to it as the *application server layer*). You can, for example, place business rules, replication schemes, and data translation rules on the middle layer. You can build the middle layer yourself using languages such as C and C++, or you can buy software designed to aid in the development of middleware. Some of the more popular middleware applications on the market include EZ-RPC, Entera, RPC Painter, and Tibco.

Interactive SQL

Before you jump into SQL and ObjectPAL, review what Paradox can do interactively with SQL. As a front end for SQL, Paradox rivals anything on the market. Your first experience may well lead you to the same conclusion. When you access SQL tables, you'll notice a few differences from using Paradox tables. The following are some of the obvious features to note:

- You can open an SQL in a table window by choosing File | Open | Table. Note that you can directly edit the data in the table.
- Creating SQL tables, adding data to a SQL table, restructuring, and so on are integrated into the standard Paradox menus. In general, you simply use the option you want and select the SQL alias you want to work with.
- You can create a quick form based on an SQL table. Press F9 to go into Edit mode. The default setting for Read-only for all tables in the data is unchecked. Leave this option turned off to edit data. Also worth mentioning is that you need to execute forceRefresh() with table frames to update data altered by other users, but not with fields.
- When you query SQL tables with the QBE, note that the SQL button shows you the equivalent QBE query in SQL. If you are familiar with Query by Example (QBE), then you might want to always use it—rather than SQL—to query both local and SQL tables. If you know SQL or have an interest in learning it, however, you can use the SQL Editor built into Paradox.
- When you use the SQL File (or query SQL tables with SQL), note that you do not put a semicolon at the end of a SQL statement as you do with other SQL Editors. Also note that you can execute only a single line of SQL at a time.
- You can use SQL statements with local tables.
- You can base a report on a SQL table or SQL statement. By now, you may have noticed that the link to SQL tables is nearly transparent. Paradox provides an extremely easy-to-use SQL front end.
- The button on the vertical scroll bar in a table frame behaves differently than with Paradox tables. While you view remote tables in Paradox, the

data is cached. Paradox reads only part of a remote table—unlike a local table. Performance would suffer if the SQL link had to ask the server for the table size and record position while scrolling through the table.

Answer Set

Whenever you access data on a SQL server, you create an answer set. When you open a table in a SQL database in a table window, you can call the data you are currently viewing an *answer set*. When you execute a specific SQL query—either through a QBE query or a SQL file—you refer to the data returned by the server as an answer set.

Note on Cached Data

Paradox may have occasional delays when accessing data. Paradox is fairly fast at retrieving data if the data is within the set of cached data. If, however, Paradox has to request a new set of records, the SQL link slows down because Paradox has to either generate a fetch or select for the new data. Using indexes—for example, a primary key on Oracle tables—greatly speeds up performance, and this issue is no longer a concern.

ObjectPAL and SQL

With ObjectPAL, you can establish a connection to a SQL server. You can use TCursor and Table variables almost exactly the same way you do with local tables. You can embed SQL code in your ObjectPAL code; this includes any server-specific extensions. For example, you can have ObjectPAL, QBE, SQL, and Oracle's PL/SQL all in one event. ObjectPAL also supports the use of transactions. You can even trap for errors.

Connecting via an Existing Alias

To connect to an existing alias, use the Database open event. The syntax for the Database open event is as follows:

```
open ( const aliasName String ) Logical
```

The following is a simple example:

```
;Button :: pushButton
method pushButton(var eventInfo Event)
   var
     dbSQL    Database
   endVar

   dbSQL.open(":Godzilla2:")
endMethod
```

In the preceding example, the user is prompted to enter his or her password. If you know the user's password, you can use it in ObjectPAL so that the user doesn't have to enter it. To enter the password for the user, use the following syntax:

open ([const ***aliasName*** String,] [const ***ses*** Session,] [const ***parms*** DynArray]) Logical

The following is another simple example of using the Database open event passing the alias a username and password:

```
;Button :: pushButton
method pushButton(var eventInfo Event)
   var
      dbSQL       Database
      dynAlias    DynArray[]  AnyType
   endVar

   dynAlias["USER NAME"]   = "guest"
   dynAlias["PASSWORD"]    = "guest"
   dbSQL.open(":Godzilla2:", dynAlias)
endMethod
```

Connecting via a New Alias

The following example demonstrates connecting to an Oracle server without a preexisting alias:

```
;Button :: pushButton
method pushButton(var eventInfo Event)
 var
```

```
        tv          TableView
        dbSQL       Database
        dynAlias    DynArray[] String
    endVar

    dynAlias["SERVER NAME"]        = "Godzilla2"
    dynAlias["USER NAME"]          = "guest"
    dynAlias["OPEN MODE"]          = "READ/WRITE"
    dynAlias["SCHEMA CACHE SIZE"] = "8"
    dynAlias["NET PROTOCOL"]       = "SPX/IPX"
    dynAlias["LANGDRIVER"]         = ""
    dynAlias["SQLQRYMODE"]         = ""
    dynAlias["PASSWORD"]           = "guest"

    addAlias("Godzilla2_guest", "Oracle", dynAlias)
    dbSQL.open("Godzilla2_guest", dynAlias)
    tv.open(":godzilla2_guest:ksmith.customer")
  endMethod
```

Disconnecting is actually quite simple. As you do with so many other objects in ObjectPAL, you simply close it. Assuming that the SQL Database variable DbSQL from the preceding example is within scope, the following line of code closes the connection:

```
dbSQL.close()
```

SQL and *TCursor* and *Table* Variables

In the preceding example, you used a TableView variable to open up a TableView of an SQL table. The following code shows that you can use TCursor and Table variables with the same techniques with which you are already familiar. A *cursor* is a pointer to a row in a SQL answer set. Cursors are implemented in ObjectPAL as a TCursor object. This next example shows you how to copy a table from the server to a local hard drive:

```
;Button :: pushButton
method pushButton(var eventInfo Event)
  var
        tc    TCursor    ;Declare a TCursor variable.
  endVar

```

```
    tc.open(":Godzilla2:rspitz.customer") ;Open table on server.
    tc.copy(":work:customer")             ;Copy table.
    tc.close()                            ;Close table.
endMethod
```

This example shows how to copy a table from your local hard drive to the server:

```
;Button :: pushButton
method pushButton(var eventInfo Event)
   var
        tc    TCursor
   endVar

   errorTrapOnWarnings(Yes)
   try
      tc.open(":work:customer.db")
      tc.copy(":godzilla2:rspitz.test")
      tc.close()
   onFail
      errorShow()
   endTry
endMethod
```

NOTE *Although TCursor and Table variables work with SQL data, for the sake of speed, using a SQL query is always better. Therefore, try to do what you want with a query first and then fall back to using a TCursor only when a SQL query is not possible.*

Executing a SQL Query in ObjectPAL

The executeSQL() method works just like the Query equivalent executeQBE(). After you define the SQL variable, then you execute it using executeSQL(). The following example shows how to execute an existing SQL file. In ObjectPAL, the technique is similar to executing an existing QBE file.

```
;Button :: pushButton
method pushButton(var eventInfo Event)
   var
      sqlEXESQL   SQL
      tvAnswer    TableView
   endVar
```

```

      sqlEXESQL.readFromFile(":WORK:EXECSQL.SQL")
      sqlEXESQL.executeSQL(db, ":PRIV:ANSWER.DB")

      tvAnswer.open(":PRIV:ANSWER.DB")
   endMethod
```


You assign a SQL variable to a SQL string in any of the following three ways: embedding SQL in ObjectPAL, reading it in from a string, or reading it in from a file. You used readFromFile() previously to read in a SQL file and execute it. The next three examples use embedded SQL, embedded SQL with a tilde variable, and readFromString() to assign a SQL variable a SQL statement and then use executeSQL() to execute it.

Embedded SQL

The capability to place SQL commands within another programming language enables you to extend that language. This capability is called *embedding SQL*, and it means that you can actually embed SQL commands inside ObjectPAL. The following example shows how to embed SQL statements into your ObjectPAL code. Again, just as you can embed query code, you can embed ObjectPAL code.

```
;Button :: pushButton
method pushButton(var eventInfo Event)
   var
      sqlVar   SQL
      tvLike   TableView
   endVar

   ;Define SQL variable.
   sqlVar = SQL

   select * from ksmith.customer

   endSQL

   ;Execute SQL variable.
   executeSQL(db, sqlVar, ":PRIV:__LIKE")

   ;View answer table.
   tvLike.open(":PRIV:__LIKE")
endMethod
```

The next SQL query example demonstrates how to use a tilde variable to pass a SQL statement some data. This process is just like passing a tilde variable to an embedded query.

```
;Button :: pushButton
method pushButton(var eventInfo Event)
   var
        sqlVar     SQL
        tvLike     TableView
        s          String
   endVar

   s = "ksmith.customer"
   s.view("Enter SQL table name")

   sqlVar = SQL

        select * from ~s

   endSQL

   executeSQL(db, sqlVar, ":PRIV:__LIKE")
   tvLike.open(":PRIV:__LIKE")
endMethod
```

This final SQL query example demonstrates how to use a SQL string. This process is just like using a query string.

```
;Button :: pushButton
method pushButton(var eventInfo Event)
   var
        s          String     ;Declare a String variable.
        sTilde     String
        sqlVar     SQL        ;Declare an SQL variable
        tv         TableView  ;Declare a TableView variable.
   endVar

   ;Assign String values.
   sTilde = "Dive"

```

```
      s = "SELECT LAST_NAME, FIRST_NAME, COMPANY, PHONE " +
          "FROM    CONTACTS " +
          "WHERE   COMPANY LIKE '%" + sTilde + "%'"

      ;Read String values into an SQL variable.
      sqlVar.readFromString(s)

      ;Execute SQL statement.
      sqlVar.executeSQL(db, ":PRIV:ANSWER.DB")

      ;Open answer table.
      tv.open(":PRIV:ANSWER.DB")
   endMethod
```

Transactions: The Protocol for Communication

Client applications such as Paradox communicate with SQL database servers with a unit of work called a *transaction*. Although a transaction is perceived as a single operation, a transaction may consist of a number of operations. For example, a single transaction could update multiple records. If you want to have some control over undeleting changes to your data, then use the following methods and procedures:

beginTransaction()	Starts a transaction on a server
commitTransaction()	Commits all changes within a transaction
rollbackTransaction()	Rolls back all changes within a transaction (undo feature)

Commit and Rollback Overview

The term *commit* is part of a concept for entering data. The idea is to enter data into a temporary table and commit, or copy, the data to a main table. The term *rollback* is also part of a concept for entering data. The idea is to enter data into a temporary table with the opportunity to empty the temporary table and to leave the main table untouched. The term *two-phase commits* applies this idea over a wide area network. With two-phase commits, you can have data entry from anywhere in the world.

In the following example, the first record 1001 is posted to the table and then undone with the rollback:

```
;Button :: pushButton
method pushButton(var eventInfo Event)
     var
          dbSQL      Database
          tc         TCursor
     endVar

     dbSQL.open(":Server1:")
     dbSQL.beginTransaction()
     tc.open(":Server1:guest.customer")
     tc.insertRecord()
     tc.(1) = 1001
     tc.(2) = "Mike Prestwood"
     tc.postRecord()
     dbSQL.rollbackTransaction()    ;Un-inserts record 1001.
     dbSQL.begintransaction()
     tc.(1) = 1002
     tc.(2) = "Lisa Prestwood"
     dbSQL.commitTransaction()      ;Commits record 1002.
     tc.close()
endMethod
```

Statement Atomicity

In ObjectPAL, all database commands are committed immediately. For example, a single QBE query, a single ObjectPAL table append, and a single edit operation are examples of commands that are executed and committed to the database immediately.

Views

A *view* is a virtual table that represents a part of the database or the whole database. The following is a list of various types of views:

- A vertical subset of columns from a single relation. This type of view limits the columns displayed.

- A horizontal subset of records from a single relation. This type of view limits the records displayed.
- A combined vertical and horizontal subset of records from a single relation. This type of view limits the number of records displayed.
- A subset of records from many relations. This type of view usually performs a join operation.

You can use a view to ensure security, and for convenience you can allow users to see only columns or values, as necessary. Views can also enable users to see the bigger picture; for example, you can simplify a complex join into a manageable package. You create a view using the SQL command create view. The syntax is as follows:

```
create view [<owner.>]<view name>
[(<column name>[, <column name>...])
as <SELECT statement>
```

Triggers and Stored Procedures

Triggers are procedures stored in the database that help you enforce both business and data relationship rules. With a trigger, you can keep summary data up-to-date, take actions based on what data a user enters, and enforce business rules such as no out-of-state checks accepted.

A trigger can occur when you either update, insert, or delete values. A trigger is like a Paradox validity check in which you can put code. In a way, triggers are analogous to events in a form, and stored procedures are analogous to custom methods.

Creating and Using a Sybase Trigger

The following is a simple example of how you might create and use a trigger in Sybase to ensure data integrity. On the SQL side, you create an update trigger on a table's column.

```
create trigger updatetrigger on sqlTableName
for update as
if update(columnName)
```

```
    begin
       raiserror 30000 'Cannot change values in this. Changes have been discarded.'
       rollback transaction
    end
```

To raise or see the error in Paradox, use the error event. For example,

```
;tableframe :: error
method error(var eventInfo ErrorEvent)
   if eventinfo.reason() = ErrorWarning then
     eventinfo.setReason(ErrorCritical)
   endIf
endMethod
```

Or, you can use errorTrapOnWarnings(Yes). This rudimentary example should help you get started using triggers.

Summary

This chapter introduced you to Paradox as a client/server development tool. You also reviewed what a user can do interactively with Paradox and how to use ObjectPAL with SQL servers. Then, you got started using SQL. Now that you are familiar with ANSI SQL, and because SQL is common to many database tools, you can begin to query many types of databases with many different types of tools.

CHAPTER 25

Paradox and the Internet

Paradox has many features that integrate, use, or support the Internet. You can add simple hyperlinks to your applications or build a complete Internet site using Paradox as a Web server. This chapter will introduce you to techniques for utilizing Paradox on the Internet.

There is a great PDF document included in the Reference Center on the Paradox CD titled jPdox Web Utilities that documents how Paradox integrates with the Internet. In addition to reading this chapter, I suggest you read that document as well.

Setting Up Hyperlinks

Paradox supports the following Internet protocols for hyperlinks:

- HTTP
- FTP
- MAILTO
- GOPHER
- NEWS
- TELNET

When you execute a hyperlink in ObjectPAL, Paradox will use the appropriate Internet protocol to follow the link (for example, HTTP will launch the default browser and MAILTO will open a new message in the default mail program).

Launching the Default Browser

You can add the ability to launch the default browser and display a Web page. This is particularly handy these days for adding options to the Help menu of your product. For example, you can add the following options to your Help menu (each pointing to a separate page on the Internet): Product Support, Product Upgrades,

FAQ, and Order Information. To add a button to a form that launches your browser to the home page of Prestwood Software & Consulting, do the following:

```
method pushButton(var eventInfo Event)
    StartWebBrowser("http://www.prestwood.net")
endMethod
```


Hyperlinking with the Text Expert

This next section will also set up a hyperlink, this time using the Text Expert. To follow this example, make sure the "Run experts when creating objects on documents" box is checked on the Experts tab of the Preferences dialog box.

Step By Step

1. Create a new form and place a text object on it. The Text Expert Wizard displays.
2. Type **PrestoNet** into the text field, as shown next. Press Next.

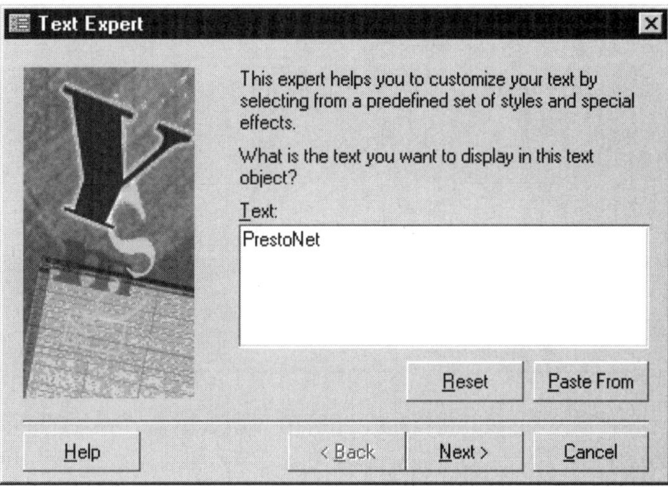

3. Set the style of the text, as shown next. Press Next.

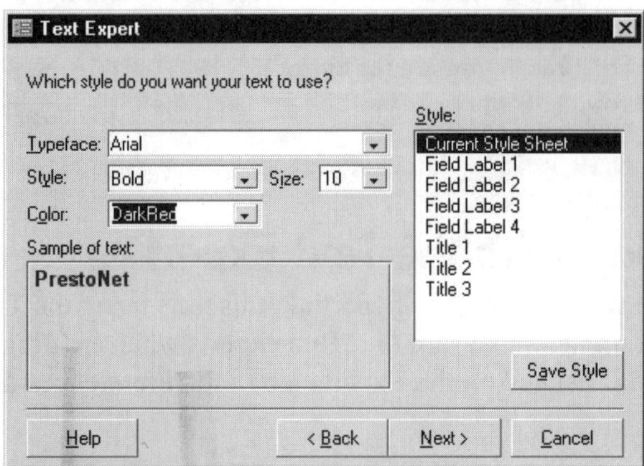

4. Select Hyperlink and type **http://www.prestwood.com**, as shown next. (Note that the whole address does not show on the screen.) Press Next, then Finish.

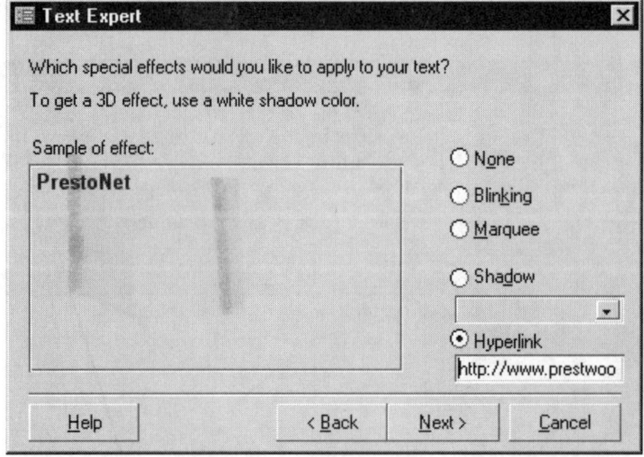

Notice the link has the default characteristics of a hyperlink. Whenever you use the experts, it is a good idea to study the ObjectPAL that was added. In this case, take a look at the mouseClick event of the text object.

Importing Data from HTML Pages

You can use the HTML Import Expert to import data in tables or lists embedded in HTML pages. To get to the HTML Import Expert, select Tools | Experts and select the HTML Import option, shown next.

Publishing to HTML

Perhaps the most common technique you will use to publish Paradox data on the Internet is to use the HTML Table Expert. This expert offers both static and dynamic publishing.

Web Server Repository

Use the Web Server Repository to store, view, and edit GXEngine templates for dynamic HTML publishing. The Web Server Repository is a set of Paradox tables located in the websrv/WebRepos folder. Whenever you use File | Publish to HTML and select a dynamically published document, it is also added to the Web Server Repository. It is a storage facility for HTML template files. Click Tools | Web Server Repository to view a list of stored templates. Choose the Template tab to view their contents.

Publishing Static Documents

Static documents are generated once as HTML and do not change. The benefit of static pages is that they can be posted to any type of Web server (NT, UNIX, Mac, etc.). Paradox can publish simple forms, tables, and reports as static documents. Use the File | Publish to HTML (forms and tables) or File | Publish As | HTML (reports) while you have either a form, table, or report open.

When you have a form open, you can publish it as a static HTML document. This feature works best with simple forms that use text, edit boxes, list boxes, radio buttons, and check boxes. Form objects such as graphics, table frames, crosstabs, notebooks, and charts do not translate statically to HTML.

When you have a table open and select File | Publish to HTML, the HTML Table Expert displays. The HTML Table Expert allows you more freedom than publishing simple forms. You can choose which fields, the HTML title, the color scheme, whether you want the document to be static or dynamic, and whether you want to save the document as an HTT document. Figure 25-1 shows the Customer table in Netscape after the table was published as a static table.

With the report in Run Mode, you must select File | Publish As | HTML to display the HTML Report Expert. The HTML Report Expert gives you more options than either static tables or form documents. When you use bands in a report, the HTML Report Expert offers you the option of having drill-down data. For example, the Customer report is grouped by Country. When you publish it to HTML, you have the option of having one page for the whole report or one page listing all the countries and one page for each country. Refer to Figures 25-2 and 25-3.

Publishing Dynamic Documents

Dynamic pages are built every time the Web page is called. Dynamic pages can use either the Corel Web Server or the Corel Report Server. Since these two servers only run on Windows-based machines, you are limited to distributing your dynamic pages to Windows-based machines like NT.

Roll Out the Paradox Internet Servers

Paradox comes with several Internet servers you can use to serve up documents to browsers, to set up servers on the Internet, or to set up your own intranet. They are

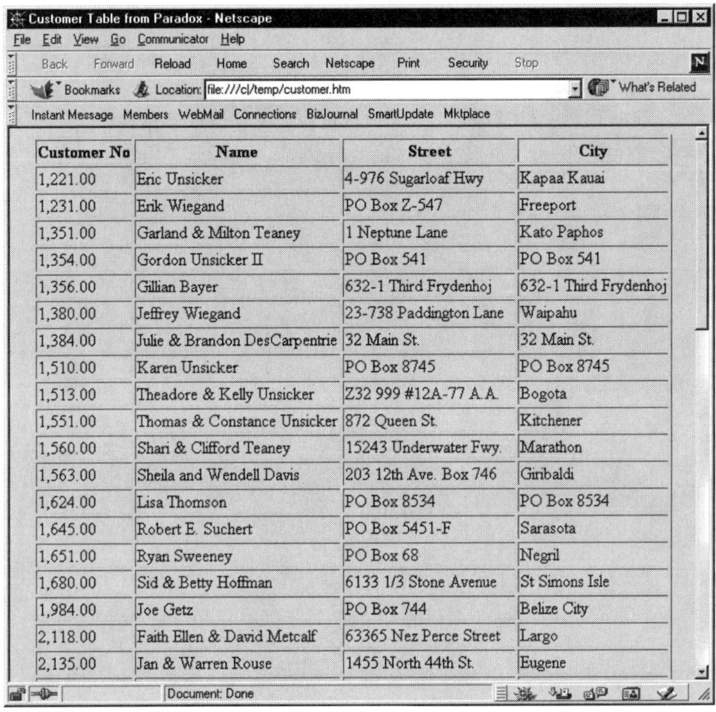

Customer No	Name	Street	City
1,221.00	Eric Unsicker	4-976 Sugarloaf Hwy	Kapaa Kauai
1,231.00	Erik Wiegand	PO Box Z-547	Freeport
1,351.00	Garland & Milton Teaney	1 Neptune Lane	Kato Paphos
1,354.00	Gordon Unsicker II	PO Box 541	PO Box 541
1,356.00	Gillian Bayer	632-1 Third Frydenhoj	632-1 Third Frydenhoj
1,380.00	Jeffrey Wiegand	23-738 Paddington Lane	Waipahu
1,384.00	Julie & Brandon DesCarpentrie	32 Main St.	32 Main St.
1,510.00	Karen Unsicker	PO Box 8745	PO Box 8745
1,513.00	Theadore & Kelly Unsicker	Z32 999 #12A-77 A.A.	Bogota
1,551.00	Thomas & Constance Unsicker	872 Queen St.	Kitchener
1,560.00	Shari & Clifford Teaney	15243 Underwater Fwy.	Marathon
1,563.00	Sheila and Wendell Davis	203 12th Ave. Box 746	Giribaldi
1,624.00	Lisa Thomson	PO Box 8534	PO Box 8534
1,645.00	Robert E. Suchert	PO Box 5451-F	Sarasota
1,651.00	Ryan Sweeney	PO Box 68	Negril
1,680.00	Sid & Betty Hoffman	6133 1/3 Stone Avenue	St Simons Isle
1,984.00	Joe Getz	PO Box 744	Belize City
2,118.00	Faith Ellen & David Metcalf	63365 Nez Perce Street	Largo
2,135.00	Jan & Warren Rouse	1455 North 44th St.	Eugene

FIGURE 25-1 A static table document

the Corel Web Server, Paradox Report Server, Paradox JDBC driver, and JDBC Proxy Server. If that isn't good enough for you, you also get a complete Web server in the form of an ActiveX control so you can write your own Web server in Paradox using ObjectPAL. (This last one is demonstrated at the end of this chapter.)

THE COREL WEB SERVER The Corel Web Server is a Windows-based application and runs on Windows platforms including Windows 95, 98, 2000, and NT. The Corel Web Server acts as an intermediary between Web browsers and Paradox. However, Paradox does not need to be running (or even installed) on the server.

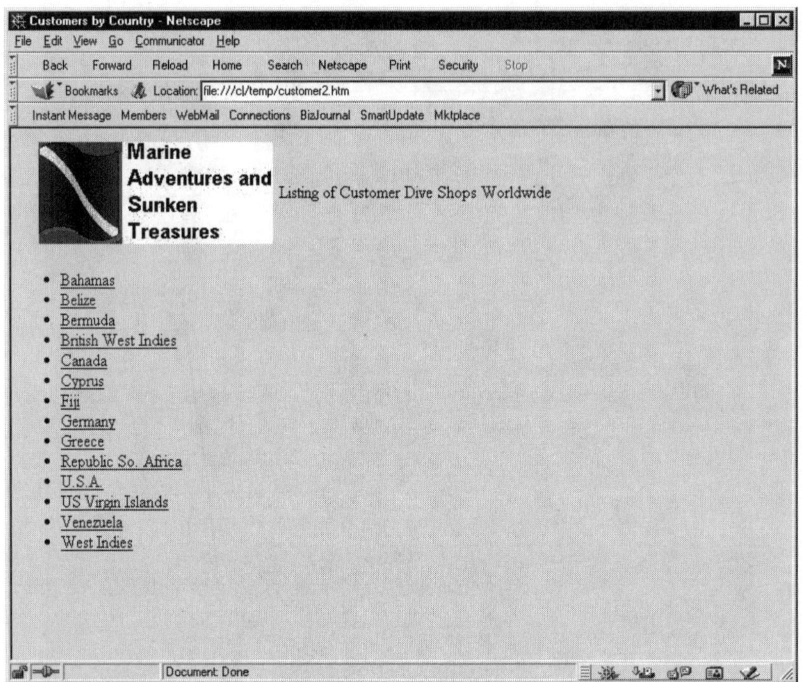

FIGURE 25-2 The first HTML page of the Country report

The BDE does need to be installed in order to retrieve dynamic reports from the web repository, which is a set of Paradox tables. The Corel Web Server is a fully functional Web server with the following features:

- HTTP support (version 1.0 and many 1.1 elements)
- File caching
- Contact (access) logging using the CERN/NCSA Common Log Format plus transaction logging
- Custom MIME types
- Multithreaded (supports multiple IntraBuilder sessions)

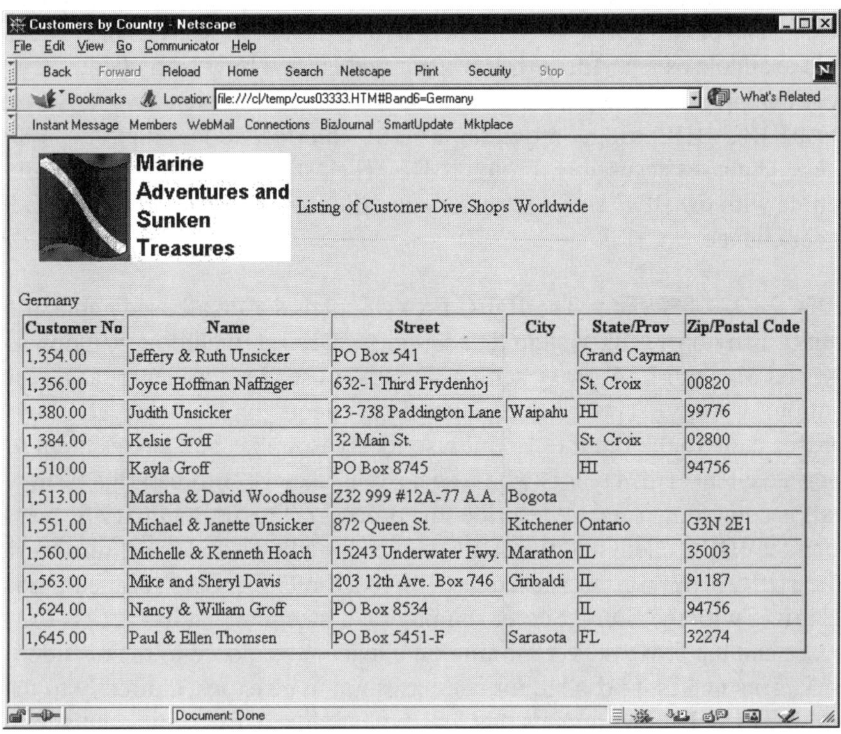

Customer No	Name	Street	City	State/Prov	Zip/Postal Code
1,354.00	Jeffery & Ruth Unsicker	PO Box 541		Grand Cayman	
1,356.00	Joyce Hoffman Naffziger	632-1 Third Frydenhoj		St. Croix	00820
1,380.00	Judith Unsicker	23-738 Paddington Lane	Waipahu	HI	99776
1,384.00	Kelsie Groff	32 Main St.		St. Croix	02800
1,510.00	Kayla Groff	PO Box 8745		HI	94756
1,513.00	Marsha & David Woodhouse	Z32 999 #12A-77 A.A.	Bogota		
1,551.00	Michael & Janette Unsicker	872 Queen St.	Kitchener	Ontario	G3N 2E1
1,560.00	Michelle & Kenneth Hoach	15243 Underwater Fwy.	Marathon	IL	35003
1,563.00	Mike and Sheryl Davis	203 12th Ave. Box 746	Giribaldi	IL	91187
1,624.00	Nancy & William Groff	PO Box 8534		IL	94756
1,645.00	Paul & Ellen Thomsen	PO Box 5451-F	Sarasota	FL	32274

FIGURE 25-3 One of the linked pages from the Country report

PARADOX REPORT SERVER The Paradox Report Server is a Java 1.2-based application that *must* run in a Windows environment. It receives requests from the Paradox Servlet running on a Web server (which may be running on the same machine or another machine) and returns the appropriate dynamic HTML Web page back to the Web server. The Report Server forwards Web page requests to GXPublish.dll, which then produces the HTML page generated dynamically from Paradox tables. Because the Report Server works with GXPublish.dll, which then works with the BDE, the Report Server must run on the same machine that Paradox is installed on.

Contrast this with the Paradox Servlet (dynpub.jar)—which is also Java based—that may run in any environment with a Web server that supports the Servlet API.

THE PARADOX JDBC DRIVER The Paradox Java Database Connectivity (JDBC) driver consists of two parts: the JDBC client and the JDBC server. The JDBC client is available as a jar file, PdxJDBC.jar and is used by a Java client application/applet to access databases through the JDBC server. The JDBC driver acts as a JDBC-BDE bridge, providing a JDBC interface to Paradox. It can be used to access databases accessible through BDE. The JDBC server must be running on a machine with the BDE and is necessary for all transactions involving Web Form Designer clients.

THE JDBC PROXY SERVER The JDBC Proxy Server is a Java-based application and runs on any operating system that supports JDK 1.2, including Windows, UNIX, and Macintosh. A proxy server is a server used by companies as a security precaution. A proxy server takes requests from clients (typically a Web browser) and passes them to the Internet, and it also receives replies and passes them to the appropriate client. This layer is where security is usually enforced (the term firewall is commonly used to describe this process). The JDBC Proxy Server sits between the JDBC client and the JDBC server and allows you to set up security.

The JDBC Proxy Server is used to enforce a three-tier setup for the Paradox JDBC driver with the JDBC Server running on a machine that has access to databases and the proxy server running on a machine exposed to the outside network. This makes it possible for databases not to be exposed directly to the outside world and allows applets that use the Paradox JDBC components to be set up on a different machine, which is running the Web server. The proxy server takes all requests from the JDBC client and passes them to the JDBC server, making it appear to the clients that it is the JDBC server. The proxy server is also necessary when the BDE and JDBC servers are located on a machine other than the machine the Web server is installed on. The Web form, which is a Java applet, makes a direct connection to the JDBC server once loaded. The Java security model, under normal circumstances, does not allow for connections to machines other than the one where the applet came from, so we need the proxy server on the Web server machine to pass the requests to the JDBC server.

This servlet runner responds to requests for dynamic documents based on the URL by passing that request to the servlet runner (JRun). The servlet runner then responds by running the Paradox Servlet, which then makes contact with the Report Server. This allows you to separate browser calls from Paradox and the

BDE. The Paradox Servlet (dynpub.jar) requires a servlet runner that works in conjunction with a Web server. JRun is a third-party Web server plug-in that provides the necessary environment to run servlets. The Web Server, which can run on any operating system (Windows, UNIX, Macintosh), supports the Java Servlet API (such as JRun). The benefit of doing this is that now you can have two- or three-tier applications. Two-tier development would consist of the client browser on any platform and a Windows-based server (Web Server, Paradox, and BDE). Three-tier could consist of the client browser on any platform, the Web Server integrated with JRun running on any platform, and the Paradox/BDE server running on a Windows-based server.

Creating and Using Dynamic Documents

You create dynamic documents the same way you create static documents. You use either the HTML Table Expert or the HTML Report Expert. As stated earlier, these experts are available when you have either a table or report open. Most of the dynamic documents I create are created using the HTML Report Expert because it is more powerful, supporting such features as drill-down (discussed earlier), banding (grouping), and calculated fields.

Using a dynamic document is simple. Run the Corel Web Server on the machine that you want to serve up the documents (see next). Paradox does not need to be running. The Corel Web Server interacts directly with the HTML document you created and the database engine to create an updated HTML document.

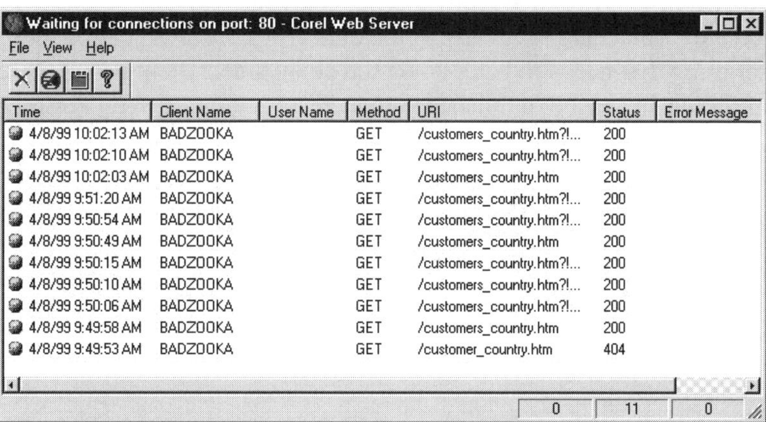

The Corel Web Server has most of the usual settings you would expect in a Web server, including HTTP port, minimum and maximum connections, timeout, default page, and logging. You can view the properties, shown here, by right-clicking on the Corel Web Server Tray icon and selecting Properties.

The Web Form Designer

The Web Form Designer allows you to use Java browser applets to create HTML documents that any Java-enabled browser running on any platform—including Windows, Macintosh, and UNIX—can use. You create Web forms using the Web Form Designer and embedding JavaBeans, without writing a single line of code.

As long as the server is a Windows-based machine and has the BDE installed, you can create forms that access any of the data types the BDE can. There is no custom scripting that needs to be done on the client side. Client browsers require the Java 1.2 plug-in to view published forms created with the Web Form Designer.

The ActiveX Web Server Control

With the ActiveX Web Server control, you can create your own Web server written in Paradox. This ActiveX control is a fully functioning Internet server with these features:

- HTTP 1.0 support (plus some features of HTTP 1.1)
- File caching
- Logging using the CERN/NCSA Common Log Format
- Custom MIME types
- Support for cookies (sessions)
- Support for multithreaded containers, such as Delphi
- OGI programming interface

Because Paradox forms support OLE controls as containers, you can use the ActiveX Web Server control by placing it in a form. The form is notified when an HTTP GET, POST, or HEAD method is requested by a Web browser client. The Corel Web Server Control supplies its container with an OGI (OLE Gateway Interface) event. An OGI event is an ActiveX control connection point event. This allows the container to execute an event-handling procedure in its native code. Custom event behavior can be programmed or the default HTTP response can be accepted.

Using the Web Server Control with Other Programs

Does the Corel ActiveX Web Server work with other products like VB and Delphi? Yes it does. It should work with any product that supports OLE controls as containers.

A Paradox Web Server

This final example demonstrates creating a Web server written in Paradox. This example will combine ObjectPAL, SQL, and HTML. Once completed, you will be able to use an Internet browser to select a city from the Customer table and, upon pressing a button, display all the customers in that city. You can do this on one machine, or you can install Paradox on your server and then call the server machine name from a client machine running a Web browser.

First, we will build our Web server.

Step By Step

1. Create a blank form and place a Corel Web Server control on it, as shown here. The Corel Web Server control is available from the ActiveX toolbar.

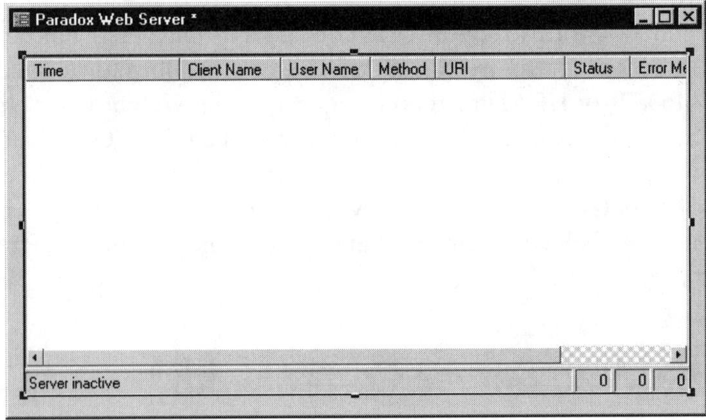

2. Alter the Var window of the form as follows:

```
Var
   strPath  String
endVar
```

3. Alter the Init event of the form as follows:

```
method init(var eventInfo Event)
   var
```

```
      dynFile  DynArray[] String
   endVar

   ;Get the current path of the form.
   splitFullFileName(getFileName(), dynFile)
   strPath = dynFile["DRIVE"] + dynFile["PATH"]

   ;The server is set to the path in strPath in the DoStartup
   ;of the ServerOCX object.
endMethod
```


4. Alter the DoStartup event of the ActiveX Web Control as follows:

```
method DoStartUp(var Cancel Logical)
   ; This is where we set the BasePath.
   ; This allows the form to be run from
   ; any directory.
   self.BasePath = strPath

   ;Set the default HTML document.
   self.DefaultPage = "index.htm"
endMethod
```

5. Alter the OnGetRequest event of the ActiveX Web Control as follows:

```
method OnGetRequest(Request OleAuto, Response OleAuto)
   var
      resultstr   String
      tcCustomer  TCursor
   endvar

   ;The Get_Customers below is what the HTML form passed
   ;to the server from an HTML form's get method.
   if (Request.URI = "/GET_CITIES") then
      ;Construct first part of html page (header).
      resultstr = "<HTML>" + chr(13)
```

```
resultstr = resultstr
   + "<!DOCTYPE HTML PUBLIC \"-//W3C//DTD HTML 3.2//EN\">"
   + chr(13)
resultstr = resultstr + "<html>" + chr(13)
resultstr = resultstr + "<head>" + chr(13)
resultstr = resultstr + "<title>Customer Example</title>" +
; chr(13)
resultstr = resultstr + "</head>" + chr(13)
resultstr = resultstr + "<body BGCOLOR=\"#FFFFFF\">" +
; chr(13)
resultstr = resultstr
   + "<h1 ALIGN=\"CENTER\"><b>Select a City</b></h1>"
   + chr(13)
resultstr = resultstr + "<hr>" + chr(13)
;Build first half of drop box. Notice the action
;is find_customers and the method is post. We trap for the
;find_customers value in OnPostRequest.
resultstr = resultstr + "<form method=\"POST\"
; action=\"find_customers\">"
resultstr = resultstr + "<p><select name=\"City\"
; size=\"1\">"
;Open Customer table and scan through
;table adding each city to the Drop Down box. If you
;have duplicates, you could sort by a secondary index.
tcCustomer.open("customer.db")
;Add city to list box of HTML form
scan tcCustomer:
   resultstr = resultstr+"<OPTION VALUE=\"" +
; tcCustomer."City" + "\">"
      + tcCustomer."City" + "</OPTION>" + chr(13)
endscan
;Build rest of drop box.
resultstr = resultstr + "</select><br>"
```

```
      resultstr = resultstr + "<input type=\"submit\"
      ;  value=\"Retrieve\" name=\"City\"></p>"
      resultstr = resultstr + "</form>"

      ;Build last portion of page (footer).
      resultstr = resultstr + "<hr>"
      resultstr = resultstr + "</body>"
      resultstr = resultstr + "</html>"

      ;Return to browser.
      Response.ResultString = resultstr

      tcCustomer.close()
   endIf
endMethod
```

6. Alter the OnPostRequest event of the ActiveX Web Control as follows:

```
method OnPostRequest(Request OleAuto, Response OleAuto)
   var
      tcCustomer   TCursor
      resultstr    String
      strSQL       String
      CDSQL        SQL
      db           Database
   endvar

   if (Request.URI = "/find_customers") then
      ;Construct first part of html page (header).
      resultstr = "<HTML>" + chr(13)
      resultstr = resultstr + "<!DOCTYPE HTML PUBLIC \"-//W3C//DTD
      ; HTML 3.2//EN\">" + chr(13)
      resultstr = resultstr + "<html>" + chr(13)
      resultstr = resultstr + "<head>" + chr(13)
      resultstr = resultstr + "<title>Customer Example</title>" +
      ; chr(13)
      resultstr = resultstr + "</head>" + chr(13)
      resultstr = resultstr + "<body BGCOLOR=\"#FFFFFF\">" +
      ; chr(13)
```

```
resultstr = resultstr + "<h1 ALIGN=\"CENTER\"><b>Customer
; Info</b></h1>" + chr(13)
resultstr = resultstr + "<hr>" + chr(13)

;Construct SQL statement. Notice the use
;of GetField which gets the value from the
;HTML form request.
strSQL = "SELECT * FROM Customer "
strSQL = strSQL + "where City = \"" +
; Request.GetField("City") + "\""

;Read string into SQL variable, open database, and execute
; sql.
CDSQL.readFromString(strSQL)
db.open(":work:");this will open the connection to the local
; table or SQL table via the alias
CDSQL.executeSQL(db, tcCustomer) ;execute the SQL statement
; into an answer table

;// Create HTML Table Header
resultstr = resultstr + string(
   "<P><TABLE BORDER=2>",
   "<TR><TH>No</TH>",
   "<TH>Name</TH>",
   "<TH>Street</TH>",
   "<TH>City</TH>")

;// Fill in HTML Table Contents
scan tcCustomer : resultstr = resultstr + string(
   "<TR>",
   "<TD>", tcCustomer."Customer No", "</TD>",
   "<TD>", tcCustomer."Name", "</TD>",
   "<TD>", tcCustomer."Street", "</TD>",
   "<TD>", tcCustomer."City", "</TD>" + chr(13))
```

```
        endScan

        ;Build rest of table.
        resultstr = resultstr + "</TABLE>" + chr(13)

        ;Build page footer.
        resultstr = resultstr + "<hr>" + chr(13)
        resultstr = resultstr + "</body>" + chr(13)
        resultstr = resultstr + "</HTML>\r\n" + chr(13)

        ;Send back response.
        Response.ResultString = resultstr
    endIf
endMethod
```

7. Save the form as **web_server.fsl** and run the form. Leave this server running for the next part. This illustration shows the web_server.fsl form after receiving several requests.

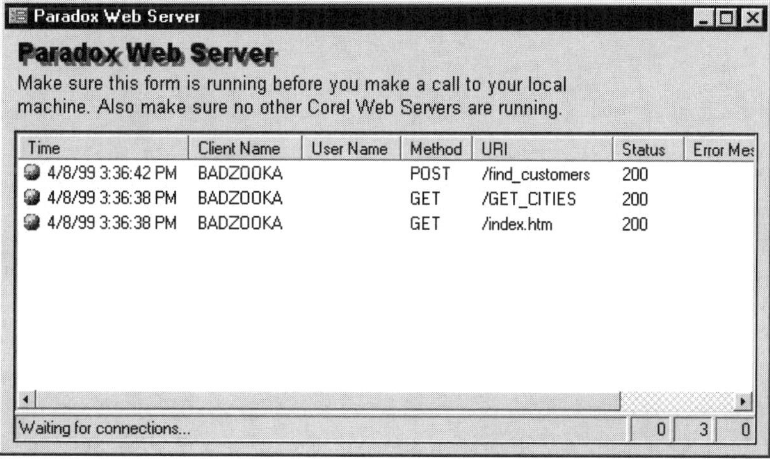

Now that the server has been created, we need to create an initial HTML page that gets us into the system. Let's keep this simple. Type the following into any text editor (Notepad, PrestoEdit, Wordpad, for example) and save it as **index.htm**. (Make sure you change the machine name of **badzooka** to the name of your machine.)

```
<html>
<head>
<title>Customer Example</title>
</head>
<body bgcolor="#FFFFFF">

<center>
<h1>
<b>Using a Paradox form as a Web Server</b></h1></center>

<hr>
<p><a href="http://badzooka/GET_CITIES">Query Example</a>
<br>
<hr>
</body>
</html>
```

Notice the HREF in the link simply says GET_CITIES. The Web server OCX embedded in the web_server.fsl form intercepts this request. The form takes care of processing the request and generating the HTML to return. This is done in the OnGetRequest event of the OCX, which is embedded in the form. You can also use HTML postform events to send to the OCX, and those can be trapped for in the OnPostRequest event. I could have easily used get_cities.html in place of GET_CITIES if I wanted the request to feel more like a static page.

The final step is to load your favorite browser and open your page. On my machine, the server is called Badzooka, so I type the following URL into the browser:

```
http://badzooka/index.htm
```

Because I have index.htm specified as my default page, I could just use the following:

```
http://badzooka
```

Figures 25-4, 25-5, and 25-6 show the pages in Netscape.

Summary

Paradox integrates well with the Internet. You can import and export to static HTML documents, or you can publish your data dynamically using the various Web servers included.

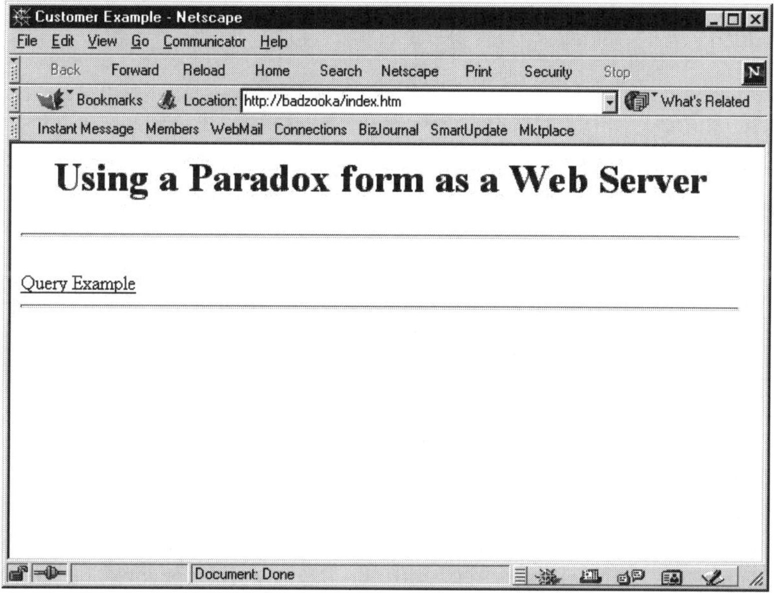

FIGURE 25-4 Initial Web page

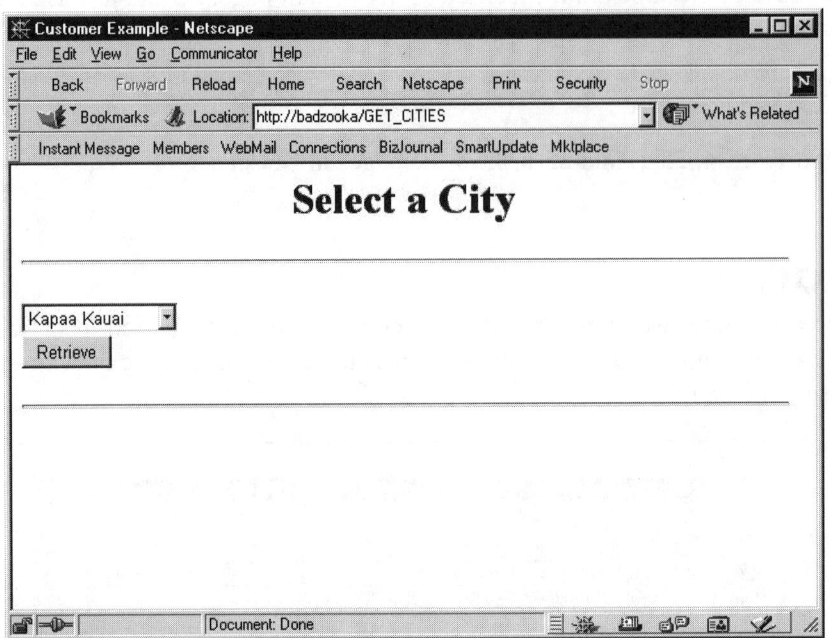

FIGURE 25-5 Choose a city

With both the Corel Web Server and Paradox Report Server, you can display data in Web browsers that were created with either the HTML Table Expert or the HTML Report Expert. The Corel Web Server is a Windows-based machine and therefore runs on Windows platforms such as Windows NT. The Paradox Report Server, on the other hand, is Java based and is platform independent.

For interactive Web-based applications for use with Java-enabled browsers, you can use the Web Form Designer, which allows you to embed JavaBeans into HTML documents that will interface with the BDE on the server. The server must be a Windows-based server with the BDE installed, but the client browser just needs to be Java enabled.

If all of the servers that come bundled with Paradox are not enough for you, you can write your own Web server using the Web Server ActiveX control

FIGURE 25-6 The customers in that city are displayed

included. This is a great way to take full advantage of Paradox and all of its features, including ObjectPAL, TCursors, queries, and SQL. With this solution, you must build the HTML documents in your code, but you have the freedom and power to do anything ObjectPAL can do. This final solution does not require a Java-enabled browser but the server must be a Windows-based server running Paradox or Paradox Runtime.

CHAPTER 26

Using the Application Framework

In this chapter, we will introduce the Application Framework. The Application Framework consists of an additional feature to the Project Viewer, a new Application Event Expert, an Application Menu, the Framework Launcher, and several special aliases.

About the Application Framework

Versions of Paradox prior to version 8 had a major problem—there was no easy way to create global menus. Imagine you've created your opening form to your application and you've put on it a menu that will open up other forms. The problem is that the control for the menuAction event is in your opening form and will have to be duplicated in every form where you wish to use the global menu. A good solution to this particular problem is to pass the eventInfo to a library routine and let it handle the menu processing. This means adding code in the menuAction event of every form that uses the menu. The Application Framework solves this problem by implementing this technique for you. That is just one example, and there are many more that you'll discover as you explore the Application Framework.

Exploring the Application Framework

Perhaps the best way to learn about the Application Framework is to jump right in and explore its capabilities. In this section, you'll create a new Application Framework application and explore the default .EXE, .INI, aliases, script, forms, tables, libraries, and menus that are automatically created for every Application Framework application.

Creating an Application Framework Application

The following steps document how to create a new Application Framework application.

Step By Step

1. Open the Project Viewer and select the Applications icon.
2. Right-click on the Applications icon and select New, as shown next. The New Application dialog box displays.

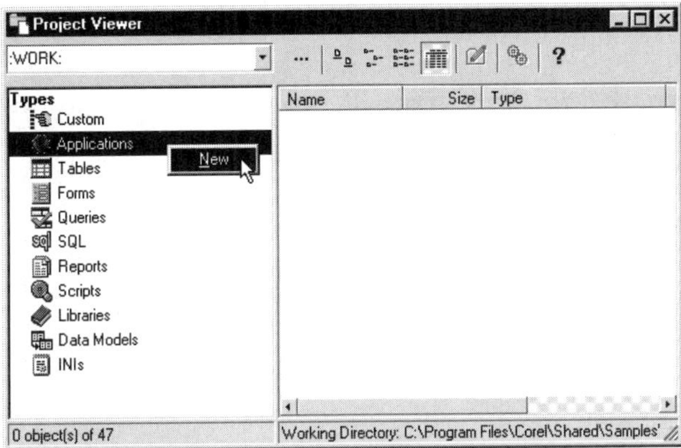

3. Specify the values in the New Application dialog box, as shown next. The folder you specify must *not* already exist. Paradox creates it for you.

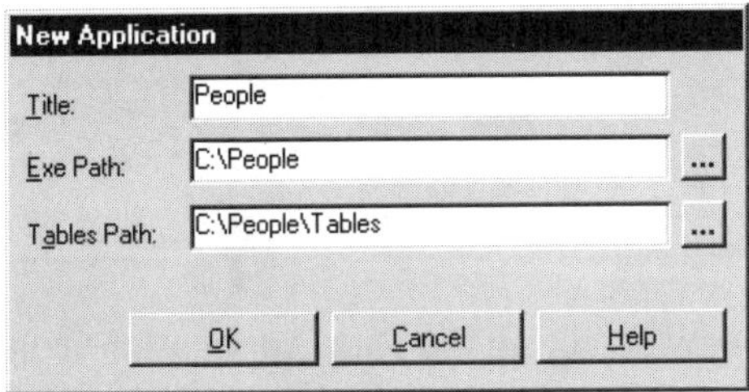

You have just created your first Application Framework application that is now ready to run. Granted, it's just a shell of an application, but it is a complete application.

Running Your Application from the Development Environment

Running an Application Framework application from the development environment is easy, but before we do that, let's set some application-level parameters. Using the Project Viewer, select the Applications icon and set the Author Company, Author Copyright, Author Name, Author Version, and Description. An example is shown next.

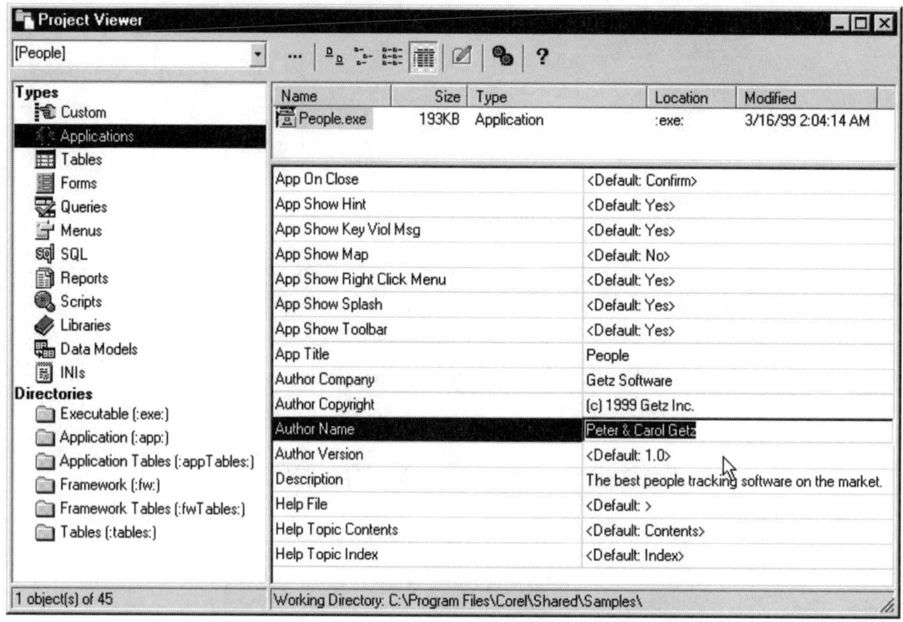

Run the application by selecting the Run Application icon, as shown next.

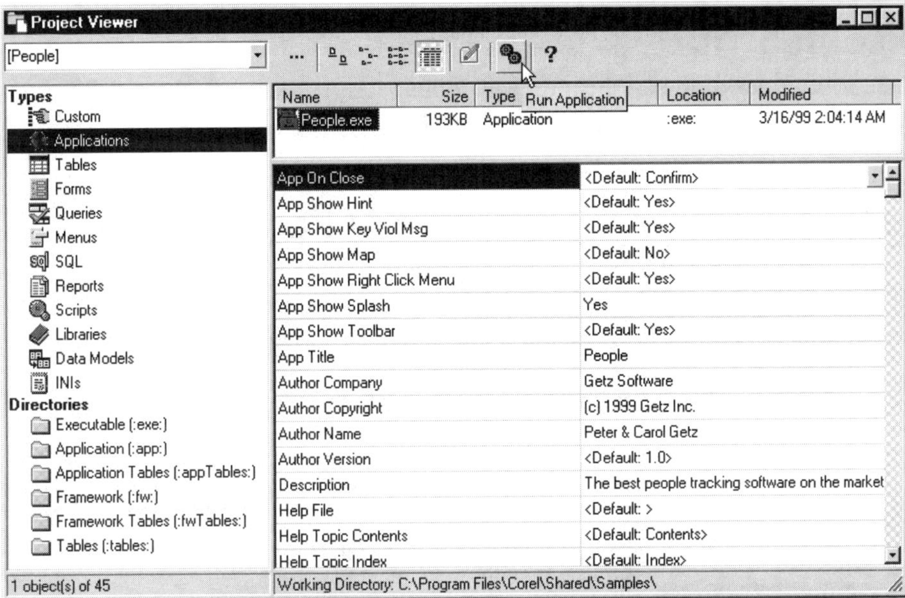

Notice that the application title, splash screen, and the Help | About dialog box automatically use the application-level data we entered.

Running Your Application Outside of Paradox

The nice thing about the Application Framework is that it sets up your application ready to run outside of the Paradox environment. Your application still requires Paradox, but it feels more like a regular Windows application than traditional Paradox applications do. To see what I'm talking about, exit Paradox, open the Windows Explorer and double-click on the .EXE you created earlier (C:\People\People.exe if you followed the screen shots).

Default Script

In the root folder of the application is a default script created by the Application Framework. This script is called by the .EXE.

Reopening Your Application in Paradox

To reopen an Application Framework application, open Paradox and from within the Project Viewer select your application. All the Application Framework applications are grouped together and bracketed, as shown next.

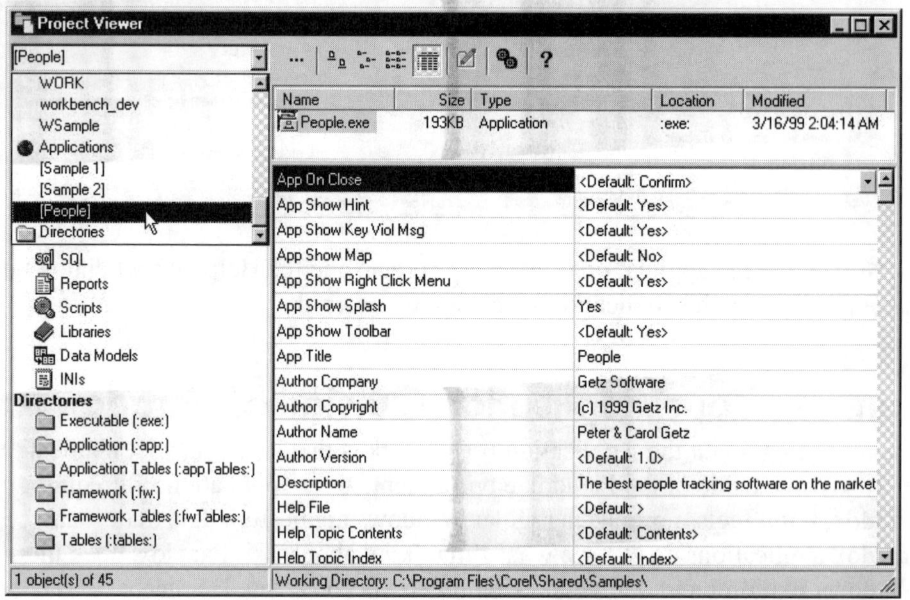

Framework Aliases

The Application Framework creates several aliases for use with your application. These aliases allow you to easily manage all of the objects required for your application. The following table lists the aliases:

Alias	Description
exe	Points to the executable folder, which contains the .EXE and .INI files and the startup script for an application.
app	Points to your application folder, which contains all of the code used by your application. This is where you place all of your application objects (forms, reports, libraries, and scripts).
appTables	Points to the application tables folder, which contains all of the code-related tables used by an application.
fwTables	Points to the Application Framework tables folder, which contains all of the tables shared across applications.
fw	Points to the Application Framework folder that contains all of the code shared across applications.
tables	Points to the tables folder, which contains all of the data tables used by an application. This is where you put your data.

In general, *do not* modify the files in the appTables, fwTables, or fw aliases directly. Only use the various interfaces provided by the Application Framework. The two aliases you will use most in your code are the app and tables aliases.

Default Forms

All of the default forms the Application Framework creates are located in the fw folder. Feel free to alter any of them, but keep in mind these forms are common to all applications you develop. The following table lists the default forms:

Form	Description
appAbout.fsl	Your Help | About dialog box for this application. Feel free to modify this form to your hearts delight.
appDesk.fsl	This form file contains the Desktop form (main window) used by your application.
appmap.fsl	This form file contains the map form used by the application. A map form contains a series of buttons that open forms and reports in the application and is a shortcut to using menus. When you close the default map form, you close your application.
appsplash.fsl	This form file contains the splash screen used by the application. The splash form is not an Application Framework form. Therefore, it doesn't contain all of the form-level code that integrates a form with the rest of the Application Framework.
fwerr.fsl	Your error dialog box.

Application Framework Coding Levels

The Application Framework adds two coding levels above the traditional Paradox application: the application and framework levels. The code for these two levels is stored in traditional ObjectPAL libraries. To access both the application and framework levels, use the Application Event Expert, shown next, available by selecting Tools | Application Event.

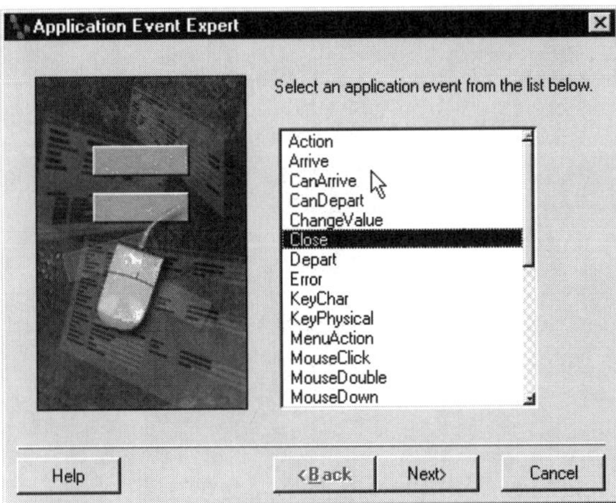

The application level is used for code that you want to apply to all objects within this application, but to only this application. Application-level code is stored in the :app:app.lsl and :app:apptools.lsl libraries. These two libraries are created in the app folder for every Application Framework application you create.

The framework level is used for code that you want to apply to all Application Framework applications you develop. Framework-level code you create is stored in the :fw:fw.lsl and :fw:fwglbl.lsl libraries. These two libraries are in the fw folder, and there is only one fw folder for Paradox. Also included in this folder are several delivered ObjectPAL libraries that are used with the Application Framework, and because they are delivered, you can't modify them.

Using the Application Event Expert

To add code to an event at the application or framework level, select Tools | Application Event. The Application Event Expert displays. Select which event you wish to alter, as shown next, then press Next.

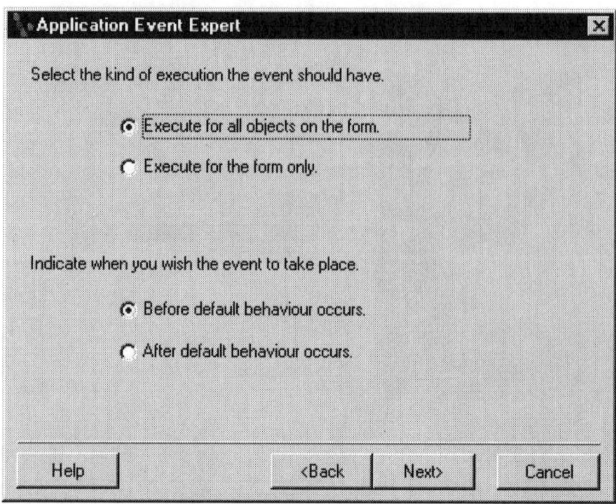

Next, choose if you want the event to execute in all forms in all applications (the highest level), all forms for the current application (global to the application), or only for the specified form, as shown next.

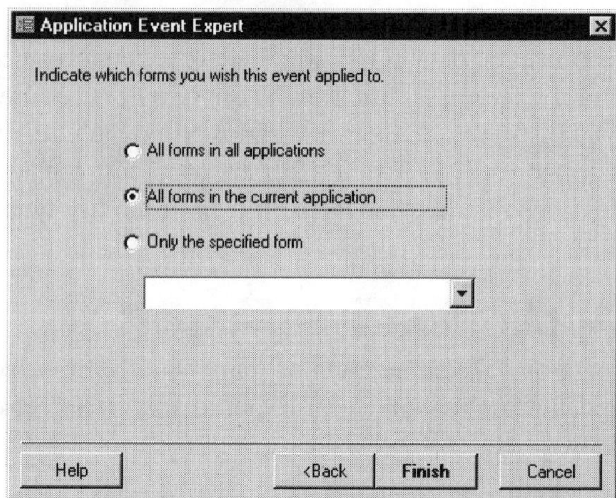

When you click Finish, the ObjectPAL Editor will be opened to the correct event or method.

Application Framework Menus

Figure 26-1 shows the Application Menu dialog box showing the File | Exit option. This dialog manipulates tables in your appTables folder. By default, the Application Framework creates three menus. The App menu is used while no forms or reports are specified or if you choose not to display either the Form or Report menu. The Form menu is merged with the App menu when a form is displayed, and the Report menu is merged with the App menu when reports are displayed. Forms and reports have a Menu property where you can specify which menu will be displayed when the object is selected from the menu. When adding options, pay particular attention to the Merge ID property. The Merge ID determines the location of the option when the menu is merged.

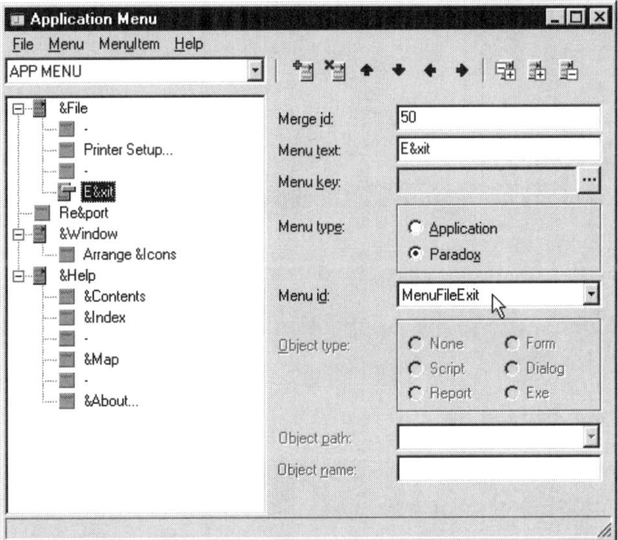

FIGURE 26-1 The Application Menu

Upgrading from Nonframework Applications

Unfortunately, there isn't an automatic way to upgrade your Paradox forms and reports to use the Application Framework. You could simply add them as a menu option, but you will not get all the default code. The only way to get the default code in your existing forms is to create a new Application Framework, then re-create your forms, reports, libraries, and scripts within it. Although you do have to re-create them, you don't have to start over. Here are surefire procedures for moving objects into a new Application Framework.

Importing Tables

Your tables don't need to change. If you used an alias to refer to them, then just keep using the alias. If you left them in the same folder as your forms and reports, then move them to the app folder (the folder titled app that the Application Framework created as a subfolder to the base folder you chose).

Importing Forms

Here is the procedure I use to move a form to the Application Framework:

1. Open the old form and save the data model in the new app folder.
2. Create a new form in the Application Framework using the data model you saved in step 1 (a .DM file).
3. Copy and paste the page(s) from the old form to the new form.
4. Merge the old form-level code (events, methods, and properties) with the default form-level code added to your new form by the Application Framework.

NOTE *You may wish to open two instances of Paradox in order to make copying and pasting easier.*

Another technique is to simply add the needed code to your existing forms. All framework forms have the same default methods and declarations at the form level. You can copy the following events from a framework form to the old form. Then, manually add the form to the menu.

- TYPE
- USES
- VAR
- MENUACTION
- OPEN

Summary

The Application Framework allows you to create Windows applications that look and feel like other Windows applications. Just as Visual Basic requires various DLLs, your Application Framework applications still require Paradox. You can distribute your applications with the full version of Paradox or just the Runtime. If you use the Paradox Distribution Expert (PDE) that comes with the Paradox Runtime, your applications will be compressed and installed with a slick installation program custom-created for your application.

APPENDIX A

Prestwood's Coding Convention: Paradox Edition

A coding convention consists of the rules that you use to type your code, names, objects, and so on. Every programming language is flexible in how you use it. For example, the idea to use the built-in object variables self, subject, and container as much as possible can be part of a coding convention. How you personally or your business decides to use these flexible areas of the language is your coding convention—for example, what names you choose to name variables, UIObjects, forms, and so on. Developing a consistent coding convention is very important. With a good, consistent coding convention, your code is much easier to read and maintain. In the long run, it saves you time. In order for programmers to use it, a coding convention needs to be simple and easy to remember. Prestwood's Coding Convention is comprised of the coding convention used by Prestwood Software & Consulting, and is the coding convention adopted by many other businesses.

An updated version of PCC is available on the Prestwood Software & Consulting Internet site. Go to http://prestwood.net/pcc.

You are free to adopt PCC as a whole or adapt it into your own coding convention.

Adopting PCC

You are free to adopt and use PCC as a whole as long as you don't change anything and as long as you leave the name intact. If you choose this path, then to make changes, additions, or deletions to the coding convention, you'll go through a formal process with Prestwood Software & Consulting. Send proposed changes and additions to

Fax: 1 (916) 726-5676
Internet Mail: pcc@prestwood.com
Internet proposal form: http://prestwood.net/cs/pcc.html

Adapting PCC

When you adapt a coding convention, you tailor it to your needs by adding and deleting standards and guidelines. You are free to borrow specific parts and sections from PCC to create your own coding convention. Optionally, you can give credit to PCC and Prestwood Software & Consulting.

Standard Versus Suggestion

Throughout this document, you will see the terms "standard" and "suggestion" used carefully. A standard is a coding convention that you must follow for your application to be PCC compliant. A suggestion is just that, a suggestion. Although following the suggested coding convention is wise, there will be plenty of exceptions.

Business Objects and Structured Programming

Although the use of business objects and structured programming deals more with program design and architecture and is slightly out of the scope of any coding convention, both are something that every programmer should study and strive for, and are therefore included in PCC. This section gives you a very short introduction to using business objects and structured programming. Its intent is to encourage you to study program design and how it relates to your coding convention.

Use Business Objects Standard

The technique of using business objects to help design the architecture of your application is really an object-oriented approach to designing software. In common practice, business objects have some type of relationship with the database. Business objects have two functions. They allow you to focus much of the database access of an application into business objects and they allow you to store the business rules in the object. The idea is to store data in tables in your database and to store the code that retrieves, manipulates, and uses that data in an appropriate business object. (Business objects are sometimes referred to as business entity objects for this reason.) For example, you could have a Customer table that stores the data for each customer and a **Customer** business object that retrieves, manipulates, and uses the data. The business object would store the business routines (the business rules). Some designers of software go so far as to create one business object per table. PCC does not recommend that approach—it seems too rigid.

When designing the architecture for your Paradox application, it is a common practice to create a library to store frequently used routines. Sometimes these libraries become very large and hard to use. A better approach is to break down routines by business objects. Figure A-1 shows a sample class hierarchy from Rational Rose showing a base **Person** class with two descendant classes: **Customer** and **Employee**. ObjectPAL doesn't support inheritance yet, so you can't create a base class with a descendant class. You can't, for example, create a base **Person** class and a descendant **Customer** class that inherits all the attributes and functionality of the **Person** class. Even with this restriction, you can still use this object-oriented approach to software design and create the lower **Customer** and **Employee** business objects (use one business object per ObjectPAL library).

The following simple example will demonstrate converting a typical **pushButton**-level routine into using a business object. You'll notice that it takes a little more effort to code this way, but the benefits of reusing the code later warrant the extra time spent now. The following code displays the number of orders a customer has placed. This might be useful, for example, if your client has a business rule that specifies the customer gets a discount on every 10 orders.

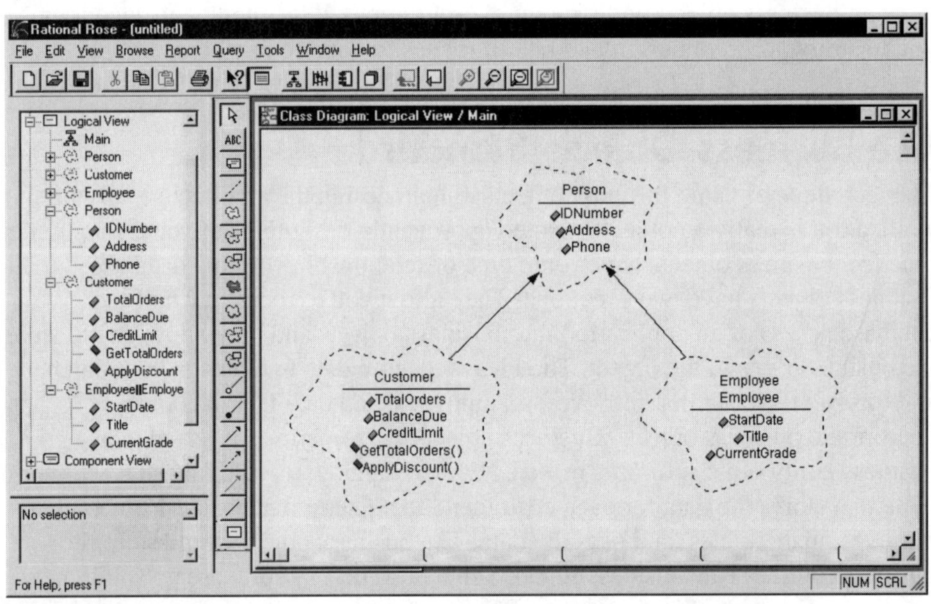

FIGURE A-1 A sample class hierarchy

The following code on the pushButton event of a button accomplishes the task in a traditional, code as low as you can, technique.

```
; Button :: pushButton
method pushButton(var eventInfo Event)
   const
      TBLCUSTOMER = "Customer"
   endConst
   var
      tcCustomer     TCursor
      dynCustomer    DynArray[] AnyType
      liOrders       LongInt
      nRemainder    Number
    endVar

   dynCustomer["Customer No"] = "1231"

   tcCustomer.open(TBLCUSTOMER)
   if not tcCustomer.setGenFilter(dynCustomer) then errorShow() endIf
      liOrders = tcCustomer.cCount("Customer No")
      nRemainder = liOrders.mod(10)

   if nRemainder = 0 then
      msgInfo("Customer Discount", "Give customer a 10% discount.")
   else
      msgInfo("Customer Discount",
      "No discount this time. Customer has " + String(SmallInt(10 -
      ; nRemainder)) + " orders to go before they get the discount.")
   endIf
endMethod
```

Taking this code and translating it into using a business object requires creating and then using a library. The following is the translated business object (in the form of a library), starting with the Var window of the library:

```
;Library :: Var
Var
   tcCustomer TCursor
endVar
```

The following is the Const window of the library:

```
;Library :: Const
Const
   TBLCUSTOMER = "Customer"
endConst
```

The following is the open event of the library:

```
;Library :: open
method open(var eventInfo Event)
   tcCustomer.open(TBLCUSTOMER)
endMethod
```

The following is the first of two custom methods for this new business object. This custom method gathers the total orders for a customer. Since this part of the code was a good candidate for reuse, it was made into its own custom method.

```
;Library :: cmGetTotalOrders
method cmGetTotalOrders(CustomerNumber String) LongInt
  var
    dynCustomer DynArray[] AnyType
    liOrders         LongInt
  endVar

  dynCustomer["Customer No"] = CustomerNumber

  if not tcCustomer.setGenFilter(dynCustomer) then errorShow() endIf

  liOrders = tcCustomer.cCount("Customer No")

   return(liOrders)
 endMethod
```

The following is the second custom method. It makes use of the cmGetTotalOrders custom method and returns a True or False.

```
;Library :: cmApplyDiscounts
method cmApplyDiscount(CustomerNumber String) Logical
   var
```

```
      liOrders    LongInt
      nRemainder  Number
   endVar

   liOrders = cmGetTotalOrders(CustomerNumber)

   nRemainder = liOrders.mod(10)

   if nRemainder = 0 then
      return(True)
   else
      return(False)
   endIf
endMethod
```


Once you have created this library, you can then use it. The following is the code that uses the business object starting with the Uses window of the form:

```
;Form :: Uses
Uses ObjectPAL
   "CustomerObject.lsl" ;Customer business object.
endUses
```

The following is the Var window of the form. It's a good idea to declare library variables at the form level.

```
;Form :: Var
Var
   libCustomerObject Library
endVar
```

The following is the init event of the form. It's a good idea to open all global libraries in the form's init event.

```
;Form :: Init
method init(var eventInfo Event)
   libCustomerObject.open(":files:CustomerObject")
endMethod
```

The following is the actual code that uses the library. It is in the button's pushButton event.

```
;Button :: pushButton
method pushButton(var eventInfo Event)
  var
    sCustomerNumber String
  endVar

  sCustomerNumber = "1231"

  if libCustomerObject.cmApplyDiscount(sCustomerNumber) then
     msgInfo("Customer Discount", "Give customer a 10% discount.")
  else
     msgInfo("Customer Discount",
     "No discount this time. Customer has " + String(10 -
     ; libCustomerObject.cmGetTotalOrders(sCustomerNumber)) +
     ; " total orders.")
  endIf
endMethod
```

As you study the technique of using business objects more, you might be tempted to put all the functionality of retrieving the data from a table into the appropriate business object and use the business object exclusively. PCC doesn't recommend that technique. Encapsulating all the functionality of retrieving data from a table into the business object would require you to abandon the use of a form's data model. To me, that is too big a sacrifice. The data model is a powerful tool and should be used. Use business objects in conjunction with the data model. In other words, for displaying data on a form, use a data model with defined fields and table frames. When you want to use a TCursor, open a table, find a value, and use it. That is a routine that is a prime target to move to a business object.

Once you become accustomed to thinking in business objects, you'll find this technique quite natural. When you need to accomplish a task (add a routine to your application), you'll find yourself stepping back and thinking, "What business object does this routine belong to?" As your application grows, you'll find that you can reuse your code more efficiently than ever.

Structured Programming

Structured programming is a programming technique used in the design and coding of computer programs. The approach assumes the disciplined use of a few basic coding structures and the use of top-down concepts to decompose large blocks of code into smaller blocks of code, making the overall program management easier to debug and maintain. Structured programming is concerned with improving the programming process through better organization of code.

Top-Down Programming and Design

Top-down programming is a way of organizing your code so that it begins with the most general statement of a program and divides it into increasingly more detailed routines. With most applications, you start by writing down the main goal of the application. After all parties agree on the main goal of the application, you start to form sections of tasks. For example, say that your goal is as follows:

> "The invoicing application is going to generate and print invoices for our company. In addition, it will keep track of all customers, vendors, and stock."

The next step is to break down this statement into sections: Track customers, vendors, and stock. Allow data input of invoices, and data output to a printed invoice. In Paradox, these sections can directly translate into forms and reports. The next step is to break down each section even further into subsections. For example, "Track customers" can be broken down into data input and data output into a Customer table. In turn, data input can be broken down into input name and address, buying patterns, and so on. In an event-driven environment such as Paradox, not all of these low subsections will translate into code. Only after you have listed all the subsections for a section and all the sections of an application should you decide which subsections are to be translated into code and interactive features.

High Cohesiveness Suggestion

Each custom method and custom procedure that you write should do one thing only. Determining what that one thing is can be difficult, but the time you spend up front, logically breaking up large routines into smaller ones, will pay off in the long term. Moving these routines into business objects will allow for even greater reuse later.

Low Coupling Suggestion

Each custom method or custom procedure should be as independent as possible from all other custom methods/procedures. If a custom method is called only by another custom method, for example, then the called custom method should be moved to the calling custom method and translated into a custom procedure. The following two custom methods, cmProcessNumber and cmMyMethod, can be combined into a single custom method. Only when cmProcessNumber is needed by other custom methods should it become a custom method.

```
;Custom Method :: cmProcessNumber
method cmProcessNumber(n Number) Number
   ;Do something wonderful with n.
   return n
endMethod
;Custom Method :: cmMyMethod
method cmMyMethod()
   cmProcessNumber(fldEnterNumber.value)
   ;Do something else wonderful with n.
endMethod
```

Because cmProcessNumber is not needed by any other custom method, it should be moved to within cmMyMethod, as in the following example:

```
;Custom Method :: cmMyMethod
proc cpProcessNumber(n Number) Number
   ;Do something wonderful with n.
   return n
endProc
method cmMyMethod()
   cpProcessNumber(fldEnterNumber.value)
   ;Do something else wonderful with n.
endMethod
```

The exception is if cmProcessNumber is likely to be reused elsewhere. If it is, leave it higher in the containership path or in a business object.

Avoid a Large Number of Private Custom Procedures Standard

As you are writing code in a single method, you will often move parts of code to above the method. When you get above five or six private custom procedures, then analyze the private custom procedures that you are creating and see whether any of them are generic enough to use with other methods. If they are generic enough for possible future reuse, then move them to a custom method. If the new custom method belongs to a business object, then move it to the appropriate business object library.

Avoid Copy-and-Paste Programming Suggestion

Whenever possible, take the time to combine reusable code into custom methods and access those custom methods from multiple spots. Do this even when the custom method must behave slightly differently in two different situations. The analysis needed to make this custom method generic will pay for itself later in reuse.

Limit the Size of Routines Standard

Limit the size of methods, custom methods, and custom procedures. Some experts in structured programming suggest limiting the number of lines of code to between 5 and 10. Some say between 10 and 25 is acceptable. This decision is up to you. In PCC, we limit the number of lines for a single routine to 25. As the number of lines for a single method grows above 10, however, start thinking about breaking parts of it into a custom procedure or custom method.

Limit the Number of Arguments Standard

Avoid more than three or four arguments (parameters) per custom method or custom procedure. More than three or four is a strong indication that your method, custom method, or custom procedure is trying to do too much. The PCC limit is eight. That is, no custom method or procedure can have more than eight parameters. If you need more than eight parameters, then you must use an array or record structure and pass it.

Avoid Using Flags Suggestion

Flags are sometimes necessary when you are stumped, but, in general, avoid them.

Avoid Global Variables Suggestion

Avoid the use of variables declared at the form level Var window. Many times they are useful and necessary, but don't overuse them—particularly when two variables declared lower in the containership hierarchy would be better. There are many notable exceptions to this suggestion, including the declaration of business object library variables.

Avoid Using Literals Standard

Using constants rather than literals can save on maintenance. For example, if you have a tax constant set up and the tax rate changes, you have only one place to change the value. The standard here is to make a literal a constant when it is used more than once. For example, take the following code snippet:

```
var
    tcCustomer     TCursor
    tvCustomer     TableView
endVar

tcCustomer.open(":App:Customer")
;Use tcCustomer here.

tvCustomer.open(":App:Customer")
```

Notice the string literal is used twice. This code should be rewritten so the string literal is a constant as follows:

```
const
TBLCUSTOMER = ":App:Customer"
endConst
var
    tcCustomer     TCursor
    tvCustomer     TableView
endVar

tcCustomer.open(TBLCUSTOMER)
;Use tcCustomer here.

tvCustomer.open(TBLCUSTOMER)
```

Use Switch over Nested If Statements Standard

A switch block is always preferred over nested if statements even if the nested if statements are only two deep.

Application Framework Standard

The PCC standard is that all new Paradox applications must use Paradox's Application Framework.

Application Checklist Suggestion

Whenever you start a new project, you should develop an application checklist. Usually, you do this before you start to code. A checklist guides you through an application. It enables you to step back and look at the features that you want to include in your application. A checklist helps you develop clearer, more professional applications. Here is a checklist that you can follow:

1. Use a splash screen.
2. Use either a main menu form as a navigator style button form or a menu system (preferably using the Application Framework menu system).
3. Either the splash screen, the main menu form, or a script should check for all needed aliases at application startup, and add them if possible.
4. If possible, set the correct working directory in the init event. If your application depends on objects in the current working directory, then you should either change the working directory for the user (if necessary) or at least check and automatically close with an error.
5. Use a consistent color and object scheme. Using a single style sheet per application will go a long way to achieving this goal.
6. Supply a help system for your application—preferably a Windows help file with context-sensitive help.

7. If you include a text file or a Microsoft Write file, include a button—or some other easy way—to launch the file with Notepad or Write. For example:

```
if isFile("TEXTFILE.WRI") then    ;Check for TEXTFILE.WRI.
   execute("WORDPAD TEXTFILE.WRI") ;If it is there, open it.
else
  beep()                          ;If it is not, let the user
  message("File not found")       ;know.
endIf
```

8. Include a button or menu option to exit the application. Having the user double-click on the Close box in the upper-left corner of the form isn't sufficient for full applications.

Gradually, you will develop your own application checklist and even a few template forms to speed your developing time. Your goal is to create a master checklist that you can use to develop applications that are Windows 95/98 compliant and have your own style stamped on them.

One Style Sheet per Application Suggestion

Use only one style sheet for forms and one style sheet for reports per application. This alone will go a long way to giving your application a consistent look and feel.

Main Directory Naming Suggestion

Use a descriptive name for the main directory of your application. Use names such as SECRETS, DESKTOP, and INVOICE. Do not use names such as DATA, WORK, WORKING, or FORMS.

Main Form Naming Suggestion

Name the main form in the directory the same name as the directory. For example, INVOICE.FSL is the main form in the INVOICE directory.

Documenting a Form Standard

If you have general comments about a particular form, then put them above the init event.

Documenting a Library Standard

If you have general comments about a particular library, then put them above the open event.

Commenting Suggestion

Comment your code liberally. Use a complete sentence starting with a capital and ending with a period. Seeing normal English in code really sets your remarks apart from your code.

White Space and Formatting Standard

Use white space to make your code easier to read. In ObjectPAL, white space does not matter. For example, you can place more than one command per line, as in the following:

```
var s1, s2 String endVar s1 = "Monica" s2 = "Arias-LaRheir"
; msgInfo("Name", s1 + " " + s2)
```

The preferred way to write the preceding line, however, is as follows:

```
var
   sFirst String
   sLast  String
endVar

sFirst = "Monica "
sLast = "Arias-LaRheir"
msgInfo("Name", sFirst + " " + sLast)
```

Here is an example of code that is hard to read because its syntax style is inconsistent:

```
method pushButton(var eventInfo Event)
VAR s     String  EndVar
s="Enter your name" s.VIEW()
if  s.isBlank() or s="Enter your name" Then
MSGStop("Operation Stopped","You must type in your name.")
return else msgInfo("","Hello "+s)  EndIf
Message("Goodbye " + s)
endMethod
```

s is used for a string variable. In this case, that's not so bad because *s* is the only variable. When you have three or more variables, however, nondescriptive variable names make the code difficult to read.

The formatting in this example is poor. The capitalization and formatting are inconsistent. Whether you choose to capitalize some characters and not others is not important. Whether you choose to tab sections of code or insert several spaces to set off sections of code also is not important. What is important is that you remain consistent.

Here is the same piece of code formatted in a consistent style:

```
method pushButton(var eventInfo Event)
   var
      str     String
   endVar

   str = "Enter your name"
   str.view()

   if str.isBlank() or str = "Enter your name" then
     msgStop("Operation Stopped","You must type in your name.")
     return
   else
     msgInfo("","Hello " + str)
   endIf
   message("Goodbye " + str)
endMethod
```

How much faster can you figure out what this second piece of code does? It's much easier to read and understand. The variable has a new name. Tabs are used in sections of code and the capitalization is consistent. White space is also used.

Now, add comments and the Prestwood Coding Convention (PCC) to the code to help others read it—or to refresh your memory later:

```
method pushButton(var eventInfo Event)
   ;This code demonstrates using view() for input
   var
      sName      String               ;Declares sName as a String.
   endVar

   sName = "Enter your name"          ;Setup variable to prompt user.
   sName.view()                      ;Shows user the current value. Also
                                      ;prompts user.

   ;Test user input.
   if sName.isBlank() or sName = "Enter your name" then
     msgStop("Operation Stopped","You must type in your name.")
     return                          ;If bad data, displays above
                                     ;message and aborts.
   else
      msgInfo("","Hello " + sName) ;Displays message.
   endIf
   message("Goodbye " + sName)        ;Says goodbye.
endMethod
```

Obviously, this version of the code is the clearest. Sometimes, though, you don't have time to remark a piece of code this heavily, but try to at least comment the sections of code. You should, however, always have time to format it, because you can do this as you go. If you're working under a deadline, you might set aside these good programming techniques in order to get the job done. Usually, however, you can afford to spend a little time now to document your code in order to save yourself and others a lot of time later. Here's a good rule of thumb: If you are writing code that others will see or that you might reuse, take the time to format and comment it fully; otherwise, comment as much as is appropriate.

Use Compiler Warnings and Compile with Debug Standard

Every form, library, and script should have Compiler Warnings and Compile with Debug checked. These two options allow for better warning messages, making developing and debugging in ObjectPAL much easier and therefore more enjoyable.

Use an Alias for Your Data Directory Standard

If you are using the Application Framework, then all your local data will be in a directory referred to by the Paradox generated Tables alias. If you are not using the Application Framework, place all your data in a separate directory from your application and refer to it through a single alias (preferably named Tables).

Code Header Standard

Many times, you will forget how a custom method or procedure works, and perhaps even what it does. Even if you're the one who wrote it, you might have to study it as if someone else wrote it. You can avoid this problem if you take a little extra time while developing to format and comment your code.

It is not code that obfuscates readability; it is the programmer. ObjectPAL has the potential to be very comprehensible. The use of consistent programming standards can make code quite easy to read. If you format your code consistently, and use common sense when naming variables, others will be able to understand your code—and so will you. The PCC standard is to place a flower-style comment box above every routine and to comment every line of code that is not self-explanatory. The flower-style comment box can be of any style, but should be consistent within each application. The following is the flower box created when you use the third-party Paradox tool Paradox Workbench:

```
{----------------------------------------------------------
Title: MyForm::MyButton::pushButton
By: Mike Cottle
Date: 12:45:14 PM, 3/15/1999
Company Name: Prestwood Software & Consulting
Description:
Modification History:
----------------------------------------------------------}
```

Camel Cap Method Names Standard

Although method and procedure names are not case sensitive, be consistent. For methods, procedures, and variables, stick with the capitalization that the manuals use. Except for the first word of the name, the first letter of every word is capitalized, as in setMouseShape(), setMouseScreenPosition(), play(), and msgYesNoCancel(). Take advantage of descriptive variable names—for example, tblOrders, arNames, and nCounter. Being consistent with your code increases its readability.

Use errorTrapOnWarnings Suggestion

Unless you can think of a good reason not to, every form should have errorTrapOnWarnings(True) in the form init event. This raises warning errors to critical errors and makes developing in ObjectPAL much easier. One notable exception is when your are using Paradox's Application Framework. The Application Framework was coded in such a way as to make using errorTrapOnWarnings() impossible, so this suggestion applies to non-Application Framework applications only.

Form-Level Coding Suggestion

In general, avoid putting code at the form level. When you put code at the form level, ObjectPAL executes the method for every object, even when you don't use the prefilter level. In general, consider putting code that does not require the prefilter at the page level. The code still executes when the event bubbles. Do not confuse the form level with the prefilter level. The prefilter level is still a great location for writing generic routines. The one exception to this rule is the init event, which was added in version 7 so that you can move code from the open event and put it in the init event so that the form will open faster.

Menu Trapping Suggestion

When building menus, the preferred way to trap for user selection is to use menu IDs (not strings) and to offset your user-defined menu IDs with the built-in ObjectPAL UserMenu constant. The first number represents the position of the menu, while the following two numbers represent the menu option's position under the main menu option. For each cascading menu, add a number. The following example of a typical menu system illustrates:

Menu Option	Menu Constant ID	Notes
File | Open	UserMenu + 101	The first 1 is for File (File is in the first position). The 01 is because Open is the first option under File.
Separator	None	Separators are not included in this numbering convention.
File | Exit	UserMenu + 102	The 02 is because Exit is the second option under File.
Edit | Cut	UserMenu + 201	The 2 is because Edit is in the second position.
Edit | Copy	UserMenu + 202	
Edit | Paste	UserMenu + 203	
Record | Insert	UserMenu + 301	
Record | Delete | Field Value	UserMenu + 3021	The added 1 is for Field Value, which is the first option under Delete.
Record | Delete | Record	UserMenu + 3022	
Help | About	UserMenu + 401	

Don't Use Reserved Words for Names Standard

The names of commands, keywords, functions, system variables, and operators are all reserved words. These words should not be used as object variable names. Even though you can use reserved words in certain circumstances and not get an error—for example, you are permitted to name an object array—don't. Sometimes your code can pass the syntax checker but still cause a run-time error. Also, it's confusing to read code in which you can't distinguish the names of objects and variables from the names of commands. For example, although you could use <u>to</u> as the name of an object, you couldn't use it in ObjectPAL. If you used <u>to</u> as the name of an object and typed the following command, you would get the message Error: Identifier expected error:

```
to.moveTo()     ;to is incorrectly named. You can't use keywords
                ;for names of objects.
```

You also might get a run-time error in addition to immediate syntax errors. At the very least, your code will be hard to read.

Avoid the use of keywords to name objects. It's good programming practice to make sure that you don't name objects the same name as a method or procedure (or any language element). Avoid using the names of methods and procedures for object names (even though it's permitted). For example, in the following,


```
moveTo.moveTo()
```

the first moveTo is the name of an object. This is permitted, but the code is confusing.

Use Real Names Standard

Paradox goes along way to being self-documenting if you use real names for variables and object names. The capability to use real names in ObjectPAL shouldn't be taken lightly. Easy-to-read code is very helpful when several people are developing an application or when an application becomes very large. Resist using archaic computer initials. For example, decide which of the following you consider clearer:

```
1:   x = x + 1
2:   Counter = Counter + 1
```

Obviously, the Counter version, line 2, is a much clearer use of a variable name. You might remember that, in algebra, x is used to substitute for numbers. That familiarity might lead you to overuse x as a variable name. For the sake of clarity, resist the temptation to use arcane variables. Use descriptive variable names and descriptive object names.

Built-In Object Variables Suggestion

Use the built-in object variables as much as possible. In general, using the built-in variables promotes generic code and generic code is often more reusable.

Use the Value Property Standard

When referring to the value of an object, it is always preferred to use the value property. This one is not mandatory, but it does make your code more readable, because you and the compiler can tell at a glance that you are looking at a UIObject. Table A-2 that appears later shows a few examples.

Referring to Fields with a TCursor Standard

When using a TCursor to refer to fields in a table, always use quotation marks, or dereference with parentheses. There are two ways to refer to a field using a TCursor—*tc.Last_Name*, *tc."Last_Name"*—and a third for dereferencing: *tc.(2)*. The preferred usage for referencing a field is with quotation marks. For example, in *tc."Name"*, it is clear that *Name* is a field.

Referring to Columns with Local SQL Standard

Since single quotes are not allowed when referring to fields using a TCursor, the PCC standard for referring to fields using both local SQL or a TCursor is to use quotation marks (sometimes referred to as double quotes). The following SQL statement abides by the PCC standard:

```
select o."City"
from Orders o
```

The following usage of a TCursor abides by the PCC standard:

```
var
    tcCustomer TCursor
endVar

tcCustomer.open("Customer")
msgInfo("", tcCustomer."City")
```

Notice the use of double quotes in the previous two examples to refer to the City field even when quotes (single or double) was not required.

Use True in Place of Yes Standard

For a logical, ObjectPAL allows both True and Yes. For example, the following two lines of code are equivalent:

```
errorTrapOnWarnings(True)
errorTrapOnWarnings(Yes)
```

Since True is more standard throughout the industry, the PCC standard is to always use True.

Be Specific Suggestion

When you have an option and there is no clear reason to do otherwise, use specific coding. For example, although tc.open("CUSTOMER") will open a Paradox table, the preferred syntax is tc.open("CUSTOMER.DB"). One other example: when executing action() and menuAction(), be specific. Do not use action(Constant); instead, use active.action(Constant).

DisableDefault Versus SetErrorCode() Suggestion

In general, use setErrorCode(UserError) rather than disableDefault to disable the built-in behavior whenever possible.

Button Tab Stop Standard

The tab stop property for buttons should be set to True. Because the default for Windows applications is to allow the user to move from button to button with the TAB key, so should the applications you develop in Paradox.

Wide Scroll Bar Standard

Use the wide scroll bar only—the thin default scroll bar just isn't standard.

Naming Convention Suggestion

By looking at your code, you should be able to easily distinguish between objects and variables. Furthermore, you should be able to distinguish between UIObjects that you have named and the UIObjects that Paradox has named. Use any naming convention you wish. Just be consistent.

The following are some naming rules and warnings:

- Generally, name an object only if you reference it in your ObjectPAL code or for clarity.
- Do not reference noise names. Noise names are the default names that Paradox gives objects—they always start with #. There are several reasons for not using noise names in your ObjectPAL code. One of them is that the names change with foreign versions of Paradox. For example, #Page2 becomes #Sida2 in the Swedish version.
- Names of objects and variables are limited to 64 characters. Shorter is better, however.
- The first character must be a letter A–Z, a–z, or an underscore.
- After the initial character, you can use letters, digits, extended ANSI, and any of the following three characters: $, !, _. Although you can use $, !, and _, avoid them.
- No spaces or tabs are allowed.
- Object and variable names are case insensitive.
- Generally, it is considered good programming not to duplicate language elements. Do not use date, time, method, var, and so on to name objects or variables.

Naming Variables Standard

Hungarian notation is a variable naming scheme. All variables of a given type should start with a lowercase prefix. The system PCC uses is a variation on the Hungarian notation style of naming objects.

1. Start with a lowercase descriptor (a character or characters that represent the variable or object type); for example, *s* for string, *si* for small integer, *tc* for TCursor, *mnu* for a menu variable, *sec* for secondary indexes, and so on. This descriptor should be one to three characters and as consistent with the *ObjectPAL Reference Guide* as possible (although it is not always consistent).

2. Follow the variable descriptor with a short description of the variable in camel caps—for example, *sFirstName*, *siCounter*, *tcCustomer*, *fOrders*, *secState*, and so on.

3. If you need two or more variables with similar names, increment the descriptor—not the short description (*tc1Customer*, *tc2Customer*).

4. Use common sense when naming objects. After the initial 1- to 3-character beginning, use a common-sense, camel-caps description. For example, use the table name for Table and TCursor variables (*tcOrders*, *tcCustomer*, *tc1Lineitem*, *tc2Lineitem*). Use the name of the table or field to name objects that are defined to a table or a field (*tfOrders, fldLast_Name*).

5. Use full English words for the short camel-cap description, but also keep it short—for example, *tblOrders* and *fldLastName*. In addition, avoid useless extra characters such as *siCounterVariable* (instead, use *siCounter*). As one final example, if you have a field UIObject with a label of *Working Directory*, do not use *fldWorkingDirectory* (instead, use *fldWorking*, or, better yet, *fldWork*). Remember, a coding convention should save you time in the long run; shorter names are preferred.

Naming Scratch Variables Standard

If you have to use scratch or temporary variables, the preferred naming convention for temporary variables is to just use the descriptor only. If you declare a variable within a method, it is acceptable to use only the descriptor. This may seem as if it is making your code more ambiguous, but in the long run, it helps the programmer code fast. For example:

```
method pushButton(var eventInfo Event)
  var
     s1, s2    String   ;Strings start with s.
     si        Smallint ;Small integers start with si.
     tc        TCursor  ;TCursors start with tc.
  endVar

  s1 = "CUSTOMER.DB"
  tc.open( s1 )

  si = 3
  s2 = tc.(si)               ;Note in this line you can easily
  s2.view()                  ;tell what each variable type is.
endMethod
```

Note several conventions in the preceding text that were used to make the code easier to read. In the preceding example, all code is indented a single tab inside a code block. All code inside the method block is indented an additional tab. Also, the variable declarations are indented one more tab than the var block. Note also that when two string variables were needed, *s1* and *s2* were used.

Naming Objects Standard

Naming UIObjects requires a little different naming convention than naming variables. The following are the rules used with PCC when naming an object:

1. If you rename an object, start it with a lowercase descriptor and use camel caps after the descriptor, just as with variables—for example, fldName, boxHeaderFrame, tfOrders, and recOrders.

2. Do not rename objects that Paradox names for you. Renaming objects unnecessarily is a waste of time and energy. For example, when you define a field object to a field in a table, Paradox names the field object the same name as the field.

3. Only rename objects if you use them in your ObjectPAL code. Renaming objects from noise names unnecessarily is a waste of time and energy. The symbol table holds variables and object names.
4. Never refer to noise names in your ObjectPAL code. Object noise names can be reshuffled when you deliver your form. This includes record objects of TableFrames and MROs. If you need to distinguish among the various duplicated record objects during View Data mode, then use the rowNo property of the record object.

Tables A-1 through A-5 show you many examples of naming variables and objects in ObjectPAL.

Object	Example	Description
AnyType	anyUserInput	Start with any
Array	arNames	Start with ar
Binary	bCorelDrawing	Start with b
Currency	cTotal	Start with c
Date	dBeginDate	Start with d
DateTime	dtFileStamp	Start with dt
DynArray	dynSysInfo	Start with dyn
Graphic	gEmployee	Start with g
Logical	lFlag	Start with l
LongInt	liCounter	Start with li
Memo	mNotes	Start with m
Number	nCounter	Start with n
OLE	oWinword	Start with o
Point	pBoxPosition	Start with p
Record	recCustomerInfo	Start with rec
SmallInt	siCounter	Start with si
String	sLastName	Start with s
Time	tBeginTime	Start with t

TABLE A-1 Prestwood's Coding Convention for Data Variables

Preferred	Acceptable
fldName.value = "Greg Unsicker"	fldName = "Greg Unsicker"
Cust_No.value = 12	Cust_No = 12
btnToggleDates.value = True	btnToggleDates = True
txtReportTitle.value = "Sales Report"	txtReportTitle = "Sales Report"

TABLE A-2 Using the Value Property Is Preferred

One of the problems with many naming conventions is that they are cumbersome and overwhelming. Some naming conventions actually slow the programmer down. The nice thing about the naming convention used in PCC is that you can still use simple 1- to 3-letter variable names if you wish and still stay within all the rules. For example, you can still use *tc* for a TCursor and *s* for a string. Yet, when you need to be more descriptive, you can add the short description. For example, you can use *tcOrders* and *tcCustomer* for descriptive variables. The PCC naming convention even has the power to have many similarly named objects. For example, if you need several TCursor variables all pointing to the Customer table, you would use *tc1Customer*, *tc2Customer*, *tc3Customer*, and so on. In addition, you can easily tell the difference between UIObject names and variables. When reading your code weeks later, you instantly know whether you are looking at a string, TCursor, form, report variables, or a specific type of UIObject such as a field or a table frame.

Object	Example	Description
Application	app	Just use app (you never need more than one)
Database	dbOracle	Start with db and follow with type of database
DDE	ddeWinword	Start with dde and follow with server name
FileBrowserInfo	fbi	Start with fbi
FileSystem	fs	Start with fs
Form	fOrders	Start with f and follow with form filename

TABLE A-3 Prestwood's Coding Convention for Object Variables

Object	Example	Description
FormOpenInfo	fiOrders	Start with fi and follow with form filename
Library	libSecrets	Start with lib and follow with filename
Menu	mnuMain	Start with mnu
PopUpMenu	popEdit	Start with pop and follow with menu name
Query	qOrders	Start with q and follow with first table name
Report	rOrders	Start with r and follow with report filename
ReportOpenInfo	riOrders	Start with ri and follow with report filename
Session	ses	Start with ses
SQL	sqlCommit	Start with sql and follow with SQL filename
Table	tblCustomer	Start with tbl and follow with table name
TableView	tvOrders	Start with tv and follow with table name
TCursor	tcCustomer	Start with tc and follow with table name
TextStream	tsAutoexecBat	Start with ts and follow with filename
Toolbar	tbStandard	Start with tb and follow with toolbar name
UIObject	uiTargetStart	UIObject variables with ui

TABLE A-3 Prestwood's Coding Convention for Object Variables *(continued)*

Object	Example	Description
Custom methods	cmCalculateTotal	Start custom methods with cm
Custom procedures	cpCalculateTotal	Start custom procedures with cp
Custom actions	caCalculateTotal	Start with ca (see postAction)
Secondary indexes	secLast_Name	Start Paradox secondary indexes with sec
Indexes	iLASTNAME	Start dBASE indexes with i
Constants	kPi	Start user-defined constants with a k
Types	TPassArray	Start user-defined types with a capital T

TABLE A-4 Prestwood's Coding Convention for Miscellaneous Objects

Object	Example	Description
Field	fldLastName	Start field objects with fld
Button	btn	Start button objects with btn
TableFrame	tf	Start table frame objects with tf
MultiRecord Object	mro	Start multirecord objects with mro
Record	rec	Start record objects with rec
Crosstab	ct	Start crosstab objects with ct
Text	txt	Start text objects with txt
Box	box	Start box objects with box
Ellipse	cir	Start ellipse objects with cir
Graph	gph	Start graph objects with gph
Grouped Objects	grp	Start grouped objects with grp
Line	lin	Start line objects with lin

TABLE A-5 Prestwood's Coding Convention for UIObjects

To keep from filling up the symbol table, you may occasionally need to change an object's name back to its original noise name. To revert back to an object's noise name, delete the name you gave it.

Database Naming Standard

What you choose to name the tables of your database and the fields of your tables is as important as your own personal coding convention. What follows in this section are the PCC standards and suggestions for naming tables and columns.

Table Naming Standard

1. Use descriptive names for all tables.
2. Use camel caps to name your tables. For example, Customer, Orders, StockItems, and CustomerHistory.

3. Detail tables should have the same name as their master table, but end with the word "Details." For example, OrderDetails.
4. All lookup tables (reference tables) should use the same filenaming convention as master tables, but end with the word "Lookup"—for example, ZipLookup.

Column Naming Standard

1. Field names must be consistent throughout a database. For example, if you use Emp No as a field name, then stick with it throughout all tables. Do not allow yourself to use Employee Number, Emp Nu, or Emp #. Also, do not mix pieces of a field name. If you use No to mean number, then stick with it for all field names that require number as part of the field name (for example, Dept. No, Med. No, Phone No, and so on).
2. Use camel caps to name columns—for example, CustomerNumber, LastName, FirstName, and ZipCode.

Summary

The subjective part of every language can add to programmer confusion unless the programmer adopts a methodology for developing software. As an individual developer, you can be more creative in your naming convention. Large companies with many divisions will probably end up with a more strict and cryptic naming convention that, once you learn, will save you hours of time.

It's easy to get swept up in standards and overimplement them, creating huge, hard to use (perhaps ambiguous) standards that programmers use only because they are told to—not because they agree. All of the standards in a coding convention should be natural and easy to follow. A good test for "natural and easy" is to examine throwaway applications that were created quickly and for temporary reasons—which standards do they apply? The standards your best programmers apply on their throwaway applications are generally the gems. All other standards should be scrutinized carefully. Not that a standard should be thrown out just because the standard is not used, that is not the point. The standard still may be very necessary and better enforcement may need to be applied.

APPENDIX B

Debugging

Until now, it's been assumed that you are an excellent typist. Occasionally, you might have typed a routine incorrectly. In those cases, you had to spot the typo and debug the routine. This next section formally introduces the debugger. It gives you the tools you need to debug your code with confidence.

ObjectPAL offers an advanced debugging tool called the ObjectPAL debugger. The debugger is a set of features built into the ObjectPAL Editor that helps you debug your application. With the debugger, you can inspect variables, list the events called, step through code, and monitor various elements of your application.

Using the Debugger

The debugger included in Paradox is very powerful. You can view your running application using the following debugger windows: Breakpoints, Call Stack, Watches, Tracer, and debugger, as shown here:

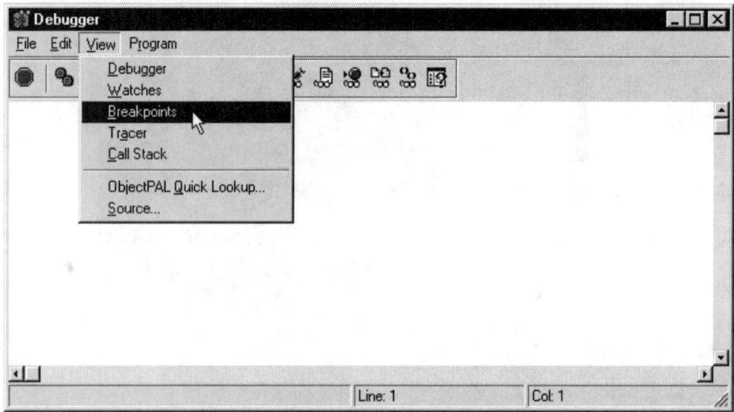

Entering and Exiting the Debugger

Any time you are in the ObjectPAL Editor, you can open any of the five ObjectPAL debugger windows from the View menu or with the appropriate toolbar icons. If your form or script is running, you can enter the debugger in three ways:

- If Compile with Debug is checked, add a debug() procedure to your code and run the form.

- If Enable CTRL+Break is checked, use CTRL+Break when the form is running.
- Set a breakpoint and run the form.

Placing a debug() statement in a method has the same effect as setting a breakpoint at a line. The advantage of debug() is that it is saved with the source code, so you don't have to keep resetting it as you would with a breakpoint. The setting for Compile with Debug is saved with the form and determines if debug() statements are ignored. When this option isn't checked, debug() statements are ignored. There is no need to uncheck this option before you deliver a form because the compiler strips out all debug() statements before it compiles. Using the debug() statement will not interrupt execution when the user runs the form.

To use the debug() procedure, follow these steps:

1. Place debug() in your code.
2. Make sure that Compile with Debug is checked.
3. Run the form.

One advantage of using the debug() procedure instead of setting a breakpoint is the ability to use it conditionally. For example:

```
if siCounter > 100 then
   ;Execute code.
else
   debug()
endIf
```

When using a debug() statement in a library, the Compile with Debug option must be selected from within the library for it to take effect.

The Breakpoints Window

One of the most effective techniques for debugging an application is to set a breakpoint and then step through your code. A *breakpoint* is a flag that you can set in your code that stops a form during run time and enters the debugger. The debugger enables you to inspect variables, step through your code, and much more. A common way of entering the debugger is by setting a breakpoint. When you choose Program | Toggle Breakpoint, the visual minus sign appears next to the active line, as shown next. Go ahead and type the code that you see in the illustration, put the cursor on the second msgStop(), and select Program | Toggle Breakpoint. In addition to selecting Toggle Breakpoint, you can double-click to the left of the line of code where you wish to place a breakpoint.

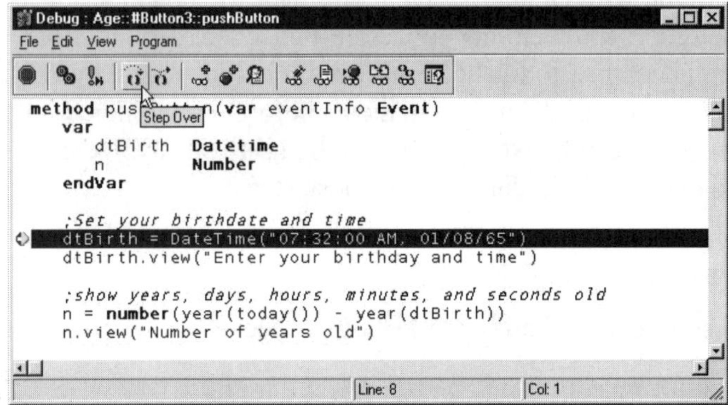

To see the currently set breakpoints, toggle the Breakpoints window open by selecting View | Breakpoints, as shown next. Right-click the Breakpoints window to gain access to its menu. When you run the form, execution stops right where you placed the breakpoint.

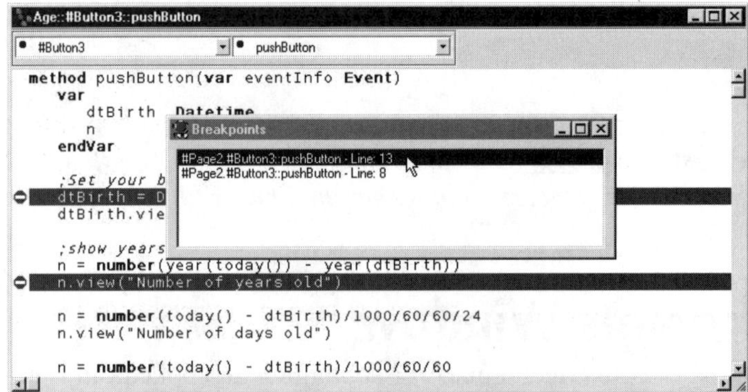

When you are in Debug mode, you have many options. For now, just select Program | Run or press F8 to continue execution. To use breakpoints, follow these steps:

1. Select the editor window where you want to put a breakpoint—for example, pushButton, newValue, Var, cmMyCustomMethod, and so on.
2. Place the cursor on the line on which you want the breakpoint to occur.
3. Select Program | Toggle Breakpoint.
4. Run the form.
5. To view the current breakpoints, select View | Breakpoints to display the Breakpoints windows.

The Call Stack Window

The Call Stack window is used after execution stops at a breakpoint. Select View | Call Stack to toggle the Call Stack window open. The Call Stack window lists all the events, custom methods, and custom procedures called since the form started running. The most recently called routine and its caller are listed first. This process continues all the way back to the first method or procedure.

The Call Stack window is most useful when you want to know where you are. For example, if you've called several custom methods in your code and you want to verify that a certain custom method was called, use View | Call Stack. To use the Call Stack window, follow these steps:

1. Set a breakpoint at the place in your code from which you want to start viewing the stack.
2. Run the form.
3. When the breakpoint occurs, select View | Call Stack. A list of all the called methods appears. Right-click the Call Stack window to view its menu.

The Watch Window

The Watch window allows you to watch variables as your form executes. To toggle the Watches window open, select View | Watches. To add a watch, select Program | Add Watch, or right-click on the Watch window, which is shown here:

The Tracer Window

ObjectPAL offers a powerful tracing utility that enables you to view the behind-the-scenes activity of your application. You can start the tracer before you run your form while in the Editor. The tracer is a window that logs all the activity of your code as the code executes.

The Properties | Tracer On option in the Tracer window toggles the tracer on. When the form is open, a window will display that traces the form, script, or report.

The Properties | Show Code option in the Tracer window toggles on and off when the Tracer lists each line of code as it executes.

The Properties | Built-In Events option in the Tracer window allows you to select any events that you wish to trace. If you check the Properties | Trace On option and you haven't selected any events to trace, the ObjectPAL tracer opens a window and lists each line of code as it executes. Use this method to trace only the code that you write. This is a wonderful way to find the location of a problem. To trace your code, follow these steps:

1. Make sure that Program | Compile with Debug is checked in the main Paradox menu.
2. Select Properties | Trace On from the Tracer menu. Make sure that no events are checked.
3. Make sure Properties | Show Code is checked from the Tracer menu.
4. Run the form.

The tracer requires that you have Program | Compile with Debug checked in order to trace your code. Compile with Debug has no effect on tracing built-in events.

Tracing Built-In Events

In addition to tracing only your code, you can trace your code and the events. If you check the View | Tracer | Properties | Built-In Events and then select some events to trace, the ObjectPAL tracer opens a window and lists each line of code and each event as it executes.

Checking an event indicates that you want that event traced; unchecked events are not traced. It doesn't matter whether the event has code attached to it. If you check the event, it will be traced. Figure B-1 shows the Select Built-In Events for Tracing dialog box with the action event selected. The action event is perhaps the most important event to trace.

When the box labeled Form Prefilter is checked, events are traced as they execute for the form and for the intended target object. Otherwise, events are traced only for the target object. Your settings for these options are saved with the form, so you don't have to check them every time you want to trace execution. When the tracer is open, execution proceeds normally. ObjectPAL provides

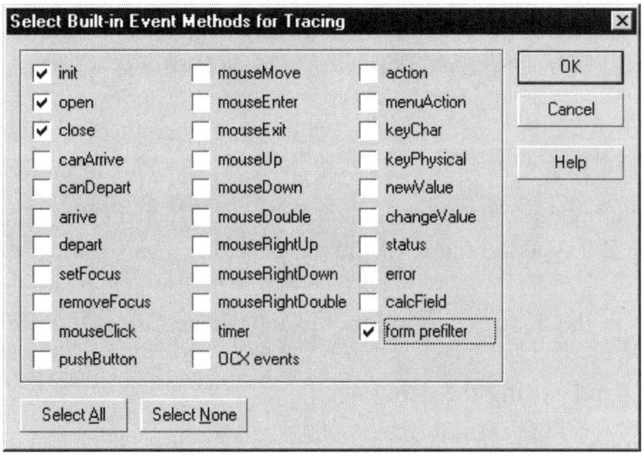

FIGURE B-1 The Select Built-In Events for Tracing dialog box

procedures for controlling the tracer. To trace your code and the events, follow these steps:

1. Select Properties | Built-In Events. Choose the built-in events that you want to trace (see Figure B-1). You can check any combination of events, but the fewer you check, the better. It will be easier to follow.
2. Make sure Properties | Trace On is checked.
3. Run the form.

You also can use the tracerOn() procedure in your ObjectPAL code, but you still have to manually select the combination of events that you want to trace.

The Debugger Window

You can get into and out of the debugger, but what can you do with it? When execution stops at a breakpoint, you can inspect variables. Paradox has a built-in way to check a variable's value at a certain point in your code. To check a value, set a break at the point in your code at which you want to check a variable, and run the form. When your program breaks, select Program | Inspect to inspect as many different variables as you want.

There are three steps in inspecting a variable:

1. Set a breakpoint at the place in your code where you want to view a variable.
2. Run the form.
3. When the breakpoint occurs, select Program | Inspect from the Debug window and type the name of the variable that you want to see.

The options in the debugger window fall into these four categories:

- Entering and exiting the debugger
- Inspecting variables
- Stepping through the application
- Monitoring the application

The following paragraphs describe the more important options in the debugger.

- **Program | Run** You can select this option before or after you set breakpoints or while you're in the debugger. If you haven't set any breakpoints, Run does nothing extra. After you set breakpoints, select Program | Run to run the form. Paradox saves all attached events, compiles the code, and runs the form. When Paradox encounters a breakpoint, execution halts and a debugger window opens. In effect, this is how you enter the debugger. When you're in a debugger window, this option enables you to continue execution from the breakpoint.
- **Program | Step Over** Select Program | Step Over to step through your code line by line. You can use this option after execution stops at a breakpoint.
- **Program | Step Into** Select Program | Step Into to step through every line in a custom procedure. You can use this option after execution stops at a breakpoint.
- **Program | Stop Execution** Select Program | Stop Execution to exit the debugger. This option halts execution and closes any debugger windows. You can use this option after execution stops at a breakpoint.
- **Program | Inspect** Select Program | Inspect to display and change the value of a variable. You can use this option when execution stops at a breakpoint.
- **Program | Origin** Select Program | Origin to return to the event that contains the current breakpoint. The cursor will appear on the line that contains the breakpoint. You can use this convenient feature when execution suspends at a breakpoint and your screen becomes cluttered.
- **Program | Compile with Debug** Check Program | Compile with Debug to stop execution whenever the debug() statement is encountered. Placing a debug() statement in an event has the same effect as setting a breakpoint at that line. Both can be saved to disk, but unlike a breakpoint, the debug() procedure is part of your code. This option tells Paradox to provide more detailed error information. In most situations, I recommend that you leave Compile with Debug checked—even if you never use the debug() statement.

NOTE *When do you want to uncheck Compile with Debug? Breakpoints can be saved in code. Leaving Compile with Debug on during development is OK, but it is recommended that you turn it off if you plan to distribute nondelivered forms, libraries, or scripts. With Compile with Debug checked, your form, library, or script is about 1/3 bigger and runs slower. For best performance, turn off Compile with Debug if you distribute undelivered forms, libraries, or scripts.*

- **Enable CTRL+Break** If you check Enable CTRL+Break, pressing CTRL+Break in the ObjectPAL Preferences dialog box, execution suspends and opens a debugger window that contains the active event, method, or procedure. This operation is similar to setting a breakpoint. If Enable CTRL+Break to enter the debugger isn't checked, pressing CTRL+Break still works, but it only halts execution. Although CTRL+Break halts the execution of ObjectPAL methods and procedures, other operations, such as queries, are not affected.

  It is also important to note that Enable CTRL+Break will stop execution when CTRL+Break is pressed, but you must also check Compile with Debug in order for CTRL+Break to enter the debugger.

TIP *Here is an undocumented tip. If you're like most programmers, the default error messages make sense most of the time, but not always. Select Program | Compile with Debug to get better error messages from the compiler. This applies even if you don't use the debug() procedure.*

The Enable CTRL+Break Option

To get into the debugger easily, use the Enable CTRL+Break option and press CTRL+Break. This technique suspends execution when your form is running. It enables you to decide on the fly whether—and where—you want to interrupt execution. Although this technique is less precise than setting a specific breakpoint or using the debug() procedure, you'll like its flexibility. To use CTRL+Break, follow these steps:

1. Select the Tools | Settings | Developer Preferences and check the Enable CTRL+Break option on the General tab.
2. Run the form.
3. Press CTRL+Break when you want to move into the debugger.

Stepping Through Your Application

Selecting Program | Step Over enables you to step through your code line by line. Selecting Program | Step Into enables you to step through every line in a event and through every line in a custom procedure that it calls.

To step through your code, follow these steps:

1. Set a breakpoint at the place in your code that you want to start stepping through.
2. Run the form.
3. When the breakpoint occurs, select Program | Step Into or Program | Step Over to execute the next piece of code.

If you want to try this, make sure that Compile with Debug is checked. Place the following code on a button and run the form:

```
;Button :: pushButton
method pushButton(var eventInfo Event)
   debug()

   message("1")
   message("2")
   message("3")
   message("4")
endMethod
```

After you run the form, click the button. The debugger window opens. Select Program | Step Into repeatedly to step through the messages.

Debugging Without the Debugger

The debugger is wonderful. Often, however, it's just as easy to debug code without the debugger as it is to set a breakpoint and go into the debugger. This section discusses general debugging techniques.

Debugging means locating the places where your application or routine doesn't work—but also the places where it does. If you're debugging, you're at a place where your application doesn't work, and you need to get to a place where it does work. One popular technique is to strip code and objects until something works, and then rebuild. ObjectPAL offers several ways to debug without the debugger.

Types of Errors

A *logic error* is an error in thinking. Often, you try to code something that doesn't make sense because it's a logic error. Logic errors are among the most difficult types of errors to diagnose. If you knew that your thinking was wrong, you wouldn't try to implement the code in the first place! A *run-time error* is an error that occurs while a form is being run, even though the routine has passed a syntax check. A *syntax error* is an error that occurs because of an incorrectly expressed statement. Syntax errors usually occur when you mistype a command or when you attempt to use a command that doesn't exist.

TIP *If you want tighter, cleaner code, turn on the Compiler Warnings option. It gives you better control over your code. For example, not declaring variables slows down your code. The Compiler Warnings option catches undeclared variables and warns you. To turn on this option, go into the ObjectPAL Editor and select Program | Compiler Warnings.*

Warning and Critical Errors

In ObjectPAL, two levels of errors occur: warning errors and critical errors. Because warning errors aren't critical errors, they display nothing during run time, or, at most, a message in the status bar. A key violation error is an example of this type of error. If you want to include a higher level of error trapping in your applications, use one of the following techniques:

- If the method or procedure returns a Logical, use it in an if statement.
- Use errorShow() to display the built-in error messages.
- Use a try structure to trap for errors.

Warning errors do not stop execution, whereas critical errors do. To illustrate, type the following code into the pushButton event of a button:

```
;btn1 :: pushButton
method pushButton(var eventInfo Event)
  var
```

```
      tc  TCursor
   endVar

   errorTrapOnWarnings(No)      ;Make sure warning errors
                                ;stay warning errors.

   msgInfo("", "Before error")
   tc.open("123xyz")            ;123xyz does not exist.
   msgInfo("", "After error")   ;This message does appear.
endMethod
```

Now, raise the warning error to a critical error. Type the following:

```
method pushButton(var eventInfo Event)
   var
      tc  TCursor
   endVar

   errorTrapOnWarnings(Yes)     ;Raise warning errors to
                                ;critical errors.

   msgInfo("", "Before error")
   tc.open("123xyz")            ;123xyz does not exist.
   msgInfo("", "After error")   ;Note that this message never appears.
endMethod
```

This is an important part of dealing with errors. Note that warning errors do not stop execution of code, whereas critical errors do.

Using the Built-In *error* Event

So far, I haven't discussed the built-in error event. Despite what you might think, the built-in error event is not the preferred place to put code. The reason is that the built-in error event is always called after the error occurs. Most of the time, you are going to want to know before the error occurs so that you can take appropriate steps. Sometimes, however, you will want to simply add to or alter an error message.

Use an *if* Statement to See Whether a Routine Is Successful

A technique commonly used for error checking is to use an if statement. Many methods and procedures return a Logical, and display or do one thing when a routine succeeds and another when it fails. For example, type the following into the pushButton event of a button:

```
;Button :: pushButton
method pushButton(var eventInfo Event)
  if isFile("AUTOEXEC.BAT") then   ;If exists, then
    message("File exists")          ;display "File exists".
  else                              ;If not,
    message("File does not exist") ;display "File does not".
  endIf
endMethod
```

I used a variation of the preceding error-checking routine in the form open routines in an earlier chapter:

```
if f.attach("My Form") then  ;MY FORM is a title.
  f.moveTo()
else
  f.open("MYFORM")           ;MYFORM is a filename.
endIf
```

You can use an if structure for many methods and procedures to give the user a better user-oriented message than the programmer-oriented, built-in error messages. For example, type the following code into the pushButton event of a button:

```
;Button :: pushButton
method pushButton(var eventInfo Event)
   var
      tbl  Table
   endVar

```

```
      if isTable("WORLD.DB") then
         tbl.attach("WORLD.DB")
      else
         msgStop("Oops!",
      "Could not find WORLD.DB. Check your working directory")
      endIf
   endMethod
```

Table.attach() returns True if the Table variable is associated with the table name. It doesn't report whether it is a valid table, or even that the file exists!

Use *errorShow()* in an *if* Statement

With Paradox, you can utilize the built-in error stack. To do this, you use the errorShow() procedure. The errorShow() procedure displays the Error dialog box with the current error information from the error stack. For example, type the following code into the pushButton event of a button:

```
;Button :: pushButton
method pushButton(var eventInfo Event)
   var
      tc TCursor
   endVar

   if not tc.open("xyz") then
      errorShow("Table xyz is missing or corrupt",
      "Try rebuilding or reinstalling")
   endIf
endMethod
```

If the open event fails for any reason, an error message is displayed. You won't see benefits of this type of error checking while you develop. Instead, the benefits come when users use your program. Without this extra code, you might get a telephone call from a user who says, "The program doesn't work. When I click this button, nothing happens." With the extra code, the user would get a specific message—for example, an error saying that a table doesn't exist (as shown next). The user could check whether the table exists on the disk, and you would be spared the telephone call.

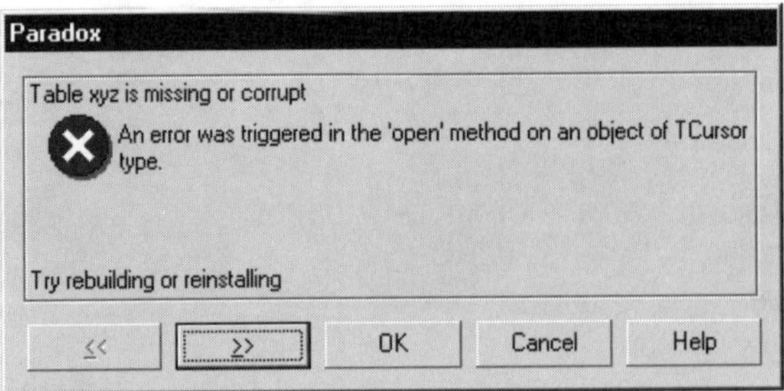

The errorShow() procedure also can accept two optional string parameters that you can use to add text to the error box. When you use hundreds of errorShow() procedures in a large project, adding text to the error box can really help. The following is the complete syntax for errorShow():

errorShow([const ***topHelp*** String, [const ***bottomHelp*** String]])

You can use topHelp and bottomHelp for anything you wish, but here is a suggestion. Use topHelp for the name of the object followed by the path to the code, and bottomHelp for extra information. For example:

```
if not tc.open("LINEITEM") then
  errorShow("Secrets.fsl :: button1 :: pushButton", "Open
; routine failed")
endIf
```

Using the *try* Structure

To deal with errors yourself, you can place a try structure around your code. If an error is detected, you can use reTry, execute optional code, or display an error message that's better or more complete than the built-in error message. The following code uses a variation of this technique. It displays the built-in error messages, which normally wouldn't be triggered:

```
errorTrapOnWarnings(yes)
try
  ;Your code here
onFail
  msgStop( errorCode(), errorMessage() )
  ;You could also use errorShow()
endTry
```

Use errorTrapOnWarnings(Yes) to raise warning errors to critical. If you wish to write really tight ObjectPAL code, do the following three things:

- Use errorTrapOnWarnings(Yes) in the open event of every form.
- Make sure that Properties | Show Compiler Warnings is checked for every form.
- Make sure that Properties | Compile with Debug is checked for every form.

Sometimes, however, you will want to turn off errorTrapOnWarnings(). The most common time is when you are using the warning error in an if statement.

Another technique to raise warning errors to critical is with setReason(). Suppose that you wish to use setReason() to raise warning errors to critical. You might wish to use this technique when filtering out reasons. Add lines 2–4 to the error event of the form.

```
1:    ;Form :: Error Prefilter
2:    method pushButton(var eventInfo Event)
3:       if eventInfo.reason() = ErrorWarning then
4:          eventInfo.setReason(ErrorCritical)
5:       endIf
6:    endMethod
```

The errorTrapOnWarnings(Yes) makes warning errors critical errors. Specifically, it has the effect of the following:

- The built-in error event will be called.
- The standard Error dialog box will be shown.
- onFail will be called in a try structure.
- The next line of code will not execute.

Use *view()* to View a Variable

Sometimes, it's convenient to use view() to view a variable in your code. view() also provides a stopping point that can help you narrow down a problem. For example, type the following into the pushButton event of a button:

```
;Button :: pushButton
method pushButton(var eventInfo Event)
```

```
        var
            s1, s2, s3 String
        endVar

        s1 = " Julia"
        s1.view()
        s2 = "Wiegand"
        s2.view()
        s3 = s1 + " " + s2
        s3.view()
    endMethod
```

This code doesn't shed light on any problems because it has no bugs. The code demonstrates, however, how view(), heavily used, breaks a large piece of code into smaller parts. If a problem existed, you might get a view box before the problem appeared. That would enable you to get closer to the problem. The closer you are to a problem, the easier it is to fix. You also can turn on the Compile with Debug option to receive better error messages.

Use the *fullName* Property

If you're having trouble with scope or the containership hierarchy and you need to know the full containership path of an object, use the following example. It assumes that an object named theBox is on a form:

```
;Button :: pushButton
method pushButton(var eventInfo Event)
   message("Full containership path is " + theBox.fullName)
endMethod
```

Sometimes you'll be surprised about the full path of an object. Using the fullName property involves checking yourself. Some people call this type of debugging a reality check because you test your own perception of what's going on. If you're absolutely positive that an object has a certain path, do a reality check with fullName.

Use the Object Tree

Another way to check an object's path is to use the Object Tree inspector. The Object Tree is part of the Object Explorer and is a visual hierarchical display of a form and its containers. The Object Tree is most valuable when you come back to your own old code or analyze someone else's application. It's also a valuable everyday tool for opening many methods and for accessing stacked objects more easily. You can even print the Object Tree for a permanent printed record (see Figure B-2).

Summary

In this chapter, you learned that all programmers have their own ways of debugging. Now that you have the basics down, you can develop a style of your own. When problems arise, you'll be able to isolate them quickly. You'll be able to correct your mistakes, straighten out your logic, or find a solution that works around the problem.

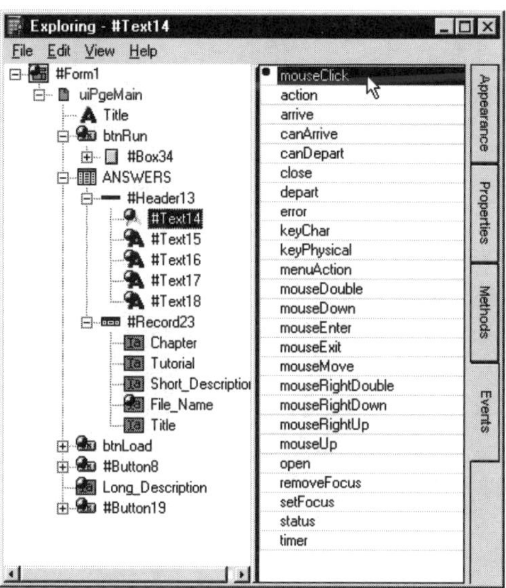

FIGURE B-2 The Object Tree allows you to see all the objects

Index

A

D

E

F

G

Q

R

S

T

U